New Perspectives on

MICROSOFT® EXCEL 2002 WITH VISUAL BASIC® FOR APPLICATIONS

Advanced

LISA FRIEDRICHSEN
Johnson County Community College

THOMSON

COURSE TECHNOLOGY™

Australia • Canada • Mexico • Singapore • Spain • United Kingdom • United States

THOMSON

COURSE TECHNOLOGY

New Perspectives on Microsoft® Excel 2002 with
Visual Basic® for Applications—Advanced

is published by Course Technology

Managing Editor:
Rachel Crapser

Technology Project Manager:
Amanda Young

Composition:
GEX Publishing Services

Senior Editor:
Donna Gridley

Marketing Manager:
Sean Teare

Text Designer:
Meral Dabcovich

Senior Product Manager:
Kathy Finnegan

Developmental Editor:
Jane Pedicini

Cover Designer:
Efrat Reis

Product Manager:
Melissa Hathaway

Production Editor:
Kristen Guevara

ISBN 0-7600-6435-0

Preface

Course Technology is the world leader in information technology education. The New Perspectives Series is an integral part of Course Technology's success. Visit our Web site to see a whole new perspective on teaching and learning solutions.

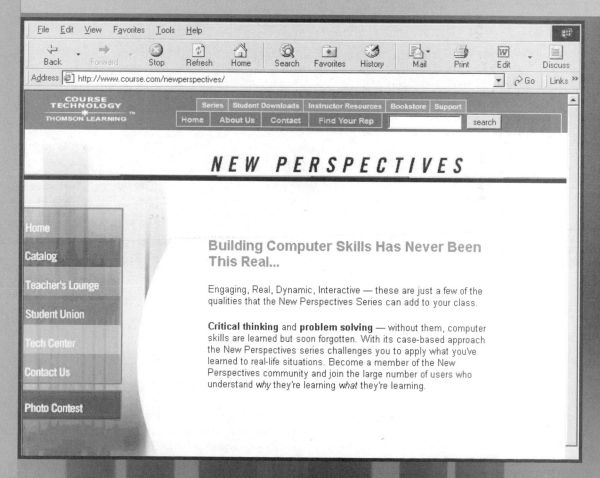

New Perspectives—Building Computer Skills Has Never Been This Real

Why New Perspectives will work for you.

Critical thinking and **problem solving**—without them, computer skills are learned but soon forgotten. With its **case-based** approach, the New Perspectives Series challenges students to apply what they've learned to real-life situations. Become a member of the New Perspectives community and watch your students not only **master** computer skills, but also **retain** and carry this **knowledge** into the world.

New Perspectives catalog
Our online catalog is never out of date! Go to the Catalog button on our Web site to check out our available titles, request a desk copy, download a book preview, or locate online files.

Complete system of offerings
Whether you're looking for a Brief book, an Advanced book, or something in between, we've got you covered. Go to the Catalog link on our Web site to find the level of coverage that's right for you.

Instructor materials
We have all the tools you need—data files, solution files, figure files, a sample syllabus, and ExamView, our powerful testing software package.

How well do your students know Microsoft Office?
Find out with performance-based testing software that measures your students' proficiency in the application. Click the Tech Center link to learn more.

Get certified
If you want to get certified, we have the titles for you. Find out more by clicking the Teacher's Lounge button.

Interested in online learning?
Enhance your course with any one of our online learning platforms. Go to the Teacher's Lounge to find the platform that's right for you.

**Your link to the future is at
www.course.com/NewPerspectives**

What you need to know about this book.

- ExamView testing software gives you the option of generating a printed test, LAN-based test, or testing over the Internet.

- All cases are NEW to this edition!

- The first half of the book covers advanced Excel applications in the areas of business decision support management, data management, and effective graphical representations of data.

- Advanced features of Excel such as Web queries, PivotTables, PivotCharts, conditional formatting, advanced chart types, add-ins, workbook customization, and workbook automation are covered.

- An extensive number of functions within each function category are used in a wide variety of scenarios. Other complex formula issues including absolute cell referencing issues, formulas that concatenate text and values, and formula error value detection and correction techniques are explored.

- The second half of the book provides an excellent introduction to Visual Basic for Applications (VBA) as it is used within Excel applications. VBA is used to create macros, event handlers, custom functions, and custom forms with a wide variety of controls.

- Macro security and digital certificates, VBA variables, logic structure, looping structures, and debugging techniques are explored.

- The book concludes with a tutorial on sharing Excel data with other programs, such as Access and the Web.

- Review Assignments and Case Problems provide hands-on reinforcement with the skills learned in each tutorial.

CASE	TROUBLE?	SESSION 1.1	QUICK CHECK	RW
Tutorial Case Each tutorial begins with a problem presented in a case that is meaningful to students. The case sets the scene to help students understand what they will do in the tutorial.	**TROUBLE? Paragraphs** These paragraphs anticipate the mistakes or problems that students may have and help them continue with the tutorial.	**Sessions** Each tutorial is divided into sessions designed to be completed in about 45 minutes each. Students should take as much time as they need and take a break between sessions.	**Quick Check Questions** Each session concludes with conceptual Quick Check questions that test students' understanding of what they learned in the session.	**Reference Windows** Reference Windows are succinct summaries of the most important tasks covered in a tutorial. They preview actions students will perform in the steps to follow.

BRIEF CONTENTS

TABLE OF CONTENTS

Tutorial 7 EX 359

Creating Custom Functions

Developing Custom Functions for GVR

Tutorial 8 EX 411

Creating Custom Forms

Developing Customized Forms for GVR

Tutorial 9 — EX 479

Examining Variables and Ranges and Controlling Code Execution

Tutorial 10 — EX 529

Sharing Excel Data with Other Programs

Importing, Linking, and Using VBA to Share Excel Data with Access Databases and the Web

Acknowledgments

I want to thank the fabulous Course Technology team that helped create this book: Rachel Crapser, Managing Editor; Donna Gridley, Senior Editor; Melissa Hathaway, Product Manager; Kristen Guevara, Production Editor; and John Bosco's excellent team of Quality Assurance testers, especially Harris Bierhoff, Shawn Day, Ashlee Welz, Danielle Shaw, and Serge Palladino. I also want to thank Jane Pedicini, the Developmental Editor; Kevin Campbell, the Copy Editor; and the staff at GEX.

In addition, I want to acknowledge and thank the dedicated team of reviewers. Their extensive knowledge provided numerous suggestions and improvements. Roy Ageloff, University of Rhode Island; Harlan Brewer, Utah State University; Anthony Briggs; Elaine Folkers, Asnuntuck Community College; Don Hoggan, Solano Community College; Earl Rosenbloom; and Jack Stevenson, Rogue Community College.

And of course, I couldn't write a book like this without the love and support from my own family, Doug, Kelsey, and Aaron.

This book is dedicated to my students. ☺

—Lisa Friedrichsen

New Perspectives on

MICROSOFT®
EXCEL 2002
WITH VBA

Read This Before You Begin

To the Student

Data Files and Data Disks

To complete the exercises in the Tutorials, Review Assignments, and Cases of this book, you need Data Files. The Data Files are organized into three folders per tutorial. The folders are named so that you know which files you need for the exercises in the Tutorial, Review Assignments, and Cases for each tutorial. For example, the Data Files for Tutorial 1 are organized in the following folder structure:

Tutorial.01\Tutorial
Tutorial.01\Review
Tutorial.01\Cases

If your school provides a copy of the Data Files on a local computer, file server, or Web site, your instructor will tell you how to locate that site and copy the Data Files. You can also download the Data Files by going to www.course.com and following the instructions printed in the back inside cover of this book on how to download Data Files.

If you use floppy disks to store your Data Files, you'll need to organize them so that you will have enough disk space to complete all of the exercises. Your instructor will either provide you with these Data Disks or ask you to make them. If you are making your own Data Disks, you will need **three** blank, formatted high-density disks for each tutorial. Copy only one folder (Tutorial, Review, or Cases) to each Data Disk for each tutorial. And, of course, label each Data Disk with the tutorial number and folder name so that you can easily locate which Data Disk you need when working through the exercises.

Note that the Tutorial, Review Assignment, and Case exercises in Tutorial 10 require that an extra folder that contains database files be copied to each Data Disk too. Look for these database files in a folder named T10. Refer to the "File Finder" chart at the back of this book for a complete list of the Data Files that are used in each exercise of each tutorial.

Using Your Own Computer

If you are using your own computer, you will need a current version of the Windows operating system, and a complete installation of either Microsoft Excel 2000 or Microsoft Excel 2002 (XP). Some exercises require that you have an Internet connection and use Internet Explorer 5.0 or higher. In Tutorial 10, Access 2000 or Access 2002 (XP) is used.

Visit Our World Wide Web Site

You can find more information on this book and other Course Technology products at www.course.com.

To the Instructor

The Data Files, Solution Files, test banks, and an instructor's manual are available on the Instructor's Resource Kit CD. Contact your sales representative for a copy of the CD, or go to www.course.com and download what you need from the Instructor Resources area of the Web site. You are granted a license to copy the data files to any computer or computer network used by students who have purchased this book.

OBJECTIVES

In this tutorial you will:

- Learn about decision support models

- Use general management decision support models, including what-if analysis, weighted criteria analysis, and scenario analysis

- Use correlation and prediction models, including regression analysis, forecasting, and scatter diagram analysis

- Set workbook protection features, such as cell locking and passwords

- Work with relative, absolute, and mixed cell references

- Apply conditional formatting to formulas

- Set advanced printing options, including gridlines and column and row headings

USING
EXCEL AS A DECISION SUPPORT TOOL

Modeling, Analyzing, and Supporting Common Business Decisions Using Excel

CASE

Green Valley Recreation

Green Valley Recreation, GVR, is a community agency that organizes hundreds of programs, such as soccer, swimming, tennis, and performing arts, which help build physical and mental skills for the residents of Green County, Illinois. GVR started as a girls-and-boys summer softball/baseball league in 1995, with over 300 children enrolling in the league that year. Currently, over 5000 individuals participate in GVR activities each year.

Due to the enormous response from the public, fast growth, and large numbers of enrollments, the GVR Board of Directors has had to make many important financial decisions in the past two years, such as setting new budgets, investing in land and other capital improvements, hiring program directors, and predicting future growth.

Lynn Tse, the director of GVR, hired you as a business analyst. Lynn has gathered financial information and wants you to organize and analyze it in preparation for the decisions that will be made at the board's next meeting. As your manager, Lynn will rely on your Excel skills to help her structure, analyze, and present management decisions that involve numeric analysis.

In this tutorial, you will use many Excel features to organize and analyze data to support the many decisions facing the GVR Board of Directors. You will address various business problems with appropriate decision support models using Excel. You will also use advanced Excel features, such as scenario analysis, conditional formatting, regression analysis, and scatter charts, to effectively organize and analyze data so that Lynn can present information that will help GVR's board make informed and appropriate decisions.

SESSION 1.1

In this session, you will learn about decision support models and how you can use Excel as a decision support tool. You will learn about the general management models, including the what-if, weighted criteria, and scenario analysis models. You will also apply conditional formatting to highlight key findings that result from the implementation of the decision support models.

Decision Support Systems

A **decision support system** (**DSS**) is a computer system that supports the decision-making needs of a typical business professional. A DSS consists of three parts: a quantitative model, a computer tool, and a business problem to which the DSS is being applied.

A **model** is a simplified representation of something, created for a specific purpose. For example, you might put together a model car that you purchased as a kit at a toy store. If your purpose in putting together the model car were to show the general color, shape, and exterior details of that vehicle, you would probably achieve your goal. If your purpose in putting together the model were to learn how an internal combustion engine works, you would probably need a different model. There are often many different types of models of the specific thing, and the challenge is to choose the one that supports your specific goal.

In business, there are several **quantitative models** (models that use numbers to describe reality) that can be used to simplify, support, and communicate many of the typical decisions that a business professional must make. You will explore many quantitative models in this tutorial. They include general management, statistical, and financial models:

- General management models:
    - What-if analysis, also called sensitivity analysis
    - Scenario analysis
    - Weighted criteria analysis
- Statistical models:
    - Regression analysis
    - scatter chart analysis
    - Forecasting
- Financial models:
    - Interest calculations
    - Depreciation calculations
    - Time value of money calculations

Although you could implement any of these models using only a pencil and paper, using Excel as the tool to organize and present the data within the model provides a tremendous number of benefits:

- Speed: Calculations are completed much faster.
- Accuracy: When formulas and raw data are entered correctly, calculations are correct as well.
- Consistency: Each time the formula calculates, it uses a consistent process.
- Accessibility: Information can be quickly and easily shared with others.
- Security: Information can be password protected, backed up, and recovered if necessary.
- Flexibility: Information can be charted or analyzed in new ways.

Two of the most important characteristics of a successful manager are the ability to make fast and fair decisions and the ability to communicate those decisions to others. Being able to create and use effective decision support systems directly affects both characteristics.

What-If **Analysis**

What-if analysis, also called **sensitivity analysis**, is a decision support model in which you analyze the effect of changing one or more assumption values. It is one of the most common decision support models, and you've probably used it before, even if you've never heard it called by either of these terms. Examples of business problems that can be supported within this model include the following:

- What will happen to profits if the minimum wage for entry-level employees is increased by 10%?
- What will happen to profits if the price of a product is increased by 5%?
- What will happen to our market share if we decrease the cost of shipping by 6%?

A key issue in implementing a successful what-if model in Excel (actually, this is an important issue for any successful spreadsheet but is particularly true for the what-if model) is to make sure that all assumption values are referenced as separate values in individual cells and not entered in formulas themselves. **Assumption values** are the values used by formulas, that is, the raw data used to calculate new information. For example, if you were to multiply the cost of an existing product by a growth factor of 10%, both the cost of the existing product and the growth factor of 10% would be considered raw data and should be entered into their own cells in the workbook (rather than typed directly into the formula).

Figure 1-1 shows two examples of how you might create a worksheet to project the cost of your products if increased by 10%. Although there doesn't appear to be any difference in the formulas in range C5:C9 versus range C17:C21 by looking at the results of the formulas, you can examine the worksheet in Figure 1-2 to see the difference in the way the formulas were constructed.

Figure 1-1	COMPARING THE RESULTS OF FORMULAS

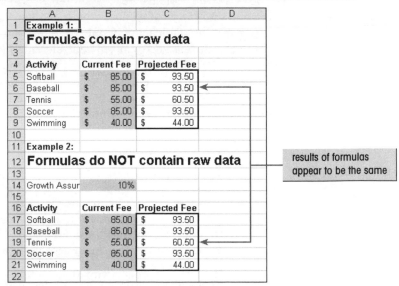

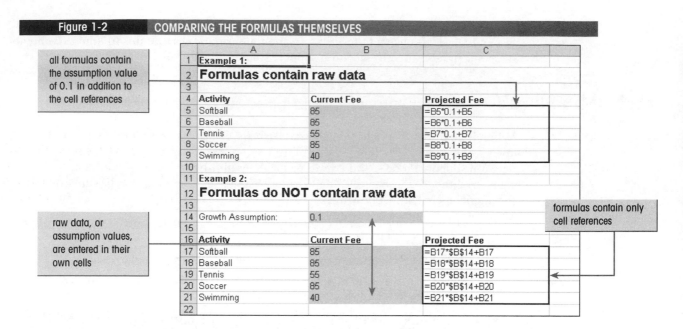

Figure 1-2   COMPARING THE FORMULAS THEMSELVES

all formulas contain the assumption value of 0.1 in addition to the cell references

raw data, or assumption values, are entered in their own cells

formulas contain only cell references

The formulas in Example 1 use cell references to refer to the current fee for that activity, but they also contain raw data (0.1). The 10% (or 0.1) figure is the growth assumption value. It is multiplied by the current fee to find the appropriate increase and then added back to the current fee to calculate the projected fee. Other ways to enter the formula in cell C5, which all give the same result but would inappropriately contain raw data, include:

$=85*0.1+85$

$=85*1.1$

$=B5*1.1$

The formulas shown in Example 2 contain only cell references and will, therefore, automatically recalculate if any of the values in the referenced cells change. The formulas shown in Example 2 also contain an absolute cell reference as indicated by the dollar signs ($) within the cell reference. For example, in cell C17, the reference to cell B14 is entered as $B$14 in the formula =B17*$B$14+B17. Whether or not an absolute cell reference is entered into the formula doesn't change the result of the formula nor its inherent ability to automatically recalculate if one of the assumption values changes. Whether you use absolute cell references, mixed cell references (a cell reference that contains a dollar sign before either the column letter or the row number, for example $B14 or B$14), or the default relative cell reference (a cell reference that does not have any dollar signs, for example B14) is determined by how you want the formula to change when you copy it. Other ways to appropriately enter the formula in cell C17 using only cell references include:

$=B17*B14+B17$

$=B17*(1+B14)$

$=B17*(1+\$B\$14)$

None of these examples contains raw data, and, therefore, each example preserves the ability of the formula to automatically recalculate if one of the assumption values changes. The benefits of creating your formulas using only cell references (Example 2) versus entering assumption values in your formulas (Example 1) include the following:

■ Increased productivity: If you want to ask "What if fees increase by 8%?", you only have to update one cell value in Example 2 (cell B14) versus updating all of the formulas that reference this assumption value in Example 1 (range C5:C9).

■ Improved accuracy: By creating formulas that reference a cell address, you are less likely to forget to update the formulas that use the assumption values.

Next, you'll explore improper versus proper construction of a what-if workbook.

Exploring an Improperly Constructed What-If Workbook

To understand the value of the correct implementation of the what-if model, you'll work with a small cash flow worksheet that is *not* set up properly. Then, you'll compare and contrast it to a what-if worksheet that is set up properly.

Lynn has created a cash flow projection worksheet, but she gets frustrated when her formulas don't work properly. She has asked that you look at the worksheet and then reenter the formulas so they always show up-to-date, accurate values.

> *To do a what-if analysis on a worksheet that is not properly set up:*
>
> 1. Start Excel and open the **CashFlow-1** workbook located in the Tutorial.01\Tutorial folder on your Data Disk. The Cash Flow worksheet contains actual revenue and cost values for the year 2003 and projected revenue and cost values for the years 2004 through 2009. Although all of the calculated values were created using Excel formulas, some of them contain raw data, which make the worksheet difficult to use as a what-if analysis model. The assumption values for the worksheet are in the shaded cells in column B: B6, B7, B10, B12, and B13.
>
> 2. Click cell **C6** and observe the formula in the Formula bar, and then click cell **C12** and observe the formula in the Formula bar. See Figure 1-3. Both cells C6 and C12 contain assumption values in their formulas. In cell C6, the formula =B6*1.1 multiplies the 2003 participants value in cell B6 by 1.1 to project a value that is a 10% increase from year to year. In cell C12, the field rental expense is calculated using the formula =C10*100, or the number of games in cell C10 multiplied by $100 per game.

Figure 1-3   **CASH FLOW WORKSHEET**

formula in cell C12 contains an assumption value

assumption values are shaded

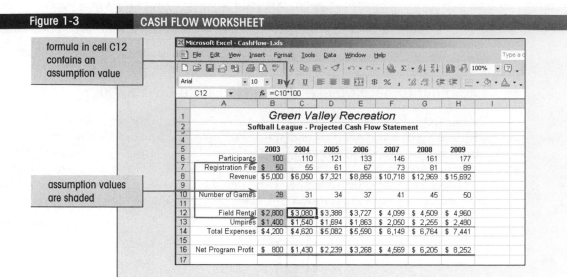

3. Click cell **C13** and observe the formula in the Formula bar. In cell C13, the formula *=C10*2*25* multiplies the number of games in cell C10 by 2 umpires per game times $25 per game. Cells C7 and C10 have similar problems; their formulas contain assumption values.

   What if the field rental expense changes to $110 per game? What if the cost for an umpire changes to $35 per game? What effort is involved to make this change in this worksheet? You will edit the formulas in cells C12 and C13 to enter the new assumption values.

4. Click cell **C12**, type **=C10*110**, and then press the **Enter** key.

5. In cell **C13**, type **=C10*2*35** and then press the **Enter** key.

   With the new assumptions entered for the year 2004, you will copy both formulas through the year 2009 columns in one motion.

6. Select the range **C12:C13**, and then drag the fill handle, which appears as a black cross in the lower-right corner of a selected cell, to the right across the range **D12:H13** to copy both the formulas. See Figure 1-4. The assumption values of $110 per game for field rental and $35 per game for an umpire have now been updated for every year from 2004 through 2009 so that you can see the updated profit values displayed in row 16.

| Figure 1-4 | COPYING FORMULAS IN THE CASH FLOW WORKSHEET |

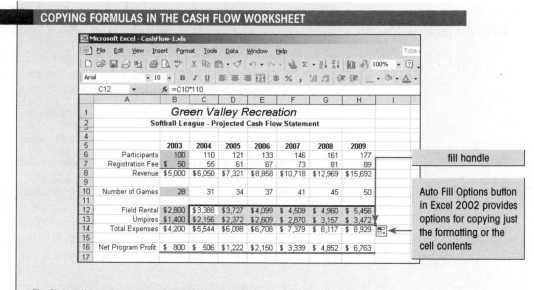

7. Save the changes to the workbook.

Although you were able to answer both of the what-if questions by modifying all of the formulas that were affected by these new assumptions, you also created the following issues:

- In order to know what assumption values were used, you must examine the formulas in each cell.
- Changing each formula that references an assumption value is a time-consuming process.
- Changing each formula that references an assumption value is an error-prone process.

By using a worksheet that has been set up to use assumption values, you will be able to avoid these problems.

Exploring a Properly Constructed What-If Workbook

When raw data is already used within a formula, you have some work to do to separate the assumption values from the formulas. You will be a faster, more accurate, and better decision maker by isolating the raw data from the formulas. So setting up a properly constructed what-if workbook, even when it requires fixing an existing workbook that was designed improperly, is well worth the effort if the workbook is going to be used more than once.

You decide to add new rows at the top of the worksheet to store additional assumption values that will help Lynn do what-if analysis in a clear, productive, and accurate way. It's also common to store assumption values on their own worksheet. In this case, however, you want Lynn to be able to see the assumption values and the results of the formulas at the same time, so you will put all of the information on one worksheet.

To redesign the what-if worksheet so that assumption values are isolated from their formulas:

1. Select the row headings for rows **5** through **11**, right-click the selection, and then click **Insert** on the shortcut menu. Seven rows are inserted above the year column headings. You will use newly inserted rows for the assumption values.

   First, you'll enter labels to identify the assumption values.

2. Click cell **A5**, type **Participant Growth %**, and then press the **Enter** key.

3. In cell A6, type **Reg Fee Growth %**, and then press the **Enter** key.

   TROUBLE? If the selection box doesn't automatically move down one cell, you can set an option so that the selection box will move down (or up, left, or right) one cell when you press the Enter key. Click Tools on the menu bar, click Options, click the Edit tab, select the Move selection after Enter check box, make sure "Down" appears in the Direction list, and then click the OK button.

4. Enter the labels in cells **A7:A10** as shown in Figure 1-5.

Figure 1-5	ASSUMPTION VALUE LABELS

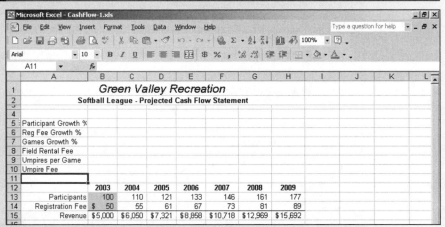

With the labels in place, you'll enter the corresponding assumption values in column B.

5. Enter **10%** in cells B5, B6, and B7.

6. In cell B8, type **110** and press the **Enter** key, type **2** in cell B9 and press the **Enter** key, and then type **35** in cell B10 and press the **Enter** key. The values in cells B8, B9, and B10 are automatically formatted as percentages since the prior entries in column B were formatted as percentages.

   You want the values in cells B8 and B10 to be formatted with a dollar sign and no cents, and the values in cell B9 to appear as a whole number.

7. Click **B8**, press and hold the **Ctrl** key, click **B10**, click the **Currency Style** button [$] on the Formatting toolbar, and then click the **Decrease Decimal** button [.00→.0] on the Formatting toolbar twice to remove the digits to the right of the decimal point.

   TROUBLE? If the values in cells B8 and B10 do not appear as $110 and $35, type $110 in cell B8 and $35 in cell B10.

8. Click cell **B9**, click the **Comma Style** button 🔳 on the Formatting toolbar, and then click 🔳 twice to remove the digits to the right of the decimal point.

TROUBLE? If the value in cell B9 does not appear as 2, type 2 in the cell, press the Enter key, and then repeat Step 8.

Another formatting enhancement that will make it easier for the users performing a what-if analysis is to format the assumption values differently from the formulas. You will apply a 25% gray fill color to the assumption values in range B5:B10 to format them similarly to the other raw data values in column B.

9. Select the range **B5:B10**, click the **list arrow** for the Fill Color button 🔳 on the Formatting toolbar, and then click the **Gray-25%** square (fourth row down, last column on the right). See Figure 1-6.

Figure 1-6	FORMATTING ASSUMPTION VALUES

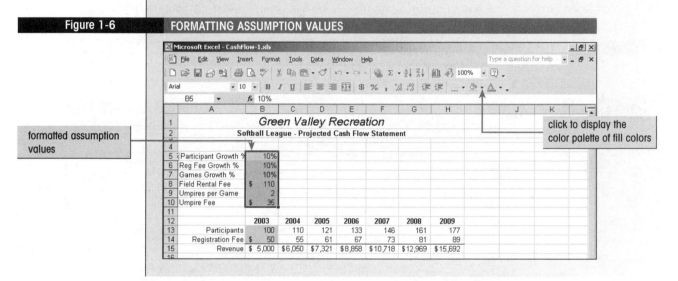

formatted assumption values

click to display the color palette of fill colors

Now that all of the assumption values are entered in individual cells, you're ready to fix the formulas so that they will include cell references rather than contain raw data. Keeping all assumption values in their own cells and shading them will give Lynn a visually enhanced way to perform what-if analysis. Before you can give the workbook to Lynn, you will fix the formulas in rows 13, 14, 17, 19, and 20 so that they reference the new assumption value cells that you added to the workbook.

To enter formulas that include cell references rather than raw data:

1. Click cell **C13**, click in the Formula bar, and then change the entry =B13*1.1 to **=B13*B5+B13**. Note that this formula multiplies the number of participants by 10% and then adds the result to the number of participants to calculate the projected increase for 2004.

When you enter formulas, you don't have to enter the cell references in upper-case letters. If you type lowercase letters within your cell references, Excel will automatically convert them to uppercase letters when you press the Enter key or click the Enter button ✓ on the Formula bar.

2. Change the formula in cell C14 to **=B14*B6+B14**.

Note that from this point on, the steps instructing you to enter a formula in a cell will be written as "enter **=B13*B5+B13**". Use the technique that works best for you: typing the formula directly from the keyboard, typing in the Formula bar, or using the point-and-click method.

With the formulas updated for both cells C13 and C14, you can copy and paste those formulas across columns D through H using the fill handle.

3. Select the range **C13:C14**, and then drag the fill handle to the right to copy the formulas across range **D13:H14**. See Figure 1-7. Although the formulas were copied successfully, they did not produce the correct results. The values in row 13 for years 2004 through 2009 are all 110, and the values in row 14 for years 2004 through 2009 are all 55. None of the values for years 2005 through 2009 were increased by the growth percentage entered in cells B5 and B6.

Figure 1-7	COPYING FORMULAS

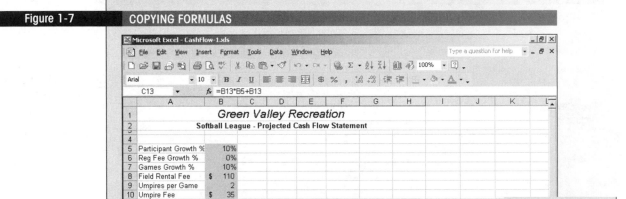

To help you troubleshoot formula problems, you can use Excel's Edit mode. In **Edit mode**, Excel color codes the borders of the cell references used in the formula. The colors of the cell borders match the color of the corresponding cell reference in the formula in the Formula bar. This visual cue can help you identify the source of the problem. If you are working in Edit mode you must finish the edit before you can do something else. To return to Ready mode, press the Enter key or click the Enter button ✓ on the Formula bar.

4. Click cell **D13** and then click in the Formula bar to examine the cell references in the formula. See Figure 1-8. By examining the formula for cell D13, you can see why the formula returned a value of 110. The formula in cell D13 multiplies the value in cell C13 (110) by the value in cell C5 (which contains no value) and adds that result back to the value in cell C13 (110). Nothing plus 110 equals 110. Instead, you want the formula to read =C13*B5+C13 so that the 10% assumption value in cell B5 is always used to calculate the increase, and so that the formula becomes *11+110=121*. You will fix the formula next. For now, just return to Ready mode.

Figure 1-8   TROUBLESHOOTING A FORMULA

cell references are
color coded

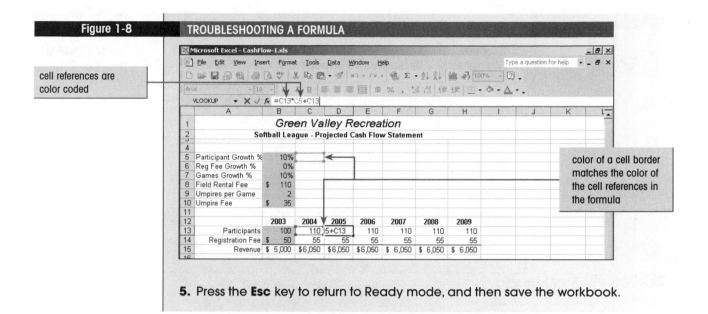

color of a cell border
matches the color of
the cell references in
the formula

5. Press the **Esc** key to return to Ready mode, and then save the workbook.

Although you could fix the formulas for each cell in the range D13:D18 so that the formulas correctly reference the 10% assumption value in cell B5, a faster way of fixing the problem is to use absolute cell references.

Relative, Absolute, and Mixed Cell References

By default, when you enter a cell reference in a formula, Excel makes several assumptions about that cell reference. First, Excel assumes that the cell is on the same worksheet and in the same workbook as the cell in which you are entering the formula. (You'll build formulas that reference cell references on other worksheets and in other workbooks later.) Second, Excel assumes that the reference is a **relative cell reference**. The term *relative* is used because the cell references change when you copy them. Cell references in a formula change in the same relative way as cell references change between the copy and paste locations. The examples in Figure 1-9 help illustrate this.

Figure 1-9 COPYING FORMULAS CONTAINING RELATIVE CELL REFERENCES

Copy Cell Reference	Paste Cell Reference	Relative Difference Between Copy and Paste Cell References	Formula Being Copied	Final Formula in the Paste Cell Reference
C5	D6	add one column add one row	=A2	=B3
C5	E10	add two columns add five rows	=SUM(A2:A10)	=SUM(C7:C15)
C5	D10	add one column add five rows	=A2*D3	=B7*E8
C5	B1	subtract one column subtract four rows	+E10+F11	=D6+E7

An absolute cell reference in a formula does not change as you copy the formula. You can change a relative cell reference to an absolute cell reference by adding a dollar sign ($) in front of the row and column of the cell reference. Using the dollar signs indicates that this row and column will not change when the formula is copied. The examples in Figure 1-10 demonstrate how the formula that contains absolute cell references changes when it is copied.

Figure 1-10 COPYING FORMULAS CONTAINING ABSOLUTE CELL REFERENCES

Copy Cell Reference	Paste Cell Reference	Relative Difference Between Copy and Paste Cell References	Formula Being Copied	Final Formula in the Paste Cell Reference
C5	D6	add one column add one row	=$A$2	=$A$2
C5	E10	add two columns add five rows	=A2+$A$2	=C7+$A$2
C5	D10	add one column add five rows	=$A$2*$D$3	=$A$2*$D$3
C5	B1	subtract one column subtract four rows	=$E$10+F11	=$E$10+E7

A **mixed cell reference** in a formula is a combination of relative and absolute cell references. In a mixed cell address, you set either the column or the row as an absolute cell reference, but you allow the other half of the cell reference to change in a relative way to the copy and paste locations. Figure 1-11 shows how mixed cell references work.

| Figure 1-11 | COPYING MIXED CELL REFERENCES |

Copy Cell Reference	Paste Cell Reference	Relative Difference Between Copy and Paste Cell References	Formula Being Copied	Final Formula in the Paste Cell Reference
C5	D6	add one column add one row	=$A2	=$A3
C5	E10	add two columns add five rows	=A2+A$2	=C7+C$2
C5	D10	add one column add five rows	=$A2*D$3	=$A7*E$3
C5	B1	subtract one column subtract four rows	=$E$10+F11	=$E$10+E7

It is very important to realize that the relative versus absolute versus mixed cell reference issue does not affect the way a formula calculates. In other words, the formula =A1*B1 would calculate the same answer as =$A$1*$B$1, =$A1*$B1, =A$1*B$1, or any other combination of mixed cell references for A1 and B1. Whether a cell reference is relative, mixed, or absolute does not affect the way the formula calculates. However, the relative/absolute/mixed cell reference issue is only important when you *copy* a formula. By using the appropriate type of cell reference, you can increase your productivity because the copy process will create formulas that do not need to be edited any further to be correct. Of course, anything you can do to make sure that the formulas are copied correctly will make your workbook more reliable, too. Not understanding how relative versus absolute versus mixed cell references work is probably the second most common problem (after not separating assumption values into their own cell references) that you will encounter in existing workbooks that attempt to support the what-if model.

You will change the cell references in the formulas in the range C13:H14 to include the appropriate type of cell reference so that as you copy the formulas, they will be correct. To change a relative cell reference to an absolute or mixed reference, you can use the F4 key, which switches between the cell reference types without your having to retype them.

To enter formulas that include the appropriate type of cell reference:

1. Click cell **C13**, click **B5** in the Formula bar, press the **F4** key three times, and then click the **Enter** button ☑ on the Formula bar. The formula now reads *=B13*$B$5+B13*. In this case, you do *not* want the reference to cell column B to change for cell B5 as the formula is copied.

2. Drag the fill handle across the range **D13:H13** to copy the formulas for projecting the number of participants through the year 2009.

3. With range C13:H13 still selected, drag the fill handle down one row to copy the formulas to the cells in range **C14:H14**. See Figure 1-12. By making only the column, and not the row, an absolute cell reference in cell C13, you were able to copy and paste this formula to create accurate calculations through row 14.

Figure 1-12   COPYING FORMULAS WITH MIXED CELL REFERENCES

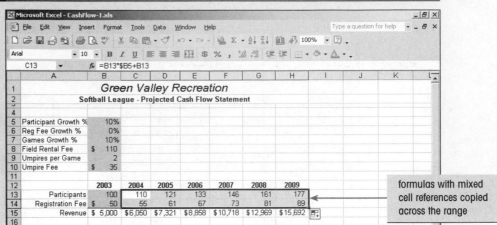

formulas with mixed cell references copied across the range

To indicate that row 15 for Revenue is subtotal, you will add a bottom border to the selected range of cells.

4. With range **C13:H14** still selected, click the **list arrow** for the Borders button on the Formatting toolbar, and then click the **Bottom Border** option (first row, second column) in the border gallery.

TROUBLE? If the icon on the Borders button already presents the border option that you want, you can click the button to apply that border rather than choose it from the list. The same rule applies to the Fill Color button and Font Color button.

Now you will edit the formula in cell C17 that projects the number of games for the year 2004.

5. Click cell **C17** and then change the formula to **=B17*$B$7+B17**. In this case, you could have correctly used *either* the mixed cell address of $B7 or the absolute cell address of $B$7 to reference the 10% assumption value in cell B7. Since this formula will not be copied to another row, the only thing to worry about is making sure that the *column* reference to cell B7 in the formula =B17*$B$7+B17 is entered as an absolute reference.

6. Click cell **C17** and then drag the fill handle across range **D17:H17** to copy the formula.

The last formulas you need to edit are the ones that project the costs for the field rental and umpires expenses. First, you will edit the formula in cell C19 and then the formula in cell C20.

7. Click cell **C19** and then change the formula to **=C17*$B$8**.

8. Click cell **C20** and then change the formula to **=C17*$B$9*$B$10**.

9. Select the range **C19:C20**, and then drag the fill handle across the range **D19:H20** as shown in Figure 1-13.

Figure 1-13	FINISHING THE FORMULAS FOR THE WHAT-IF ANALYSIS MODEL

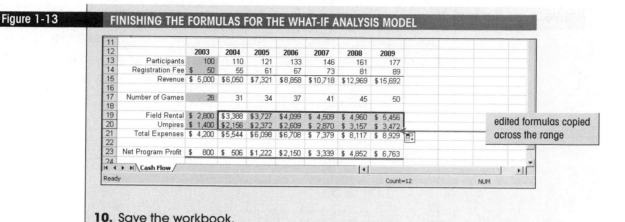

		2003	2004	2005	2006	2007	2008	2009	
11									
12		2003	2004	2005	2006	2007	2008	2009	
13	Participants	100	110	121	133	146	161	177	
14	Registration Fee	$ 50	55	61	67	73	81	89	
15	Revenue	$ 5,000	$6,050	$7,321	$8,858	$10,718	$12,969	$15,692	
16									
17	Number of Games	28	31	34	37	41	45	50	
18									
19	Field Rental	$ 2,800	$3,388	$3,727	$4,099	$ 4,509	$ 4,960	$ 5,456	edited formulas copied
20	Umpires	$ 1,400	$2,156	$2,372	$2,609	$ 2,870	$ 3,157	$ 3,472	across the range
21	Total Expenses	$ 4,200	$5,544	$6,098	$6,708	$ 7,379	$ 8,117	$ 8,929	
22									
23	Net Program Profit	$ 800	$ 506	$1,222	$2,150	$ 3,339	$ 4,852	$ 6,763	
24									

Cash Flow

Ready   Count=12   NUM

10. Save the workbook.

Now that the worksheet has been updated, you are ready to test its ability to quickly and accurately perform a what-if analysis. Lynn has several what-if questions she wants to test, including the following:

- What if registration fees remain fixed? Can the GVR still make a profit on this program without raising the fees each year?
- What if an official scorekeeper is required for each game, bringing the total number of umpires per game to three?

You will enter the new assumption values to test the what-if analysis model for Lynn.

To use the what-if analysis model to test new assumption values:

1. Click cell **B6**, type **0**, and then press the **Enter** key. The entire workbook automatically recalculates, and the new projected profit figures appear on row 23. See Figure 1-14. The worksheet shows that given the other assumptions, if the registration fee doesn't increase from $50 per participant, the program will not break even because the net program profit values in row 23 are negative.

Figure 1-14   **WHAT IF THE REGISTRATION FEE DOESN'T INCREASE?**

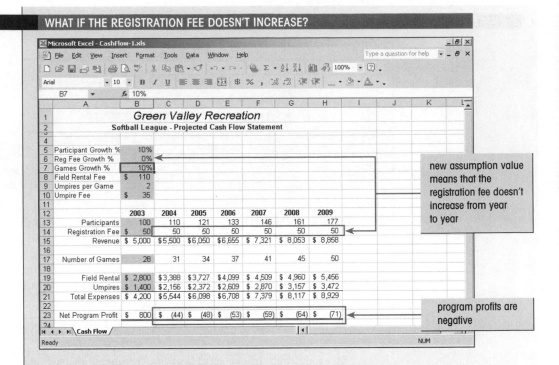

You decide to reapply the 10% registration fee assumption before entering the next assumption value.

2. Click the **Undo** button [image] on the Standard toolbar so that the value in cell B6 returns to 10%, click cell **B9**, type **3**, and then press the **Enter** key. The worksheet automatically recalculates, and the new projected profit figures appear on row 23. See Figure 1-15. The worksheet shows that given the other assumptions, if three umpires are required, the program will not break even in the year 2004. However, as participation and revenue increase in years 2005 through 2009, the additional cost of the extra umpire can be covered through additional revenue.

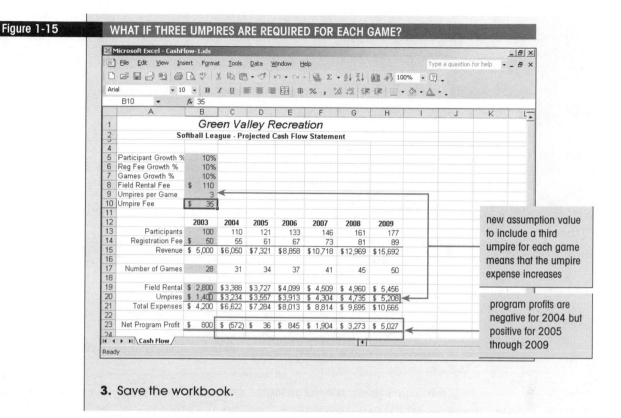

Figure 1-15 **WHAT IF THREE UMPIRES ARE REQUIRED FOR EACH GAME?**

new assumption value to include a third umpire for each game means that the umpire expense increases

program profits are negative for 2004 but positive for 2005 through 2009

3. Save the workbook.

With two very fast and easy entries, you were able to perform what-if analysis without first analyzing and then reentering formulas. You also did not have to figure out if or where the formulas needed to be copied in order to apply the new assumption to the rest of the projected values. The key difference between these two experiences is that in the properly structured worksheet, the formulas contain *no* assumption values. Rather, all assumption values are entered in separate cells, and all formulas that use the assumption values reference back to those cells.

Viewing Formulas

Because the proper construction of formulas is such a vital part of any effective worksheet, and especially a what-if analysis worksheet, knowing how to quickly view and print the formulas for the entire workbook is a handy skill.

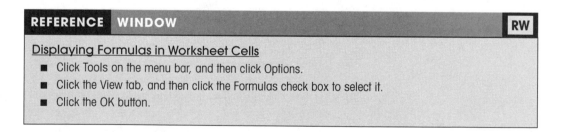

REFERENCE WINDOW   **RW**

Displaying Formulas in Worksheet Cells
- Click Tools on the menu bar, and then click Options.
- Click the View tab, and then click the Formulas check box to select it.
- Click the OK button.

In addition to viewing the formulas in a what-if analysis worksheet, you can also display gridlines on the printout of the analysis. In large or very complicated worksheets, gridlines can help the user find related data quickly and easily. In this case, printing gridlines will enable Lynn to find cell references faster.

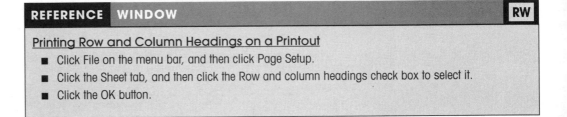

REFERENCE WINDOW   **RW**

Printing Gridlines on a Printout
- Click File on the menu bar, and then click Page Setup.
- Click the Sheet tab, and then click the Gridlines check box to select it.
- Click the OK button.

Another Page Setup option is the ability to print the row and column headings on a worksheet printout. Printing the row and column headings will help Lynn find cell references and understand the formulas faster.

REFERENCE WINDOW   **RW**

Printing Row and Column Headings on a Printout
- Click File on the menu bar, and then click Page Setup.
- Click the Sheet tab, and then click the Row and column headings check box to select it.
- Click the OK button.

You have presented the updated CashFlow-1 workbook to Lynn, and she has used it for what-if analysis. She is curious about how it works and has never worked with absolute and mixed cell references. To help her understand how the workbook is constructed, you will show her how to study all of the formulas in the workbook at the same time, rather than view them individually in the Formula bar. You will print the workbook with the formulas displayed, gridlines, and row numbers and column letters.

To view the formulas and to print the worksheet with grid-lines and headings:

1. Click **Tools** on the menu bar, and then click **Options**. The Options dialog box opens.

2. Click the **View** tab (if it is not already selected), click the **Formulas** check box in the Window options pane, and then click the **OK** button. See Figure 1-16. Note that the Gridlines option in the Options dialog box toggles on and off the gridlines on the screen (not on a printout).

   TROUBLE? If the Formula Auditing toolbar appears, close it. You won't need to use this toolbar for now.

Figure 1-16 | **VIEWING FORMULAS**

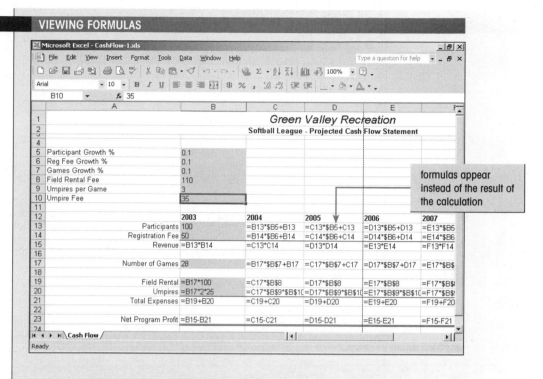

formulas appear instead of the result of the calculation

Viewing the formulas on the screen allows you to see them all at once, as opposed to one at a time in the Formula bar. You will print this workbook so Lynn can study and analyze the formulas. By printing the workbook with the gridlines and row and column headings displayed, she can more easily find specific cells and see how the workbook was constructed.

3. Click **File** on the menu bar, and then click **Page Setup**.

4. Click the **Sheet** tab, click the **Gridlines** check box to select it, and then click the **Row and column headings** check box to select it. With these two options selected, gridlines will appear on the printout (but not on the screen), and the row and column headings (that is, the row numbers and column letters) will also appear on the printout.

   Next, you will change the page orientation to landscape and the scaling to force the printout to fit within the margins of a single page.

5. Click the **Page** tab, click the **Landscape** option button, and then click the **Fit to 1 page(s) wide by 1 tall** option button.

   To identify your printout, add your name to the left section of the worksheet header.

6. Click the **Header/Footer tab**, click the **Custom Header** button, type your name in the Left section box, click the **OK** button, click the **Print Preview** button, and then zoom in on column A. See Figure 1-17.

Figure 1-17   PRINTING FORMULAS WITH GRIDLINES AND COLUMN AND ROW HEADINGS

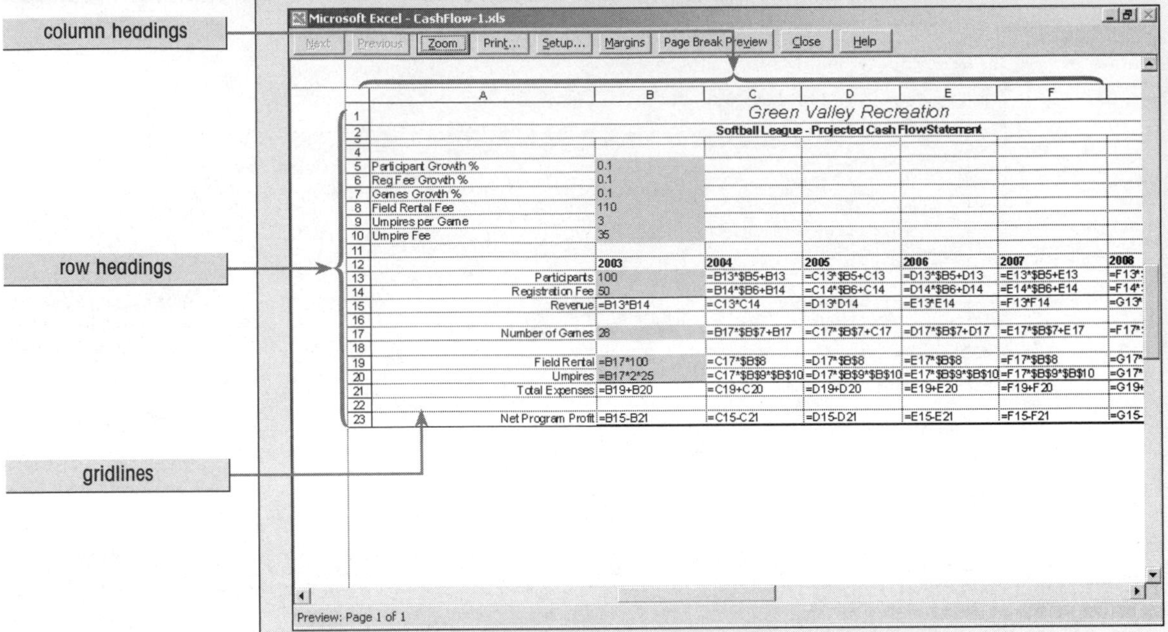

column headings →

row headings →

gridlines →

Microsoft Excel - CashFlow-1.xls

Next | Previous | Zoom | Print... | Setup... | Margins | Page Break Preview | Close | Help

	A	B	C	D	E	F
1			*Green Valley Recreation*			
2			Softball League - Projected Cash Flow Statement			
3						
4						
5	Participant Growth %	0.1				
6	Reg Fee Growth %	0.1				
7	Games Growth %	0.1				
8	Field Rental Fee	110				
9	Umpires per Game	3				
10	Umpire Fee	35				
11						
12		2003	2004	2005	2006	2007	2008
13	Participants	100	=B13*$B5+B13	=C13*$B5+C13	=D13*$B5+D13	=E13*$B5+E13	=F13*
14	Registration Fee	50	=B14*$B6+B14	=C14*$B6+C14	=D14*$B6+D14	=E14*$B6+E14	=F14*
15	Revenue	=B13*B14	=C13*C14	=D13*D14	=E13*E14	=F13*F14	=G13*
16							
17	Number of Games	28	=B17*$B$7+B17	=C17*$B$7+C17	=D17*$B$7+D17	=E17*$B$7+E17	=F17*
18							
19	Field Rental	=B17*100	=C17*$B$8	=D17*$B$8	=E17*$B$8	=F17*$B$8	=G17*
20	Umpires	=B17*2*25	=C17*$B$9*$B$10	=D17*$B$9*$B$10	=E17*$B$9*$B$10	=F17*$B$9*$B$10	=G17*
21	Total Expenses	=B19+B20	=C19+C20	=D19+D20	=E19+E20	=F19+F20	=G19+
22							
23	Net Program Profit	=B15-B21	=C15-C21	=D15-D21	=E15-E21	=F15-F21	=G15-

Preview: Page 1 of 1

7. Click the **Print** button on the Print Preview toolbar, and then click the **OK** button in the Print dialog box.

   TROUBLE? If necessary, select the printer you need to print to before clicking the OK button. If you do not know which printer to select, ask your instructor or technical support person for assistance.

8. Press **Ctrl + `** (grave accent key) to toggle off the Formula view option.

   TROUBLE? The grave accent key is usually the key directly above the Tab key on the keyboard. Do not confuse this key with the apostrophe key.

9. Save your changes to the workbook.

There are many ways to organize your workbook so that the assumption values are separated from the formulas. For example, you could separate the assumption values into their own section at the top or bottom of the worksheet, or you could use multiple worksheets, one devoted to storing the assumption values. No matter how the assumption values are separated in a workbook, however, if you apply a different cell fill color to those values, the color can also serve as a visual cue for the user as to which values they should change in order to do what-if analysis.

Protecting a Worksheet That Contains Assumption Values

Another helpful feature that helps users work with assumption values is called worksheet protection. When you **protect** a worksheet, users cannot enter or change values in any cell, except for those that are not locked. By default, all cells are locked, but by removing the locks on the assumption values before you apply worksheet protection, users will then be able to change the assumption values in the unlocked cells. The users, however, will not be able to overwrite or change any formulas or labels in the locked cells.

REFERENCE WINDOW   `RW`

<u>Protecting a Worksheet Containing Assumption Values</u>
- Select the cell or range that contains the assumption values.
- Click Format on the menu bar, and then click Cells.
- Click the Protection tab, and then click the Locked check box to deselect it.
- Click the OK button.
- Click Tools on the menu bar, point to Protection, and then click Protect Sheet.
- Select the activities that you want to allow users to access.
- Enter a password (optional).
- Click the OK button.

The purpose of unlocking assumption cells and then applying worksheet protection is to prevent the user from making entries into cells that should not be changed. If you are concerned that someone may intentionally damage a worksheet or workbook, you should also consider password protecting your worksheet or the entire workbook. A **password** is a secret code that restricts access to a range, worksheet, or workbook. Your password can include up to 255 characters. Passwords should not be obvious, such as your name, the name of the file, or the name of the company. Ideally, they should include both letters and numbers to make them harder to guess and decrypt. The password you use should be easy to remember, but not trivial, so that it isn't easy to guess.

A note of caution: If the worksheet (or workbook) is password protected, you will also be prompted for the password when you try to work with it. If you forgot the password, it cannot be retrieved. You will not be able to change the worksheet or open the workbook.

REFERENCE WINDOW   `RW`

<u>Setting a Worksheet Password</u>
- Click Tools on the menu bar, point to Protection, and then click Protect Sheet.
- Enter the password you want to apply to the worksheet, and then click the OK button.
- Type the password in the Reenter password to proceed text box, and then click the OK button.

Lynn has mentioned that several people may be using the CashFlow-1 workbook and has asked if there is a way to make sure that they don't overwrite the existing formulas. You will use cell protection and a worksheet password so that only the assumption values can be modified, and only those who know the password can open the file.

To protect the Cash Flow worksheet:

1. Select the range **B5:B10**.

   To unlock these assumption values, you will use the Format Cells dialog box.

2. Click **Format** on the menu bar, click **Cells**, and then click the **Protection** tab.

3. Click the **Locked** check box to deselect it. See Figure 1-18.

| Figure 1-18 | UNLOCKING CELLS |

deselecting this option enables the user to work with cells when the worksheet is protected

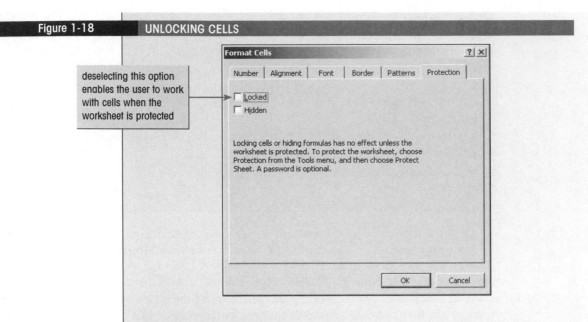

4. Click the **OK** button.

   Now you will protect the worksheet.

5. Click **Tools** on the menu bar, point to **Protection**, and then click **Protect Sheet**. The Protect Sheet dialog box opens. See Figure 1-19. This dialog box provides options that you can use to determine exactly what actions a user is allowed and not allowed to perform on this worksheet.

| Figure 1-19 | PROTECT SHEET DIALOG BOX |

password is optional

deselecting this option enables a user to select specified cells

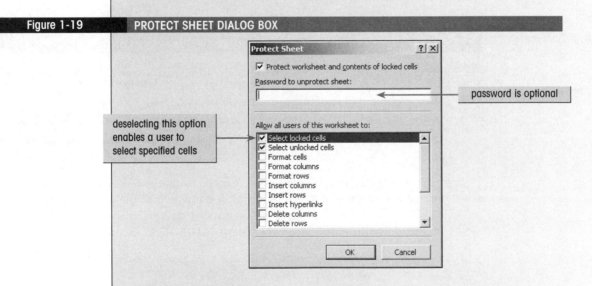

EXCEL 2000: The Protect Sheet dialog box in Excel 2000 is different from the Protect Sheet dialog box in Excel 2002. In Excel 2000, you do not have the option of enabling a user to select a locked cell in a protected sheet; therefore, skip Step 6 and continue with Step 7.

Because users will not be making any entries in any of the cells that are locked (every cell in the worksheet except for the assumption values in cells B6:E8), there's no need to allow them to select the locked cells, either.

6. Click the **Select locked cells** check box to deselect it.

To prevent users from unprotecting the worksheet, you will enter a password.

7. Click in the Password to unprotect sheet text box, type **poiuytrewq** (the top row of letters on the keyboard, from right to left), and then click the **OK** button.

8. Type **poiuytrewq** in the Reenter password to proceed text box, and then click the **OK** button.

TROUBLE? Excel worksheet passwords are case sensitive. If you have the Caps Lock key on while entering a password, you must reenter it using all capital letters as well.

9. Click any cell outside the range of assumption values. Because you chose not to allow users to select locked cells, you are unable to select any cell outside of the assumption values.

You also need to test the values in the assumption section of the worksheet.

10. Click cell **B5**, type **12%**, and then press the **Enter** key. The workbook automatically recalculates the protected participant, revenue, and profit values in rows 13, 15, and 23. See Figure 1-20.

Figure 1-20	USING A PROTECTED WORKBOOK

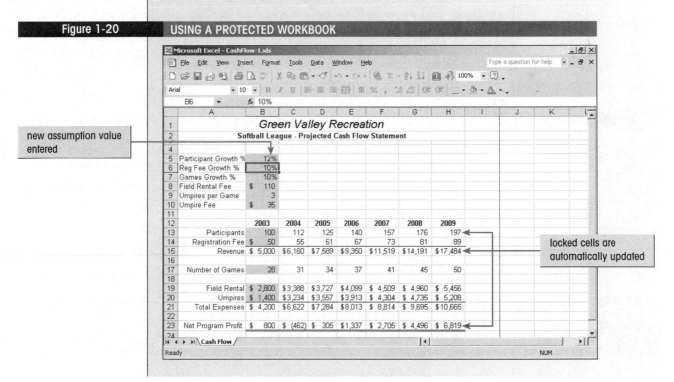

new assumption value entered

locked cells are automatically updated

If you needed to make additional changes to any cells outside of the range B5:B10, you would first have to unprotect the workbook.

You have completed your work with the CashFlow-1 workbook, so you can close the workbook and then exit the program.

To close the workbook and exit Excel:

1. Click the **Close** button ☒ on the title bar.

2. If prompted, click the **Yes** button to save your changes to the workbook before the program closes.

If you want different users or groups of users to have different permissions, you can grant permissions at the user level by using the Allow Users to Edit Ranges and the Protect and Share a Workbook options. These options are found on the Tools Protection submenu and will be covered in a later tutorial.

Session 1.1 QUICK CHECK

1. What are the three parts of a decision support system?

2. Why do business decision support systems often use quantitative models?

3. What is the key issue involved in implementing a successful what-if analysis model in Excel?

4. How can you view all of a worksheet's formulas on the screen at the same time?

5. When you protect a worksheet, which values do you typically unlock first?

SESSION 1.2

In this session, you will learn about scenario analysis and weighted criteria analysis, two common management decision support tools. You'll also learn to use conditional formatting, so that the important results of your analyses are more clearly displayed.

Scenario Analysis

Once you have a properly constructed workbook, you can quickly and easily enter as many new assumption values as you want and continue doing what-if analysis until you get the results you're looking for. However, only the last set of assumptions that you entered are stored with the workbook. Excel offers another decision support tool called **scenario analysis** that allows you to save multiple sets of what-if assumption values with the workbook. In scenario analysis, the assumption values that you change from scenario to scenario are called the **changing cells**. By saving the sets of assumption values, the changing cells, with a scenario name within the workbook, you can quickly reapply and analyze that scenario at a later time.

REFERENCE WINDOW **RW**

Saving a Scenario

- Select the assumption values that will be part of the scenario.
- Click Tools on the menu bar, and then click Scenarios to open the Scenario Manager dialog box.
- Click the Add button, and then enter a name for the scenario.
- Verify that the Changing cells reference box displays the assumption values that you selected, or use the Collapse Dialog Box button to select the assumption values.
- Modify the description of the scenario (optional), and then click the OK button.
- Verify or change the assumption values for each of the changing cells listed in the Scenario Values dialog box, and then click the OK button.
- Click the Close button.

GVR sells T-shirts for the many different sports programs they coordinate. Lynn tells you that the T-shirt sales you are currently projecting in the T-Shirts-1 workbook reflect a best case sales volume projection based on the high enrollment values. Lynn wants you to create a scenario that reflects the worst case sales volume projection based on low enrollment values as well. By using Excel's scenario analysis feature, you will save the low enrollment and high enrollment values as scenarios and then reapply them so Lynn can see and compare the best case and worst case sales volume projections.

To create the High Enrollment and Low Enrollment scenarios:

1. If you took a break after the last session, start Excel and then open the **T-Shirts-1** workbook located in the Tutorial.01\Tutorial folder on your Data Disk. The T-Shirts-1 workbook calculates the revenue and expense for GVR T-shirt sales for the softball, baseball, and golf programs.

2. Select the range **B8:E8**. The sales volume assumption values in row 8 are the ones that you will use to determine the high enrollment and low enrollment projections. Right now, the high enrollment numbers are already entered in the workbook, so you will define the High Enrollment scenario first.

3. Click **Tools** on the menu bar, and then click **Scenarios**. The Scenario Manager dialog box opens and shows that no scenarios are currently defined.

4. Click the **Add** button, type **High Enrollment** in the Scenario name text box, and then edit the comment text to display your name and the current date (if not already specified). See Figure 1-21. The Add Scenario dialog box allows you to name the scenario, identify the changing cells, and describe the scenario. Because you selected the assumption value range of B8:E8 before you opened the Scenario Manager dialog box, those cells were already selected as the changing cells. The Collapse Dialog Box button to the right of the Changing cells range allows you to edit or add more assumption values to those already selected. The Protection options allow you to prevent changes to the scenario or to hide it, if worksheet protection is later applied.

Figure 1-21   ADD SCENARIO DIALOG BOX

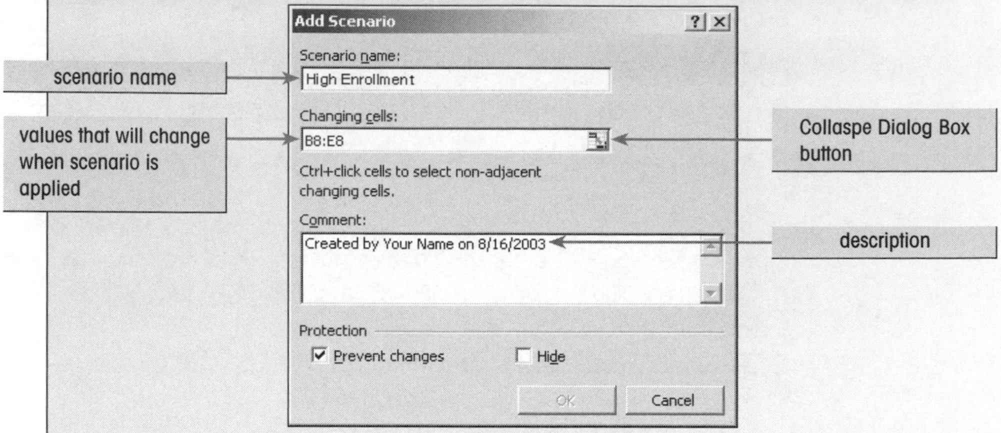

scenario name →

values that will change when scenario is applied →

Add Scenario   ? X

Scenario name:
High Enrollment

Changing cells:
B8:E8

Ctrl+click cells to select non-adjacent changing cells.

Comment:
Created by Your Name on 8/16/2003

Protection
☑ Prevent changes   ☐ Hide

OK   Cancel

← Collaspe Dialog Box button

← description

5. Click the **OK** button. The Scenario Values dialog box opens. The changing cells are listed with absolute cell references and display the values that are currently entered in those cells. Because the changing cells currently contain the values for the High Enrollment scenario, you do not need to edit them before saving them.

6. Click the **OK** button to accept the current values in the Scenario Values dialog box. The Scenario Manager dialog box redisplays with the High Enrollment scenario listed.

   Now that the High Enrollment scenario is created, you need to enter the assumption values for the low enrollment, or worst case, scenario.

7. Click the **Add** button, type **Low Enrollment** in the Scenario name text box, edit the comment text to display your name and the current date (if not already specified), and then click the **OK** button. The Scenario Values dialog box opens. It still displays the changing cells for the High Enrollment scenario with their corresponding assumption values.

   Now you will change the assumption values displayed for each changing cell so the values present the low enrollment numbers.

8. Type **50**, press the **Tab** key, type **100**, press the **Tab** key, type **40**, press the **Tab** key, and then type **30** as the low enrollment values for assumption cells B8, C8, D8, and E8. See Figure 1-22.

Figure 1-22   ENTERING THE LOW ENROLLMENT SCENARIO ASSUMPTION VALUES

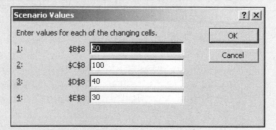

Scenario Values   ? X

Enter values for each of the changing cells.

1:    $B$8   50   OK
2:    $C$8   100   Cancel
3:    $D$8   40
4:    $E$8   30

9. Click the **OK** button to accept the new values for the Low Enrollment scenario. The Scenario Manager dialog box reappears listing both scenarios.

10. Click the **Close** button ☒ in the Scenario Manager dialog box, click cell **A1**, and then save the T-Shirts-1 workbook.

Once a scenario is created, you can return the worksheet to that set of assumption values at any time.

Now that both the Low Enrollment and High Enrollment scenarios are created, you will show Lynn how to apply a scenario.

To apply the Low Enrollment and High Enrollment scenarios to the worksheet:

1. Click **Tools** on the menu bar, click **Scenarios**, click **Low Enrollment** in the Scenarios list (if it is not already selected), click the **Show** button, and then click the **Close** button in the Scenario Manager dialog box. The low enrollment assumption values are applied to cells B8:E8 as shown in Figure 1-23.

Figure 1-23   APPLYING THE LOW ENROLLMENT SCENARIO ASSUMPTION VALUES

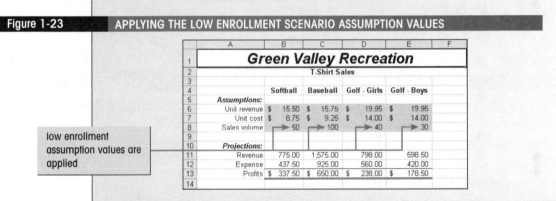

low enrollment assumption values are applied

Lynn wants a copy of the Low Enrollment scenario to study, so you will print a hard copy.

2. Print the T-Shirts-1 workbook with your name in the left section of the header.

Lynn will be presenting this information at the next board meeting and wants to begin the discussion on T-shirt revenue with the High Enrollment scenario, so you will reapply these assumption values. Depending on the discussion at the meeting, however, she can quickly apply the Low Enrollment scenario, rather than type each assumption value individually, if needed.

3. Click **Tools**, click **Scenarios**, double-click the **High Enrollment** scenario to reapply the values, and then click the **Close** button in the Scenario Manager dialog box. Double-clicking the scenario is the same as selecting the scenario and then clicking the Show button.

4. Save your changes to the workbook, and then close it.

Because the volume of T-shirt sales is highly dependent upon program participation, as well as the design of the T-shirt, you might want to create other scenarios as well. Using scenario analysis you can create as many scenarios for Lynn as she needs to save and analyze.

Weighted Criteria Analysis

Weighted criteria analysis is one of the simplest, yet most powerful, decision support models because it helps evaluate and rank alternatives that are evaluated using multiple, subjective decision criteria. For example, the following business decisions all present some degree of subjective analysis and would be good candidates to model using the weighted criteria analysis model:

- Hiring a new employee
- Promoting one employee to a new position
- Choosing a new accounting software system
- Choosing the best health insurance provider

No single quantitative value is widely available to indicate the best candidate, employee, software system, or health insurance provider. Subjective criteria, such as experience in the industry, ability to learn quickly, and personal communication style, are important parts of each decision. The weighted criteria analysis model helps you quantify and communicate the importance of subjective criteria upon the final decision. It is particularly helpful when trying to bring a group of people or a committee with various strong feelings about different subjective criteria to a consensus.

A sample weighted criteria analysis model implemented in Excel used to evaluate three candidates for a new job opportunity is shown in Figure 1-24.

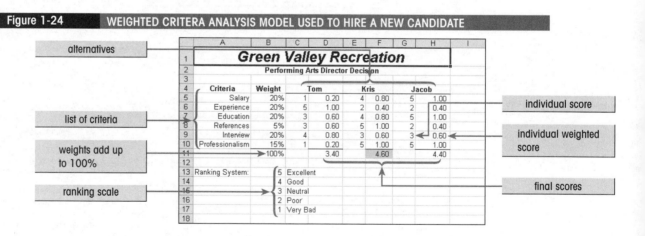

Figure 1-24   WEIGHTED CRITERA ANALYSIS MODEL USED TO HIRE A NEW CANDIDATE

The parts of a weighted criteria analysis model include the following:

- **Alternatives**, sometimes called **choices**. The goal of the weighted criteria analysis model is to help you pick the best alternative for a particular decision.
- **Criteria**. The issues you consider when making a decision.
- **Weights**. The relative importance of each criterion as they relate to each other. Weights must add up to 100%, or 100% of the issues you determine are worthy to consider in making this decision. Weights should be determined considering the relative importance of the criteria (for example, all criteria with a 20% weight should be of equal importance to the decision).
- **Ranking scale**. The scale you use for each individual score.

- **Individual score.** The number you give to each alternative as evaluated against each criterion.
- **Weighted score.** The weight for that criterion multiplied by the individual score for that alternative.
- **Final scores.** The sum total of weighted scores for that alternative.

REFERENCE WINDOW | **RW**

Creating a Weighted Criteria Analysis Model

- Identify the problem.
- Identify alternative solutions.
- Identify criteria by which to evaluate the alternative solutions.
- Weight the criteria by importance.
- Determine a ranking scale, such as 1 to 3, 1 to 5, or 1 to 10.
- Score each alternative as it relates to each criterion.
- Calculate weighted scores by multiplying the weight for each criterion by the individual score for that alternative.
- Add up the weighted scores to determine the final scores for each alternative.

As you can imagine, the majority of the work involved in using this model for a real-world business situation isn't calculating the simple formulas that are used in the final steps. The majority of the work involved in using this model is in determining which alternatives, criteria, weights, and scores should be entered. By using this model to clarify and organize your thoughts, you will not only make more logical and carefully considered decisions, you will be able to more clearly communicate that process to others.

GVR needs to expand their softball facilities. They must choose from one of these alternatives:

- Expand the current site
- Purchase land, known as Miller's Farm
- Purchase government ground formerly set aside for flood control

Lynn has organized and entered the appropriate alternatives, criteria, weights, ranking system, and scores in the Expansion-1 workbook. She wants you to complete the formulas required to make the final computations and to help determine which site is the best candidate.

To enter the formulas for the weighted criteria analysis model:

1. Open the **Expansion-1** workbook located in the Tutorial.01\Tutorial on your Data Disk. Note the weights in column B. The more important the criteria are, the larger the weight. The weights for this analysis indicate that the Initial Cost criteria, given a 40% weight, is eight times more important than Traffic, Scenery, or Dirt Work, which are all given a 5% weight. Also note the rating system in range B13:C17. As indicated by the descriptive labels in range C13:C17, 1 is very low on the scale, and 5 is the highest on the scale. The ratings in this analysis indicate that the initial cost for the "Expand Current Site" alternative is extremely high, because that item received a 1, (Terrible) rating. The Initial Cost for the "Purchase Gov. Ground" alternative is extremely low because that criterion received a 5 (Ideal) rating, giving that alternative a higher final score.

First, you will enter the formula that will calculate the individual weighted score of the Initial Cost criteria for the Expand Current Site alternative.

2. Click cell **D5** and then enter **=B5*C5** to calculate the individual weighted score.

Because you'll need to copy this formula to columns F and H, you'll change the reference for cell B5 so that it is an absolute cell reference so the references in column B will not change as the formula is copied.

3. Click cell **D5**, click **B5** in the Formula bar, press the **F4** key three times, click the **Enter** button ☑ on the Formula bar, and then examine the formula. See Figure 1-25. The final formula for cell D5 is =$B5*C5.

| Figure 1-25 | CREATING A WEIGHTED SCORE FORMULA |

mixed cell address in formula will always reference column B when the formula is copied

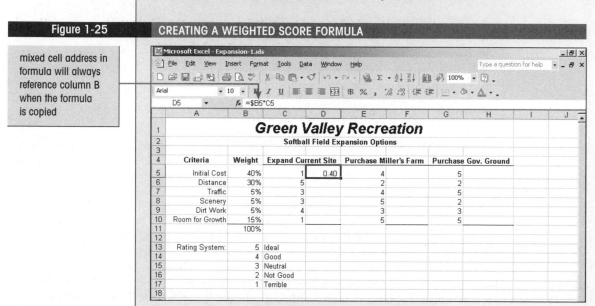

Now, as you copy this formula, the column reference for cell B5 will not be adjusted.

4. Drag the fill handle down through range **D6:D10**.

5. With range D5:D10 still selected, click the **Copy** button 🖺 on the Standard toolbar, click cell **F5**, press and hold the **Ctrl** key, click cell **H5**, and then click the **Paste** button 🖺 on the Standard toolbar.

Now that the formulas that calculate the weighted scores are properly entered into the workbook, you will total them to create final scores.

6. Click cell **D11**, click the **AutoSum** button Σ on the Standard toolbar, and then press the **Enter** key to accept =SUM(D5:D10) as the formula entry.

You will add borders to cell D11 to indicate that it is the final score for the first alternative.

7. Click cell **D11**, click the **list arrow** for the Borders button ⬚▾ on the Formatting toolbar, and then click the **Top and Double Bottom Border** option ⬚ (second row, fourth column from the left) in the border gallery.

Now that the final score for the first alternative is calculated and formatted correctly, you will copy and paste it to the final score formula and formatting to total the scores for the other two alternatives.

8. Copy cell **D11** and then paste it to cells **F11** and **H11**. See Figure 1-26.

Figure 1-26   FINAL WEIGHTED CRITERIA ANALYSIS

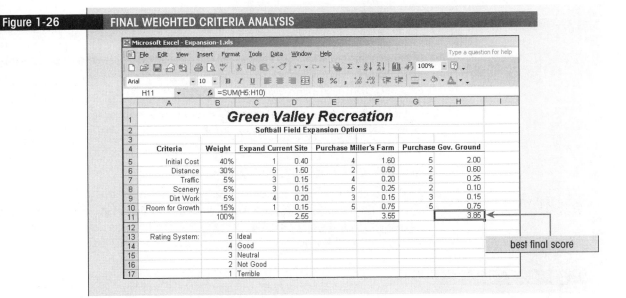

Using the 1–5 ranking scale where 5 is the "ideal," the Purchase Gov. Ground alternative appears to be the best alternative, because it has the highest final score. Although the final scores as individual numbers are not significant, the number as compared to the other final scores tells you which alternative, considering all weighed factors, is the best choice. One way to make the best final score more obvious, though, is to use conditional formatting.

Using Conditional Formatting to Highlight the Best Alternative

Conditional formatting is a way to format a cell or range of cells to enhance information depending on whether a set of conditions is true or false. Conditional formatting is especially useful when using the weighted criteria analysis model because it helps highlight the alternative with the highest score (the alternative that is best).

Lynn likes to use weighted criteria analysis to analyze the land expansion project. As she makes changes to the weights and ratings, however, she notices that sometimes the ideal alternative, the one with the highest final score, changes. She wants to know if there is a way to make the highest final score obvious at a glance. You explain that by using conditional formatting, you can apply a bright yellow fill color to the highest score, which will make the winner obvious at all times. The condition, or test that will be applied, will determine which cell (D11, F11, or H11) contains the largest number. If it is true that D11 (or F11, or H11) contains the largest value of the three, the yellow fill color will be applied to that cell.

To apply conditional formatting to the weighted criteria analysis model:

1. Click cell **D11**, click **Format** on the menu bar, and then click **Conditional Formatting**. The Conditional Formatting dialog box opens. You will use the AND function in a formula for the first condition. The **AND** function allows you to enter a number of tests and then returns a value of either TRUE or FALSE, depending on the outcome of each test. If the formula returns TRUE, the conditional format will be applied. If the formula returns FALSE, the conditional format will not be applied.

TROUBLE? If the Office Assistant appears, right-click it, and then click Hide on the shortcut menu.

In this case, you want the tests to determine if the value in cell D11 is greater than cell F11 *and* if the value in cell D11 is greater than cell H11. If both tests are true, the conditional format will be applied to cell D11.

2. Click the **list arrow** for Condition 1, click **Formula Is**, press the **Tab** key and then type **=AND(D11>F11,D11>H11)**. You have specified the condition, or the test, that must be true for the formatting to be applied.

Now you will specify the formatting.

3. Click the **Format** button, click the **Patterns** tab, click the **yellow** square (fourth row, third column) in the color palette, click the **Font** tab, click **Bold** in the Font style list, and then click the **OK** button to close the Format Cells dialog box. The first conditional format is completed. See Figure 1-27.

| Figure 1-27 | CONDITIONAL FORMATTING SPECIFIED FOR CELL D11 |

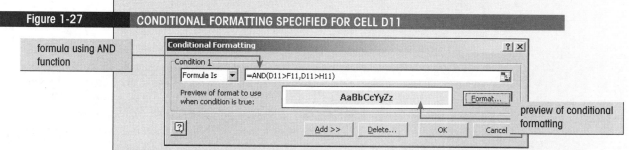

formula using AND function

preview of conditional formatting

4. Click the **OK** button to see if the selected cell meets the criterion for the conditional formatting. Because the value in cell D11 is *not* greater than the values in both cell F11 and cell H11, the conditional formatting was not applied to cell D11.

Now you will now set the conditional formatting for cell F11 to see if the value in cell F11 in greater than the values in both cell D11 and H11.

5. Click cell **F11**, click **Format**, and then click **Conditional Formatting**.

6. Click the **list arrow** for Condition 1, click **Formula Is**, press the **Tab** key, and then type **=AND(F11>D11,F11>H11)**.

7. Click the **Format** button, click **Bold** in the Font style list, click the **Patterns** tab, click the **yellow** square, click the **OK** button, and then click the **OK** button to close the Conditional Formatting dialog box. Again, because the value in cell F11 is *not* greater than the values in both cell D11 and cell H11, the conditional formatting was not applied to cell F11.

After you set the conditional formats for all three cells, you'll see how the feature improves the weighted criteria analysis model.

8. Click cell **H11**, click **Format**, and then click **Conditional Formatting**.

9. Click the **list arrow** for Condition 1, click **Formula Is**, and then press the **Tab** key and type **=AND(H11>D11,H11>F11)**.

10. Click the **Format** button, click the **yellow** square, click the **Font** tab, click **Bold** in the Font style list, click the **OK** button, and then click the **OK** button again. The yellow fill color and bold font style have been applied to cell H11 because both parts of the AND formula are true. Now, if any of the scores were changed in a way that would cause a different alternative to have the highest score, the conditional format would immediately highlight the new winner.

Lynn just learned that GVR cannot purchase the portion of the government ground they had originally wanted. The new tract of ground available from the government will more than double the initial cost. Lynn asks you to change the score from 5 to 2 for the Initial Cost criterion for the Purchase Gov. Ground alternative.

11. Click cell **G5**, type **2**, and then press the **Enter** key. The final score for the third alternative has fallen below the final score for the Purchase Miller's Farm alternative. The condition for cell F11 now returns a value of TRUE; thus the conditional formatting is applied to cell F11. See Figure 1-28.

| Figure 1-28 | USING CONDITIONAL FORMATTING TO HIGHLIGHT THE BEST ALTERNATIVE |

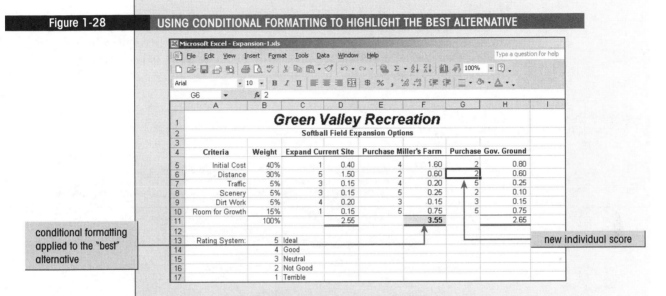

conditional formatting applied to the "best" alternative

new individual score

12. Add your name to the left section of the header, and then print the worksheet in landscape orientation.

13. Save and close the workbook, and then close Excel.

Other Applications of the Weighted Criteria Analysis Model

There is no limit to the number of business and personal decisions you face on a regular basis to which the weighted criteria analysis model can be applied. For example, sometime during your life you will probably be faced with these types of personal decisions:

- What college to attend
- What career to pursue
- Whether or not you should take a job promotion that requires a major relocation
- What house to purchase
- Where to go on vacation

From a business standpoint, you might need to make the following types of decisions at GVR:

- Which copy machine to purchase
- Which advertising agency to use
- Where to relocate the office
- What type of computer hardware or software to purchase
- Which employee should be given new responsibilities

Each example presents multiple decision considerations, or criteria, and each decision criterion should be evaluated against each possible alternative. How will you keep your thought processes organized? Use the weighted criteria analysis model. The power of the model is not in Excel's ability to quickly and accurately multiply, add, or conditionally format numbers. You can implement the weighted criteria analysis model fairly quickly using only pencil and paper, although you would have to redo the math each time you changed a weight or score. Still, the math involved in this model is very basic.

So the real power of the weighted criteria analysis isn't in the DSS tool or Excel, but in the model's great ability to organize the decision process and clearly communicate how a final decision was made. The more subjective or emotionally charged the decision, the more valuable is a tool that quantifies and validates the process used to make the final decision. Remember, two hallmarks of a good manager are the ability to make fair decisions and the ability to communicate those decisions to others. The weighted criteria analysis model will help you in both areas.

Session 1.2 QUICK CHECK

1. What Excel feature allows you to save multiple sets of what-if assumption values?

2. What are the assumption values called within the scenario analysis model?

3. In a weighted criteria analysis, how is the weighted score calculated?

4. In a weighted criteria analysis, which alternative is considered the best choice?

5. Why is the weighted criteria analysis such a powerful management tool?

SESSION 1.3

In this session, you will learn about regression analysis, a set of correlation and prediction models that help determine if one variable correlates closely with another, and if so, how to use one variable to predict another. You will create an XY scatter chart to visually present the correlation between two variables and will add trendlines to the scatter chart to help visualize the relationship between two variables. You will also add information to the scatter chart, such as the R-squared value and linear equation that best represents the data, to use in statistical analysis and prediction. Finally, you will use the FORECAST function to predict future values.

Regression Analysis

Regression analysis is used to find relationships among variables that, in turn, help predict something. You use the regression analysis tools to model any business problem in which you are seeking to determine if one variable can be used to predict another. The two variables are called the **independent variable** and the **dependent variable**. The dependent variable is the variable you are attempting to predict based on the value of the independent variable. You can use regression analysis to analyze these types of business questions:

- Does temperature have a strong relationship to sales?
- Does precipitation have a strong relationship to sales?
- Is customer age related to the types of products customers purchase?

- Does household income relate to the way an individual will vote on a particular issue?
- Does the Dow Jones average predict sales for particular products?

Linear regression determines the equation for a straight line that most closely determines how the two variables correlate. To help perform statistical analysis on data, Excel provides about 70 special statistical functions that range in complexity from AVERAGE to STDEV (standard deviation) to POISSON (Poisson distribution). In addition, Excel provides the **Analysis ToolPak**, an additional set of data analysis tools to complete complex statistical and engineering analyses that include such tools as Anova, exponential smoothing, and Fourier analysis. For many typical business problems, however, applying a simple scatter chart and basic correlation analysis for two variables can provide tremendous value.

Using the XY (Scatter) Chart

An **XY** or **scatter chart** is a chart that enables you to graph two variables, one on the x-axis and one on the y-axis, to visually determine if a strong correlation exists between the two variables. It is a helpful tool when your business problem involves determining if there is a correlation between two variables in order to make a prediction. If the plotted points form a straight line, a linear relationship exists between the two variables, as shown in Figure 1-29.

Figure 1-29	SCATTER CHART OF A LINEAR RELATIONSHIP

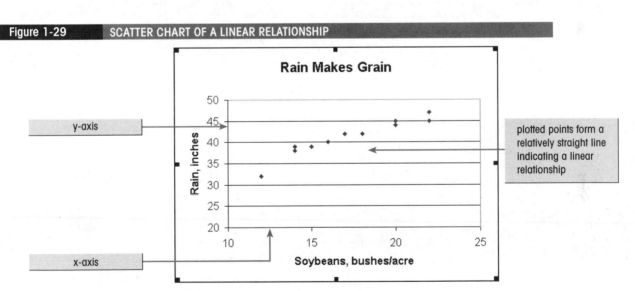

Creating a Scatter Chart
- Select the cells that contain the x- and y-axis variables that you want to chart.
- Click the Chart Wizard button on the Standard toolbar.
- Click XY (Scatter) in the Chart type list in the first Chart Wizard dialog box.
- Step through the remaining Chart Wizard dialog boxes to further define and complete the scatter chart.
- Click the Finish button.

One of the biggest management issues at GVR during the summer months is providing an adequate staff at the golf course and swimming pool facilities. Depending on the weather, GVR might need from 10 to 50 employees at each facility. Although GVR maintains a base staff of employees at each facility each day no matter how much the weather does or does not cooperate, they also have the ability to call in seasonal help on a daily basis as needed. Right now their daily staffing decisions are largely based on the personal feelings of the facility managers. Although the facility managers do a great job of hiring enough staff to support the patrons, at times they run into unexpected staff shortages or slow periods when money is wasted.

Lynn needs to present to the GVR Board of Directors an approach to staffing that is more efficient and equitable. You explain to Lynn that you can use Excel as a regression analysis tool to analyze the variables of temperature and attendance. If there is a high correlation between the two variables, Lynn will suggest that GVR facility managers use this information to help plan the appropriate staff levels needed.

To create a scatter chart using the pool statistics:

1. If you took a break at the end of the last session, start Excel and then open the **PoolStats-1** workbook located in the Tutorial.01\Tutorial folder on your Data Disk. This workbook contains the high temperatures and pool attendance levels for the months of June, July, and August of the year 2002. See Figure 1-30.

Figure 1-30   **TEMPERATURE AND ATTENDANCE STATISTICS FOR GVR POOL**

independent variables — dependent variables

	A	B	C	D	E	F	G	H
1			*Green Valley Recreation*					
2			2002 Pool Statistics					
3								
4	Date	High Temp	Attendance					
5	6/1/2002	85	560					
6	6/2/2002	88	565					
7	6/3/2002	88	599					
8	6/4/2002	86	604					
9	6/5/2002	80	600					
10	6/6/2002	78	488					
11	6/7/2002	79	489					
12	6/8/2002	81	499					
13	6/9/2002	82	523					
14	6/10/2002	82	555					
15	6/11/2002	84	548					
16	6/12/2002	84	598					
17	6/13/2002	85	597					
18	6/14/2002	84	585					
19	6/15/2002	80	572					
20	6/16/2002	79	463					
21	6/17/2002	82	536					
22	6/18/2002	84	524					
23	6/19/2002	85	555					

2002Data / Sheet2 / Sheet3 /

The High Temp variable is the independent variable, and the attendance values are the dependent variable. If you find a high correlation between these two variables, you will be able use this information to predict future attendance based on weather forecasts and to provide a more appropriate and cost-effective staffing level for the GVR pool.

2. Select the range **B5:C96**, and then click the **Chart Wizard** button 📊 on the Standard toolbar. The first Chart Wizard dialog box opens. In this dialog box, you select an appropriate chart type and if necessary a subtype.

3. Click **XY (Scatter)** in the Chart type list, and then click the **Next** button. The second wizard dialog box presents a preview of your chart, as shown in Figure 1-31.

Figure 1-31   **SECOND CHART WIZARD DIALOG BOX**

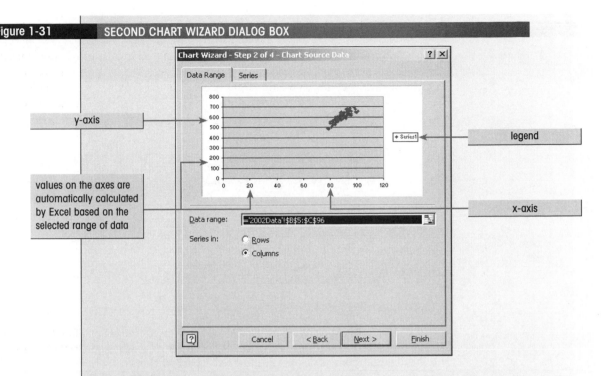

At this point, the chart doesn't appear very valuable. One of the reasons that the data is hard to read is that both the x-axis and y-axis scales start at 0, yet there is no data plotted between 0 and 60 on the x-axis, and there is no data plotted between 0 and 400 on the y-axis. You can change the scale and other chart elements to more clearly present the data after you complete the Chart Wizard, but first you need to complete the rest of the steps of the Chart Wizard.

4. Click the **Next** button, click in the Chart title text box, and then type **Does temperature predict attendance?**

5. Click in the Value (X) axis text box, and then type **Temp - Fahrenheit**.

6. Click in the Value (Y) axis text box, and then type **Attendance**. The preview of the chart changes to show the titles you have entered.

Since the legend doesn't provide any additional information for this chart, you will remove it.

7. Click the **Legend** tab, click the **Show legend** check box to deselect the option, removing it from the chart area, and then click the **Next** button. The fourth and final wizard dialog box appears.

You want to put the chart on a separate sheet in the workbook so that it will be easy for Lynn to find and print.

8. Click the **As new sheet** option button, and then click **Finish**. The final scatter chart appears on its own sheet, as shown in Figure 1-32. If the Chart toolbar automatically appears, dock it on the left side of the screen for now.

Figure 1-32   SCATTER CHART

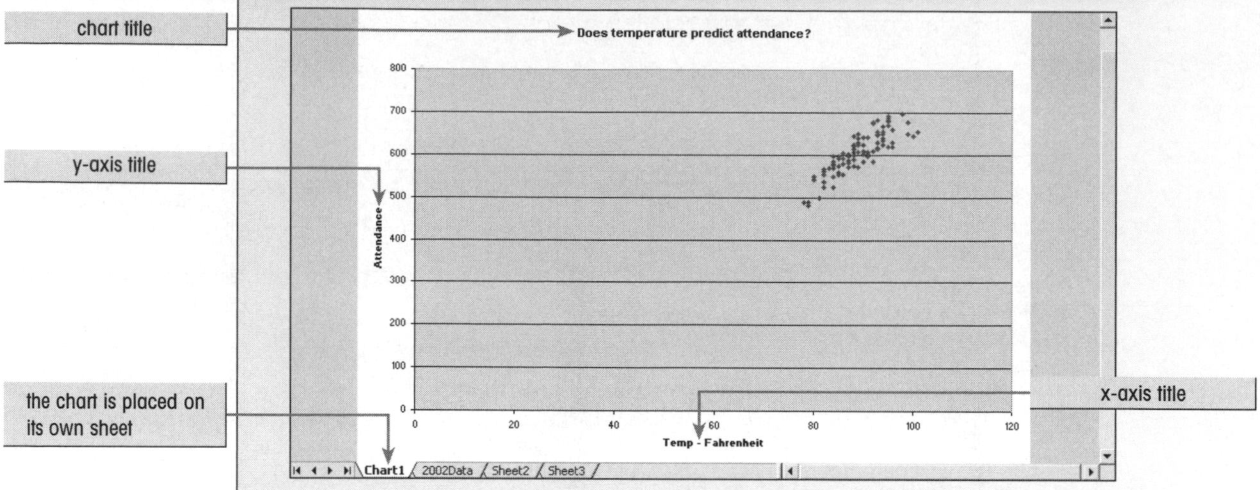

chart title

y-axis title

the chart is placed on
its own sheet

x-axis title

Does temperature predict attendance?

Temp - Fahrenheit

Chart1 / 2002Data / Sheet2 / Sheet3 /

Right now, the data points are crowded in the upper-right corner of the graph. To better see the relationship between the temperature and attendance values, you will modify the x-axis and y-axis scales to eliminate the part of the axes where no data is plotted. This modification will give the existing data more room to "stretch out" across the graph, making it easier to determine if there is a relationship between the variables.

To modify the scatter chart:

1. Double-click any value on the x-axis to open the Format Axis dialog box.

   The minimum temperature that you need to accommodate the data on the chart is 70 degrees Fahrenheit. Therefore, you will use 70 as the starting value for the x-axis.

2. Click the **Scale** tab, double-click **0** in the Minimum text box, and then type **70**. See Figure 1-33. Note that the values on your screen may differ.

Figure 1-33   FORMAT AXIS DIALOG BOX

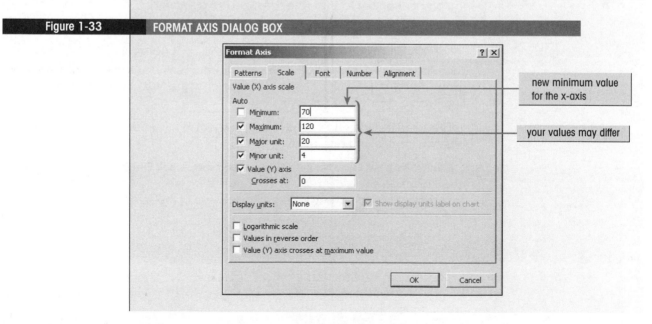

new minimum value
for the x-axis

your values may differ

You will also increase the font size of the values on the x-axis.

3. Click the **Font** tab, scroll and click **14** in the Size list, and then click the **OK** button.

Now that the x-axis is formatted in a way that makes the data much easier to read, you will work on the y-axis.

4. Double-click any value on the **y-axis** to open the Format Axis dialog box.

Because the minimum attendance that you need to accommodate on the chart is 400 people, you will start the y-axis with this value.

5. Click the **Scale** tab, double-click **0** in the Minimum text box, and then type **400**.

You will change the font size of the values on the y-axis to 14, too.

6. Click the **Font** tab, scroll and click **14** in the Size list, and then click the **OK** button.

As a final formatting improvement, you will increase the size of the chart title and change the color of the plot area so that the data points are easier to view.

7. Click the chart title, click the **list arrow** for the Font Size button 10 ⌄ on the Formatting toolbar, and then click **20**.

8. Click the plot area, click the **list arrow** for the Fill Color button ⌄ on the Formatting toolbar, and then click the **white** square (lower-right corner) in the color palette. See Figure 1-34.

Figure 1-34   FORMATTED SCATTER CHART

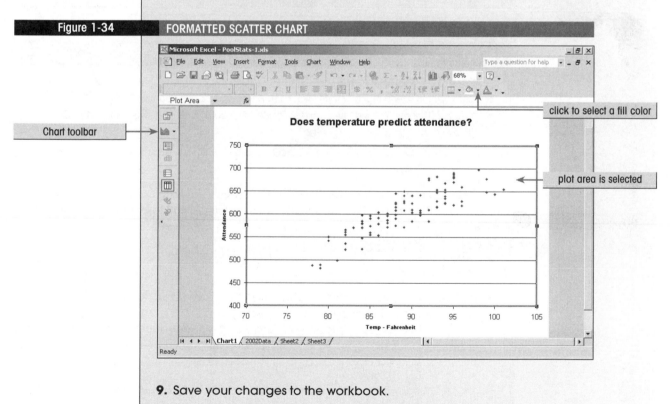

9. Save your changes to the workbook.

The formatted scatter chart now shows the individual temperature and attendance data points much more clearly. You can see that the two variables have a linear relationship because the data points are roughly arranged along a straight line. The relationship between temperature and attendance, however, isn't a perfect linear correlation because the points don't form a straight line.

Determining Correlation

The strength or the degree of the relationship is called **correlation**. You can use a scatter chart to determine correlation by applying a **trendline**, the line that most closely resembles the relationship between the data points on the chart. You can also add the R-squared value to a scatter chart to help determine whether one variable predicts another. The **R-squared value** is a statistical measurement of the strength of correlation between the two points and ranges from 0 to 1. An R-squared value close to 0 means that there is no correlation between the two variables. The scatter chart for variables with a very low R-squared value would look like a random series of dots dropped on the chart. An R-squared value close to 1 means that there is a very high degree of correlation between the two variables. If there is any sort of "pattern" to the dots (line or curve), there is some sort of correlation between the two variables. The data points on a scatter chart for variables with a linear relationship and a very high R-squared value would simulate a straight line.

REFERENCE WINDOW

Adding a Linear Trendline to a Scatter Chart
- Right-click the data points, and then click Add Trendline on the shortcut menu.
- Select the type of trendline that you want to add to the scatter chart.
- Click the OK button.

REFERENCE WINDOW

Adding the R-squared Value to a Scatter Chart
- Right-click the trendline, and then click Format Trendline on the shortcut menu.
- Click the Options tab, and then click the Display R-squared value on chart check box to select it.
- Click the OK button.

To help show more clearly the correlation between the temperatures and the attendance, you will add a linear trendline to the scatter chart for the 2002 pool data statistics.

To add a linear trendline and R-squared value to the scatter chart:

1. Right-click any one of the data points in the diagram, and then click **Add Trendline** on the shortcut menu. The Add Trendline dialog box opens, as shown in Figure 1-35. Depending on your knowledge of advanced mathematical and statistical operations, you can apply many different types of regression lines. In this case, you will apply the default linear trendline.

   TROUBLE? There are many elements on a chart, and sometimes it is difficult to select the specific item you want to examine. If the Add Trendline option does not appear on the shortcut menu, press the Esc key or click away from the shortcut menu to close it, and then try Step 1 again.

Figure 1-35   ADD TRENDLINE DIALOG BOX

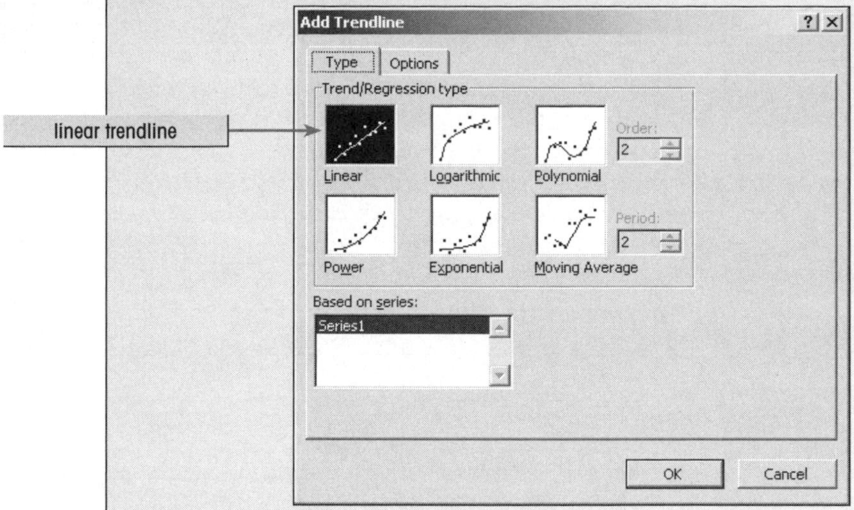

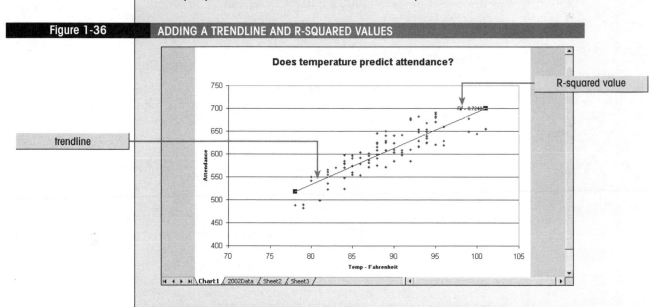

linear trendline

2. Click the **Options** tab to view the other options available when applying the trendline.

3. Click the **Display R-squared value on chart** check box to select it, and then click the **OK** button. See Figure 1-36. A trendline and R-squared value are displayed on the scatter chart, but the R-squared value is hard to read.

Figure 1-36   ADDING A TRENDLINE AND R-SQUARED VALUES

R-squared value

trendline

4. Click the **R-squared value**. Clicking the R-squared value is like clicking any other object on a chart. The R-squared value appears in a text box with selection handles.

5. Click the **list arrow** for the Font Size button 10 on the Formatting toolbar, and then click **14**.

6. Point to the border of the R-squared value text box (between the selection handles), drag it down so that it is clearly visible, and then click on the gray edge that surrounds the chart so that no chart element is selected. See Figure 1-37.

| Figure 1-37 | SCATTER CHART WITH LINEAR TRENDLINE AND R-SQUARED VALUE |

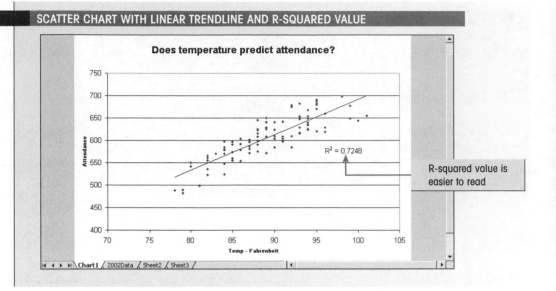

Although an R-squared value above 0.9 is generally viewed as a "very strong correlation" between two variables and can be used to make confident predictions, the value of 0.7248 does indicate a positive correlation between the two variables. A positive correlation means that you can use this information to help predict attendance. The closer the R-squared value is to 1, the more confident you can be about your prediction. Lynn will show this diagram to the Board to show how adequate staffing can be improved using correlation statistics such as this.

Making Predictions

Now that you've charted the temperature and attendance variables as a scatter chart, applied a linear trendline, and calculated the R-squared statistic that indicates that the correlation between the two variables is fairly strong, you can use additional Excel features to make future predictions.

A straight line can be defined by the general mathematical formula $y = mx + b$, where y is the variable you are attempting to predict (in this case, attendance), m is the slope of the line (how fast it goes up or down), x is the variable you know (in this case, temperature), and b is the y-intercept, or the point at which the line would cross the y-axis if x were equal to 0. Fortunately, you don't have to know or remember many rules of math in order to predict future attendance at the GVR pool, but sometimes background information does help you understand how the calculation is made. Just like the R-squared value, the equation that defines the line can be added to the scatter chart by modifying trendline options.

REFERENCE WINDOW   **RW**

Adding the Straight Line Equation to a Trendline
- Right-click the trendline, and then click Format Trendline on the shortcut menu.
- Click the Options tab, and then click the Display equation on the chart check box to select it.
- Click the OK button.

Now that you know that temperature and attendance have a strong correlation, Lynn wants to know if there is an easy way to predict attendance based on temperature. If so, then facility managers can predict attendance and make better staffing decisions. You explain that using the $y = mx + b$ equation to the trendline gives you the formula you need to make such predictions.

To add the straight line equation to the trendline:

1. Right-click the **trendline**, and then click **Format Trendline** on the shortcut menu.

2. Click the **Options** tab (if it's not already selected), click the **Display equation on chart** check box to select it, and then click the **OK** button. The equation *y = 7.926x - 99.944* appears just above the R-squared value. See Figure 1-38. This equation describes the linear trendline created by this set of data points. In this equation, *x* represents temperature in degrees Fahrenheit and *y* represents attendance.

Figure 1-38	STRAIGHT LINE EQUATION ADDED TO LINEAR TRENDLINE

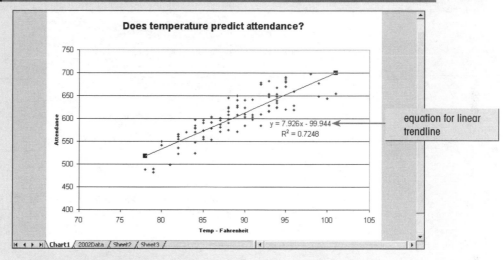

To demonstrate to Lynn how she can use this equation to predict future attendance based on predicted temperatures, you will first transfer this formula to Sheet2 and then set up the worksheet to predict the temperature for tomorrow as an example.

To use the linear equation to predict the temperature for the next day:

1. Select the **y = 7.926x - 99.944** formula within the text box (do *not* select the text box, but the formula within the text box), and then click the **Copy** button on the Standard toolbar.

2. Click the **Sheet2** tab, make sure cell A1 is the active cell, and then click the **Paste** button on the Standard toolbar.

   With the formula entered in cell A1, you can easily isolate the *m* (slope) and *b* (y-intercept) values, which you will modify.

3. Click cell **A2** and type **m**, click cell **B2** and type **7.926**, click cell **A3** and type **b**, and then click cell **B3** and type **-99.944**. Be sure to enter the *b* value in cell B3 with a leading negative sign (–).

Now you will add some labels to the worksheet to clarify the information.

4. Click cell **A5**, type **Date**, click cell **B5**, type **Forecasted Temp**, click cell **C5**, type **Predicted Attendance**, and then widen all columns so that all information in each cell is visible.

Your favorite weather forecaster claims that tomorrow's high temperature will be 85 degrees Fahrenheit. You will use this information to predict attendance based on that temperature.

5. Click cell **A6**, type the date for tomorrow, click cell **B6**, type **85**, click cell **C6**, enter **=B2*B6+B3**, and then if necessary click cell **C6** to examine the formula in the Formula bar. See Figure 1-39. According to this calculation, you can expect between 573 and 574 people to come to the pool if the temperature is 85.

| Figure 1-39 | USING THE LINEAR EQUATION TO MAKE A PREDICTION |

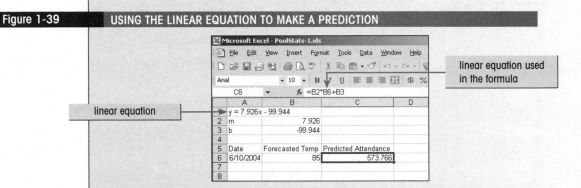

TROUBLE? If your formula didn't calculate correctly, make sure that you entered the *b* value as a negative 99.944 rather than as a positive number.

6. Save your changes to the workbook.

The formula that you used predicted that about 574 people would come to the pool if the temperature were 85 degrees Fahrenheit. Although this calculation is correct, Lynn thinks the process is somewhat tedious. Also, if she had to change or correct any of the initial 2002 values on the 2002Data worksheet that were used to create this prediction, the linear equation that describes the relationships between these two variables would change. The prediction you just made to determine how many people would come to the pool on an 85-degree day, however, would not. She asks you if there is another way to simplify predicting the attendance based on the linear equation. Fortunately, Excel provides a function that solves these problems. It is appropriately called the FORECAST function.

The FORECAST Function

The **FORECAST** function uses linear regression to predict future values given an existing set of x-axis and y-axis values. In other words, the function also uses the $y = mx + b$ linear equation model to predict a future value. The function, however, has two important benefits over the method you just used to predict pool attendance. You don't need to know or enter the slope (*m*) or y-intercept (*b*) values into the worksheet, and the FORECAST function is tied directly back to the original x- and y- variables. This means that if any of the original x- or y-axis data changes, the FORECAST function automatically recalculates, providing a new and updated forecast.

The general structure of the FORECAST function is *FORECAST(x value, known y values, known x values)*. You'll use the FORECAST function to predict attendance for a temperature of 85 degrees. For an 85-degree forecast, the function should return the same attendance prediction, 573 to 574, as you calculated manually.

Lynn wants to see how the FORECAST function works, so you will enter a formula using this function on a separate worksheet in the current workbook.

To use the FORECAST function:

1. Click the **Sheet3** tab, enter **Temp** in cell A1, enter **Attendance** in cell B1, enter **85** in cell A2, and then click cell **B2**.

   Now you will enter the formula that will forecast the attendance figure based on the historical temperature in column C and attendance statistics in column B on the 2002Data sheet.

2. Enter **=FORECAST(A2,'2002Data'!C5:C96,'2002Data'!B5:B96)** in cell B2, and then if necessary click cell **B2** to examine the formula in the Formula bar. See Figure 1-40. The formula calculated an answer between 573 and 574, the same number that you predicted using the actual linear equation.

| Figure 1-40 | USING THE FORECAST FUNCTION |

cell A2 contains the temperature value for which the forecast will be made

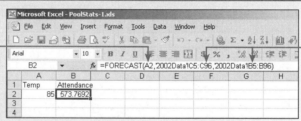

the known *y* and *x* vales are cell references located on the 2002Data worksheet

Now you will modify the workbook to extend the temperature values and FORECAST formula so that you have a predicted attendance for temperatures between 75 and 105 degrees Fahrenheit.

3. Enter **75** in cell A2, and then enter **76** in cell A3.

4. Select range **A2:A3**, and then drag the fill handle down across the range **A4:A32** so that the temperatures from 75 through 105 degrees are entered in column A.

   Now you will copy the formula in column B through cell B32 to calculate the forecast for the temperatures in column A. First, though, you have to change the known *x* and *y* values cell references to absolute references so that they do not change as you copy the formula.

5. Click cell **B2**, click **C5** in the Formula bar, press the **F4** key, click **C96** in the Formula bar, press the **F4** key, click **B5** in the Formula bar, press the **F4** key, click **B96** in the Formula bar, press the **F4** key, and then press the **Enter** key.

6. Click cell **B2** again so that you can examine the updated formula in the Formula bar. See Figure 1-41.

Figure 1-41   FORECAST FORMULA WITH ABSOLUTE CELL REFERENCES

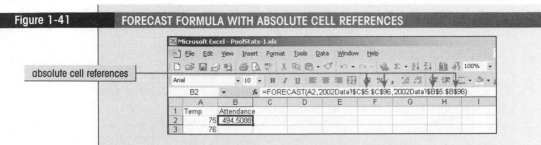

absolute cell references

7. Drag the fill handle down across the range **B3:B32** so that the FORECAST formula is copied for all temperatures.

To make the attendance numbers easier to read, you will format the cells using the Comma Style and not display digits to the right of the decimal point.

8. With the range B2:B32 still selected, click the **Comma Style** button on the Formatting toolbar, and then click the **Decrease Decimal** button on the Formatting toolbar twice to format the forecasted attendance values as whole numbers.

You will also change the tab names to more accurately reflect their contents.

9. Double-click the **Sheet2** tab, type **Linear Equation**, and then press the **Enter** key.

10. Double-click the **Sheet3** tab, type **Forecast**, and then press the **Enter** key.

The benefit of using the FORECAST function is that it is tied back to the original x-axis and y-axis values, so if that data is updated or corrected, the FORECAST formulas will be updated as well. Lynn wants you to correct the attendance number for June 30. Instead of 645, the number should be 605. The value is in cell C34 on the 2002Data worksheet.

To update the known y-axis values and observe the impact on the FORECAST function:

1. Click the **2002Data** tab, click cell **C34**, type **605**, and then press the **Enter** key.

Now you will check the chart to see if the FORECAST formula has been updated.

2. Click the **Chart1** tab, and if a chart element is still selected, click on the gray area beside the chart so that you can clearly see the equation and R-squared value on the chart. Because the chart is tied to the data on the 2002Data worksheet and the linear equation and R-squared value are tied to the chart, both the equation and R-squared value have automatically changed. See Figure 1-42. The new R-squared value, 0.7335, shows a higher correlation between temperature and attendance than the old value of 0.7248. This means that you can be slightly more confident of the values on the Forecast tab as well.

Figure 1-42   **UPDATED LINEAR EQUATION AND R-SQUARED VALUE**

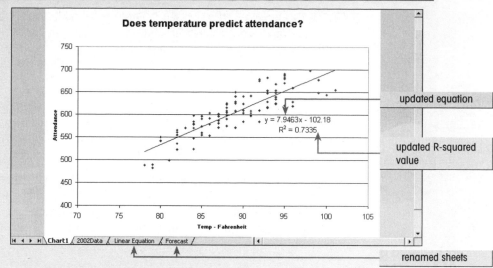

3. Save your changes to the workbook, add your name to the left section of the header on the Chart1 sheet, and then print the chart.

Other Types of Trendlines

The Add Trendline dialog box provides other types of trendlines that can be used to describe a set of data including Logarithmic, Polynomial, Power, Exponential, and Moving Average (see Figure 1-43). Each of these trendlines (except Moving Average) will calculate an R-squared value, and each can display the R-squared value and associated equation used to describe the line and predict *y* values.

Figure 1-43   **ADD TRENDLINE DIALOG BOX**

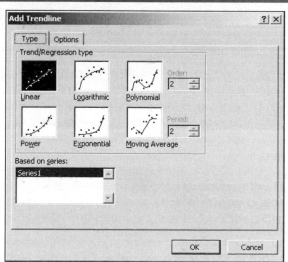

REFERENCE WINDOW   **RW**

Changing the Type of Trendline Displayed on a Scatter Chart
- Right-click the existing trendline, and then click Format Trendline on the shortcut menu; or if no trendline currently exists, right-click the data points, and then click Add Trendline on the shortcut menu.
- Click the Type tab.
- Click the new Trend\Regression type that you want to display in the scatter chart.
- Click the OK button.

Although attendance at the pool is fairly well described with a linear equation because attendance increases with the temperature, attendance at the golf course might also rise with the temperature, but then drop off as the temperature gets too hot. You will show Lynn how a scatter chart in which the dots create a curved line might be a better way to present the data.

To change the type of trendline used on the scatter chart:

1. Right-click the **trendline** and then click **Format Trendline** on the shortcut menu.

2. Click the **Type** tab, click the **Power** type, and then click the **OK** button. The new trendline is applied to the scatter chart, and the equation that describes it uses the exponent x to the 1.1981th power. Just like the linear equation, the power trendline equation can be used to predict future values. The R-squared value for this trendline is 0.7446, which is slightly higher than when the data was described with a simple linear equation, so the prediction made with the power trendline equation, is slightly more reliable than that made with the linear equation. You decide to compare the forecasts made with the linear equation to those made with the power trendline equation.

3. Click the **Forecast** tab, click cell **C1**, type **Power**, and then press the **Enter** key.

    To make a forecast using the power trendline equation, you will have to enter a formula directly in the worksheet. There is no Excel function that calculates the forecast using the Power equation as the FORECAST function did for the linear equation.

4. In cell C2, enter **=2.7901*A2^1.1981**, press the **Enter** key, and format the result in C2 using a comma style with no digits to the right of the decimal place. Examine the formula in the Formula bar as shown in Figure 1-44. The attendance forecast using the Power trendline equation is 492, two less than the forecast using linear trendline equation, 494.

Figure 1-44 | **FORECASTING WITH THE POWER TRENDLINE EQUATION**

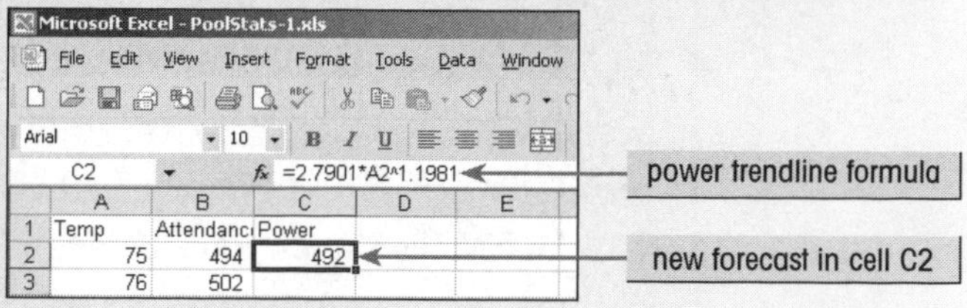

Now you will format and copy the new formula through the entire range of temperatures.

5. Drag the fill handle down through the range **C3:C32**.

The new forecast using the power trendline equation with the higher R-squared value provides a slightly better forecast for this set of data. If you changed the original *x* and *y* values, however, you would have to reenter the formulas in column C of the Forecast worksheet because that formula is not directly tied back to the original data (as opposed to the Forecast Linear trendline formulas entered in column B, which would automatically recalculate if the original *x* and *y* values were changed).

6. Add your name to the left section of the Forecast worksheet, save the workbook and then print it.

7. Close the workbook, and then exit Excel.

Regression analysis is a very powerful model because it helps determine the degree to which one variable influences another. Given a strong relationship determined by the R-squared calculation, an equation can be created that helps predict values. Based on these predictions, a wide variety of better business decisions can be made. For example, you might use regression analysis to help determine if these types of variables are related at GVR:

- Is education level related to the types of programs individuals participate in?
- Do advertising dollars spent in radio affect certain activities more than others?
- How does the distance the participant has to drive to the activity affect participation?

When you find a strong correlation between two variables, you can then use the equation that best describes that line to make future predictions. When you can confidently predict business outcomes from attendance or purchasing tendencies, you can spend advertising, payroll, and other business expenses in the areas that have the greatest positive impact. Regression analysis is at the heart of some very powerful business trends today, such as data mining. **Data mining** is the process of finding previously unknown correlations between variables for the purpose of making better business decisions.

A scatter chart helps to visually present the data points of two variables. Using Excel to create a scatter chart also allows you to apply the R-squared statistic and equation for many different types of trendlines, such as linear, logarithmic, and power. If you find a linear relationship among the variables, you can use the FORECAST function to predict future values.

Session 1.3 QUICK CHECK

1. In a regression analysis, what is the relationship between the independent and dependent variable?

2. What are the primary and secondary goals of regression analysis?

3. An XY chart is also called a(n) _____ chart.

4. If one variable has a strong influence on another, the variables are said to have a strong _____ .

5. An R-squared value of 0.95 would indicate what?

6. What is the general equation for a straight line, and what does each part of the equation mean?

7. What function can be used to predict values for a linear equation?

8. Other than a linear trendline, what other types of trendlines can Excel apply to a set of data points on a scatter chart?

REVIEW ASSIGNMENTS

The GVR Board of Directors has several decisions to make, and Lynn wants your help to model and analyze the necessary information in Excel. She has entered some of the raw data into an Excel workbook.

First, Lynn wants you to use a what-if analysis to project GVR income and expense values for the next several years. She also wants you to create the best case and worst case scenarios for this projected growth. Lynn also needs to determine which candidate is best qualified for the summer head lifeguard position. She wants your help to do a weighted criteria analysis for this decision. Finally, Lynn needs some help analyzing the correlation between the amount of radio ads and the revenue generated by those ads. She has the data for a linear regression study, but needs your help to finish it.

To complete this task:

1. Start Excel and open the **Analysis-1** workbook located in the Tutorial.01\Review folder on your Data Disk. The Growth worksheet presents a summarized income and expense what-if analysis projection for GVR through the year 2011.

2. Examine the formulas in the range B8:C15. Right now, the formulas contain assumption values. The assumption values are also entered in cells B2 and B3.

3. Edit the formulas in cell B8 and cell C8 so the formulas use cell references instead of raw data to calculate the expected income and expenses values for the year 2004.

4. Copy the updated formula in cell B8 through the range B9:B15 and the formula in cell C8 through the range C9:C15. Examine the formulas in cell B8 and C8, and then edit them to use mixed or absolute cell addresses so that when you copy the formulas, the correct formula is entered through row 15.

5. Copy the formulas in cells B8:C8 through row 15. Although there isn't any noticeable difference in the values that display on the worksheet, enter 10% in cell B2 and then enter 10% in cell B3. If your formulas are correct, the projected 2011 income should be 384 and the projected 2011 expenses should be 234.

6. Select cells B2 and B3, and create a scenario with the name "Aggressive Growth." Modify the values of the changing cell so the value for cell B2 is 15% (0.15) and the value for cell B3 is 9% (0.09).

7. Add another scenario with the name "Slow Growth." Modify the values for the changing cell B2 so the value for cell B2 is 10% (0.10). The value for cell B3 should remain at 9% (0.09).

Explore

8. In the Scenario Manager dialog box, click the Summary button, select the range B15:C15 on the workbook as the Result cells, and then click the OK button. Excel creates a new worksheet with the name "Scenario Summary." The scenario names are displayed in row 3. It's easier to understand the report if the cell references in column C are replaced with descriptive labels. You will enter formulas in cell C6, C7, C9, and C10 of the Scenario Summary worksheet to link to labels used on the Growth worksheet.

Explore

9. Click cell C6 on the Scenario Summary worksheet, type = (an equal sign to begin the formula), click the Growth tab, click cell A2, and then press the Enter key. Using this method, enter a formula in cell C7 of the Scenario Summary worksheet that references cell A3 on the Growth worksheet, in cell C9 of the Scenario Summary worksheet that references cell B6 of the Growth worksheet, and in cell C10 of the Scenario Summary worksheet that references cell C6 of the Growth worksheet. Resize column C so that all labels are completely visible.

10. On the Scenario Summary worksheet, enter your name in the left section of the header. Enter "Projections for the year 2011" in the right section of the header, and then print the worksheet.

11. Display the formulas on the Growth worksheet, and then print the range A1:C15 with gridlines and column and row headings displayed and your name in the left section of the header.

12. Switch to the Lifeguard worksheet, and then examine the weighted criteria analysis worksheet. This worksheet will help determine which candidate will be hired for the summer head lifeguard position.

13. Enter the following values for the three candidates:

    C3: Teresa
    E3: Slim
    G3: Aaron

14. Enter the following values as the weights for each criteria item:

    B4: 20%
    B5: 20%
    B6: 10%
    B7: 20%
    B8: 30%

15. Enter a formula in cell B9 that calculates the total weights in the range B4:B8.

16. Based on the information in Figure 1-45, enter appropriate individual scores for each candidate. Enter Teresa's scores in the range C4:C8, Slim's in range E4:E8, and Aaron's in range G4:G8. (*Hint*: The specific individual score isn't as important as how it relates to the scores for other candidates. For example, Aaron should receive the highest individual score for the Credentials category because he has the most credentials. Teresa's and Slim's scores in that category should be the same.)

Figure 1-45

	Teresa	Slim	Aaron
Experience	Worked as a lifeguard at the city pool for three summers	Worked as a lifeguard at the city pool for one summer	None
Credentials	Water Safety Instructor	Water Safety Instructor	Water Safety Instructor CPR Certified
References	Average	Excellent	Excellent
Swim Test	Average	Excellent	Average
Interview	Late for interview; no eye contact; sullen attitude	On time for interview; average communication skills	On time for interview; excellent communication skills

17. In the ranges D4:D8, F4:F8, and H4:H8, enter the appropriate formulas to multiply the individual scores by the appropriate weights. (*Hint*: If you reference in range B4:B8 using an absolute cell reference for column B (that is $B4, $B5, $B6, $B7, and $B8) in the formulas you create for range D4:D8, copying and pasting the formulas to ranges F4:F8 and H4:H8 for the other two candidates will be easier.)

18. In cells D9, F9, and H9, enter the appropriate formulas to determine the final scores for the three candidates.

19. Apply conditional formatting cells D9, F9, and H9 so that the largest value of the three is formatted with bold text and a yellow fill color.

20. Change the criteria weights so that Credentials are worth 10% and the Swim Test is worth 30%, display the formulas on the worksheet, and then print the worksheet in landscape orientation.

21. Switch to the Advertising worksheet, and then create an XY scatter chart using the range B4:B15 as the x-axis values and the range C4:C15 as the y-axis values. Enter "Does airtime affect sales?" as the chart title, and then enter "Radio Ads" as the x-axis title. Place the chart on the Advertising worksheet.

22. Move the chart to the right of the data on the worksheet and enlarge the chart to comfortably fit on the screen. Delete the legend. Modify the x-axis so that the scale starts at 40. Modify the y-axis so that the scale starts at 300,000.

23. Add a linear trendline, the linear equation, and the R-squared value to the scatter chart.

24. In cell C16, use the FORECAST function to forecast revenue for the x-axis value of 100 in cell B16.

25. Enter your name in the left section of the header, and then print the Advertising worksheet in landscape orientation.

26. Save and close the workbook, and then exit Excel.

| CASE PROBLEMS |

Case 1. Using What-If Analysis to Analyze New Business Profits As a business analyst for a small company, you've been asked by the president and CFO (Chief Financial Officer) to create some profit projections for a new business opportunity. You will use Excel to create a what-if analysis to analyze projected profits. Then you will save various scenarios based on the assumptions that both the president and CFO want to analyze, so that you can reapply assumption values quickly when you meet with them.

To complete this task:

1. Start Excel and open the **ProfitLoss-1** workbook from the Tutorial.01\Cases folder on your Data Disk.

2. Display the formulas on the workbook and notice that many cells including the ranges D4:G4, D6:G8, and C10:G10 (rows 4, 6, 7, 8, and 10) contain assumption values that need to be corrected.

3. Enter your name in the left section of the header, use the scaling option to scale the printout to 1 page, and then print the formulas in landscape orientation.

Explore 4. Redisplay the values, and then using the information from the printout, in cells B4, B6, B7, B8, and B10, enter the appropriate percentages at which the values are currently growing. Use a % (percent sign) format. (*Hint*: The percentages at which the values are currently growing are correct, but they are now entered with raw values within the formulas in that row.)

Explore 5. Edit the formulas in the range D4:G4 to include cell references rather than assumption values in the formulas. Use absolute or mixed cell references to make it easier to copy the formulas to rows 6, 7, and 8. (*Hint*: Refer to Figure 1-2 for a similar example.)

6. Copy the formula in cell D4 to the range E4:G4, and then copy the formulas in range D4:G4 to the ranges D6:G6, D7:G7, and D8:G8.

Explore 7. In cell C10, edit the formula that calculates the appropriate tax liability to include a cell reference. Use an absolute or mixed cell reference in the formula to make it easier to copy C10 to the range D10:G10.

8. Copy the formula in cell C10 to the range D10:G10.

9. Print the worksheet with the updated formulas displayed in landscape orientation.

Explore 10. Save the current scenario with the name "President". The changing cells are B4, B6:B8, and B10, and the current values should be saved.

11. Add another scenario with the name "CFO". Use the same changing cells with these values:
    $B$4: 0.20
    $B$6: 0.25
    $B$7: 0.25
    $B$8: 0.1
    $B$10: 0.33

12. Show the CFO scenario, and then print the updated worksheet in landscape orientation.

13. Save and close the workbook, and then exit Excel.

Case 2. Using Weighted Criteria Analysis to Help Plan Your Career Weighted criteria analysis can provide support to tough, personal decisions. The more difficult the decision is, the more valuable the tool, because it gives you a way to organize and prioritize the many facets of a difficult decision. For example, making an important personal decision, such as which school to attend, which major to declare, which job to take, or which home to buy, can be overwhelming without some sort of aid. In this exercise, you will build a weighted criteria analysis from scratch to help you determine which of three potential job offers you should take.

To complete this task:

1. Open your local newspaper and go to the want ads. Find three comparable jobs that you would like to have, and cut them out. If you have access to the Internet, go to www.monster.com or www.jobs.com or any other online career development site, find three comparable jobs that you would like to have, and print the descriptions.

2. Start Excel and open a blank workbook.

3. Based on the weighted criteria analysis models you've used in this tutorial, develop one from scratch to help determine which of the three jobs would be best for you. The three jobs will be the alternatives. You should include at least five criteria, and the weights should not all be the same between the five criteria items. The weights should add up to 100%.

4. Create a ranking scale, evaluate each alternative against each criterion, and enter the individual scores. Be sure to apply the ranking scale consistently. For example, if "Commute" is a criteria item, the job opportunity with the longest commute would have the lowest score (assuming that the ranking scale indicates that a higher number is a better score).

5. Create the formulas for the weighted scores and final scores.

6. Enter your name in the left section of the header, display the formulas for the worksheet, and then print the worksheet in landscape orientation.

7. Apply conditional formatting to display the best final score in a bold, italic, red text color.

8. Print the final worksheet in landscape orientation.

9. Save the workbook with the name **JobAnalysis-1** in the Tutorial.01\Cases folder on your Data Disk.

Case 3. Using a scatter chart to Predict Crop Yields You work for an agricultural magazine and have been asked to produce a graphic to go along with a news story with the headline "Rain Makes Grain". You have a workbook that logs the growing season's rainfall in inches, as well as the average soybean yield in bushels per acre for your area. You will analyze this data using a scatter chart, linear trendline, and the R-squared statistic to determine if the "Rain Makes Grain" phrase is accurate based on this data.

To complete this task:

1. Start Excel and open the **RainGrain-1** workbook located in the Tutorial.01\Cases folder on your Data Disk.

2. Use the rainfall data in the range B2:B12 and harvest statistics in the range C2:C12 to create an XY scatter chart to determine if rainfall in inches was highly correlated to harvest yields.

3. Enter "Rain Makes Grain!" as the chart title, "Rainfall, inches" as the title of the x-axis, and "Soybeans, Bushels/Acre" as the title of the y-axis.

4. Embed the chart on the worksheet. Move the chart to the right of the data and enlarge the chart. Delete the legend, change the minimum on the scale of the x-axis to 10, and change the minimum on the scale of the y-axis to 20.

5. Add a linear trendline to the data, and display the linear equation and R-squared value. (*Hint*: If necessary, reposition and enlarge the linear equation and R-squared value.)

6. In cell A14, enter the label "Prediction", and then in the range B15:B25, enter the numbers 15 through 25.

7. In cell C15, enter the formula using the FORECAST function to predict the rainfall for 15 inches of rain. Use absolute cell references to identify the known *y* and known *x* arguments. Format cell C15 using the Comma Style format.

8. Copy the formula in cell C15 to the range C16:C25.

9. Enter your name in the left section of the header, display the formulas for the worksheet, and then print the worksheet in landscape orientation.

10. Print the final worksheet in landscape orientation.

11. Save and close the workbook. Exit Excel.

QUICK | CHECK ANSWERS

Session 1.1

1. The three parts of a decision support system are a quantitative model, a computer tool, and a business problem for which the DSS is being applied.

2. Quantitative models use numbers to describe reality, and there are few business decisions made without analysis of some sort of numbers (sales, profits, expenses, and so forth).

3. The key issue in implementing a successful what-if model in Excel is to make sure that all assumption values are referenced as separate values in individual cells and not entered in formulas themselves.

4. Click Tools, click Options, click the View tab, click the Formulas check box to select it, and then click OK.

5. You typically unlock the assumption values so that users can still enter new values in them.

Session 1.2

1. Scenario analysis allows you to save a set of what-if assumption values with the workbook and quickly apply them at a later time.

2. changing cells

3. The weighted score is the weight for that criteria multiplied by the individual score for that alternative.

4. The alternative with the highest (or lowest) final score is considered the best candidate. The ranking scale determines whether the highest or lowest score is "best."

5. The real power of the weighted criteria analysis is the model's great ability to organize the decision process and clearly communicate how a final decision was made, two important factors for a successful manager.

Session 1.3

1. The dependent variable is the variable you are attempting to predict based on the value of the independent variable.

2. The primary goal is to determine the strength with which two variables are related. If the relationship is strong, the secondary goal of regression analysis is to help predict future values.

3. scatter chart

4. correlation

5. The value would indicate that the two variables have an extremely strong correlation.

6. The general equation for a straight line is $y = mx + b$, where y is the dependent variable you are trying to predict, m is the slope of the line, x is the independent variable, and b is the y-intercept.

7. FORECAST

8. Logarithmic, Polynomial, Power, Exponential, and Moving Average

In this tutorial you will:

- Use a Web query to import data from the World Wide Web into an Excel workbook

- Analyze imported data to determine what steps are necessary to create a flexible Excel list

- Use the Find and Replace feature of Excel to create a workable Excel list

- Use the advanced text management features of Word to scrub text fields

- Use formulas with Text functions to manage text in an Excel list

- Create, format, and change the field structure of a PivotTable to analyze data

- Create, format, and modify a PivotChart to analyze data

- Work with filtered and grouped records in a PivotTable

- Create custom calculations for a PivotTable

- Use the drilldown feature of a PivotTable

USING
EXCEL AS A LIST MANAGEMENT TOOL

Converting, Using, and Analyzing Lists of Data Using Excel

CASE

Green Valley Recreation

Lynn Tse has been gathering information regarding the programs that Green Valley Recreation (GVR) sponsors. She wants to be able to analyze the information so she can better assess the current and proposed GVR programs. Lynn has a great deal of information, but she isn't sure how to use Excel to summarize the data so it is easier to analyze. As your manager, Lynn will rely on your Excel skills to help her change this information into easy-to-use and easy-to-understand Excel lists.

In this tutorial, you will learn how to structure and use Excel lists to analyze data. You will use many of the import, text management, and list management tools in Excel to organize the information that Lynn has gathered. You will import data from the World Wide Web into an Excel workbook and then manipulate the data into a properly constructed Excel list. You'll also use Microsoft Word's advanced text management tools to further manipulate the data. Finally, you'll use the PivotTable and PivotChart features of Excel to create summarized and graphic presentations of GVR data stored in Excel lists.

SESSION 2.1

In this session, you will use Excel's list management tools to organize information for easy and quick analysis. You will learn how to convert a table on a Web page into an Excel list and modify the converted table into a list that Excel can analyze. Converting raw data into a workable list is often called "scrubbing" and includes such activities as using Excel's Find and Replace feature, using Word for advanced text manipulation activities, and using Excel formulas to manipulate text.

List Management

Excel provides many list management tools that you can use to sort, filter, subtotal, and analyze information that is presented in the form of a list. In Excel, a **list** is any contiguous range of cells that contains a single category of information in each column and describes a single entity in each row. The list must be a contiguous range. In other words, there cannot be any completely blank columns or blank rows in a list (although an Excel list can contain blank cells). In a list of data, a column is called a **field**, and a row is called a **record**. An Excel list is shown in Figure 2-1. In this case, each record describes a book, and each field describes a characteristic of the book.

| Figure 2-1 | AN EXCEL LIST |

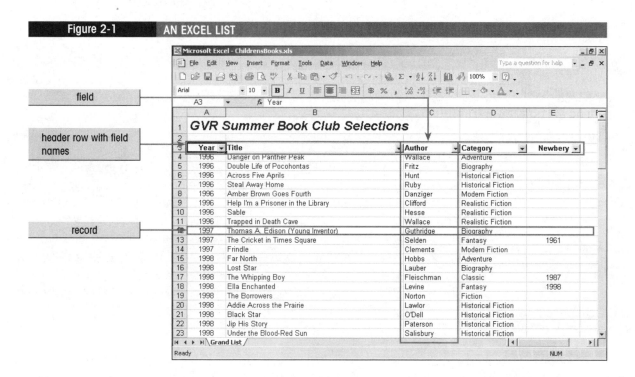

Because presenting data in the form of a list is such a common data management model, you've probably already used some of Excel's list management tools for decision support purposes. For example, you may have already used Excel's sort, filter, subtotal, and PivotTable tools to analyze data presented as a single list. In order for those Excel features to work correctly, though, you need to structure your list with certain guidelines in mind.

Guidelines for Building an Excel List

To successfully sort, filter, subtotal, and analyze an Excel list, you need to build your Excel list using the following guidelines.

- The first row of the list should contain field names. The field names should be unique. Field names describe the different characteristics of each item represented by the records within the list. The first row that contains the field names is sometimes called the **header row**.
- The field name entries in the header row should be in a single row.
- There should not be a blank row between the header row and the first record of data. Excel's list management tools assume that a blank row or blank column identifies the edge of the list. If there is a blank row between the header row and first record of data, Excel will not interpret the header row as part of the list. Rather, Excel will assume that the first record of data is the header row, which will create problems when you sort, filter, or otherwise attempt to analyze the data because the row that is assumed to be the header row doesn't become part of the sorted or filtered records. Although you can sort and filter all of the records in a list that does *not* include a header row, you have to first specify that the list has no header row. To do this, click Data on the menu bar, click Sort, and then click the No header row option button in the Sort dialog box.
- There should not be a blank row or column anywhere within the list. If you put a blank row or column anywhere within the list, Excel will interpret that blank column or row as the edge of the list.
- You can put other information in an Excel worksheet that contains a list, but the list must be separated from the other information in the Excel worksheet with a blank column or blank row.
- Each column of the list should contain one and only one piece of information. For example, you should enter first names in one column and last names in another column. Otherwise, you will limit your ability to find, sort, filter, and analyze the information. (For example, how do you sort records by author last name if names were entered in one column with entries such as Jay Allee, P. D. Chow, Mary Anne Walker, and Fred Scott Jr.?)
- Enter all values consistently. For example, do not enter "Bio" in one record and "Biography" in another. Using different entries that represent the same information limits your ability to find, sort, filter, and analyze the information.

Exploring an Improperly Constructed List

To understand the value of a properly constructed Excel list, you'll work with a list that is *not* set up properly. Then you'll modify the list so that it follows the guidelines for building an Excel list.

Lynn has created a workbook that logs all of the books selected for the GVR summer reading club, but she has been frustrated because she can't sort or filter the information and get the results that she wants. She has asked if you'll take a look at the workbook and "fix" it so that she can work with the data more efficiently.

To work with a list that is not properly constructed:

1. Start Excel and open the **ChildrensBooks-2** workbook located in the Tutorial.02\Tutorial folder on your Data Disk. This workbook contains the GVR summer book club selections for the years 1996 through 2004. There are several columns (fields) of data and 93 rows (records). There are many structural problems with the list. See Figure 2-2.

Figure 2-2   IMPROPERLY STRUCTURED LIST

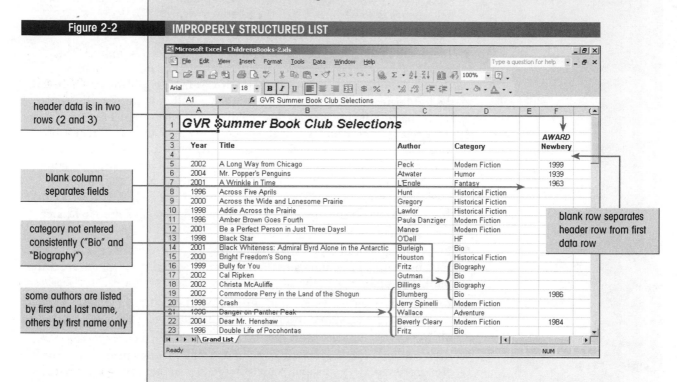

header data is in two rows (2 and 3)

blank column separates fields

category not entered consistently ("Bio" and "Biography")

some authors are listed by first and last name, others by first name only

blank row separates header row from first data row

2. Scroll down the list to view its contents, and then press **Ctrl + Home** to move back to the top of the worksheet.

Lynn told you that she wasn't able to successfully sort the records by author. You'll repeat that task to re-create the problem.

3. Click any author entry in column **C** (in range cell C5:C98), and then click the **Sort Ascending** button 🔼 on the Standard toolbar. Sorting a list that is improperly structured creates multiple problems—some of which are obvious, and some of which may not be obvious. See Figure 2-3.

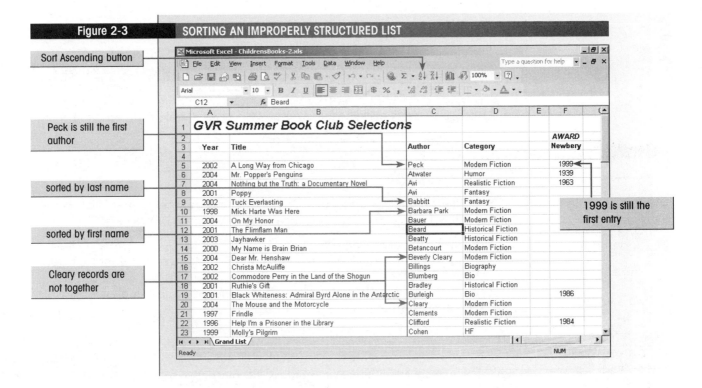

Figure 2-3   **SORTING AN IMPROPERLY STRUCTURED LIST**

Sort Ascending button

Peck is still the first author

sorted by last name

sorted by first name

Cleary records are not together

1999 is still the first entry

The following problems occurred during the sort because the list is not properly structured.

- Because there is a blank line between the header row (row 3) and the first row of data (row 5), the first row of data was treated as the header row. Therefore, row 5 didn't reorder itself when you applied an ascending sort order to the values in column C.

- Because column E is blank and separates the list from the field of data in column F, the values in column F are not part of the records and did not sort with the rest of the fields.

- The Author field, column C, doesn't contain consistent data in each record. Some records contain the author's last name, and some contain both the author's first and last names. Therefore, the records were not sorted consistently. Some records are sorted by first name and others by last name. Also, some individual author names have been entered in different ways. For example, the author Beverly Cleary is entered as both "Beverly Cleary" and just "Cleary." As a result, the records for this individual author do not appear together when you sort on the Author field.

- Some of the entries in the Category field are not entered consistently. Therefore, you would have to search for both "Biography" and "Bio" to show all of the records that are in that category.

Because you will often be presented with a list of data with structure problems, you need to be able to recognize them, and you need to know how to fix a list so that it can be easily manipulated within Excel. You will begin to fix the structure of the list by deleting the blank rows and columns within the list.

To fix the improperly developed list of data:

1. Click the **Undo** button 🔄 to restore the list to its original condition.

   One of the first things you will do to fix the structure of the list is delete the blank row that appears between the header row and the first row of data.

2. Right-click the **row heading** for row **4**, and then click **Delete** on the shortcut menu.

   Next, you will make sure that there is only one row used as the header row.

3. Click cell **F2** and then press the **Delete** key to delete the AWARD label, which is no longer needed.

   Because a blank row and a blank column define the boundaries of an Excel list, you will delete the blank column between columns D and F.

4. Right-click the **column heading** for column **E**, and then click **Delete** on the shortcut menu. The fact that the new column E contains several blank cells is not a problem for an Excel list. Now the blank rows (currently rows 2 and 98) and blank columns (currently column F and the left edge of the worksheet) define the boundaries of the list.

The problem of having more than one field of data in a single column is more difficult to resolve. Fortunately, all of the data in column C fits one of two patterns: "Beverly Cleary" or "Cleary". In other words, when both the first and last names are entered into the field, they are separated by a single space.

Using **Excel's Find and Replace**

Excel's Find and Replace feature can help you prepare data in an Excel list so you can work with the data more efficiently and effectively. In addition to finding and replacing occurrences of specific words or numbers, you can also find occurrences of special characters, such as tab stops or spaces. You can use a wildcard character, such as the asterisk (*), to find a string of characters, versus just a word or number. Therefore, you can use the Find and Replace feature to fix the inconsistent entries, making the data easier to sort and filter.

You discuss the list with Lynn and ask her if having author first names recorded in this list is important. If so, you need to create a new field of data for first names and then separate the first names from the last names in the current Author field. She doesn't think she will need the first names—the last name is all she will need. This makes your job a little easier: Instead of breaking out the data into two columns, all you have to do is eliminate the extra text (the first name) when it appears in the Author column. You can use the Find and Replace feature to accomplish this task.

Note: Excel 2000 does not have the advanced Find and Replace feature used to accomplish the next task. If you are using Excel 2000 for this tutorial, skip this set of steps, and complete the next set, which will enable to you accomplish the task of removing the first names from the Author column.

To remove first names from the Author column:

1. Click the **column heading** for column **C** to select the column, click **Edit** on the menu bar, and then click **Replace**. The Find and Replace dialog box opens.

   To find all of the occurrences of entries in the Author column with first and last names, you will use a wildcard followed by a space.

2. Type * (asterisk) and then press the **spacebar** in the Find what text box.

   TROUBLE? Be sure to enter the asterisk *before* the space in the Find what text box rather than *after* the space.

   Because you don't want first names in the Author column, you will not specify any replacement text in the Replace with text box.

3. Click the **Find All** button. The Find and Replace dialog box expands to display a list of items in column C that matches the search criteria that you entered in the Find what text box.

4. Drag the bottom border of the Find and Replace dialog box down to display the 19 items found, and then point to the third entry for **Beverly Cleary**. See Figure 2-4. Note that the items in the list work as links. When you point to an item in this list, the pointer changes to 🖑, and when you click an item, its cell reference is automatically selected on the appropriate worksheet.

Figure 2-4	FIND AND REPLACE DIALOG BOX

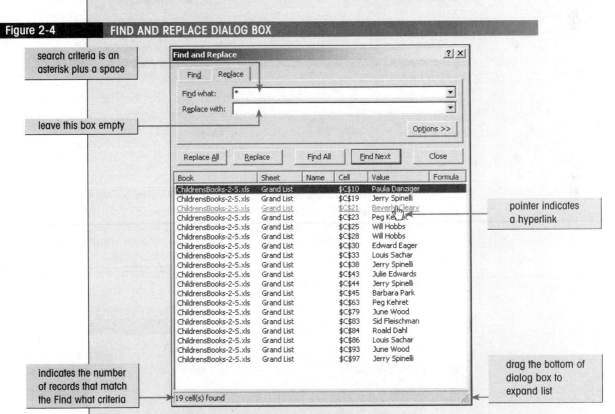

- search criteria is an asterisk plus a space
- leave this box empty
- pointer indicates a hyperlink
- drag the bottom of dialog box to expand list
- indicates the number of records that match the Find what criteria

Because you want only last names displayed in the Author column, you will replace all occurrences of first names followed by a space with nothing (remember that you did not enter anything in the Replace with text box).

5. Click the **Replace All** button, click the **OK** button when Excel completes the search, and then click the **Close** button. Clicking the Replace All button replaced *all* occurrences of the search criteria with nothing throughout the *entire* worksheet, including the Title field. See Figure 2-5.

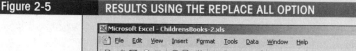

Figure 2-5   RESULTS USING THE REPLACE ALL OPTION

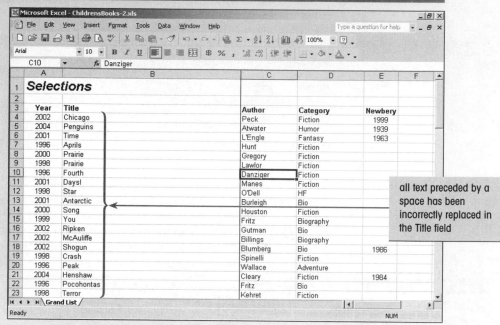

Understanding all of the options in the Find and Replace dialog box will help you use this feature in a way that gives you the results you want. In this case, to get the results you want, first restore the list to its original contents.

6. Click the **Undo** button on the Standard toolbar to restore the list to its previous condition.

7. Select column **C**, click **Edit**, and then click **Replace**. The Find and Replace dialog box opens with the last Find what criteria entry (an asterisk plus a space) still presented. The Replace with criteria is still nothing (sometimes referred to as a **null** entry).

Instead of replacing all the occurrences of text followed by a space, you will find all the occurrences in column C first.

8. Click the **Find All** button, and then check the status bar of the Find and Replace dialog box to make sure that the same 19 entries are found.

TROUBLE? Do not expand the dialog box at this time. If necessary, you can move the dialog box over to the left of the worksheet so column C is visible.

By default, Excel will still try to replace the occurrences of text and a space in each row (which includes the titles in column B) even though you previously selected column C. To address this, you need to change the direction of the search so Excel will first search and replace text in the column with the active cell, before attempting to find and replace text in other areas of the worksheet.

9. Click the **Options** button, click the **Search** list arrow, and then click **By Columns**.

10. Click the **Replace** button three times. See Figure 2-6. The Value column in the Find and Replace dialog box displays the cells that were found and indicates how the replacement process is progressing. You can see that the first name and space were removed so that "Paula Danziger" has become "Danziger," "Jerry Spinelli" has become "Spinelli," and "Beverly Cleary" has become "Cleary."

Figure 2-6   **USING FIND AND REPLACE OPTIONS**

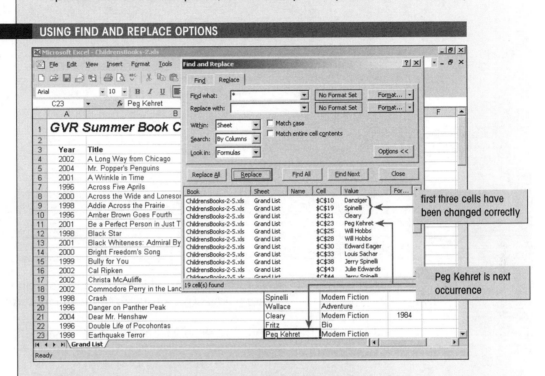

Although clicking the Replace button for each replacement is a much slower process than using the Replace All button, you need to be able to monitor the cells that you are replacing so that you don't go beyond the values in column C. You can scroll down the Find and Replace dialog box or resize it so that you can see each replacement as it is being made. You will then know when to stop clicking the Replace button.

11. Click the **Replace** button enough times to remove the first names from the entries in the Author column so only the last names remain. See Figure 2-7. Because you specified that the search should progress "By Columns," the next value that is found is the "Modern Fiction" entry in cell D1.

| Figure 2-7 | ONLY LAST NAMES OF AUTHORS DISPLAYED |

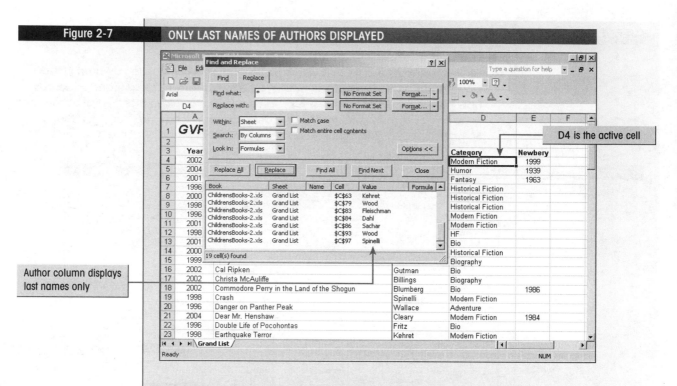

12. Click the **Close** button.

TROUBLE? If you replaced some of the entries in column D, click the Undo button as many times as is required to undo the changes to column D.

13. In column C, click any cell within the list, and then click the **Sort Ascending** button on the Standard toolbar to sort the list again. Because there are no blank rows between the header row and data records and because all of the data in the Author column is entered consistently, the records sorted correctly. See Figure 2-8.

Figure 2-8 **LIST SORTED BY AUTHOR**

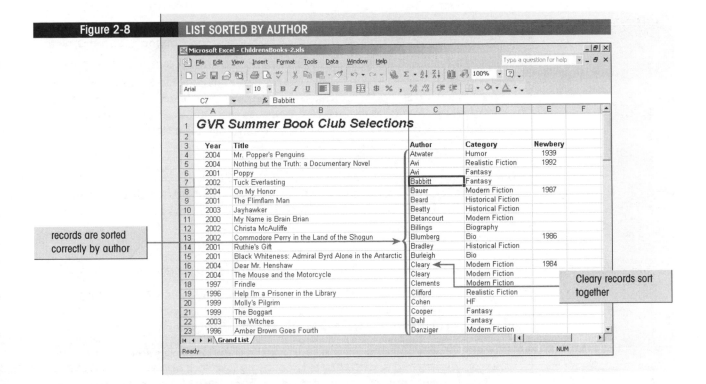

records are sorted correctly by author

Cleary records sort together

Note: If you are using Excel 2000 for this tutorial, complete this set of steps to remove the first names from the Author column.

To remove first names in the Author column:

1. Click the **column heading** for column **C** to select the column, click **Edit** on the menu bar, and then click **Replace**. The Replace dialog box opens.

   To find all the occurrence of entries in the Author column with first and last names, you will use a wildcard followed by a space.

2. Type * (asterisk) and then press the **spacebar** in the Find what text box.

   TROUBLE? Be sure to enter the asterisk *before* the space in the Find what text box rather than *after* the space.

   Because you don't want first names in the Author column, you will not specify any replacement text in the Replace with text box.

3. Click the **Find Next** button. The Formula bar identifies the cell reference and entry that matches the first entry in column C that matches the Find what criteria (any character followed by a space).

4. Keep clicking the **Find Next** button until you move through all of the entries in column C and return to the first entry in column C that matches the criteria, Paula Danziger, found in cell C10.

   Because you want only last names displayed in the Author column, you will replace all occurrences of first names followed by a space with nothing (remember that you did not enter anything in the Replace with text box).

5. Click the **Replace All** button. Note that by clicking the Replace All button *all* occurrences of text followed a space in the selected column, column D, were replaced by nothing!

6. In column C, click any cell within the list, and then click the **Sort Ascending** button ![AZ arrow icon] on the Standard toolbar. Because there are no blank rows between the header row and data records and because all of the data in the Author column is entered consistently, the records sorted correctly. (See Figure 2-8.)

The last problem you need to tackle is to make sure that the data in the Category column has been entered consistently from record to record. Now that the list contains no blank columns or rows, you can sort the list by category so you can easily find the inconsistent data in that field.

To fix the problem of inconsistent data in the Category field:

1. Click any cell in column D within the list, and then click the **Sort Ascending** button ![AZ arrow icon] on the Standard toolbar. Now that the data in the Category field is sorted in alphabetical order, you can see the inconsistencies.

Figure 2-9 identifies the inconsistent data and the appropriate entry for each inconsistency in column D. There is no single step that can fix all of these problems. If the inconsistency were entered in only one cell, you could just retype the entry. Therefore, depending on how many inconsistent entries, you will probably want to use the fill handle, the Copy and Paste buttons, or the Find and Replace commands to eliminate the inconsistencies rather than reentering the correct value for each item.

Figure 2-9	FIXING INCONSISTENT ENTRIES

INCONSISTENT DATA ENTRY	CORRECT DATA ENTRY VALUE
Adv	Adventure
Bio	Biography
HF	Historical Fiction

2. Change all occurrences of inconsistent values to their correct values by using whatever Excel techniques are the easiest for you, and then sort the list again in ascending order by category. Note that the entry for the category "Biographical Fiction" should not be replaced with "Biography."

Another problem that you want to correct is in the Fiction category. First, move to the beginning of the Fiction category.

3. Scroll down the list so cell D38, which contains the first occurrence of the category "Fiction," is visible at the top of the worksheet window, and then click cell **D38**. Five records have been entered with the generic category entry of "Fiction." Because the rest of the fiction books in this list have been further categorized into the categories of "Classic," "Modern Fiction," "Historical Fiction," and "Realistic Fiction," you want to edit the generic "Fiction" entries so that they are parallel with these categories. Based on a phone call to the local library, you will recategorize the fiction titles as shown in Figure 2-10, using the existing, more descriptive categories.

Figure 2-10   **CHANGING "FICTION" TO AN EXISTING CATEGORY VALUE**

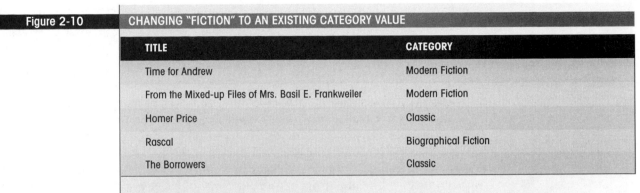

TITLE	CATEGORY
Time for Andrew	Modern Fiction
From the Mixed-up Files of Mrs. Basil E. Frankweiler	Modern Fiction
Homer Price	Classic
Rascal	Biographical Fiction
The Borrowers	Classic

4. Change all occurrences of "Fiction" to the categories shown in Figure 2-10.

   Now that all of the entries in the Category field have been entered consistently from record to record, the list can be sorted using this field.

5. Click cell **D9**, and then click ![sort icon] to sort the list. See Figure 2-11.

Figure 2-11   **LIST SORTED CORRECTLY BY CATEGORY**

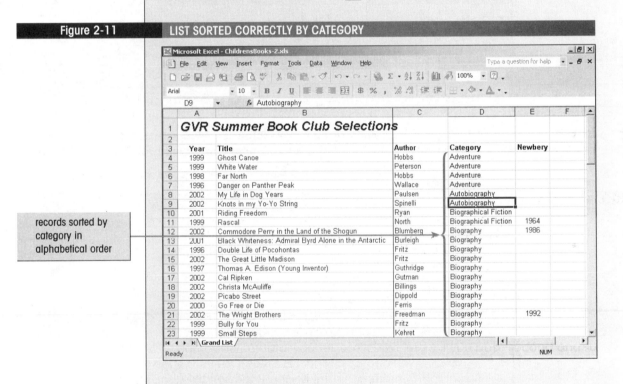

records sorted by category in alphabetical order

6. Save the ChildrensBooks-2 workbook, and then close it.

Now that you've reorganized this data into a workable Excel list, Lynn can use the book list to sort, filter, find, and analyze the data successfully. The effort involved in successfully setting up your list directly relates to the current state of the data, as well as your own skills in working with advanced Excel features.

Understanding how a user might work with a list should greatly influence how you organize the list. For example, in this case, you didn't need to save the first names that were entered in the Author field. If the users of this list needed or used that information, however, you obviously wouldn't want to delete it. Also, because this list was only used for GVR's internal tracking purposes, you recategorized the "Fiction" books based on the opinion of a local librarian. If used for other purposes, however, you might need to research a more specific literary standard by which to categorize each book.

Converting World Wide Web Tables to Excel Lists

If you are experienced with the World Wide Web, you will notice that facts and data are often presented in a tabular format. As a business manager, you might want to use data that you've found in a Web page table to help support a decision. If you are using Excel 2002 and Internet Explorer version 5.0 or later, you can use a new Excel feature called a **Web query** to help you import data from a Web page into an Excel workbook. Although you can also copy and paste information from a Web page into an Excel workbook, using a Web query also retains information about the location of the Web page so that if the data on the Web page changes, the data in the Excel workbook can be easily refreshed.

REFERENCE WINDOW   **RW**

Importing Data from a Web Page
- Start Internet Explorer version 5.0 or later.
- Go to the Web page that presents the data as a table that you want to import.
- Right-click the table, and then click Export to Microsoft Excel on the shortcut menu.

GVR is considering sponsoring a new summer event, a marathon. Lynn asks you to gather some statistics about marathons for some preliminary research on the topic.

Note: You must be using Excel 2002 and Internet Explorer version 5 or higher to complete Steps 1 through 8. If you do not have access to these programs, read Steps 1 through 8, open the BostonLists-2 workbook located in the Tutorial.02\Tutorial folder on your Data Disk, and then continue with Step 9.

To import tables of marathon-related information from the Web into a workbook:

1. Make sure Excel is running, and open a blank workbook.

2. Start Internet Explorer, connect to the Internet (if using a dial-up connection), and then enter the URL **www.bostonmarathon.org**.

   TROUBLE? If you cannot connect to the Internet or connect to the Boston Marathon Web site, open the BostonLists-2 workbook located in the Tutorial.02\Tutorial folder on your Data Disk, read Steps 2 through 8, and then continue with Step 9.

3. If necessary, scroll down the navigation pane on the left side of the Web page, click the **History** link, and then click the **Past Marathon Champions** link. The Web page presenting the marathon champions appears, as shown in Figure 2-12. The data that lists the winners starting from the year 1897 is presented in the form of a table, even though the borders of the table are not visible. If you see information lined up in columns on a Web page, there's a very good chance that it is organized by using HTML (HyperText Markup Language) **table tags**, which can be used to organize information in columns and rows that can be directly imported into Excel.

TROUBLE? Although Web sites change often, you'll probably find the History and Past Marathon Champions links in the navigation pane on the left side of the Web page. If not, search the site to find this page.

Figure 2-12	BOSTON MARATHON CHAMPIONS WEB PAGE

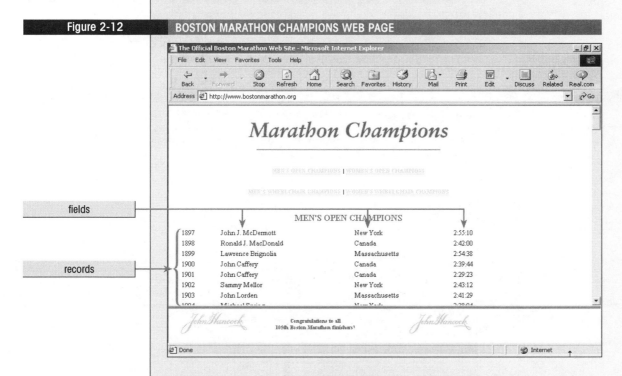

4. Right-click the **table** and then click **Export to Microsoft Excel** on the shortcut menu. The table is imported into a blank Excel workbook. See Figure 2-13. The External Data toolbar appears. This toolbar provides buttons that allow you to control the connection between the Web page and the worksheet.

   TROUBLE? If you don't see the Export to Microsoft Excel option on the shortcut menu, make sure that you are using Internet Explorer as your browser and that you are pointing within the table of data itself when you right-click the table.

Figure 2-13	BOSTON MARATHON DATA IMPORTED INTO AN EXCEL WORKBOOK

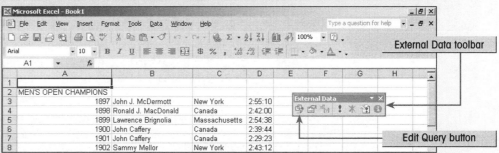

5. Press **Ctrl + End** to move to the end of the worksheet to see how many rows were imported.

   To import the other tables on the Web page, you will use the Edit Web Query dialog box.

6. Click the **Edit Query** button ⬚ on the External Data toolbar. The Edit Web Query dialog box opens. See Figure 2-14. The green check mark icon ✓ indicates that the selected information is defined as part of the Web query import process.

TROUBLE? If you don't see the External Data toolbar, right-click any existing toolbar, and then click External Data on the shortcut menu.

Figure 2-14   EDIT WEB QUERY DIALOG BOX

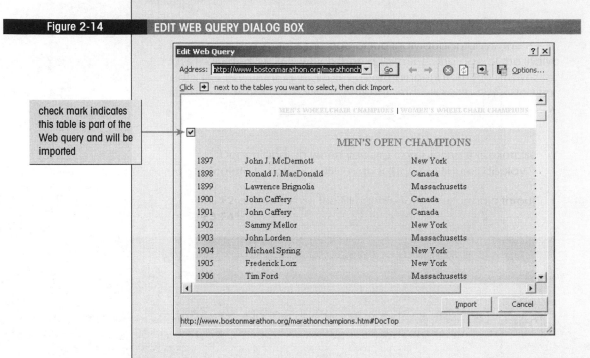

check mark indicates this table is part of the Web query and will be imported

7. Scroll down the Edit Web Query dialog box until you reach the WOMEN'S OPEN CHAMPIONS title. A yellow arrow icon ➡ indicates that the table is not defined as part of the Web query import process. You want to add this table to the former Web query definition.

8. Click ➡ for the WOMEN'S OPEN CHAMPIONS table, scroll down the Edit Web Query dialog box, click ➡ for the MEN'S WHEELCHAIR CHAMPIONS table, scroll down the Edit Web Query dialog box, click ➡ for the WOMEN'S WHEELCHAIR CHAMPIONS table, and then click the **Import** button. The edited Web query has now imported all four tables from this Web page instead of just one table. The Web query has also been automatically saved with the workbook. If data were changed or added to these tables on the Boston Marathon Web page, you could click the Refresh Data ❗ button on the External Data toolbar to import the data again.

9. Press **Ctrl + End** to move to the last field of the last record. See Figure 2-15. Approximately 200 records of data have been imported via this Web query.

Figure 2-15	ALL FOUR BOSTON MARATHON CHAMPIONS TABLES IMPORTED INTO EXCEL

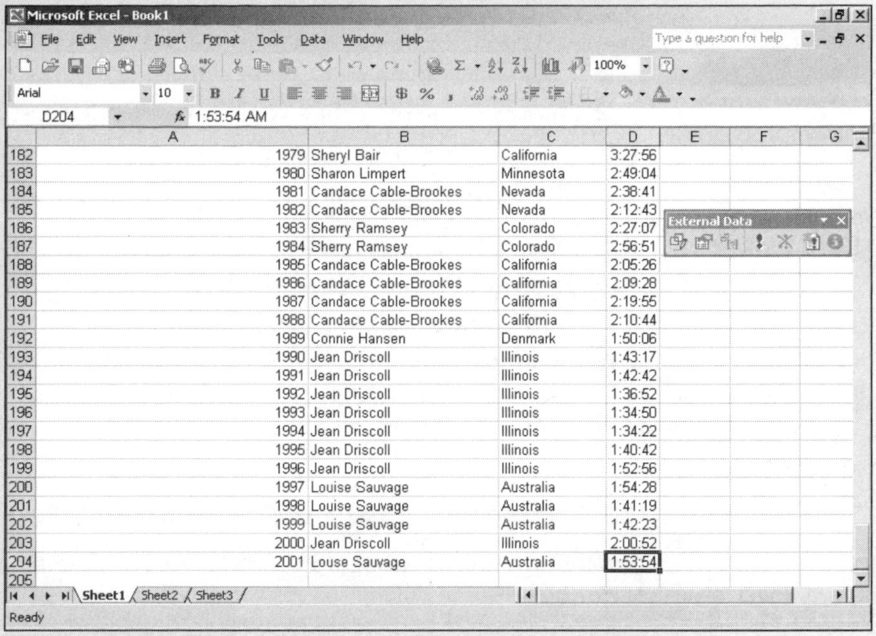

Because you will not be editing the Web query link and there is no need to refresh this data, you no longer need the External Data toolbar.

10. Click the **Close** button ☒ on the External Data toolbar to hide it.

11. Close Internet Explorer and then disconnect from the Internet if you are using a dial-up connection.

The tables of information that you have downloaded will be very helpful to Lynn and her assessment of the potential success of a marathon sponsored by GVR. As you explain to Lynn that although importing data from a Web site is easier, faster, and more accurate than rekeying data, there will often be a need to modify imported data so it can be presented as a single list within Excel. For example, if you want to analyze the Boston Marathon winners as a single list, you will need to eliminate the blank rows between the four lists. Furthermore, if you want to easily sort and find data by the winner's last name, you will need to separate the first and last names into their own fields.

Data Scrubbing

Unless the owner of a Web page followed the guidelines for building successful Excel lists, you will probably have to work with the data that you import from a Web page before you can use Excel's list management tools. The process of improving a list of data that will work best with Excel is called **data scrubbing**.

Scrubbing a list of data in Excel first requires that you analyze the list to see what needs to be improved, as explained in the following steps. You will recognize many of these activities as the same steps you took to make the data in the ChildrensBooks-2 workbook into a properly constructed Excel list.

1. Analyze the structure of each column.

   ■ Does the list have a single header row that contains the field names for each column?
   ■ Does each column contain the same category of information?
   ■ Does each column contain only one piece of data?
   ■ Are the values in each column formatted consistently?

2. Look for and delete blank rows or columns within the list.

3. Using Excel's list management tools, such as sort, filter, and find and replace, analyze the data for errors or inconsistent entries, and then fix them.

Now that you've imported the data you want to analyze, you need to organize it as a single list. You want to combine the four lists of marathon champions into one list that can be analyzed. To do that, however, you will need to change the columns so that each contains only one field of data. You will also need to delete the blank rows between the four lists.

To analyze and modify the structure of each column:

1. Scroll down the worksheet to view the four lists of data. You recognize at least two more columns of information that will need to be added to this list: Gender (Male or Female) and Race Type (Open or Wheelchair).

2. Right-click the **column heading** for column **A**, click **Insert** on the shortcut menu, and then press the **F4** key. Two new columns are inserted. Note that in Excel pressing the F4 key performs two actions, depending on what you are currently doing. Pressing the F4 key when the insertion point is in the Formula bar changes the cell reference between relative, absolute, and mixed cell references. When you are not currently making a cell entry (when you are in Ready mode), pressing the F4 key repeats the last action performed.

   You will use the two newly inserted columns for the Gender and Race Type fields.

3. Enter the field names, **Gender** and **Race Type**, in the header row (row 2), and then resize the columns as needed. See Figure 2-16.

Figure 2-16	INSERTING NEW FIELDS

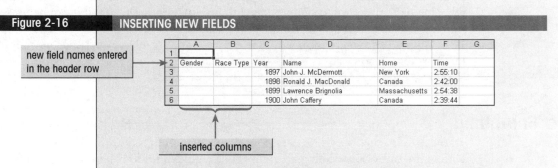

You'll enter the appropriate gender and race type in the first two columns before you delete the extra rows that separate the four lists (so that you still know where each list begins and ends).

4. Click cell **A3**, type **Male**, click cell **B3**, type **Open**, select the range **A3:B3**, and then drag the fill handle down over the range **A4:B107** to copy those values through the last row for the men's races.

TROUBLE? Depending on when you do this exercise, the results for the 2002 or 2003 Boston Marathon may have been added to the table, which means that you will need to work with different rows.

5. Select the **row headers** for rows **108** through **110** (located between the men's and women's open champions if the last row for the men's open champions is the year 2001), right-click the selection, and then click **Delete** on the shortcut menu.

TROUBLE? Depending on when you do this exercise, you might need to delete different rows between the men's and women's results. The women's race statistics start with Roberta Gibb for the year 1966.

At this point, you would to need enter and copy the appropriate entries for the Gender and Race Type fields for the women's open champions, the men's wheelchair champions, and the women's wheelchair champions, as well as delete the extra blank rows between the other lists in order to make this into a single Excel list. Fortunately, that work has already been done for you.

6. Save the workbook without saving the changes, and then open the **BostonLists-2B** workbook located in the Tutorial.02\Tutorial folder on your Data Disk.

7. Press the **Page Down** key several times. All of the data has been combined into a single list.

You will sort the list of the champions in alphabetical order.

8. Click any cell in column D within the list and then click the **Sort Ascending** button ![Sort Ascending icon] on the Standard toolbar. The list is sorted in ascending order by name. Note that because both the first and last names for each marathoner were entered into this single column, the entries are sorted by first name.

Although you were able to quickly and easily combine the four lists of information into one by adding two new columns and deleting the extra rows between the lists, your list isn't yet optimized for analysis. When multiple pieces of information are stored in the same field, you severely limit your ability to sort, find, filter, and analyze the data. Lynn has also decided that she wants you to preserve the first names of the marathoners, so you need to work with a few new data scrubbing tools to separate the first and last names into their own columns.

Separating Fields into Their Own Columns

Entering multiple pieces of information in the same field is a very common list management problem. The most common culprits are the name and address fields. Unless a name is separated into multiple fields, such as FirstName, MiddleInitial, and LastName, you will not be able to do such common and simple list management tasks such as sorting by the last name. Putting the address, city, state, and zip code fields into one column creates the same type of list management problem.

Because you will often want to analyze data that has been imported from external sources, such as Web pages, mainframes, and other applications over which you have no control, you need to know how to separate fields into their own columns once the data resides within Excel. To separate the data into multiple columns, the first thing you must do is make the data in the field as consistent as possible from record to record.

In the BostonLists-2B workbook, you will separate the information in column H into two new fields: FirstName and LastName. Also, some of the Name fields contain the text "(unofficial)," (which indicates that this champion was not an official Boston Marathon winner); therefore, you will need to remove that text.

To erase unnecessary data in column D:

1. Scroll down the worksheet to scan the data in column D, the Name column.

   If you wanted to track whether a winner was "official" or not, you would need to create a new field to store that information for each record. Because Lynn doesn't care about this designation, you will delete that text from the current Name field.

2. Select column **D**, click **Edit** on the menu bar, and then click **Replace**.

3. Type **(unofficial)** in the Find what text box, press the **Tab** key, and then press the **Delete** key several times to make sure that there is nothing in the Replace with text box.

   EXCEL 2000: Because Excel 2000 automatically highlights any entry that might be present in the Replace with text box, you don't have to press the Delete key more than once as instructed in Step 3.

4. Click the **Find Next** button. The first occurrence of "(unofficial)" is found in the Name column.

   TROUBLE? If you are presented with a message indicating that Excel cannot find the data that you are searching for, click the OK button. Repeat Steps 2 through 4, making sure you spell the search criteria correctly in the Find what text box.

5. Click the **Replace All** button to replace all occurrences of "(unofficial)" in the worksheet.

6. Click the **OK** button when Excel completes the search and has made six replacements, and then click the **Close** button to close the dialog box.

   EXCEL 2000: Because the Replace dialog box in Excel 2000 closes at the end of the process, you don't click the OK and Close buttons as instructed in Step 6.

The next inconsistency you need to tackle is breaking out the names in the Name field into two fields: FirstName and LastName. This task is difficult because some names contain first and last names, some contain first name, middle initial, and last name, and some have two last names separated by a space. Because the data was not entered consistently, there is no single-step way to break it out. In the absence of knowing how to write a program to separate the text into separate fields, you will use the tools within the Microsoft Office XP suite to get the job done.

Although Excel is the best tool for building formulas to calculate values within Office XP, Word is the program that best manipulates text. Because the problem of breaking out the fields of information within the Name field involves manipulating strings of text, you will use Word to help manipulate the text, and then copy and paste the individual fields back to Excel.

Using **Word** to Parse Text

The process of breaking a string of text into smaller pieces or fields is called parsing text. In order to **parse** a string of text into more than one field, you must be able to identify a rule by which the string should be separated into multiple fields. For example, if you were attempting to parse the first five digits from a ZipCode field, you would be able to use the Excel LEFT function to specify that you wanted to return the first five characters in the field. An example of a formula using the LEFT function would be *=LEFT(A5,5)*, where *A5* contained the zip code entry.

If you are attempting to parse text that does not have the same number of digits in each field, however, you need a different rule by which to determine how the data within the string will be parsed into multiple fields. One way to do this is to separate the parts of the string with a special character, such as a tab or paragraph mark, that can be used to identify where the fields within the string start and stop. Excel, however, does not provide the ability to find and replace for special characters. Instead, you can use Word, which provides advanced Find and Replace features not available in Excel. For example, in Word you can find and replace special characters such as tabs and paragraph marks. Word also provides powerful text-to-table and table-to-text conversion tools that will help you parse a string of text into separate columns of data.

You need to separate the first and last names from the Name column. Because this is a text parsing issue that involves a variable number of characters, you will use Word to help with the task. First, you need to copy the Name column of data from the Excel workbook into a Word document. When you copy data from Excel to Word, the data is displayed in Word as a table. You will then use Word's table conversion tools to separate the text into two separate columns so that the first and last names are separated.

To copy information from Excel to Word:

1. Right-click the **column heading** for column **D**, and then click **Copy** on the shortcut menu. This selection is placed on the Clipboard, which makes the selection available to other programs.

2. Click the **Start** button on the taskbar, point to **Programs**, and then click **Microsoft Word**. A blank Word document appears.

3. Close the New Document Task pane if it appears, and then click the **Paste** button on the Word Standard toolbar. The column of information from Excel is pasted into the blank Word document as a table. (This might take a few seconds.) See Figure 2-17.

Figure 2-17   **EXCEL DATA PASTED IN A WORD DOCUMENT**

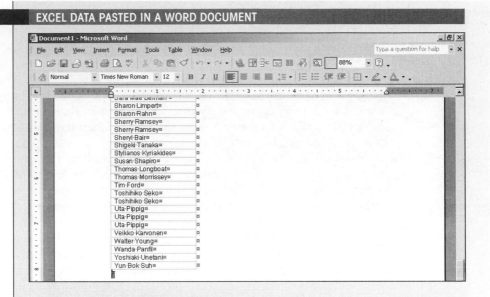

TROUBLE? Depending on the document view, zoom percentage, and other Word settings, your screen might look slightly different.

Your first task will be to strip away all text after the first space, leaving only the first name. To do that, you will convert the table to text, replace the spaces with tabs, and then convert the text back to a table using the tab character to separate the columns of the table so that the first name data is isolated in the first column.

To parse the data in the Name column to isolate the first names:

1. Click any cell in the table, click **Table** on the menu bar, point to **Convert**, click **Table to Text**, and then click the **OK** button to separate text with paragraph marks, which will put paragraph marks after each row of the table.

    Now you'll convert the text back into a table, but this time you will use spaces to separate the information into multiple columns in order to isolate the first name data in its own column.

2. With the text still selected, click **Table**, point to **Convert**, click **Text to Table**, make sure the Number of columns option is set to **4**, click the **Other** option button, and then press the **spacebar** to enter a space as the character to use to separate the text. See Figure 2-18.

    TROUBLE? If the text is not selected, press **Ctrl + A** to reselect it, and then repeat Step 2.

Figure 2-18 CONVERT TEXT TO TABLE DIALOG BOX

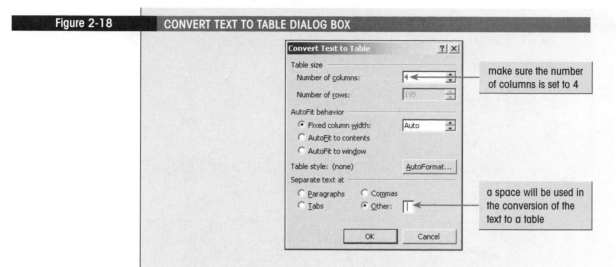

make sure the number of columns is set to 4

a space will be used in the conversion of the text to a table

3. Click the **OK** button and then click anywhere within the table to deselect the text. The text is converted back to a table with four columns. See Figure 2-19. Each part of the name was separated into its own column, which means that the first column now contains only the champion's first name.

Figure 2-19 TEXT CONVERTED TO A TABLE WITH COLUMNS SEPARATED BY SPACES

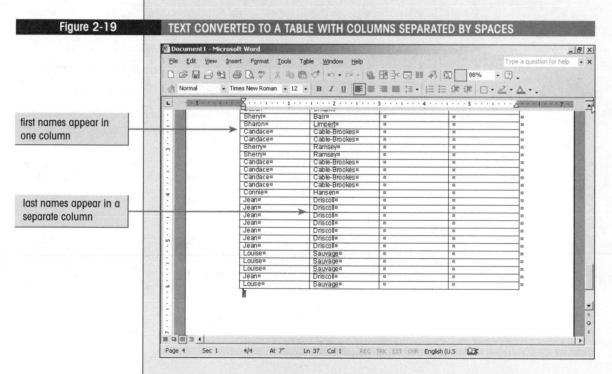

first names appear in one column

last names appear in a separate column

4. Scroll to the top of the document, click just above the first column with ↓ to select the column, and then click the **Copy** button 🗐 on the Standard toolbar to copy the selection to the Office Clipboard.

5. Click the **BostonLists-2B.xls** program button on the taskbar, select column **G**, click the **Paste** button 🗐 on the Excel Standard toolbar, and then click the **OK** button when prompted that the data on the Clipboard is not the same size as the selected area. The first names are pasted into the Excel workbook in column G. See Figure 2-20.

Figure 2-20   **PASTING FIRST NAME DATA FROM WORD INTO EXCEL**

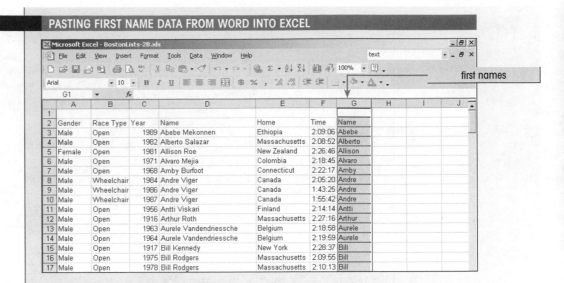

first names

6. Click cell **G2**, type **FName**, and then press the **Enter** key to give the column a unique field name.

TROUBLE? When you press the Enter key, the *N* in the label might automatically become lowercase due to an AutoCorrect setting. To change the letter *N* to uppercase, edit it in the Formula bar.

TROUBLE? To change an AutoCorrect setting, click Tools on the menu bar, click AutoCorrect, and then change the setting on the AutoCorrect tab.

Column G isn't formatted in the same way as the other columns, but you can easily deal with this formatting issue later.

7. Save your changes to the workbook.

Using Word's Find and Replace

Word's Find and Replace feature allows you to search for text and replace it with special characters. By inserting a special character, such as a tab, between characters in a single string of text, you can then use Word's table conversion features to break a single string of text into multiple fields.

Now that the first names are parsed from the Name column, you will work on the last names. Because some names include a middle initial, the last name isn't consistently displayed in the column; therefore, parsing the last names will require a few more steps than it took to parse the first names.

To further parse the Name column so only last names without spaces appear in the column:

1. Click the **Document1 – Microsoft Word** program button on the taskbar.

To make working with the data easier, you will remove the first column.

2. Click in any cell in the first column, click **Table** on the menu bar, point to **Delete**, and then click **Columns**.

With the first names out of the way, the middle initials and last names will be easier to separate. First, however, you need to convert the table back to text.

3. Click **Table**, point to **Select**, and then click **Table**.

4. Click **Table**, point to **Convert**, click **Table to Text**, make sure the Tabs option button is selected, and then click the **OK** button. The fields of text are separated by tabs.

5. Scroll down the document to examine it.

Before you begin parsing the remaining text in the Word document, you need to see any special formatting characters that might exist in the document. In Word, special formatting characters are called **nonprinting characters**, which include spaces and tab stops, for example. If you can see characters, in addition to the text on your screen, you do not have to turn on the nonprinting characters options as instructed in Step 6.

6. Click the **Show/Hide ¶** button ¶ on the Standard toolbar.

You need to delete all middle initial entries. Because the middle initials include a period, you will use another wildcard, the question mark (?), followed by a period as the search criteria and then replace it with nothing.

7. Click **Edit** on the menu bar, click **Replace**, and then press the **Delete** key to delete any existing entry in the Find what list box. Because a space might exist in either the Find what or Replace with list box, you must make sure that any existing entries in those text boxes are deleted.

8. If necessary, click in the Find what list box, click the **More** button to expand the dialog box, and then click the **Special** button. See Figure 2-21. Note that the More button changes to the Less button when the dialog box is expanded.

Figure 2-21   FIND AND REPLACE SUBMENU OF SPECIAL CHARACTERS

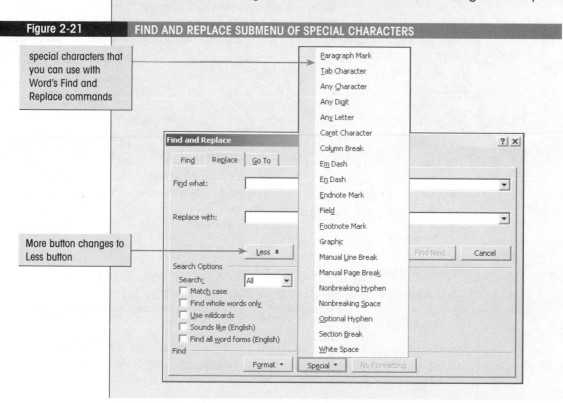

special characters that you can use with Word's Find and Replace commands

More button changes to Less button

9. Click **Any Character** (which inserts the characters ^? into the Find what list box), type . (a period), click the **Special** button, and then click **Tab Character** (which insert the characters ^t). The question mark (?) is a wildcard character that stands for any character. In other words, you want to find any character followed by a period and a tab character, which will find all middle initials.

   You'll replace this series of characters with nothing, which in effect will remove the middle initials from the document.

10. Press the **Tab** key and then press the **Delete** key to make sure that nothing is in the Replace with list box. See Figure 2-22.

| Figure 2-22 | USING SPECIAL CHARACTERS AS SEARCH CRITERIA |

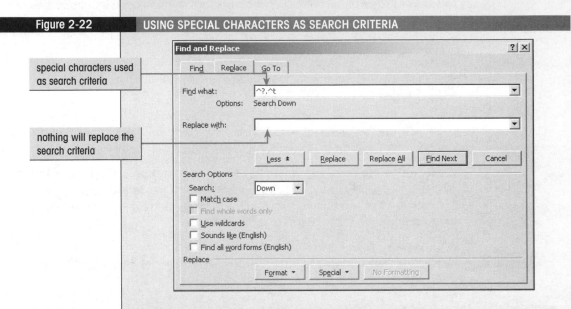

11. Click the **Replace All** button, click the **Yes** button if prompted to search the remainder of the document, and then click the **OK** button when prompted that Word has finished searching the document.

12. Click the **Close** button, and then scroll down the document to examine it.

The last inconsistency you need to deal with is a last name that has two names, such as "Yong Ham," or two parts, such as "de Castella." Because you formerly replaced spaces with tab characters, these two-part last names have been separated as if they are two fields. You need to put them back together by replacing tabs with spaces. Once again, you need to use Word's advanced search and replace features because you are working with the special tab character that cannot be easily manipulated within Excel.

To replace tab characters with spaces:

1. Click **Edit** on the menu bar, click **Replace**, press the **Delete** key to delete the current entry in the Find what list box, click the **Special** button, and then click **Tab Character**.

2. Press the **Tab** key to move to the Replace with list box, press the **Delete** key to make sure that there is no entry in the Replace with list box, and then press the **spacebar**.

3. Click the **Replace All** button, click the **OK** button, and then click the **Close** button. One column of data that consists of only the champions' last names remains.

4. Press **Ctrl + A** to select the entire document, click **Table** on the menu bar, point to **Convert**, click **Text to Table**, type **1** in the Number of columns text box, click the **Paragraphs** option button to separate the text, and then click the **OK** button to convert the text into a single-column table.

5. With the column still selected, click the **Copy** button 📋 on the Standard toolbar, click the **BostonLists-2B.xls** program button on the taskbar, select column **H**, click the **Paste** button 📋 on the Standard toolbar, and then click the **OK** button when prompted that the data on the Clipboard is not the same size as the selected area.

   With the last name pasted into column H, you will add a field name and format the new data like the rest of the worksheet.

6. Click cell **H2**, type **LName**, and then press the **Enter** key.

   TROUBLE? When you press the Enter key, the *N* in the label might automatically become lowercase due to an AutoCorrect Option setting. To change the lowercase letter to an uppercase letter, edit it in the Formula bar.

7. Click the **column heading** for column **E**, click the **Format Painter** button 🖌 on the Standard toolbar, and then drag the pointer across the **column headings** for columns **G** and **H**. See Figure 2-23.

| Figure 2-23 | FORMATTED BOSTONLISTS-2B WORKBOOK |

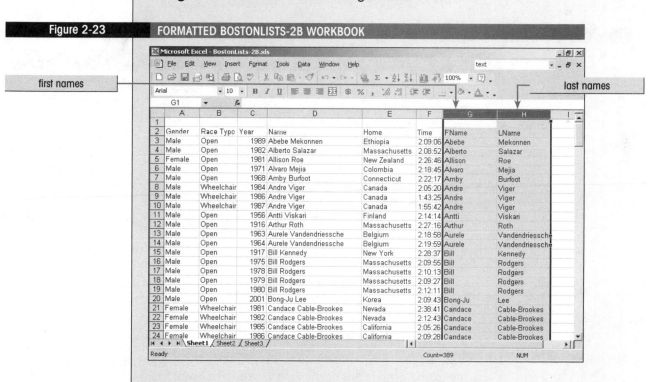

8. Click any cell to deselect the columns.

9. Right-click the **Document1 – Microsoft Word** program button on the taskbar, click **Close** on the shortcut menu, and then click the **No** button to close Word without saving the document.

You might have noticed while you were using Word that the entries in the LName field contain spaces after the name entry. If you wanted to delete extra trailing spaces in the LName field, you could use either Excel or Word's Find and Replace feature to do that. You would need to eliminate extra spaces after a name if you were merging this data into a form letter or report and didn't want the trailing spaces to appear after you inserted the LName data. For your list management activities, however, the trailing spaces don't create any problems.

Because Excel will open almost any PC file format, you may find yourself using Excel as an intermediate file format to open, view, and scrub data that will ultimately be sent to an Access database or some other file format. Excel can handle a list of up to 256 columns (fields) and over 65,000 records (rows) of data in one worksheet.

Now that you've separated the first and last names of the marathon winners into their own separate columns, Lynn will be able to sort or find data using either piece of information.

Combining Multiple Fields into One Column

There may be times when you want to combine multiple fields into one column. For example, if the marathon data had been given to you with the first and last names in separate columns, you might want to combine them to appear as one entity just because you like the way the full name appears on a printout.

To combine multiple fields into one column, you can use an Excel formula or an Excel function. Using an Excel formula or function to add pieces of text to one another is called **concatenating** text. You can use either the CONCATENATE function or the & (ampersand) character to accomplish the task. Figure 2-24 provides an example of equivalent formulas that concatenate text. For the examples, assume that cell A1 contains 100 and cell A2 contains 5.

Figure 2-24	CONCATENATION FORMULA EXAMPLES

FUNCTION AND FORMULA	RESULT
=CONCATENATE("Tim went ",A1/A2," mph.")	Tim went 20 mph.
="Tim went "&A1/A2&" mph."	Tim went 20 mph.

Lynn understands the benefits of breaking each field into its own column. She is, however, worried that she will be unable to create a report without big gaps between the first and last names, which won't be as aesthetically pleasing as the presentation of a complete name with only a single space between the names. You explain that Lynn can join the first and last names using a formula. By using a formula to join the name, you do not create a copy of the data, but link back to the original text values. Therefore, if either the first name or last name entries change, the formula that combines the two automatically updates as well.

To create the text formula that combines the FName and LName values:

1. Click cell **I2**, type **Full Name**, and then press the **Enter** key.

   Now that the field name is entered, you will enter the formula that combines the data from the first name field in column G with the data in the last name field in column H with a space.

2. In cell I3, type **=G3&" "&H3** (making sure to include a space between the quotation marks), and then click the **Enter** button ☑ on the Formula bar. Expand column **I** and examine the formula in the Formula bar, as shown in Figure 2-25.

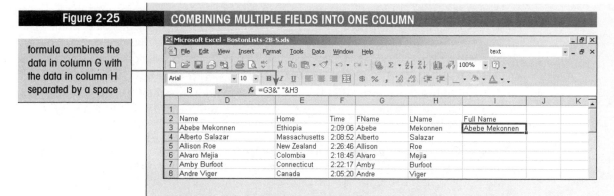

Figure 2-25   COMBINING MULTIPLE FIELDS INTO ONE COLUMN

formula combines the data in column G with the data in column H separated by a space

3. Use the fill handle to copy the formula down to the end of the list, and then widen the column as shown in Figure 2-25.

   At this point, you no longer need the original name data in column D. Once you are sure that you've broken out the first and last names successfully, you should delete redundant data to clarify and simplify the list.

4. Press **Ctrl + Home** to move to the top of the worksheet, right-click the **column heading** for column **D**, and then click **Delete** on the shortcut menu.

5. Save and close the workbook, and then exit Excel.

No doubt you'll need to analyze data organized in the form of a single list over and over again for many business and personal reasons. Knowing how to scrub data so that your list contains a single, consistent piece of data will enable you to use Excel's list management features to summarize and analyze that data. Now that you've successfully scrubbed the Boston marathon champions list, Lynn can use Excel's list management features to sort, filter, and find data easily.

Other Data Scrubbing Examples

The ways that you scrub data are as varied as the sources and types of data themselves. Any time you import, link to, or copy data from an external source into an Excel workbook, you will have to analyze the data and probably will have to do some scrubbing in order to make it work best for your purposes. While it's impossible to cover every situation you might encounter because the potential sources and formats for data are almost endless, a few of the most common data scrubbing issues and techniques have been presented in this tutorial. Excel provides many other functions to help you scrub data though, and a few more examples are worth mentioning.

■ If a date is imported as text, such as "8/27/2003," "27-AUG-2003," or "2003/08/27," it can be converted to a serial number using the **DATEVALUE** function. By default, Excel stores dates as serial numbers by assigning 1 to the date 1/1/1900, 2 to the date 1/2/1900, and so forth. By using the DATE-VALUE function to convert text dates to numeric dates, you can then sort the dates sequentially, use them in calculations, and format them with predefined Date number formats.

■ Once a date is converted to a numeric date, if you want to isolate a part of a date, such as the day, month, or year, Excel provides several functions to help you. For example, you can use the **WEEKDAY** function to determine the day of the week (1 through 7), the **DAY** function to determine the day of the month (1 through 31), the **WEEKNUM** function to determine the week of the year (1 through 54), the **MONTH** function to determine the month of the year (1 through 12), and the **YEAR** function to isolate the year.

■ If text is imported in all uppercase or lowercase letters, it can be converted to proper case (where the first letter of each word in the text string is capitalized) using the **PROPER** function. In addition, the **UPPER** function converts all text to uppercase characters, and the **LOWER** function converts all text to lowercase characters.

No doubt you will run into even more data scrubbing issues as you attempt to use Excel to analyze data from another electronic source. Because you can use Excel to open and read a wide variety of file formats, data scrubbing is an extremely useful tool, even if the final destination for the data is not the Excel workbook itself.

Session 2.1 QUICK CHECK

1. What guidelines should you consider when creating a field of information in a single Excel column?

2. Describe how blank columns or rows are interpreted when Excel is analyzing a list of information.

3. What browser allows you to import tabular data on a Web page into an Excel workbook?

4. Identify three common problems that require you to scrub data after it is imported into Excel.

5. What two features of Word help you parse text?

SESSION 2.2

In this session, you will use a PivotTable and PivotChart to analyze a list of information. You will learn how to select the data source that will be used for the PivotTable and PivotChart. You will learn how to control the formatting and grouping aspects of each and how to create custom calculations and formulas.

Analyzing a List with PivotTables and PivotCharts

When the data you want to analyze is in the form of a long list of information, and you want to create and compare multiple summary statistics, such as subtotals, averages, or counts, using different combinations of fields, you can use a PivotTable and a PivotChart. A **PivotTable** is a summary of a subset of the fields and records in an existing list. The fields used in a PivotTable are the same fields as those presented in the original list, but in an organization that allows you to summarize and analyze groups of records. A sample PivotTable is shown in Figure 2-26. The PivotTable toolbar is also displayed.

Figure 2-26 SAMPLE PIVOTTABLE

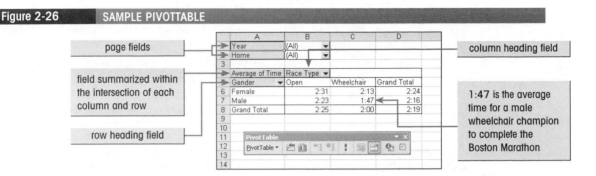

In this example, the Gender field is used as a PivotTable row heading, the Race Type field is used as the column heading, and the Time field is averaged for all records of that Race Type and Gender within the body of the PivotTable. The Year and Home fields are used as page fields, which allow you to filter the data presented by the PivotTable. Although you can use Excel's subtotal feature to create subtotals based on *one* field, a PivotTable allows you to summarize data using *multiple* fields placed in the column and row positions. The page fields are used to filter the records to determine which records should be used within the body of the PivotTable.

A PivotTable is **interactive**, which means that you can apply filters, sorts, and other customizations that automatically cause the PivotTable to automatically recalculate. Therefore, a PivotTable is a flexible and popular data analysis tool.

A **PivotChart** is a graphical representation of a PivotTable. You can create a PivotChart based on an existing PivotTable or create a PivotChart directly from an Excel list. When you create a PivotChart first, an underlying PivotTable is automatically created. Figure 2-27 shows a PivotChart presentation of the same data displayed in the PivotTable shown in Figure 2-26. PivotCharts use chart terminology to refer to the field positions. Therefore, when you create a PivotChart from a PivotTable, the row field of a PivotTable becomes the category field of a PivotChart, and the column field of the PivotTable becomes the series field of the PivotChart.

Figure 2-27 SAMPLE PIVOTCHART

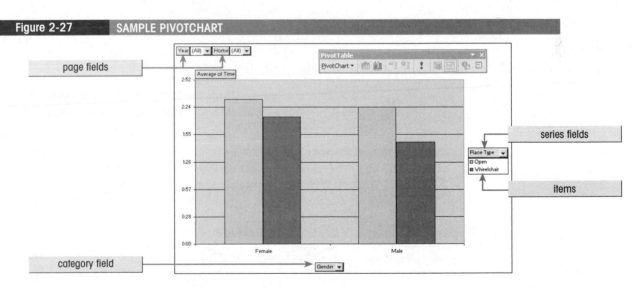

The **source data** for either a PivotTable or a PivotChart can be a single list within an Excel worksheet, multiple data ranges, and also external sources of data, such as a Microsoft Access database or an OLAP (On-Line Analytical Processing) source. **OLAP** is a technology used to organize and improve the performance of data analysis. By connecting an Excel workbook to an OLAP data source, such as Microsoft SQL Server database, you can use the extensive data manipulation features of Excel, including PivotTables and PivotCharts to analyze very large amounts of data stored in external databases.

If the source data changes after a PivotChart or PivotTable is created, you must refresh the PivotTable and PivotChart in order to see the most up-to-date data. To refresh a PivotChart or PivotTable, click the Refresh Data button on the PivotTable toolbar, or right-click the PivotTable and click the Refresh Data button on the shortcut menu.

REFERENCE WINDOW   **RW**

Analyzing a List with a PivotChart

- Click any cell in the Excel list.
- Click Data on the menu bar, and then click PivotTable and PivotChart Report.
- Click the PivotChart report (with PivotTable report) option button, and then click the Next button.
- Follow the steps of the PivotTable and PivotChart Wizard to define the PivotChart.
- Drag the fields that you want to show on the chart to the appropriate drop areas of the PivotChart.

GVR recently completed a survey to gather long-term planning data. The survey consisted of five questions:

- What city do you live in?
- What is your gender?
- What is your birth date?
- If GVR were to invest in *either* additional swimming or golf facilities, which would you prefer?
- What amount would you pay for a season pass to our existing public facilities?

Lynn has entered the feedback from the first 50 surveys into an Excel workbook, and she wants several types of summary statistics on this data. You recognize this to be a good application for a PivotTable and PivotChart to help Lynn with her analysis.

To start the PivotTable and PivotChart Wizard:

1. If you took a break after the last session, start Excel and then open the **Survey-2** workbook located in the Tutorial.02\Tutorial folder on your Data Disk.

2. Click any cell in the list, click **Data** on the menu bar, and then click **PivotTable and PivotChart Report**. The first Wizard dialog box opens. It lists the source data options in the top half and the report options in the bottom half. Your PivotChart will come from the existing Excel list, so the correct source data option is already chosen. Because you created the PivotChart from a list, Excel will automatically create a PivotTable that the PivotChart uses to determine which data to use and how to present it.

3. Click the **PivotChart report (with PivotTable report)** option button, and then click the **Next** button. The second Wizard dialog box opens.

   Excel 2000: Click the **PivotChart (with PivotTable)** option button.

4. Click the **Next** button to accept *$A$1:$E$41* for the range, and then click the **Finish** button to create a new worksheet with the PivotChart and PivotTable. A

blank PivotChart appears, as shown in Figure 2-28. Note that there are two new worksheets in the workbook: Chart1 and Sheet1. Chart1 contains the PivotChart, and Sheet1 contains the associated PivotTable, which you will work with shortly.

Figure 2-28	BLANK PIVOTCHART

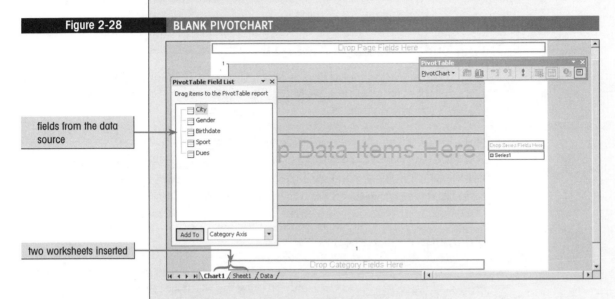

fields from the data source

two worksheets inserted

TROUBLE? If necessary, drag the PivotTable toolbar or PivotTable Field List to another area on the screen to clearly view all of the elements.

EXCEL 2000: The PivotTable toolbar in Excel 2000 displays the actual field names on the bottom portion of the toolbar, but you can toggle the field names on and off by clicking the Display Fields/Hide Fields button 🔲 on the PivotTable toolbar. Therefore, when you add fields to a PivotTable or PivotChart in Excel 2000, you drag them from the PivotTable toolbar as opposed to dragging them from the PivotTable Field List.

There are four **drop areas** on a PivotChart. You drag a field from the Field List to one of the blue outlined drop areas to lay out the PivotChart. The **Field List** is a small window that displays all of the field names from the list used as the source of data for the PivotChart. Figure 2-29 describes the PivotChart drop areas, as well as how they correspond to the drop areas on a PivotTable. As you design either a PivotChart or PivotTable, the other view of the data is being automatically modified as well.

Figure 2-29	DROP AREAS

DROP AREA	DESCRIPTION
Page	Fields in the Page drop area are used to filter the presentation of data in the PivotTable and PivotChart.
Category (x-axis)	Fields in the Category drop area are used as labels for the x-axis of the PivotChart.
Series (legend)	Fields in the Series drop area are used in the legend of the PivotChart.
Data Item	Fields in the Data Item drop area are presented as bars, the value of which is displayed on the y-axis of the PivotChart

Lynn wants to compare the average value in the Dues field by gender as well as by sport and city so you will use those fields on the PivotChart. Because you can move the fields from one drop area to another, you will go ahead and build the PivotChart with the fields you need, and then you can move them around to analyze the data in new ways.

To create the survey PivotChart:

1. Drag the **Gender** field from the Field List to the Drop Category Fields Here area.

> **EXCEL 2000:** Drag all fields from the bottom portion of the PivotTable toolbar. Also, in Excel 2000, the Drop Category Fields Here area is the Drop More Category Fields Here area.

2. Drag the **City** field to the Drop Page Fields Here area.

3. Drag the **Dues** field to the Drop Data Items Here area. Note that the SUM function is the default Excel function used. Also note that field names are bold in the Field List if they have been used on the PivotChart.

> **EXCEL 2000:** Note that a field name does not appear in bold after being dragged to a drop area.

4. Drag the **Sport** field from the Field List to the Drop Series Fields Here area, and then click the **Hide Field List** button ▣ on the PivotTable toolbar to hide the PivotTable Field List. See Figure 2-30.

> **EXCEL 2000:** Drag the **Sport** field from the PivotTable toolbar to the Drop More Series Fields Here area, and then click the **Hide Fields** button ▣ on the PivotTable toolbar to hide the field names. For the remaining steps, click ▣ when instructed to hide or display the Field List.

| Figure 2-30 | INITIAL PIVOTCHART |

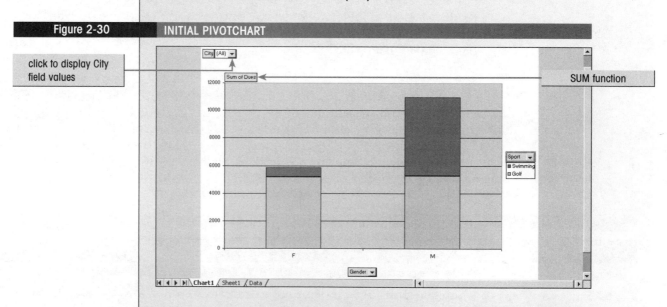

click to display City field values

SUM function

TROUBLE? If you drag a field to the wrong drop area, drag the field to another drop area or off the chart altogether.

Right now, the information in the PivotChart shows a stacked column chart that summarizes the dues by gender and sport. Because the number of men and women who took the survey is not equal and because the subtotals of all of dues represented by the stacked bar aren't meaningful numbers, you need to modify the PivotChart to provide better information. Lynn wants to see an average of the dues broken down by gender and by sport. Therefore, you need to change the chart type so that the data for each sport is not stacked on top of each other (making it more difficult to compare golf to swimming), and you also need to change the way the Dues field is being summarized. Instead of subtotaling the dues values, you want to average them.

To modify the survey PivotChart:

1. Click the **Chart Wizard** button 📊 on the PivotTable toolbar, make sure the Column chart type is selected, click the **Clustered Column** sub-type (top left icon in Chart sub-type gallery), and then click the **Finish** button. Now that the PivotChart shows each sport as an individual column (rather than as stacked columns), you're ready to change the way the Dues field is summarized.

2. Double-click the **Sum of Dues** field button to open the PivotTable Field dialog box, click **Average** in the Summarize by list, and then click the **OK** button. The average dues for each gender and sport are now represented in the PivotChart. See Figure 2-31. This PivotChart clearly shows that of those surveyed the average amount of annual dues that men are willing to pay is slightly higher than that for women. Moreover, the PivotChart shows that those who want GVR to expand their golf facilities are willing to pay a higher annual fee for public services.

| Figure 2-31 | REVISED PIVOTCHART |

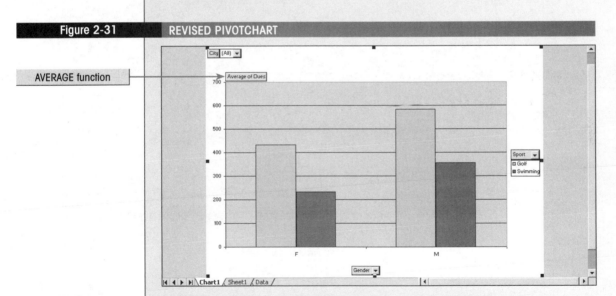

AVERAGE function

You also want to see the actual data values on the PivotChart.

3. Double-click the **data marker** in the Golf series to open the Format Data Series dialog box, click the **Data Labels** tab, click the **Value** check box, and then click the **OK** button. The values appear above the Golf series columns.

   EXCEL 2000: In the Format Data Series dialog box, click the **Show value** check box.

4. Double-click a **data marker** in the Swimming series to open the Format Data Series dialog box, click the **Value** check box on the Data Labels tab, and then

click the **OK** button. The data values for the Golf series appear above each column. With the specific data values on the chart, understanding the bar values is easier. Because the values are small and appear with a distracting number of digits to the right of the decimal point, however, you will format the values to improve their readability.

EXCEL 2000: In the Format Data Series dialog box, click the **Show value** check box.

You will use the Formatting toolbar to format these items on the PivotChart just as you would format values in a worksheet.

5. Click one of the data values for the Golf series, click the **list arrow** for the Font Size button ⟨10 ▾⟩ on the Formatting toolbar, click **16** in the Font Size list, click the **Comma Style** button ⟨,⟩, and then click the **Decrease Decimal** button ⟨.00→.0⟩ twice. Applying the Comma Style format automatically decreases the number of digits to the right of the decimal place to two, but in this case, you want the values rounded to the nearest whole number.

6. Click one of the data values for the Swimming series, click ⟨10 ▾⟩, click **16**, click the ⟨,⟩, and then click the ⟨.00→.0⟩ twice. See Figure 2-32.

Figure 2-32	FORMATTED PIVOTCHART

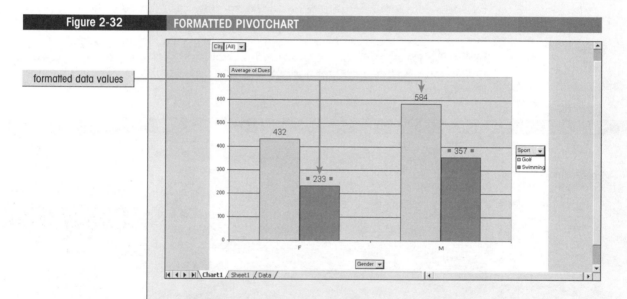

formatted data values

7. Save the workbook, and then print the formatted PivotChart with your name in the left section of the header.

The number of formatting improvements you can make to a PivotChart is vast. For example, you could also change the attributes of the axes, bar colors, and titles by double-clicking the particular chart element that you want to modify and then making the appropriate changes in the element's Format dialog box. At this point, however, you want to work with the PivotChart's associated PivotTable.

Working **with PivotTables**

Any time you create a PivotChart, a PivotTable is automatically created and used as the source of data for the PivotChart. As you make field modifications to the PivotChart, those changes are automatically applied to the PivotTable as well.

You will look at the PivotTable that was created when you created the PivotChart so you can show Lynn how the fields on a PivotChart correspond to a PivotTable.

To view and modify the survey PivotTable:

1. **Click the Sheet1 tab.** The same fields are used in the PivotTable as those used in the PivotChart. See Figure 2-33.

| Figure 2-33 | INITIAL PIVOTTABLE |

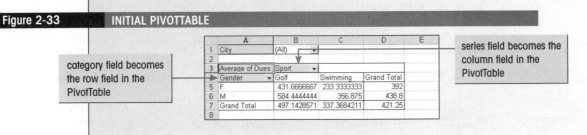

category field becomes the row field in the PivotTable

series field becomes the column field in the PivotTable

When you make structural changes to a PivotChart, such as adding or moving a field, the same corresponding change is made to PivotTable view. In this case, the PivotChart Category field, Gender, is the row field on the PivotTable. The PivotChart Series field, Sport, is the column field on the PivotTable. Figure 2-34 shows how the drop areas of the PivotChart and PivotTable correspond. Adding fields to either view changes the corresponding drop area of the other view.

| Figure 2-34 | CORRESPONDING PIVOTTABLE AND PIVOTCHART DROP AREAS |

PIVOTTABLE	PIVOTCHART
Page	Page
Row	Category (x-axis)
Column	Series (legend)
Data Item	Data Item

Formatting changes, such as font sizes and number formats, are not linked between the two views of data, though.

Formatting Values on the PivotTable

You can format the values on your PivotTable to improve their appearance and make them easier to read. Formatting changes that you make in a PivotChart are not automatically applied to the same values as they appear on the PivotTable and vice versa. However, you can easily format the values on the PivotTable using the Format Cells dialog box.

> **REFERENCE WINDOW**   **RW**
>
> Formatting a Data Field in a PivotTable
> - Double-click the data field button to open the PivotTable Field dialog box.
> - Click the Number button.
> - Select a category, and specify any category-related options in the Format Cells dialog box.
> - Click the OK button in the Format Cells dialog box, and click the OK button in the PivotTable Field dialog box.

You can also format values in a PivotTable by selecting them like any other Excel cells and then clicking the appropriate buttons on the Formatting toolbar or using desired options from the Format menu.

Lynn wants you to format the numbers on the PivotTable so that they are rounded to the nearest integer, which will make the values easier to read.

> ### To format the number values on the PivotTable:
>
> 1. With the PivotTable still displayed, double-click the **Average of Dues** field to open the PivotTable Field dialog box.
>
> 2. Click the **Number** button to open the Format Cells dialog box, click **Number** in the Category list, and then change the value for the Decimal places option to **0**.
>
> 3. Click the **OK** button, and then click the **OK** button to close the PivotTable Field dialog box.

There are still some changes you want to make to the PivotTable. Structural changes, such as changing the arrangement of fields or the summary statistics (average, sum, or count) for the data file that you make in a PivotTable, are automatically reflected in a corresponding PivotChart and vice versa.

Changing the Field Structure of a PivotTable

There are many different structural changes you can make to a PivotTable, including changing the field positions, deleting fields from the PivotTable, and adding fields to the PivotTable. Structural changes that you make in either PivotTable or PivotChart View are automatically displayed in the other.

<u>Changing the Structure of a PivotTable</u>

- Drag existing fields from one drop area to another (to move them) or off the PivotTable (to delete them).

or

- Click the PivotTable button on the PivotTable toolbar, click Wizard, and then click the Layout button.
- Drag the fields to the appropriate locations in the PivotTable and PivotChart Wizard—Layout dialog box.
- Click the OK button, and then click the Finish button.

or

- Click the Show Field List button on the PivotTable toolbar to display the PivotTable Field List.
- Drag a field from the PivotTable Field List to a drop area on the PivotTable diagram, or use the Add To button in the PivotTable Field List to add the fields to a drop area on the PivotTable.

Now Lynn wants to know how many people participated in the survey from each city, broken down by gender. To generate the analysis Lynn wants, you will change the structure of the PivotTable.

To change the structure of the PivotTable to generate a new analysis of the data:

1. Drag the **Sport** field button to the right, away from the PivotTable, which will remove the field. The new analysis will not use this field in its calculations. Note how the pointer changes to indicate where the field is being moved.

2. Drag the **City** field button from the Page field position down to the column field position (cell B3), which is to the right of the Average of Dues field position. When you release the mouse button, the city-related field data appears in columns B through G.

3. Double-click the **Average of Dues** field button to open the PivotTable Field dialog box, click **Count** in the Summarize by list, and then click the **OK** button. The PivotTable now shows how many people by gender participated in the survey from each city. See Figure 2-35. Note that if you wanted to count the number of records within a PivotTable, you would need to use a field that contains an entry for each record. For example, if the Dues field contained a null value (nothing) for one of the records, that record would not be included in the count statistics within the PivotTable.

Figure 2-35   **PIVOTTABLE THAT COUNTS SURVEYS FOR EACH CITY AND GENDER**

COUNT function

City field is in the column field position

	A	B	C	D	E	F	G	H
1								
2								
3	Count of Dues	City						
4	Gender	Apache	Oxford	Pawnee	Rosehill	Sunflower	Grand Total	
5	F		1	5	2	7	15	
6	M	8	5	1	10	1	25	
7	Grand Total	8	6	6	12	8	40	
8								
9								

You can also use the PivotTable and PivotChart Wizard to modify the structure of the PivotTable.

4. Click anywhere in your PivotTable, click the **PivotTable** button on the PivotTable toolbar, click **Wizard**, and then click the **Layout** button. See Figure 2-36. The PivotTable and PivotChart Wizard – Layout dialog box shows you the structure of your current PivotTable and allows you to modify the PivotTable structure by dragging fields to new locations in the PivotTable diagram. This dialog box also gives you easy access to the other fields in the data source, which are not used for this particular PivotTable.

| Figure 2-36 | PIVOTTABLE AND PIVOTCHART WIZARD – LAYOUT DIALOG BOX |

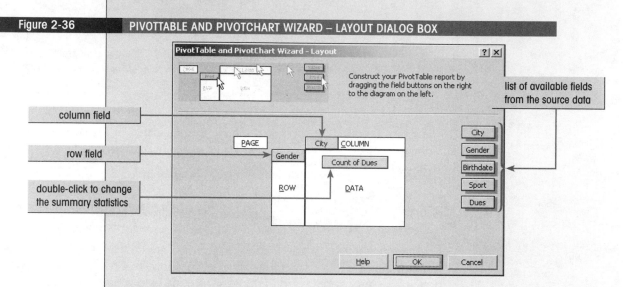

EXCEL 2000: If the PivotTable toolbar is not displayed, click **View** on the menu bar, point to **Toolbars**, and then click **PivotTable**. If the PivotTable toolbar is displayed, but the field names are hidden, click the **Display Fields** button on the PivotTable toolbar.

5. Drag the **Sport** field to the Page area, click the **OK** button in the PivotTable and PivotChart Wizard – Layout dialog box, and then click the **Finish** button. The Sport field now appears at the top of the PivotTable.

6. Click the **Chart1** tab to display the PivotChart, and then close the Field List. The PivotChart bars now represent a count of surveys for each city. Note that the Series field (in the legend position) is now the City field, which you modified in the PivotTable.

7. Click the **City** field list arrow, click the **Show All** check box to deselect all the cities, click the **Oxford** and **Pawnee** check boxes to select them, and then click the **OK** button. The PivotChart now shows you that only one female and five males took the survey from Oxford, and five females and one male took the survey from Pawnee. See Figure 2-37.

EXCEL 2000: Because there is no Show All option in the field list, deselect all the cities *except* Oxford and Pawnee.

Figure 2-37   **FILTERING A PIVOTCHART**

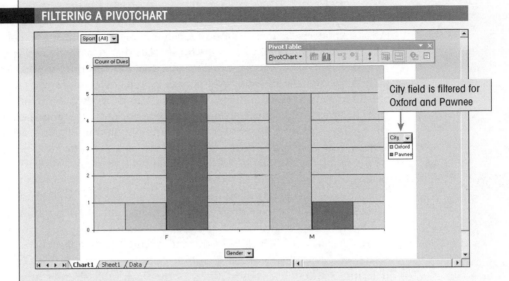

City field is filtered for Oxford and Pawnee

8. Click the **Sheet1** worksheet tab. The PivotTable is also filtered for only the cities of Oxford and Pawnee. As you filtered for specific data in the PivotChart, the PivotTable is automatically filtered, too.

   Renaming worksheets will help to clarify what they contain.

9. Double-click **Sheet1**, type **PivotTable**, double-click **Chart1**, type **PivotChart**, and then press the **Enter** key.

10. Save the workbook.

Another way to modify the structure of a PivotTable is to use the PivotTable Field List. You can either drag a field button from the PivotTable Field List to the PivotTable or use the Add To button at the bottom of the Field List to add fields from the source data to the PivotTable.

Regardless of what field organization you use for your PivotTable, however, remember that the PivotChart will always reflect the current organization of fields displayed on the PivotTable. Also, if you filter records in one view, they are automatically filtered in another view.

Using **Advanced PivotTable and PivotChart Features**

There are a number of advanced formatting and organizational changes that you can apply to a PivotTable and PivotChart. For example, you can show or hide detail on a PivotTable, use AutoFormats to professionally present PivotTable information, and add a number of custom calculations. If you are working with date fields, there are a number of special grouping options that allow you to organize the PivotTable by various spans of time including days, months, and years. There are also a number of PivotTable options that you can set to change the structure of the entire PivotTable that affect the grand totals. Other advanced options affect the way a PivotTable is updated, or refreshed. For example, you can change a setting so that the PivotTable is automatically refreshed with any data that has been entered in the source data.

Yet another PivotTable feature is the ability to drill down. Because each value in the body of a PivotTable represents a summarization of records, you may want to know which individual records were used to create that statistic. By drilling down a value within a PivotTable, you create a copy of the records from the original list that were used to create the summarized value on the PivotTable.

Showing and Hiding Details on a PivotTable

As you know, every intersection of a column and row on a PivotTable represents a value that summarizes all of the records in the source data that also have matching values for the given row and column field values. You can use more than one row or more than one column field to show subgroupings, details, within a group. For example, you might want to use both the Gender and the Sport field as row headings so that you can show each sport subgrouping within both the male group and the female group. When you put more than one field in the row heading area, the field on the left is the first grouping level. If you wanted gender subgroupings within Sport groups, you would place the Sport field as the far left row heading field.

If you use more than one row or column field, you can choose to show or hide subgrouping details by using the Hide Detail button and Show Detail button on the PivotTable toolbar. Therefore, showing or hiding details is another way to change the presentation of data on the PivotTable. An advantage of showing and hiding details over adding and removing fields from the PivotTable is that showing and hiding does not remove the data from the PivotTable, but simply displays or hides it. Showing and hiding is also different from filtering in that filtering selectively determines which *records* are displayed on the PivotTable. Showing and hiding determines whether or not the body of the PivotTable shows summary statistics for each field on the PivotTable.

REFERENCE WINDOW   **RW**

Showing or Hiding Detail on a PivotTable
- Click the row or column field for which you want to show or hide detail.
- Click the Show Detail or Hide Detail button on the PivotTable toolbar.

or

- Right-click the row or column field name for which you want to show or hide detail.
- Point to the Group and Show Detail option, and then click Hide Detail or Show Detail.

Lynn wants to analyze the survey data to determine if there is a big difference between the number of men and women who prefer golf and swimming. You explain that by using the Show Detail and Hide Detail options, Lynn can add the Sport field as a row heading to the existing PivotTable and, therefore, show golf and swimming subgroupings within each gender.

To show and hide detail on the survey PivotTable:

1. Switch to the **PivotTable** sheet, click the **Gender** field button on the PivotTable, and then click the **Show Detail** button 🔲 on the PivotTable toolbar. The Show Detail dialog box opens, prompting you for the field containing the detail you want to show.

   EXCEL 2000: If the PivotTable toolbar is not displayed, click **View** on the menu bar, point to **Toolbars**, and then click **PivotTable**. If the PivotTable toolbar is displayed, but the field names are hidden, click the **Display Fields** button 🔲 on the PivotTable toolbar.

2. Click **Sport** and then click the **OK** button. Adding the Sport field to the PivotTable in this way gives you the same results as if you had used the PivotTable Field List or PivotTable and PivotChartWizard – Layout dialog box to add the field to the PivotTable.

With the Sport field added as a second row heading, Lynn has the flexibility to show or hide Sport details within Gender, depending on what information she is trying to analyze.

3. Click the **Gender** field button, and then click the **Hide Detail** button on the PivotTable toolbar. The Sport details are hidden, but now that the Sport field is positioned to the right of the Gender field in the row area, which will make it easier for Lynn to expand those details at a future time.

4. Click . See Figure 2-38. When you click the Show Detail button for a field in a PivotTable, if a field already exists as a subgroup, the details of that field will display on the PivotTable. As you saw in Step 1, however, if you click the Show Detail button for a field on the PivotTable for which no subgrouping field exists, you are presented with the Show Detail dialog box to choose a subgrouping field.

| Figure 2-38 | SHOWING AND HIDING DETAILS |

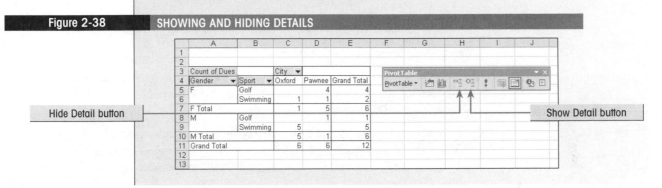

Hiding the detail on a PivotTable is different from hiding the field altogether. You will show Lynn the difference.

To hide the Sport field on the survey PivotTable:

1. Right-click the **Sport** field button, and then click **Hide** on the shortcut menu. The Sport field is removed from the PivotTable. Hiding a field is the same as dragging it off the PivotTable. There is no "unhide" command. To add the field back to PivotTable, you have to add it as if it were a new PivotTable field.

2. Click the **Undo** button on the Standard toolbar.

Once your PivotTable is structured to show the data you want to analyze, you will probably want to improve its appearance by formatting the data.

Using AutoFormats

Excel provides many **AutoFormats**, predesigned formatting schemes, which include font, color, and shading choices to enhance the presentation of your PivotTable. The first 10 AutoFormats that Excel provides in the AutoFormat dialog, named Report 1 through Report 10, are in an indented format layout. An **indented** format moves a column field to the first field in the row. In addition, an indented format aligns all values in the last column of the PivotTable. There are also 10 AutoFormats that are **nonindented** formats in which the PivotTable structure does not change when the AutoFormat is applied.

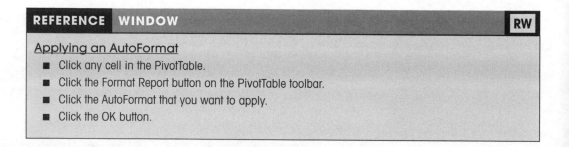

Lynn would like to improve the way the data in the PivotTable is formatted. You will show her both the indented and nonindented AutoFormats so she can decide which one she likes best.

To apply an AutoFormat to the survey PivotTable:

1. Click in any cell in the PivotTable.

2. Click the **Format Report** button 📄 on the PivotTable toolbar to open the AutoFormat dialog box, make sure the **Report 1** AutoFormat is selected, and then click the **OK** button.

3. Click any cell in the report so that you can observe the indented Report 1 AutoFormat. See Figure 2-39. The City field, formerly in the column field, has been moved to the first field in the row field. All values are aligned in the last column of the PivotTable.

Figure 2-39	APPLYING AN INDENTED AUTOFORMAT

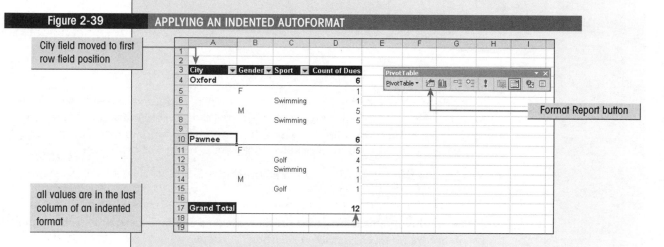

You show Lynn the indented format and compare it to a nonindented format.

4. Click 📄, scroll about halfway down the list box, click the **Table 2** AutoFormat, and then click the **OK** button.

5. Click any cell in the worksheet so that you can observe the nonindented Table 2 AutoFormat. See Figure 2-40. The structure of the PivotTable remains the same as it was originally created with the City field in the column area. This is the format that Lynn likes the best.

Figure 2-40 APPLYING A NONINDENTED AUTOFORMAT

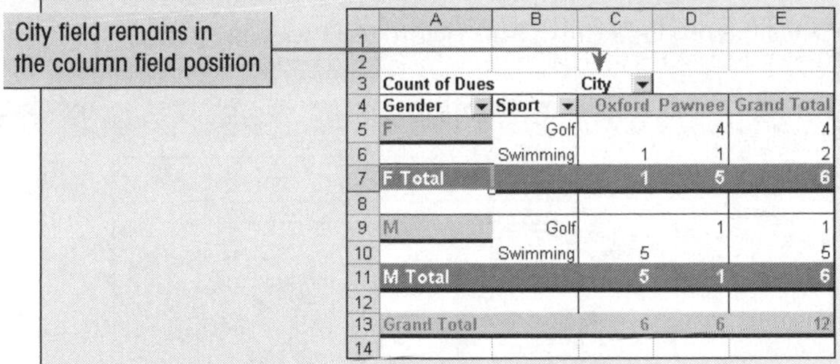

City field remains in the column field position

	A	B	C	D	E
1					
2					
3	Count of Dues		City		
4	Gender	Sport	Oxford	Pawnee	Grand Total
5	F	Golf		4	4
6		Swimming	1	1	2
7	F Total		1	5	6
8					
9	M	Golf		1	1
10		Swimming	5		5
11	M Total		5	1	6
12					
13	Grand Total		6	6	12
14					

6. Save your changes to the workbook, and then print the PivotTable worksheet with your name in the left section of the header.

You can change the field organization, filter, or show and hide details on a PivotTable with an AutoFormat applied just as if the format was not applied.

Working with Date Fields in a PivotTable

When you add a field that contains dates to a PivotTable, you may not be interested in individual dates (such as birth dates), but ranges of dates. For example, if your list consisted of sales records, you may not need detailed sales totals for each day, but you may want to summarize the sales values by week, month, or year. PivotTables allow you to group fields with date values in these increments of time or in custom increments of time that you define.

Lynn has asked you to analyze whether the age and gender of the person seems to affect the data in the Dues field. You will create a second PivotTable to answer this question.

To create a second PivotTable:

1. Click the **Data** tab, click any cell in the list, click **Data** on the menu bar, and then click **PivotTable and PivotChart Report**.
2. Click the **Next** button to create a PivotTable based on the Excel list, and then click the **Next** button to accept the *$A$1:$E$41* range. A Microsoft Excel message box appears. As stated in this box, if two PivotTables are based on the same source data, you will use less memory if you base second and subsequent PivotTables on the first one. Because the second PivotTable that you want to create will use the same source data as the existing one, the suggested option works for you.
3. Click the **Yes** button. A different second wizard dialog box appears. The source of the data is now displayed as the location of the single existing PivotTable report on which you will be basing the new one.
4. Click the **Next** button, and then click the **Finish** button to place the new PivotTable in a new worksheet. The new worksheet is inserted before the Data sheet.
5. Double-click the new sheet tab and then type **AgeAnalysis** as the new worksheet name.

   To analyze how age and gender of the person are related to the values in the Dues field, you will use the Gender, Birthdate, and Dues fields on the new PivotTable.

6. Drag the **Gender** field to the Drop Column Fields Here area, drag the **Birthdate** field to the Drop Row Fields Here area, and then drag the **Dues** field to the Drop Data Items Here area. See Figure 2-41 for the layout of the new PivotTable.

Figure 2-41   LAYING OUT THE PIVOTTABLE WITH THE BIRTHDATE FIELD

	A	B	C	D	E
1		Drop Page Fields Here			
2					
3	Sum of Dues	Gender			
4	Birthdate	F	M	Grand Total	
5	5/3/1939	100		100	
6	5/1/1941		820	820	
7	11/15/1943		400	400	
8	12/24/1944	400		400	
9	3/2/1945	1000		1000	
10	10/3/1945		910	910	
11	3/10/1946		1000	1000	
12	7/2/1949		500	500	
13	10/4/1950	820		820	
14	11/5/1951	400		400	
15	5/12/1960	910		910	
16	4/1/1961	400		400	
17	5/2/1963		450	450	
18	8/19/1963		730	730	
19	3/2/1964		640	640	
20	4/26/1965	550		550	
21	9/14/1965		100	100	
22	4/20/1966		500	500	
23	5/20/1966	200		200	
24	8/10/1967		250	250	

PivotChart / PivotTable \ AgeAnalysis / Data /

Ready

Although the PivotTable shows all of the data you requested, viewing the Dues value for each birthday doesn't help you analyze how different age groups responded to the Dues question on the survey. You want to group people of similar ages together to get a feel for how each age group responded. To do this, you need to group records based on the values in the Birthdate field.

Grouping Records in a PivotTable

As the PivotTable is presented now, unless two people had the same birthday, each record would represent an individual survey. In this case, you don't want to analyze the Dues by individual dates, but rather, by a range of dates. To do this, you will use the PivotTable's **grouping** feature. The grouping feature allows you to group multiple records by defining a range of values for the grouping field. Date fields are common grouping fields because you are often more interested in summarizations over a period of time rather than information about specific dates.

In order to summarize this data by age groups as Lynn requested, you will group the data by year so that the PivotTable summarizes the information for each year rather than each individual birthdate.

To group records by year based on the Birthdate field:

1. Right-click the **Birthdate** field button on the PivotTable, point to **Group and Show Detail**, and then click **Group**. The Grouping dialog box opens. You can use this dialog box to group date and time information by a set of predetermined intervals.

EXCEL 2000: Point to **Group and Outline** on the shortcut menu.

2. Click **Months** to deselect this option, scroll down the list, and then click **Years**.

3. Click the **OK** button. See Figure 2-42. Now the records in the Birthdate field are summarized by years, beginning with the earliest year (or in other words, the oldest person who took the survey).

TROUBLE? If the PivotTable on your screen does not look like the one in Figure 2-42, you may have inadvertently selected another grouping option. Right-click the Birthdate field button, point to Group and Show Detail (for Excel 2000 users, point to Group and Outline), and then click Ungroup. Repeat Steps 1 and 2, making sure that only the Years option is selected in the By list.

Figure 2-42   **GROUPING BY THE BIRTHDATE FIELD**

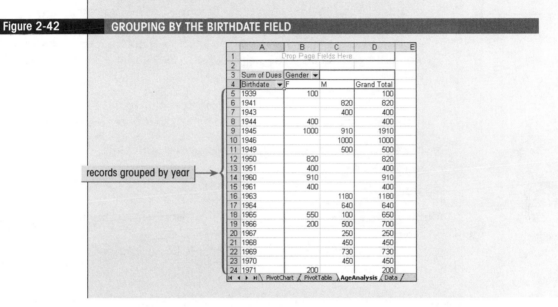

records grouped by year →

Although summarizing the Dues values by year, versus by individual birthdates, does help summarize the data by age, it's still not clear how various age groups responded to the Dues question on the survey. Lynn wants to know how people in their 20s, 30s, 40s, and so on responded to this survey. To create this information, you will calculate each person's age in a new field in the original list, add the field to the PivotTable, and then create grouping intervals so that the records are summarized in 10-year age brackets.

Adding a New Field to the Source Data

The source data of a PivotTable or PivotChart changes when you enter, delete, or modify data on the existing list. You can also change the source data by adding a new field. A new field may consist of an entirely new category of information for each record, such as ZipCode, EducationLevel, or IncomeLevel, or it may be something that you can calculate from an existing field. In this case, you will create an Age field that can be calculated from the existing Birthdate field.

Lynn wants the records grouped together so that all of the records for each age group are presented as a single row. Lynn wants the age groups broken out in groups of 10 years. To accomplish this, you first need to determine the individual ages for the original records of the source data. You will add a new field to the source data that consists of a formula that calculates the ages of those who took the survey, and then you will add it to the PivotTable.

To create a new field in the source data:

1. Click the **Data** worksheet tab, click cell **F1**, type **Age**, and then press the **Enter** key.

   The Excel functions that you will use are the TODAY() function, which returns today's date (based on the computer's battery) and the INT function, which converts the resulting value to an integer. You will also use the Birthdate values in column C in the formula.

2. In cell F2, type **=INT((TODAY()-C2)/365)**, and then press the **Enter** key. The formula subtracts the date in cell C2 (the individual's birth date) from the current date, which determines the age of the individual in days. The total number of days is divided by 365, which then determines the age of the individual in years. The INT function truncates all remainders from the answer so that the age will always display as a whole number and will not be rounded up. In other words, if the actual age of an individual is 39.9 years, the formula will return 39 as their age.

   TROUBLE? Depending on when you are completing this exercise, some ages may calculate to values a little higher than the figures display.

3. Click cell **F2** and then use the fill handle to fill the formula through the range **F3:F41**.

With the new field created in the source data, you are now ready to add it to the PivotTable.

Changing the Range of the Source Data for the PivotTable

As you work with the source data that is used by a PivotTable, you need to make sure that the range of the source data for the PivotTable is still correct. For example, if you add new records or fields to the source data, it is *not* automatically added to the range for the PivotTable and, therefore, is *not* automatically analyzed by the PivotTable. Fortunately, it is easy to double-check and to change the source data for a PivotTable.

REFERENCE WINDOW   **RW**

Changing the Range of the Source Data for the PivotTable

- Click any cell in the PivotTable.
- Click the PivotTable button on the PivotTable toolbar, and then click Wizard.
- Click the Back button to go to the PivotTable and PivotChart Wizard—Step 2 of 3 dialog box.
- Type the new range in the Range text box, or use the Range Finder button to enter a new range.
- Click the Finish button.

Now that a new field containing the individual's age has been added to the source data, you need to expand the range of the source data for the PivotTable to include this new column of data.

To add the Age field to the PivotTable:

1. Click the **AgeAnalysis** tab, and then click any cell in the PivotTable.

2. Click the **PivotTable button** on the PivotTable toolbar, and then click **Wizard**. The third step of the PivotTable and PivotChart Wizard appears, which provides the Layout button. You want to change the range of source data, which is identified in the second step of the PivotTable Wizard.

3. Click the **Back** button, edit the entry in the Range text box so that it becomes **Data!$A$1:$F$41**, and then click the **Finish** button. The Age field is automatically added to the PivotTable Field List, which means that you can now add it to the PivotTable.

   Because the Age field has all of the information you need, you don't need the Birthdate field on the PivotTable anymore and can, therefore, remove it from the PivotTable.

4. Drag the **Birthdate** field off the PivotTable, and then drag the **Age** field from the Field List to the Row area just below the Sum of Dues field. See Figure 2-43.

   TROUBLE? If the PivotTable on your screen does not look like the one in Figure 2-43, you may have moved the Age field to the wrong location. Click the Undo button on the Standard toolbar, and then drag the Age field from the Field List to the Row area, releasing the mouse button when the field is positioned at cell A4.

| Figure 2-43 | ADDING A FIELD BASED ON A FORMULA TO THE PIVOTTABLE |

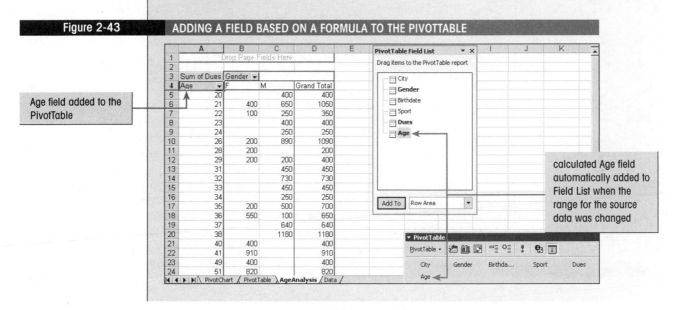

Age field added to the PivotTable

calculated Age field automatically added to Field List when the range for the source data was changed

The PivotTable now displays the ages of those who took the survey. Now you need to use this data to group in 10-year ranges.

Grouping Data on a Numeric Field

Grouping data on a numeric field is different from grouping a date field because Excel does not provide any predefined groups, such as months and years, from which you can choose. When you group the records on a numeric field, you must define the upper and lower ranges for the group, as well as the value by which the groups will increment.

Lynn's original request was to group the values in the PivotTable by 10-year age groups, so that the PivotTable summarizes the surveys for those in their 20s, 30s, 40s, and so forth.

To group a numeric field on a PivotTable:

1. Right-click the **Age** field button on the PivotTable, point to **Group and Show Detail**, and then click **Group**. For a numeric field, the Grouping dialog box requires three values: the start value (the bottom value of the range for the first group), the end value (the top value for the range for the last group), and the increment value (that determines the size of each group).

   EXCEL 2000: Point to **Group and Outline** on the shortcut menu.

   You want the groups to increment by 10, starting at 20 and ending at 89. To make sure that these start and end values never change, even if the birthdate values in the list are modified, you will remove the Auto options and specify the start and end values yourself.

2. Click the **Starting at** check box to remove the Auto option, click the **Ending at** check box to remove the Auto option, double-click **62** in the Ending at text box, and then type **89**. You don't need to modify the By option because, by default, the increment value is already 10. See Figure 2-44.

Figure 2-44	GROUPING BY A NUMERIC FIELD

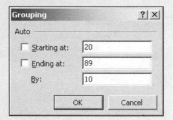

3. Click the **OK** button in the Grouping dialog box.

4. Double-click the **Sum of Dues** field button, click **Average** in the Summarize by list, click the **Number** button, click **Number** in the Category list, change the value in the Decimal places option to **0**, click the **OK** button in the Format dialog box, and then click the **OK** button in the PivotTable Field dialog box. The final PivotTable is shown in Figure 2-45.

Figure 2-45	GROUPING BY THE AGE FIELD

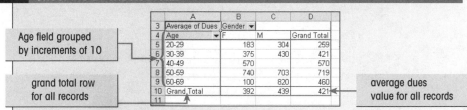

Age field grouped by increments of 10

grand total row for all records

average dues value for all records

	A	B	C	D
3	Average of Dues	Gender ▾		
4	Age ▾	F	M	Grand Total
5	20-29	183	304	259
6	30-39	375	430	421
7	40-49	570		570
8	50-59	740	703	719
9	60-69	100	820	460
10	Grand Total	392	439	421
11				

TROUBLE? Depending on when you are completing this exercise, some ages may calculate to values a little higher than the figures display.

5. Save the workbook, and then print the AgeAnalysis worksheet with your name in the left section of the header.

You can also create a field directly on the PivotTable without adding a column that contains a formula to the source data. In a PivotTable, a field whose contents are dependent upon another field of data is called a **calculated field**. To create a calculated field, click the PivotTable button on the PivotTable toolbar, point to Formulas, and then click Calculated Field. You define a calculated field similarly to how you define a formula in Excel. If you did not have direct access to the source data (for example, if the data was physically stored in an external database and you were using Excel only as a front-end analysis tool), this would be your only method of creating new calculated fields to use in the PivotTable. PivotTable calculated fields are more limited than Excel formulas, however. For example, calculated fields cannot use certain functions, such as RAND (generates a random number) or TODAY (returns today's date), that return variable results. So in this case, responding to Lynn's request by expanding the source data with a new field based on a formula was your best option for adding this data to the PivotTable.

Creating Custom Calculations

A **custom calculation** in a PivotTable is an advanced method of analyzing values in the data area of a PivotTable. For example, you may want to know how each value compares as a percentage of the row, as a percentage of the column, or as a percentage of the total.

Custom calculations differ from calculated fields in this way: Calculated fields create a new value for each record in the data source, are displayed in the Field List, and are manipulated within the PivotTable just like the original fields of the source data. Custom calculations, however, do not create new fields; rather, custom calculations change the way the values from the Data Item field are summarized.

As you have already learned, the most common ways to summarize the Data Item field is to sum, count, or average its values. Using custom calculations, though, you display the Data Item field values as a percentage of the row, column, or total, or as compared to a base value. A **base value** is a value used for comparison purposes. Base values are stored in a field identified as the **base field**. For example, if you were comparing budget values from year to year and organized the data as an Excel list, you could use a PivotTable and custom calculation to show the difference between each year's budget values as compared to a "base" budget.

REFERENCE WINDOW   **RW**

<u>Creating a Custom Calculation</u>
- Click the Data Item field in the PivotTable, and then click the Field Settings button on the PivotTable toolbar.

or
- Double-click the Data Item field.

or
- Right-click the Data Item field, and then click Field Settings on the shortcut menu.
- Click the Options button in the PivotTable Field dialog box.
- Click the Show data as list arrow, and then click the appropriate custom calculation.
- Click appropriate choices in the Base field and Base item lists as appropriate.

Although the PivotTable currently shows that the total average Dues value is $421, and you can mentally compare each group to $421 to determine whether the group's average is higher or lower than the total average, Lynn would like to know the specific percentages for this comparison. You will apply a custom calculation to the Average of Dues field to determine how the age groups compare to the overall average.

To create a custom calculation:

1. Double-click the **Average of Dues** field, and then click **Options**. The PivotTable Field dialog box expands to show the custom calculation options.

   First, you will select the option for displaying the data that you want to calculate as a percentage of the data in the column of dues.

2. Click the **Show data as** list arrow, and then click **% of column**. See Figure 2-46. If you choose a calculation, such as "Difference From" or "% Difference From," you also have to specify a base field and base item.

Figure 2-46	CREATING A CUSTOM CALCULATION

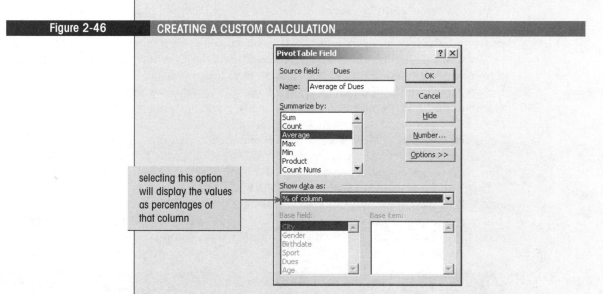

selecting this option will display the values as percentages of that column

3. Click the **OK** button. See Figure 2-47. The average Dues values are now shown as a percentage of the column. Values above 100% are above the average for the total column, and values below 100% are below the average for the total column.

Figure 2-47	VALUES SHOWN AS A PERCENTAGE OF THE COLUMN

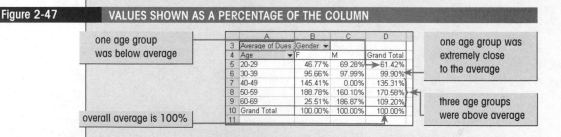

one age group was below average

one age group was extremely close to the average

three age groups were above average

overall average is 100%

	A	B	C	D
3	Average of Dues	Gender		
4	Age	F	M	Grand Total
5	20-29	46.77%	69.28%	61.42%
6	30-39	95.66%	97.99%	99.90%
7	40-49	145.41%	0.00%	135.31%
8	50-59	188.78%	160.10%	170.58%
9	60-69	25.51%	186.87%	109.20%
10	Grand Total	100.00%	100.00%	100.00%
11				

TROUBLE? Because ages are calculated using the NOW() function, your percentages may be slightly different than those shown in Figure 2-47.

Using a custom calculation, you can quickly see that one age group (20-29) reported dues that were much lower than the average for the entire survey, one age group (30-39) reported dues that were about equal to the total average, and three age groups (40-49, 50-59, and 60-69) reported dues higher than the average. People in the 50-59 age group reported the highest dues, at more than 170% higher than the overall average.

Changing PivotTable Options

The PivotTable itself has a number of options that help you identify the PivotTable and present and manage the data. For example, you can use the PivotTable options to add or remove the grand total column or row, to rename the PivotTable itself, or to change the way that the data is refreshed.

REFERENCE WINDOW   **RW**

Changing PivotTable defaults
- Right-click the PivotTable.
- Click Table Options on the shortcut menu.
- Make the appropriate choices in the PivotTable Options dialog box.
- Click the OK button.

By default, data in a PivotTable is not automatically updated if edits to the source data are made. Lynn asks if there is a way to refresh the data in the PivotTable and PivotChart automatically. You will use PivotTable Options to investigate this request.

To investigate how to automatically refresh data in a PivotTable and PivotChart:

1. Right-click any cell in the PivotTable, and then click **Table Options** on the short-cut menu. The PivotTable Options dialog box opens. The options that you select in this dialog box apply to the PivotTable as a whole.

2. Type **AgeGroups** in the Name text box. When you create a new PivotTable, Excel assigns it a default name of "PivotTable" plus a digit that indicates how many PivotTables have been created in this workbook during this session. Although you do not have to rename the PivotTable, a descriptive name can help you identify the PivotTable with which you are working, especially in situations where the PivotTable's name is displayed (for example, in the PivotTable and PivotChart Wizard Step 2 of 3 when you create a new PivotTable based on an existing one).

   To determine if there are any PivotTable options that provide Lynn with the automatic refresh capability that she requested, you will use the What's This? pointer to get more information on the Refresh on open feature.

3. Click the **Help** button ⟨?⟩ in the upper-right corner of the PivotTable Options dialog box, and then click the **Refresh on open** check box with ⟨?⟩. See Figure 2-48.

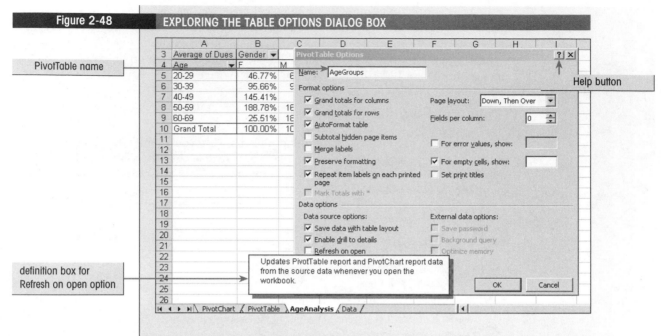

Figure 2-48   EXPLORING THE TABLE OPTIONS DIALOG BOX

You explain to Lynn that you can make the PivotTable automatically refresh every time the workbook is opened, but as data is edited or changed, she needs to manually refresh the PivotTable using the Refresh Data button on the PivotTable toolbar or by right-clicking the PivotTable and then selecting Refresh Data on the shortcut menu.

4. Click the **Refresh on open** check box, and then click the **OK** button.

Lynn is very excited with the analysis capabilities of PivotTables, but some of the statistics that you have calculated using PivotTables have raised even more questions. She asks if there is an easy way to isolate or view the records that are used for a particular calculation within the PivotTable. You explain that the drill down feature of a PivotTable provides that functionality.

Drilling Down in a PivotTable

Drill down means to quickly find, copy, and present the detail records that are used to develop a summarized value in a PivotTable. You drill down in a PivotTable by double-clicking any value in the Data Item area. The individual records that are used in that calculation will be copied and pasted to a new worksheet.

Lynn is very curious about the value in the Grand Total cell for the 50-59 age group. She asks you if there is a quick way to determine from which cities those surveys came. You explain that by double-clicking any value in the Data Item area of a PivotTable, she can drill down and quickly view the details she is looking for.

To drill down in a PivotTable:

1. Double-click cell **D8** in the Grand Total column for the 50-59 age group. Excel creates a new sheet with just the information relating to this age group.

2. Click any cell in the new worksheet so that you can view the data. See Figure 2-49. Lynn can see the specific records that are responsible for these high dollar values in the Dues column.

   TROUBLE? Because ages are calculated using the NOW() function, your results might be slightly different.

Figure 2-49	DRILL DOWN RESULTS

	A	B	C	D	E	F	G
1	City	Gender	Birthdate	Sport	Dues	Age	
2	Rosehill	F	12/24/1944	Golf	400	56	
3	Sunflower	F	3/2/1945	Golf	1000	56	
4	Sunflower	F	10/4/1950	Golf	820	50	
5	Apache	M	11/15/1943	Golf	400	57	
6	Apache	M	7/2/1949	Swimming	500	52	
7	Rosehill	M	10/3/1945	Golf	910	55	
8	Rosehill	M	3/10/1946	Golf	1000	55	
9							

3. Print the results of the drill down worksheet with your name in the left section of the header.

4. Save and close the workbook, and then exit Excel.

Using PivotTables and PivotCharts, you can summarize and analyze a list of data in many ways. Now that you've showed Lynn how to use PivotTables and PivotCharts, she is confident that she will be able to analyze the results of the final survey in any way she wants.

Session 2.2 QUICK CHECK

1. Describe the four drop areas of a PivotChart.

2. What is the relationship between a PivotTable and a PivotChart?

3. What are the acceptable types of source data for a PivotTable?

4. Identify four techniques to change the fields in a PivotTable.

5. What does drill down mean?

6. Describe two ways to add a calculated field to a PivotTable.

REVIEW ASSIGNMENTS

Green Valley Recreation wants to import and analyze data on women's tennis champions for an upcoming event. You will import the data and then work with the PivotTable and PivotChart to analyze it.

To complete this task:

1. Start Excel and Internet Explorer, and then go to **http://sports.yahoo.com/ten/stats/womoney.html**.

2. Import the table showing the women's professional leading money winners using a Web query. Enter your name in the left section of the header, and then print the worksheet in landscape orientation. Close the workbook without saving the changes.

3. Open the **Tennis-2B** workbook from the Tutorial.02\Review folder on your Data Disk. All the fields were imported into a single column within Excel. You will use tools within both Excel and Word to parse the data and create a correctly structured list of information.

4. Insert a new row 4 to be used as a header row. Enter the following field names in the following cells:

   A4:   Rank

   B4:   FName

   C4:   LName

   D4:   Country

   E4:   Earnings

Explore   5. Because you can easily re-create the rank data using Excel's Auto Fill feature, delete the numbers (and periods) from the current list using Excel's Find and Replace feature. (*Hint*: Use appropriate wildcard characters to find two numbers followed by a period, and replace the Find what criteria with nothing.)

6. Move the existing list in the range A5:A29 into the range G5:G29, and then enter a numerical series beginning with "1" in cell A5 and ending with "25" in cell A29. Now that the ranking data has been separated into its own column, you will work on the other four fields.

7. Copy the data in the range G5:G29, and then paste it into a blank Word document. It will paste into the Word document as a table with one column.

8. Convert the table to text, separating the text with paragraph marks, and then replace multiple spaces with a single space to get each record as consistent as possible. (*Hint*: Search for two spaces and replace it with one space. Continue this process until zero replacements can be made.)

Explore   9. Search for the character that indicates the beginning of the earnings field, a dollar sign ($), and replace it with a tab character plus a dollar sign ($). Select the list and convert it back to a table with two columns using tabs to separate the columns.

10. The income data should now be separated in the second column. Copy and paste the second column into column E of the Tennis-2B workbook, starting at cell E5.

11. In the Word document, delete the second column of income data, and then convert the existing table that contains first name, last name, and country information back into text, separating the text with paragraph marks.

12. To separate the Country data, find a comma (,) followed by a single space, and then replace both characters with just one tab character.

13. With all text still selected, convert the list back to a table with two columns using tabs to separate the columns. The country data should now be separated in the second column. Copy and paste the second column into column D of the Tennis-2B workbook, starting at cell D5.

14. In the Word document, delete the second column of country data, and then convert the existing table that contains first name and last name back into text, separating the text with paragraph marks.

15. Find a single space and replace it with a tab character.

16. With all text selected, convert the list back to a table with three (if a tab character was inserted before each first name) or four (if some names, such as Chris Everett Lloyd, have three parts) columns using tabs to separate the columns. The first name data should now be separated in the second column (if a tab character was inserted before each first name which creates a blank first column). Fix any inconsistent records. Copy and paste the first name data into column B of the Tennis-2B workbook, starting at cell B5.

17. In the Word document, delete the column of first name data, and if there is an extra blank column as the first column, delete it as well. Then convert the existing table that contains last names only, back into text, separating the text with a space character (if some last names are in two columns) or paragraph marks (if all last names are already in one column).

18. Copy and paste the last name data into column C of the Tennis-2B workbook, starting at cell C5. (*Note*: Because there is only one column of data at this point, you don't need to first convert it to a table before copying and pasting it back into Excel.)

19. Use the Format Painter to copy the format from column F to columns A through E. Then resize the columns as necessary to view all of their entries. See Figure 2-50 for the final list. Use column G to make sure all entries were pasted correctly before you continue. Note that depending on your Excel 2002 SmartTag settings, you might see SmartTag indicators in the corner of some of the cells, such as those that contain names of countries.

Figure 2-50

	A	B	C	D	E	F	G H I	J	K
3									
4	Rank	FName	LName	Country	Earnings				
5	1	Jennifer	Capriati	United States	994528		Jennifer Capriati, United States	$994,528	
6	2	Martina	Hingis	Switzerland	926451		Martina Hingis, Switzerland	$926,451	
7	3	Venus	Williams	United States	774306		Venus Williams, United States	$774,306	
8	4	Amelie	Mauresmo	France	612786		Amelie Mauresmo, France	$612,786	
9	5	Lindsay	Davenport	United States	574178		Lindsay Davenport, United States	$574,178	
10	6	Serena	Williams	United States	552345		Serena Williams, United States	$552,345	
11	7	Jelena	Dokic	Yugoslavia	309093		Jelena Dokic, Yugoslavia	$309,093	
12	8	Amanda	Coetzer	South Africa	283163		Amanda Coetzer, South Africa	$283,163	
13	9	Meghann	Shaughnessy	United States	278037		Meghann Shaughnessy, United States	$278,03	
14	10	Kim	Clijsters	Belgium	276242		Kim Clijsters, Belgium	$276,242	
15	11	Arantxa	Sanchez-Vicario		245388		Arantxa Sanchez-Vicario	$245,388	
16	12	Lisa	Raymond	United States	227372		Lisa Raymond, United States	$227,372	
17	13	Magdalena	Maleeva	Bulgaria	221061		Magdalena Maleeva, Bulgaria	$221,061	
18	14	Elena	Dementieva	Russia	215361		Elena Dementieva, Russia	$215,361	
19	15	Paola	Suarez	Argentina	213194		Paola Suarez, Argentina	$213,194	
20	16	Conchita	Martinez	Spain	210618		Conchita Martinez, Spain	$210,618	
21	17	Nathalie	Tauziat	France	210150		Nathalie Tauziat, France	$210,150	
22	18	Justine	Henin	Belgium	195787		Justine Henin, Belgium	$195,787	
23	19	Elena	Likhovtseva	Russia	183610		Elena Likhovtseva, Russia	$183,610	
24	20	Ai	Sugiyama	Japan	176713		Ai Sugiyama, Japan	$176,713	
25	21	Sandrine	Testud	France	176255		Sandrine Testud, France	$176,255	
26	22	Anna	Kournikova	Russia	169572		Anna Kournikova, Russia	$169,572	

Sheet1 / Sheet2 / Sheet3 /

20. Create a PivotChart in a new worksheet from the data in the list. Use Earnings in the Data Items area, Country in the Page Fields area, and LName in the Category Fields area. Filter for the United States in the Country field.

21. Enter your name in the left section of the header, and then print the PivotChart in landscape orientation. Switch to the Sheet1 worksheet, enter your name in the left section of the header, and then print the list in landscape orientation.

22. Switch to the worksheet that includes the PivotTable, and then use whatever PivotTable structure modification technique you like best to switch the Earnings and LName field positions. Earnings will now be in the row heading area, and LName will be counted in the data item area. Remove the Country field from the Page area.

23. Group the records so that you count how many players are in income groupings. Start the groupings at 100,000, end them at 1,000,000, and increment the groups by 100,000.

24. Show detail records for each Earnings category by adding the LName field as a second row heading.

25. Apply a Report 2 AutoFormat, and then print the worksheet with the PivotTable. See Figure 2-51 to view a portion of the completed PivotTable.

Figure 2-51

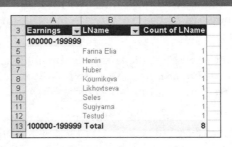

26. Save and close the workbook, and then exit Excel. Close any open Word documents without saving them, and then exit Word.

CASE PROBLEMS

Case 1. Building a List of the U.S. House of Representatives You're building a directory of the U.S. House of Representatives members for an upcoming political science project. You will go to the Web to find a list of members and then scrub and analyze the data in Excel.

To complete this task:

1. Start Excel, open your Web browser, go to **http://www.house.gov/**, and then search for the Web page that lists the current U. S. House of Representatives.

Explore

2. If the list of representatives is not in the form of a table that you can import using a Web query, you can still create a static copy of the information on the Web page and paste it into an Excel workbook. Select the list of representatives, click Edit on the menu bar in your browser, and then click Copy. Start Word, and then click the Paste button on the Standard toolbar.

3. Study the list. Is there a consistent set of characters that could be used to separate the fields? Since some of fields, such as first name, last name, and state, contain more than one word in that field (Capito, Shelley Moore, West Virginia, 2nd or Clay Jr., William "Lacy," Missouri, 1st), you can't use the space character alone to determine how to separate the fields. You do notice, however, that the fields are consistently separated by a comma and a space. Therefore, search for and replace all occurrences of a comma followed by a space with a tab character. (*Hint*: To find these special nonprinting characters in a Word document, make sure the Show/Hide button on the Standard toolbar is toggled on.) Enter your name in the header, and then print the first page. Close the document without saving it.

4. Open the **Representatives-2B** document from the Tutorial.02\Cases folder on your Data Disk.

5. Select the entire list, and then use the Table menu options to convert the list to a table with four columns, using the comma character to separate the text.

6. With each field in its own column in a form of a Word table, you can easily copy and paste the entire list back to Excel. Select the entire table, and then copy and paste it into a blank Excel workbook starting at cell A1 of the first worksheet.

7. Return to the Word document, and close it without saving it. Exit Word.

8. In the Excel workbook, insert a header row as a row with the field names of Last, First, State, and District.

9. Use the Format Painter to copy the formatting from column F to columns A through D, and then resize columns A through D so that all of the data in each column is clearly displayed.

10. Save your workbook with the name **Representatives-2B** in the Tutorial.02\Cases folder on your Data Disk, then scroll through your list of representatives in Excel. If any of the records are stored inconsistently (for example, if the State and District data is in the same field), fix those entries manually. In a new Word document, explain why some of the records did not convert to four consistent fields in the Excel workbook.

11. Create a PivotTable from the data that counts the number of representatives by state. Place the PivotTable in a new worksheet. Use the State field as the row heading, and use the Last name as the data field.

Explore ▷ 12. Sort the PivotTable in descending order based on the Count of Last field.

Explore ▷ 13. Rename the Count of Last field name to "Number of Reps."

Explore ▷ 14. Add the Last field to the Data Item area a second time, and rename the field to "Percent of Total."

Explore ▷ 15. Using Options button in the PivotTable Field dialog box for the Percent of Total field, add a custom calculation so that this data is shown as a % of the total. A portion of the PivotTable is shown in Figure 2-52.

Figure 2-52

	A	B	C	D
1	Drop Page Fields Here			
2				
3	State ▼	Data ▼	Total	
4	California	Number of Reps	52	
5		Percent of Total	11.82%	
6	New York	Number of Reps	31	
7		Percent of Total	7.05%	
8	Texas	Number of Reps	30	
9		Percent of Total	6.82%	
10	Florida	Number of Reps	23	
11		Percent of Total	5.23%	
12	Pennsylvania	Number of Reps	21	
13		Percent of Total	4.77%	
14	Illinois	Number of Reps	20	
15		Percent of Total	4.55%	
16	Ohio	Number of Reps	19	
17		Percent of Total	4.32%	
18	Michigan	Number of Reps	16	
19		Percent of Total	3.64%	
20	New Jersey	Number of Reps	13	
21		Percent of Total	2.95%	
22	North Carolina	Number of Reps	12	
23		Percent of Total	2.73%	

16. Save the workbook, add your name to the left section of the header, and then print the worksheet that contains the PivotTable.

17. Close the workbook. Exit Excel.

Case 2. Managing Census Data There is a large amount of free census data on the Web that you can use for various business planning purposes. Even though it is often a few years old (the age of the data depends upon the date of the last U.S. census) the data is used by many businesses as the most accurate representation of population statistics available. For example, suppose that one of your company's products (such as a home appliance or a life insurance policy) is highly correlated with the birth rate for an area. You can use census data to determine which states have the fastest growing populations due to new births and focus your marketing dollars in those states.

To complete this task:

1. Start Excel and Internet Explorer. Go to **http://www.census.gov** and explore the site.

Explore

2. Use a Web query to import the census data into a new Excel workbook. Print the first page with your name in the header, and then close the file without saving it.

3. Open the **Census-2B** workbook located in the Tutorial.02\Cases folder on your Data Disk. Because you only want to evaluate data by state, not by region, delete rows 17 through 30.

4. Click cell A17, the new first row of the list, for Alabama, and look in the Formula bar. The entire record is entered in cell A17. Right now, only spaces separate the field values. You will use Word to help scrub this data.

5. Select rows 17 through 67 (all 50 states), and then paste them into a new Word document. They will paste into Word as rows in a single-column table.

6. Convert the entire table to text, separating the records with paragraph marks.

Explore

7. To convert the records into individual fields, you have to determine what common character separates the fields. Unfortunately, you can't use a single space because some field values (New York, North Dakota) also contain a single space. The presence of two or more spaces, however, does indicate that a field has ended. Find and replace all

occurrences of two spaces, and replace the search criteria with a tab character. Then find and replace for all occurrences of two tab characters, and replace the search criteria with a single tab character. Continue replacing two tab characters with a single tab character until Word prompts you that there are no more replacements to be made.

8. With the records scrubbed so that there is a single tab character between fields, convert the rows back to a Word table with nine columns using the tab character as the field separator.

9. Select the entire table, and then paste it into Sheet2, starting at cell A2 of the Excel workbook. Close the Word document without saving it, and then exit Word.

10. Rename Sheet1 as "RawData" and Sheet2 as "StateData."

11. Enter the following field names in row 1 of the StateData worksheet as the row header values:

   A1:   State

   B1:   1999

   C1:   1998

   D1:   Growth

   E1:   % Growth

   F1:   Births

   G1:   Deaths

   H1:   International

   I1:   Domestic

Explore ▷ 12. The data in both columns D and E can be computed using an Excel formula. By using a formula to compute this information, you ensure that it is correct as compared to the population statistics reported for 1999 and 1998 in column B and C. Because you never want to use raw data for any value that can be calculated in an Excel workbook, enter formulas in cells D2 and E2 to calculate the correct values, and then copy those formulas through all of the state records.

13. Format the values in column E so that they appear as percentages with one digit to the right of the decimal point.

14. Sort the data in descending order based on the highest number of births. Give the cells with the 10 highest birth values a yellow fill color.

15. Sort the data in descending order based on the % Growth values. Give the cells with the 10 highest % Growth values a turquoise fill color.

16. Based on the data that you highlighted, which states appear to have both the most births as well as the highest growth rates? Give the state cells (column A) that met both criteria a bright green fill color.

Explore ▷ 17. You are also very interested in migration statistics and whether or not your product is also correlated to the international migration value. To get a feel for how many states have a large migration population, create the PivotTable shown in Figure 2-53. (*Hint*: The International field is used in both the data and row areas. The row field is grouped by increments of 10,000).

Figure 2-53

	A	B	C
1			
2			
3	Count of International		
4	International ▼	Total	
5	0-9999	37	
6	10000-19999	7	
7	20000-29999	1	
8	30000-39999	1	
9	40000-49999	1	
10	80000-89999	2	
11	100000-109999	1	
12	240000-249999	1	
13	Grand Total	51	
14			

18. Drill down to find out which state had between 240,000 and 249,999 international migrants between the years 1998 and 1999.

19. Print the worksheet with the PivotTable with your name in the left section of the header. Also print the first 11 rows of the StateData worksheet with your name in the left section of the header.

20. Save and close the Census-2B workbook. Exit Excel.

Case 3. Analyzing Sales Performance You are in the process of analyzing sales performance for your company, a small technology distributor. The sales results for the first four months of the year have been entered into an appropriate Excel list. You will use Excel's PivotTable and PivotChart features to create several reports.

To complete this task:

1. Start Excel and then open the **TechnologyStore-2** workbook located in the Tutorial.02\Cases folder on your Data Disk.

Explore

2. Create and print the clustered bar PivotChart shown in Figure 2-54. Note that the font size for the legend and axes has been increased so that the information is easier to read. Be sure to enter you name in the left section of the header. Use the Chart Wizard to change the chart type.

Figure 2-54

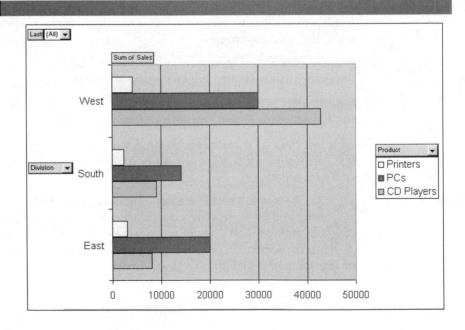

3. Create and print the PivotChart shown in Figure 2-55. Note that the font size for the legend and axes has been increased so that the information is easier to read. Be sure to enter you name in the left section of the header.

Figure 2-55

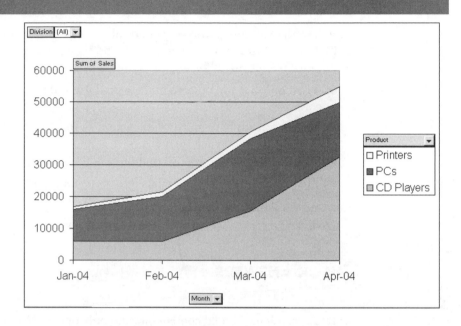

4. Based on these two charts, what conclusions can you make? Record your thoughts in a Word document. Write a paragraph of analysis for each PivotChart.

5. Use the existing PivotTables and PivotCharts to analyze the data to answer the following questions:

   ■ Why were the Apr-04 sales so high for the company?

   ■ What divisions, products, and salesmen were responsible for this performance?

6. Print the PivotTable and PivotChart that help support your answers for these questions. Be sure to enter your name in the left section of the header.

7. Save and close the workbook. Exit Excel

Case 4. Preparing a List for a Children's Book Club   You're in charge of developing a list of high-quality books to recommend for a children's summer reading club for an elementary school in your hometown. You'll use the PivotChart, PivotTable, and drill down capabilities to create a list of the books in the Fantasy category.

To complete this task:

1. Start Excel and then open the **BookClub-2** workbook located in the Tutorial.02\Cases folder on your Data Disk.

2. Create a PivotChart placing the chart on its own sheet. Place Author in the Page drop area, Category in the Category drop area, and Title in the Data Item drop area.

Explore

3. Enter "Book Club Selections" as the title for the PivotChart, and increase the font size of the title and values on the y-axis to 16. Enter your name in the left section of the header of the PivotChart worksheet, and then print it.

4. Rename the worksheet with the PivotTable as "PivotTable."

5. Drill down in the PivotTable to display the Fantasy books.

6. Rename the Sheet2 tab as "Fantasy." Enter your name in the left section of the header of the Fantasy worksheet, and then print it.

7. Switch to the PivotTable sheet, and then use the Show Detail button to show Title details within the Category row heading. Apply a Report 4 AutoFormat.

8. Switch to the Selections worksheet to display the original list, note the entry of 1986 in cell E12 for the Commodore Perry book, and then sort the records in ascending order by author. Answer the following questions:

   ■ Based on what you observe in the sorted list, did the values in column E sort correctly?

   ■ Not all records have an entry in column E, the Newbury field. How did this change the way the list sorted?

   ■ What are the left, right, top, and bottom edges of this list?

   ■ What are two reasons that a header row is important to an Excel list?

9. Save and close the workbook. Close Excel.

QUICK | CHECK ANSWERS

Session 2.1

1. Each column should contain one and only one piece of information. Also, enter all values in the column consistently.

2. Blank rows or columns mark the boundaries of the Excel list. Therefore, there should not be any blank rows or columns within a list. There should be a blank row above the header row, to separate the list from other data in the worksheet.

3. Internet Explorer

4. There is no header row, or the header row does not contain clear field names. Each column contains more than one piece of data. There are blank rows or columns within the data. The data hasn't been entered consistently from record to record (for example, IL vs. Illinois).

5. Word enables you to search and replace special text characters such as tabs. Word also enables you to convert information that is separated by a specific character, such as a space or a tab, into a table, using the special character to separate the columns.

Session 2.2

1. The drop areas of a PivotChart are

   ■ Page: Fields in the Page drop area are used to filter the presentation of data in the PivotTable and PivotChart.

   ■ Category (x-axis): Fields in the Category drop area are used as labels for the x-axis of the PivotChart.

   ■ Series (legend): Fields in the Series drop area are used in the legend of the PivotChart.

   ■ Data Item: Fields in the Data Item drop area are presented as bars, the value of which is displayed on the y-axis of the PivotChart.

2. PivotCharts are based on PivotTables. You cannot have a PivotChart without also creating a PivotTable. You can have a standalone PivotTable.

3. The source data for either a PivotTable or a PivotChart can be a single list within an Excel worksheet, multiple data ranges, and also external sources of data, such as an Access database or an OLAP (On-Line Analytical Processing) source.

4. To change the fields in a PivotTable, you can use any of the following techniques:

   ■ Drag existing fields from one field area to another.

   ■ Click the PivotTable button on the PivotTable toolbar, click Wizard, click the Layout button, and then drag the fields to their desired locations in the PivotTable and PivotChart Wizard – Layout dialog box.

   ■ Click the Show Field List button on the PivotTable toolbar to display the PivotTable Field List, and then drag the fields from the PivotTable Field List to the desired location.

   ■ Click the Show Field List button on the PivotTable toolbar to display the PivotTable Field List, and then use the Add To button in the PivotTable Field List to add the fields to the desired PivotTable location.

   ■ Use the Show Detail button on the PivotTable toolbar to add more detail to a PivotTable.

5. Drill down means to quickly find the detail records that are used to develop a summarized value in a PivotTable. To drill down in a PivotTable, double-click a value and the individual records used in that calculation are copied and pasted to a new worksheet.

6. To add a calculated field to a PivotTable, add a field that contains a formula to the source data, or create the calculated field within the PivotTable itself.

In this tutorial you will:

- Select the best chart type for your business needs

- Work with the Chart Wizard to create and modify charts

- Compare how various chart types communicate different messages

- Change values in a data series

- Format chart elements

- Create a custom chart

- Change the default chart type

USING EXCEL CHARTS TO MAKE BUSINESS DECISIONS

CASE

Green Valley Recreation

Green Valley Recreation (GVR) is a community agency that organizes hundreds of programs, such as basketball, golf, and music lessons, which help build the physical and mental skills of the residents of Green County, Illinois. As a business analyst for GVR, you are responsible for collecting, organizing, and presenting data to support various decisions at several levels. Your supervisor, Lynn Tse, has requested that you use charts to summarize the numeric information that you have gathered in preparation for several upcoming GVR Board meetings. You already use Excel to organize and analyze data to support the many decisions facing the GVR Board of Directors. Now, however, you will add a visual component to each presentation of data using Excel's extensive charting capabilities. You will use charts to more clearly and quickly emphasize the significance of the data rather than require the reader to analyze columns and rows of numbers. For example, GVR has received a significant number of calls from residents of surrounding counties. Based on the calls received, you will present charts of data that will help clarify which counties are interested in GVR services and to evaluate how the call volumes are increasing over time.

You will also compare and contrast the chart types so that you will know which chart type to use for the data you have, as well as for the message you want to present. For example, one of GVR's programs, the billiards tournament, has had great success, and Lynn needs to go to the Board with a special request for new billiards tables that aren't currently in the budget. She needs your help to clarify both the rate of overall growth of the tournament and the fact that the tournament is now becoming popular among a wider range of members. You will examine the effectiveness of several chart types and formatting options to clarify various messages.

SESSION 3.1

In this session, you will learn about different chart types and sub-types, and you will work with the extensive features within the Chart Wizard to create and modify charts. You will move, edit, and resize charts, and you will also learn how to control what data the chart is presenting by working with the data series and x-axis (category axis) labels.

Emphasizing Information with a Chart

In Excel, a **chart** is a graphical presentation of data. A chart is also commonly called a graph. Figures 3-1 and 3-2 present income statement and projection data for We Make It Right, a small manufacturer. Figure 3-1 shows the data as a spreadsheet of numbers, and Figure 3-2 presents two of the significant findings in charts. Which of the two do you think is easier to read and understand?

Figure 3-1 | **2003 INCOME STATEMENT AND 2004 INCOME PROJECTIONS**

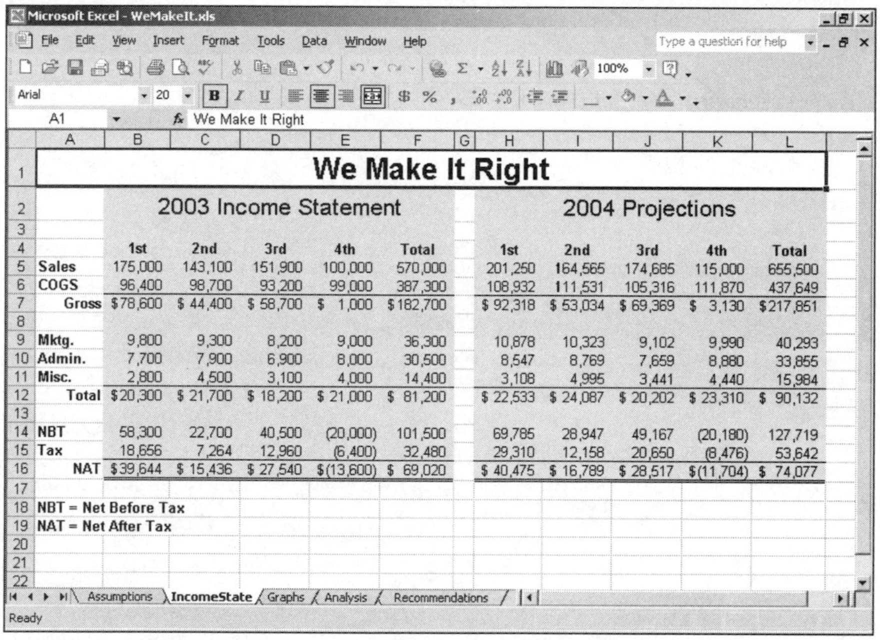

We Make It Right

	2003 Income Statement						2004 Projections				
	1st	2nd	3rd	4th	Total		1st	2nd	3rd	4th	Total
Sales	175,000	143,100	151,900	100,000	570,000		201,250	164,565	174,685	115,000	655,500
COGS	96,400	98,700	93,200	99,000	387,300		108,932	111,531	105,316	111,870	437,649
Gross	$78,600	$ 44,400	$ 58,700	$ 1,000	$182,700		$ 92,318	$ 53,034	$ 69,369	$ 3,130	$217,851
Mktg.	9,800	9,300	8,200	9,000	36,300		10,878	10,323	9,102	9,990	40,293
Admin.	7,700	7,900	6,900	8,000	30,500		8,547	8,769	7,659	8,880	33,855
Misc.	2,800	4,500	3,100	4,000	14,400		3,108	4,995	3,441	4,440	15,984
Total	$20,300	$ 21,700	$ 18,200	$ 21,000	$ 81,200		$ 22,533	$ 24,087	$ 20,202	$ 23,310	$ 90,132
NBT	58,300	22,700	40,500	(20,000)	101,500		69,785	28,947	49,167	(20,180)	127,719
Tax	18,656	7,264	12,960	(6,400)	32,480		29,310	12,158	20,650	(8,476)	53,642
NAT	$39,644	$ 15,436	$ 27,540	$(13,600)	$ 69,020		$ 40,475	$ 16,789	$ 28,517	$(11,704)	$ 74,077

NBT = Net Before Tax
NAT = Net After Tax

Figure 3-2   **TWO GRAPHICAL REPRESENTATIONS OF INCOME STATEMENT DATA**

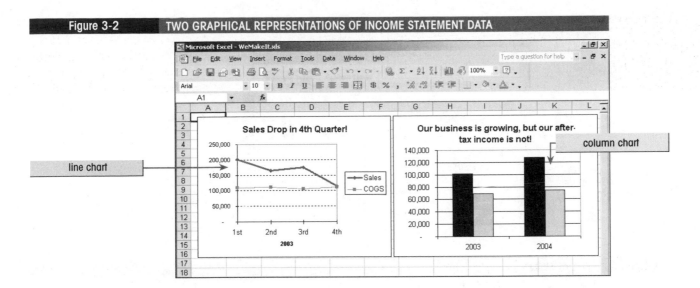

Even though all of the information presented in Figure 3-2 is also presented in Figure 3-1, the information is much easier to read and understand when presented in charts.

Of course, the purpose of a chart isn't to replace the need for detailed analysis of raw data. Rather, a chart should be used in conjunction with traditional workbook data to further enhance, summarize, and communicate key points. By providing a chart of the significant trends, findings, or issues, you have gone beyond the mechanics of creating correct formulas and are now working to analyze and summarize the important information within the data.

Creating a chart isn't a difficult task, but sometimes creating an *effective* chart—one that clearly and accurately conveys the intended meaning or message—can be challenging. To create an effective chart, first determine what you want to chart, and then display those findings in the form of an appropriate chart. Sometimes, you will already know the significant trends, comparisons, and findings in the data before you attempt to chart it, but other times, the chart itself will help identify and clarify that information. There is really no easy or automated way to determine the significant information, because what is "significant" often hinges on business knowledge that is not part of the data within Excel. For example, if We Make It Right ran a huge sale in the fourth quarter to intentionally clean out existing inventory, the line chart shown in Figure 3-2 might not be alarming or even particularly significant. At any rate, knowing more about how to use the charting tools within Excel, and which chart types support which types of information, will help you determine where you can use charts to more effectively analyze and communicate information. You've heard the phrase, "a picture is worth a thousand words." In Excel, a chart is worth a thousand numbers.

Understanding **the Chart Terminology and Chart Types**

Excel supports 14 standard types of charts, over 70 sub-types (variations of the 14 standard types), and about 20 custom chart types that you can use to present numeric data. For business data, the most common chart types are the column, line, area, and pie charts. Using the sample chart shown in Figure 3-3 as a reference, review the basic chart terminology provided in Figure 3-4.

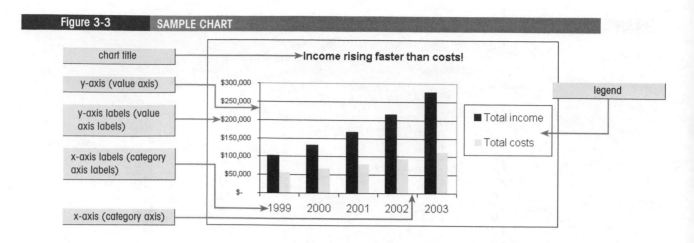

Figure 3-3   SAMPLE CHART

Figure 3-4   CHART TERMINOLOGY

CHART ITEM	DESCRIPTION
X-axis	Also called the **category axis**. The x-axis is the horizontal axis on a column chart and the vertical axis on a bar chart. The x-axis displays the **x-axis labels**.
X-axis labels	Also called the **category labels**. The x-axis labels are labels placed along the x-axis to identify the categories represented on the graph.
Y-axis	Also called the **value axis**. The y-axis is the vertical axis on a column chart and the horizontal axis on a bar chart. The y-axis displays numbers that identify the size of the bars.
Legend	Area that displays the color and pattern used for the bars of each data series.
Data series	In a column or bar chart, a set of bars for the same subject. A data series will have one corresponding data point for each x-axis label.
Data point	In a column or bar chart, the value of one bar. One data point corresponds to one value in a cell of a worksheet.
Data marker	The graphical item that represents the data point. In a column or bar chart, the data marker is a bar.
Gridline	Vertical or horizontal lines that extend from an axis to the other side of the chart to make the chart easier to read. In a column chart, horizontal gridlines are commonly used to help identify the size of the columns.

Because these are the terms that Excel uses to identify the components of a chart, knowing the terminology will improve your productivity when creating and modifying charts.

The Column Chart

The **column chart**, shown in Figure 3-5, is probably the most common chart type. The general public sometimes calls this chart a "bar chart"; however, in Excel, a **bar chart** is a separate chart type that displays values in horizontal bars, as shown in Figure 3-6. Therefore, in this textbook, the term *column chart* will be used to describe a chart with values in vertical columns, and bar chart will be used to describe a chart with values in horizontal bars.

Figure 3-5	SAMPLE COLUMN CHART

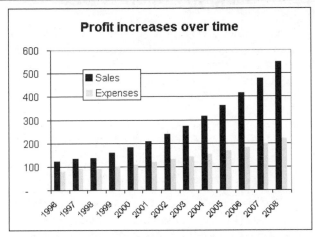

Figure 3-6	SAMPLE BAR CHART

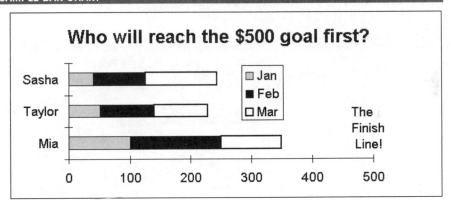

Both column and bar charts are appropriate chart types to use when you are trying to compare values against each other. Whether you use a column or bar chart is partly determined by your own personal preference, but the vertical orientation of column charts is more common than the horizontal orientation of bar charts. You might want to use a bar chart, however, when you want to emphasize values that "move forward" through time. In Figure 3-6, for example, the bar chart is used to show how sales representatives are progressing against a sales goal.

There are many sub-types of column and bar charts. For example, in Figure 3-5, the column chart is actually a clustered column chart because the values in each data series, Sales and Expenses, are clustered, side-by-side, for each category label. The bar chart in Figure 3-6 is more precisely called a stacked bar chart, because the data series (Jan, Feb, and Mar) are stacked to create a sum total for each category. (In a bar chart, the x-axis is vertical.) To change the chart type or sub-type for new or existing charts, you can use the Chart Wizard.

The **Chart Wizard** is an Excel tool that you can use to quickly create or modify an existing chart. The Chart Wizard offers hundreds of options, some of which depend on the type of chart you select. Before you start the Chart Wizard, though, you should select the data you want to chart. Although you can select the data you want to chart after you start the Chart Wizard, making the data selection first gives you access to several benefits inherent in the Wizard, including being able to preview the actual chart data with several different chart types.

Creating a Chart Using the Chart Wizard

Green Valley Recreation has had many calls from other counties, requesting information about GVR's activities and facilities. You have been logging these calls in an Excel workbook so that Lynn can use this data with the Board of Directors as part of a study on whether or not GVR should expand the GVR facilities to non-Green County residents. You will use the Chart Wizard to analyze the call volumes with a column chart.

To create a column chart using the Chart Wizard:

1. Start Excel and open the **CallAnalysis-3** workbook from the Tutorial.03\Tutorial folder on your Data Disk.

2. Select the range **A4:E8** (making sure not to include the total values in column F), and then click the **Chart Wizard button** 📊 on the Standard toolbar. The Chart Type dialog box of the Wizard opens. See Figure 3-7. The first step in creating a chart is choosing one of the 14 chart types. Because column charts are the most common, it is the default chart for Excel and is already selected. Seven column chart sub-types are also displayed.

| Figure 3-7 | CHART WIZARD – STEP 1 OF 4 – CHART TYPE |

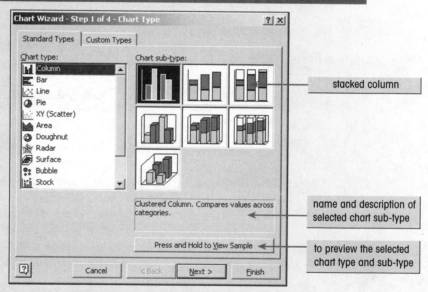

Because you selected the range of data you wanted to chart before starting the Chart Wizard, you can preview the data in any chart type that you might be curious about. For example, you wonder how this data would appear as a line chart.

3. Click **Line** in the Chart type list, click the **Line with markers displayed at each data value** chart sub-type (first column on the left, second row), and then click the **Press and Hold to View Sample** button. See Figure 3-8. Note that if you do not select the data that you want to chart before starting the Chart Wizard, the Chart Wizard cannot show you a preview of how your data will appear.

TROUBLE? If your chart doesn't look like the one in Figure 3-8, you may have selected a range other than A4:E8 as specified in Step 2. To correct this, click the Cancel button in the Chart Wizard, and then repeat Step 2.

Figure 3-8	PREVIEWING A CHART TYPE

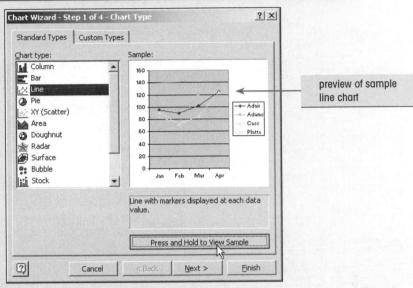

Because you are mostly interested in the cumulative call volume for all four counties for a particular month, you will preview the data as a stacked column chart. Although the line chart emphasizes trends over time for individual counties better than a stacked column chart, a stacked column chart will better display the cumulative call volume totals for that month.

4. Click **Column** in the Chart type list, click the **Stacked Column** chart sub-type, (middle column, first row), and then click the **Press and Hold to View Sample** button. This is the chart type you want to use because, at this point, Lynn isn't concerned with trends for individual counties (which would be best illustrated with a line chart) or with comparing call volumes between the four counties (which would be best illustrated with a clustered column chart). Rather, she's trying to show the cumulative call volumes for all four counties for four months.

5. After you have studied the chart, release the mouse button, and then click the **Next** button.

Modifying the Source Data Ranges Using the Chart Wizard

Once you've determined the appropriate chart type and sub-type, you can use the second step of the Wizard, the Chart Source Data dialog box, to work with the **source data**, which is the data plotted by the chart. If you did not select the range of data that you want to chart before starting the Chart Wizard, or if the original range that you selected does not include all of the data series ranges you need, you can add or modify the data ranges in Step 2 of the Chart Wizard. If you selected a data range before starting the Chart Wizard, the entry appears in the Data range reference box as shown in Figure 3-9.

| Figure 3-9 | CHART WIZARD – STEP 2 OF 4 – CHART SOURCE DATA |

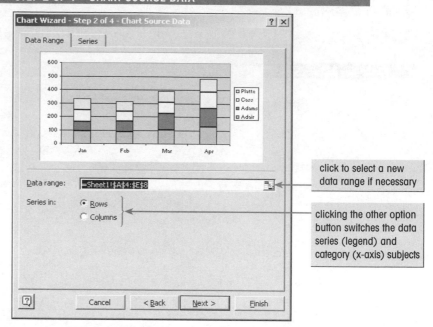

In addition to the data range, Step 2 of the Chart Wizard presents the Rows and Columns option buttons, which you can use to determine the orientation of data from the selected range data. As shown in Figure 3-9, each row (that is, each county) is currently graphed as a data series and is identified in the chart legend. Clicking the Columns option button would switch the chart so that each column of data (that is, each month) is represented as a data series.

Another way to think about the Columns and Rows options buttons is to realize that when you click the option button that isn't currently selected, the entries in the legend and the x-axis labels will switch places. Also realize that there is no single "right" way to present the data (in rows or in columns). The best presentation depends on what message you are trying to communicate. For example, if you are trying to communicate the cumulative growth of call volumes over four months, the information is best presented as it is currently displayed. If you were more interested in comparing the total call volume for one county versus another, however, then you would want to switch the legend and x-axis values so that the county names were in the x-axis label position and the months were in the legend position. This arrangement would stack the monthly values for one county in one column, so the totals for each county could be easily compared.

You are curious as to how the total call volumes compare for each county. You will switch the data series to Columns to analyze your data from that perspective.

To redisplay the data series by columns:

1. Click the **Columns** option button, and then observe that columns (months) are now used as the data series and each column (month) has an entry in the legend.

   Being able to see how the data charted by columns emphasizes the cumulative totals by county versus the cumulative totals by month, you are now confident that displaying the data series by rows is a better option.

2. Click the **Rows** option button.

3. Click the **Series** tab. See Figure 3-10.

Figure 3-10	SERIES TAB IN THE CHART SOURCE DATA DIALOG BOX

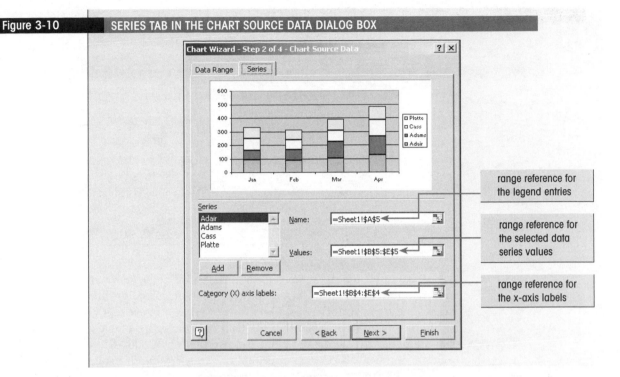

Having selected the data range and how it will be charted, you can use the Series tab in the Chart Source Data dialog box to modify the individual data series, legend entries, and x-axis (category axis) labels. Because the Platte County residents already have their own recreational facilities, and most of those inquiries would not translate to additional customers should GVR open up memberships to people outside of Green County, Lynn has asked that the calls from Platte county not be included in the chart.

To remove the Platte county data series:

1. Click **Platte** in the Series list.

2. Click the **Remove** button. The preview of the chart changes, removing the Platte data markers and legend entry.

3. Click the **Next** button.

Changing Chart Options Using the Chart Wizard

The third step of the Chart Wizard provides six tabs, as shown in Figure 3-11, which deal with the many chart options, including titles, axes, gridlines, the legend, data labels, and the data table. You can use these options to further clarify and improve your chart.

Figure 3-11   **CHART WIZARD – STEP 3 OF 4 – CHART OPTIONS DIALOG BOX**

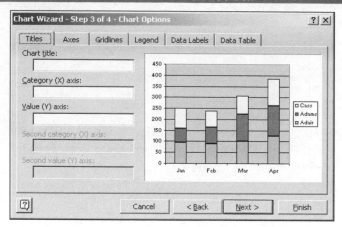

For example, adding an appropriate chart title helps summarize and communicate the main point of the chart to the reader. Adding appropriate gridlines helps the reader differentiate and compare bar sizes. **Data labels**, values or text that are added to the bars, help clarify the category or value that the data markers represent. Of course, adding too many chart options may actually detract from, rather than add to, the value of the chart. For example, if the labels on the x-axis or y-axis are already self-explanatory (for example, if the x-axis labels were Jan, Feb, Mar, and so forth), it would be unnecessary to add an axis title that identified the labels as "Months." Furthermore, axis labels use some of the space formerly occupied by the chart itself, making the chart smaller to accommodate the additional information. Fortunately, the Chart Wizard gives you a preview of each chart option as you apply it so you can evaluate the effect the option has on the chart. If you don't like the result of the option, you can remove it.

You know that you want to add a clarifying chart title to the chart, but you also want to experiment with the other chart options to determine which ones truly enhance the chart.

To use chart options to improve your column chart:

1. Click in the Chart title text box, type **Call volumes are growing!** and then press the **Tab** key so you can see the title above the chart in the preview window.

If the values on the y-axis needed to be clarified, you could enter a y-axis title. For example, if the values on the y-axis represented gallons or mileage, you might want to add a label to the y-axis that identified the nature of the values. In this case, though, the values on the y-axis represent the actual number of calls and do not require additional clarification. You can also enter a Category (X) axis, but in this case, the three-letter abbreviation for each month clearly identifies the categories on the chart. Before continuing with the Wizard, you want to see how the options on the Gridlines tab affect the presentation of the data on the chart.

2. Click the **Gridlines** tab, click the **Category (X) axis Major gridlines** check box to select it and observe the change, click the **Category (X) axis Minor gridlines** check box to select it and observe the change, and then click the **Value (Y) axis Minor gridlines** check box to select it and observe the change. You want enough gridlines to clearly differentiate the bars and provide a visual guide between the y-axis and the size of the bars, but too many gridlines can detract from the chart itself.

3. Clear the **Category (X) axis Minor gridlines** and **Value (Y) axis Minor grid-lines** check boxes to deselect these options, and then click the **Value (Y) axis Major gridlines** check box to select it (if it is not already selected), as shown in Figure 3-12.

   EXCEL 2000: The Value (Y) axis Major gridlines check box should already be selected. Do not click the check box again or you will deselect the option.

| Figure 3-12 | APPLYING THE GRIDLINES |

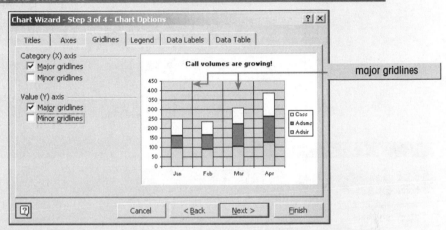

You also want to see what options are available that affect the legend.

4. Click the **Legend** tab, and then click the **Show legend** check box to deselect this option. You decide that removing the legend from this chart is not a good idea. Without the legend, you don't know what the colors in the bars represent. If you are only graphing one data series, this information is often provided in the title of the chart, and the legend is not necessary. When using multiple data series, however, you need some way to identify what the various colors for each data series represents, and a legend is the most common way to communicate that information.

5. Click the **Show legend** check box to select it again, click each of the **Placement** option buttons to observe how the legend appears in the various locations, and then click the **Bottom** option button to position the legend below the chart.

   Next, you will check out the options available on the Data Labels tab.

6. Click the **Data Labels** tab, click the **Series name** check box to select it, and then observe the series names that appear in each data marker. When using multiple data series, you can use series name data labels as another way to identify what each color represents within each bar. Because you are already using a legend to communicate this information, you don't also need to place the Series names within the data markers.

   EXCEL 2000: There is no Series name check box on the Data Labels tab of the Chart Wizard dialog box. Continue to Step 7.

7. Click the **Series name** check box to deselect it, and then click the **Category name** check box. Now the names of the months appear on the bars. Because the x-axis already displays the category name labels, you don't need to place the category names within the columns.

EXCEL 2000: There is no Series name check box or Category name check box on the Data Labels tab of the Chart Wizard dialog box. Instead, click the **Show label** option button to display the x-axis labels above the columns.

8. Click the **Category name** check box to deselect it, and then the click **Value** check box. See Figure 3-13. The value that each data marker represents displays within the data marker.

EXCEL 2000: There is no Category name check box or Series name check box on the Data Labels tab of the Chart Wizard dialog box. Click the **Show value** option button to display the numeric values above the columns. Click the **None** option button to deselect the option and remove the values.

Figure 3-13	ADDING LABELS TO DATA MARKERS

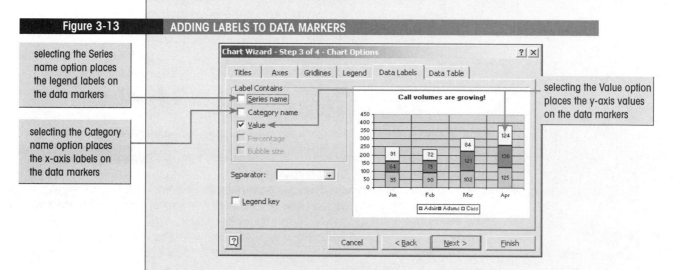

selecting the Series name option places the legend labels on the data markers

selecting the Category name option places the x-axis labels on the data markers

selecting the Value option places the y-axis values on the data markers

The Separator option determines whether a space or comma, for example, is used to separate multiple labels on one bar, and the Legend key option places a legend within the data markers. Neither option is needed for your chart because you have only placed one data value element in each data marker. Finally, you want to see what options are available on the Data Table tab.

9. Click the **Data Table** tab, click the **Show data table** check box to select it, and then click the **Show legend keys** check box to observe the change.

EXCEL 2000: The Show legend keys check box should already be selected.

The data table is yet another way to clarify the values of each data marker. Because you've added the values to the bars themselves, there's no need to add this information as a data table as well.

10. Click the **Show data table** check box to deselect it, which in turn deselects the Show legend keys option, and then click the **Next** button. The last step of the Wizard appears.

The last step of the Chart Wizard prompts you for information on where to place the chart, as a new sheet in the workbook, or as an object in an existing sheet. A chart that is inserted as an object on an existing worksheet is called an **embedded chart**. No matter whether the chart is embedded on an existing worksheet or added as a new chart worksheet, it is bound to the data on the original worksheet. That means that if the values in the worksheet change, the chart will automatically update as well.

If you insert the chart on an existing worksheet, you can print the chart and the worksheet data together on the same page, or print the chart by itself. If you insert the chart as a new sheet, you can't print the chart and worksheet data side by side on the same piece of paper. Therefore, you'll accept the default option and insert the chart as an object in the current sheet.

To complete the Chart Wizard and place the chart on the current worksheet:

1. Click the **Finish** button. See Figure 3-14. The data series and x-axis labels are identified by colored borders on the worksheet data. You could resize the borders in the worksheet to redefine what data is presented on the chart. The final column chart shows, however, that over the months of January through March, the combined call volumes for the three counties are growing, so there is no need to make any other changes to the chart at this time.

| Figure 3-14 | COLUMN CHART AFTER THE LAST STEP OF THE CHART WIZARD |

colored borders outline the data on the chart

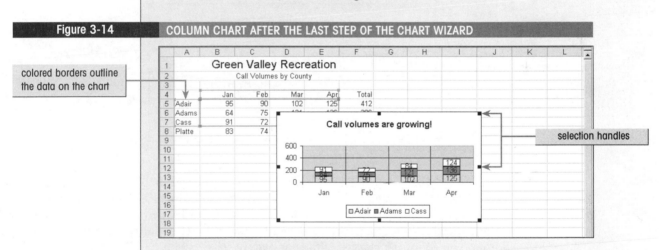

selection handles

TROUBLE? The y-axis scale automatically adjusts, depending on the physical size of the chart. A taller chart has more room to display more values on the y-axis and therefore can support smaller increments between values.

TROUBLE? The Chart toolbar appears by default. You can choose to hide the toolbar by clicking View on the menu bar, pointing to Toolbars, and then clicking Chart to remove the check mark.

Once a chart is added to a workbook, either as an embedded chart, or on its own worksheet, the chart is automatically connected to the data within the workbook. Any changes to the data automatically update all charts that use that value.

2. Click cell **B5**, notice the change in the border of the chart (the border no longer displays selection handles, which means that the chart is no longer selected), type **45**, and then press the **Enter** key. The chart is automatically updated with the new value.

You can change any of the chart options that you specified with the Chart Wizard after the chart is already created. Once the chart is created, you can also make many additional chart modifications that are not available from the Chart Wizard (such as resizing or changing the color of various chart elements). The more options that you specify correctly during the initial chart creation process, however, the less work you will have to do later. To access chart options from the menu system on an existing chart, click Chart on the menu bar, and then click Chart Options.

Selecting, Moving, and Resizing a Chart

Moving and resizing embedded charts are two of the most common improvements you will want to make to a chart. To move a chart, you simply drag the entire chart by dragging the chart area to the desired new location. You must be careful that you do not drag an item within the chart (such as the title or the legend), or you will move only that item and not the entire chart. Fortunately, Excel provides **ScreenTips** that identify what you are pointing to. For example, if you were to drag the chart while pointing to the chart area as shown in Figure 3-15, you would move the entire chart and not an element within the chart. While dragging the chart, the Move Object pointer ✛ will appear.

Figure 3-15   **CHART AREA SCREENTIP**

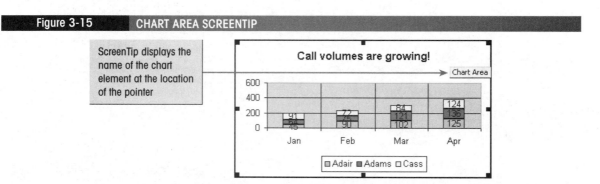

To resize a chart, it must be selected. You select a chart by clicking it, and you know when a chart is selected because it displays **selection handles**, the black squares, on the edges of the object. If a chart is not selected, a smooth black border without selection handles will outline the chart. Once a chart is selected so that it displays selection handles on the chart border, you resize the chart by dragging one of its selection handles in the direction you want the new shape to become.

To select, move, and resize the chart:

1. Click the **chart** to select it, point to the **Chart Area** on the chart, and then drag the chart up and to the right. See Figure 3-16.

Figure 3-16	MOVING A CHART

outline of the chart being moved

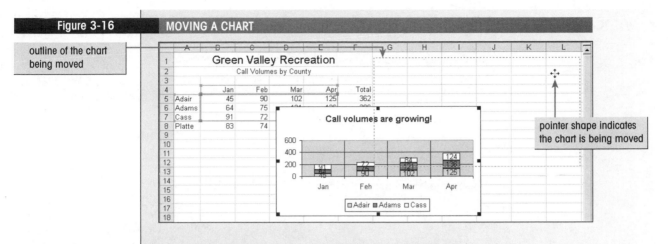

pointer shape indicates the chart is being moved

2. Position the pointer over the bottom middle selection handle so that the pointer changes to ↕, and then drag the selection handle down to expand the chart to the available size of the screen. See Figure 3-17.

Figure 3-17	CHART MOVED AND RESIZED

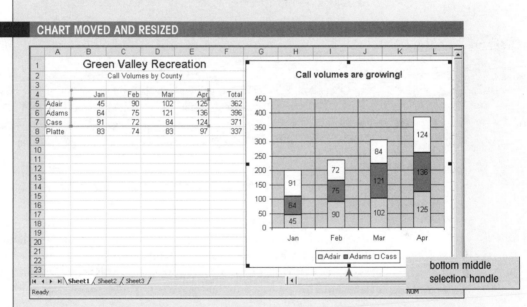

bottom middle selection handle

3. Enter your name in the left section of the worksheet header, save the CallAnalysis-3 workbook, and then print it in landscape orientation so that both the data and chart are on the printout.

TROUBLE? If an embedded chart is selected, Excel assumes that you want to print only the chart. If an embedded chart is not selected, Excel will print the chart beside the data, just as it appears on the screen.

4. Save and close the CallAnalysis-3 workbook.

Now that the chart is large enough to clearly show all data, you will modify it in a variety of ways to present exactly the information you want to communicate.

Modifying Source Data Ranges for an Existing Chart

When creating a chart, you should select the data you want to chart before starting the Chart Wizard so that you can take full advantage of the preview screens within the Chart Wizard. Presenting the right data on the chart is essential to conveying the right message. In some cases, though, the chart doesn't turn out the way you want it to look, you inherit an existing chart that needs to be modified, or your needs change after you've created the chart. In these cases, you need to know how to modify the data series and other chart elements after the chart is created. You can use the Chart Wizard to modify an existing chart. You can also use the Source Data option from the Chart menu or the right-click method to modify the data series or x-axis labels on your chart.

REFERENCE WINDOW   **RW**

Modifying the Data Series or X-Axis Labels on an Existing Chart
- Click the chart to select it, and then click the Chart Wizard button on the Standard toolbar.
- Click the Next button to go to Step 2 of 4 of the Chart Wizard.
- Click the Series tab, and then enter the cell or range references for the name, values, and x-axis labels for the selected series using your mouse pointer or the Collapse Dialog Box button.
- Click the Finish button.

or
- Click the chart to select it, click Chart on the menu bar, and then click Source Data (or right-click the chart and then click Source Data on the shortcut menu) to open the Source Data dialog box.
- Click the Series tab, and then enter the cell or range references for the name, values, and x-axis labels for the selected series using your mouse pointer or the Collapse Dialog Box button.
- Click the OK button.

GVR has sponsored a billiards tournament since 1997. The popularity of the event has been growing, and you've been keeping the participation totals in an Excel workbook. Lynn is requesting funds for new billiards tables, and she tried to create a chart that graphically presents the growth of the program to justify this expense. She's having trouble with her chart, though, and asked if you could help troubleshoot the problem.

To modify the data series and x-axis labels of an existing chart:

1. Open the **Billiards-3** workbook from the Tutorial.03\Tutorial folder on your Data Disk, and then click the **chart** to select it. See Figure 3-18. Lynn wanted to graph the attendance values for the Men and Women categories for all years, but instead, she has created a column chart with three data series, the first of which appears to have a value of 2000 for each data marker.

Figure 3-18   CLUSTERED COLUMN CHART WITH DATA SERIES AND X-AXIS LABEL PROBLEMS

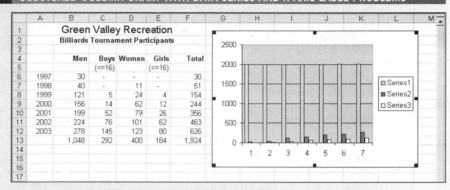

2. Click **Chart** on the menu bar, and then click **Source Data** to open the Source Data dialog box. Excel interpreted the values in range A6:A12 to be a data series rather than the values that identify the x-axis labels.

3. Click the **Series** tab, click **Series1** in the Series list (if not already selected), and then click the **Remove** button. You can see from the preview of the chart that the first data series has been removed, and the y-axis scale has changed to accommodate values between 0 and 300 rather than values through 2000. Now it's much easier to see that Series2 represents the Men data series and Series3 represents the Women data series. The next thing that you will do, however, is add the A6:A12 range back to the chart, but in the x-axis label position rather than as a data series.

4. Click in the Category (X) axis labels reference box, and then select the range **A6:A12** on the workbook. The preview of the chart now shows the years 1997 through 2003 in the x-axis label position. With the x-axis labels clarified, you're ready to modify the data series themselves so that the legend displays the actual name of the data series rather than the generic entries of "Series2" and "Series3".

TROUBLE? If column A is visible, you can use your pointer to select the range. If column A is not visible, you can move the dialog box and select the column using your pointer, or you can use the Collapse Dialog Box button 📉 to select the range.

5. Click **Series2** in the Series list (if it's not already selected), click in the Name reference box, click cell **B4** on the workbook, and then click **Series3** in the Series list. Note that the entry in the legend and in the Series list box now appears as "Men," the label from cell B4, rather than "Series2".

6. With Series3 still selected, click in the Name reference box, click cell **D4** on the workbook, and then click **Men** in the Series list to update the preview window. See Figure 3-19.

TROUBLE? If necessary, move the Source Data dialog box so you can click cell D4, or use the Collapse Dialog Box button 📉 to select cell D4.

Figure 3-19   MODIFYING THE DATA SERIES AND X-AXIS LABELS FOR AN EXISTING CHART

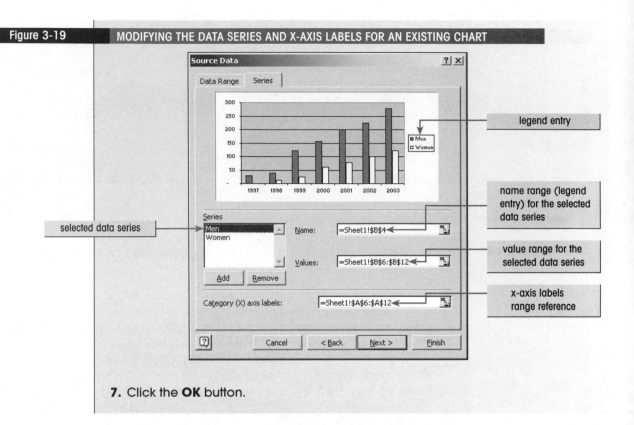

7. Click the **OK** button.

Adding a New Data Series Using the Chart Wizard

Although the major interest in the billiards program is from adults, Lynn has asked you to add the Boys and Girls data to the same chart to see how that data compares to the existing data for the Men and Women series. One way to create that chart would be to start over. The speed with which you can create a new chart using the Chart Wizard makes that a tempting option. If, however, you had applied extensive formatting changes to this chart, changes that would have to be reapplied to a new chart, it would probably be faster to add the new data series to this chart than to start over. There are many techniques for adding a data series to an existing chart, including using the Chart Wizard and using the Source Data option from the Chart menu.

Adding a New Data Series Using the Chart Wizard

- Click the chart to select it, and then click the Chart Wizard button on the Standard toolbar.
- Click the Next button to go to Step 2 of 4 of the Chart Wizard, and then click the Series tab.
- Click the Add button to add a new series, and then enter the cell or range references for the name and values for the selected series using your mouse pointer or the Collapse Dialog Box button.
- Click the Finish button.

or

- Click the chart to select it, click Chart on the menu bar, and then click Source Data (or right-click the chart and then click Source Data on the shortcut menu) to open the Source Data dialog box.
- Click the Series tab, click the Add button to add a new series, and then enter the cell or range references for the name and values for the selected series using your mouse pointer or the Collapse Dialog Box button.
- Click the OK button.

or

- Select the data you want to add to the chart, and then click the Copy button on the Standard toolbar.
- Click the chart, and then click the Paste button.

You decide to use the Chart Wizard technique to add the Boys data series to the existing chart.

To add the Boys data series to the chart using the Chart Wizard:

1. With the chart still selected, click the **Chart Wizard** button 🔲 on the Standard toolbar, click the **Next** button, and then click the **Series** tab.

2. Click the **Add** button to add a new series to the list, click in the Name reference box, and then click cell **C4**.

   TROUBLE? If you typed the cell reference C4 instead of clicking the cell on the worksheet, "C4" will be interpreted as a label for the series instead of as the cell reference itself. To correct this problem, click the Undo button 🔙 on the Standard toolbar, and then click cell C4.

3. Select the entry in the Values reference box, click the **Collapse Dialog Box** button 📑, select range **C6:C12**, and then click the **Expand Dialog Box** button 📇. See Figure 3-20. The Boys data series has been added.

   TROUBLE? If there is an existing entry in the Values reference box, you must delete it before selecting a new range.

Figure 3-20	ADDING A DATA SERIES USING THE CHART WIZARD

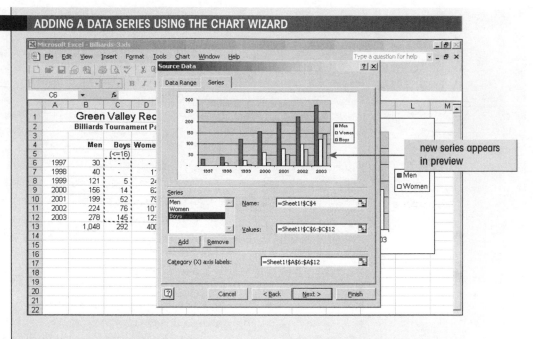

4. Click the Finish button.

Adding a New Data Series Using Copy and Paste

Another way to add a new data series is to copy and paste it to the graph. You must be careful to select a data series that is consistent with the other series on the graph, though. In other words, in order to use the copy and paste technique to add a data series to the chart, you must select a name and value range for the new series that is consistent with the existing series on the chart. If you click any data series on the graph, a colored border will surround the corresponding range of cells on the worksheet so that you can study the structure of the existing data series.

To add the Girls data series to the chart using copy and paste:

1. Click any bar in the **Women** series. See Figure 3-21. Selection handles appear in each column of the series indicating that the entire data series is selected. A purple border surrounds cells A6:A12, the range used for the x-axis labels, a green border identifies cell D4 that stores the data series name, and a blue border is used for cells D6:D12, the values for the data series itself.

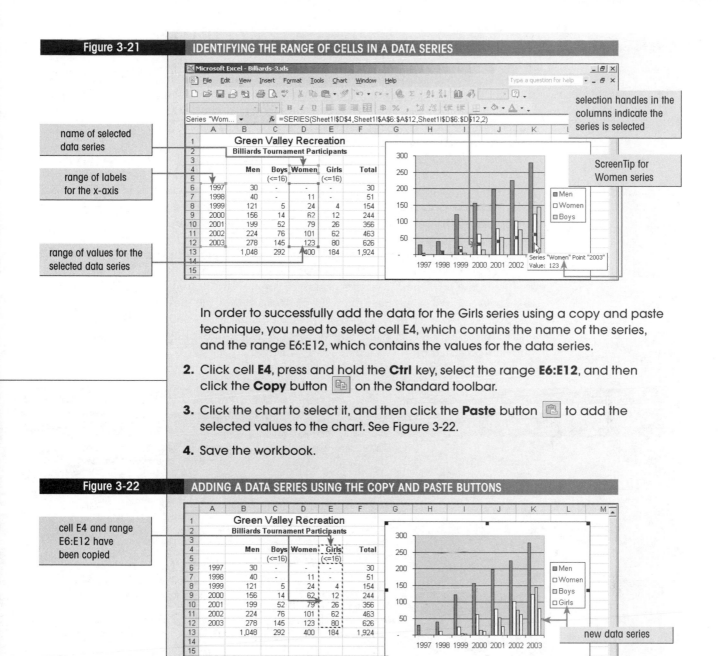

Figure 3-21   IDENTIFYING THE RANGE OF CELLS IN A DATA SERIES

Figure 3-22   ADDING A DATA SERIES USING THE COPY AND PASTE BUTTONS

In order to successfully add the data for the Girls series using a copy and paste technique, you need to select cell E4, which contains the name of the series, and the range E6:E12, which contains the values for the data series.

2. Click cell **E4**, press and hold the **Ctrl** key, select the range **E6:E12**, and then click the **Copy** button on the Standard toolbar.

3. Click the chart to select it, and then click the **Paste** button to add the selected values to the chart. See Figure 3-22.

4. Save the workbook.

Using the Chart Wizard to add or modify the data series or x-axis labels is easy once you understand the terminology of charts and how the dialog boxes work. Using the copy and paste buttons is also an easy way to add data to a chart, but each data series must contain a consistent number and type of cells in order for the chart to interpret the data correctly. To delete a series, click any bar in the series to select the entire series, and then press the Delete key.

Changing a Chart Type or Sub-Type to Present a New Point of View

Each chart type and sub-type is useful, but the appropriateness of the chart type or sub-type is dependent upon the message you are trying to communicate. In general, you use the column, bar, cylinder, cone, and pyramid charts in very similar situations, that is, to compare values. The choice between these chart types is largely due to personal preferences. The line chart is used to show trends over time and, because of this, usually requires that the x-axis labels be a measurement of time. The area chart is similar to the line chart in that it also shows trends over time. The difference, however, is that on an area chart, the lines are stacked one on top of the other to show cumulative versus individual trends for the data. In that respect, an area chart is similar to a stacked column chart in that both are best at comparing cumulative totals rather than comparing individual values.

The pie chart can support only one data series. There is only one axis in a pie chart, and it is used as the circumference of the pie. As such, you can graph only one column or one row of values on a pie chart. The values in that column or row become the single data series, the wedges in the pie. The XY (scatter) chart, as you saw in Tutorial 1, is used to show correlations between two values, and the stock chart is used for the purpose of showing high, low, and average data over time. Figure 3-23 further summarizes and describes the 14 standard chart types. The bubble, radar, and surface charts are much less common, but they create powerful presentations of data for specific situations.

Figure 3-23	CHART TYPES		
ICON	**CHART TYPE**	**PURPOSE**	**BUSINESS EXAMPLE**
	Column	To compare values as vertical bars	Comparing the sales of five different products for three different regions
	Bar	To compare values as horizontal bars	Comparing the average SAT scores for several local high schools
	Line	To show trends using lines to connect data points recorded at different points in time	Showing income and expense trends over several months
	Pie	To compare the size of parts of a whole as wedges of a pie	Comparing overall income contribution from three major products
	XY (Scatter)	To determine how or if one variable correlates to another	Determining if education level has a correlation to the type of music purchased
	Area	To show the cumulative effect of several contributing parts over time	Determining total sales by stacking monthly contributions from four regions on top of each other
	Doughnut	To compare the size of parts of a whole as parts of a ring	Comparing overall income contribution from three major product lines for two corporate divisions
	Radar	To compare the sum of multiple values between several data series	Comparing the total math, science, and reading standardized scores for several schools

| Figure 3-23 | CHART TYPES (continued) | | |

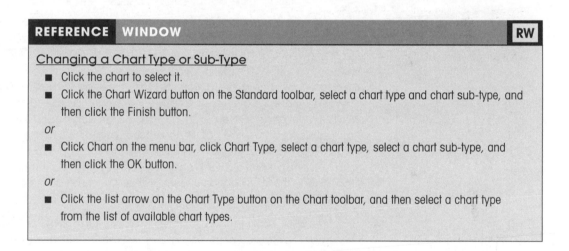

ICON	CHART TYPE	PURPOSE	BUSINESS EXAMPLE
	Surface	To find a desired range of values based on two numeric variables	Showing the combinations of temperature and rainfall that result in an acceptable crop yield
	Bubble	To determine how or if three variables correlate to one another	Determining if both age and gender have a strong correlation to soft drink preference
	Stock	To illustrate how the high, low, and close price of a stock varies over time	Showing how a stock performs over time
	Cylinder	To create a column chart using three-dimensional (3-D) cylinders for the data markers	Comparing the number of contributions to five local charities
	Cone	To create a column chart using three-dimensional (3-D) cones for the data markers	Comparing the fastest keyboarding speed by ten different students
	Pyramid	To create a column chart using three-dimensional (3-D) pyramids for the data markers	Comparing the total value of a $100 investment after one year as determined by the performance of seven different stocks

---

REFERENCE WINDOW   **RW**

<u>Changing a Chart Type or Sub-Type</u>

- Click the chart to select it.
- Click the Chart Wizard button on the Standard toolbar, select a chart type and chart sub-type, and then click the Finish button.

or

- Click Chart on the menu bar, click Chart Type, select a chart type, select a chart sub-type, and then click the OK button.

or

- Click the list arrow on the Chart Type button on the Chart toolbar, and then select a chart type from the list of available chart types.

You will experiment with these chart types to see if different presentations of the same data help you emphasize the growth of the billiards program better than the existing column chart.

To change the chart type and chart sub-type:

1. Click the chart to select it (if it is not already selected), and then click the **Chart Wizard** button ⊞ on the Standard toolbar. One advantage of using the Chart Wizard to change the chart type or sub-type is that the Wizard provides access to all possible chart types and subtypes, of which there are over 70. If you change the chart type using the Chart Type button on the Chart toolbar, you have access to only 18 chart type choices.

2. Click **Line** in the Chart type list, click the first sub-type on the second row (if it is not already selected), and then click the **Next** button twice to move to the third step of the Wizard.

3. Click the **Titles** tab (if it is not already selected), click in the Chart title text box, type **Billiards Tournament Growth**, and then click the **Finish** button. On a line chart the data marker appears as a symbol, such as a small square, triangle, or diamond. The data marker and associated color are identified in the legend. Lines connect the data markers and illustrate trends within that data series. Because the x-axis is a measurement of time, this chart shows the trend for each data series over time, as shown in Figure 3-24.

Figure 3-24   **LINE CHART**

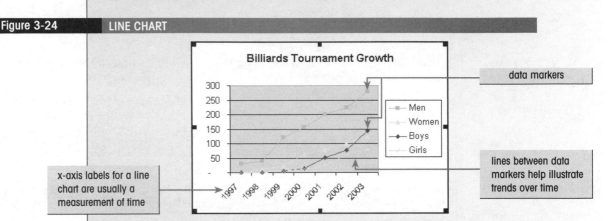

data markers

x-axis labels for a line chart are usually a measurement of time

lines between data markers help illustrate trends over time

Although it is a little more difficult to compare the values for each data marker between different categories using a line chart (as compared to the bar chart), a line chart more clearly shows the growth trends for each category. Also, note that if you are not using a color printer, it can be difficult to differentiate between different data markers and line styles using only black and white colors. Although the growth trends for each series are interesting, you are more interested in the cumulative growth trend. An area chart can best provide this information.

4. Click 📊, click **Area** in the Chart type list, click the **Stacked Area** sub-type (first row, second column), and then click the **Finish** button. When the values are stacked on top of each other in an area chart, as shown in Figure 3-25, it is very difficult to compare the values from one data series to the next. However, it is much easier to see the cumulative growth for all series combined. In this case, the area chart most clearly shows the trend in growth for all billiards tournament participant numbers.

Figure 3-25	AREA CHART

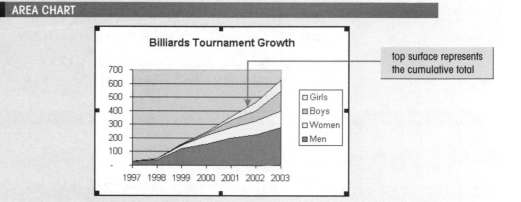

One more chart that you are curious about exploring at this time is the 100% stacked column chart.

5. Click [icon], click **Column** in the Chart type list, click the **100% Stacked Column** sub-type (first column on the right, first row), and then click the **Finish** button. Any time a chart shows a percentage as the y-axis, you must be extremely careful that you are interpreting the chart correctly. A 100% stacked column chart shows each data series as a percentage of the contribution to the total number of participants for each year. In 1997, for example, the entire tournament consisted of players in the Men category. By 2003, however, Men constituted a little over 40% of the players, and Girls, Boys, and Women posted healthy percentages as well. This chart, however, tells you nothing about the actual numbers of participants or growth from year to year. In fact, you could get the same chart with *declining* participation from year to year, as long as the percentages between the categories were the same. However, Lynn has expressed an interest in showing the board that this program is becoming more popular to a wider audience, so you will save this chart and apply some of the available chart options to clarify the intended message.

6. Click [icon], click the **Next** button twice to move to the third step of the Wizard, and then click the **Titles** tab (if not already selected). Charts are intended to clarify, not obscure, information. One of the easiest ways to make sure that your chart is giving the reader the intended message is to clarify the message with a meaningful chart title.

7. Change the text in the Chart title text box to **Billiards is a Family Sport**. This title clarifies the point of this graph—that both genders, including both children and adults, represent a significant percentage of overall participants in the billiards tournament.

8. Click the **Data Labels** tab, and then click the **Value** check box. If you wanted to also show the actual numbers of participants within each bar, you could use this option to do so. Of course, the more elements you put on one graph, the more cluttered it becomes. In this case, you will save this chart without the values added to the chart. You want the chart to show the fact that the sport is becoming more and more appealing to a wider audience over time. You can then create a separate chart, such as the line chart, to depict individual category growth or an area chart to depict cumulative growth.

Excel 2000: There is no Value check box on the Data Labels tab of the Chart Wizard dialog box. Click the **Show value** option button. Click the **None** option button to deselect the option and remove the values.

9. Click the **Value** check box to deselect it, and then click the **Finish** button. Your 100% stacked bar chart should look like Figure 3-26.

Figure 3-26   100% STACKED BAR CHART

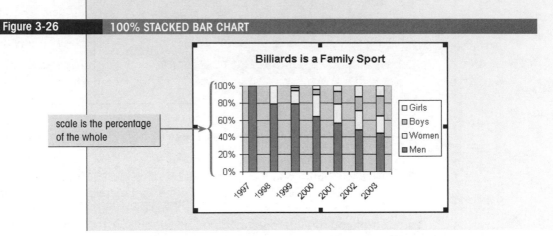

scale is the percentage of the whole

Charting the same data in different ways will help you convey different aspects of the information. If you have one chart that contains the data you want to duplicate and apply a different chart type to, you can copy and paste the entire chart to speed up the process.

To display the same data using three different type charts:

1. With the chart still selected, click the **Copy** button on the Standard toolbar.

2. Click the **Sheet2** tab, make sure cell A1 is the active cell, and then click the **Paste** button on the Standard toolbar.

3. Click cell **G1** and click , click cell **A17** and click , and then click cell **G17** and click . You now have four copies of the chart.

   TROUBLE? Depending on the size of your monitor and your screen resolution, you might need to select different cells to paste the four charts. The goal is to create four copies of the same chart on Sheet2 that you can modify.

4. Using the Chart Wizard, modify each of the charts to show the chart type and chart titles shown in the Figure 3-27.

Figure 3-27	FOUR FINAL CHARTS

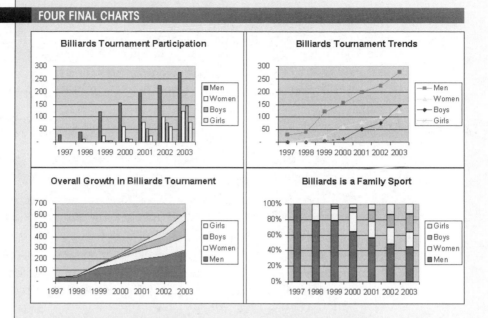

5. Rename Sheet1 as **Data** and Sheet2 as **Charts**.

6. On the Charts sheet, click any cell that is not occupied by a chart to deselect all of them, add your name to the left section of the header of the Charts worksheet, and then print the Charts worksheet in landscape orientation.

7. Save the Billiards-3 workbook.

Because the source data for all five charts references the same data on the Data worksheet, any change made to the original data in cells A4:E12 will now automatically change five charts, one on the Data worksheet and the four you just modified on the Charts worksheet.

Modifying Chart Values

All charts are inherently linked to the original cell values used to create the chart. If the cell values change, then the chart or charts that present the data automatically change. You can change the values in the worksheet, or you can change the values in the chart itself. To change a value in a chart, you select the data marker whose value you want to change and then drag the selection handle up or down to increase or decrease the value of the data marker. When you change a value, the change is reflected in both the chart and worksheet.

REFERENCE WINDOW	RW

Modifying Chart Values
- Click the cell that contains the original chart value, and then enter the new value.

or
- Select the data marker on the chart that represents the chart value, and then drag the selection handle of the data marker to the new value.

Lynn explains that the values in the Men series might change later, after all of the walk-in registrations from the actual tournament are tallied. She asks you to show her how changes in the data affect the charts. You will modify the chart values of the Billiards-3 workbook to see how the worksheet data and chart data markers are linked.

To modify the chart values to test the linked data:

1. Click the **Data** tab, click cell **B12**, type **100**, and then press the **Enter** key. Notice the change in the stacked bar chart on the Data worksheet.

2. Click the **Charts** tab. Notice that the data markers for the Men series for the year 2003 have been automatically updated to reflect a value of 100 in each chart.

   Although Lynn is clear on how changes in the data source stored on a worksheet affect the chart, you also want to show her how changes in the chart affect the data source on the worksheet.

3. In the column chart in the upper-left corner of the worksheet, click any column in the Men series, and then click the **2003 column** to select only that data marker. With a single column data marker selected, you can drag a selection handle to change the value it represents.

   TROUBLE? If you double-clicked the column and the Format Data Series dialog box opened, close the dialog box, and then click the 2003 column for the Men series to select only that data marker.

4. Position the pointer over the upper selection handle in the 2003 Men series data marker until the pointer changes to ↕, and then drag the selection handle up until the ScreenTip displays the value of **200**. Notice that every other chart now displays a value of 200 for the 2003 Men data point as well.

5. Click the **Data** tab. Notice that cell B12 shows a value of 200, the value that you changed by dragging the data marker on the chart. Because not all users are aware that they can actually change the source data from within the chart, they sometimes do this by mistake without realizing it. Lynn thanks you for the excellent tips, but she now wants to return the value for the Men 2003 data point to its original value.

6. Click the **Undo** button 🔄 on the Standard toolbar twice to remove the data value changes made to cell B12 and restore it to its original value of 278.

7. Save and close the workbook, and then exit Excel.

Usually, you use the worksheet itself to enter and edit the data. Dragging data markers in the chart is probably a less efficient way to change or correct a data value than using the traditional method of clicking the original cell and retyping the value. It's important that you realize, however, that values can be changed directly within the chart. You want to be aware of this because it can easily happen by mistake when you are trying to format chart elements but unintentionally drag a data marker instead.

Session 3.1 QUICK CHECK

1. In most chart types, the x-axis is also called the _____ axis, and the y-axis is also called the _____ axis.

2. Explain the difference between the terms data series, data marker, and data point.

3. How does the legend relate to the data series?

4. Briefly describe the decisions made in the four steps of the Chart Wizard.

5. Which chart type would you use to show the performance of several sales representatives over several months?

6. Which chart type would you use to show the cumulative performance of several sales representatives over several months?

SESSION 3.2

In this session, you will format the elements on a chart, including the x-axis, plot area, and legend, to make the chart easier to read. You will also learn how to change the default chart type and to create a custom chart type.

Formatting a Chart to Support a Business Decision

Formatting a chart means to change the outward appearance of it. There are many formatting options that you can apply to the individual elements that make up the chart, such as changing the color or borders of data markers or modifying the font and size of the titles. Changing the chart type itself is a type of formatting, too, since chart types change only the appearance of the chart and not the values that are being charted. You can also format the individual elements that make up a chart.

To format a chart element, you first need to select the element that you want to modify. To select a chart element, you can click it or select from the Chart Objects list box on the Chart toolbar. When a chart element is selected, selection handles appear, but sometimes they are not very obvious. For example, in Figure 3-28, the x-axis is selected as evidenced by the selection handles at the start and end of the x-axis.

Figure 3-28   X-AXIS IS SELECTED

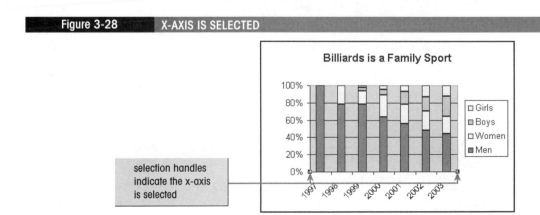

selection handles indicate the x-axis is selected

Excel provides the following methods to help you know which element of a chart you are selecting:

- When you point to any element on a chart, a ScreenTip appears that identifies the element.
- When you click a chart element, selection handles appear within that element to visually identify the element.
- When you are having trouble selecting the correct chart element, you can use the Chart Objects list on the Chart toolbar to select the specific chart element you want to modify.
- When you right-click any element on a chart, the shortcut menu will identify the name of the element within the Format shortcut menu option.
- When you double-click any element on a chart, you open the Format dialog box for that element. The title bar of the dialog box will identify which item you are currently formatting.

Note that when you want to select just one column (one data marker), you must first click any column within the data series and then click the specific data marker you want to change within the selected series.

You can make formatting changes to a chart element using the toolbars and menu options. You can also see a complete list of all formatting choices for a particular chart element by opening its Format dialog box. The title bar of the Format dialog box identifies which item you are currently formatting.

REFERENCE WINDOW   **RW**

Formatting a Chart Element Using Its Format Dialog Box
- Double-click the chart element that you want to format.

or

- Right-click the chart element that you want to format, and then click Format on the shortcut menu.

or

- Select the chart element that you want to format, and then click the Format button on the Chart toolbar
- Make the appropriate formatting change in the Format dialog box.
- Click the OK button.

You need to print a chart from the Billiards-3 workbook on a black and white printer. You will format the chart so that the data series are clearly distinguished using only black and white colors.

To format the data series using the Formatting toolbar:

1. If you took a break at the end of the last session, make sure Excel is running and then open the **Billiards-3** workbook from the Tutorial.03\Tutorial folder on your Data Disk.

2. Right-click the chart, click **Chart Type** on the shortcut menu, click the **Stacked Column** (first row, second column) in chart sub-type list, and then click the **OK** button.

3. Position the pointer over the gray area between the gridlines until the ScreenTip displays "Plot Area," and then click to select this chart element.

4. Click the **list arrow** for the Fill Color button 🖌▾ on the Formatting toolbar, and then click the **White** square (lower-right square) in the color palette as shown in Figure 3-29.

Figure 3-29 FORMATTING THE PLOT AREA

plot area is selected

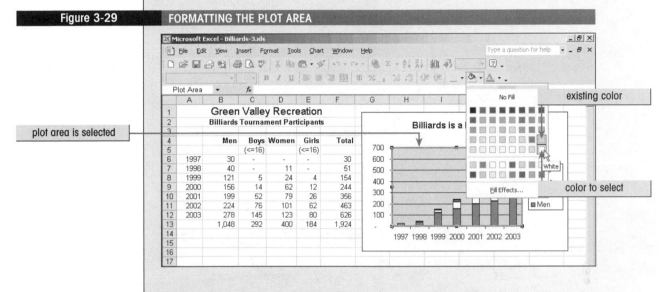

5. Click any **Light Turquoise** data marker for the Girls series, click the **list arrow** for the Fill Color button 🖌▾, and then click the **Black** square (first row, first column from the left).

6. Click any **Periwinkle** data marker for the Boys series, click the **list arrow** for 🖌▾, and then click the **White** square.

7. Click any **Ivory** data marker for the Women series, click the **list arrow** for 🖌▾, and then click the **Gray – 25 %** square (directly above the White square).

It's difficult for a black-and-white printer to distinguish more than three column or bar colors—black, white, and gray. To discriminate a fourth type of column or bar, you will need to use a fill pattern.

8. Click any **Plum** data marker for the Men series, click the **list arrow** for 🖌▾, and then click **Fill Effects**. The Fill Effects dialog box provides the options that you can use to change many aspects of the fill color, including what color or colors are used for the fill, how the colors will be mixed and shaded, and whether or not you want to apply a texture, pattern, or picture to the fill area. In this case, you want to use a black and white striped pattern to identify the third data series.

9. Click the **Pattern** tab, click the **Foreground** list arrow, click the **Black** square (first row, first column), and then click the **Wide upward diagonal** pattern in the pattern gallery, as shown in Figure 3-30.

Figure 3-30 APPLYING A PATTERN TO THE FILL AREA

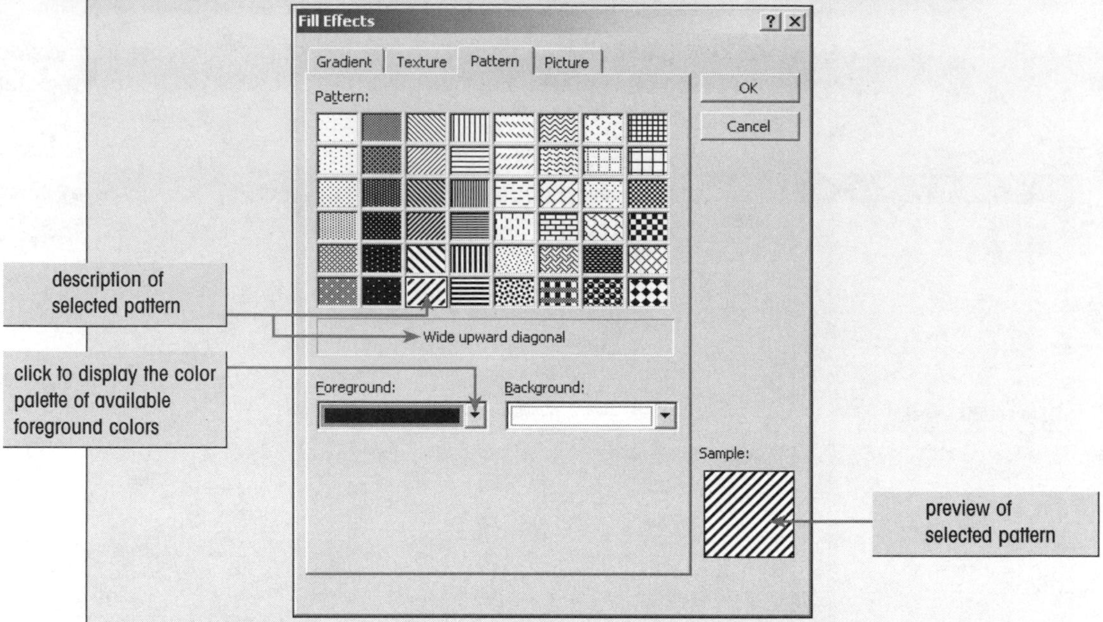
Fill Effects
Gradient
Texture
Pattern
Picture
Pattern:
OK
Cancel
description of selected pattern
Wide upward diagonal
click to display the color palette of available foreground colors
Foreground:
Background:
Sample:
preview of selected pattern

10. Click the **OK** button to apply the new pattern to the Men series.

You notice that the color boxes in the legend would be clearer if they were bigger. The size of the color boxes corresponds to the size of the legend text, so you will increase the font size of the legend to increase the size of the color boxes.

To format the legend using the Format Legend dialog box:

1. Right-click the legend and then click **Format Legend** on the shortcut menu to open the Format Legend dialog box.
2. Click the **Font** tab and then scroll down the Size list box and click **14**.
3. Click the **OK** button.

   You can also move the legend so that the rest of the chart can use the space more effectively.

4. Using Figure 3-31 as a guide, move the legend to the left and resize the plot area to more effectively use the chart space.

Figure 3-31 **MOVING THE LEGEND AND RESIZING THE PLOT AREA**

legend formatted in a
14-point font size and
moved to a new location

plot area is resized

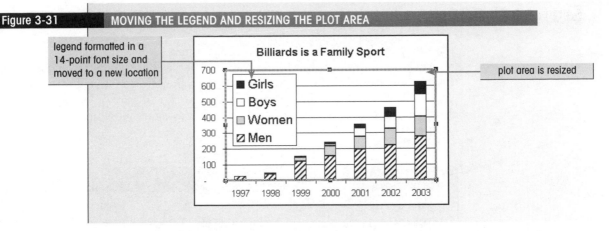

Your goal for the year 2004 is to have 800 people enrolled in the billiards tournament. Therefore, you want to change the top value of the y-axis (value axis) scale to 800 to clarify the delta between the 2003 total and the goal of 800 participants for the year 2004.

To format the scale on the y-axis and the labels on the x-axis:

1. Click the **Chart Objects** list arrow on the Chart toolbar, and then click **Value Axis**.

   TROUBLE? If your Chart toolbar is docked along the left side of the Excel window, the Chart Objects list arrow may be hidden. Move the Chart toolbar to another location.

2. Click the **Format Axis** button on the Chart toolbar to open the Format Axis dialog box. Note that the name of this toolbar button changes, depending on the chart element that you have selected.

3. Click the **Scale** tab. The y-axis scale automatically adjusts to accommodate the smallest and largest values it is charting. By default, the y-axis starts at 0 unless you specify a different Minimum value. In this case, you will change the Maximum value to 800 to clarify the shortfall between the largest number and the goal of 800 participants.

4. Double-click **700** in the Maximum text box, type **800**, and then click the **OK** button.

   As a final formatting embellishment, you will bold the labels on the x-axis.

5. Click any year label on the x-axis, and then click the **Bold** button on the Formatting toolbar. The final chart, formatted for a black and white printer, is shown in Figure 3-32.

Figure 3-32 **FINAL FORMATTED CHART**

maximum value on
the y-axis (value
axis) is 800

labels on the x-axis
(category axis) are bold

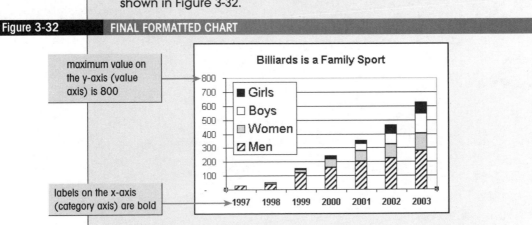

Creating a Custom Chart Type

You can save the formatting choices that you have applied to a chart so that they can be quickly applied to another chart in other workbooks. For example, you might want the first three columns or bars of your chart to default to the colors of blue, green, and yellow versus Microsoft's first three color choices of plum, ivory, and periwinkle. By adding the current chart's formatting options to the custom list, you can choose and apply those options to other charts very quickly.

REFERENCE WINDOW   **RW**

Creating a Custom Chart Type

- Create and format a chart with the formatting options you want to save.
- Select the chart.
- Click Chart on the menu bar, and then click Chart Type.
- Click the Custom Types tab, click the User-defined option button, and then click the Add button.
- Enter a name for the new custom chart type.
- Enter a description for the custom chart type (optional).
- Click the OK button twice.

You decide to save the black and white formatting scheme that you applied to the stacked column chart in case you need to format another chart in a similar way in the future.

To save the black and white formatting scheme as a custom format:

1. Select the stacked column chart if it is not already selected.

2. Click **Chart** on the menu bar, and then click **Chart Type**. The Chart Type dialog box opens.

3. Click the **Custom Types** tab, and then click the **User-defined** option button as shown in Figure 3-33.

Figure 3-33   **CREATING A CUSTOM CHART TYPE**

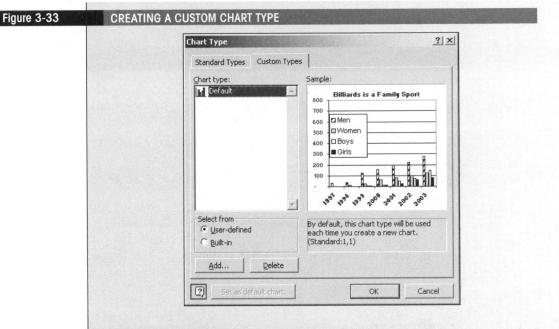

4. Click the **Add** button, type **BWSC** in the Name text box, press the **Tab** key, type **Black and white stacked column chart** in the Description text box, and then click the **OK** button. The new chart type and its description appear on the Custom Types tab.

5. Click the **OK** button.

Applying a Custom Chart Type to an Existing Chart

Now that you have defined and stored the new BWSC custom chart type, you can use it to quickly format existing or new charts in this or other workbooks.

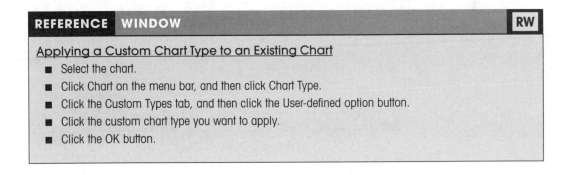

REFERENCE WINDOW   RW

Applying a Custom Chart Type to an Existing Chart
■ Select the chart.
■ Click Chart on the menu bar, and then click Chart Type.
■ Click the Custom Types tab, and then click the User-defined option button.
■ Click the custom chart type you want to apply.
■ Click the OK button.

You will apply the new BWSC custom chart type to one of the other billiards-related charts.

To apply the BWSC chart type to one of the Billiards charts:

1. Switch to the **Charts** sheet, and then click one of the charts to select it.

2. Click **Chart** on the menu bar, and then click **Chart Type**.

3. Click the **Custom Types** tab (if not already selected), click the **User-defined** option button, click **BWSC** in the Chart type list, and then click the **OK** button. The chart is immediately formatted with all of the series, axes, title, and legend changes that were stored in the BWSC custom chart type.

Changing the Default Chart

Formatting a chart requires a lot of work because there are so many chart elements and so many formatting choices for each element. If you decide that you would prefer to have new charts default to a particular chart type or formatting scheme rather than the one provided by Microsoft, you can change the default chart type or sub-type. For example, you might want all new charts to default to the clustered column with 3-D visual effect chart sub-type.

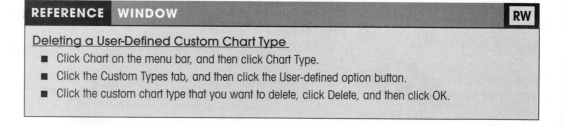

REFERENCE WINDOW	RW

Changing the Default Chart Type
- Select the chart.
- Click Chart on the menu bar, and then click Chart Type.
- Click the new chart type or sub-type, and then click Set as default chart.
- Click the OK button.

Because so many people at GVC use Excel on the computer you are using, you will not change the default chart type.

Deleting a Custom Chart Type

Custom chart types are available for all new and existing charts in the current workbook, as well as any other workbook you open. Therefore, if you're working on a computer shared by other users, you need to delete the custom chart type you just created and tested.

REFERENCE WINDOW	RW

Deleting a User-Defined Custom Chart Type
- Click Chart on the menu bar, and then click Chart Type.
- Click the Custom Types tab, and then click the User-defined option button.
- Click the custom chart type that you want to delete, click Delete, and then click OK.

If you were working at GVR, you would use this BWSC custom chart type to improve your productivity. You may also want to keep this custom chart type if you are using your own computer to complete this exercise. If you are not using your own computer to complete this exercise, you need to delete the BWSC custom chart type so that it doesn't interfere with the next user's activities.

To delete the BWSC custom chart type:

1. Click any chart to select it.

2. Click **Chart** on the menu bar, and then click the **Chart Type** option.

3. Click the **Custom Types** tab (if not already selected), click the **User-defined** option button, click **BWSC** in the Chart type list, click the **Delete** button, and then click the **OK** button.

4. Click the **Cancel** button. By clicking the Cancel button, you didn't apply a new chart type or sub-type to the existing chart.

   TROUBLE? If you click the OK button in the Chart Type dialog box and the selected chart type was applied to your chart, click the Undo button ⟲ on the Standard toolbar. You do not have to reopen the dialog box; the BWSC was deleted.

5. Save and close the Billiards-3 workbook, and then exit Excel.

The charts that you have created tell a great deal about the events sponsored by the GVR. The information that is graphically represented will help the GVR Board of Directors make several decisions about upcoming events.

Session 3.2 QUICK CHECK

1. List at least three of the features that Excel provides to help you format a chart.

2. List at least two different techniques that you can use to format a chart.

3. Identify several formatting changes that you would apply to a chart to distinguish the series on a black and white printer.

4. What is the benefit of creating a custom chart type?

REVIEW ASSIGNMENTS

Lynn has entered the program registration data into an Excel workbook. She wants you to chart the data corresponding to each county's registrations for 12 months and then chart the data using a pie chart that shows the total registrations for all four counties.

To complete this task:

1. Start Excel and open the **Registrations-3** workbook from the Tutorial.03\Review folder on your Data Disk.

2. Based on the data presented, create and format a stacked area chart that shows the data for each county's registrations for all 12 months (but not the totals) with the title "Total Registrations for the Year". (*Hint*: make sure the x-axis is a measurement of time.) Place the chart in a new worksheet named "TotalReg".

Explore

3. Work with the data series order so that the counties appear in alphabetical order in the legend.

Explore   4. Create a line chart that presents the same data, but shows only the total values, not the individual stacked county data series, in the chart. Use the same title "Total Registrations for the Year", and place the chart in a new worksheet named "TotalReg2".

5. Print the stacked area chart on the TotalReg worksheet and the line chart on the TotalReg2 worksheet with your name in the left section of the headers.

6. On a separate piece of paper, identify two benefits of each chart as compared to the other.

7. Create a pie chart that shows the total registrations for all four counties. Title the chart "County Comparison". Embed the chart in the RegistrationData worksheet, to the right of the numbers in columns A through F.

8. Copy and paste the pie chart, so that a second copy exists just below the first, and then change the chart type to a column chart. Print the RegistrationData worksheet with your name in the left section of the header.

Explore   9. On a separate piece of paper, identify two reasons why you would use the pie chart to present this information, and two reasons why you would use the column chart to present this information.

10. Select the pie chart on the RegistrationData worksheet, and then change the color of each wedge of the pie to a primary color as identified below:

Periwinkle to Blue
Light Turquoise to Bright Green
Plum to Red
Ivory to Yellow

11. Using the pie chart, add a user-defined custom chart type called "Primary Colors" to the available chart types. Enter "Pie chart that uses blue, green, red, and yellow as the first four wedges of the pie" in the Description text box.

12. Create another pie chart that shows just the July data for the four counties, title the chart "July Registrants", add the chart as a new sheet named JulyReg. Apply the Primary Colors custom chart type to the July Registrants pie chart.

13. Print the JulyReg worksheet with your name in the left section of the header. Delete the Primary Colors custom chart type.

14. Save and close the Registrations-3 workbook, and then exit Excel.

CASE PROBLEMS

Case 1. Using Charts to Illustrate Academic Performance You're a teacher at a local community college and have entered the grades for your class in a worksheet. Now you want to create some charts to illustrate their performance.

To complete this task:

1. Start Excel and open the **Grades-3** workbook from the Tutorial.03\Cases folder on your Data Disk.

2. Enter your name in cell C1, a school name in cell C2, and the current date in cell C3. Resize columns if necessary.

3. Enter a formula in cell N6 that calculates the total weighted score for the first student. Copy the formula in N6 through the range N7:N20.

4. Enter a formula in cell O6 that uses a VLOOKUP function to lookup the total weighted score in column N, uses the lookup table in Q6:R14 to determine the final grade, and returns the appropriate final letter grade to cell O6. Copy the formula in cell O6 through the range O7:O20.

5. Create a clustered column chart using the range N6:N20 as the single data series and range A6:A20 as the x-axis labels. Add the chart as an embedded chart to the right of the data on the Final Grade sheet.

6. Remove the legend, and then change the scale on the y-axis to start at 1 and end at 4.

7. Click any cell in the range N6:N20, and then sort the student grades from highest to lowest.

8. Click any column in the column chart to select the entire series, and then individually select and change the fill color for the columns that represent grades in the B range to bright green, for the column(s) that represent grades in the C range to yellow, and for the column(s) that represent grades in the D or F range to red.

9. Change the font size of the x-axis and y-axis to 12 points, and then resize the chart so that all of the labels on box axes are clearly displayed. Title the chart "Grade Distribution."

Explore   10. Open the Format Axis dialog box for the x-axis, and set the alignment of the text at a positive 45-degree angle. You may need to enlarge the size of the chart to display all of the x-axis labels in this orientation.

11. Save the Grades-3 workbook, and then print the worksheet in landscape orientation. Write a brief statement commenting on ways that the graph clarifies information about the grades that are not as readily apparent without the graph.

12. Close the Grades-3 workbook, and then exit Excel.

Case 2. Analyzing Business Performance Using Charts Column and line charts are two of the most common ways to present key business measurements. You are consulting with a small manufacturer of office supplies named "We Make It Right." You have been asked to create both a column chart and a line chart that the president needs to analyze key business trends and measurements for the upcoming season.

1. Start Excel and open the **WeMakeIt-3** workbook from the Tutorial.03\Cases folder on your Data Disk.

2. Complete the IncomeState worksheet by using the Assumptions sheet and formulas to build a projected income statement for 2003. (*Hint*: The projected total sales for 2003 will be $655,500, and the total NAT will be $74,077.)

3. Using Figure 3-34 as a guide, create the line chart and column chart shown in the figure based on the data in the IncomeState sheet. The charts should be placed on a new worksheet named "Graphs".

Figure 3-34

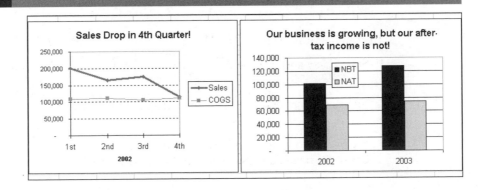

4. Save the WeMakeIt-3 workbook, add your name to the left section of the header for the Graphs worksheet, and then print the worksheet in landscape orientation. Write a brief statement commenting on the message that each graph communicates to you.

5. Close the WeMakeIt-3 workbook, and then exit Excel.

Case 3. Charting Kentucky Derby Winnings   It's your turn to develop and present a short speech on a favorite topic for your monthly breakfast club. You are a horseracing fan and decide to create a chart that illustrates how much money was won by the winners of the Kentucky Derby from 1976 through 2001 to use as a visual aid for your presentation.

To complete this task:

1. Start Excel and open the **KentuckyDerby-3** workbook from the Tutorial.03\Cases folder on your Data Disk. (*Hint*: If the External Data toolbar appears, close it.)

2. Select the nonadjacent range A2:A27;J2:J27 to create the line chart shown in Figure 3-35. Add the chart title "Kentucky Derby Winnings", and place the chart in a new sheet named "Winnings". (*Hint*: Do not format of the chart as you work through the Chart Wizard. You will be instructed to format the chart in the steps that follow.)

Figure 3-35

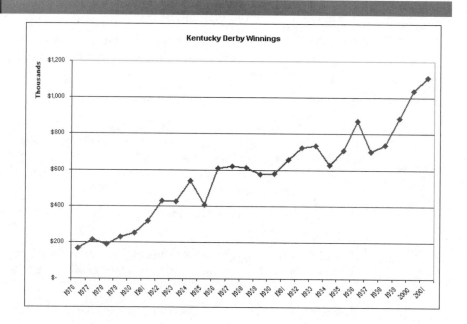

Explore

3. Change the values on the y-axis so they appear in thousands, and then change the values on the x-axis to show the units of measurement in years. (*Hint*: Change the Base unit to Year(s) on the Scale tab in the Format Axis dialog box.)

4. Remove the legend, and then format the plot area with a white color and the line series to a thicker weight so that the graph is easier to read.

5. Save the KentuckyDerby-3 workbook, add your name to the left section of the header for the Winnings worksheet, and then print the line chart worksheet. Write a sentence or two commenting on what information the graph reveals to you.

6. Save and close the KentuckyDerby-3 workbook, and then exit Excel.

Case 4. Charting Turnover You work as a business analyst in the personnel department for a large company and are helping the VP of Personnel prepare for an annual "state of the business" meeting. Specifically, you have been asked to develop a chart that shows how the various divisions within your company compare in regard to turnover rates.

To complete this task:

1. Start Excel and open the **Turnover-3** workbook from the Tutorial.03\Cases folder on your Data Disk.

2. Create the chart shown in Figure 3-36. Embed the chart in the HRData worksheet. Move the chart to the right of the data.

Figure 3-36

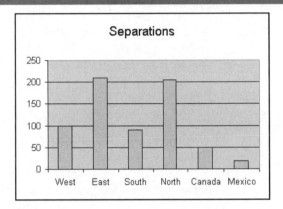

3. Create the chart shown in Figure 3-37. Embed the chart in the HRData worksheet, and then move the chart so it appears just below the first chart. Format the word "rates" in the title with a red color.

Figure 3-37

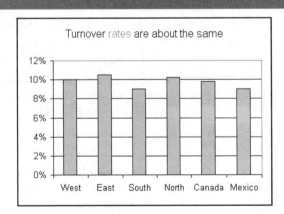

4. Print the HRData worksheet. Be sure to include your name in the left section of the header.

Explore 5. Write a paragraph in which you compare and contrast the two column charts. The charts use the same data yet support different conclusions. Why?

6. Save and close the Turnover-3 workbook, and then exit Excel.

QUICK | CHECK ANSWERS

Session 3.1

1. category, value

2. A data marker is the graphical item that represents the data point. In a column or bar chart, the data marker is a bar. The size of the data marker is determined by the data point. A data point is a value that corresponds to one cell of the worksheet. A data series is a set of bars, of data markers, for the same subject.

3. The legend is the area of the chart that displays the color and pattern used for the bars of each data series.

4. The Chart Wizard presents four basic steps:

   a. Select the chart type and sub-type.

   b. Confirm the overall data range, the range for each data series and data series name, and the range for the x-axis (category axis labels).

   c. Specify title, axes, gridline, legend, data labels, and data table options.

   d. Determine the location of the final chart, either as an embedded object in an existing worksheet or as a chart in a new worksheet.

5. A line chart shows trends over time.

6. An area chart shows cumulative trends over time.

Session 3.2

1. The features that Excel provides for formatting a chart include three of the following:

   ■ When you point to any element on a chart, a ScreenTip appears that identifies which element you are pointing to.

   ■ When you click any element on a chart, selection handles appear within that element to visually identify which item you are working with.

   ■ If you are having trouble selecting the correct chart element, you can use the Chart Objects list on the Chart toolbar to select the specific chart element you want to modify from the list of available chart items.

   ■ When you right-click any element on a chart, the shortcut menu will identify the name of the element within the Format shortcut menu option.

   ■ When you double-click any element on a chart, the Format dialog box for the selected element opens. The title bar of the dialog box identifies which element you are currently formatting.

   ■ If you format the wrong element, Excel allows you to undo that action.

2. The following are techniques for formatting a chart:

   ■ Select the element on the chart that you want to format, and then make the appropriate formatting change using the options on the Formatting and Chart toolbars or the options on the Format and Chart menus.

   ■ Right-click the element on the chart that you want to format, and then click Format on the shortcut menu to open the Format dialog box for the selected element. Make the appropriate formatting changes and then click the OK button.

   ■ Double-click the element on the chart that you want to format, make the appropriate formatting changes in the Format dialog box for the selected element, and then click the OK button.

- ■ Select the element on the chart that you want to format, click the Format button on the Chart toolbar, make the appropriate changes, and then click the OK button.
- ■ Select the chart, click the Chart Wizard button on the Standard toolbar, make the appropriate formatting change using the cap options available in the Chart Wizard, and then click the Finish button to close the Wizard and apply the changes

3. Applying a white color to the plot area helps differentiate the color of the bars. Changing the background color of the bars to solid black or white also helps clarify data series when printed on a black and white printer.

4. You can apply a saved custom chart type, and all of its formatting features, to any other chart in that or any other workbook.

USING EXCEL FOR ADVANCED CHARTING

Communicating Information Using Advanced Charts in Excel

Green Valley Recreation

The success of the Green Valley Recreation (GVR) community agency has resulted in additional requests for information at several levels. You and your supervisor, Lynn Tse, have been organizing data to support the decisions that the GVR Board of Directors is considering. You have also been gathering data to help Lynn communicate important information in her monthly staff meetings.

At its last quarterly meeting, the board proposed several initiatives. One of those initiatives requires that referees and umpires pass a standardized test before they can officiate GVR-sponsored sports events. Another program is studying the time management skills of the GVR managers. In addition to these initiatives, the board asked Lynn to provide an update on the accident rate and financial status of the Southside pool. They also want an update on the profitability of the GVR T-shirt shop over its five-year history. The board has also requested a report on the daily average attendance of GVR employees at the Sundance and Copper golf courses.

You and Lynn have been using Excel to organize and analyze data, and you want to add a visual component to each presentation of data using Excel's extensive charting capabilities. In this tutorial, you'll work with many of Excel's less common chart types, including various types of three-dimensional (3-D) charts. You will compare pie and doughnut charts and line and ribbon charts. Finally, you will work with radar, surface, and stock charts.

SESSION 4.1

In this session, you will learn about three-dimensional (3-D) charts, including their strengths and weaknesses, and the terminology associated with them. You will learn to modify the chart elements specific to 3-D data, and you will use pyramid, cone, and cylinder charts. You will also compare a pie chart to a doughnut chart to determine the benefits of each chart type. Finally, you will add a data table to a chart.

Deciding Which Chart Type Is Best for Your Data

Being able to produce a meaningful graphic of numeric information can help to make you a more effective communicator and decision maker. Now that you are comfortable with several of the most common types of Excel charts, you decide to study some of the lesser-known chart types to expand your awareness of the types of business decisions that you can support and clarify using a chart. Figure 4-1 provides a short description of the chart types you are presented with in the first step of the Chart Wizard, as well as an extra tip for each one.

Figure 4-1		CHART TYPES AND TIPS	
CHART TYPE	**ICON**	**DESCRIPTION**	**TIP**
Column		Use a column chart when you want to compare the size of values in a series. A column chart is the most common chart type because it accomodates a wide assortment of data.	Switch the series names in the legend with the labels on the x-axis by clicking the By Row button or By Column button on the Chart toolbar.
Bar		Use a bar chart when the horizontal orientation of the bar also represents progress toward a final goal.	In Excel, a bar chart displays in a horizontal orientation. A column chart displays bars in a vertical orientation.
Line		Use a line chart to show trends over time. As such, the x-axis of a line chart is usually a measurement of time.	If you have more than two data series, the line chart is not effective in black and white because distinguishing between more than two lines without using multiple colors might be difficult.
Area		Use an area chart when you want to show the cumlative effect of several series over time. As such, the x-axis is usually a measurement of time.	Because data series are stacked, it is easy to see the cumlative effect of the data series, but very difficult to compare one data series to another.
Pie		Use a pie chart when you want to show proportions of a whole. Make sure that the wedges of a pie add up to 100% of one thing.	A pie chart generally communicates best when there are only a few wedges, and the wedges are dramatically different in size.
Doughnut		Use a doughnut chart to show the relationship of parts to a whole for multiple series.	If there is only one series of wedges, a doughnut chart is the same thing as a pie chart except that the center of the pie is removed.
XY (scatter)		Use an XY (scatter) chart when you want to show the degree of correlation between two numeric variables.	Right-click the data series on an XY (scatter) chart, and then click Insert Trendline to add a trendline. Use the Format Trendline option to add the R-square value or correlation equation to the chart

Figure 4-1		CHART TYPES AND TIPS (continued)	
CHART TYPE	**ICON**	**DESCRIPTION**	**TIP**
Bubble		Use the bubble chart when you want to show the correlation between three numeric variables.	The bubble chart is an XY (scatter) chart with a third variable represented by the size of the data points (the bubbles).
Surface		Use the surface diagram to show how two numeric factors combine to create a third numeric measurement.	You might need to change the elevation or rotation of the chart so that you can see the entire surface.
Radar		Use a radar chart to compare the cumulative value of several data series.	The data series are represented by axes that radiate from a central point, creating a "radar" effect.
Cylinder Cone Pyramid		Use the cylinder, cone, and pyramid charts any time you would use a 3-D column chart.	The only difference between the Cylinder, Cone, and Pyramid charts is the shape and style of the data marker.

In addition to exploring the applicability of new chart types, Lynn wants you to create highly professional charts for the board. She wants you to examine how three-dimensional charts might support her upcoming board presentations.

Working with Three-Dimensional Charts

A typical chart presents data in two dimensions, height and width, and therefore uses only two axes. **Three-dimensional**, or **3-D**, **charts** present three dimensions—height, width, and depth—and therefore use three axes. Within Excel, most two-dimensional (2-D) chart types, including bar, column, pie, line, and area charts, also provide one or more 3-D sub-types. A 3-D chart is generally used to increase the visual interest or perceived professionalism of the information. In a 3-D chart, the data markers are often more visually interesting, because they appear as three-dimensional shapes rather than "flat" areas of color or simple lines. You can change an existing 2-D chart to a 3-D chart using the Chart Wizard, Chart menu, or Chart Type button on the Chart toolbar.

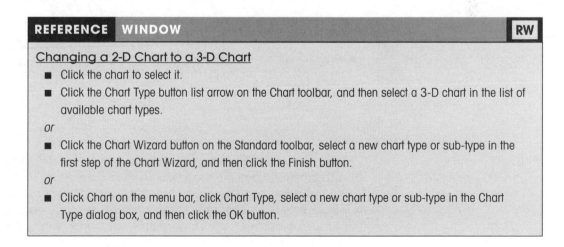

REFERENCE WINDOW   **RW**

Changing a 2-D Chart to a 3-D Chart
- Click the chart to select it.
- Click the Chart Type button list arrow on the Chart toolbar, and then select a 3-D chart in the list of available chart types.

or
- Click the Chart Wizard button on the Standard toolbar, select a new chart type or sub-type in the first step of the Chart Wizard, and then click the Finish button.

or
- Click Chart on the menu bar, click Chart Type, select a new chart type or sub-type in the Chart Type dialog box, and then click the OK button.

You should use 3-D charts with caution because they can cause unforeseen presentation issues. For example, 3-D charts require extra space for the third dimension on the screen or printout. Also, depending on the order of the data series, larger data markers in the front of a 3-D chart can hide or obscure those in the back of the chart. In addition, it's not always obvious where the tops of the data markers intersect with the y-axis. Therefore, creating effective 3-D charts requires additional charting skills.

GVR requires new referees and umpires to pass examination tests before they can referee a game. Not everyone who takes the test passes it. For the past year you have logged the number of tests given and the number who have passed the test into an Excel workbook. Lynn wants to create a chart to show how many applicants took the test and how many passed for each sport to determine whether or not GVR should offer additional study courses. You'll work with the data to determine how to best present it as a 3-D chart.

To apply a 3-D visual effect to the existing clustered column chart:

1. Start Excel and then open the **Tests-4** workbook located in the Tutorial.04\Tutorial folder on your Data Disk. The sport, number of tests given, and number of tests passed data are presented in columns A, B, and C. Column D contains a formula that calculates the pass rate percentage. The existing Test Results 2-D column chart shows how many individuals took the test compared with how many passed.

2. Click the chart to select it, click the **Chart Wizard** button on the Standard toolbar, click the **Clustered column with a 3-D visual effect** chart sub-type (second row, first column from the left), and then click the **Finish** button to accept the rest of the existing choices in the Chart Wizard. See Figure 4-2.

Figure 4-2	CLUSTERED COLUMN CHART WITH A 3-D VISUAL EFFECT

Chart toolbar

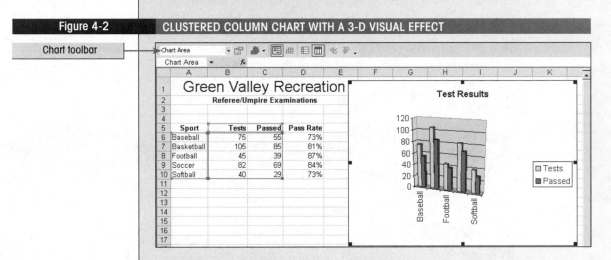

TROUBLE? If the Chart toolbar is not visible, right-click any visible toolbar, click Chart, and then dock the toolbar below the Formatting toolbar at the top of your screen. By default, the Chart toolbar appears whenever the chart is selected. But if the previous user hid the toolbar when the chart was selected, the Chart toolbar will not reappear until you perform the commands to display it. The Chart toolbar may also appear docked or floating, again determined by the choices of the previous user.

Lynn asks if there are other 3-D column charts that emphasize the third dimension a little more clearly. You will use the Chart Wizard again to explore the other 3-D column chart options.

To switch from a 3-D visual effect to a 3-D Column chart type:

1. With the chart still selected, click the **Chart Wizard** button 🗐 on the Standard toolbar, click the **3-D Column** sub-type (third row), and then click the **Finish** button to accept the rest of the existing choices in the Chart Wizard.

2. Resize the chart so that it fills the available space on the screen as shown in Figure 4-3.

Figure 4-3	3-D COLUMN CHART

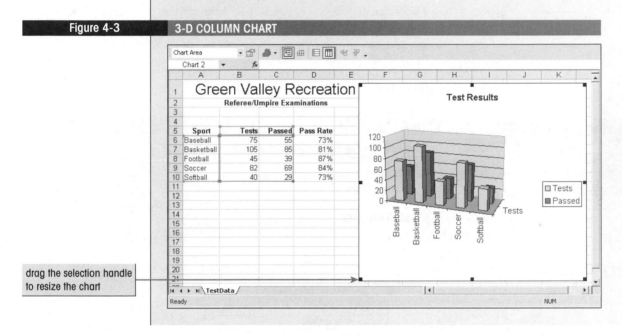

drag the selection handle to resize the chart

The 3-D column chart places the columns in a front-to-back versus side-by-side orientation. Therefore, the chart emphasizes the feeling of depth, but unfortunately it might create new problems if the data markers "in front" obscure the data markers "in back." Resizing the chart to give it more room on the screen is one way to clarify a 3-D chart, but sometimes you will need to change the order of the data series so that one series of bars does not obscure another.

REFERENCE WINDOW	RW

Changing the Data Series Order

- Right-click any data marker in the series, and then click Format Data Series on the shortcut menu; or double-click any data marker in the series to open the Format Data Series dialog box.
- Click the Series Order tab on the Format Data Series dialog box.
- Click the choice in the Series order list that you want to move, and then click the Move Up or Move Down button.
- Click the OK button.

Lynn likes the visual interest and perception of depth provided by the 3-D column chart, but although this chart type might be more visually exciting than a 2-D column chart, Lynn thinks it might be harder to read, especially since the columns for the number of tests taken partially hide the columns for the number of tests passed. Because the values represented by the Passed data series will always be the same or less than the Tests data series, you'll switch the order of the data series to clarify this 3-D chart.

To change the data series order:

1. Double-click any column in either series to open the Format Data Series dialog box, and then click the **Series Order** tab.

   TROUBLE? If you double-click a chart element other than a column, that element's Format dialog box opens. Close the dialog box and repeat Step 1, making sure that you are pointing to a column in one of the data series.

2. Click **Tests** in the Series order (if it is not already selected), and then click the **Move Down** button. See Figure 4-4.

| Figure 4-4 | CHANGING THE ORDER OF THE DATA SERIES |

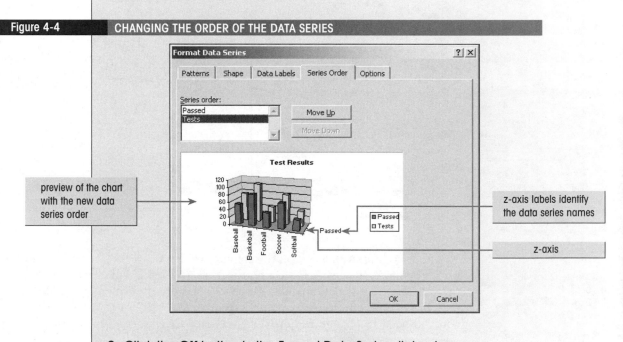

3. Click the **OK** button in the Format Data Series dialog box.

With the shorter Passed series data markers in front, the chart is easier to read, and it's easier to visually gauge how many tests were taken versus how many were passed. There are other elements of a 3-D chart that you can change to improve its overall appearance. For example, Lynn feels that it's still hard to see where the tops of the columns intersect with the y-axis, and you have also noticed that the data series labels that automatically appear on the z-axis to help identify the two data series do not both appear. When the Tests data series was in front, the z-axis showed the Tests label, and now that the data series have been switched, only the Passed label appears.

Changing the 3-D View

The **3-D view** of the chart is the angle from which you are viewing the chart. This view is directly related to how clearly the data markers are presented. The current default view places you in a position that is slightly above and to the right of the front of the chart. The 3-D view of the chart is controlled by several measurements, including rotation, elevation, and perspective. **Rotation** defines how much the chart swings around a vertical axis through its center. By default, the 3-D column chart is rotated by 20 degrees to the left. **Elevation** defines how the chart swings around a horizontal axis, also going through the middle of the chart. By default, the 3-D column chart is elevated down by 15 degrees.

Perspective is a number between 0 and 100 that reshapes the chart so that there is a sense of distance from the front to the back of the chart. The higher the number, the farther away the front and back are designed to appear. The **Height** measurement fine-tunes the perspective. This measurement is a number between 5 and 500, which represents how tall the chart will be as a percentage of its base. A number greater that 100 "stretches" the chart to make it taller, and a number less than 100 does the opposite.

By default, perspective is set to 30. Not all 3-D charts have perspective or height values, however. Perspective and height are only available when you are *not* using **right angle axes**, a situation in which the x- and y-axes are set at a right angle, just as they are set when you use a 2-D column chart.

REFERENCE WINDOW   **RW**

Applying Right Angle Axes
- Click the chart to select it.
- Click Chart on the menu bar, and then click 3-D View to open the 3-D View dialog box.
- Click the Right angle axes check box, and then click the Apply button.
- Click the Close button.

One of Lynn's concerns is that she is having trouble seeing where the tops of the bars cross the y-axis. You'll apply right angle axes to this 3-D chart to explore whether this option helps address this problem.

To apply right angle axes to the current 3-D column chart:

1. Click the chart (if it's not already selected), click **Chart** on the menu bar, and then click **3-D View**. The 3-D View dialog box with the default 3-D view settings opens as shown in Figure 4-5. The default elevation, rotation, and perspective values are displayed.

Figure 4-5   3-D VIEW DIALOG BOX

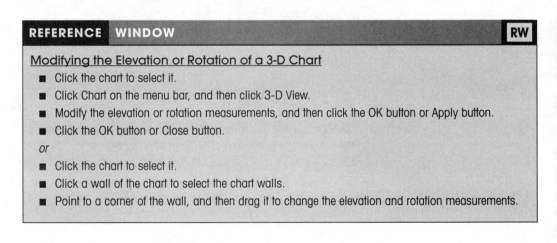

2. Click the **Right angle axes** check box. Note that the Perspective option is no longer available.

3. Click the **OK** button. The Right angle axes option is applied to the existing chart so that the x- and y-axes now form a right angle.

   TROUBLE? Not all of the category labels appear on the x-axis. Don't worry about this now; this problem will be resolved later in this session.

You feel that this option makes it slightly easier to see where the tops of the bars cross the y-axis, but you are anxious to explore some of the other 3-D view measurements as well. You can make modifications to the rotation and elevation 3-D view measurements by using either the 3-D View dialog box or by directly manipulating the chart with your pointer. To use your pointer to modify the 3-D view, you drag the corners of the 3-D chart, defined by the floor and the walls of the chart. The **floor** of a chart is the bottom surface from which the data markers start, and the **walls** are the sides that surround the chart.

REFERENCE WINDOW   **RW**

Modifying the Elevation or Rotation of a 3-D Chart
- Click the chart to select it.
- Click Chart on the menu bar, and then click 3-D View.
- Modify the elevation or rotation measurements, and then click the OK button or Apply button.
- Click the OK button or Close button.

or
- Click the chart to select it.
- Click a wall of the chart to select the chart walls.
- Point to a corner of the wall, and then drag it to change the elevation and rotation measurements.

Before presenting the chart to Lynn, you want to work with the elevation and rotation of the 3-D chart to see if you can improve it any further. One problem that still exists is that the z-axis doesn't have room to clearly display both data series labels. But since both the z-axis labels and the legend identify the data series, you don't need both of them on the chart. So first, you will remove the legend so there is room to expand the size of the chart.

To change the elevation and rotation of a 3-D chart using the pointer:

1. Click the legend to select it, and then press the **Delete** key.

2. Click a wall of the chart to select that chart element. See Figure 4-6. Selection handles appear at the corners of all of the walls to indicate that the walls have been selected. By dragging the corners of the walls, you are, in effect, changing the rotation (left-to-right orientation) and elevation (top-to-bottom orientation) of the chart. As you drag a selection handle, Excel presents an outline of the chart to help you see how much you are changing the view.

Figure 4-6   **SELECTING THE WALL OF A 3-D CHART**

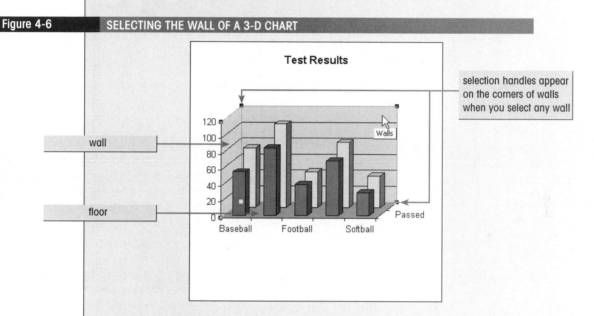

3. Click the upper-right selection handle so that the pointer changes to ┼, and then drag the handle to the right. See Figure 4-7. Dragging a selection handle left or right changes the rotation of the chart.

   TROUBLE? If your chart does not look like the one in the figure, click the Undo button ↺ on the Standard toolbar, and then repeat Step 3, making sure you drag the handle to the right, but not up or down.

Figure 4-7   **CHANGING THE ROTATION OF A 3-D CHART USING THE POINTER**

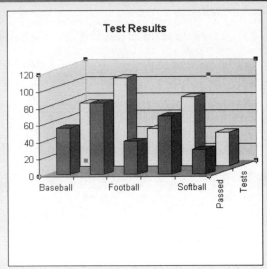

4. Position the pointer over the upper-right selection handle so that the pointer changes to ┼, press and hold the **Ctrl** key, and then drag the handle up (appropriately two rows) to change the elevation of the cube. Pressing the Ctrl key while dragging a wall selection handle shows the outline of the data markers in addition to the outline of the walls. Dragging a wall selection handle up or down changes the elevation measurement of the 3-D view.

Using the pointer to change the view of a 3-D chart can be quick and easy, but you may have noticed that there is a limit to the amount of elevation and rotation that you can apply using the pointer. At some point, whether you are rotating left, right, up, or down, the pointer simply will not rotate or elevate the chart any further. If you want to enter precise rotation and elevation measurements or measurements that go beyond those that can be applied using the pointer, you have to use the 3-D View dialog box.

To change the 3-D view measurements using the 3-D View dialog box:

1. Click the chart to select it, click **Chart** on the menu bar, and then click **3-D View**. The 3-D View dialog box opens.

2. Experiment with the increase elevation, decrease elevation, rotate to the left, and rotate to the right buttons, and observe the changes to the chart presented by the preview area.

3. When finished experimenting, type **17** in the Elevation text box, and then type **32** in the Rotation text box, as shown in Figure 4-8.

Figure 4-8 | CHANGING THE ELEVATION AND ROTATION OF THE CHART

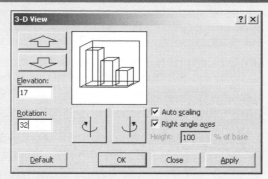

4. Click the **OK** button in the 3-D View dialog box to observe the changes on the chart. Now you can clearly see the Passed and Tests series labels on the z-axis.

Working with the Cylinder, Cone, and Pyramid Charts

The cylinder, cone, and pyramid charts are 3-D versions of column and bar charts that use interesting data markers in the form of cylinders, cones, and pyramids. The difference between the data markers used for the cylinder, cone, and pyramid shapes for your chart is really a personal decision. Depending on the nature of your data, however, one shape might be more meaningful than another. Cylinders, for example, might work well to illustrate measurements such as gallons, megabytes, or kilograms. Cones might be a good way to visually represent points or scores. Pyramids could be used to visually represent growth or achievement values. You can apply the cylinder, cone, or pyramid chart type to an existing chart using the Chart Type button on the Chart toolbar, the Chart Type option on the Chart menu, or the chart type options in the Chart Wizard.

REFERENCE WINDOW   **RW**

Applying a Cylinder, Cone, or Pyramid Chart Type to an Existing Chart
- Click the chart to select it.
- Click the list arrow for the Chart Type button on the Chart toolbar, and then select the 3-D Cylinder Chart, 3-D Cone Chart, or 3-D Pyramid Chart options in the Chart Type list.

or
- Click Chart on the menu bar, click Chart Type, select the Cylinder, Cone, or Pyramid options in the Chart type list, and then click the OK button.

or
- Click the Chart Wizard button on the Standard toolbar, click the Cylinder, Cone, or Pyramid option in the Chart type list, and then click the Finish button.

Although the existing 3-D chart is visually interesting and easy to read, you still wonder how the 3-D Cylinder, 3-D Cone, or 3-D Pyramid chart types might improve it. Once you examine these chart types using the existing data, you and Lynn will choose the one you like best to display the Test Results data.

To apply a 3-D Cylinder, Cone, or Pyramid chart type to the Test Results chart:

1. Select the chart (if it is not already selected).

2. Click the **list arrow** for the Chart Type button 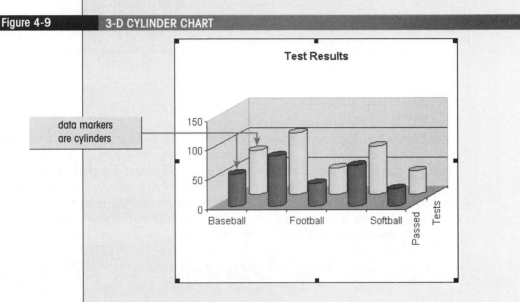 on the Chart toolbar, and then click the **3-D Cylinder Chart** icon in the chart gallery. The data markers now take the shape of cylinders. See Figure 4-9. Also note that the Chart Type button on the Chart toolbar displays the icon for the last chart type chosen.

   Trouble? Depending on the size of your chart, the values and increments on the y-axis may be different. Resize your chart so that it looks like Figure 4-9.

Figure 4-9   3-D CYLINDER CHART

data markers are cylinders

Test Results

150 —
100 —
50 —
0 —

Baseball   Football   Softball   Passed   Tests

---

3. Click the **list arrow** for , and then click the **3-D Cone Chart** icon in the chart gallery.

4. Click the **list arrow** for , and then click the **3-D Pyramid Chart** icon in the chart gallery. You like the visual impact that the 3-D pyramid data markers provide for this chart, but you need to make one final change to the chart. You need to change the angle of the text on the x-axis so that all of the labels are visible and easy to read.

5. Click any label on the x-axis, and then click the **Angle Counterclockwise** button on the Chart toolbar. The labels on the x-axis appear on an angle (and now all the labels appear). See Figure 4-10.

   Excel 2000: Click the **Angle Text Upward** button on the Chart toolbar.

Figure 4-10   **3-D PYRAMID CHART**

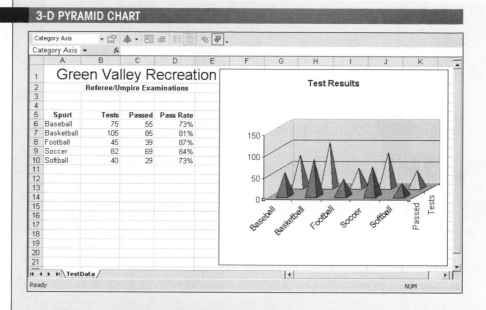

When an embedded chart is selected and you initiate a print command (either by clicking the Print button on the Standard toolbar or choosing the Print or Page Setup option from the File menu), the resulting printout will contain only the selected chart, sized to fill the paper. If you want the printout to contain both the worksheet data and the chart, click a cell on the worksheet so that the chart is not selected before initiating a print command. Print just the chart with your name in the header.

6. Click the chart, click **File** on the menu bar, click **Page Setup**, click the **Header/Footer** tab, click the **Custom Header** button, and add your name to the left section of the header, click the **OK** button, and then click the **Print** button.

7. Save the Tests-4 workbook, and then close it.

Most charting choices are a matter of personal preference. If you can quickly apply many different chart types, sub-types, and formatting options to the same data, though, you can test many variations and then use the options that help communicate your message best.

Working with Pie Charts

A pie chart presents only one series of numbers (that is, one data series), each number represented by a slice in the pie. Each **slice** (wedge) in the pie is therefore a data marker for that chart type and represents one data point within the data series. You can chart only one data series on a typical pie chart because the chart has only one axis that forms the circumference of the pie. Often, when users have trouble creating a pie chart, they are trying to chart more than one series of data on a single chart. A sample pie chart is shown in Figure 4-11.

Figure 4-11   SAMPLE PIE CHART

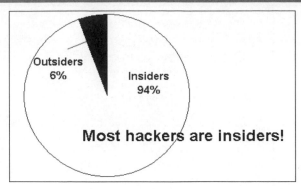

Also note that an effective pie chart typically does not display a large number of slices. Multiple small slices are hard to differentiate in color and in size. But if you have a few data points that represent the whole of something, and the point of your chart is to show a dramatic difference between the contributions of each category, a pie chart is a good choice.

Pie Chart Sub-Types

There are two general types of pie chart sub-types that you might want to use: an exploded pie or a pie chart with extracted values. An **exploded pie** emphasizes individual values by sliding one or more slices of the pie away from the center to emphasize those data points. An exploded pie chart can be either two- or three-dimensional. You create an exploded pie by applying an exploded pie chart type (which explodes all slices). You can also create an exploded pie by starting with a regular pie chart and selectively dragging the slice(s) that you want moved away from the main pie using the pointer. Figure 4-12 shows a sample exploded 3-D pie chart.

Figure 4-12   SAMPLE EXPLODED 3-D PIE CHART

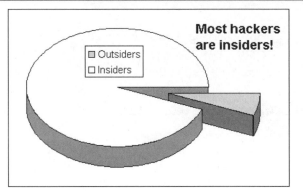

A pie chart with extracted values can be used to further illustrate pieces of one slice. In other words, one slice is extracted into smaller pieces. The **extracted values** are displayed as bars or as a smaller pie beside the slice that they further describe. Therefore, the extracted values pie charts are called the **bar of pie** and **pie of pie** charts within Excel. In Figure 4-13, the Outsiders slice is further extracted into two bars that illustrate the two categories within the Outsiders slice: For Fun and Criminal Intent.

Figure 4-13   SAMPLE BAR OF PIE CHART

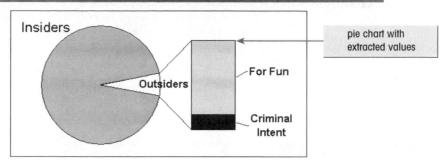

Creating an Exploded Pie Chart

Creating an exploded pie chart isn't much different from creating any other chart; however, organizing and selecting the data for any pie chart can be tricky, because the data for a pie chart involves only one data series. One data series means that there can be only one column or one row of numeric values. If you have multiple columns or rows of numeric values, you need to use a chart type other than a pie chart to graphically display that much data at one time.

REFERENCE WINDOW   **RW**

Creating an Exploded Pie Chart
- Select the single data series that you want to chart.
- Click the Chart Wizard button on the Standard toolbar.
- Choose an exploded pie chart sub-type in the first step of the Chart Wizard, and then complete the remaining Chart Wizard steps.
- Click the Finish button.

In an effort to use existing personnel more effectively, GVR went through an internal reorganization. As part of that process, they surveyed all management-level employees to determine what proportion of an eight-hour day they spent doing four basic duties: working on customer issues, attending internal meetings, dealing with employee issues, and completing administrative work both before and after the reorganization. Lynn has entered the results of those surveys in an Excel workbook and has asked you to create a graphical representation of how GVR management spent their time before the reorganization. Since she wants only one data series, and the values add up to 100% of a day, the data is a good candidate for a pie chart. Since there are only four data points, you'll experiment with an exploded pie chart type to see how this chart type supports this data.

To create an exploded pie chart using the management survey data:

1. Open the **MgmtSurvey-4** workbook located in the Tutorial.04\Tutorial folder on your Data Disk.

2. Select the range **A4:B8**, and then click the **Chart Wizard** button 📊 on the Standard toolbar.

3. Click **Pie** in the Chart type list, click **Exploded pie with a 3-D visual effect** chart sub-type (second row, second column), and then click the **Next** button twice to accept the source data choices and to display Step 3 of the Chart Wizard.

4. Double-click the text in the Chart title text box, type **Are our managers productive?** as the chart title, click the **Next** button, and then click the **Finish** button to insert the chart as an embedded object in the SurveyData worksheet.

5. Move and resize the chart so that it looks like Figure 4-14.

| Figure 4-14 | EXPLODED 3-D PIE CHART |

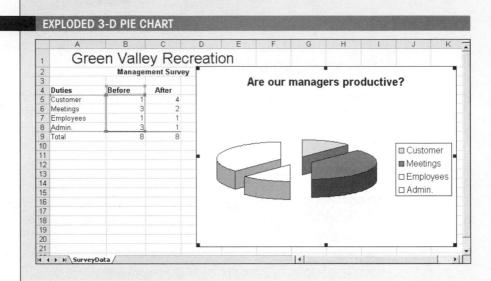

Formatting Pie Chart Slices

Because pie charts have only one data series and because those data markers are presented as the slices of a pie instead of as columns or bars, the color of the data markers on a pie chart are formatted using different assumptions than those used for a column chart. On a pie chart, since there is only one data series, every data marker in the series (every slice) is given a different color to differentiate the slices. On a column or bar chart, however, every data marker in the same series is formatted with the same color. Therefore, the colors of the slices on a pie chart emphasize the difference between values in one data series, whereas the colors on a bar or column chart emphasize the difference between the values of one entire data series versus another.

Formatting an individual slice of a pie chart is similar to formatting an individual column in a column chart. First you must single-click any slice to select the entire series, and then single-click the slice that you want to modify. Once a single slice is selected, you open the Format Data Point dialog box by either double-clicking the selected slice or by clicking the Format Data Point button on the Chart toolbar. If you double-click a slice of a pie *before* an individual slice is selected, you'll open the Format Data Series dialog box for the entire series instead of the Format Data Point dialog box for a single slice.

Lynn wants to emphasize the low amount of time that GVR managers were spending with customers. You'll emphasize this data point by adding data labels to the Customer data marker, so that more information and attention are focused on that slice.

To format the Customer slice of the exploded pie chart:

1. Click any slice in the pie to select the entire data series. Note that one selection handle appears on each slice of the series, indicating that all slices are currently selected.

2. Click the **Customer** slice. Now only that data marker is selected.

   TROUBLE? If you double-clicked the Customer slice instead of single clicking, close the Format Data Series dialog box and repeat Step 2.

3. Click the **Format Data Point** button 🖼 on the Chart toolbar to open the Format Data Point dialog box, as shown in Figure 4-15. You can also open the Format Data Point dialog box by double-clicking the selected item. But selecting the chart item you want to format before you click the Format Data Point button 🖼 on the Chart toolbar is probably the most precise way to make sure that you are opening the Format dialog box for the desired item, because you can see which item is selected at all times, and you don't double-click another chart item by accident.

| Figure 4-15 | FORMAT DATA POINT DIALOG BOX |

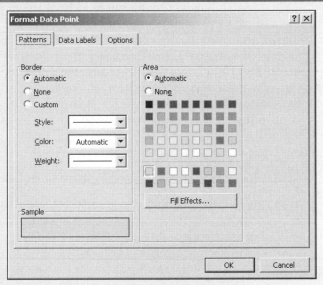

4. Click the **Data Labels** tab, click the **Series name** check box, click the **Category name** check box, click the **Value** check box, click the **Percentage** check box, click the **Separator** list arrow, click **, (Comma)**, and then click the **OK** button. See Figure 4-16. The series name "Before," the category name "Customer," the value "1," and the percentage "13%" appear above the selected slice, each separated by a comma.

   Excel 2000: The options on the Data Labels tab in the Format Data Point dialog box are different. Click the **Show label and percent** option button. Note that there is no Separator option; therefore, the chart on your screen will not match Figure 4-16 exactly.

Figure 4-16   ADDING DATA LABELS TO A PIE SLICE

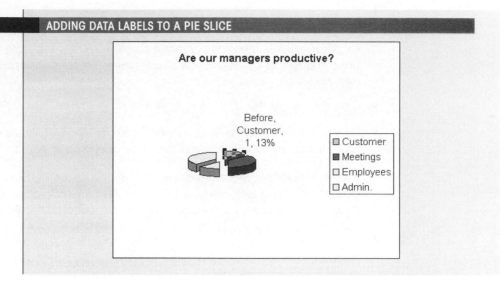

Resizing the Slices of a Pie Chart

When you add more information to a chart, the rest of the elements sometimes automatically resize to accommodate the additional element. This adjustment can make the slices of the pie chart very small. To expand the slices, you have to expand the size of either the chart area or the plot area. In a pie chart, the plot area is an invisible square upon which the wedges of the pie chart rest. To expand the size of the plot area, you first have to select it and then drag one of the corner selection handles.

Because the chart area is already as large as your screen will allow, you'll expand the plot area of the chart in an attempt to make the slices of this pie larger without expanding the chart area itself.

To enlarge the slices of the pie by expanding the plot area:

1. Position the pointer in the middle of the pie slices until the ScreenTip "Plot Area" appears, and then click to select this chart element. See Figure 4-17. Selection handles appear on each corner of the plot area.

Figure 4-17   SELECTING THE PLOT AREA OF THE PIE CHART

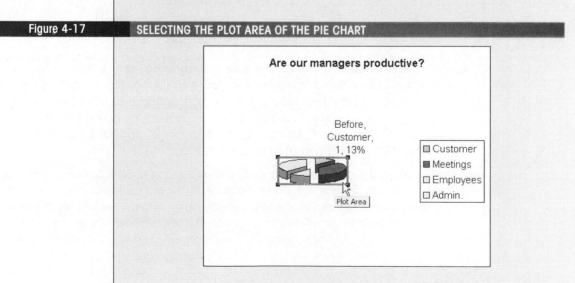

2. Drag the upper-left selection handle of the plot area up and to the left edge of the chart area, and then drag the lower-right selection handle of the plot area down and to the right edge of the chart area so that the slices of the pie fill the chart area. Now that you've expanded the size of the plot area, the data labels have become too large to fit in the chart area.

TROUBLE? Make sure that you drag the lower-right selection handle over to the right edge of the chart area. Enlarging the plot area will not affect the legend.

3. Double-click any part of the data labels for the Customers wedge to open the Format Data Labels dialog box, click the **Font** tab, click **10** in the Size list, and then click the **OK** button.

4. Click the legend to select it, and then drag the legend to a position on the chart so that all chart elements are clearly visible, as shown in Figure 4-18.

Figure 4-18	RESIZING AND MOVING CHART ELEMENTS

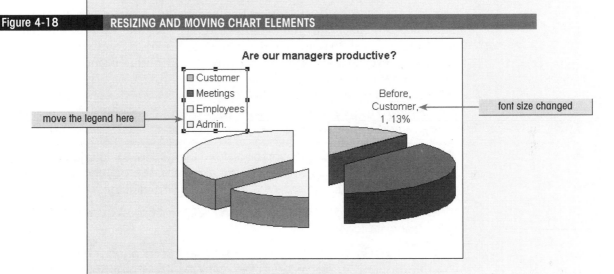

5. Save your changes, and then print the SurveyData worksheet in landscape orientation with your name in the left section of the header.

6. Close the MgmtSurvey-4 workbook.

Lynn likes the exploded 3-D pie chart that you created. It clearly shows how managers responded to the time management survey before the reorganization. She will ask you to create more charts to compare the Before and After survey data at a later time. Right now, though, she asks you to set this project aside to work on an even higher priority. A special committee is meeting to examine the expenses for the Southside Pool, and she needs your immediate help to chart this expense information.

Creating an Extracted Pie Chart

To create an extracted pie chart, you start with the same basic organization of data (a single column or row of values) as you do with a regular pie chart. Some of the values in the series, however, should be parts of a category that constitute a single slice. For example, you might want to create an extracted pie chart of the sales for several regions, using the slices of the main pie chart to represent the sales in each region. Then for one particular region, you might want to extract its slice into smaller increments, such as products or sales managers, that make up the total value of that slice. Therefore, the key design issue is that the pieces of the extraction must constitute the whole value of the slice that you are extracting.

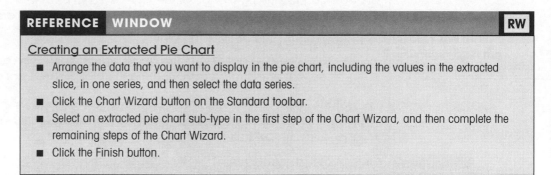

REFERENCE WINDOW   RW

Creating an Extracted Pie Chart
- Arrange the data that you want to display in the pie chart, including the values in the extracted slice, in one series, and then select the data series.
- Click the Chart Wizard button on the Standard toolbar.
- Select an extracted pie chart sub-type in the first step of the Chart Wizard, and then complete the remaining steps of the Chart Wizard.
- Click the Finish button.

Lynn wants you to create a chart to illustrate the swimming pool expenses for the new Southside pool. She wants you to use a chart that will emphasize the different kinds of utility expenses that she has listed in the workbook. You'll use an extracted pie chart so that the total utility expense category can be compared to the other major expenses, and so that the individual utility expenses can also be itemized.

To create an extracted pie of pie chart for Southside pool's swimming expenses:

1. Open the **Southside-4** workbook from the Tutorial.04\Tutorial folder of your Data Disk. You want to graph these expenses as a pie chart, with the utility wedge extracted to show the individual utility values in A7:B9.

2. Select the range **A4:B10**, and then click the **Chart Wizard** button 📊 on the Standard toolbar.

3. Click **Pie** in the Chart type list, make sure the Pie chart sub-type (first chart in the first row) is selected, and then click the **Press and Hold to View Sample** button. See Figure 4-19. Compared to the other slices, the Electricity, Water, and Telephone slices are so small they are barely visible. Because you can combine these three slices in one category called Utilities, this data provides a good opportunity to apply an extracted pie chart.

| Figure 4-19 | PREVIEWING A PIE CHART |

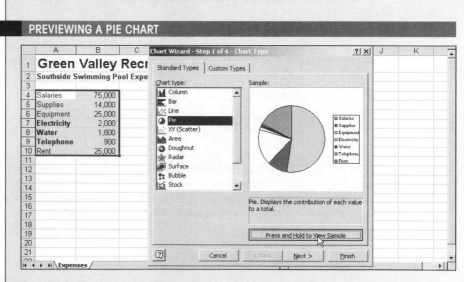

4. Click **Pie of Pie** chart sub-type (first row, first column on the right), and then click the **Next** button. At this point, the extracted pie doesn't appear to be illustrating the utility values of Electricity (2,000), Water (1,800), and Telephone (900) because one wedge is so much larger than the other two. Unfortunately, you can't use the Chart Wizard to specify which values will be in the main pie and which will be in the extracted pie, so you'll continue through the steps of the Chart Wizard and modify the pie of pie chart wedges after that.

5. Click the **Next** button, type **Southside Expenses** as the chart title, click the **Next** button, and then click the **Finish** button to insert the chart as an embedded object in the Expenses worksheet.

6. Move and resize the chart so that it looks like Figure 4-20.

| Figure 4-20 | PIE OF PIE CHART |

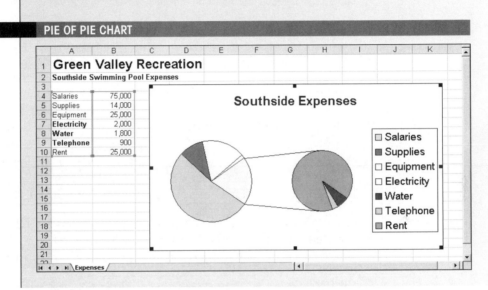

By default, a pie of pie chart type determines which values are going to be extracted by the position they occupy in the data series. By default, the last three values in the selected data series become the wedges of the extracted pie, regardless of their value. You can change the way that the data series is split in a pie of pie chart or bar of pie chart by choosing to extract all data points with a value less than a given number or a percent value less than a given percentage. You can also manually choose which data points go in the main pie and which go in the extracted pie or extracted bar chart.

Also, by default, the wedge on the main pie that is extracted is given the Category name "Other." You can view the data labels (Series name, Category name, Value, and Percentage) for any data marker of any chart by pointing to it and reading the information in the ScreenTip. To move the data points to the correct pie, you need to work with the Format Data Series dialog box.

REFERENCE WINDOW   RW

Moving the Data Points in an Extracted Chart:

■ Click any wedge in the data series to select the entire series, and then click the Format Data Series button on the Chart toolbar; or double-click any wedge in the data series to open the Format Data Series dialog box.

■ Click the Options tab.

■ Click the Split series by list arrow, and then click the option that indicates how you want to split the series. To manually move the slice(s) between the pies, click Custom.

■ Click the OK button in the Format Data Series dialog box.

■ To manually move the slice(s), drag a slice from the main pie to the extracted pie or extracted bar chart (or vice versa) until the chart matches the data that you are presenting.

Right now, the pie of pie chart extracted the last three data points of the data series (the Water, Telephone, and Rent values) and used them to develop the extracted pie. You want the three utility expenses (the Electricity, Water, and Telephone values) to comprise the extracted pie. Therefore, you'll have to manually move the Rent slice from the extracted pie back to the main pie and the Electricity slice from the main pie to the extracted pie.

To move the Rent and Electricity data points to the correct pies:

1. Double-click any slice in the pie to open the Format Data Series dialog box.

TROUBLE? If the Format Data Point dialog box opens, you double-clicked a single slice instead of the entire data series. Close the Format Data Point dialog box, click away from the selected slice, and then try Step 1 again.

2. Click the **Options** tab to display the extraction options. See Figure 4-21. The default options show that the split is completed by Position, and that the second plot (the extracted pie) contains the last three values. Another option specifies that the size of the second plot is 75% of the first. To define which values are in the main pie and which in the extracted pie (or second plot), you need to choose Custom for the Split series by option.

Figure 4-21 **FORMAT DATA SERIES DIALOG BOX**

click to display the options that you can use to split the data

number of data points in the extracted pie

size of the extracted pie

extracted pie

Format Data Series

Patterns | Axis | Data Labels | Options

Split series by: Position

☑ Series lines
☑ Vary colors by slice

Second plot contains the last: 3 values

Size of second plot: 75   Gap width: 100

Southside Expenses

☐ Salaries
■ Supplies
☐ Equipment
☐ Electricity
■ Water
☐ Telephone
■ Rent

OK   Cancel

3. Click the **Split series by** list arrow, click **Custom**, and then click the **OK** button. Each slice in each pie, the entire data series, is still selected. Now that the Split series by option is set to Custom, you are allowed to move wedges by dragging them to the appropriate pie.

4. Drag the **Rent** slice from the extracted pie on the right to the main pie on the left. The Rent slice is inserted in the main pie.

TROUBLE? If you don't drag the slice between the pies correctly, your action might resize or explode the wedges of the pie. If this happens, click the Undo button, and then repeat the step. Use the ScreenTip that appears above the slice when you hover the pointer over the slice to help select the correct slice.

5. Drag the **Electricity** slice from the main pie to the extracted pie. See Figure 4-22.

Figure 4-22 **MOVING SLICES BETWEEN THE MAIN AND EXTRACTED PIES**

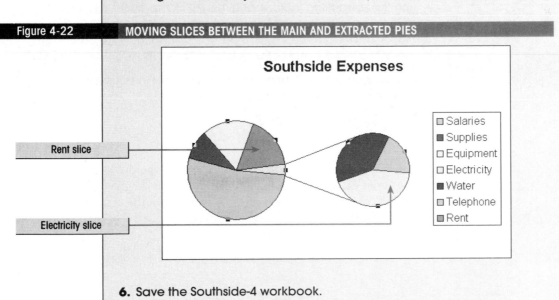

Rent slice

Electricity slice

Southside Expenses

☐ Salaries
■ Supplies
☐ Equipment
☐ Electricity
■ Water
☐ Telephone
☐ Rent

6. Save the Southside-4 workbook.

Changing Slice Colors

When you create pie charts, Excel colors each slice with a new color, but you might want to modify them to fit a particular color scheme or to show more or less contrast between the wedges.

REFERENCE WINDOW   **RW**

Changing a Slice Color
- Click the data series to select it, and then click the individual slice that you want to modify to select only that slice.
- Double-click the selected slice or click the Format Data Point button on the Chart toolbar, click the Patterns tab, click the color you want to apply to the slice, and then click the OK button.

or

- Click the list arrow for the Fill Color button on the Formatting toolbar, and then click the color that you want to apply.

Lynn wants you to change the color of two of the slices in the main pie chart to distinguish them more clearly from the other slices of the main pie. You will change the color of the Rent slice in the main pie to light green and the color of the slice that represents the total utilities to white.

To change the color of the Rent and Other slices:

1. Click the main pie to select it, click the **Rent** slice to select it and then double-click it to open the Format Data Point dialog box.

2. Click the **Patterns** tab, click the **Light Green** square (fifth row, fourth column) in the color palette, and then click the **OK** button.

3. Click the **Other** slice in the main pie, click the **list arrow** for the Fill Color button on the Formatting toolbar, and then click the **White** square (fifth row, last column) in the color palette. The advantage of using the Fill Color button rather than the Format Data Point dialog box to change the slice color is that when you point to a color in the color palette, a ScreenTip identifies the color's name.

4. Save your changes, and then print the worksheet in landscape orientation with your name in the left section of the header.

5. Close the Southside-4 workbook.

The Southside pool expenses are now illustrated in the pie of pie chart. With the total value of the utilities category shown as a single wedge on the main chart, and the three utility expenses that comprise the utility category clarified in the extracted pie chart, Lynn can clearly show the relationship of the total utility category to the other expenses, as well as the composition of the utility category itself.

Working **with Doughnut Charts**

A **doughnut chart** is similar in appearance to a pie chart. The big difference between the two is that a doughnut chart can show multiple data series as separate rings. Because a doughnut chart can be used to show more than one series of data, it can be interchanged with column or bar charts that chart more than one series. The center of a doughnut chart is open to emphasize the rings of the chart. Doughnut charts are rare, though. They are not used to emphasize the area of the ring sections themselves, but rather to emphasize how the proportions of an item (represented as a section of each ring) change over time. The doughnut chart shown in Figure 4-23 illustrates how the ratio of fat to muscle improved after participants went through a fitness program.

Figure 4-23 | **SAMPLE DOUGHNUT CHART**

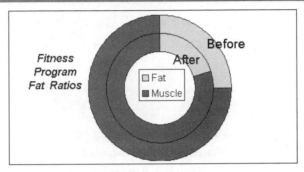

Creating a Doughnut Chart

Now that you've finished the Southside pool expenses chart, Lynn wants you to continue working on the management survey data. Lynn likes the way the wedges of the pie chart represent the time the managers spend in each of the four categories, but she wants to know if you can add the After series to the pie chart, too. The After series represents the results of the same survey after GVR restructured to allow managers to spend more time with customers. You explain to Lynn that while a pie chart can only support one series of values, a doughnut chart is similar to a pie chart and supports multiple sets of values (multiple data series). You'll copy the pie chart, change the copy into a doughnut chart, and add the new data series to it.

To copy the pie chart and change the copy into a doughnut chart:

1. Open the **MgmtSurvey-4** workbook from the Tutorial.04\Tutorial folder on your Data Disk.

2. Click the chart to select it (if it isn't already selected), click the **list arrow** for the Chart Type button 🔽 on the Chart toolbar, and then click the **Doughnut Chart** icon 🔘 in the chart gallery. When there is only one series of data, a doughnut chart is a pie chart with the center missing. Now you will add the second series of data to the chart.

   TROUBLE? The icon on the Chart Type button changes to reflect the last chart type selected.

3. Select the range **C4:C8**, click the **Copy** button 🖺 on the Standard toolbar, click the chart, and then click the **Paste** button 📋 on the Standard toolbar. The Before series is the inner ring of the chart, and the After series is the outer ring of the doughnut chart. Note the change in the Customer slices between the rings. The outer (After) ring is significantly larger than the inside ring (Before) ring.

4. Move the legend as necessary, so that your chart looks like Figure 4-24.

Figure 4-24	A NEW DATA SERIES ADDED TO A DOUGHNUT CHART

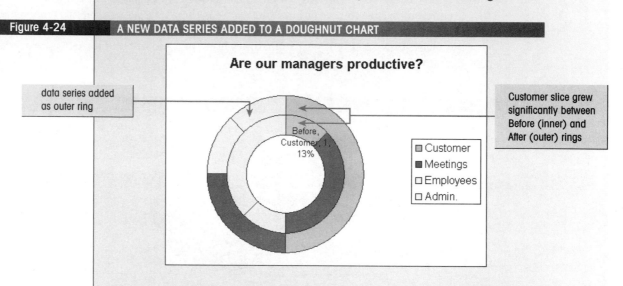

5. Click the **Before, Customers, 1, 13%** label, and then press the **Delete** key.

TROUBLE? If you deleted the wrong element, click the Undo button 🔄 on the Standard toolbar. Repeat Step 4, making sure that the ScreenTip for the selected item reads: "Before" Point "Customer" Data Label.

6. Click cell **A1** to deselect the chart, and then save the MgmtSurvey-4 workbook.

Reorganizing the Data Points on a Doughnut Chart

Although a doughnut chart is not a common chart type, you can use it successfully if you make sure that you have organized all of the data points so that they are as easy to understand as possible. For example, in the doughnut chart that you created, it's a little difficult to compare the slices between the Meetings and Employees slices because they are not in the same position on the two rings. Notice that the first data points for the Customer values start at 12 o'clock on the chart and expand in a clockwise direction. Because the Customer data for the inner ring (Before) is one hour and the Customer data for the outer ring (After) is four hours, the slices are dramatically different in size, which undermines the alignment of the rest of the slices in each ring.

Lynn has pointed out that the Employees data and the Meetings data are hard to compare between the Before and After series. The time that the managers reportedly spent with employees before the restructuring was one hour, and the time they spent with employees after the restructuring was one hour. With this in mind, you explain to Lynn that you could start the pie chart with those data points, and then the rest of the colors might align better between the inner and outer rings. In effect, you want to start the doughnut chart with the values that have the least difference between the inner and outer rings and progress to the values with the largest difference so that the colors stay as aligned as possible.

To accomplish this, you first need to determine the difference between the Before and After values. To determine the difference between the values, you will use the ABS (absolute) function. This function will return the difference between two values as a positive value.

To change the data series of the doughnut chart:

1. Reduce the size of the chart slightly and move it to the right so that you can clearly see the entire chart and all of column D.

2. Click cell **D4**, type **Difference**, and then press the **Enter** key.

3. In cell D5, enter **=ABS(B5-C5)** and then use the fill handle to copy the formula in cell D5 through range **D6:D8**.

4. Click in any cell in the range **D4:D8**, and then click the **Sort Ascending** button ⟨⟩ on the Standard toolbar. See Figure 4-25. Sorting the data series in ascending order based on the difference between the values better aligns the slices for comparison on the doughnut chart.

| Figure 4-25 | REORDERING THE DATA POINTS ON A DOUGHNUT CHART |

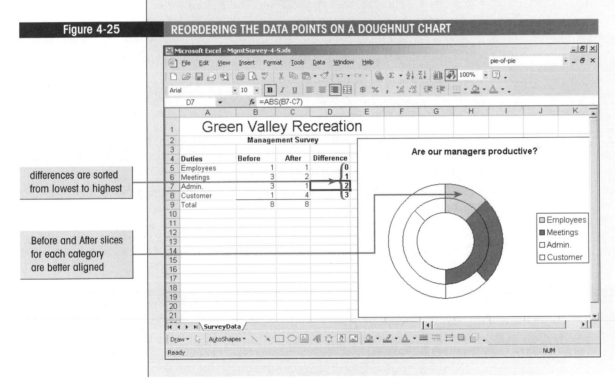

Now that the two rings are better aligned, you can see more clearly how the Before and After values have changed. Lynn is most interested in the Customer data series, presented as the last slice of each ring. Because both slices stop at the same place (the top of the circle), you can clearly compare those slices and see the big difference between the inner (Before) and outer (After) series for the customer category.

Adding Data Point Labels to a Doughnut Chart

Although you know that the inner ring represents the Before series and the outer ring represents the After series, without labels your readers won't know this. Therefore, you will add labels with the series names Before and After to the Customer slices in order to identify the rings and draw attention to the big change in this category.

Note: If you are using Excel 2000, the Format Data Point dialog box does not provide the same options as in Excel 2002. Read through Steps 1 through 6, and then complete Step 7.

To add the Before and After labels to the Customer slices:

1. Click any slice in the outer ring of the chart to select the After series, and then click the **Customer** slice in the After series to select just that slice. Selection handles surround the Customer slice of the outer series to indicate that only this data marker is selected.

2. Click the **Format Data Point** button 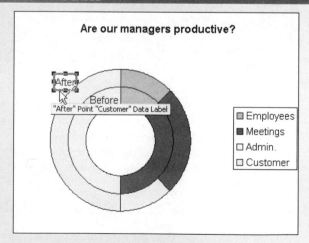 on the Chart toolbar, click the **Data Labels** tab, click the **Series name** check box, and then click the **OK** button. The After series name label is added to the outer ring.

   TROUBLE? If the label is too large, double-click the label to open the Format Data Labels dialog box, click the Font tab, click 10 in the Size list box, and then click the OK button.

3. Click any slice in the inner ring to select the Before series, and then click the **Customer** slice in the Before series to select just that slice.

4. Click the **Format Data Point** button in the Chart toolbar, click the **Series name** check box on the Data Labels tab, and then click the **OK** button.

   TROUBLE? If the label is too large, double-click the label to open the Format Data Labels dialog box, click the Font tab, click 10 in the Size list box, and then click the OK button.

   Now that the After and Before series labels are added to the appropriate slices to clarify and draw attention to that part of the doughnut chart, you will move the labels to a location that makes them easier to read.

5. Click the **After** series name label to select it, and then drag the label up and to the left as shown in Figure 4-26.

   TROUBLE? If the After series name label is too large or too small, right-click the label to open the Format Data Labels dialog box, click the Font tab, click 12 in the Size list box, and then click the OK button.

Figure 4-26   MOVING A SERIES NAME LABEL

6. Click the **Before** data series label, and then drag it to the middle of the doughnut chart.

> **7.** Save your changes to the MgmtSurvey-4 workbook, and then print the SurveyData worksheet in landscape orientation with your name in the left section of the header.

The first time you see any new graph, it might take a while to understand it. Because you want to make sure that all charts you create are truly effective ways to communicate information, ask a trusted colleague or your manager to review how you have used them.

You're not sure that a doughnut chart will be well received, so you suggest to Lynn that you might try creating a 100% stacked column or 100% stacked bar chart instead. All three of these charts compare percentages across multiple series of data.

Creating a 100% Stacked Column Chart

You use a 100% stacked column chart when you want to compare the percentage each value contributes to a total across series. As with the doughnut chart, you are not evaluating the data marker size itself but rather how that data marker size varies from series to series.

By now, you're very familiar with the process of changing a chart type from one to another. To change a chart type, you can use the Chart Wizard, the Chart menu option, or the Chart Type button on the Chart toolbar. The 100% stacked column chart type is not, however, one of the 18 chart types provided by the Chart Type button on the Chart toolbar, so you must use either the Chart menu or the Chart Wizard to apply this chart type.

To change the doughnut chart into a 100% stacked column chart:

1. Click the chart to select it, click the **Copy** button 🖺 on the Standard toolbar, click cell **L2**, and then click the **Paste** button 🖺 on the Standard toolbar to paste a copy of the chart to the right of the original doughnut chart. You'll change the chart type of this copy so that you can compare how various chart types communicate the same data.

2. Click the **After** label and press the **Delete** key, and then click the **Before** label and press the **Delete** key.

3. With the second chart selected, click **Chart** on the menu bar, click **Chart Type**, click **Column** in the Chart type list, click the **100% Stacked Column** chart subtype (first row, third column), and then click the **OK** button. Because the 100% stacked column chart presents a legend that identifies the colors of the columns, you don't also need the series name labels for the Customers data markers.

4. Move the legend so it appears above the Customer bar. See Figure 4-27.

   TROUBLE? Depending on the size of your chart, there may not be enough room to show all of the labels on the x-axis. Resize your chart so that it matches Figure 4-27.

Figure 4-27 | 100% STACKED COLUMN CHART

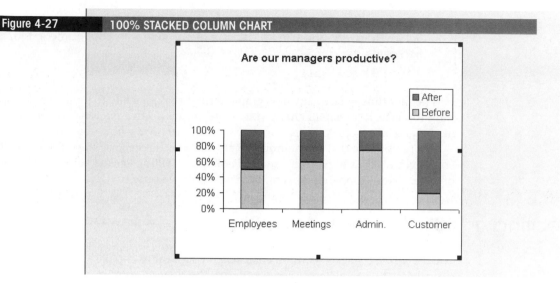

Because the y-axis shows percentages, you know that you are not comparing actual values, but rather proportions of a whole. Although this chart does a good job of comparing the relative size of the Before and After values for each category, the chart does not provide information about the actual time the managers spent in each category. In other words, you do not know how much time they spent in the Customer category, but you can clearly see that they spent much more time with customers in the After series as compared to the Before series.

Adding a Data Table to a Chart

As you've already experienced, one way to make sure that the data in a chart is clearly identified is to use data labels. You can add data labels that identify the name of a series, category, and value for a particular data series, or you can label individual data markers. Another way to identify the data values in a chart is to include a data table. A **data table** is a grid of values that correspond to the data markers on the chart.

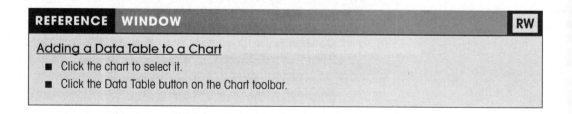

REFERENCE WINDOW | RW

Adding a Data Table to a Chart
- Click the chart to select it.
- Click the Data Table button on the Chart toolbar.

After discussing the management survey chart with Lynn, you suggest adding a data table to the 100% stacked column chart so that the actual values represented by the data markers are presented as part of the chart.

To add a data table to the stacked column chart:

1. Click the chart to select it (if it is not already selected).

2. Click the **Data Table** button 🖩 on the Chart toolbar. A grid of values appears beneath the chart. The grid displays the actual data that was used to create the proportional bars on the chart. Because the data table also serves as a legend, you no longer need the legend element.

3. Delete the legend and expand the size of the plot area to resize the chart so that the y-axis has room to display more values as shown in Figure 4-28.

Figure 4-28	ADDING A DATA TABLE TO THE CHART

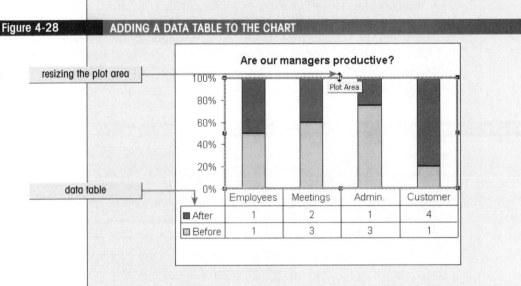

4. Save your changes, and then print the SurveyData worksheet on one page in landscape orientation.

5. Close the MgmtSurvey-4 workbook, and then exit Excel.

These charts will help Lynn communicate to the board how the restructuring process affected middle management.

Session 4.1 QUICK CHECK

1. Discuss the reasons to use a 3-D chart as well as potential problem areas you need to be aware of while you are creating them.

2. The cylinder, cone, and pyramid charts apply a 3-D data marker to what type of chart?

3. What are two fundamental differences between the pie and doughnut charts?

4. What do the columns on a 100% stacked column chart represent?

5. Describe two ways to show the actual data values on a 100% stacked column chart.

SESSION 4.2

In this session, you will learn about the relationship between an XY (scatter) chart and a bubble chart. You will also work with line charts and their 3-D counterparts, ribbon charts. Finally, you will work with radar, surface, and stock charts.

Analyzing an XY (Scatter) Chart

The **XY (scatter) chart** shows the relationship between two numeric variables. Because this type of chart measures two values and plots them according to the scales on two different axes, the chart has two value axes. In other words, both the x- and y-axes are considered value axes on an XY (scatter) chart. (In contrast, on a column chart, the y-axis is the only value axis and the x-axis is the category axis.) Whether or not the values that are plotted on the XY (scatter) chart form a line depends on how closely one variable correlates with the other. An example of an XY (scatter) chart and the data that was used for the diagram is shown in Figure 4-29.

Figure 4-29   SAMPLE XY (SCATTER) CHART

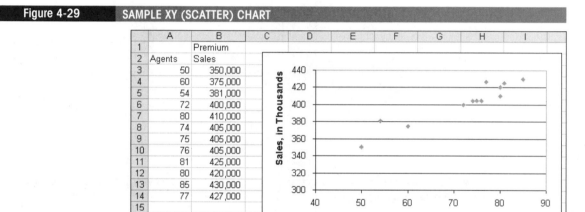

In this example, you would expect that the more agents you have (as plotted on the x-axis), the more sales you would have (plotted on the y-axis). You might also expect this relationship to be linear, which means that the plotted points form a straight line. By recording, plotting, and analyzing the data in an XY (scatter) chart or using some other statistical measures, you can find out much more about this relationship than you can by simply looking at the list of values. Sometimes what you expect to be closely correlated is actually not, whereas seemingly unrelated variables, such as rainfall and sales, may be highly correlated for unknown reasons. Knowing that one variable is highly correlated with another, even if you don't know why the correlation exists, helps you make predictions and better business decisions.

Comparing an XY (Scatter) Chart with a Bubble Chart

A **bubble chart** is really just an XY (scatter) chart with a third numeric dimension. The third dimension is represented by the size of the bubble. Figure 4-30 shows an example of a bubble chart.

Figure 4-30   SAMPLE BUBBLE CHART

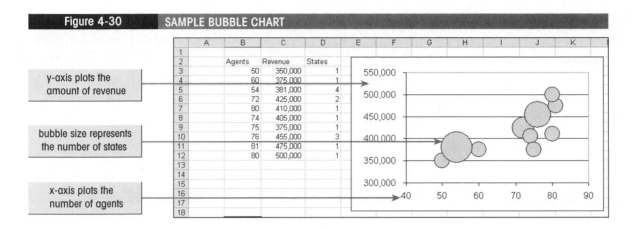

y-axis plots the amount of revenue

bubble size represents the number of states

x-axis plots the number of agents

You use a bubble chart in the same way that you might use an XY (scatter) chart, that is, to determine whether there is a strong correlation between the values plotted along the x- and y-axes. If there were a correlation, the bubbles would form a line. The size of the bubble measures a third numeric variable—in this case, the number of states recorded in column D.

The board is very concerned about pool safety and is asking Lynn to analyze whether the current plan to reduce accidents, adding more lifeguards, is working. After reviewing related statistics over a 10-week period, Lynn suspects that the number of accidents is not directly related to the number of lifeguards on duty, but rather to the number of pool visitors. She is searching for a way to prove her hunch and show the board why increasing the number of lifeguards does not, in and of itself, directly reduce the number of pool accidents. She is asking for your help to graphically present this data. Because you need to compare three numeric variables at one time (average number of lifeguards, number of weekly patrons, and number of accident incidents per week), you'll apply the bubble chart type to this data to see if any correlations between the three numeric variables can be made.

To create and format a bubble chart:

1. Open the **LifeguardReport-4** workbook located in the Tutorial.04\Tutorial folder on your Data Disk. This workbook logs the average number of lifeguards on duty, the total number of patrons for that week, and the total number of accident incidents for that week.

2. Select the range **B5:D14**, and then click the **Chart Wizard** button 📊 on the Standard toolbar.

   A bubble chart automatically creates the values for the x-axis based on the first data series (in this case, column B), the y-axis based on the second series (column C), and the bubble sizes based on the third series (column D).

3. Click **Bubble** in the Chart type list, and then click the **Next** button twice to move to accept the current choices for the source data and to move to the third step of the Wizard.

4. Click the **Titles** tab (if it is not already selected), type **Lifeguard Accident Report** as the chart title, type **Avg # of Lifeguards** as the title on the x-axis, and type **Weekly Swimmers** as the title on the y-axis.

Because the legend doesn't provide any valuable information, you will delete it, and thus expand the plot area, providing more room for the data markers, which will clarify the information on the chart.

5. Click the **Legend** tab, click the **Show legend** check box to deselect it, and then click the **Next** button.

6. Click the **Finish** button to embed the chart as an object in the Accidents worksheet.

7. Move and resize the chart so that it looks like Figure 4-31.

| Figure 4-31 | BUBBLE CHART |

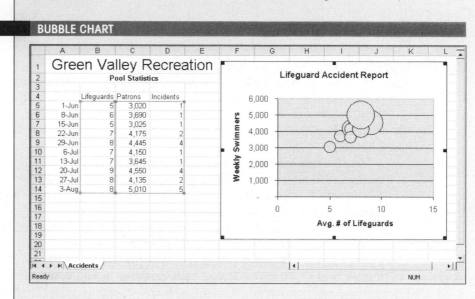

Formatting a Bubble Chart

As you can see in Figure 4-31, the initial bubble chart is somewhat difficult to read because some of the data markers cover other data markers. To improve the clarity of this information, you will give the bubbles more room on the chart by shortening the scales on the x- and y-axes.

To change the scales on the x- and y-axes:

1. Double-click any value on the x-axis to open the Format Axis dialog box, click the **Scale** tab, double-click the value in the Minimum box to select it, type **4**, and then click the **OK** button. With the x-axis starting at 4 instead of 0, there is more horizontal space in which the bubbles are displayed.

You will start the y-axis at 2,000 to increase the amount of vertical space on the plot area.

2. Double-click any value on the y-axis to open the Format Axis dialog box, click the **Scale** tab, double-click the value in the Minimum box to select it and type **2000**, click the **Display units** list arrow, and then click **Hundreds**. See Figure 4-32.

TROUBLE? Depending on the size of your chart, the values on the y-axis and in the default values for the Major unit and Minor unit scale may be different.

| Figure 4-32 | CHANGING THE UNIT OF MEASUREMENT DISPLAYED ON THE Y-AXIS |

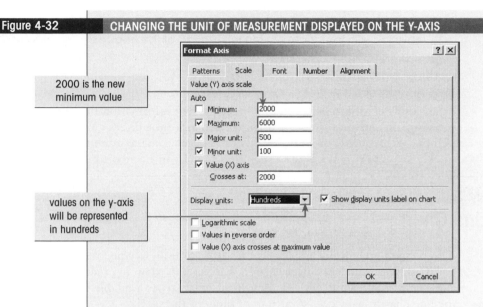

2000 is the new minimum value

values on the y-axis will be represented in hundreds

3. Click the **OK** button.

As a final formatting change, you want the values on the x-axis that represent the average number of lifeguards to increment by 1 instead of by 2.

4. Double-click any value on the x-axis to open the Format Axis dialog box, click the **Scale** tab (if it is not already selected), double-click the value in the Major unit box to select it, type **1**, and then click the **OK** button. See Figure 4-33. The bubble chart shows a somewhat linear relationship between weekly swimmers on the y-axis and lifeguards on the x-axis. If, however, the number of lifeguards on duty lowered the number of accidents as the Board of Directors had hoped, the size of bubbles, which represent the number of incidents, would be smaller as the number of lifeguards increased. Instead, the opposite is true. The bubble sizes appear to have more to do with the number of weekly swimmers than the average number of lifeguards, because the bubble sizes get larger as the number of weekly swimmers grows.

EXCEL 2000: If the value in the Major unit box is already set to 1, no action is necessary. Click the **OK** button.

| Figure 4-33 | FINAL BUBBLE CHART |

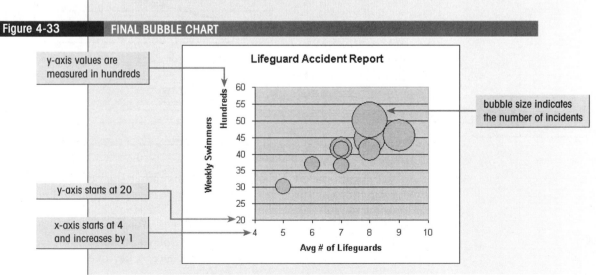

y-axis values are measured in hundreds

bubble size indicates the number of incidents

y-axis starts at 20

x-axis starts at 4 and increases by 1

5. Save your changes, and then print the Accidents worksheet in landscape orientation with your name in the left section of the header.

6. Close the LifeguardReport-4 workbook.

A bubble chart can help you to visually present information that includes three numeric variables. In this case, it shows that accidents do not directly correlate with the average number of lifeguards on duty, but instead appear to have more to do with the number of weekly swimmers. This is the conclusion that Lynn needed to illustrate for the Board of Directors.

Using the Line Chart

A line chart graphically displays trends over time by connecting data points recorded at equal intervals with lines. Because trends are so important in predicting future performance, a line chart is often one of the most valuable chart types available. To show trends over time, the line chart usually uses some unit of time for the x-axis.

In Figure 4-34, the lines show the trend for the corresponding data series, Sales or Expenses, over a period of several years. The chart dramatically shows the growing gap between the two lines. The gap represents profits. The gap is increasing because the **slope**, the steepness of the line, measured as the amount of **rise** (change in y) over **run** (change in x), is increasing faster for the Sales line than it is for the Expenses line. Unfortunately, on a black and white printer, it is difficult to create effective line charts because the lines are hard to differentiate. You can vary the thickness and style (solid, dotted, dashed) of each line, but your chart will quickly lose its value if the reader has to concentrate very hard to understand it.

Figure 4-34 — EXAMPLE OF THE APPROPRIATE USE OF A LINE CHART

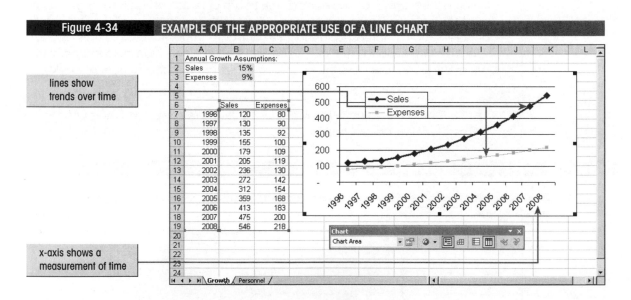

lines show trends over time

x-axis shows a measurement of time

If the data measures the value of separate items rather than the value of the same item over time, the line chart is probably an inappropriate chart type to use. Figure 4-35 displays an inappropriate use of the line chart. The order of the labels on the x-axis is random. This means that if the labels were listed in a different order, the line would be completely different. Therefore, the line itself has no meaning, displays no meaningful trend, and actually detracts from the information presented in this chart. A key question to ask yourself after you create a line chart is "Does each point on the line represent a real value?" For the line chart in Figure 4-34 the answer would be "Yes, each point on the line represents an estimated value for that point in time." In other words, the point on the line halfway between the 2003 and 2004 values estimates sales and expenses halfway through the year 2003, June of 2003. For the line chart in Figure 4-35 the answer would be "No, the point on the line halfway between Don and Harold, for example, doesn't represent anything meaningful."

Figure 4-35	EXAMPLE OF THE INAPPROPRIATE USE OF A LINE CHART

the line itself doesn't mean anything nor does it illustrate a meaningful trend

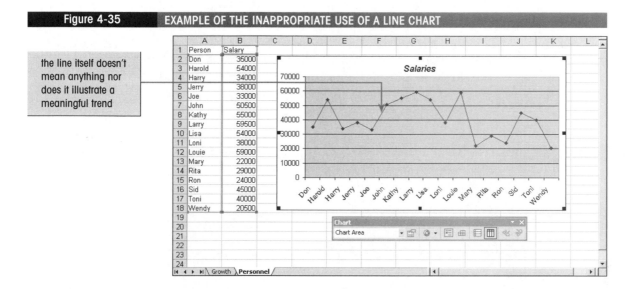

A better way to present the data in Figure 4-35 would be to sort the salaries in ascending order and then present the information in a column or bar chart. But even with the salaries sorted in ascending order, a line chart would not be appropriate because, once again, the points on the lines between the actual data points would not represent anything.

Creating a Line Chart

Lynn has created a workbook with financial information about the GVR T-shirt shop for the past five years. Because of the nature of the data (that is, sales over time), you suggest that this information be displayed as a line chart. A line chart will help show sales trends over the five-year period.

To create and format a line chart for the T-shirt sales data:

1. Open the **T-ShirtShop-4** workbook located in the Tutorial.04\Tutorial folder on your Data Disk, and then navigate through the workbook by pressing **Ctrl + End** to move to the bottom of the worksheet quickly and then pressing **Ctrl + Home** to return to the top of the worksheet.

   Now that you have quickly scanned the data in the workbook, you will graph total income versus the total costs in a line chart. Total income is in row 7, and total costs are in row 27. The values you want to add as the x-axis labels are the years, which appear in row 4.

2. Select the nonadjacent range **A4:F4;A7:F7;A27:F27**, and then click the **Chart Wizard** button 📊 on the Standard toolbar. Even though cell A4 is an empty cell, the Chart Wizard will not be able to interpret your selected values correctly unless you select the same number of cells for each range.

TROUBLE? To select nonadjacent ranges of cells, select the first range, and then press and hold the Ctrl key while you select the other range(s).

3. Click **Line** in the Chart type list, click **Line** in the Chart sub-type list (first row, first column on the left), and then click the **Next** button twice to accept the existing source data entries and to display the third step of the Chart Wizard.

4. Click the **Titles** tab, type **T-shirt profits are rising!** as the chart title, and then click the **Next** button.

Because the income statement data on the existing Income worksheet covers a large range of cells (which would make it difficult to print an embedded chart next to the income statement data), you'll insert this chart on a new sheet.

5. Click the **As new sheet** option button, type **Profit Line Chart** as the new sheet name, and then click the **Finish** button. See Figure 4-36.

| Figure 4-36 | LINE CHART INSERTED ON ITS OWN SHEET |

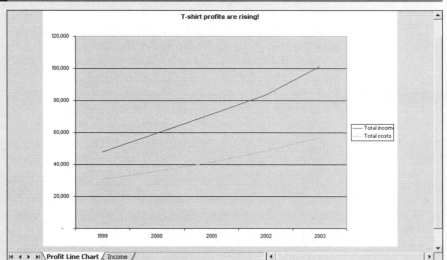

TROUBLE? If you can't see the entire chart on the screen, move the Chart toolbar from its current position and dock it at the top of the screen.

The line chart clearly shows upward trends for both lines. It also illustrates the positive fact that the slope is greater for the Total income line than the Total costs line. In other words, income is growing at a faster rate than costs.

Formatting a Line Chart

There are several formatting attributes that you can apply to a line chart to make it easier to read. The gray plot area, for example, eliminates some of the contrast between the lines. You'll change it to white to allow greater contrast.

To format the plot area of the line chart:

1. Double-click the plot area to open the Format Plot Area dialog box, click the **White** square (fifth row, last column on the right) in the color palette, and then click the **OK** button.

   TROUBLE? If the wrong Format dialog box opens (as evidenced by the information in the title bar of the dialog box), close it and then repeat Step 1, making sure to double-click the gray plot area, and not another chart element.

   You also feel that if the lines were thicker, they would be easier to see.

2. Double-click the **Total income line** to open its Format Data Series dialog box, click the **Patterns** tab (if it is not already selected), click the **Color** list arrow, click the **Black** square (first row, first column), click the **Weight** list arrow, and then click the last option in the list. Note that a preview of the new line appears in the Sample pane. See Figure 4-37. You can also use the options on this tab to remove or change the style of the line. In the Marker area of the dialog box you can add data markers to the lines and change their style (for example, diamond, square, or circle), foreground color (border color), background color (interior color), and size. Depending on your access to a color printer, these options can dramatically emphasize the line.

Figure 4-37   USING THE FORMAT DATA SERIES DIALOG BOX TO FORMAT THE LINE CHART

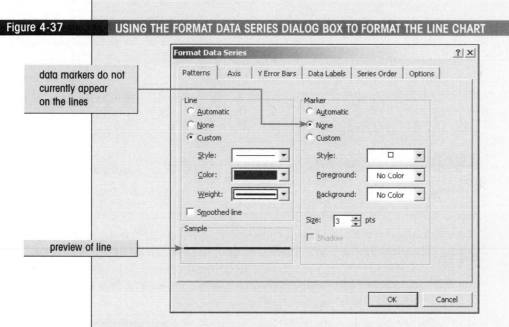

Another formatting embellishment to consider is the use of **drop-lines** (which appear as thin vertical lines extending from the selected data series line to the x-axis), **high-low lines** (which appear as thin vertical lines between the data series lines), and **up/down bars** (which appear as thick vertical bars between the data series lines).

3. Click the **Options** tab, click the **Drop lines** check box to observe that formatting embellishment in the preview sample, click the **Drop lines** check box to unselect it, click the **High-low lines** check box to observe that formatting change in the preview sample, click the **High-low lines** check box to unselect it, and click the **Up/down bars** check box to select this option. Because the bars between the Total income and Total costs data series lines represent profits, you decide that the thick up/down bars best emphasize these important values. You can modify the thickness of the bars by modifying the gap width value.

   EXCEL 2000: Click the **Up-down bars** check box on the Options tab.

4. Click the **Gap width** up arrow to change the value to 200. See Figure 4-38. The Gap width value represents the number of pixels (picture elements) between the bars. The larger the number, the larger the gap.

Figure 4-38   CHANGING THE GAP WIDTH BETWEEN THE UP/DOWN BARS

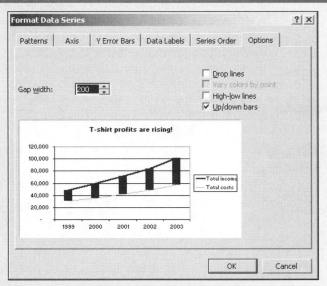

5. Click the **OK** button. Now that you've added up/down bars to the chart, you can format them just as you would format any other chart element. For example, if you wanted to change the color of the up/down bars, double-click any bar to open the Format Down Bars dialog box, and then choose the color you desire for the bars.

   You also need to format the Total costs line, which currently displays in a pink color on your monitor. Because you want to print this chart on a black and white printer, you need to format the Total costs data series in a way that will differentiate it from the Total income data series line using only black and white colors.

6. Double-click the **Total costs** line to open the Format Data Series dialog box, click the **Patterns** tab, click the **Style** list arrow, click the short dashed option (third from the top), click the **Color** list arrow, click the **Black** square (first row, first column) in the color palette, click the **Weight** list arrow, click the last example in the list, and then click the **OK** button.

   As a final formatting improvement, you'll increase the size of the legend, x-axis labels, and y-axis labels.

7. Click the legend, click the **list arrow** for the Font Size button on the Formatting toolbar, and then click **16**. Increasing the font size of the legend not only increases the size of the text in the legend, but also increases the size of the line color and style samples.

8. Click any label on the x-axis to select the axis, click the **list arrow** for , and then click **16**.

9. Click any label on the y-axis to select the axis, and then press the **F4** key to apply the 16-point font size to the y-axis labels. Remember that the F4 key performs different functions in Excel, depending on what you are doing. In this case, pressing the F4 repeated your last action.

10. Click the chart title, click the **list arrow** for , and then click **24**.

11. Click the **list arrow** for the Font button  on the Formatting toolbar, and then click **Comic Sans MS** in the list. Comic Sans is a font that simulates printed letters and is very easy to read.

TROUBLE? If the Comic Sans MS font is not available, select another font that is very easy to read.

12. Click in the gray border outside the chart so that no chart element is selected, and then save your changes. See Figure 4-39.

Figure 4-39	FORMATTED LINE CHART

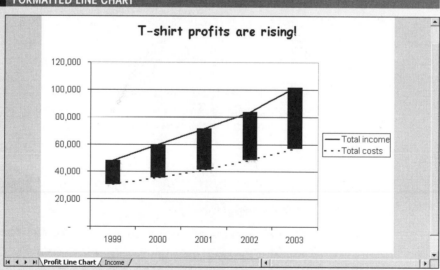

13. Print the Profit Line Chart worksheet with your name in the left section of the header for the worksheet.

14. Save the T-ShirtShop-4 workbook.

Line charts can reveal trends over time, and because of this, they are among the most influential chart types. An effective line chart will communicate information many times faster and better than a column of numbers. Yet line charts are sometimes difficult to successfully create because the lines are difficult to select and format, and they are sometimes applied to data that doesn't support this chart type. Here is a good rule of thumb for deciding whether a line chart applies to your data: If the x-axis represents a measurement of time, the line chart is probably a good chart type for that set of data. If you have more than two data series, you should use color to differentiate the lines.

Working with a Ribbon Chart

A **ribbon chart** is a three-dimensional version of a line chart (see Figure 4-40). The ribbon chart offers the same benefits as other 3-D charts: a more visually interesting presentation of data and the option to chart the series in three dimensions instead of two. But it also suffers from the same potential problems that all 3-D charts have: It is more difficult to see where the data points cross the y-axis, it requires more physical space to present the data in three dimensions, and depending on the size of the ribbons and orientation of the chart, data may be hidden or obscured.

Figure 4-40	SAMPLE RIBBON CHART

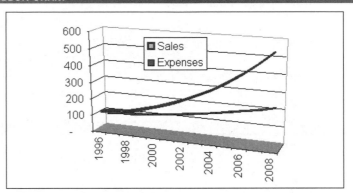

Although GVR itself is a nonprofit organization, the T-shirt shop is run as a standalone, profit-generating business. Lynn also wants you to create a chart to illustrate the tax implications of this status for the past five years. You will create a ribbon chart to show the trend between before- and after-tax income.

To create a ribbon chart of before- and after-tax data:

1. Click the **Income** tab.

2. Select the nonadjacent ranges **A4:F4;A29:F29;A31:F31**, and then click the **Chart Wizard** button on the Standard toolbar.

3. Click **Line** in the Chart type list, click **3-D Line** in the Chart sub-type list (third row), and then click the **Next** button twice to accept entries for the chart source data and to display the third step of the Chart Wizard.

4. Click the **Titles** tab (if it is not already selected), type **Tax Analysis** as the chart title, and then click the **Next** button.

5. Click the **As new sheet** option button, type **Tax Analysis** as the new sheet name, and then click the **Finish** button.

Because the legend and the z-axis labels provide the same information, you don't need both chart elements.

6. Right-click the **Profit after taxes** label, and then click **Clear** on the shortcut menu. See Figure 4-41. The gap between the lines represents the amount of money paid in taxes. This chart helps illustrate why the impressive increase in profit before taxes over the five years did not equate to a similar gain in after-tax profits.

Figure 4-41 | **TAX ANALYSIS RIBBON CHART**

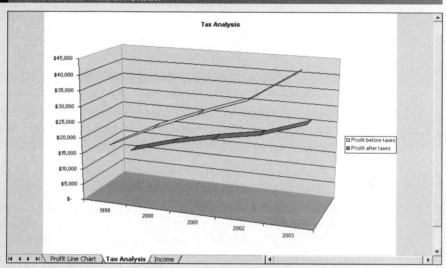

7. Save your changes, and then print the Tax Analysis sheet with your name in the left section of the header.

8. Close the T-ShirtShop-4 workbook.

At this point, you could further format the 3-D line chart (ribbon chart) by modifying the fonts, colors, and sizes of various chart elements to improve the visibility of the information. As with all chart types, to format any element on a ribbon chart, you first select the item and then open its Format dialog box. Because the ribbon chart is a 3-D chart, it must respect all of the rules of sound 3-D chart construction, and because it is a modified line chart, it is best at showing trends over time.

Working **with a Radar Chart**

A **radar** chart compares the cumulative values of a number of data series. This chart type can often be interchanged with a stacked bar chart or a stacked line chart, because those types are also used to show cumulative totals for multiple data series. Because the radar chart isn't very common, you should use it with caution and make sure that your audience is comfortable evaluating data in this arrangement. Figure 4-42 shows an example of a filled radar chart.

Figure 4-42   SAMPLE RADAR CHART WITH FILL EFFECT

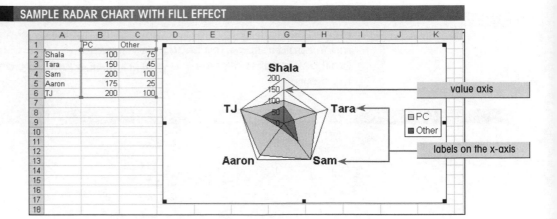

On a radar chart, the labels on the x-axis go around the chart, and each label creates its own value axis that starts in the middle of the chart and increases as it moves out. The data series that are identified by the legend are plotted along the axis for each label. The larger the value, the farther out the data point is placed, and the greater amount of surface area is covered. In a radar chart, the lines between the data points are not significant. For example, the point halfway between Shala and Tara for the PC data series is not significant. What is significant, however, is the area represented by each color (each data series) and the length of each cumulative data point on each x-axis label. In the sample radar chart, you see that the area that represents the PC series is much larger than the area of the Other series. You can also see that TJ and Sam have the largest cumulative values.

Lynn has logged the daily average golf course attendance at the Sundance and Copper golf courses in an Excel workbook. Because you are interested in the cumulative attendance for each course, you will chart this information as a radar chart.

To create and format a radar chart using the golf course attendance data:

1. Open the **GolfCourses-4** workbook located in the Tutorial.04\Tutorial folder on your Data Disk.

2. Select the range **A4:C9**, click the **Chart Wizard** button 🔲, click **Radar** in the Chart type list, click the **Radar with markers at each data point** chart sub-type (second column) if it is not already selected, and then click the **Next** button.

   In order to more clearly understand how a radar chart works, you will examine the ranges used for the data series.

3. Click the **Series** tab. The Series list shows two data series, Sundance and Copper. The x-axis labels are found in the range A5:A9. The x-axis labels go around the outside of the radar chart. If you had four x-axis labels, the radar chart would have only four axes coming out of the middle. If you had six x-axis labels, you would see six axes, and so forth.

4. Click the **Next** button, click the **Titles** tab (if it is not already selected), type **Strong attendance in June!** as the chart title, and then click the **Finish** button, which will embed the chart on the Attendance worksheet.

5. Move and resize the chart area, the plot, and the title area so that your radar chart looks like Figure 4-43.

Figure 4-43   **RADAR CHART**

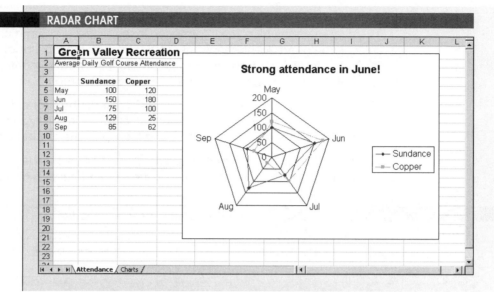

The outermost pentagon of the radar chart represents a value of 200. The value decreases by 50 as the pentagons move to the center of the radar chart. Pink lines represent the Copper golf course attendance figures, and blue represent the Sundance course. The relative sizes of the areas of the shapes give you a feel for the popularity of the two courses. Copper outperformed Sundance every month except for August, and June was the strongest month for both courses.

Although you can read the radar chart, you know that it is not the most common chart available. You will experiment with other chart types that could present the same message as does the radar chart, and then you will let Lynn choose the charts she thinks will work best for her presentation.

To compare the radar chart to more common chart types:

1. Click the chart to select it (if it is not already selected), click the **Copy** button 📋 on the Standard toolbar, click the **Charts** tab, press **Ctrl + Home** to make cell A1 the active cell, and then click the **Paste** button 📋 on the Standard toolbar.

2. Resize the chart so that it fills one fourth of the available room on the screen (approximately 6 columns by 12 rows), and then copy and paste it three more times, so that you have four copies of the same radar chart.

    Using these four charts of the same data, you'll apply different chart types to each of them to compare the message of each.

3. Right-click the second chart, click **Chart Type** on the shortcut menu, click **Column** in the Chart type list, and then click the **OK** button.

4. Resize the plot area, format the axes labels, or move the legend as necessary to clearly view all of the information in the column chart.

    You will find it easier to compare the individual values using a bar chart. If you're more interested in cumulative values than in the individual values of each data series, then you might want to use a stacked bar chart.

5. Right-click the third chart, click **Chart Type** on the shortcut menu, click **Column** in the Chart type list, click the **Stacked Column** chart sub-type (first row, second column), and then click the **OK** button.

6. Resize the plot area, format the axes labels, or move the legend as necessary to clearly view all of the information in the stacked column chart. The stacked column chart doesn't show the comparison of the individual values very well, but it clearly compares the cumulative totals for each month. Yet another chart that shows cumulative totals well is the stacked area chart.

7. Right-click the fourth chart, click **Chart Type** on the shortcut menu, click **Area** in the Chart type list, click the **Stacked Area** chart sub-type (first row, second column) if not already selected, and then click the **OK** button.

8. Resize the plot area, format the axes labels, or move the legend as necessary to clearly view all of the information in the stacked column chart. See Figure 4-44.

| Figure 4-44 | FOUR CHARTS DISPLAYING THE SAME DATA BUT COMMUNICATING DIFFERENT MESSAGES |

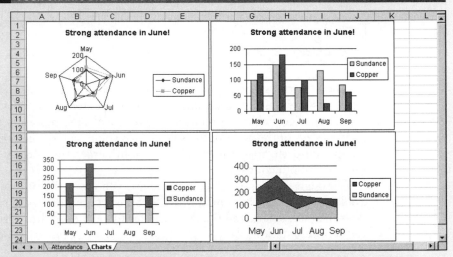

9. Save your changes, and then print the Charts worksheet with your name in the left section of the header.

10. Close the GolfCourses-4 workbook.

Radar charts are sometimes used to compare the cumulative area of one data series against another. By using other more common chart types, however, you might be able to more clearly communicate the same message in a more common format.

Working with a Surface Chart

A **surface chart** is a 3-D chart that you can use to evaluate a combination of numeric variables that, when measured at the same time, meet an important criterion. For example, GVR is evaluating a policy that states that if the wind chill is below a certain value, outside events are canceled. The wind chill is a combination of wind and temperature, both of which can be represented by numeric values. Figure 4-45 shows a sample surface chart that plots temperature in Fahrenheit degrees against wind speed in miles per hour to record wind chill on the surface of the graph.

Figure 4-45 **SAMPLE SURFACE CHART**

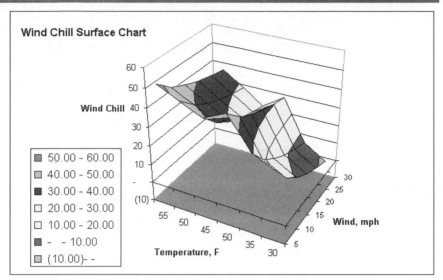

The colder the temperature and the faster the wind speed, the more the wind chill plummets. Yet the wind chill does not have a linear relationship with either temperature or wind speed. The surface of the surface diagram shows just how much wind chill can vary for one temperature or for one wind speed based on the value of the other variable. A surface chart has three axes: the x-axis (category axis), the y-axis (which represents each series of data and is called the series axis on a surface chart), and a z-axis (which represents the values plotted for each x- and y-value and is called the value axis). The purpose of the surface chart is to visually depict how two numeric variables affect the value of a third numeric measurement.

GVR is offering free body mass index screenings during the month of September. The body mass index is calculated using a special ratio of height to weight and is used to track body fat. The healthy range for a BMI score is from 19 to 24. A BMI score of 25 to 29 is considered overweight, and a score over 30 is considered obese. You'll use a surface diagram to visually present this information.

To create and modify a surface chart using the body mass index data:

1. Open the **BMI-4** workbook located in the Tutorial.04\Tutorial folder on your Data Disk. The data is arranged in a way that supports a surface chart because two numeric variables, Weight in column A and Height in row 6, are used to calculate BMI scores displayed in cells B7:G18. See Figure 4-46. The values in range B7:G18 will form the contour of the surface chart.

Figure 4-46 | **DATA FOR THE SURFACE CHART**

height will appear
on the y-axis

weight will appear
on the x-axis

BMI scores will create
the contour of the
surface of the chart

	A	B	C	D	E	F	G	H	I	J	K
1		Green Valley Recreation									
2		Body Mass Index Calculator									
3											
4											
5	Weight, lbs	Height, inches							BMI Scores		
6		60	62	64	66	68	70				
7	100	19.5	18.3	17.2	16.1	15.2	14.3		Normal	19-24	
8	110	21.5	20.1	18.9	17.8	16.7	15.8		Overweight	25-29	
9	120	23.4	21.9	20.6	19.4	18.2	17.2		Obese	30-34	
10	130	25.4	23.8	22.3	21.0	19.8	18.6		Extremely Obese	>35	
11	140	27.3	25.6	24.0	22.6	21.3	20.1				
12	150	29.3	27.4	25.7	24.2	22.8	21.5				
13	160	31.2	29.3	27.5	25.8	24.3	23.0				
14	170	33.2	31.1	29.2	27.4	25.8	24.4				
15	180	35.1	32.9	30.9	29.0	27.4	25.8				
16	190	37.1	34.7	32.6	30.7	28.9	27.3				
17	200	39.1	36.6	34.3	32.3	30.4	28.7				
18	210	41.0	38.4	36.0	33.9	31.9	30.1				
19											
20											
21	Note:	BMI = (Weight*0.4535)/((Height*0.0254)^2)									
22											
23											

Sheet1 / Sheet2 / Sheet3 /

2. Select the range **A6:G18**, click the **Chart Wizard** button, click **Surface** in the Chart type list, click **3-D Surface** chart sub-type (first row, first column) if not already selected, and then click the **Next** button.

3. Click the **Series** tab to examine how the chart is organized. Each column of data in the workbook, represented by height in inches starting with 60 inches in column B, is used as a series and is plotted along the y-axis, which is on the right side of the chart. The weight values in column A are used for the category axis labels.

4. Click the **Next** button, type **BMI Calculator** as the chart title, type **Weight, lbs** as the category axis title, type **Height, in** as the series axis title, type **BMI** as the value axis title, and then click the **Next** button.

   In order to give the chart as much room on the screen as possible, you'll put the chart on its own worksheet.

5. Click the **As new sheet** option button, type **BMI Surface Chart**, and then click the **Finish** button.

Figure 4-47 | **BMI SURFACE CHART**

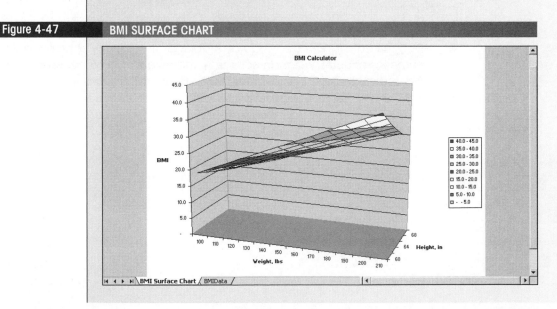

Formatting a Surface Chart

The contour of the surface of the chart that illustrates the different BMI ranges is not distinct. But, because BMI values do not go below 15, you can start the value axis at 15 to see if this improves the readability of the surface chart.

To change the z-axis scale in the surface chart:

1. Double-click any value on the value axis to open the Format Axis dialog box, click the **Scale** tab (if it is not already selected), double-click **0** in the Minimum text box and type **15**, double-click **45** in the Maximum text box and type **40**, and then click the **OK** button. Because you forced the value axis scale to remain within the values of your chart, the surface and BMI ranges are easier to distinguish. You'll also increase the size of the plot area to expand the size of the surface chart.

2. Click the plot area for the surface chart (click just beyond the gray walls), and then drag the upper-right selection handle of the plot area up and to the right to expand the surface chart as large as room will allow. The final surface chart with expanded plot area is shown in Figure 4-48.

Figure 4-48 **FINAL SURFACE CHART**

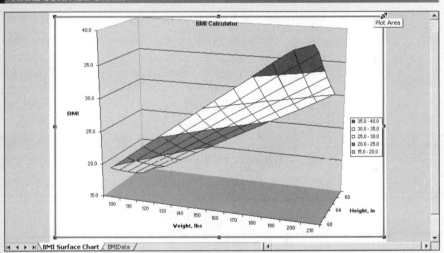

3. Save your changes, and then print the BMI Surface Chart worksheet with your name in the left section of the header.

4. Close the BMI-4 workbook.

When you need to chart a numeric result based on two numeric variables, the surface chart may be the best way to display this data.

Working **with a Stock Chart**

As the name implies, a stock chart lets you track stock prices over time. There are four stock chart sub-types that show various amounts of stock price detail on each chart. The variables that you can chart on the available stock charts include these: **volume** (number of shares traded that day), **open** (the opening price for the stock for that day), **high** (the highest price for the stock for that day), **low** (the lowest price for the stock for that day), and **close** (the closing price for the stock for that day). You can use the Chart Wizard to organize your data and determine which of the available stock chart sub-types best suits the data you are presenting.

You've started an investment club at GVR and have been asked to research the stock price of Quality Automotive Mechanics, which trades under the symbol QAM. You have been tracking the stock for the first six months and have entered the volume, high, low, and closing prices for the stock into an Excel spreadsheet. Now you will use a stock chart to graphically show how the stock has performed over the last month.

To chart QAM stock performance for a period of one month:

1. Open the **StockWatch-4** workbook from the Tutorial.04\Tutorial folder of your Data Disk.

2. Select the range **A4:E24**, click the **Chart Wizard** button on the Standard toolbar, click **Stock** in the Chart type list, and then click each chart sub-type and read the chart sub-type description. The description for each stock chart not only describes the chart but also explains the precise order in which to organize the series values.

3. Click the **Volume-High-Low-Close** Chart sub-type (second row, first column), and then click the **Next** button twice to accept existing source data entries and to display the third step of the Chart Wizard.

4. Click the **Titles** tab (if it is not already selected), type **QAM January Performance** as the chart title, press the **Tab** key twice, type **(in millions)** in the Value (Y) axis text box, press the **Tab** key twice, and then type **Stock Price** in the Second value (Y) axis text box. See Figure 4-49. When you are charting both volume and stock price on the same chart, you use two y-axes to measure them.

Figure 4-49	LABELING THE AXES OF THE STOCK CHART

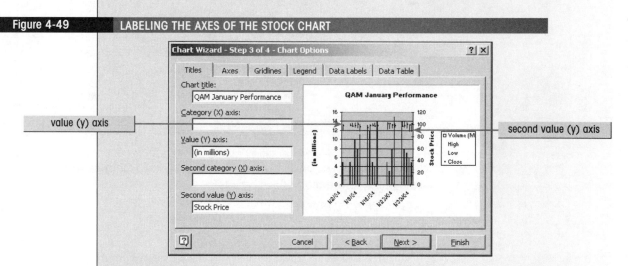

5. Click the **Next** button, click the **As new sheet** option button, type **Jan**, and then click the **Finish** button. See Figure 4-50. The large light turquoise columns represent the volume of stock traded on that day, as measured by the values on the first y-axis. The high-low line represents the high and low stock price for that particular day, and the close marker represents the price at which the stock closed on that day.

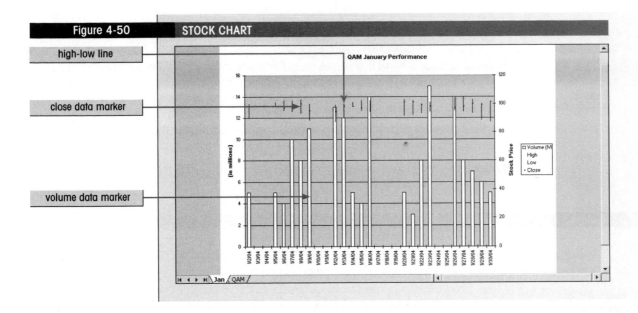

Figure 4-50   STOCK CHART

- high-low line
- close data marker
- volume data marker

QAM January Performance

When you create a chart using dates along the x-axis, Excel automatically applies a time-scale axis so that the intervals between the data points are correct from a chronological measurement, even if you don't have data for each value. In this case, you didn't have data for the Saturday or Sunday of any date in January, yet the time-scale axis shows those dates so that the gaps between the data points represent the correct amount of elapsed time. Other time-scale options include months or years. The months or years time-scale options work well when you have data for every day for several months or years, but you want the x-axis to consolidate that information using the larger time increments.

Formatting a Stock Chart

You feel that the information on the stock chart would be a little clearer if the plot area was white and the High, Low, and Close data markers were more distinct. Therefore you'll format the QAM stock chart to more clearly display the information before you present it to your investment club.

To format the QAM stock chart:

1. Click the plot area to select it, click the **list arrow** for the Fill Color button on the Formatting toolbar, and then click the **White** square (fifth row, last column on right) in the color palette. Now that the plot area is white, there is more contrast between the plot area and the high-low lines.

You also want the high-low lines to be more pronounced. You can stretch them out by starting the stock price y-axis, the second y-axis, at a higher value.

2. Double-click the second y-axis for the stock price to open the Format Axis dialog box, click the **Scale** tab (if not already selected), double-click **0** in the Minimum box to select that value, type **50**, and then click the **OK** button.

In addition to increasing the size of the high-low lines, you also want to make them thicker and more distinct.

3. Double-click one of the high-low lines to open the Format High-Low Lines dialog box, click the **Weight** list arrow, click the last line style in the list, and then click the **OK** button.

Finally, you'd like to make the Close value a little clearer. You'll use both a new shape and a new color to make it stick out.

4. Double-click one of the Close data markers to open the Format Data Series dialog box, click the **Patterns** tab (if it is not already selected), click the **Style list** arrow in the Marker pane and click the **diamond** shape, click the **Foreground** list arrow and click the **Red** square (third row, first column) in the color palette, click the **Background** list arrow and click the **Red** square, click the **Size up** arrow to change the size to **6** pts, and then click the **OK** button.

5. Click the gray area to the left or right of the chart so that nothing is selected. See Figure 4-51.

| Figure 4-51 | FORMATTED STOCK CHART |

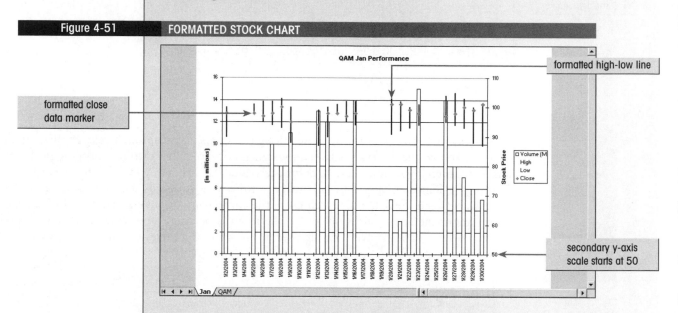

6. Save your changes, and then print the Jan worksheet with your name in the left section of the header.

7. Close the StockWatch-4 workbook, and then exit Excel.

This stock chart will help you present QAM's January performance to the new investment club. If you kept tracking QAM's performance over time, the stock chart would present trends in the stock that would help you decide when to purchase and sell it.

Lynn is pleased that you have shown her so many new chart types, including the bubble, ribbon, radar, surface, and stock charts. She knows that although these charts are not as common as column, line, area, and pie charts, they are extremely useful in specific situations and can help support important decisions. Furthermore, she is pleased that you have also charted the same data using different chart types as a way of determining which chart types support the message you are trying to communicate. She knows that as you become more skilled with charts, she will become a better communicator and decision maker.

Session 4.2 QUICK CHECK

1. What is the basic difference between an XY (scatter) chart and a bubble chart?

2. For what type of data do you use a line or ribbon chart?

3. What is the basic difference between the line and ribbon charts?

4. What do the shapes on a radar chart represent?

5. What is the purpose of a surface chart?

6. What types of data can you chart on a stock chart?

REVIEW ASSIGNMENTS

The Board of Directors of Green Valley Recreation is considering hiring Canby and Associates, a small programming, teaching, and consulting group, to do some custom programming. Lynn has asked you to evaluate the financial status of this small organization. She wants you to create several charts based on several worksheets of data that she has prepared for analysis.

To complete this task:

1. Start Excel and open the **Consult-4** workbook from the Tutorial.04\Review folder on your Data Disk.

2. On the Income sheet, create the 3-D clustered column chart and stacked line chart shown in Figure 4-52 and Figure 4-53 using the guidelines that follow. Embed the charts on the Income sheet. After completing the charts, print each chart with your name in the left section of the header. Then, in a brief statement, indicate which chart you think better communicates the intended message, and explain why.

Figure 4-52

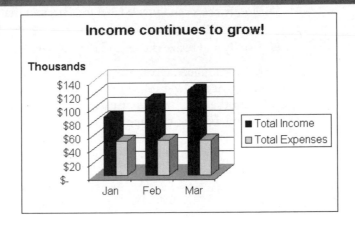

Figure 4-53

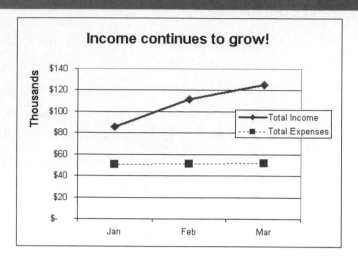

Guidelines for creating the 3-D column and line charts:

- Use the total income values in row 9 and the total expenses values in row 15 as the data series for each chart. Use the month labels in row 5 as the category (x-axis) labels.
- Resize the chart area and plot area as needed.
- Use a 30-degree elevation, a 40-degree rotation, and right-angle axes 3-D options for the 3-D column chart.
- Modify the scale on the y-axis to display values as thousands.
- Format the y-axis values with dollar signs but no digits to the right of the decimal point. (*Hint*: To format the y-axis values as shown, select the axis, and then use the Currency Style and Decrease Decimal buttons on the Formatting toolbar.)
- Modify the bar and line colors so that they can be clearly distinguished using only black and white colors.
- Modify the line widths and styles so that they can be clearly distinguished using only black and white colors.
- Modify the x- and y-axis label font sizes so that they clearly display the values shown in the figures.
- Modify and resize the legend as necessary.

3. On the Income sheet, create the stacked area chart shown in Figure 4-54 using the guidelines that follow. Embed the chart on the Income sheet. After completing the chart, print the chart with your name in the left section of the header. In a brief statement, summarize the message that is communicated with the chart.

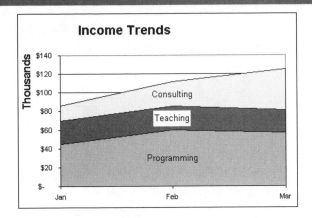

Guidelines for creating the stacked area chart:

- ■ Use the Programming, Teaching, and Consulting range for Jan, Feb, and Mar (range A5:D8) as the data series for the chart.

- ■ Remove the legend and add the series name labels to the chart.

- ■ Resize the chart area and plot area as necessary.

- ■ Format the series name labels so that they are all 10 points in size, and fill the Teaching data point with a white fill color so that the black text is legible against the dark background of the data marker.

- ■ Modify the y-axis to display values as thousands without dollar signs or digits to the right of the decimal point. Apply a 10-point font size to the Thousands label.

4. On the Income sheet, create the 100% stacked column charts shown in Figure 4-55 and Figure 4-56 using the guidelines that follow. Embed the charts on the Income sheet. After completing the charts, print just the charts with your name in the left section of the header. The purpose of creating these charts is to determine if Canby and Associates has a diversified income stream that would protect it against a downturn in any one of their three income categories. Print each chart with your name in the left section of the header. In a brief statement, indicate which chart you think best clarifies this issue, and explain why.

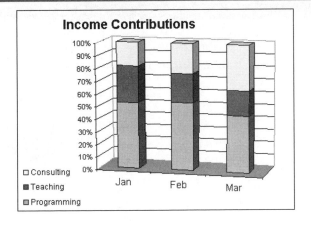

Figure 4-56

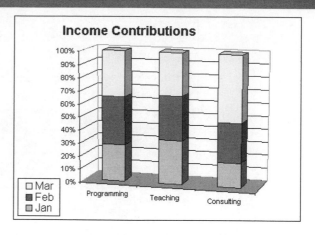

Guidelines for creating the 100% stacked chart with a 3-D visual effect:

■ Use the Programming, Teaching, and Consulting range for Jan, Feb, and Mar (range A5:D8) as the data series for the chart.

■ Use the 100% stacked column chart with a 3-D visual effect chart type for each chart.

Explore

■ Use a 10-degree elevation, a 15-degree rotation, and a value of 15 for the perspective value for each chart. The height should be 75% of the base.

■ Note that both charts show the same data, but that the series names in the legend and the x-axis labels are switched between the two figures.

■ Modify the x- and y-axis label font sizes so that they clearly display the values shown in the figures.

■ Modify and resize the legend, plot area, and chart area as necessary.

Explore

■ Remove the border of the legend (for the chart shown in Figure 4-55) by selecting the None option in the Format Legend dialog box.

5. On the Programmers sheet, create the doughnut chart shown in Figure 4-57 using the guidelines provided below. Embed the chart on the Programmers sheet. After completing the chart, print the chart with your name in the left section of the header. In a brief statement, summarize the message that is communicated with the chart.

Figure 4-57

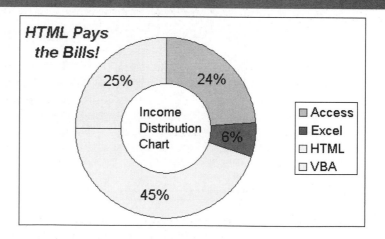

Guidelines for creating the doughnut chart:

- Use the range B5:E5 for the x-axis labels, and use the range B10:E10 for the series values.
- Add percentage data labels to the slices.
- Resize the chart object and plot area of the chart to display the slices more clearly.

Explore
- Format the chart title as shown in the figure, and move it to the upper-left corner of the chart area to make more room to expand the plot area of the chart.

Explore
- Add a text box in the center of the doughnut chart with the text "Income Distribution Chart".

6. On the Programs sheet, create the 3-D column chart shown in Figure 4-58 using the guidelines that follow. Embed the chart on the Programmers sheet. After completing the chart, print just the chart with your name in the left section of the header. In a brief statement, summarize the message that is communicated with the chart.

Figure 4-58

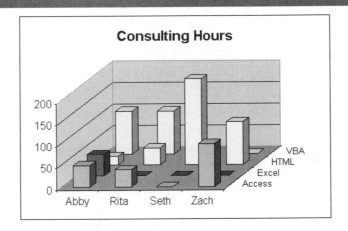

Guidelines for creating the chart:

- Use the range A5:E9 as the data series.
- Display the data series by columns.
- Apply the right angle axes and adjust the evaluation and rotation as necessary.
- Decrease the size of the labels on the axes, remove the legend, and increase the size of the chart and plot area so that all labels are clearly visible.

7. Save and close the Consult-4 workbook.

8. Each spring Green County holds its Annual Green County Tulip Festival. Because GVR has so many outdoor facilities, they have their own landscaping department and take great pride in providing many beautiful displays of tulips throughout their sports fields. In an effort to determine which tulip supplier provided superior products, they logged the cost, average size, and a color rating for the tulips provided by nine different suppliers. Now they need your help to determine if there are any significant correlations within this data. Open the **Research-4** workbook from the Tutorial.04\Review folder on your Data Disk.

9. On the Research1 sheet, create the XY (scatter) charts and bubble chart shown in Figure 4-59, Figure 4-60, and Figure 4-61 using the guidelines that follow. Embed the charts on the Reseach1 sheet. Print the charts with your name in the left section of the header. In a short paragraph, compare and contrast how each chart answers the question posed by the chart title.

Figure 4-59

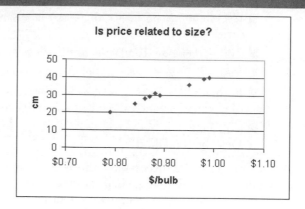

Figure 4-60

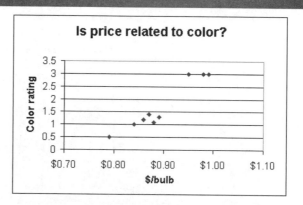

Figure 4-61

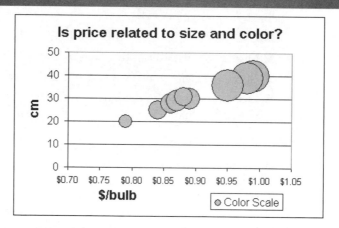

Guidelines for creating the charts:

- Use the values in the range B6:D14 for the charts. In Figures 4-59 and 4-60, only two data series are compared in XY (scatter) charts. In Figure 4-61, all three data series are used, and the values in C6:C14 are used for the bubble sizes.

- Modify and resize the titles for the chart, the x-axis, and the y-axis, as well as the scale for the x-axis.

- For the bubble chart in Figure 4-61, add the legend, and use the value in cell D5 as the name for that series so that the legend identifies the data illustrated by the size of the bubbles.

- For each chart, remove the shading on the plot area so that the data points are easier to see.

10. Also, in the Research-4 workbook, the Research2 sheet shows data collected by a survey that summarizes estimated usage of a new fitness center. The data was gathered for three townships within Green County and is broken into five demographic groups. Create the filled radar chart shown in Figure 4-62 to illustrate this information using the guidelines that follow. Embed the chart on the Research2 sheet. After completing the chart, print the chart with your name in the left section of the header. In a brief statement, summarize the message that is communicated with the chart.

Figure 4-62

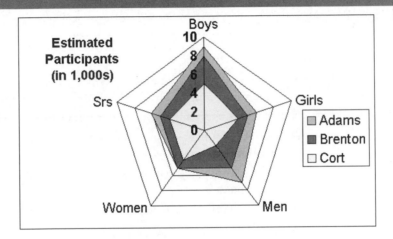

Guidelines for creating the filled radar chart:

- Use the values in the range A5:F8 for the chart. Range A6:A8 contains the series names, and range B5:F5 contains the range for the x-axis labels.

- In the chart, modify and resize the titles for the chart, the x-axis, and the y-axis, and adjust the scale for the x-axis.

Explore

- Move and resize the chart elements so that the numbers on the value axis increment by 2. Bold the numbers on the value axis.

- Modify the chart title according to the figure.

11. Your final research project is presented on the WindChill sheet. GVR has considered implementing a policy to cancel outdoor activities if the wind chill factor reaches a certain level. Using the following guidelines, create and print the 3-D surface chart shown in Figure 4-63 that shows how wind speed in miles per hour and temperature in degrees Fahrenheit combine to create the wind chill factor. Embed the chart on the WindChill sheet. Print only the chart with your name in the left section of the header. In the brief statement, summarize the message that is communicated with the chart.

Figure 4-63

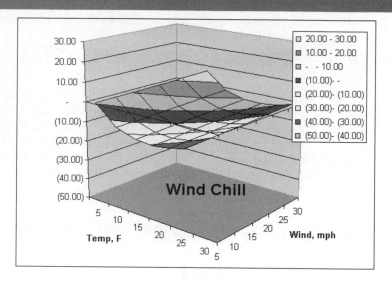

Guidelines for creating the surface chart:

- Use the values in the range A7:G13 for the chart. Range B7:G7 is used for the x-axis labels, and range A8:A13 contains the data series names.
- Resize the chart and plot area to present the data clearly.
- Modify the font size for each axis, the axis titles, and the chart title to present the information clearly.
- Select a corner of the chart, and rotate the cube so that all of the values on the y-axis appear.
- Move and resize the legend as necessary.

12. Save and close the workbook, and then exit Excel.

CASE PROBLEMS

Case 1. Charting Sales Performance for a National Bicycle Company You're the marketing manager for National Bike Accessories, a nationwide distributor of bicycle accessories. You manage nine sales representatives who cover three regions, two reps per region. You want to create some charts to graphically present their sales performance.

To complete this task:

1. Start Excel and open the **SalesPerformance-4** workbook located in the Tutorial.04\Cases folder on your Data Disk.

2. In column G, total the sales values for the first three quarters for each marketing representative. Add an appropriate label above the totals.

Explore

3. In column H, calculate each representative's attainment as a percentage of quota through the first three quarters of sales. Format the column so that the values are formatted as whole number percentages. Add an appropriate label above the values. (*Hint*: The attainment for the first representative, Dehart, should calculate to 75%.)

4. Create a clustered column chart with the names of the sales reps on the x-axis and the attainment percentage on the y-axis. Embed the chart on the Sales worksheet just below the data.

Explore 5. Using the Chart Wizard, change the chart type to a Line – Column on 2 Axes custom chart, and then add a data series with the name "Quota" found in cell C5 and with values found in range C6:C14. Change the series name label for the attainment values as well.

6. Using the final chart shown in Figure 4-64, format the axes as needed.

Figure 4-64

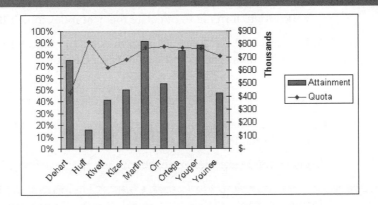

7. Save your changes, and then print the Sales worksheet with your name in the left section of the header. Based on the information provided by the chart, write a paragraph summarizing your findings.

8. Close the SalesPerformance-4 workbook, and then exit Excel.

Case 2. Charting Bakery Income Figures You work for Baker Brothers Bakers, a small family-owned business. You have been organizing the financial data for the bakery over the last five years in an Excel workbook. You want to present the income statement figures to the owners using charts so they can see their company's profitability over time.

To complete this task:

1. Start Excel and open **Baker-4** from the Tutorial.04\Cases folder of your Data Disk.

Explore 2. Create a chart that summarizes why the net income is not rising as fast as sales. Create the chart on its own chart sheet named Profitability. (*Hint*: If you select a 3-D column chart type, consider applying the right angle axes, and then adjust the evaluation and rotation as necessary.) Format the labels on the axes if necessary, and adjust the values on the y-axis as needed. Add an appropriate title and format the legend, making sure the series names are displayed.

Explore 3. Copy the worksheet, and then change the chart type to present the same data using a different chart type (for example, using a line chart with high-low lines).

4. Save your changes to the workbook, and then print both chart sheets with your name in the left section of the header.

5. On a piece of paper, discuss why you chose the data you chose to clarify why net income is not rising as fast as sales. Discuss how each chart communicates this message.

6. Close the Baker-4 workbook, and then exit Excel.

Case 3. Measuring the Heat Index You're a coach at a local high school. You want to develop a heat index chart that will help students to understand and be wary of dangerous heat index levels during periods of high heat and humidity.

To complete this task:

1. Go your favorite search engine, and search for ways to calculate the heat index. Print the page that shows the heat index formula.

2. Start Excel and open the **HeatIndex-4** workbook located in the Tutorial.04\Cases folder of your Data Disk.

Explore ▷ 3. Use the World Wide Web to research the formula to calculate the heat index. Enter the appropriate formula to calculate the heat index in cell B5, and then copy to range B5:J12.

4. Create a 3-D surface chart from the data in range A4:J12, and place the chart in its own sheet. Rename the worksheet "Surface Chart".

Explore ▷ 5. Make sure that the x-axis, y-axis, and z-axis are correctly labeled with descriptive labels, and that all of the font sizes are large enough to clearly read.

6. Save your changes to the workbook, and then print the Surface Chart sheet with your name in the left section of the header.

7. Close the HeatIndex-4 workbook, and then exit Excel.

Case 4. Using the Web to Find Stock Charts There are many Web sites that help you track financial portfolios. They also provide graphical representations of stock performance using stock charts. In this exercise, you'll use the World Wide Web to find and create stock charts.

To complete this task:

Explore ▷ 1. Go to www.quicken.com, and use the links on the site to create the chart shown in Figure 4-65. (*Hint*: The dates and numbers will vary of course, depending on when you do this exercise.)

Figure 4-65

2. Print the Web page that displays the stock chart, and then identify where the volume data, as well as the stock price high, low, and close values are shown.

3. Explore the rest of the www.quicken.com Web site at your own pace. Be sure to explore the types of charts that the site will create for you. Print another chart of your choice,

and in a brief statement, explain why you chose this chart, and why you thought it was a valuable presentation of data.

Explore 4. Go to www.nasdaq.com, and use the links on the site to create the chart shown in Figure 4-66.

Figure 4-66

5. Print the Web page that displays the stock chart, and then identify where the volume data, as well as the stock price high, low, and close values are shown.

6. Explore the rest of the www.nasdaq.com Web site at your own pace. Be sure to explore the types of charts that the site will create for you. Print another chart of your choice, and in a brief statement, explain why you chose this chart and why you thought it was a valuable presentation of data.

QUICK CHECK ANSWERS

Session 4.1

1. Three dimensional (3-D) charts are more visually exciting than their 2-D counterparts. As such, 3-D charts might be perceived as more professional or important. Also, the 3-D data markers, such as cones or pyramids, can help communicate information about the data that you are charting.

   Three-dimensional (3-D) charts create extra challenges, including these:

   - Extra physical space on the monitor or paper is required to illustrate the third dimension, so 3-D charts need more space to show the same amount of data as a 2-D chart.

   - Depending on the order of your data series, larger bars in the "front" of a 3-D chart can hide data in the "back."

   - Depending on the size of the third dimension, it is sometimes difficult to see where the tops of the data markers (tops of the bars) intersect with the y-axis.

2. The cylinder, cone, and pyramid charts are really 3-D versions of the column chart with specially shaped data markers.

3. A pie chart supports only one data series, whereas the doughnut chart can support multiple series presented as concentric rings. A pie chart presents a solid pie, whereas the doughnut chart presents rings instead of slices, so there is no center to a doughnut chart.

4. The individual pieces of the columns on a 100% stacked column chart represent the proportion of that value to the whole value of the column.

5. To show actual values on a 100% stacked column chart, you can either use a data table or add the data values as labels to the columns.

Session 4.2

1. A bubble chart plots three variables instead of only two. The third variable in a bubble chart determines the size of the bubbles. In an XY (scatter) chart, the bubbles are merely dots, because there are only two variables to plot, one that is measured along the x-axis, and one that is measured along the y-axis.

2. You use the line and ribbon charts when you want to show trends over time.

3. A ribbon chart is simply a 3-D version of a line chart.

4. The shapes on a radar chart represent the cumulative value of the data points in one data series.

5. The purpose of a surface chart is to find a range of values that meet a desired level or criterion based on the measurement of two other numeric variables.

6. You can chart trading volumes data, as well as several stock prices (high, low, open, close) on a stock chart.

OBJECTIVES

In this tutorial you will:

- Identify error values that identify formula and formatting problems

- Use the Trace Error

- Use test values and the R1C1 reference style feature

- Use advanced Financial functions

- Use advanced Database functions

- Enter criteria using different values, specifying And and Or criteria, and using wildcards

- Use advanced Date and Time functions

- Use Statistical functions

- Use advanced Math and Trigonometry functions

- Use Engineering functions

- Use advanced Lookup and Reference functions

- Use advanced Information functions

- Use advanced Text functions

TROUBLESHOOTING
FORMULAS AND USING ADVANCED FUNCTIONS

Correcting Errors in Formulas and Using Complex Functions at GVR

Green Valley Recreation

Green Valley Recreation (GVR) is a community agency that organizes hundreds of programs, such as soccer and swimming. Because of your proven success and experience with Excel, you handle most of the questions and requests for help from other GVR employees regarding Excel worksheets. Often, those requests are funneled through your manager, Lynn Tse. In this tutorial, you will help others untangle Excel problems that result in error value messages. You'll also assist users in a wide range of workbook applications that cover almost every Excel function category. For example, you'll help the accounting department analyze various depreciation methods, you'll help the new health club analyze equitable club dues payment plans, and you'll apply time value of money concepts to analyze the financial impact of various plans to raise money for a future building project.

You'll work with Dfunctions to analyze data within a list, and you will use various Date and Time functions to convert dates from one form to another. You'll use Statistical functions to analyze the season's pitching statistics, and you'll assist the Math Camp teacher with curriculum development. Finally, you'll also learn how to build formulas that manipulate text, which are handy for scrubbing data and presenting it more clearly.

SESSION 5.1

In this session, you will learn how to troubleshoot and correct common formatting and formula errors. You'll examine and correct error values in a workbook, use auditing features to find and correct errors, and work with test values to check the accuracy of calculations.

Workbook Errors

It is often said that the primary benefit of using an Excel workbook is its ability to automatically recalculate formulas when assumption values change. Therefore, your ability to build correct formulas is directly tied to your success with Excel. Yet in creating new workbooks, you've probably run into a few situations when the formulas didn't work as you had intended. Or you may have been asked to troubleshoot a workbook for someone else and soon found yourself trying to untangle complex formulas that didn't work correctly.

Because formulas are the heart of a workbook, formula problems appear in a wide range of situations and have a wide variety of causes. Furthermore, depending on the problem, the troubleshooting technique that you choose will have a big impact on how fast you solve the problem. Therefore, you might find it very helpful to review the types of formula problems you might encounter, as well as the troubleshooting techniques you can use to fix these problems. Generally, the hardest part about fixing a problem formula is diagnosing it. Once you understand why the problem exists, the "fix" is generally straightforward. For example, do you remember your reaction the first time you saw pound signs (########) in a cell? Having experienced this problem several times, by now you quickly recognize that error message for what it is—a mere formatting problem with a very easy solution. You need to widen the column to display the entire value. Fortunately, Excel will not allow you to display a portion of a number, because viewing numbers where portions of them are hidden would be extremely confusing and misleading. The first time you encountered this error, however, you may have thought that the formula itself was to blame. You may have wasted time examining or reentering what was already a correct formula.

Because formulas are so varied, though, there's no single approach that can be used to successfully troubleshoot every problematic formula. In general, there are at least three major categories of formula problems as identified in Figure 5-1. Recognizing which category your problem fits into helps you choose the troubleshooting technique that most quickly addresses the problem.

Figure 5-1	FORMULA PROBLEM CATEGORIES AND EXAMPLES
CATEGORY	**EXAMPLES**
Formatting	• Zeros that appear as dashes instead of zeros or vice versa • Numbers that are not vertically aligned in a column • Numbers that appear as percentages instead of digits or vice versa • Numbers that appear as dates instead of digits or vice versa • Pound signs that appear instead of numbers • Numbers that appear in scientific notation, for example 8.6E+05
Formula	• Error messages, such as #VALUE!, #DIV/O!, #N/A, #NAME?, #REF!, #NUM!, or #NULL!, that appear in cells • Numbers that appear as negative values instead of positive values
Result	• A formula calculates, but the result is not correct

Of the three, the Result category creates the errors that are the hardest to find and resolve because there are no visual indicators to help you find this problem. Without careful analysis of your workbook, these errors can easily go undetected.

Lynn inherited a workbook from a previous director that projects the youth sports fees into the future. The workbook uses actual growth percentages between the years 2002 and 2003 as well as a static 12% growth goal to project fees for 2004. Unfortunately, there are many problems with the workbook, and Lynn isn't sure how to handle them. She asks for your help. You decide to undertake the formatting problems first.

Formatting Errors

Formatting problems affect how a value appears in the workbook, not how a formula is constructed. Because formatting problems have nothing to do with the calculation itself, they are generally the easiest of all problems to resolve if you recognize them for what they are. Because some formatting problems can dramatically change how the values are presented, you might find formatting errors difficult to recognize unless you've had previous experience with the problem.

You explain to Lynn that you've decided to handle the formatting problems first, as they are the easiest issues to resolve.

To diagnose and fix the formatting problems in the GVRGrowth-5 workbook:

1. Start Excel and open the **GVRGrowth-5** workbook located in the Tutorial.05\ Tutorial folder on your Data Disk. See Figure 5-2. This workbook shows the fees for several youth sports for the years 2002 and 2003 in columns B and C. In column D, the growth from the year 2002 to 2003 is calculated as a percentage. Columns E and F project 2004's fees using two different methods. In column E, the 2004 projected fees are supposed to be calculated by projecting the current growth rate in column D for that particular sport another year. The values in column F are supposed to be calculated by adding 12% to all corresponding 2003 values.

Figure 5-2	INITIAL GVR YOUTH SPORTS FEES WORKBOOK WITH ERROR VALUES

	A	B	C	D	E	F	G
1	GVR Youth Sports Fees						
2	#NAME?						
3					2004	2004 at	
4	**Name**	**2002**	**2003**	**Growth**	**Projected**	**12%**	
5	Baseball	5,005	5,500	(0)	4,956	#REF!	
6	Softball	3,500	3,489	(0)	3,478	#REF!	
7	Golf (Girls)	1,245	1,875	1	2,824	#REF!	
8	Golf (Boys)	2,670	4,544	70.19%	7,733	#REF!	
9	Football	2,356	2,458	4.33%	2,564	#REF!	
10	Soccer (Girls)	7,546	8,578	13.68%	9,751	#REF!	
11	Soccer (Boys)	9,568	9,578	0.10%	9,588	#REF!	
12	Basketball (Girls)	3,526	4,145	17.56%	4,873	#REF!	
13	Basketball (Boys)	5,445	6,544	20.18%	7,865	#REF!	
14	Tennis (Girls)		589	#DIV/0!	#DIV/0!	#REF!	
15	Tennis (Boys)		850	#DIV/0!	#DIV/0!	#REF!	
16							
17	TOTALS:	42,863	#####		#DIV/0!	#REF!	
18							
19	Last Updated:	38,352.00					

Callouts: Select All button; error in the value being calculated; alignment problem; column too narrow to display contents of cell; should display as a date; values do not appear as percentages; errors in values being calculated

However, there are also several error values in the workbook. You will eventually solve all of the formula problems, but for now, you'll tackle the easiest problems to resolve, the formatting issues. The first problem you'll resolve are the pound signs, which indicate a formatting error, in cell C17.

2. Click the **Select All** button to select all columns and all rows, and then double-click any line that separates two column headings. When all of the columns are selected, double-clicking any line that separates two column headings will automatically adjust all columns to as wide as needed to accommodate the widest entry in that column. By changing the width of column C, you eliminate the pound signs in cell C17 because the column is wide enough to display the widest value in that column.

There is still a formatting error in column D. All of the values in column D are supposed to be formatted as percentages, but the values in cells D5, D6, and D7 are not. As decimal numbers, percentages between 0% and 100% are values between 0 and 1. Therefore, percentages between 0% and 50% round to 0, and those between 50% and 100% round to 1 when the Comma, Currency, Number, or Accounting format is applied to the values.

3. Click the column heading **D** to select the entire column, click the **Percent Style** button [%] on the Formatting toolbar, and then click the **Increase Decimal** button [.00] twice to show two digits to the right of the decimal point. Now all numeric values in column D are formatted similarly.

The value in cell B19 is supposed to represent a date. Excel interprets date entries as the number of days since January 1, 1900. A quick mental calculation (100 years * 365 days/year) indicates that the current date is greater than 36,500 days. Based on the label in cell A19 and the fact that the value in cell B19 is 38,352, you suspect that the value should actually be a date but is currently given an incorrect format.

4. Click cell **B19**, click **Format** on the menu bar, click **Cells**, click the **Number** tab (if it is not already selected), click **Date** in the Category list, click **3/14/01** in the Type list, and then click the **OK** button. The number 38,352 represents the date 12/31/04.

EXCEL 2000: Click **3/14/98** in the Type list.

The last formatting issue that you'll resolve is aligning the values in column B on the decimal point. The values in range B5:B8 appear to be slightly to the right of the values in range B9:B13.

5. Select the range **B5:B15**, click **Format** on the menu bar, click **Cells**, and then click **Number** in the Category list. See Figure 5-3.

| **Figure 5-3** | **FORMAT CELLS DIALOG BOX** |

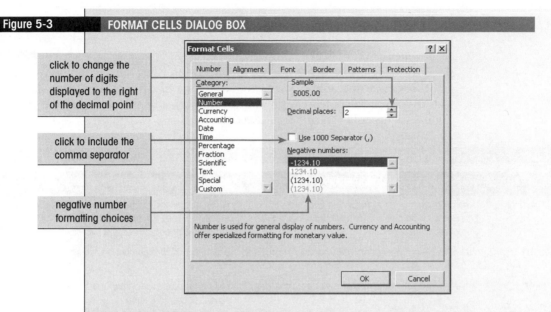

click to change the number of digits displayed to the right of the decimal point

click to include the comma separator

negative number formatting choices

Not all numeric formats format negative numbers in the same way or color. One numeric formatting option is to use a minus sign to indicate a negative number, and another is to use parentheses. If you choose a format that uses parentheses, the number is moved slightly to the left, to make room for the right parenthesis. (And even if the number is positive, it is moved slightly to the left to accommodate an eventual right parenthesis, should the value become negative.) In order to make values align properly on the decimal point, you need to choose a format for all numbers in the column that either uses parentheses for negative values or doesn't, even if no negative values exist in the list.

6. Click the **Decimal places** down arrow twice to change the value to **0**, click the **Use 1000 Separator (,)** check box, click the black **(1,234)** in the Negative numbers list, and then click the **OK** button. All of the numbers in column B are now aligned on the decimal point.

The decimal point alignment formatting problem is fairly common because all cells are given a General number format that by default shows negative values with a minus sign. If you use either the Currency Style or Comma Style button on the Formatting toolbar, you apply a format that displays negative values in parentheses, which shifts the formatted values slightly to the left to accommodate the eventual need for the right parenthesis. Because of this, you may want to click the Select All button and globally format a worksheet with a Comma Style before you do the rest of your numeric formatting. The Comma Style formatting will ensure that all values are displayed with the comma separator, that all values are moved slightly to the left, and that if you selectively format other cells with the Currency Style, all values will still be aligned on the decimal point.

Now that the formatting issues are handled, you'll turn your attention to the errors that indicate problems in the values in the worksheet cells.

Formula **Errors**

If a formula cannot calculate properly, it will display an error value such as #REF!. Although the error value names might not be completely intuitive, the fact that you have a calculation error in your workbook is obvious because the cell displays an error value that is easy to spot. All error values start with a pound sign (#), and the error name is in capital letters. Figure 5-4 describes the different Excel error values.

Figure 5-4	EXCEL ERROR VALUES	
ERROR VALUE	**WHEN DOES THIS ERROR APPEAR?**	**WHAT ARE THE POSSIBLE SOLUTIONS?**
########	When a column is not wide enough to display the contents or when a date or time format is applied to a negative value	Widen the column or change the format of the value so that it is smaller. (For example, display fewer digits to the right of the decimal point or use a smaller font size.)
#VALUE!	When the wrong type of data (text, number, logical, or cell reference) has been entered for an argument	Determine which argument is referenced incorrectly, and edit it.
#DIV/0!	When a number is divided by zero or by a blank cell	Edit the formula so that zero or a blank cell is not used as the divisor, or use an IF function to prevent the error from displaying if the divisor is zero or a blank cell.
#NAME?	When unrecognized text is used in a formula	Determine which text entry in the formula is unrecognized, and correct it.
#N/A	When an argument is missing from a function within a formula	Determine which argument is missing, and add it to the formula.
#REF!	When an invalid cell reference is used in a formula	Determine which cell reference is invalid, and correct it.
#NUM!	When invalid numeric values are used in a formula	Determine which numeric value is invalid, and correct it.
#NULL!	When you specify a range reference using a space between the first and last cell reference instead of a colon	Determine which range reference is entered inappropriately, and add the missing colon.

At this point, you still see three types of error values in the GVRGrowth-5 workbook, #NAME?, #DIV/0!, and #REF!. You'll use a variety of troubleshooting techniques to determine what is wrong with each formula so that you can correct them.

#NAME?

The #NAME? error value will occur when a function, range name, or worksheet reference is misspelled, the colon was omitted from a range reference, parentheses were omitted from a function, or text used in the formula was not enclosed in quotation marks. You also may be using a function that is not recognized unless an add-in such as the Analysis ToolPak Add-In is installed. You decide to analyze and correct the #NAME? error in the worksheet.

To correct the #NAME? error in the worksheet:

1. Click cell **A2** and examine the formula in the Formula bar. Although the function name, TODAY, is spelled correctly, this function requires parentheses, even if there are no arguments.

2. Click to the right of **=today** in the Formula bar, type **()** (left and right parentheses), and then press the **Enter** key. The current date appears in cell A2.

Sometimes, you can troubleshoot and correct formulas by simply examining and editing them in the Formula bar. Excel offers many features to help you diagnose a formula that isn't working properly.

#DIV/0!

The #DIV/0! error value occurs when you try to divide by zero or by an empty cell. You decide to analyze and correct the #DIV/0! errors in the workbook.

To correct the #DIV/0! errors in the workbook:

1. Click cell **D14**, and then click the formula in the Formula bar. As you've already experienced, Excel color codes the cell references in the Formula bar with the borders of the actual cells in the workbook. This step is all you really needed to take to see why the #DIV/0! error is occurring. Cell B14 is obviously empty, which means that you can't divide by B14 to determine the growth from year to year for this line item.

   To address this problem of an empty cell, you will use both the IF and the AND functions in this formula. You need to test for the possibility of an empty cell or a cell that contains a 0 and apply a different formula in those cases.

2. Edit the formula for cell D14 in the Formula bar so that the formula reads **=IF(AND(B14<>"",B14<>0),(C14-B14)/B14,"")**, and then click the **Enter** button ☑ on the Formula bar. See Figure 5-5. The *AND(B14<>"",B14<>0)* portion of the formula is the test for the IF function by comparing the value in cell B14 to "" (which indicates an empty cell, also referred to as **null**) and to 0. If both of these conditions are true (if B14 contains something other than null or 0), the original formula is executed. However, if either of these conditions is false (if cell B14 contains either null or 0), a null entry is entered into the cell.

Figure 5-5 USING THE IF AND THE AND FUNCTIONS TO CORRECT ERRORS

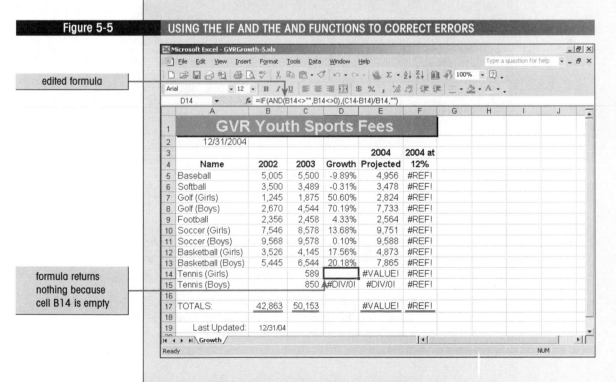

edited formula

formula returns nothing because cell B14 is empty

3. Copy the formula in cell **D14** to cell **D15**.

Once again, you were able to troubleshoot the problem and correct it using the Formula bar. A large number of formula errors can be handled this way. Sometimes, though, you will need to know about other Excel tools that help you analyze formulas, such as those available on the Formula Auditing toolbar (which is called the Auditing toolbar in Excel 2000).

#VALUE!

The #VALUE! error occurs when one of the arguments used in a function is supplied with an incorrect type of data. For example, you cannot multiply with text, so if cell B3 contained the formula =B1*B2 and cell B1 contained your name, cell B3 would display the #VALUE! error.

Tracing Errors

To help you track down the source of errors in cells E14, E15, and E17, you will use the Trace Error feature in Excel. The **Trace Error** feature places **tracer arrows** in the workbook to help you identify the cell or cells that are used by the formulas. Red tracer arrows identify precedent cells, and blue tracer arrows identify other precedent cells. A **precedent cell** is any cell that is used in the formula of the current cell.

If the Trace Error feature finds a precedent cell, it becomes the active cell, and you can click the Trace Error button again to continue the process of identifying precedent cells. Often, fixing an error found in a precedent cell will automatically correct other error values that depend on that cell, so start with the "last" error value in a series of connected errors in order to maximize your productivity. (For example, if you see an error value in both a subtotal and a grand total, start the Trace Error process with the grand total.)

REFERENCE WINDOW   **RW**

<u>Tracing Errors</u>
- Click View on the menu bar, point to Toolbars, and then click Formula Auditing to display the Formula Auditing toolbar. (In Excel 2000, click Tools on the menu bar, point to Auditing, and then click Show Auditing Toolbar.)
- Click the cell that contains the error value you want to trace, and then click the Trace Error button on the Formula Auditing toolbar.
- Continue clicking the Trace Error button until you find the first error value in the series of connected errors.

You will trace the errors for the #VALUE! errors in the workbook.

To trace errors for the #VALUE! errors:

1. Click **View** on the menu bar, point to **Toolbars**, click **Formula Auditing** to display the Formula Auditing toolbar, and then dock it under the existing toolbars at the top of the window.

   EXCEL 2000: The Formula Auditing toolbar is called the Auditing toolbar in Excel 2000. To display the toolbar, click **Tools** on the menu bar, point to **Auditing**, and then click **Show Auditing Toolbar**.

2. Click cell **E17**, and then click the **Trace Error** button ◈ on the Formula Auditing toolbar. Two arrows appear on the worksheet. A red trace arrow points from cell E14 to cell E17 because cell E14 also contains an error value. Cell E14 is the source of the error in cell E17. A blue arrow has been added to cells C14 and D14—these are precedent cells that, in this case, do not contain errors. Note also that cell E14 has become the active cell, which indicates that cell E14 also contains an error value. To find the source of the error in cell E14, you can use the Trace Error feature again.

TROUBLE? If you trace the errors for the wrong cell, click the Remove All Arrows button ☒ on the Formula Auditing toolbar to remove all trace arrows, and then repeat Step 2.

3. Click ◈. Another precedent cell, cell B14, has been found and is identified with a blue trace arrow. Because no more value errors have been found, though, the active cell has not changed (cell E14 is still the active cell). If you keep clicking the Trace Error button at this point, Excel will beep to indicate that you have found the first error value in this chain of error values.

As you analyze the formula for cell E14, you see that the formula is trying to multiply by cell D14, which contains a null text entry, "". To correct this problem, you'll use another IF statement.

4. Edit the formula for cell **E14** in the Formula bar so that the formula reads **=IF(D14<>"",C14*D14+C14,C14*1.1)**, and then click the **Enter** button ✓ on the Formula bar. See Figure 5-6. The calculated value, 648, is the result of multiplying C14 by 1.1 which represents a 10% increase in growth. The False argument (the third argument) of the IF statement was used to calculate this value because the test (the first argument) was false.

Figure 5-6	TRACING AND CORRECTING ERRORS

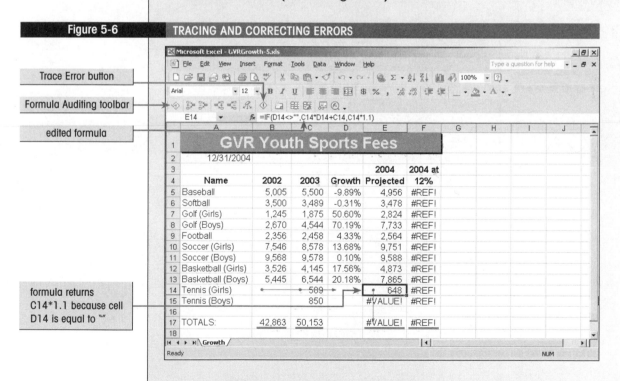

Trace Error button

Formula Auditing toolbar

edited formula

formula returns C14*1.1 because cell D14 is equal to ""

5. Copy the formula in cell **E14** to cell **E15**. Once the error value was corrected in cell E15, the error value in cell E17 automatically corrected itself.

The Trace Error feature is particularly helpful when you're working with a large workbook in which formulas reference cells in areas of the worksheet or workbook that you cannot currently see on the screen.

#REF!

The #REF! error value occurs when a formula is referencing an invalid cell reference. For example, if you have entered the formula =B1*B2 in cell B4, and then delete row 1, the reference to B1 in the deleted row will create a #REF! error because that row no longer exists.

You will trace the errors to find the source for the #REF! errors. You can fix #REF! errors by starting with any #REF! error you can find and eliminating the problems one by one. Because all values in column F are obviously totaled in cell F17, you'll improve your productivity by starting with the "final" error and using the Trace Error feature to help you find the precedent errors.

To trace errors for the #REF! errors:

1. Click cell **F17** and then click the **Trace Error** button ◈ on the Formula Auditing toolbar. A precedent cell is identified with a red trace arrow, and cell F5 is now the active cell, indicating that there is an error in this cell as well. See Figure 5-7. Looking at the Formula bar you can see that the formula in cell F5 also contains a #REF! error. Cell C5 is identified as a precedent cell with a blue trace arrow.

Figure 5-7	TRACING A #REF! ERROR VALUE

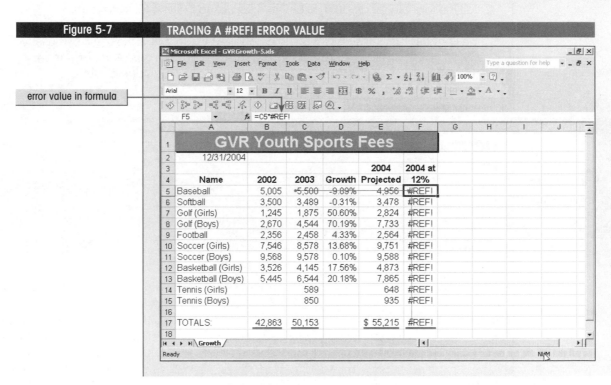

In this case, you want the formula to multiply the corresponding 2003 value in column C by 12% represented in cell F4. You could correct the formula in cell F5 using an absolute cell reference to cell F4 so that as you copied the formula down column F the reference wouldn't change. If you give cell F4 a range name and use the range name in the formula, the range name acts as an absolute cell address as well. The benefit of using a range name in this case is that it makes this formula easier for you to explain later to Lynn. You will assign the range name FixedGrowth to cell F4 and use the range name to correct the formula in cell F5.

2. Click cell **F4**, click the **Name Box**, type **FixedGrowth**, and then press the **Enter** key.

3. Click cell **F5**, edit the formula in the Formula bar to read **=C5*FixedGrowth**, and then use the fill handle to copy the formula through the range **F6:F15**.

4. Widen column **F** as necessary to display the total value in cell F17. See Figure 5-8.

Figure 5-8	USING A RANGE NAME IN A FORMULA

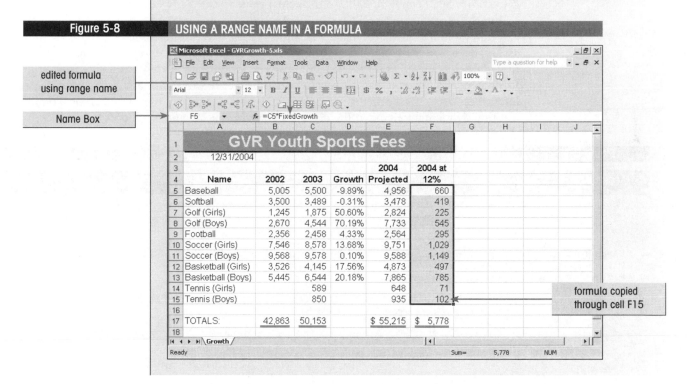

edited formula using range name

Name Box

formula copied through cell F15

Although you have corrected all of the formatting and calculation errors that display error values, you're still not confident that all of the formulas in this workbook are correct. A quick scan down column F tells you that something is wrong with the formula even though it no longer shows error values. None of those numbers are large enough to represent 2004 fees, given a 12% increase over the 2003 values. Also, a quick scan down column D tells you that something is wrong there, too. The growth for Baseball in row 5 should yield a positive growth percentage in column D, not a negative one.

These errors are typical of the third category of errors, result errors. Result errors are the hardest to spot because they occur when your formula calculates without error values, but still displays the wrong result. Finding and troubleshooting result errors requires additional Excel skills.

Troubleshooting **Result Errors**

There are many troubleshooting techniques to detect result errors, and some of the most useful techniques do not involve Excel, but rather common sense. For example, any time you create a formula, ask yourself if it passes the "Reasonableness Test". The Reasonableness Test asks this question: Is the result reasonable? If not, you know that you have some sort of result error to work out. For example, you know that the value in cell F5 must be greater than 5500, the value in cell C5. Also, you know that if there are more participants in 2003 than there were in 2002 (if C5 is greater than B5), the percentage in cell D5 should be positive as well.

The Reasonableness Test requires that you make some mental calculations to determine whether or not an answer is reasonable. For example, to apply the Reasonableness Test to cell B17, you might scan and count the values in column B that are used in that total, and say to yourself, "There are nine numbers in column B, and 5000 appears to be an average value. Nine times 5000 equals 45,000, so the actual value in cell B17, 42,863, seems reasonable."

But the Reasonableness Test, while practical, of course isn't foolproof. And if you aren't extremely familiar with the data you are working with, your ability to apply reasonable assumptions is not strong. Therefore, you need other tools to determine whether the formulas are actually giving you the right answers. Although clicking a cell and analyzing the formula in the Formula bar is probably the most common way of analyzing formula problems, there are several other workbook techniques that you can use to find errors you might not find by merely looking at the data. These techniques are identified in Figure 5-9.

Figure 5-9	TECHNIQUES TO FIND AND EVALUATE FORMULA ERRORS
TECHNIQUE	**DESCRIPTION**
Test values	Make a copy of the worksheet, and then enter easy-to-understand test values in place of all existing raw values in the copied worksheet so that you can anticipate and visually check whether the formulas are calculating correctly or not.
Display formulas	Display the formulas in the workbook itself. Press Ctrl + grave accent (`) to toggle the display of formulas on and off.
R1C1 reference style	Use the R1C1 reference style to check copied formulas.
Auditing	Use the buttons on the Formula Auditing toolbar (Auditing toolbar in Excel 2000) to display trace arrows to the precedent cells and dependent cells of a formula.
Validation	Use Excel's data validation features to define the type of data and limits for the data you can enter in a cell.
Watch Window (Excel 2002 only)	Use the Watch Window to view the value of cells and their formulas.
Formula evaluator (Excel 2002 only)	Use the Formula evaluator to see the result of various parts of a nested formula.
Formula error checking (Excel 2002 only)	Set error-checking rules to flag certain types of errors using an indicator symbol in the corner of the cell. Excel 2002 will automatically display error indicators in the corners of affected cells for a variety of conditions. Click Tools on the menu bar, click Error Checking, and then click the Options button in the Error Checking dialog box to view those conditions.

Test Values

Test values are simple values such as 1, 5, or 10% that when entered in assumption value cells help you determine if your formulas are working properly or not. A good test value is any value that helps you check the validity of your formula. For example, if you were trying to troubleshoot why the values in column F are incorrect, you might enter values in cells B5 and C5 that would produce an easy-to-compute value for cell F5, and then you can compare the expected value to the actual value. You will enter the value of 100 in cell C5, which should result in the value of 112 (a 12% increase over 100) in cell F5.

To enter test values in the Growth worksheet:

1. Click cell **C5**, type **100**, and press the **Enter** key. Instead of getting the expected value of 112 in cell F5, the formula calculated the value 12.

2. Click cell **F5** and examine the formula in the Formula bar. Now it's easier to see that the formula calculates only the growth itself. To get the total expected value for the year 2004, you need to add the growth to the fees for the year 2003.

3. Click in the Formula bar, edit the formula so that it is **=C5*FixedGrowth+C5**, and then click the **Enter** button ☑ on the Formula bar. The expected value, 112, appears in cell F5. Another way to enter the formula would be *=C5*(1+FixedGrowth)*. Both alternatives are correct, and the one you choose just depends on which formula makes more sense to you.

4. Use the fill handle to copy the formula in cell **F5** through the range **F6:F15**, and widen column **F** as necessary to display all values.

5. Click cell **C5**, type **5500**, and then press the **Enter** key to change the test value back to the original value. The value in cell F17 should be $53,928.

Now that you've fixed the problems in column F, you'll turn your attention to column D. You know that the growth percentage in cell D5 should be a positive value.

R1C1 Reference Style

R1C1 reference style is an alternative system to the A1 (column A row 1) system of identifying cell references. R1C1 reference style can be used to refer to cells based on their location relative to the current cell. "R" stands for row and "C" for column. The numbers represent the position of the references relative to the current cell. For example, if your current cell is A1 and it contains the formula =B2+B3, the R1C1 reference to that formula would be =R[1]C[1]+R[2]C[1]. In other words, add the value that is one row below and one column to the right of the current cell to the value that is two rows below and one column to the right of the current cell. If the current cell is F5 and it contains the formula =SUM(F1:F4), the R1C1 reference to that formula would be =SUM(R[-4]C[0]:R[-1]C[0]). Negative numbers are used to reference cells above the current row and to the left of the current column.

If the formula contains absolute cell references, the R1C1 reference to that cell uses the actual row and column numbers to refer to the cell reference. For example, no matter what the current cell is, if it contained the formula =$A$2*$B$4, the R1C1 reference to that formula would be =R2C1*R4C2.

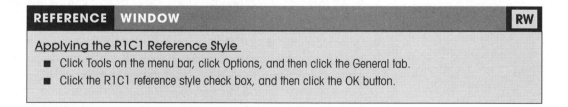

REFERENCE WINDOW	RW

Applying the R1C1 Reference Style

- Click Tools on the menu bar, click Options, and then click the General tab.
- Click the R1C1 reference style check box, and then click the OK button.

You will apply the R1C1 reference style to the Growth worksheet to see if it helps you understand the formulas in column D.

To apply R1C1 reference style to the Growth worksheet:

1. Click cell **D5**, click **Tools** on the menu bar, click **Options**, and then click the **General** tab. See Figure 5-10. The General tab of the Options dialog box contains default settings that apply to a wide range of issues including how many files appear in the recently used file list (at the bottom of the File menu), how many sheets automatically are created in a new workbook, the default font choices, and the default saved files location.

Figure 5-10	GENERAL SETTINGS IN THE OPTIONS DIALOG BOX

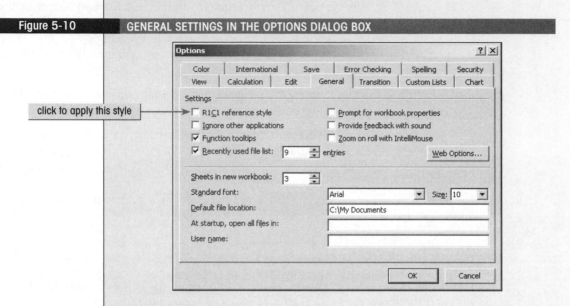

click to apply this style

EXCEL 2000: The Options dialog box has been expanded in Excel 2002 to include new tabs and new options on each tab. For example, the Security, International, and Error Checking tabs are new.

TROUBLE? The default settings, such as number of entries for the Recently used file list options, may be different on your screen. The differences will not affect the steps.

2. Click the **R1C1 reference style** check box, and then click the **OK** button. Note that the column headings have changed from letters to numbers and that the formula in the Formula bar now displays the formula for cell R5C4 (formerly called cell D5) using the R1C1 reference style. Using the R1C1 reference style in combination with displaying formulas on the screen will help you compare the formulas in the column.

3. Click **Tools** on the menu bar, click **Options**, click the **View** tab, click the **Formulas** check box, and then click the **OK** button.

4. Widen column **4** so that you can see all of the formulas in the column, and click the **scroll right arrow** to see the entire column. Because the R1C1 reference style displays cell references in a way that is relative to the current cell, you can see that the formula in R5C4 is inconsistent with the other formulas in the column. See Figure 5-11. The cell references used to determine the difference from 2002 to 2003 value are switched.

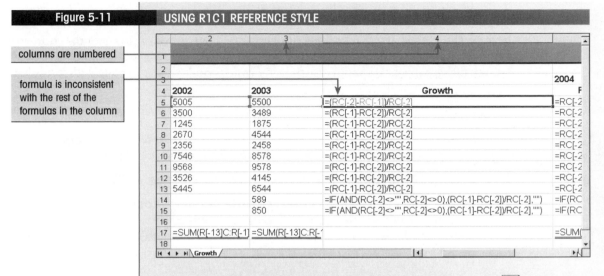

Figure 5-11 | **USING R1C1 REFERENCE STYLE**

columns are numbered

formula is inconsistent with the rest of the formulas in the column

5. Click cell **R6C4** (row 6 column 4), click the **Copy** button on the Standard toolbar, click cell **R5C4** (row 5 column 4) and then click the **Paste** button on the Standard toolbar.

6. Press **Ctrl + ` (grave accent)** to toggle off the formula view of the workbook, and then double-click the column separator between columns **4** and **5** to resize column 4 to be only as wide as it needs to be. The new growth percentage, 9.89%, seems much more reasonable. Because the fees grew from 5,005 in 2002 to 5,500 in 2003, the Reasonableness Test tells you to expect the growth percentage to be very close to 10%.

You should also copy the formula to the other cells in the column (range R14C4:R15C5). To make the entire column consistent, you'll copy the formula in cell R14C4 that you have modified with an IF function to better accommodate missing data, and to keep the formulas consistent, which also helps you find and correct errors.

To copy the formula from cell R14C4 through the range R5C4:R13C4:

1. Click cell **R14C4** (row 14 column 4), click the **Copy** button on the Standard toolbar, select the range **R5C4:R13C4**, and then click the **Paste** button on the Standard toolbar.

2. Click cell **R5C4**, and press the ↓ key to move through the entire range of formulas in column 4.

   Now all of the formulas are consistent in this column, which will make the formulas more flexible and easier to modify. You will also be able to spot errors between the formulas more quickly.

3. Click **Tools** on the menu bar, click **Options**, click the **General** tab (if it is not already displayed), click the **R1C1 reference style** check box to deselect it, and then click the **OK** button to return to the A1 reference style.

Even though you've already determined that the total value in cell B17 passes the Reasonableness Test, and you've fixed the formulas in columns D, E, and F, you're still not comfortable that all of the formulas are correct. You'll use test values to check the entire workbook. Because you'll be entering so many values, you'll copy the existing raw data to another area of the workbook so that it's easy to reenter when you're done working with test values.

To enter test values in the Growth worksheet:

1. Select the range **B5:C15**, click the **Copy** button 🔲 on the Standard toolbar, click cell **H5**, and then click the **Paste** button 🔲 on the Standard toolbar.

2. Click cell **B5** and type **75**, and then click cell **C5** and type **100**.

3. Select the range **B5:C5**, and then use the fill handle to copy the values through the range **B6:C15**. See Figure 5-12. Although the resulting formulas based on these test values are easier to mentally evaluate than the original raw data, you would prefer to use 75 as the test value for each program in the year 2002, and 100 as the test value for each program in the year 2003. You can accomplish this by changing the **step value**, the value by which the series grows, to zero.

| Figure 5-12 | COPYING TEST VALUES |

	A	B	C	D	E	F	G	H	I	J
1	GVR Youth Sports Fees									
2	12/31/2004									
3					2004	2004 at				
4	Name	2002	2003	Growth	Projected	12%				
5	Baseball	75	100	33.33%	133	112		5,005	5,500	
6	Softball	76	101	32.89%	134	113		3,500	3,489	
7	Golf (Girls)	77	102	32.47%	135	114		1,245	1,875	
8	Golf (Boys)	78	103	32.05%	136	115		2,670	4,544	
9	Football	79	104	31.65%	137	116		2,356	2,458	
10	Soccer (Girls)	80	105	31.25%	138	118		7,546	8,578	
11	Soccer (Boys)	81	106	30.86%	139	119		9,568	9,578	
12	Basketball (Girls)	82	107	30.49%	140	120		3,526	4,145	
13	Basketball (Boys)	83	108	30.12%	141	121		5,445	6,544	
14	Tennis (Girls)	84	109	29.76%	141	122			589	
15	Tennis (Boys)	85	110	29.41%	142	123			850	
16										
17	TOTALS:	2,882	3,158		$ 1,516	$ 1,294				
18										

Growth

4. With the range B5:C15 still selected, click **Edit** on the menu bar, point to **Fill**, click **Series**, and then enter **0** as the step value. See Figure 5-13. By default, the step value is 1, which means that numbers will automatically increment by 1 when you use the fill handle to fill a range. In this case, though, you do not want the series to change.

| Figure 5-13 | SERIES DIALOG BOX |

Series

Series in
- Rows
- Columns

Type
- Linear
- Growth
- Date
- AutoFill

Date unit
- Day
- Weekday
- Month
- Year

☐ Trend

Step value: 0   Stop value:

OK   Cancel

5. Click the **OK** button in the Series dialog box. The range is filled with a series starting in cells B5 and C5 and incremented using 0 as the step value. As expected, the Growth percentage for each row calculates to 33.33%, the 2004-projected fee for each row in column E calculates to 133, and the 2004-projected fee for each row in column F calculates to 112. The only other formulas you need to check are those in row 17. Because there are 11 programs, you expect the value in cell B17 to be 11*75 or 825, and the value in cell C17 to be 11*100 or 1100. Obviously, something is wrong.

6. Click cell **B17**, and then click the formula in the Formula bar. See Figure 5-14. Excel applies the same color to the cell references used in the formula to the border of those cells in the worksheet. In this case, there is only one reference to the range of cells B4 through B16, so only one color, blue, is used. The border makes it clear why the formula is still incorrect, though. The year in cell B4 was incorrectly included in the range, possibly because someone created the formula using the AutoSum button and didn't notice that cell B4 was also included in the range used by the formula. You can drag the handles in the corners of the border to adjust the cell reference in the formula.

| Figure 5-14 | CHANGING FORMULAS USING BORDER HANDLES |

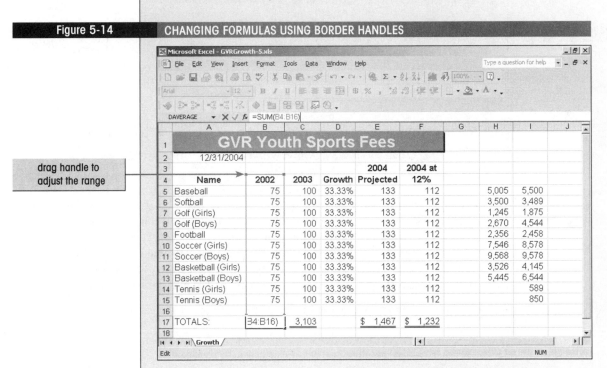

drag handle to adjust the range

7. Drag the top-right corner blue border of the range down one row to adjust the formula in the Formula bar to **=SUM(B5:B16)**, and then press the **Enter** key. If you are using Excel 2002, you may see an automatic error indicator appear in the corner of cell **B17**. Click cell **B17**, point to the error indicator icon ⬦, and a ScreenTip will appear with additional information about why the error indicator is displayed.

EXCEL 2000: Because the top border of the formulas in Excel 2000 do not have handles, edit the formula in the Formula bar to read **=SUM(B5:B16)**.

8. Click cell **B17**, click the **Currency Style** button 💲 on the Formatting toolbar, click the **Decrease Decimal** button twice, and then drag the fill handle from cell **B17** to cell **C17**.

Now that all of the formulas, including row 17, display the values you expected using test values, you're ready to move the raw data back to the range B5:C15.

9. Select the range **H5:I15**, and then copy the range and paste it back to the range **B5:C15**.

10. Delete the values in range **H5:I15**, and widen any columns as necessary. The final, corrected workbook is shown in Figure 5-15.

Figure 5-15	FINAL GVRGROWTH-5 WORKBOOK

GVR Youth Sports Fees

	A	B	C	D	E	F
2	12/31/2004					
3					2004	2004 at
4	Name	2002	2003	Growth	Projected	12%
5	Baseball	5,005	5,500	9.89%	6,044	6,160
6	Softball	3,500	3,489	-0.31%	3,478	3,908
7	Golf (Girls)	1,245	1,875	50.60%	2,824	2,100
8	Golf (Boys)	2,670	4,544	70.19%	7,733	5,089
9	Football	2,356	2,458	4.33%	2,564	2,753
10	Soccer (Girls)	7,546	8,578	13.68%	9,751	9,607
11	Soccer (Boys)	9,568	9,578	0.10%	9,588	10,727
12	Basketball (Girls)	3,526	4,145	17.56%	4,873	4,642
13	Basketball (Boys)	5,445	6,544	20.18%	7,865	7,329
14	Tennis (Girls)		589		648	660
15	Tennis (Boys)		850		935	952
16						
17	TOTALS:	$40,861	$48,150		$ 56,303	$ 53,928

Growth

11. Print the workbook with your name in the left section of the header.

12. Save and close the GVRGrowth-5 workbook, and then exit Excel.

Correcting existing formula mistakes and insuring that all formulas calculate properly is a big responsibility when creating a useful workbook. The number of problems you will run into is infinite. Having exposure to some of the most common errors and being able to use the formula troubleshooting tools that Excel provides can make a big difference in your ability to detect and fix errors. Lynn is pleased that you were able to correct the errors in this workbook and commends you on your excellent Excel troubleshooting skills.

Session 5.1 QUICK CHECK

1. What types of formula errors might you encounter in Excel? Which type is the hardest to correct, and why?

2. Provide an example of a formula that uses the AVERAGE function that would produce a #NAME? error.

3. What is the most common cause of a #REF! error?

4. Explain the significance of the color of the trace arrows that appear when you are tracing an error.

5. How does the R1C1 reference style help you spot errors?

6. How do you determine what test values to use?

SESSION 5.2

In this session, you will learn about advanced functions in the Financial, Database, and Date and Time categories. You'll work with depreciation and time value of money functions in the Financial category, and you'll learn how to use the Database functions to isolate information within a list. You'll also work with Date and Time functions to isolate pieces of information about a date such as the day of the week, as well as work with date, time, and custom formats to modify the way date and time information displays in the workbook.

Financial Functions

With over 50 different functions, the Financial category is one of the largest categories of functions. If you are faced with making a calculation that has to do with investments, interest rates, or the time value of money, you may be able to simplify the calculation by using a **Financial function**.

Depreciation

Depreciation is the process of allocating the cost of a long-term asset over the period of its useful life for accounting and tax purposes. For example, if you have a small business and purchase a truck for company use, you typically can't claim the entire amount that you paid for the truck as an expense in the year that you purchased it. Instead, you must spread out the expense of the truck over a period of time such as 3, 5, or 10 years, as defined by the current tax laws (which, in turn, are based on the typical useful life of the asset). For example, some assets such as computers or furniture can be depreciated quickly, but other assets, such as buildings or land, might take 10 years to depreciate.

In general, you want to depreciate an asset as quickly as possible, because the amount of depreciation that you claim is treated as an expense against income, which thereby lowers your tax burden. But in certain situations, you may want to minimize your current year's depreciation expense. For example, if your company has a bad year and income is down, you might want to minimize your depreciation expense this year and maximize it next year, in an effort to offset next year's higher anticipated income (and higher anticipated tax bracket). No matter how much depreciation expense you claim in each year, however, the total amount of depreciation that you can claim must equal the initial cost of the asset less its **salvage value**, the amount it is worth at the end of the depreciation period. The **undepreciated balance** is the total amount of depreciation that you can take (initial cost less salvage value) less any depreciation expenses already claimed in previous years.

Excel provides functions for four different depreciation methods as described in Figure 5-16.

Figure 5-16	DEPRECIATION METHODS	
METHOD	**EXCEL FUNCTION**	**DESCRIPTION**
Straight line	SLN	A method of depreciation in which each year's depreciation expense is the same. It is calculated by dividing the initial cost of the asset less the salvage value by the number of years that you claim depreciation expense for the asset.
Sum-of-years' digits	SYD	A method of accelerated depreciation in which each year's depreciation expense is calculated by multiplying a different ratio (determined by the life of the asset) by the undepreciated balance. For example, if the life of the asset is three years, the sum of the years' digits would be $1 + 2 + 3 = 6$, the first year's depreciation would be 3/6*undepreciated balance, the second year's depreciation would be 2/6*undepreciated balance, and the third year's depreciation would be 1/6*undepreciated balance.
Fixed-declining balance	DB	A method of accelerated depreciation in which each year's depreciation is calculated by multiplying a fixed percentage against the undepreciated balance.
Double-declining balance	DDB	A method of accelerated depreciation in which the first year's straight-line depreciation amount is doubled for the first year. For subsequent years, the ratio of the first year's depreciation to the initial cost is multiplied by the remaining undepreciated balance to determine that year's depreciation.

GVR has several pieces of equipment such as tractors and lawn mowers that are used to maintain their sports facilities such as baseball and soccer fields. It also has land, buildings, and several other capital assets for which the accounting department has to calculate the appropriate depreciation expense each year. Lynn noticed that these calculations are tedious, especially because the accounting department tries to compare various depreciation methods for a new asset. She knows that Excel can help make these calculations much faster and has started a new Excel workbook to support this process. She needs your help in entering the depreciation formulas, though. You'll use the depreciation functions in the financial category to help build the formulas.

To calculate straight-line depreciation for a new capital asset:

1. Start Excel and then open the **DepreciationCalculator-5** workbook located in the Tutorial.05\Tutorial folder on your Data Disk. Lynn has already entered the labels and color-coded the input and output areas. The light yellow shading highlights the range of cells (B5:B8) that will contain the facts about a new piece of equipment. The light turquoise shading highlights the range of cells (B11:F14) that will display the depreciation expense for the given depreciation method, which is provided in the range A11:A14, and the given year, which is provided in the range B10:F10.

2. Enter the assumption values in the range B5:B8 as shown in Figure 5-17.

Figure 5-17   DEPRECIATION ASSUMPTION VALUES

	A	B	C	D	E	F	G
1	Green Valley Recreation						
2	Equipment Depreciation Calculator						
3							
4							
5	Item	Tractor					
6	Useful Life	5					
7	Purchase Price	$ 35,000					
8	Salvage Value	$ 15,000					
9							
10		1	2	3	4	5	
11	Straight Line						
12	Sum-Of-Years Digits						
13	Fixed-Declining Balance						
14	Double-Declining Balance						
15							

assumption values

Because Lynn knows that the assumption values in cells B6, B7, and B8 will be used in the depreciation formulas, she has already range named them to make them easier to reference in the formulas. B6 is named Life, B7 is named Purchase, and B8 is named Salvage.

3. Click cell **B11**, click the **list arrow** for the AutoSum button Σ ▾ on the Standard toolbar, and then click **More Functions**. The Insert Function dialog box opens.

   EXCEL 2000: Click the **Paste Function** button f_x on the Standard toolbar to open the Paste Function dialog box.

4. In the Search for a function text box, type **depreciation**, and then click the **Go** button. Five functions are found that deal with depreciation as shown in Figure 5-18.

   EXCEL 2000: Click **Financial** in the Function category list.

Figure 5-18   DEPRECIATION FUNCTIONS FOUND IN THE INSERT FUNCTION DIALOG BOX

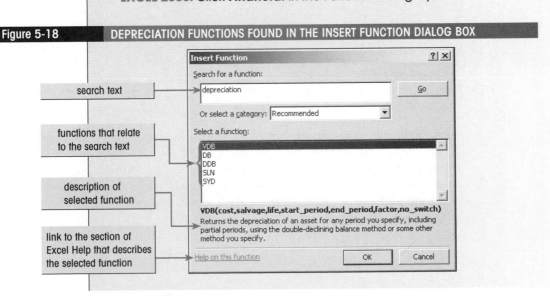

search text

functions that relate to the search text

description of selected function

link to the section of Excel Help that describes the selected function

The Insert Function dialog box provides a description at the bottom of the dialog box of the selected function. If you want a more extensive explanation of the function, click the Help link in the lower-left corner of the dialog box.

5. Click **SLN** in the list of functions, and then click the **OK** button. The Function Arguments dialog box opens with the three required arguments for calculating straight-line depreciation. A short description of the selected argument is presented at the bottom of the dialog box.

6. Click the **Collapse Dialog Box** button [icon] for the Cost argument, click cell **B7** (which was previously given the range name "Purchase"), and then click the **Expand Dialog Box** button [icon] to expand the dialog box.

7. Enter **Salvage** (the range name of B8) for the Salvage argument, enter **Life** (the range name of B6) for the Life argument, and then click the **OK** button.

8. Use the fill handle to copy the formula in cell **B11** through the range **C11:F11**. See Figure 5-19.

Figure 5-19   **CALCULATION STRAIGHT-LINE DEPRECIATION**

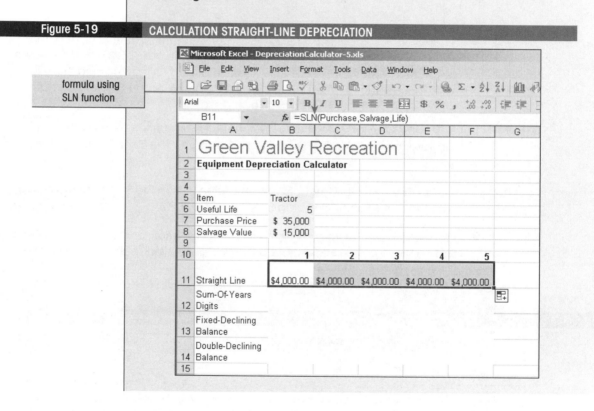

formula using
SLN function

Straight-line depreciation spread the total amount of depreciable expense ($35,000 - $15,000 = $20,000) across the five-year life of the asset, which resulted in $4000 of depreciation expense per year. Although this formula is not too difficult to calculate without using an Excel function, the other depreciation methods are less simple. Next, you'll determine the allowed depreciation expense for each of the five years using the sum-of-years' digits depreciation method.

To calculate sum-of-years'-digits depreciation for a new capital asset:

1. Click cell **B12**, click the **list arrow** for the AutoSum button ∑ ▾ , and then click **More Functions**.

   EXCEL 2000: Click the **Paste Function** button *fx* on the Standard toolbar.

   This time you'll search for the desired function by narrowing down your choices to a function category.

2. Click the **Or select a category** list arrow, click **Financial**, scroll and click **SYD** in the Select a function list, and then click the **OK** button. The sum-of-years'-digits depreciation method has four required arguments. The first three are the same as you experienced with the straight-line depreciation function, but the fourth, Per, represents the depreciation period (year 1, 2, 3, 4, or 5 if the asset has a five-year useful life).

   EXCEL 2000: Click **Financial** in the Function category list (if it is not already selected), scroll and click **SYD** in the Function name list, and then click the **OK** button.

3. Enter the arguments as shown in Figure 5-20.

Figure 5-20	ENTERING THE ARGUMENTS FOR THE SYD FUNCTION

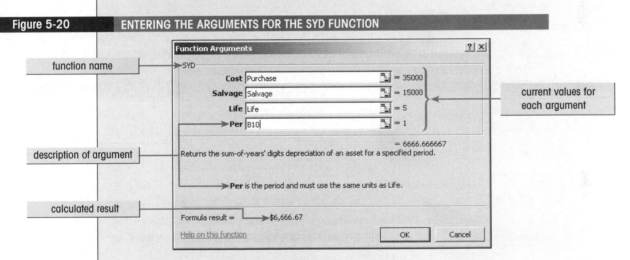

The current value for each argument is displayed to the right of the argument reference box. The calculated result of the entire formula is displayed toward the bottom of the dialog box. This information helps you determine whether or not the values for your arguments have been selected correctly. Because the sum-of-the-years'-digits depreciation method is an accelerated method of depreciation that allows you to claim higher depreciation expenses in the early part of the asset's life, the calculated first year's depreciation of $6,666.67 seems like a reasonable depreciation expense when you compare it to the $4000 value calculated by the straight-line function.

4. Click the **OK** button. The first year's depreciation, $6,666.67, is entered in cell B12.

5. Use the fill handle to copy the formula in cell **B12** through the range **C12:F12**. As expected, the sum-of-years'-digits function accelerates depreciation in the early years of the asset, which means that the expense tapers off in the later years.

To finish out the analysis, you need to insert the formulas for the other two depreciation methods: the fixed-declining balance and the double-declining balance methods.

To enter the fixed-declining balance and double-declining balance depreciation formulas:

1. Click cell **B13**, click the **list arrow** for the AutoSum button Σ ▾, and then click **More Functions**.

   EXCEL 2000: Click the **Paste Function** button fx on the Standard toolbar.

   This time you'll search for the desired function by entering the function name in the search box.

2. Type **db** in the Search for a function box, click the **Go** button, click **DB** in the Select a function list (if it is not already selected), and then click the **OK** button. The fixed-declining balance formula has four required arguments and one optional argument, Month. Recall that required arguments are bold and optional arguments are not bold in the Function Arguments dialog box.

   EXCEL 2000: Click **Financial** in the Function category list (if it is not already selected), click **DB** (if it is not already selected) in the Function name list, and then click the **OK** button.

3. Type the required arguments for the DB function as shown in Figure 5-21, and then click the **Month** argument reference box so that you can read more about this argument at the bottom of the dialog box.

Figure 5-21   **ENTERING THE ARGUMENTS FOR THE DB FUNCTION**

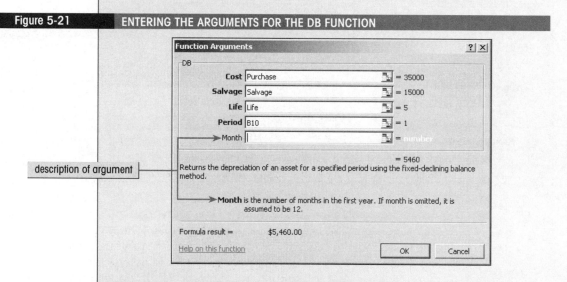

description of argument

The description of this function explains that you can omit the argument if you are calculating the depreciation expense assuming that there are 12 months in a year, which is the assumption that you are using.

4. Click the **OK** button to finish the first year's fixed-declining balance formula.

   Next you'll enter the double-declining balance for the first year.

5. Click cell **B14**, click the **list arrow** for Σ ▾, and then click **More Functions**.

   EXCEL 2000: Click fx.

6. Using either the Search for a function text box or the category list, select the **DDB** function, which calculates depreciation using the double-declining balance method, and then click the **OK** button.

   EXCEL 2000: Click **Financial** in the Function category list (if it is not already selected), click **DDB** in the Function name list, and then click the **OK** button.

7. Enter the required arguments for the DDB function as shown in Figure 5-22. Because you want to use a double-declining balance method for depreciation, you can omit an entry in the Factor argument.

Figure 5-22   **ENTERING THE ARGUMENTS FOR THE DDB FUNCTION**

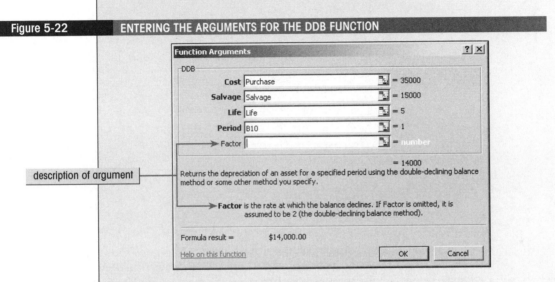

description of argument

8. Click the **OK** button, and then widen column **B** so that the entire depreciation expense is visible in cell B14.

   With the first year's depreciation calculated for the fixed-declining balance and double-declining balance methods in cells B13 and B14, you'll copy those formulas throughout each depreciation period.

9. Select the range **B13:B14**, and then use the fill handle to copy the formulas throughout the range **C13:F14**. See Figure 5-23. With the depreciation formulas entered in cells B11:F14, the accounting department can use this workbook to quickly analyze how one depreciation method compares to another.

Figure 5-23   **COPYING THE DB AND DDB FORMULAS**

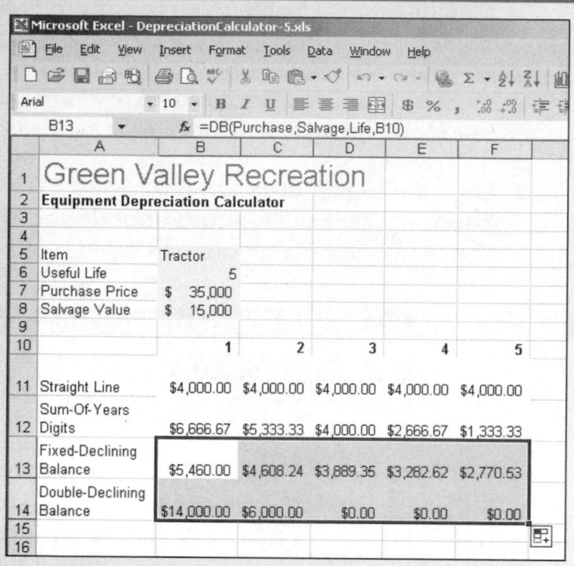

10. Save and then print the workbook with your name in the left section of the header.

11. Close the DepreciationCalculator-5 workbook.

Lynn is pleased with the speed with which you were able to compare the periodic depreciation expenses for an asset using four different depreciation methods. Now the accounting department can use this workbook to compare the periodic depreciation expenses by merely entering new assumption values (name, useful life, purchase price, and salvage value) for a new capital asset. If the asset has a 10-year useful life, the employees in the accounting department merely need to copy the entries in cells F10:F14 five more columns to the right to expand the formulas to a 10-year period instead of the current five-year period.

Time Value of Money

The **time value of money** concept deals with the theory that receiving a dollar today is more valuable than receiving a dollar in the future for two major reasons:

- In an **inflationary** economy (an economy in which goods and services cost more in the future than they do today), an item that costs one dollar today will cost more than that, for example $1.04 if the annual inflation rate was 4%, a year from now.

- If you invest a dollar today, it would draw interest and be worth more than that, for example $1.06 if the return on your investment was 6%, a year from now.

If you have ever purchased something on credit such as a house or a car, you've already made a time value of money decision. You've decided to pay more in a series of payments over a specified period of time than the amount loaned to you, in order to be able to use that money to purchase something now. Excel's PMT function helps you determine the periodic payment on a loan amount, given an interest rate and the number of periodic payments.

Figure 5-24 identifies other Excel functions that you might use to help make time value of money calculations.

Figure 5-24	TIME VALUE OF MONEY FUNCTIONS	
CONCEPT	**EXCEL FUNCTION**	**DESCRIPTION**
Periodic payment	PMT	Calculates the periodic payment on a loan, given an investment rate and number of payment periods
Future value	FV	Calculates an equivalent future value of a series of payments, given an expected interest rate and the number of payment periods
Present value	PV	Calculates an equivalent present value of a series of payments, given an expected interest rate and the number of payment periods

GVR has recently built a new community health club facility and has asked Lynn to propose at least two different membership plans. GVR wants to offer two different payment plans for a five-year membership, one based on a single lump-sum payment and one based on five annual payments. Once again, Lynn knows that Excel's extensive financial functions can be of tremendous value when analyzing the time value of money, but she needs your help to determine exactly which functions should be used and how to enter the arguments for the formulas.

To explore the PV function:

1. Open the **HealthClub-5** workbook located in the Tutorial.05\Tutorial folder on your Data Disk. Lynn has already structured the workbook for you by entering the labels, number of payments, payment amounts, and the estimated annual interest rate that she wants to use for these calculations. She needs your help to finish the present value formulas in cells B9 and C9.

   This time you will use the Insert Function button on the Formula bar. This method provides a fast way to open the Insert Function dialog box.

2. Click cell **B9** and then click the **Insert Function** button [fx] on the Formula bar.

   EXCEL 2000: Click the **Paste Function** button [fx] on the Standard toolbar.

3. Find and click **PV** in the Select a function list (it's in the Financial category), and then click the **OK** button. The arguments for the PV function are presented. PV has three required arguments (Rate, Nper, and Pmt), and two optional arguments (Fv and Type).

   EXCEL 2000: Click **Financial** in the Function category list (if it is not already selected), scroll and click **PV** in the Function name list, and then click the **OK** button.

4. Using the technique you prefer, enter **B11** (which contains the interest rate of 6%) as the value for the Rate argument, **B5** as the value for the Nper (which contains the number of payment periods) argument, and **B6** (which contains the payment value of $1000) as the value for the Pmt argument. See Figure 5-25. Unfortunately, the current formula result is not what you expected. Right now, the calculation shows that the current formula result is $(943). But you know that's not correct. The present value of $1000 is $1000. You'll explore the optional arguments to see if you can figure out why this formula isn't calculating correctly.

Figure 5-25   ENTERING THE ARGUMENTS FOR THE PV FUNCTION

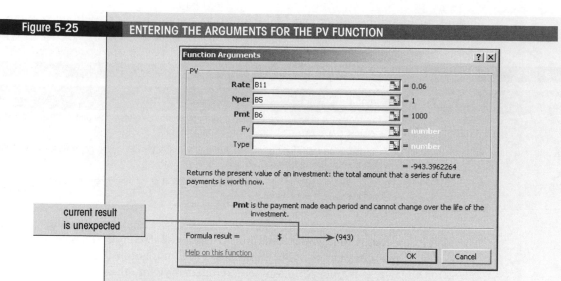

current result
is unexpected

5. Click the **Fv** argument box. Based on the information in the Function Arguments dialog box, the Fv argument determines the cash balance you want to attain after the last payment is made. Because you won't be returning any portion of the payment to the member at the end of the five-year period, this argument isn't needed.

6. Click the **Type** argument box. The Type argument determines when the payment is made, at the beginning or end of the period. By default you see that the payment is made at the end of the period. Because GVR is going to require that the payment be at the beginning of the five-year membership, you need to enter 1 in this argument.

7. Type **1** in the Type argument. Now the formula result as displayed in the Function Arguments dialog box is also $(1,000), the value you expected. But, it still shows a negative value. To change the sign of the resulting calculation, you'll insert a minus sign in front of the Pmt argument.

8. Edit the Pmt argument so that it is **-B6**, and then click the **OK** button. See Figure 5-26.

Figure 5-26   USING THE PV FUNCTION

formula using
the PV function

Insert Function button

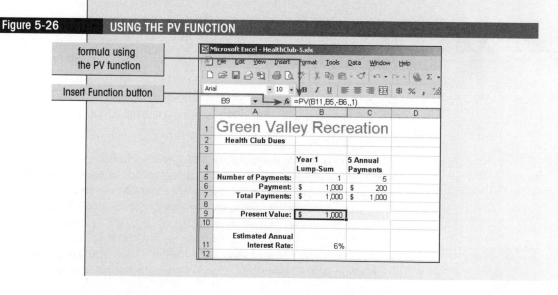

By applying the PV function to this simple case, you were better able to understand some of the complexities of using time value of money functions. First of all, in this case, you had to use an optional argument. You saw that by default, the PV function assumed that payments were made at the end of the period, and in this case, you wanted to evaluate a payment made at the beginning of a period.

Furthermore, the resulting calculation of the PV function was presented as a negative value. This has to do with how Excel interprets the arguments in time value of money functions, as **cash inflows** (positive values) or as **cash outflows** (negative values) to you. In other words, the Excel PV formula is answering this question: What would you pay today (cash outflow, a negative value to you) to purchase this amount of money (cash inflow, a positive value to you)? In this case, you determined that receiving $1000 today (inflow) would be worth paying $1000 (outflow) today. Because you want to represent both values as positive numbers, rather than cash inflows and outflows, you changed the sign of the Pmt argument to accomplish this. Other ways of converting the formula to a positive value would be to multiply the entire formula by -1 or to use the ABS function to determine the absolute value of the result of the formula.

Next you'll determine what the present value of five $200 payments would be. You expect the present value of five payments of $200 each to be a little less than $1000, because a dollar in the future is worth a little less to you than a dollar now.

To apply the PV function to analyze the present value of five annual payments:

1. Click cell **C9** and then click the **Insert Function** button f_x on the Formula bar.

   EXCEL 2000: Click the **Paste Function** button f_x on the Standard toolbar.

2. Click **PV** in the list of Financial functions, and then click the **OK** button.

3. Enter the arguments for the PV function as shown in Figure 5-27.

Figure 5-27	ENTERING ARGUMENTS FOR THE PV FUNCTION

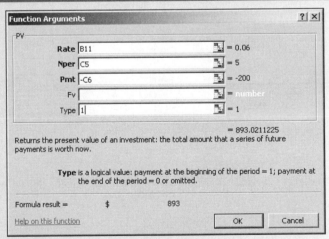

4. Click the **OK** button, and then save the workbook.

The present value of five annual payments of $200 each at a 6% interest rate is $893. This means that if you want the two plans to be equivalent using these assumptions (and assuming no inflationary impact), you should either raise the annual payment for the five-year plan to something higher than $200 or lower the lump-sum payment plan to $893. Now that you have the formulas entered so that the present value of each option is calculated correctly, you'll let Lynn test other payment options and present them to the Board of Directors.

Lynn also had a future time value of money problem that she needs your help on. On another worksheet of the current workbook she has entered some raw data that describes two plans currently being considered to raise money for a portion of the Phase II athletic club facility that GVR intends to build in seven years. Each plan requires a special assessment of funds from Green County residents, but whether the funds are assessed and deposited in GVR's bank account as a lump sum now, or as seven deposits over the next seven years depends on what the future value of each of those alternatives would be. You'll help Lynn analyze these plans using the future value function, FV.

To apply the FV function to analyze the future value of the initial assessment plan:

1. Click the **Phasell** tab, click cell **B9** and then click the **Insert Function** button ![fx] on the Formula bar.

   EXCEL 2000: Click the **Paste Function** button ![fx] on the Standard toolbar.

2. Find and click **FV** in the Financial category, and then click the **OK** button. The arguments for the FV function are similar to those for the PV function. Both functions have three required arguments (Rate, Nper, and Pmt), and two optional arguments. The optional arguments for the FV function are Pv and Type.

3. Enter the arguments for the FV function as shown in Figure 5-28.

Figure 5-28	ENTERING ARGUMENTS FOR THE FV FUNCTION

4. Click the **OK** button.

Your formula determines that $1,000,000 deposited now is equivalent to $1,503,630 in seven years, given a 6% interest rate and no inflationary considerations. Now you'll enter the formula for the second plan that deposits $170,000 at the end of each year for seven years.

To apply the FV function to analyze the future value of the seven-year assessment plan:

1. Click cell **C9** and then click the **Insert Function** button 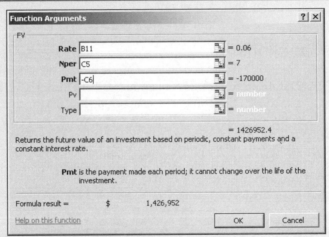 on the Formula bar.

   EXCEL 2000: Click the **Paste Function** button *fx* on the Standard toolbar.

2. Click **FV** in the list of Financial functions, and then click the **OK** button.

3. Enter the arguments for the FV function as shown in Figure 5-29. In this case, there are seven total payments (represented by the value in C5), and each payment is $170,000 (represented by the value in C6). There is no initial present value (the Pv argument) to enter, and the deposits will be made at the end of each year (therefore the Type argument was omitted).

Figure 5-29	ENTERING ARGUMENTS FOR THE SECOND FV FUNCTION

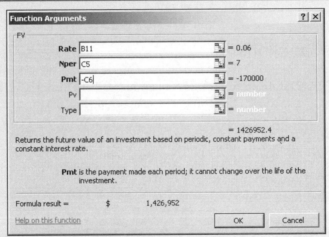

4. Click the **OK** button. See Figure 5-30.

Figure 5-30	THE FUTURE VALUE CALCULATION

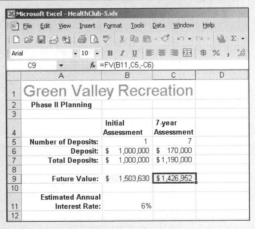

5. Save the workbook, and then print both worksheets of the workbook with your name in the left section of the headers.

6. Display the formulas on the screen, and print both worksheets a second time.

7. Close the HealthClub-5 workbook.

The future value calculations showed that even though the total amount of funds raised and deposited by using the seven-year assessment plan ($1,190,000 as displayed in cell C7) were greater than the total amount of funds raised and deposited by using the initial assessment plan ($1,000,000 as shown in cell B7), the future value of the seven-year assessment plan is about $75,000 less (C9 compared to B9) than the future value of the initial assessment plan. Considering the fact that inflation will further dilute the value of future funds, Lynn can make a strong recommendation to the Board that the initial assessment plan is more financially favorable to GVR than the seven-year assessment plan, given a 6% estimated annual interest rate.

Database Functions

Database functions, sometimes called **Dfunctions**, are used to help analyze data stored in a list. All Dfunctions are structured similarly in that they all have three arguments. In its generic form, a Dfunction is structured as follows: *Dfunction(list, field name, criteria)*.

Each of the three arguments is a reference to a cell or range of cells. The first defines the range for the *list* of data, the second defines the *field name* that the function will use for the calculation, and the third defines the range that stores the *criteria* that determine which records within the list will be used within the calculation. See Figure 5-31 for a description of popular Dfunctions.

Figure 5-31	DATABASE FUNCTIONS
FUNCTION	**DESCRIPTION**
DAVERAGE	Returns the average value for the specified field for records that are true for the given criteria
DCOUNT	Counts the values in the specified field for records that are true for the given criteria
DCOUNTA	Counts the nonblank values in the specified field for records that are true for the given criteria
DMAX	Returns the maximum value in the specified field for records that are true for the given criteria
DMIN	Returns the minimum value in the specified field for records that are true for the given criteria
DSUM	Returns the subtotal of the values in the specified field for records that are true for the given criteria

Organizing the Workbook for Dfunctions

Because all Dfunctions have three arguments that identify ranges, you might find it helpful to spend some time organizing your workbook to make it easier to find the ranges and enter the Dfunction formulas. If you enter range names for the list and criteria ranges, you will be able to highlight those areas of the workbook as well as enter your Dfunction formulas.

Lynn has asked you to help her analyze some information for the recent fundraiser. Several companies have generously donated money to GVR, and it has been designated toward one of three categories: new baseball lights, a new community center, and the general fund. Because the data is organized as a list and you need to compute individual statistics from the list based on the criteria Lynn specifies, you believe this will be a good candidate for the use of Dfunctions. First you'll specify range names for the three arguments required by a Dfunction formula.

To name range the list and criteria for Dfunction formulas:

1. Open the **FundRaiser-5** workbook located in the Tutorial.05\Tutorial folder on your Data Disk.

   The first thing you need to do is identify the list with a range name of Donations. You need to include the row that contains the field names in the range name, so your selection will start at row 6 and end when the data stops at row 26.

2. Select the range **A6:C26**, click the **Name Box**, type **Donations**, and then press the **Enter** key.

   TROUBLE? If you make a spelling error or other range name entry mistake, click the cell and reenter the correct name in the Name Box. Later, you'll get an opportunity to test, delete, and edit incorrect range names.

   Next, you'll identify the range that will contain the criteria argument. This criteria range must include both the field names and the rows that contain criteria. You will position this range above the list to make it easy to find. To create the range, you'll copy the field names from row 6 and paste them in row 3 to create the field names for the criteria range.

3. Click the **row heading** for row **6**, click the **Copy** button on the Standard toolbar, click the **row heading** for row **3**, and then click the **Paste** button on the Standard toolbar.

   For now, you'll define the range to include the field name row and one more row that will hold the actual criteria entries.

4. Select the range **A3:C4**, click the **Name Box**, type **Criteria**, and then press the **Enter** key. See Figure 5-32.

Figure 5-32	DEFINING THE CRITERIA RANGE

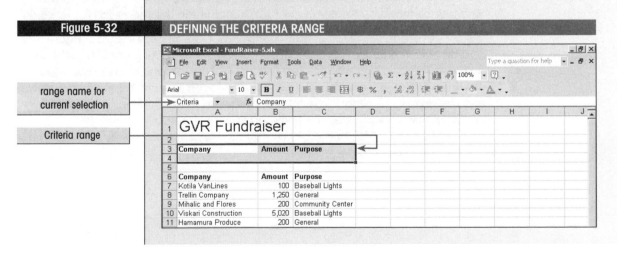

range name for current selection

Criteria range

To view the range names in this workbook or to select a range name, you can use the Range Name list.

5. To verify that the range names have been created correctly, click the **list arrow** for the Name Box, click **Donations**, click the **list arrow** for the Name Box, and then click **Criteria**. The range A3:C4 should be selected.

TROUBLE? If any of the range names are entered incorrectly, click Insert on the menu bar, point to Name, and then click Define to open the Define Name dialog box. You can use the options in this dialog box to add, delete, or edit existing range names.

Once the list and ranges are established in the workbook, you will find working with Dfunctions considerably easier. Lynn wants to be able to count, subtotal, and average the contributions within each of the three categories. She also wants those calculations to be very easy to find in the workbook. You'll enter some labels in column E to identify the Dfunctions you are about to use.

To enter labels to identify the Dfunctions:

1. Click cell **E6** and enter **Subtotal**, click cell **E7** and enter **Average**, and then click cell **E8** and enter **Count**.

2. Select cells **E7** and **E8**, and then click the **Bold** button [B] so that all three labels are bold.

With range names and function labels in place, you're ready to enter the appropriate criteria in the Criteria range and the Dfunction formulas in the range F6:F8 to determine the subtotal, average, and count of donations for the Baseball Lights fund.

To enter criteria and Dfunction formulas to analyze the Baseball Lights:

1. Click cell **C4** and enter **Baseball Lights**. This entry identifies the criteria that will be used. Only records with this value in the Purpose field will be used for the Dfunctions. Now you'll enter the actual Dfunctions in the range F6:F8.

2. Click cell **F6**, and then type **=DSUM(Donations,2,Criteria)** as shown in Figure 5-33. As you enter the range names for the arguments of the DSUM function, Excel 2002 identifies those ranges with colored borders that correspond to the colors used for the first and last arguments in the formula. The second argument, the field name, can be entered as either the number that represents the position of the field name in the list or the field name itself, enclosed in quotation marks. Therefore, =DSUM(Donations,"Amount",Criteria) would be an equivalent entry.

Figure 5-33	ENTERING THE DSUM FUNCTION

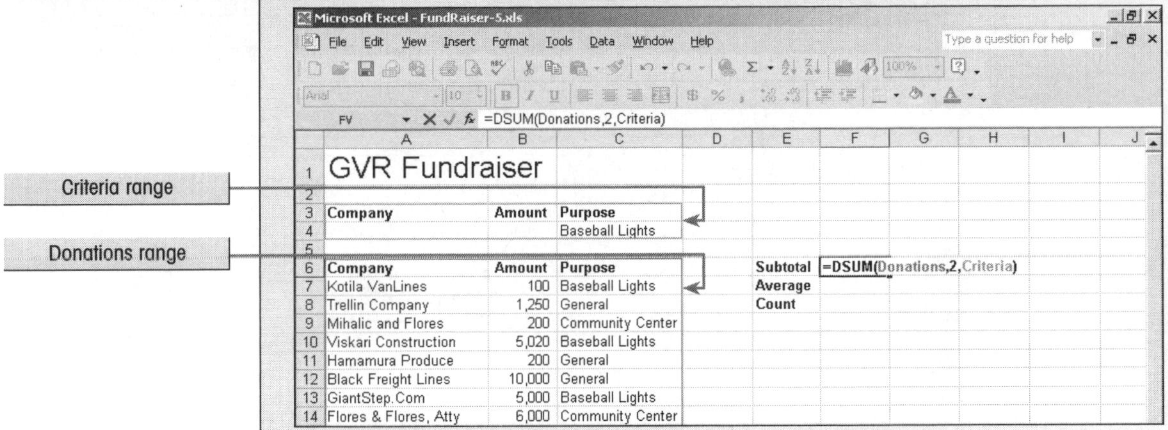

Criteria range

Donations range

3. Press the **Enter** key. The subtotal of all donations for the Baseball Lights fund, $19,620, is displayed in cell F6, but it is not formatted properly.

4. Click cell **F6**, click the **Currency Style** button [$] on the Formatting toolbar, and then click the **Decrease Decimal** button [.00] on the Formatting toolbar twice. Because the other Dfunction formulas are very similar to the DSUM formula used in cell F6, you'll copy and paste the formula in cell F6 to cells F7 and F8 and then edit the function names to determine the average and count statistics.

5. Drag the fill handle for cell **F6** through the range **F7:F8**. Another advantage of using range names for the list and criteria arguments is that range names are treated as absolute values, so the cells that those range names reference do not move as you copy a formula that contains them.

6. Double-click cell **F7**, change DSUM to **DAVERAGE**, and then press the **Enter** key.

7. Double-click cell **F8**, change DSUM to **DCOUNT**, press the **Enter** key, and then click cell **F8**.

   Because the value for cell F8 is a count rather than a monetary value, you'll remove the currency symbol.

8. Click the **Comma Style** button [,] on the Formatting toolbar, and then click [.00] twice. See Figure 5-34. These three Dfunctions subtotal, average, and count the number of donations where the Purpose field equals Baseball Lights.

Figure 5-34   DFUNCTION FORMULAS

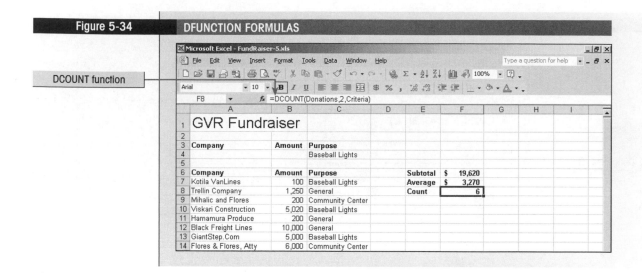

Note that criteria entries such as the one in cell C4 are not case sensitive. Therefore the entries "baseball lights", "Baseball Lights", and "BASEBALL LIGHTS" would all produce the same results. Always strive to enter data in a list using consistent capitalization, though, because consistency makes it easier to read and more professional, too.

Entering Different Criteria Values

Now that list and ranges are clearly identified in the workbook, and the Dfunction formulas are entered, you can enter different criteria values to automatically view different statistics on the list. Lynn also wants to view the subtotal, average, and count statistics for the General and Community Center funds.

To view the statistics for other Purpose values:

1. Click cell **C4**, type **General**, and then press the **Enter** key. The statistics for the General fund appear in range F6:F8. See Figure 5-35.

Figure 5-35   STATISTICS FOR THE GENERAL FUND

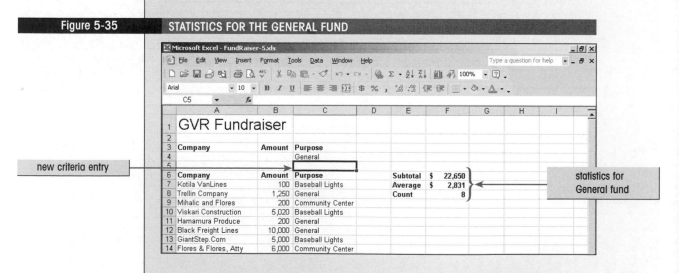

2. Click cell **C4**, type **Community Center**, and then press the **Enter** key. The statistics for the Community Center fund now appear in range F6:F8.

Entering "And" Criteria

Now that Lynn sees how easy it is to calculate different statistics from the list, she is starting to ask more complex questions. For example, now she wants to know how many donations there were for the Community Center fund that are greater than or equal to $1000. In this case, because both criteria must be true in order for the record to be used in the Dfunction formulas, the criteria are considered "and" criteria.

To enter "and" criteria:

1. Click cell **B4**, type **>=1000**, and then press the **Enter** key. You have now added "and" criteria by entering another criterion to the same row in the Criteria range. Only three donations meet both criteria with a subtotal of $13,500 and an average of $4500.

Entering "Or" Criteria

Sometimes you want to calculate statistics on the records that meet one of several different criteria. In this case, because only one of the criteria entries must be true in order for the record to be used in the Dfunction formula, the criteria are considered "or" criteria.

Lynn wants to know how many donations of $1000 or higher were made for the Community Center and the Baseball Lights funds. You'll use "or" criteria to make this determination.

To enter "or" criteria:

1. Right-click the **row heading** for row **5**, and then click **Insert** on the shortcut menu. You add "or" criteria to a different row in the Criteria range.

2. Click cell **B5**, type **>=1000**, click cell **C5**, type **Baseball Lights**, and then press the **Enter** key.

   Even though you added a second row to enter another criterion, the Dfunctions didn't recalculate. This is because the Criteria range is still defined as A3:C4. The entry you entered in row 5 has no effect on the Dfunction formulas because that row isn't part of the Criteria range. To redefine the Criteria range, you'll use the Define Name dialog box.

3. Click **Insert** on the menu bar, point to **Name**, and then click **Define**. The Define Name dialog box opens. You can use this dialog box to add, delete, or edit existing range names.

4. Click **Criteria** in the Names in workbook list, click to the right of =Donations!$A$3:$C$4 in the Refers to box, press the **Backspace** key to delete **4**, and then type **5** to extend the Criteria range through row 5 as shown in Figure 5-36.

Figure 5-36	DEFINE NAME DIALOG BOX

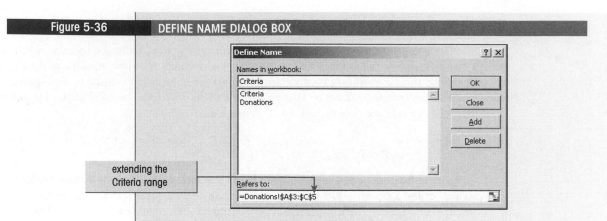

extending the
Criteria range

5. Click the **OK** button. See Figure 5-37. Now the Dfunctions in cells F7:F9 reflect the donations over $1000 for both the Community Center and Baseball Lights projects.

Figure 5-37	USING "OR" CRITERIA

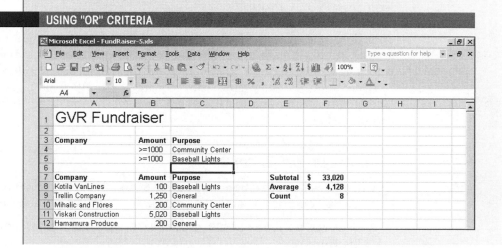

It's very important to define the Criteria range with the correct cell references. Don't forget that you can click a formula in the Formula bar to display color-coded borders around the range names for the existing arguments to help you to troubleshoot range problems in Dfunction formulas.

Using Wildcards in the Criteria Range

You can use **wildcard** characters in the Criteria range to represent any series of characters. A question mark (?) wildcard represents any single character, and an asterisk (*) represents one or many characters. GVR has issued a friendly challenge to the attorneys and CPAs in the area to see which profession will donate more money to the new facility. Lynn is curious to know which group is in the lead. You'll use wildcard characters to help you find and report on those donations.

To use a wildcard character in the Criteria range:

1. Delete the current criteria entries in the range **B4:C5**. Notice that the Dfunction statistics now report the total, average, and count for *all* records since there is no criteria that limits which records are used for these functions.

2. Click cell **A4**, type ***CPA**, and then press the **Enter** key. Because all CPA firms that are represented in this list end with these three characters, this criteria entry should help you find all of them. Unfortunately, the Dfunctions still show the statistics for all of the records. This is because the Criteria range still includes row 5, which no longer contains any criteria. Because all records are "true" for the criteria in row 5, they are all still used in each Dfunction. To correct this, you again need to modify the cell reference for the Criteria range name.

3. Click **Insert** on the menu bar, point to **Name**, and then click **Define** to open the Define Name dialog box.

4. Click **Criteria** in the list, edit the reference in the Refers to box so that the entry is **=Donations!$A$3:$C$4**, and then click the **OK** button. See Figure 5-38. Two records were true for the *CPA criteria entered in the Company field.

Figure 5-38	USING A WILDCARD IN THE CRITERIA

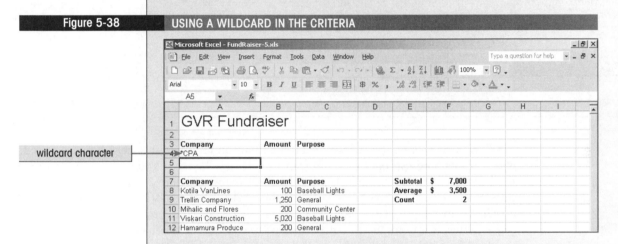

wildcard character

Now enter the appropriate criteria to see the statistics for the law firms. All Company entries for the attorneys in the area end with the Atty abbreviation.

5. Click cell **A4**, type ***Atty**, and then press the **Enter** key. Although the average CPA donation was $3500, higher than the average attorney firm donation of $2800, the total amount of the donations for the attorneys at $11,200 is higher than that of the CPAs at $7000 because four attorney groups donated whereas only two CPA firms are represented.

6. Save the FundRaiser-5 workbook, print it with your name in the left section of the header, and then close the workbook.

Dfunctions help you to calculate statistics and analyze data stored in lists. Once the list range and criteria range are organized and defined, and Dfunction formulas are entered, you can make different entries in the criteria range to see the statistics for that group of records. Remember, though, if you use "or" criteria you must be sure to expand the criteria range to include each row in which you've entered criteria. Also realize that if your criteria range includes a blank row, all records will be used in the Dfunction calculations because all records are "true" for a criteria row that contains no limiting criteria.

Date and Time Functions

The most common function in the Date and Time category is probably =TODAY(), which returns the value of today's date as maintained by your computer's battery. Many of the Date and Time functions help you convert date or time data from one format to another. For example, you might import data from an accounting system into Excel that contains dates in a different form than you want to view in Excel. By using the functions in Excel's Date and Time category, you can often convert date data to the form you desire. Figure 5-39 lists some of the less common DATE and TIME functions that you might use to convert data from one form to another.

Figure 5-39	DATE AND TIME FUNCTIONS
FUNCTION(ARGUMENTS)	**DESCRIPTION**
DATE(*year,month,day*)	Given a year, month, and day, returns the date as a single value
MONTH(*date*)	Given a date, returns the month of the year as an integer, ranging from 1 (January) to 12 (December)
WEEKDAY(*date*)	Given a date, returns the day of the week as an integer ranging from 1 (Sunday) to 7 (Saturday)
WEEKNUM(*date*)	Given a date, returns a number identifying which week of the year (1 to 52) the week falls within the year

GVR maintains a public park called Rock Road, and it relies on several volunteers to help with various landscaping and maintenance activities. When a volunteer comes to help at Rock Road, an employee records the volunteer's name, the date and the time of arrival, and the time of departure. Lynn has a copy of the workbook that GVR has used to track volunteer hours in the past with some sample data. She needs your help to analyze the dates and times better. For example, to better manage the volunteer time, Lynn would like to know the day of the week and the week of the year that the volunteer activity occurred.

To calculate the day of the week and the week of the year:

1. Open the **RockRoad-5** workbook located in the Tutorial.05\Tutorial folder on your Data Disk. In this workbook, the date has been entered in three separate parts: the month portion in column B, the day portion in column C, and the year portion in column D. In order to make date calculations easier, you need to calculate the date as a single value, stored in a single cell. You can use the DATE function for this, but first you'll enter a label to identify the date column.

2. Click cell **G4**, type **Date** for a column label, and then press the **Enter** key.

   You'll use the DATE function in cell G5 to return the date as a single value based on its parts stored in columns B, C, and D.

3. In cell G5, type **=DATE(D5,B5,C5)** and then click the **Enter** button ☑ on the Formula bar. See Figure 5-40. Now that the date is stored as a single entity in column G, you can use other types of date functions to return other types of information. For example, Lynn also wants to know the day of the week and the week of the year for each volunteer date.

Figure 5-40   **USING THE DATE FUNCTION**

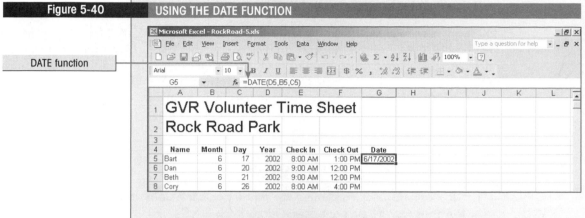

DATE function

4. Enter the label **Day of Week** in cell H4 and the label **Week of Year** in cell I4, and then widen both columns to clearly display the labels.

    With the labels in place, you're ready to use the WEEKDAY and WEEKNUM functions to return the information you need.

5. Click cell **H5**, type **=WEEKDAY(G5)**, and then click ☑. The value 2 appears in cell H5, which means that this volunteer activity occurred on Monday. By default, the WEEKDAY function begins the week at Sunday, and thus Sunday is assigned the number 1, Monday the number 2, and so forth. But if you want to start the week assigning Monday to the number 1, the WEEKDAY function supports that modification with an optional argument. Next, you'll calculate the week number (WEEKNUM function) from 1 to 52 (and sometimes 53) that the week falls within the year.

6. Click cell **I5**, type **=WEEKNUM(G5)**, and then click ☑. See Figure 5-41.

    TROUBLE? If you get a #NAME? error in cell I5, then Excel doesn't recognize the WEEKNUM function. You must install the Analysis ToolPak add-in for Excel to recognize the WEEKNUM function. To install the Analysis ToolPak add-in, click Tools on the menu bar, click Add-Ins, click the Analysis ToolPak check box, and then click the OK button. Click Yes if prompted to install it now. Repeat Step 6.

Figure 5-41   **USING THE WEEKDAY AND WEEKNUM FUNCTIONS**

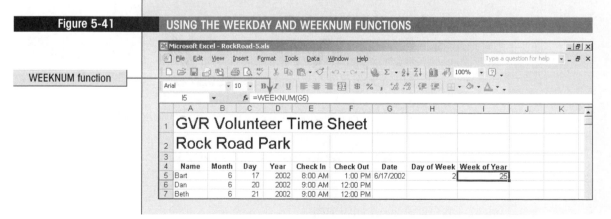

WEEKNUM function

Formatting Date and Time Data

There is a wide range of preexisting formats, such as 5/1/2004, 01-May-04, and Monday, October 4, 2004, that you can apply to date data within Excel. If you want to format date information in a format that doesn't already exist, you can use the Custom Format category in the Format Cells dialog box to customize the format you want for a specific date or time.

To make the data easier to read, Lynn wants you to format the value in cell H2 to display the name of the day of the week, Monday, instead of an integer 2, which represents the day of the week.

To format the day of the week:

1. Click cell **H5**, click **Format** on the menu bar, click **Cells**, and then click the **Number** tab (if it isn't already selected).

2. Click **Date** in the Category list, and then scroll through the preexisting date formats in the Type list. Because none of the existing formats match the way you want this date information to display, as the day of the week, you'll have to use a Custom format.

3. Click **Custom** and then enter the code for the day of the week **dddd** in the Type text box as shown in Figure 5-42.

| Figure 5-42 | CREATING A CUSTOM DATE FORMAT |

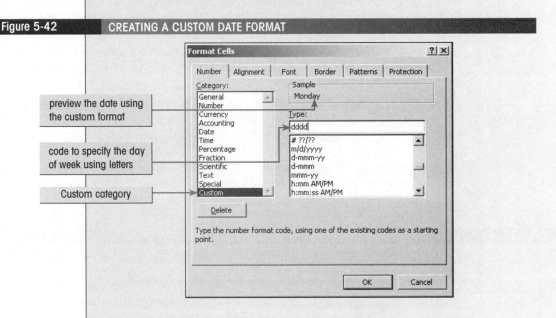

preview the date using the custom format

code to specify the day of week using letters

Custom category

4. Click the **OK** button in the Format Cells dialog box. "Monday" now appears in cell H5 instead of 2.

5. Use the fill handle to copy the formulas in cells **G5:I5** through the range **G6:I23**.

Using Times in Calculations

Excel stores dates and times as values. By default, January 1, 1900, is the number 1, January 2, 1900, is the number 2, and so forth. Times are stored as portions of a day. In other words, 1:00 AM is stored as 1/24th of a day, 0.04167. Because dates and times are really just numbers, formatted to look like date information, you can use them within calculations. For example, you can subtract one time from another to find the length of time between the entries.

Lynn is pleased with the new information you've been able to provide about the dates on the Rock Road volunteer time sheet, but she has one more request. She wants to know the number of hours of each volunteer activity. Because you have both the Check In time and the Check Out time recorded in the workbook, you can use a formula to calculate the difference between the two times.

To calculate the number of hours between two times:

1. Right-click the **column heading** for column **G**, click **Insert** on the shortcut menu, click cell **G4**, type **Hours**, and then press the **Enter** key.

2. In cell G5, type **=F5-E5** and then press the **Enter** key. The result, 5:00 AM, is shown in cell G5. Because you just need the number of hours and minutes, and do not need to display AM or PM after the entry, you need to format the value in cell G5 using a different time format.

3. Click cell **G5**, click **Format** on the menu bar, click **Cells**, click **Time** (if it is not already selected) in the Category list, click **13:30** in the Type box, and then click the **OK** button.

4. Using the fill handle, copy the formula from cell **G5** through the range **G6:G23**, and then press **Ctrl + Home** to return to cell A1. See Figure 5-43.

Figure 5-43   **THE COMPLETED TIME SHEET**

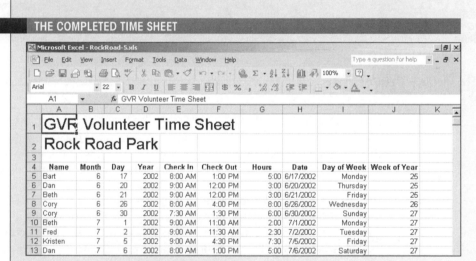

5. Save the workbook, print the worksheet in landscape orientation with your name in the left section of the header, and then close the RockRoad-5 workbook.

Sometimes when you do a calculation involving times, such as finding the elapsed time between two time entries (for example, 11:30 AM minus 8:00 AM), the resulting value appears as a decimal value, such as 0.15. In this case, the 0.15 represents the three-and-a-half-hour difference between 8:00 AM and 11:30 AM as a portion of a 24-hour day. In other words, 0.15 times 24 hours equals three and a half hours. To display this number in a mm:ss format (3:30), apply a Time format.

Remember that all dates and times are stored as numbers so that Excel can use them in calculations. Therefore, by applying various number, date, time, and custom formats to date and time values, you can control what portion of the date or time appears on the screen, as well as in what format.

Session 5.2 QUICK CHECK

1. According to Figure 5-23, which two depreciation methods would you most likely choose if your company were currently very profitable and therefore wanted to claim as much depreciation expense in the early years of the asset as possible?

2. What is the total depreciation expense that you can claim on an asset?

3. To determine whether receiving $1000 today or five annual payments of $225 is worth more to you, you would use which financial function to help you make the calculation?

4. What three arguments are used in all Dfunctions?

5. Compare "and" and "or" criteria when they are used in the Criteria range of a Dfunction.

6. If a date or time value appears as a number, for example 36,000 or 0.53 in the work-book, what does that indicate, and how would you make the value appear as a date (for example, 5/1/2004) or time (for example, 3:30 AM)?

SESSION 5.3

In this session, you will learn about advanced functions in the Statistical, Math and Trigonometry, Engineering, Lookup and Reference, Information, and Text categories.

Statistical Functions

Statistics is an area of mathematics that deals with the collection, organization, and analysis of collections of numbers that measure something. The something that you measure can be as diverse as a population study for a particular state, a measurement of high and low tem-peratures for a particular area, or the average speed of the Indy 500 champion over the life of the race. The purposes for collecting the data are just as diverse. Often, data is collected and analyzed to help businesses make better decisions and predictions, but providing better information for national security, extending the body of scientific knowledge, and analyzing numbers for recreational purposes are other good reasons to become a statistician.

With almost 80 different built-in functions, the Statistical category is the single largest cate-gory of built-in functions in Excel. Some of the statistical functions such as AVERAGE, COUNT, MAX, and MIN are quite common, but others such as BETADIST (returns the cumulative beta probability density function), FISHER (returns the Fisher transformation), and HYPGEOMDIST (returns the hypergeometric distribution) would be used in only the most advanced scientific or statistical analyses. You decide to explore the Statistical function category to gain an appreciation for the vast number of functions Excel provides within this area.

To explore the Statistical function category:

1. Open a new, blank workbook, click the **list arrow** for the AutoSum button Σ ▾ on the Standard toolbar, and then click **More Functions**.

   EXCEL 2000: Click the **Paste Function** button f_x on the Standard toolbar.

2. Click the **Or select a category** list arrow, and then click **Statistical**. The Statistical functions appear in alphabetical order in the Select a function list.

EXCEL 2000: Click **Statistical** in the Function category list, and then click **AVEDEV** in the Function name list (if it is not already selected).

3. Press the ↓ key several times to move through the list of Statistical functions. A short description of each function is provided at the bottom of the Insert Function dialog box.

4. Continue pressing the ↓ key enough times until you locate and select the **STDEV** (standard deviation) function. Standard deviation is a common statistical measurement of a list of values. You will use Help to get more information on this function.

5. Click the **Help on this function** link in the lower-left corner of the Insert Function dialog box, click the **Hide** button 🔲 on the navigation bar in the Microsoft Excel Help window if the left pane is showing, and then maximize the window. Figure 5-44 shows the Help page that describes the STDEV function.

EXCEL 2000: Click the **Help** button ❓ in the lower-left corner of the Paste Function dialog box, and then search for help on the STDEV function.

Figure 5-44 | HELP ON THE STDEV FUNCTION

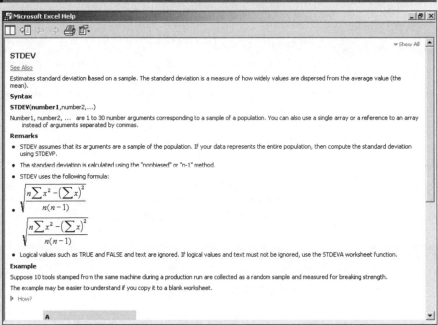

6. Read the Help page, and if you want a hard copy, print it.

7. Close the Microsoft Excel Help window, and continue exploring the other Statistical functions.

8. When finished exploring the Statistical functions, click the **Cancel** button, and then close the workbook without saving it.

In this tutorial you'll focus on other common statistical functions identified in Figure 5-45.

Figure 5-45	STATISTICAL FUNCTIONS

FUNCTION	DESCRIPTION
AVERAGE	Returns the average of the values, also called the **mean**.
MEDIAN	Returns the **median** or middle value, when the values are arranged in numerical order.
MODE	Returns the **mode**, the value that occurs most frequently.
STDEV	Returns the **standard deviation** of the values, the average distance of the values from their cumulative mean (average). If the standard deviation is small, the measurement is tightly clustered around the mean. If it is large, the values are widely scattered.
VAR	Returns the **variance** of the values, the standard deviation squared.

Over the past season, the GVR baseball league has collected pitching statistics for the pitchers in their adult competitive league. The league has asked if you can help it analyze the data. You'll apply eight of the most commonly applied statistical measures to the data that has been provided, the count, maximum, minimum, mean (average), median, mode, standard deviation, and variance for each category of data that has been collected.

To calculate statistical values for the pitching data:

1. Open the **Pitching-5** workbook located in the Tutorial.05\Tutorial folder of your Data Disk, and then scroll through the data. The player, team, number of wins, losses, earned run average **(ERA)** per game, games pitched, innings pitched, total hits, total runs, total number of times the pitcher hit the batter with a pitch, total number of times the pitcher walked the batter, and total number of times the pitcher struck out the batter are recorded for each player in columns A through M.

2. Scroll through the data, and then enter the labels in cells **A29:A36** as shown in Figure 5-46. These labels will identify the statistical formulas you'll enter for each column of statistics in cells C29:M36.

Figure 5-46	ENTERING LABELS TO IDENTIFY THE STATISTICAL VALUES

	A	B	C	D	E	F	G	H	I	J	K	L	M
1	GVR Baseball Pitching Data												
2													
3	Player	Team	Wins	Losses	ERA	Games	Innings Pitched	Hits	Runs	Home Runs	Hit by Pitch	Base on Balls	Strike-outs
25	Sturtze	Bedford	8	11	4.51	35	169.2	172	87	20	6	69	100
26	Helling	Bedford	10	9	5.17	29	182.2	220	113	32	3	56	132
27	Carpenter	Bedford	9	11	4.11	29	186.1	201	98	28	15	65	136
28													
29	Count												
30	Maximum												
31	Minimum												
32	Average												
33	Median												
34	Mode												
35	Standard Deviation												
36	Variance												
37													
38													

3. In cell C29, enter the formula **=COUNT(C4:C27)**. There are 24 pitchers in this group.

4. In cell C30, enter the formula **=MAX(C4:C27)**. The most number of wins is 19.

5. In cell C31, enter the formula **=MIN(C4:C27)**. The least number of wins is 8.

6. In cell C32, enter the formula **=AVERAGE(C4:C27)**. The average number of wins is 12.4.

7. In cell C33, enter the formula **=MEDIAN(C4:C27)**. The middle number of wins is 12.

8. In cell C34, enter the formula **=MODE(C4:C27)**. The most common number of wins is 10.

9. In cell C35, enter the formula **=STDEV(C4:C27)**. The standard deviation is 2.8 wins (the average number of wins each pitcher was away from the mean).

10. In cell C36, enter the formula **=VAR(C4:C27)**. The variance is 7.9 wins (the standard deviation squared). See Figure 5-47.

Figure 5-47 STATISTICAL CALCULATIONS FOR THE WINS COLUMN

	A	B	C	D	E	F	G	H	I	J	K	L	M
1	GVR Baseball Pitching Data												
2													
3	Player	Team	Wins	Losses	ERA	Games	Innings Pitched	Hits	Runs	Home Runs	Hit by Pitch	Base on Balls	Strike-outs
20	Mulder	P-L	17	7	3.48	29	196.1	185	79	15	3	40	134
21	Zito	P-L	12	8	3.70	30	182.1	158	84	14	13	63	173
22	Garcia	S-M	15	5	3.09	29	203.2	177	77	13	5	57	129
23	Sele	S-M	13	5	3.71	30	189.0	193	84	23	7	43	96
24	Moyer	S-M	16	5	3.48	28	178.1	163	73	23	9	36	97
25	Sturtze	Bedford	8	11	4.51	35	169.2	172	87	20	6	69	100
26	Helling	Bedford	10	9	5.17	29	182.2	220	113	32	3	56	132
27	Carpenter	Bedford	9	11	4.11	29	186.1	201	98	28	15	65	136
28													
29	Count		24										
30	Maximum		19										
31	Minimum		8										
32	Average		12.4										
33	Median		12										
34	Mode		10										
35	Standard Deviation		2.8										
36	Variance		7.9										
37													
38													

Stats

11. Select the range **C29:C36**, use the fill handle to copy the formulas through the range **D29:M36**, and then widen any columns that need to be expanded in order to be able to clearly see all the values in each column. The eight statistical calculations have been applied to each column of values.

12. Enter your name in the left section of the header, and then print the workbook in landscape orientation.

13. Save and close the Pitching-5 workbook.

Understanding a handful of statistical measurements can be of great value in understanding a series of data. And if you become a scientist, engineer, or conduct any type of research, statistical analysis will be a central part of your activities.

Math and Trigonometry Functions

The Math and Trigonometry category of functions deals with calculations in one of two categories: those that are not specific to any other category (the Math functions), and those that deal with trigonometry issues (the Trigonometry functions). Some of the common Math functions are shown in Figure 5-48. Note that these functions might be used for many different calculations within the world of finance, statistics, engineering, or for any other general business or personal purpose. Because they are not specific to any particular category of calculations, they are lumped together in the Math category.

Figure 5-48	MATH FUNCTIONS
FUNCTION	**DESCRIPTION**
ABS	Returns the **absolute value** of a number, the positive value of the number, regardless of its sign.
COUNTIF	Counts the number of nonblank cells within a range that meet the given criteria.
EXP	Returns **e**, the base of the natural system of logarithms that is approximately 2.71828, raised to the power of the given number.
FACT	Returns the **factorial** of the number, the product of the integers from 1 to the given number.
GCD	Returns the greatest common **divisor** for the given numbers, the value that can be divided evenly into each of them.
INT	Rounds a number down to the nearest **integer**, the nearest whole number.
LCM	Returns the least common **multiple** for the given numbers, the smallest value that may be divided by the given numbers with no remainder.
LOG10	Returns the base-10 logarithm of a number. **Logarithm** is the power to which a base number, such as 10, must be raised to produce a given number. For example, $10^3 = 1000$; therefore, $\log_{10} 1000 = 3$.
LN	Returns the natural logarithm (base e) of a number.
MOD	Returns the **remainder**, the number left over when one number is divided by another.
POWER	Returns the result of a number raised to a **power** (an exponent).
QUOTIENT	Returns the integer (whole number) portion of a division calculation.
RAND	Returns a random number between 0 and 1.
ROUND	Rounds a number to a specified number of digits.
SQRT	Returns the positive square root of a value. A **square root** of a value is the number that when multiplied by itself, produces that value. For example, the positive square root of 25 is 5.
SUM	Returns the sum total of the values.
SUMIF	Returns the sum total of the values selected by given criteria.

Trigonometry deals with math as it applies to angles within shapes such as circles and triangles. Common trigonometry terms include **sine** (in a right triangle, the ratio of the length of the side opposite an acute angle to the length of the hypotenuse), **cosine** (in a right triangle, the ratio of the length of the side adjacent to an acute angle to the length of the hypotenuse), and **tangent** (in a right triangle, the ratio of the length of the side opposite the acute angle to the length of the side adjacent to the acute angle). The **hypotenuse** of a right triangle is the long side of the triangle, the side opposite the right angle. Some of the common Trigonometry functions are shown in Figure 5-49.

Figure 5-49	TRIGONOMETRY FUNCTIONS
FUNCTION	**DESCRIPTION**
COS	Returns the **cosine** of an angle measured in radians
DEGREES	Converts radians to degrees
PI	Returns the value of **pi** (the ratio of the circumference of a circle to its diameter)
RADIANS	Converts degrees to radians
SIN	Returns the **sine** of an angle measured in radians
TAN	Returns the **tangent** of an angle measured in radians

GVR sponsors a summer Math Camp for students to explore additional math concepts. At the beginning and end of the camp, the students are given a test of 12 math and trigonometry questions in an effort to measure how much new material they have learned. The questions are all written as very short word problems. While the Math Camp teacher understands what math questions she wants to ask the students to evaluate their math skills, she doesn't know how to use Excel's Math and Trigonometry functions to check their answers. You'll help her apply the functions to the problems she has already entered in an Excel workbook to supply her with an answer key.

To create formulas with math and trigonometry functions:

1. Open the **MathCamp-5** workbook from the Tutorial.05\Tutorial folder of your Data Disk. The 12 questions that the Math Camp teacher wants to use for both the pre-test and the post-test are listed as word problems in column B of the workbook. She understands that Excel functions can be used to calculate the answers in column C but doesn't know how to use them.

2. In cell C4, enter the formula **=FACT(5)**. Five factorial is calculated as 5*4*3*2*1, which equals 120.

3. In cell C5, enter the formula **=GCD(100,88,60)**. The greatest common divisor, the value that can be divided evenly into each of these three values, is 4.

4. In cell C6, enter the formula **=EXP(5)**. "E" to the fifth power is 148.4132.

5. In cell C7, enter the formula **=LCM(2,5,12)**. The least common multiple for 2, 5, and 12 is 60.

6. In cell C8, enter the formula **=LN(25)**. The natural logarithm of 25 is 3.218876.

7. In cell C9, enter the formula **=LOG10(100)**. The base-10 logarithm of 100 is 2.

8. In cell C10, enter the formula **=MOD(25,4)**. The modulus of 25 divided by 4 is 1.

9. In cell C11, enter the formula **=QUOTIENT(25,4)**. The quotient of 25 divided by 4 is 6.

10. In cell C12, enter the formula **=SQRT(144)**. The square root of 144 is 12.

11. In cell C13, enter the formula **=PI()*4^2**. The area of a circle is calculated with the formula πr^2 with "r" as the length of the radius of the circle, half the distance of the diameter.

12. In cell C14, enter the formula **=RADIANS(90)**. The number of radians in a 90° angle is 1.570796.

13. In cell C15, enter the formula **=DEGREES(1.2)**. The number of degrees in 1.2 radians is 68.75494. See Figure 5-50.

Figure 5-50	MATH CAMP QUESTIONS AND ANSWERS

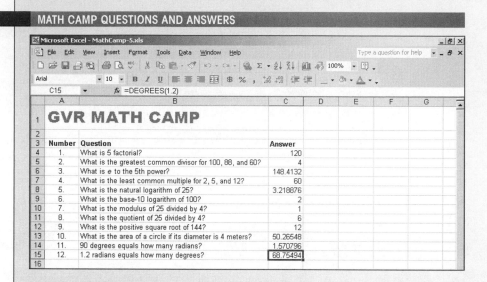

14. Save the workbook, enter your name in the left section of the header, press **Ctrl + ` (grave accent)** to display the formulas, and then print the worksheet in landscape orientation on one page.

15. Press **Ctrl + ` (grave accent)** to redisplay the values, and then close the MathCamp-5 workbook.

The Math Camp teacher is excited with the speed with which you were able to calculate the answers to her questions. By entering the formulas using the Math and Trigonometry functions, you were able to demonstrate the speed and power of these functions to her. You explain, though, that although these answers are correct for these questions, you would really like to get the chance to redesign this workbook so that the actual numbers used in the formulas are replaced by cell references. You explain that by using cell references in the formulas instead of the actual numbers, she would have a more flexible test because she could quickly and easily create a new test by entering new assumption values. If the formulas contained cell references instead of raw values, they would automatically update as she entered new assumption values. The Math Camp teacher is very intrigued by your suggestion. She sets up an appointment to meet with you next week to redesign this workbook so that she not only uses the power of advanced Math and Trigonometry functions, but also has a flexible workbook that can be used to create new tests.

Engineering Functions

The Engineering functions category contains many functions that work with **complex numbers**. Complex numbers include the **imaginary number**, *i*, which is defined as the square root of -1. Complex numbers are used in **quantum theory**, which helps to describe and predict how matter and energy interact, and therefore they have been useful for describing the behavior of natural phenomena such as electric circuits and electromagnetic waves. For example, the Engineering function of **IMDIV** returns the quotient of two complex numbers, **IMEXP** returns the exponential of a complex number, and **IMSQRT** returns the square root of a complex number. The Engineering functions that deal with complex numbers would be used by physicists or research engineers who work in the fields of electrical or nuclear energy.

Another subset of Engineering functions deals with conversions from one number system (binary, octal, decimal, or hexadecimal) to another. These functions are used by computer engineers as they convert **decimal numbers** (the common system that uses 10 digits, 0-9) to **octal systems** (a system that uses eight digits, 0-7), **hexadecimal systems** (a system that uses 16 digits, 0-9 and A-F), and **binary systems** (a system that uses two digits, 0-1). Computer engineers need these conversion systems because computers, at their most basic level, work in a binary system in that all information is identified using either a pulse or the absence of a pulse of electricity. These pulses and absences of electricity, better known as **bits**, can be represented as 1s and 0s in written form. Therefore, when a computer engineer looks at the activity within a computer circuit, he or she is examining a long string of pulses or absences of electricity, which can be symbolized by the binary system that uses only 1s and 0s. Obviously, reading a printout or screen that contains only 1s and 0s is a very tedious and difficult way to read computer instructions. Therefore, 1s and 0s are often converted into more compact numbering systems such as the octal or hexadecimal systems in order to make them easier to read. Figure 5-51 summarizes some of the functions within the Engineering category that convert numbers from one system to another.

Figure 5-51	ENGINEERING FUNCTIONS
FUNCTION	**DESCRIPTION**
BIN2DEC	Converts a binary number to the decimal number system
BIN2HEX	Converts a binary number to the hexadecimal number system
BIN2OCT	Converts a binary number to the octal number system
DEC2BIN	Converts a decimal number to the binary number system
DEC2HEX	Converts a decimal number to the hexadecimal number system
DEC2OCT	Converts a decimal number to the octal number system
HEX2BIN	Converts a hexadecimal number to the binary number system
HEX2DEC	Converts a hexadecimal number to the decimal number system
HEX2OCT	Converts a hexadecimal number to the octal number system
OCT2BIN	Converts an octal number to the binary number system
OCT2DEC	Converts an octal number to the decimal number system
OCT2HEX	Converts an octal number to the hexadecimal number system

One day of GVR Math Camp is spent learning about converting decimal numbers to other systems. Once again, the camp instructor has come to you to ask for your help in developing an answer key for the test she gives the participants to determine their comprehension of the subject. You can use Engineering functions to find these answers.

To use the Engineering functions to make number system conversions:

1. Open the **ComputerCamp-5** workbook from the Tutorial.05\Tutorial folder of your Data Disk. The Math Camp teacher wants the students to convert all of the decimal numbers in column A to their binary, octal, and hexadecimal equivalents in columns B, C, and D. While the students have to be able to do these conversions using only pencil and paper, you can use the Engineering functions to provide the teacher with an answer key.

2. In cell B5, enter the formula **=DEC2BIN(A5)**. The binary equivalent of the decimal number 1 is 1.

3. In cell C5, enter the formula **=DEC2OCT(A5)**. The octal equivalent of the decimal number 1 is 1.

4. In cell D5, enter the formula **=DEC2HEX(A5)**. The hexadecimal equivalent of the decimal number 1 is 1.

5. Select the range **B5:D5**, and then use the fill handle to copy those three formulas through the range **B6:D54**.

6. Press **Ctrl + Home** to quickly return to cell A1 and observe the values in columns B, C, and D as shown in Figure 5-52. Notice how the binary system uses only two digits, 0 and 1, to represent all values, the octal system uses eight digits, 0 through 7, and the hexadecimal system uses 16 digits, 0 through 9 and A through F, to represent numbers.

Figure 5-52   **NUMBER SYSTEM CONVERSIONS**

Decimal	Binary	Octal	Hexadecimal
1	1	1	1
2	10	2	2
3	11	3	3
4	100	4	4
5	101	5	5
6	110	6	6
7	111	7	7
8	1000	10	8
9	1001	11	9
10	1010	12	A
11	1011	13	B
12	1100	14	C
13	1101	15	D
14	1110	16	E
15	1111	17	F
16	10000	20	10

7. Enter your name in the left section of the header, scale the printout to fit on one page, and print the worksheet.

8. Save and close the ComputerCamp-5 workbook.

Just as the position of a digit is significant in the decimal system, it is significant in each of the other systems. In the decimal system, the position of the value is determined by taking that value times 10 to a power. Figure 5-53 shows you how to manually convert number systems.

Figure 5-53	CONVERTING NUMBER SYSTEMS WITHOUT USING EXCEL FUNCTIONS		
DECIMAL TO DECIMAL	**BINARY TO DECIMAL**	**OCTAL TO DECIMAL**	**HEXADECIMAL TO DECIMAL**
634 in the decimal system is:	*1001 in the binary system is:*	*31 in the octal system is:*	*15 in the hexadecimal system is:*
6 times 10 to the 2nd power = 600 *plus* 3 times 10 to the 1st power = 30 *plus* 4 times 10 to the 0 power = 4 (600 + 30 + 4 = 634)	1 times 2 to the 3rd power = 8 *plus* 0 times 2 to the 2nd power = 0 *plus* 0 times 2 to the 1st power = 0 *plus* 1 times 2 to the 0 power = 1 (8 + 0 + 0 + 1 = 9)	3 times 8 to the 1st power = 24 *plus* 1 times 8 to the 0 power = 1 (24 + 1 = 25)	1 times 16 to the 1st power = 16 *plus* 5 times 16 to the 0 power = 5 (16 + 5 = 21)

Once you understand how number systems are converted, it's much easier to use the power of Excel to do the calculations than to work them out by hand.

Lookup and Reference Functions

Lookup and Reference functions are divided into two major categories as indicated by the category name. **Lookup** functions such as **VLOOKUP** (vertical lookup) and **HLOOKUP** (horizontal lookup) help you retrieve information from a reference list of information. For example, you could create a lookup table that listed zip codes and their associated cities and states so that every time a particular zip code was entered in one area of the workbook, the associated city and state information was also automatically recorded, based on lookup formulas that retrieved the appropriate data for the given zip code. Whether you use a VLOOKUP or HLOOKUP formula depends on how the fields of the reference list are organized—that is, vertically in columns or horizontally in rows. Both VLOOKUP and HLOOKUP have three arguments in the following format:

VLOOKUP(LookupValue, LookupTable, Column(or Row)Number)

The *LookupValue* argument contains the **lookup value**. The lookup value is compared with the first column (for VLOOKUP) or row (for HLOOKUP) in the *LookupTable* argument. The **LookupTable** is a list of reference information with fields organized by columns (for VLOOKUP) or rows (for HLOOKUP). The *Column(or Row)Number* argument is the sequential number of the column (for VLOOKUP) or row (for HLOOKUP) that contains the field value that you want the function to return.

The **Reference** functions, such as ADDRESS, COLUMN, and ROW, return information about the cell reference. As you would suspect, the **ADDRESS** function returns a cell reference as a text value, the **COLUMN** function returns a column number for a specific cell reference, and the **ROW** function returns a row number for a specific cell reference. Although these functions are not often used in a workbook itself, they can be very helpful to a VBA programmer who needs to determine the specific cell address, column, or row of a given value and then send that information to another part of the program.

When GVR registers participants for their baseball leagues, much of the information about their registration is based on a single table of reference information. For example, when someone is registered for the baseball league, as soon as they are assigned to a baseball team they immediately know how much their uniform will cost, what their team colors will be, and what their coach's name is based on the team assignment. Lynn has asked you to examine the registration workbook that is used to enroll new baseball league participants to see if the entries for the uniform cost, colors, and coach can be automated based on the team assignment entry. You'll use a Lookup function to tackle this problem.

To use a Lookup function to automate baseball registration:

1. Open the **BBRegistration-5** workbook from the Tutorial.05\Tutorial folder of your Data Disk. The Registration worksheet is where information about the new participants will be entered. After entering the person's first and last names in columns A and B and making their team assignment in column C, you will want the Lookup functions to automatically enter the uniform cost, colors, and coach information in columns D, E, and F.

2. Switch to the **TeamInfo** worksheet. The TeamInfo worksheet contains the standard information for each team. This will be used for lookup purposes. Because the fields of the table are in vertical columns, you'll use the VLOOKUP function. In order to use a table for lookup purposes, it must be sorted in ascending order based on the values in the first column (the lookup values).

3. Click in any cell in the range **A3:A11**, and then click the **Sort Ascending** button on the Standard toolbar.

4. Switch to the **Registration** worksheet, and then enter sample data for the first new registrant, using *your first name* in cell **A4**, *your last name* in cell **B4**, and **Dexfield** as the team name in cell **C4**.

   You'll enter VLOOKUP formulas in cells D4, E4, and F4 to use the team name lookup entry in cell C4 to return the appropriate value for that team name from the table stored in the TeamInfo worksheet.

5. In cell **D4**, enter the formula **=VLOOKUP($C4,TeamInfo!$A$4:$D$11,2)**. In this formula, the value in $C4 (the team name) is used as the lookup value. The lookup table is found on the TeamInfo worksheet in the range $A$4:$D$11. Notice that the field names of the lookup table are not included in the lookup table argument. The column that contains the value to be returned by the function is column 2, which contains cost information. Because the cost of the Dexfield uniform is $30.50 as documented by the second column of the lookup table, 30.50 is the value returned by the function. Because you want to copy this formula throughout many rows in the Registration worksheet, entering the lookup value (which doesn't move from column C) and lookup table range with appropriate absolute values will allow you to copy the formula successfully.

6. Use the fill handle to copy the formula from cell **D4** through cells **E4:F4**.

7. In cell E4, edit the column number argument in the formula to **=VLOOKUP($C4,TeamInfo!$A$4:$D$11,3)**.

8. In cell F4, edit the column number argument in the formula to **=VLOOKUP($C4,TeamInfo!$A$4:$D$11,4)**, and then widen any columns as necessary to clearly view all data as shown in Figure 5-54.

   TROUBLE? If the lookup values on your screen differ from those in the figure, make sure that you did not skip Step 3. The lookup values in the lookup table (the first column of the lookup table) should be sorted in ascending order.

| Figure 5-54 | ENTERING VLOOKUP FUNCTIONS |

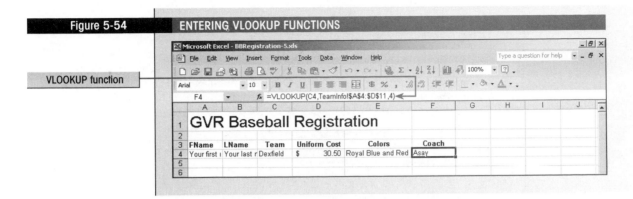

The VLOOKUP and HLOOKUP functions work well when you have a table of reference information that provides values for several records based on a lookup value. Because the values in column C, the team names, represent a fixed list of values, Lynn wants to know if there is a quick and easy way to look up the team values too.

Creating a List of Valid Cell Entries

Although the entries in the Uniform Cost, Colors, and Coach fields are best supplied from a single lookup table, the team name itself cannot be looked up because it serves as the lookup field. However, you can build a drop-down list of values for any field. By providing a list of valid cell entries for the Team field, you can improve data entry productivity and accuracy.

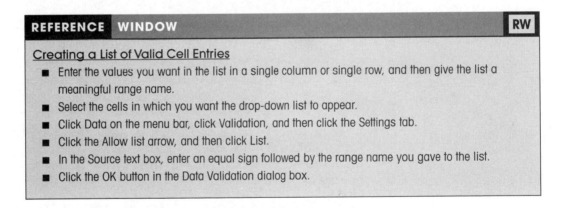

Although the VLOOKUP functions are working well, you also want to provide a list of team names from which an employee can choose. Providing a list of team names will eliminate the need to manually look up a name and the possibility of misspelling a name. You'll create a drop-down list of team names.

To create a list of valid entries for the Team field:

1. Switch to the **TeamInfo** worksheet, select the team names in the range **A4:A11**, click the **Name Box**, type **Teams** as the range name, and then press the **Enter** key.

2. Switch to the **Registration** worksheet, and then click **column heading** for column **C** to select the entire column. You'll apply data validation rules to every cell in column C so that the list will be available to every row, no matter how many baseball players you enroll.

3. Click **Data** on the menu bar, click **Validation**, and then click the **Settings** tab (if it is not already selected).

4. Click the **Allow** list arrow, and then click **List**.

5. Click in the **Source** box, and then type **=Teams** (the range name that contains the actual team names) as shown in Figure 5-55.

Figure 5-55	DATA VALIDATION DIALOG BOX

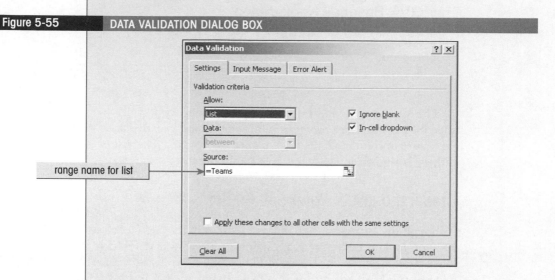

range name for list

6. Click the **OK** button, and then click cell **C4**. A drop-down arrow appears to the right of the cell.

With the list of team names now defined and available, you can test the list in conjunction with your VLOOKUP formulas.

To test the valid list of entries for the Team field:

1. Click the **Team** list arrow, and then click **Anita**. The Uniform Cost, Colors, and Coach values in range D4:F4 should have also automatically changed, based on the new choice for the lookup value in cell C4. Now test the use of the drop-down list in another row.

2. In cell A5, type **Lynn**, press the → key, type **Tse** in cell B5, and then press the → key. When cell C5 becomes the active cell, the drop-down list arrow appears.

3. Click the **Team** list arrow, and then click **Bedford**. The values in cells D5, E5, and F5 are not automatically filled in because they do not contain the lookup formulas yet.

4. Copy the formulas in range **D4:F4** to the range **D5:F24** to accommodate 20 registrations, widen the columns as necessary to view all of the data, and then click cell **A1**. See Figure 5-56. While the Uniform Cost, Colors, and Coach fields for the second registrant in row 5 are now automatically entered, the rows that contain VLOOKUP formulas but do not contain a vlookup value display #N/A error values. The #N/A error value is displayed when a formula cannot compute a value because a required argument is missing.

Figure 5-56	#N/A ERRORS INDICATE LOOKUP VALUES ARE MISSING

	FName	LName	Team	Uniform Cost	Colors	Coach
4	Your first name	Your last name	Anita	$ 33.50	Purple and White	Lahey
5	Lynn	Tse	Bedford	$ 28.75	Red and Yellow	Queck
6				#N/A	#N/A	#N/A
7				#N/A	#N/A	#N/A
8				#N/A	#N/A	#N/A
9				#N/A	#N/A	#N/A
10				#N/A	#N/A	#N/A
11				#N/A	#N/A	#N/A
12				#N/A	#N/A	#N/A
13				#N/A	#N/A	#N/A

5. Save the workbook.

Lynn sees a lot of applications for drop-down lists and Lookup functions. Anytime a workbook has a limited set of available entries for a particular cell, a drop-down list of valid entries can be created. Anytime a cell entry can be supplied from a lookup table of values, the Lookup functions should be used. Both of those features will make the workbook faster and easier to use, as well as more accurate.

Although the drop-down list is now working correctly for column C, and the VLOOKUP formulas are in place to handle the first 20 registrants, you are still unhappy with the visual presentation of the workbook. The #N/A error values make the workbook messy and give the appearance that something is wrong with the workbook. In reality, there is nothing wrong with the workbook, but any formula that doesn't have all the values it needs for each argument will display an #N/A error value. Therefore, the #N/A error values will automatically display for unfilled rows. You would like to find a way to keep the VLOOKUP formulas in place, but suppress the #N/A error values for rows that do not yet contain lookup value entries. The Information category of functions can help you detect error values in a cell.

Information **Functions**

The **Information** category of functions returns information about the contents of the cell itself. You can use an Information function in a formula to determine whether a certain condition about a cell is true. VBA programmers use information functions to determine formatting or content information about a cell or information that is used by another part of the program. Figure 5-57 identifies several Information functions.

Figure 5-57   **INFORMATION FUNCTIONS**

FUNCTION	DESCRIPTION
CELL	Returns information about the formatting, location, or contents of a cell
COUNTBLANK	Counts the number of blank cells within a range
INFO	Returns information about the current operating environment
ISBLANK	Returns TRUE if the value is blank
ISERR	Returns TRUE if the value is any error value except #N/A
ISERROR	Returns TRUE if the value is any error value
ISNA	Returns TRUE if the value is the #N/A error value
ISNUMBER	Returns TRUE if the value is a number
ISTEXT	Returns TRUE if the value is text
NA	Returns the error value #N/A
TYPE	Returns a number indicating the data type of a value

Rarely, though, do you want the worksheet cell itself to display TRUE or FALSE, which are the two possible results for many of the Information functions. Therefore, Information functions are commonly used in conjunction with the IF function (a member of the Logical category of functions) so that if the condition tested by the Information function is true, one course of action is taken, and if not, another course of action is taken.

Lynn likes the drop-down list and lookup features of the BBRegistration workbook but wonders if there is a way to suppress the #N/A error messages for those rows that contain formulas but are not yet used for registrations. You'll use the ISNA function to determine whether the result of the formulas in columns D, E, and F is #N/A. You'll surround the ISNA function with an IF function so that one course of action can be taken if the ISNA function returns true, and another if the ISNA function returns false. In effect, you want to display nothing if the result of the formula is #N/A, but otherwise, you want to display the actual result of the VLOOKUP formula.

To suppress the #N/A error values:

1. Copy the labels in the range **D3:F3** to the range **G3:I3**, and then widen the columns to display the labels clearly. You'll use columns G, H, and I to test the values in columns D, E, and F with the IF and ISNA functions.

2. Click cell **G4** and enter the formula **=IF(ISNA(D4),"",D4)**. This formula tests whether or not the value in cell D4 contains an #N/A error value, and if true, returns "" (nothing) to the cell. If cell D4 does not contain an #N/A error value, then the value of D4 itself is returned. Because D4 contains the result of a calculation and not an #N/A error value, the ISNA portion of this function is false, and the false argument of the IF function, D4, is returned.

3. Use the fill handle to copy the formula in cell **G4** to cells **H4:I4**, and then with the range G4:I4 still selected, copy the formula through the range **G5:I24**. Because rows 6 through 24 contain #N/A error values, the formulas in the range G6:I24 should return the TRUE part of the function, "", which in turn makes each cell appear as a blank cell.

4. Select the **column headings** for columns **D** through **F**, click the **Format Painter** button on the Standard toolbar, and then drag through the **column headings** for columns **G** through **I**. Now that columns G through I contain the information you want displayed on this workbook and are formatted the same as columns D through F, you can hide the extra D through F columns.

5. Select the **column headings** for columns **D** through **F**, click **Format** on the menu bar, point to **Column**, and then click **Hide**. You will enter another registration to test the workbook.

6. Enter **Mark** in cell A6, **Rozek** in cell B6, select **Dexfield** from the drop-down list in cell C6, and then click cell **G6** to observe the formula in the Formula bar. See Figure 5-58. The formulas in columns G, H, and I display nothing if the VLOOKUP formulas return the #N/A error value, and the result of the VLOOKUP formula itself if not.

Figure 5-58	USING IF AND ISNA TO SUPPRESS #N/A ERROR VALUES

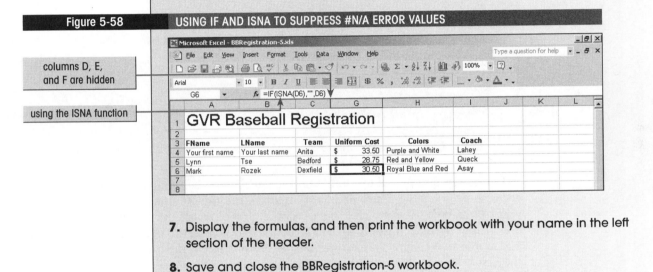

columns D, E, and F are hidden

using the ISNA function

7. Display the formulas, and then print the workbook with your name in the left section of the header.

8. Save and close the BBRegistration-5 workbook.

Using Information and Logical functions to identify certain cell conditions such as the presence of the #N/A value error helps you to further automate and clarify your workbook.

Text **Functions**

As the name implies, **Text functions** help you manipulate strings of text. Text functions are very useful for converting or scrubbing data that you have received from an external source. For example, you can use Text functions to find and replace text, to convert text from uppercase to lowercase and vice versa, or to return a number of characters on the left or right side from a cell entry. Figure 5-59 lists some Text functions you might use for a conversion effort.

Figure 5-59	TEXT FUNCTIONS

FUNCTION	DESCRIPTION
DOLLAR	Converts a number to text, using the $ (dollar) currency format
FIND	Finds one text value within a string (case sensitive)
FIXED	Formats a number as text with a fixed number of decimals
LEFT	Returns the number of leftmost characters of a value that you specify
LEN	Returns the number of characters in a text string
LOWER	Converts text to lowercase
PROPER	Capitalizes the first letter in each word of a text value
REPLACE	Replaces characters within text
RIGHT	Returns the number of rightmost characters of a value that you specify
SEARCH	Finds one text value within a string (not case sensitive)
TEXT	Formats a number and converts it to text
TRIM	Removes spaces from text
UPPER	Converts text to uppercase
VALUE	Converts a text argument to a number

GVR is sponsoring an upcoming golf tournament as a community charity event. In an effort to promote the event, Lynn has imported the top 50 money leaders for the current year from a Web page into an Excel workbook so she can use the data for promotional purposes. She has asked for your help to scrub the data so that the first and last names are separated into two columns for sorting. She also wants to convert the name data so that only the first character of the golfer's first and last names is capitalized.

To use Text functions to scrub name data:

1. Open the **Golfers-5** workbook located in the Tutorial.05\Tutorial folder on your Data Disk. This workbook shows the top 50 golfers in column A, the number of events in column B, and their total earnings in column C. You want to use Text functions to clean up the first and last name data in column A.

2. Click cell **D2**, type the formula **=PROPER(A2)**, and then press the **Enter** key. The PROPER Text function capitalizes the first letter in each word of a text value, so you can use it to convert names that have been entered in all capital or all lowercase letters. Tiger Woods's name is now listed as "Tiger Woods" instead of as "TIGER WOODS".

3. Copy the formula in cell **D2** through the range **D3:D51**, and then widen column **D** to accommodate the widest entry in that column.

4. Save the workbook.

Text functions are generally not difficult to work with, but the thought of applying an Excel function to a text string is sometimes foreign because some people are used to working with functions only as they relate to numeric calculations.

Concatenating Text to Numeric Data in a Formula

Another way that text can be used within a formula is to concatenate it to numeric data. For example, you might want to combine data from an Excel workbook with text to create a phrase or sentence that serves to summarize or clarify workbook data. As with all formulas, those that concatenate text and values start with an equal sign. The text portion of the formula is enclosed in quotation marks. A string of text is concatenated to a value or cell reference using the & (ampersand) character.

Lynn has asked that you provide an Executive Summary worksheet based on the data in the Players list. Specifically, she wants to know who the top golfer is, how many events he has played in, and how much he has earned to date. You decide to use formulas that contain both text and numeric data to make the summary read like a real sentence.

To create an Executive Summary worksheet:

1. Right-click the **Players** tab, click **Insert** on the shortcut menu, and then click the **OK** button in the Insert dialog box.

2. Double-click the new sheet tab, and then type **Executive Summary** for the new worksheet name.

3. Type **="The top golfer is "&** in cell A1, click the **Players** tab, click cell **D2**, and then press the **Enter** key. Cell A1 should display "The top golfer is Tiger Woods".

   TROUBLE? If there is not a space between the word "is" and "Tiger", edit the formula so that there is a space before the second quotation mark.

   To punctuate the sentence with a period, you have to concatenate the current entry to a period.

4. Click cell **A1** and then edit the formula in the Formula bar so that it reads **="The top golfer is "&Players!D2&"."** See Figure 5-60.

Figure 5-60	CONCATENATING TEXT IN A FORMULA

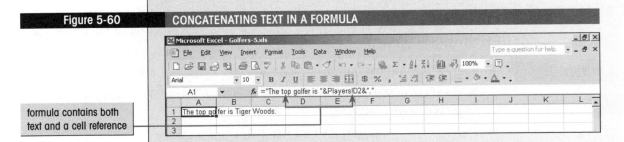

formula contains both text and a cell reference

5. Click cell **A2** and then enter the formula **=Players!D2&" has earned "&Players!C2&" to date."** Cell A2 should read "Tiger Woods has earned 5568777 to date". Unfortunately, even if you formatted the dollar values in column C of the Players worksheet to display a dollar sign and commas to make the value more readable, those formats are not preserved when used in a formula that concatenates the value with text. But you can use the Text function DOLLAR to convert the number to text using the currency format.

6. Edit the formula in cell **A2** to read **=Players!D2&" has earned "&DOLLAR(Players!C2,0)&" to date."** Cell A2 should now read "Tiger Woods has earned $5,568,777 to date".

7. Click cell **A3**, and then enter the formula **=Players!D2&" has played in "&Players!B2&" tournaments to date."** See Figure 5-61.

Figure 5-61	THE RESULT OF THREE FORMULAS THAT CONCATENATE TEXT WITH NUMBERS

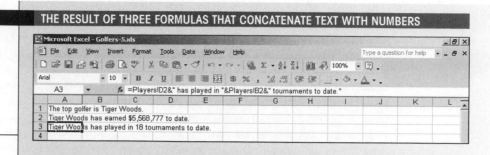

8. Switch to the **Players** worksheet, enter *your name* in cell A2.

9. Switch to the **Executive Summary** worksheet, and print the worksheet. Then, display the formulas, widen column A to show the entire formula, and print the worksheet again.

10. Save and close the Golfers-5 workbook, and then exit Excel.

By building formulas that concatenate text and values together, you can make sure that any change made to the raw data in your workbook is updated in all other locations where that data is referenced.

Excel has hundreds of built-in functions organized within several function categories such as Database, Date and Time, Engineering, Financial, Information, Logical, Lookup and Reference, Math and Trigonometry, Statistical, and Text. Although some of the functions are specific to a narrow financial or statistical need, others are used by a wide variety of business professionals in many industries.

Session 5.3 QUICK CHECK

1. If you created a formula using the STDEV function on a list of numbers whose smallest value was 25 and largest value was 100, and the result of the formula was 30, what could you conclude about that list of numbers?

2. The PI function has how many arguments?

3. Name three professions that would be most likely to use the functions in the Engineering category.

4. Compare and contrast the VLOOKUP function with the data validation criteria feature.

5. Why is the ISNA function often used with the IF function?

6. What would be the formula to concatenate the text "Created by" and your name on the Summary worksheet if your name were stored in cell A1 of the Assumptions worksheet in the same workbook?

REVIEW ASSIGNMENTS

Lynn Tse and other executives at GVR have noticed your excellent Excel skills and have asked you to form and lead an Excel users group within the company. At the first meeting, they want you to present a workbook with an example of a function in each of the major categories as a way of exposing GVR employees to the additional possibilities that built-in Excel functions provide. You have created the following exercise to allow GVR employees to experience using a function from each of the major categories.

To complete this task:

1. Start Excel and open the **UsersGroup-5** workbook located in the Tutorial.05\Review folder on your Data Disk. The workbook contains business problems that can be more easily solved using one or more built-in Excel functions.

2. Before you can demonstrate the VLOOKUP formula, you have to set up a lookup table. In the range A1:A3 of the InsuranceCoPay sheet, enter the labels "BCBS", "Cigna", and "Delta". Give the range A1:A3 the range name "Insurance". These values will be used both in the lookup table and in a list of valid entries. In cells B1, B2, and B3 enter the values 10, 20, and 25, respectively. Name the range A1:B3 "LookupTable".

3. In range C1:E1 of the InsuranceCoPay sheet, enter the labels "Name", "Insurance", and "Copayment". Select column D and set the Data Validation criteria for the range to allow only those values from the Insurance list.

4. In cell E2, enter a formula that looks up the copayment value in column B based on the insurance value choice in column D. Copy the formula in cell E2 through the range E3:E20.

5. Click cell D2, and select BCBS from the list. Based on the VLOOKUP formula in cell E2, the copayment value should be 10. Select Cigna from the list for cell D3 and Delta for cell D4. The copayments in cells E3 and E4 should be 20 and 25, respectively. If your list and VLOOKUP formulas in columns D and E are working correctly, hide columns A and B.

6. In cell F1, enter the label "Copayment", and in cell F2, enter a formula using the IF and ISNA functions so that nothing appears in the cell if ISNA is TRUE, and the result of the VLOOKUP function in cell E2 appears in the cell if ISNA is FALSE.

7. Copy the formula in cell F2 through the range F3:F20, and then hide column E.

8. In cells C7 and below, make a list of the function names and other advanced Excel features that are represented by the InsuranceCoPay worksheet.

9. Display the formulas on the worksheet, and then print it with your name in the left section of the header.

10. Switch to the Savings worksheet and enter your name in cell A1. Use a function to enter today's date in cell A2, and format it with a custom mmm-dd-yyyy format. In cells A4, A5, and A6, enter the labels "Goal", "Interest Rate", and "Term", respectively.

11. In this workbook, you're going to determine how much you need to save each month in order to purchase a vehicle that costs approximately $10,000 two years from now. In other words, you want $10,000 to be the future value of your savings. Assume that you earn a 5% annual interest rate on the monthly amount that you save. Enter "5%" in cell B5 and "24" in cell B6.

12. In cell A8, enter the label "Monthly Savings" and widen column A to clearly display the entire label. Your goal is to determine what monthly savings value you need to reach the future value of $10,000. Although there is no "reverse" future value function that helps you determine what the value of the monthly payment argument should be, you can create a formula using the FV function and then use the Goal Seek feature to determine the value for an individual argument.

13. In cell B4, enter the formula *=FV(B5/12,B6,-B8)*. Test the formula by entering various monthly savings values in cell B8, such as 100, 200, and 500, and widen column B as necessary to see the resulting future value in cell B4. You could keep guessing as to the amount you'd need to save on a monthly basis to have $10,000 in two years, or you could goal seek to find the actual value.

Explore

14. To use the Goal Seek feature to determine the monthly value that will result in a $10,000 future value, click cell B4, click Tools on the menu bar, and then click Goal Seek. Set the goal to 10,000 by changing the monthly savings value. Accept the answer provided by the Goal Seek tool.

15. Format the value in cell B8 with a Currency Style format.

16. In cells A10 and below, make a list of the function names and categories and other advanced Excel features that are represented by the Savings worksheet.

17. Switch to the Conversions worksheet and enter the labels "Temp, F" and "Temp, C" in cells A1 and B1, respectively.

18. Enter "Temp, C" and "Temp, F" in cells D1 and E1, respectively. This worksheet will demonstrate how the CONVERT function within the Engineering category can convert one temperature scale to another.

19. In cell A2, enter "-10" and enter "-9" in cell A3. Fill that pattern through cells A4:A112. Copy the values from A2:A112 to D2:D112.

20. In cell B2, enter the appropriate formula that uses the CONVERT function to convert the Fahrenheit temperatures in column A to Celsius temperatures. Copy the formula from cell B2 through the range B3:B112.

21. In cell E2, enter the appropriate formula that uses the CONVERT function to convert the Celsius temperatures in column D to Fahrenheit temperatures. Copy the formula from cell E2 through the range E3:E112.

22. Apply the Comma Style format to both columns B and E, display the formulas on the worksheet, and print the first page with your name in the left section of the header.

23. Switch to the MathCamp worksheet and use Math functions to solve the 12 problems listed in cells B2:B13. Display the formulas on the workbook, and then print the MathCamp worksheet with your name in the left section of the header.

24. Switch to the TestScores worksheet, and enter the appropriate formula using Statistical functions in the range B17:D21 for each of the tests in columns B, C, and D according to the function names identified in range A17:A21.

25. Based on the statistics provided, what conclusions can you make about the difficulty of each test? Write your answer in cell A23, and then print the TestScores worksheet with your name in the left section of the header.

26. Save and close the UsersGroup-5 workbook, and exit Excel.

CASE PROBLEMS

Case 1. Time Value of Money: 30- vs.15-Year Mortgage Each year, thousands of people finance or refinance a home mortgage. Although most people realize that the interest paid over 30 years is much greater than that paid over a 15-year mortgage, it's much easier to see the differences between mortgage options when the options are laid out side by side. In this case you'll build a workbook from scratch that helps you evaluate how the monthly loan payment, term of the loan, and time value of money affect the overall cost of home ownership.

To complete this task:

1. Start Excel and open a new, blank workbook. Rename the first worksheet "15" (to represent calculations for a 15-year mortgage), rename the second worksheet "30" (to represent calculations for a 30-year mortgage), and rename the third worksheet "Summary". Save the workbook as **Mortgage-5** in the Tutorial.05\Cases folder on your Data Disk.

2. Enter the labels, values, and first formula for the 15-year mortgage on the 15 worksheet as shown in Figure 5-62. Format the values as shown in the figure.

Figure 5-62

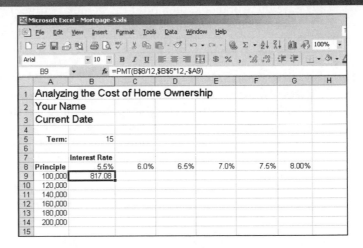

3. Copy the formula in cell B9 through the range B9:G14. Copy all of the entries on the 15 worksheet to the 30 worksheet, and then change the value in cell B5 of the 30 worksheet to 30. Widen the columns as needed.

4. On the 15 worksheet, name range B8:G8 "InterestRates".

Explore

5. Enter the labels, values, and formulas for the Summary worksheet as shown in Figure 5-63. On this worksheet, you're calculating the present value of a particular payment. You don't have to use 6% in cell B5 and 100,000 in cell B6 as shown in Figure 5-63, but if you choose different values, be sure to modify the formulas in cells B9:C10 so that the third argument, the monthly payment, represents the correct value for that interest rate and principal amount from the 15 and 30 worksheets. You'll know that you calculated the correct present value when the result of the present value formula in cells B9 and C9 equals the amount of the loan entered in cell B6.

Figure 5-63

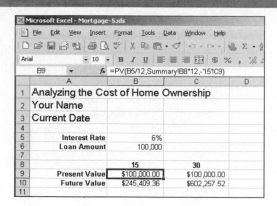

6. The formulas in cells B10 and C10 use the same arguments as those in B9:C9, except the function used is the FV function instead of the PV function. This shows you how much money you will pay, over time, based on the loan and interest rate specified. In this case, $100,000 now is worth $245,409.36 in 15 years and $602,257.52 in 30 years. The difference between the $100,000 loan and the future value is the amount you pay in interest expense.

7. Save the workbook, then print the Summary page. Display the formulas for the Summary page, and print it again.

8. Save and close the workbook, and then exit Excel.

Case 2. Improving a Business Plan You work for a CPA firm that consults with small businesses and helps them create business plans used in communication with investors, lenders, and other business partners. One of the key business plan tools you help these businesses to develop is an up-to-date income statement. Projecting the income statement into the future based on growth assumption values is one of the most common uses for an Excel workbook. Although your firm has created several income statement projects in Excel, you have noticed that if some of the formulas in the business plan were entered with concatenated text and number formulas, the formulas would be more flexible and allow the client to update them more quickly.

To complete this task:

1. Open the **BusinessPlan-5** workbook from the Tutorial.05\Cases folder on your Data Disk.

2. On the Assumptions sheet, enter *your name* in cell A1, the four digits that represent last year in cell B4, and the four digits that represent the current year in cell C4. You want all other cells in the workbook that refer to your name or these two years to use these values. The first cells that need to be updated are cells A8, A14, and A15 .

3. In cell A8, enter a formula that concatenates the value of cells B4 and C4 to text to create the phrase "2003 to 2004 Increases", for example. (*Hint*: Use the F2 key to edit the formula within the cell.)

4. In cells A14 and A15, enter appropriate formulas to concatenate the year entered in cells B4 and C4 to "Tax Rate".

5. Change the names of the 2003 and 2004 worksheet tabs to the years you entered in cells B4 and C4.

6. In cells A2 and A3 of the first year's income statement worksheet, enter the appropriate formulas to concatenate the first year's value in cell B4 of the Assumptions worksheet to the rest of the text shown in cell A2 of the first year's income statement worksheet. Likewise, concatenate your name stored in cell A1 of the Assumptions worksheet to the rest of the text shown in cell A3 of the first year's income statement worksheet.

7. Copy the formulas from the range A2:A3 of the first year's income statement to the range A2:A3 of the second year's income statement, and then modify the reference to the year in cell A2 to refer to cell C4 of the Assumptions worksheet..

Explore

8. Switch to the Analysis worksheet, and change the entries in cells A1, C4, and C7 to use formulas that concatenate text and values to display the same information in one formula. (*Hint*: You'll need to use the FIXED Text function to convert the percentages to a fixed value. You'll also need to multiply the percentages by 100 in order to display the values as a percentage rather than as a decimal number. The formula for cell C4 should be ="NBT/Sales in "&Assumptions!B4&" is "&FIXED('2003'!F15/'2003'!F6*100,0)&"%". The worksheet references to the worksheet 2003 will be replaced with the worksheet names in your workbook.)

9. Delete the entries in cells F4, F7, G7, and I7 which are no longer needed.

10. Save the changes you have made, and then print the Analysis sheet with your name in the left section of the header. Display the formulas on the Analysis sheet, and print it again.

11. Save and close the BusinessPlan-5 workbook, and then exit Excel.

Case 3. Converting Measurement Scales for a Science Lab You work as a scientist for a research facility and constantly face the need to convert numbers from one measurement system to another. You have learned that the CONVERT function within the Engineering category helps make common conversions from one measurement system to another, but you haven't used it before. You've logged some of the most common conversions that your research team uses in an Excel workbook, and you'll use the CONVERT function to determine equivalent values from one measurement system to another.

To complete this task:

1. Start Excel and open the **Conversion-5** workbook located in the Tutorial.05\Cases folder on your Data Disk. The workbook contains the initial unit of measurement in column A and the converted unit of measurement in column B. The operation to convert from one measurement scale to another is listed in column C, and the factor used within the conversion process is listed in column D. Columns F, G, and I are devoted to learning and testing the CONVERT function.

2. In cell G4, enter the formula =F4*D4 to convert 100 inches into an equivalent number of millimeters.

3. Copy the formula in cell G4 through the range G5:G10 so that the converted values appear for each conversion example.

4. Use Help to search for information on the CONVERT function. When you find the page that describes the CONVERT function, print the page to use it as a reference, and then close Help.

5. Using the information about the CONVERT function from Help, enter the correct formula in cell I4 that converts the value in cell F4 from inches to millimeters. The formula should be =CONVERT(F4,"in","mm").

Explore

6. Using the information about the CONVERT function from Help, enter the correct formulas in the range I5:I10. Use the values you previously calculated in column G to test whether the formulas in column I were entered correctly.

7. Enter *your name* in the left section of the header, and print the worksheet.

8. Display the formulas, and print the worksheet again.

9. On a piece of paper, write a few sentences to explain why you think that the values in columns G and I were slightly different in some cases.

10. Save and close the Conversion-5 workbook, and then exit Excel.

Case 4. Improving the Teaching Materials for Math Camp GVR holds a summer Math Camp that teaches a wide variety of math and trigonometry skills. The Math Camp teacher knows that Excel can be used to calculate the answers to the tests that she gives the students. The teacher needs some help setting up the functions using cell references rather than using raw data.

To complete this task:

1. Start Excel and open the **MathTest-5** workbook located in the Tutorial.05\Cases folder on your Data Disk. You want to redevelop this workbook so that as new values are entered in columns D and E, the rest of the workbook is automatically updated. To do this, you need to enter and edit several workbook entries.

2. In the range C6:C15, enter the name of the Math or Trigonometry function that you want to use to answer the questions posed in column B. The first two function names, FACT and GCD, are entered in cells C4 and C5 as an example, as shown in Figure 5-64.

Figure 5-64

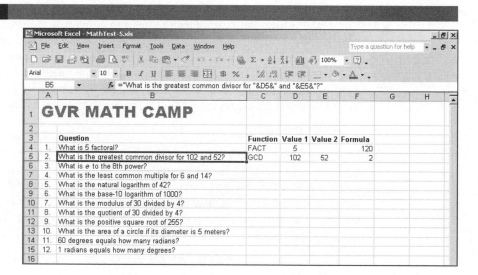

3. In columns D and E, enter the values for the arguments that you want to use within the formulas. Some functions will use one value because they use only one argument, and some will use two. The values for the first two questions have been entered in cells D4, D5, and E5 as an example.

4. In cells F6:F15, enter the formula to answer the question using the function name and argument values you have already identified. Be sure to use cell references in columns D and E for the arguments of your function rather than entering raw data into the formula. The correct formulas have been entered in F4 and F5 as an example.

5. In the range B6:B15, edit the existing entries so that a text formula is used that combines the existing text with the cell references for the raw data so that as the values within the workbook change, so do the test questions. The values for the first two questions in cells B4 and B5 have been completed as an example.

6. Save the changes you have made, display the formulas in the workbook, enter your name in the left section of the header, and then print the worksheet in landscape orientation.

7. Save and close the MathTest-5 workbook. Exit Excel.

QUICK | CHECK ANSWERS

Session 5.1

1. Formatting, Formula, and Result: Of the three, the result category creates the errors that are the hardest to find and resolve because there are no visual indicators to help you find the problems.

2. Because the #NAME? error value will occur when a function, range name, or worksheet reference is misspelled, or when any of several other conditions occurs, there are an endless number of examples that could produce this condition. "=AVG(A1:A10)" is one such example because the function AVERAGE is misspelled in the formula.

3. The #REF! error is most likely caused by deleting a column or row that contains a cell that is referenced in a formula. When that happens, the cell reference within the formula changes to #REF! and any dependent formula also shows a #REF! error value.

4. Red arrows identify precedent error values. Blue arrows identify other precedent cells.

5. The R1C1 reference style refers to cells based on their location relative to the current cell. Therefore, if you have entered a consistent formula throughout a column, when you display the R1C1 reference style, all of the formulas should be the same.

6. A good test value is any value that helps you check the validity of your formula.

Session 5.2

1. The double-declining balance and sum-of-years'-digits methods are the two types of depreciation methods with the most accelerated depreciation schedules.

2. No matter how much depreciation expense you claim in each year, the total amount of depreciation that you can claim must equal the initial cost of the asset less its salvage value, the amount it is worth at the end of the depreciation period.

3. You could use either the FV or PV function to help you make this determination, but applying the PV function to the five annual payments of $225 is the easier of the two because the $1000 value is already represented in present value dollars. If you used the FV function, you would have to take both values forward in time to determine what $1000 today is worth in five years and what $225 in five annual receipts is worth in five years.

4. All Dfunctions use three arguments: the list range, the field name upon which the calculation is to be performed, and the Criteria range.

5. "And" criteria are entered in the same row of the Criteria range. All criteria in one row must be true in order for the record to be used in the Dfunction calculation. "Or" criteria are entered in two rows of the Criteria range. The record must be true for only one row in order to be used in the Dfunction calculation.

6. If a date or time value appears as a numeric value in a workbook, a numeric format (as opposed to a date or time format) has been applied to the cell. To display a value as a date or as time, open the Format Cells dialog box, select the Date or Time category, and then select the type of format that you want to apply to the value. (To open the Format Cells dialog box, click Format on the menu bar and then click Cells.)

Session 5.3

1. The STDEV function finds the standard deviation for a list of values. The larger the number, the more widely scattered the values are from the mean (average) value. A value of 30 in a range of values from 25 to 100 would make you conclude that the numbers are widely scattered from the mean.

2. PI has no arguments and is entered as PI() in a formula. The PI() function is a fixed number that represents the ratio of the circumference of a circle to its diameter, which is always 3.14159265358979.

3. Computer engineers, scientists, physicists, or researchers who work in the field of electrical or nuclear energy would be most likely to use the functions.

4. The Lookup functions are used when one entry can be used to find and look up another. The data validation criteria feature provides a drop-down list of values for a range of cells.

5. The ISNA function returns either TRUE or FALSE. Rarely do you want the workbook to display that result. By surrounding the result of the ISNA function with an IF statement, you can take one of two courses of action depending on whether the result of ISNA is true or false.

6. ="Created by "&Assumptions!A1

OBJECTIVES

In this tutorial you will:

- Learn how Visual Basic for Applications (VBA) can improve an Excel workbook

- Run and edit a macro

- Assign a keystroke combination to a macro

- Attach a macro to a toolbar button

- Modify a toolbar button

- Use the macro recorder

- Edit a macro in the Visual Basic Editor

- Learn about the Excel Objects model

- Learn key VBA terminology

- Learn about Excel security

- Create a digital signature

- Sign a macro

INTRODUCTION
TO VISUAL BASIC FOR APPLICATIONS USING EXCEL

Exploring How VBA Can Help GVR

CASE

Green Valley Recreation

Lynn Tse, director of Green Valley Recreation (GVR), uses Excel in a wide variety of ways to help support decision making; to manage, scrub, and analyze lists of data; and to visually communicate numeric information with graphs. She recognizes the wide range of business problems that Excel can be used to automate and wants you to help others at GVR use Excel to support their work activities. Although many people at GVR currently use Excel, most of their workbooks are limited to their unique work tasks. The workbooks that Lynn wants to make available for other GVR employees deal with corporate-wide issues, such as retirement planning and budget preparation. Because a wide variety of users will be working with these workbooks, you have decided to learn Visual Basic for Applications (VBA) to make the workbooks as productive and easy to use as possible.

For example, using VBA, you can create custom buttons, toolbars, forms, and functions that are specific to the purpose of the workbook. With VBA, you can also hide the features of Excel that are not needed for that task and therefore make the workbook easier to use. You can also customize the interface so that users don't need extensive experience with Excel or training in order to successfully work with the data. VBA also helps you automate and simplify repetitive functions. By customizing Excel workbooks to simplify and automate the task at hand, you'll minimize the users' learning curve and improve their productivity.

SESSION 6.1

In this session, you will be introduced to Visual Basic for Applications (VBA). You'll learn the uses and benefits of VBA, and you will explore existing workbooks that use VBA for different purposes. You'll also learn how to attach and modify a macro.

What Is VBA?

Visual Basic for Applications (**VBA**) is a programming language that is packaged as a standard feature within many Microsoft Office XP and Office 2000 programs, such as Word, Excel, Access, and PowerPoint. VBA is not a standalone programming language (such as Visual Basic) but rather works only from within a **host application**, such as Excel, Access, or whichever Microsoft program you use to access VBA. VBA has many similarities to Visual Basic, so a user who is skilled in the Visual Basic programming language will have a considerable advantage if asked to work with VBA, and vice versa. A key difference is that VBA cannot be used independently of the host application. VBA is specifically designed to supplement the host application from within which it is accessed. VBA is used to customize, automate, simplify, and extend the capabilities of the host application. VBA is also used to help products such as Excel and Access work together.

Historically, each software program had its own macro programming language, macro recording techniques, and macro interface. Macro development skills gained in one product could not be directly transferred to another. Furthermore, there was no common interface between products to allow them to pass information back and forth. With VBA, the Microsoft Corporation has standardized the interface and language used to automate and customize its Office XP and Office 2000 programs. When you record a **macro**, a stored set of keystrokes or mouse clicks, within Excel, you are actually writing VBA code. In other words, a macro name is a name for a set of VBA statements. Each **statement** is one line of code that performs a specific task. If you need to edit a macro or write VBA from scratch, you use the Visual Basic Editor.

Some of the VBA statements that you'll be using in Excel, such as those that select a worksheet or format a range of values, are specific to Excel and do not make sense within Word or Access because documents and databases do not contain the same elements—for example, worksheets or cell ranges. However, the Visual Basic Editor, VBA terminology, and VBA programming syntax are consistent from product to product. For example, by learning what an "object" or "method" is to VBA within Excel, you'll already know what those terms mean to VBA within other Office XP or Office 2000 programs. When you learn about VBA reserved words, such as "sub" or "function," or color-coding used within the Visual Basic Editor, you can transfer that knowledge to VBA within any product from which you access it.

Why Use VBA?

VBA is a robust programming language that can be used for a wide variety of purposes. It can be used to create something simple, such as automatically adding a standard header to a worksheet, or something as complex as a custom application that prompts a user for several investment planning entries and then creates a financial statement based on that information. The following list identifies some of the common purposes of using VBA within Excel:

- To automate repetitive processes
- To make a workbook faster and easier with custom dialog boxes, menu bar options, toolbar buttons, or shortcut keys

- To make the workbook more visually appealing by changing or hiding screen elements that aren't necessary to the task at hand
- To build custom functions to simplify complex or unique calculations
- To share data with external files such as an Access database

Although some people might feel that learning VBA isn't necessary until they master all of the existing features of Excel, the truth is that very few people need to use each and every feature or function of Excel. However, almost everyone could benefit from some form of repetitive task automation or interface simplification. For example, you might find yourself typing your name, your company name, or a standard company disclaimer over and over. Using a very simple macro, you can record the actions required to do that task and then replay those actions instantly as often as you need them. Furthermore, you can ensure accuracy and consistency by using a macro instead of retyping text. Also realize that even though you may be an Excel expert, for every Excel expert there are many more business workers who are intimidated by the extensive menus, toolbars, and features of Excel. Therefore, if you build an Excel workbook for others, VBA can provide tremendous benefits by helping you simplify and customize the user interface so that others can quickly, easily, and accurately use the workbook.

Working with an Existing Macro

One of the easiest ways to get a sense of how VBA can improve your workbooks is to explore existing workbooks that incorporate VBA in various ways. To show Lynn the power of VBA, you have created a very small macro that inserts standard text into the header of a workbook. The macro consists of only a few VBA statements. To **run** a macro means to execute the VBA statements that comprise the macro. There are many ways to run a macro, such as using a keyboard shortcut or clicking a toolbar button. For now, however, you'll run macros from the Tools menu.

REFERENCE WINDOW	RW

Running an Existing Macro
- Click Tools on the menu bar, point to Macro, and then click Macros.
- Click the name of the macro you want to run, and then click the Run button.

At GVR, the name of the person who created the workbook is typically entered in the left section of the header. So the first workbook you'll show Lynn contains a macro that automatically enters text in the left section of the header. You'll run the macro within the workbook where the macro was originally created.

To run the Header macro:

1. Start Excel and then open the **Athlete-6** workbook located in the Tutorial.06\Tutorial folder on your Data Disk.

   TROUBLE? If you are prompted that the workbook contains macros, click the Enable Macros button in order to work with the workbook. Later, you'll learn more about security levels and how to protect your computer from unauthorized macros.

TROUBLE? If a message box appears, indicating that macros are disabled because security is high, click the OK button. You must change the security level to medium before opening the workbook. To set the security level to medium, click Tools on the menu bar, point to Macro, click Security, click the Security Level tab, click the Medium option button, and then click the OK button. Repeat Step 1.

2. Click the **Print Preview** button [icon] on the Standard toolbar, zoom in and out as necessary to confirm that there is no existing entry in the header, and then click the **Close** button on the Print Preview toolbar.

3. Click **Tools** on the menu bar, point to **Macro**, and then click **Macros**. Right now, the workbook only contains one macro, named Header.

4. With the Header macro selected, click the **Run** button.

To confirm that the macro worked correctly, you need to preview the worksheet again.

5. Click [icon] and then zoom in to examine the left section of the header.

6. Click the **Close** button on the Print Preview toolbar.

Lynn immediately comments on the fact that the macro inserted the text "Your Name" into the header instead of an actual name. She wants to know how hard it is to change the macro to fix this. You explain that, although you are not yet a seasoned VBA programmer, you know that to modify a macro you can use the Visual Basic Editor.

REFERENCE WINDOW   **RW**

Editing an Existing Macro
- Click Tools on the menu bar, point to Macro, and then click Macros.
- Click the name of the macro you want to run, and then click the Edit button.

You explain to Lynn that you will edit the Header macro so that the text "Your Name" within the VBA code for the Header macro is changed to her name, "Lynn Tse."

To edit the macro so that the header text is modified:

1. Click **Tools** on the menu bar, point to **Macro**, and then click **Macros**.

2. With the Header macro selected, click the **Edit** button. The Visual Basic Editor window opens. When the editor opens, you may see the Code window, the Project Explorer, and the Properties window. Right now you only need the Code window.

3. Click the **Close** button [X] for the Project – VBAProject window, and then click the **Close** button [X] for the Properties window. See Figure 6-1. There are seven lines of VBA code in the Header macro, and one line refers to the text "Your Name."

TROUBLE? If necessary, maximize the Code window.

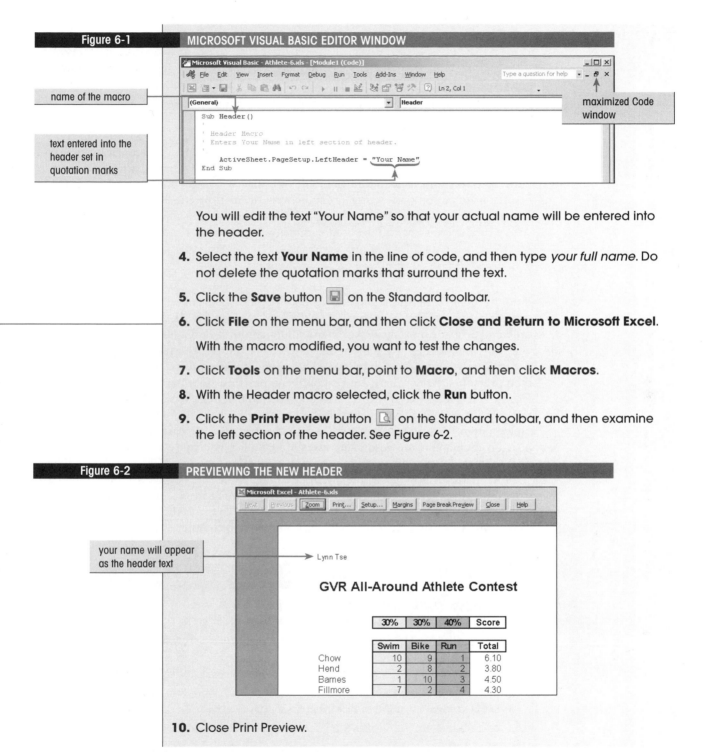

Figure 6-1   MICROSOFT VISUAL BASIC EDITOR WINDOW

name of the macro

text entered into the
header set in
quotation marks

maximized Code
window

```
Sub Header()
'
' Header Macro
' Enters Your Name in left section of header.

    ActiveSheet.PageSetup.LeftHeader = "Your Name"
End Sub
```

You will edit the text "Your Name" so that your actual name will be entered into
the header.

4. Select the text **Your Name** in the line of code, and then type *your full name*. Do
not delete the quotation marks that surround the text.

5. Click the **Save** button 🖫 on the Standard toolbar.

6. Click **File** on the menu bar, and then click **Close and Return to Microsoft Excel**.

With the macro modified, you want to test the changes.

7. Click **Tools** on the menu bar, point to **Macro**, and then click **Macros**.

8. With the Header macro selected, click the **Run** button.

9. Click the **Print Preview** button 🔍 on the Standard toolbar, and then examine
the left section of the header. See Figure 6-2.

Figure 6-2   PREVIEWING THE NEW HEADER

your name will appear
as the header text

Lynn Tse

GVR All-Around Athlete Contest

	30%	30%	40%	Score

	Swim	Bike	Run	Total
Chow	10	9	1	6.10
Hend	2	8	2	3.80
Barnes	1	10	3	4.50
Fillmore	7	2	4	4.30

10. Close Print Preview.

Lynn sees the value of the Header macro. By automating the entry of standard text at
GVR, you can standardize certain elements and increase productivity. Yet she feels that
using the Tools menu to run common macros might be obscure for some users. You explain
to Lynn that, once a macro is created, it doesn't have to be run from the Tools menu. You
explain that the macro can be attached to a keyboard combination, a toolbar button, or a
graphical icon on the workbook itself.

Making **Macros Easier to Use**

Once you have created a macro, you'll want to make it easy to use. Creating a quick keystroke combination such as Ctrl + H to run a macro or attaching it to a button is the most common way to do this. Your choice of choosing a quick keystroke, using a toolbar button, or using a graphical hotspot on the workbook to initiate a macro depends on what the macro does as well as what your users prefer. If your macro initiates a series of actions that are appropriate only for that workbook, you might want to add a command button or other graphical element to the workbook that when clicked runs that macro. (You'll use command buttons to run VBA code in Tutorial 8.) If your macro is of a global nature—that is, if it can be used in any workbook—you'll probably want to run it by attaching the macro to a button on a toolbar that can be displayed within any workbook or by assigning the macro to a keystroke combination that can be used within any workbook.

Assigning a Macro to a Keystroke Shortcut

If your users like the speed and convenience of quick keystrokes, you can assign a macro to a combination of keystrokes, such as Ctrl + M, Ctrl + Shift + M, or Ctrl + Alt + M, which is called a keyboard shortcut or keyboard combination. To execute a keyboard combination, you press and hold each key in the sequence. For example, to execute the keyboard combination Ctrl + Shift + M, you press and hold the Ctrl key, press and hold the Shift key, and then press the M key. There are keyboard combinations that have already been assigned in Excel, such as Ctrl + B (which is assigned to the bold action) and Ctrl + P (which is assigned to the print action). A complete list of all existing keyboard shortcuts can be found in the Help system when you search for "keyboard shortcuts." Be careful to avoid existing keyboard combinations, because many users are familiar with these shortcuts, and reassigning new actions to them will override the existing function.

Note that with most Microsoft keystroke combinations, the keyboard combination Ctrl + B works the same way as Ctrl + Shift + B. When assigning macro quick keystrokes, however, Ctrl + Shift + Q will not run a macro that was assigned to the keyboard combination Ctrl + Q. In fact, you can assign Ctrl + Q and Ctrl + Shift + Q to completely different macros.

REFERENCE WINDOW | **RW**

__Assigning a Macro to a Keyboard Shortcut__
- Click Tools on the menu bar, point to Macro, and then click Macros.
- Click the macro name that you want to assign the keyboard shortcut, and then click the Options button.
- In the Shortcut key text box, enter the keystrokes to add to Ctrl to create the keyboard shortcut. Use Shift to enter a capital letter.
- Click the OK button, and then click the Cancel button.

To make sure that the combination of keys that you want to assign to the Header macro are not already assigned to an action, you'll search the Help system to see if the Ctrl + Shift + H keyboard shortcut is employed for any other use.

To search for the Ctrl + Shift + H keyboard combination in Help:

1. Click **Help** on the menu bar, click **Microsoft Excel Help**, and then maximize the Microsoft Excel Help window if it isn't already maximized.

2. Click the **Show** button 🔲 if the navigation pane on the left if not visible, click the **Index** tab (if it is not already selected), type **keyboard** in the Type keywords text box, click the **Search** button, and then double-click **Keyboard shortcuts** in the list of topics. The Keyboard shortcuts Help page appears on the right.

   EXCEL 2000: If Clippit appears, type **keyboard** In the search box, click the **Search** button, and then click the **Keyboard shortcuts** link.

3. Click the **Show All** link in the upper-right corner of the Help menu to display all of the existing keyboard shortcut assignments.

   To determine if a specific combination has already been assigned to another action, you can scroll through the list in the Help window. Because there are so many preexisting keystroke combinations, this process could be time-consuming. To quickly find out if the keyboard combination you want to use has already been assigned, you can use the Find dialog box to search for a string of text on the Help page. You can open the Find dialog box using an existing keyboard combination.

4. Click in the Help page (but do not click on a hyperlink), and then press **Ctrl + F** to open the Find dialog box.

5. Type **Ctrl+H** (no spaces) in the Find what text box, click the **Find Next** button, and then continue to click the **Find Next** button and as you move through the list of keyboard shortcuts watch for any occurrence of the Ctrl + H keyboard combination.

   EXCEL 2000: To search for other occurrences of keyboard shortcuts that use Ctrl + H, you would have to search each link on the Keyboard shortcuts page. Read Steps 5, 6, and 7, which explain how to search for text in Help, and then continue with Step 8.

6. When the search is complete, click the **OK** button. The Ctrl + H keyboard combination is used in the context of Ctrl + Home and in Ctrl + Hyphen, but the Ctrl + H combination itself has been not assigned to a specific action.

7. Type **Ctrl + Shift + H** in the Find what text box, click the **Up** option button, click the **Find Next** button until you are prompted that the search is finished, click the **OK** button, and then click the **Cancel** button. You did not find any occurrences of the Ctrl + Shift + H combination of keys.

8. Close the Microsoft Excel Help window.

Convinced that Ctrl + Shift + H would not interfere with any other existing keyboard shortcut, you are ready to assign it to the Header macro.

To assign the keyboard combination Ctrl + Shift + H to the Header macro:

1. Click **Tools** on the menu bar, point to **Macro**, and then click **Macros** to open the Macro dialog box.

2. Make sure the Header macro is still selected, and then click the **Options** button. The Macro Options dialog box opens.

3. Press **Shift + H**. The shortcut key value changes to Ctrl+Shift+H. See Figure 6-3.

Figure 6-3	ASSIGNING A KEYBOARD COMBINATION TO A MACRO

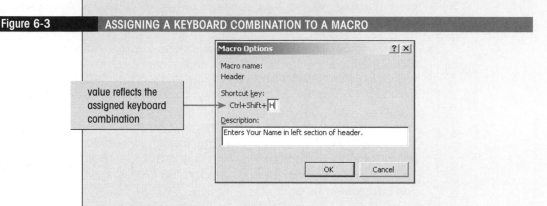

value reflects the assigned keyboard combination

4. Click the **OK** button, and then click the **Cancel** button.

Now you will test the Header macro using the keyboard shortcut you have assigned. First, you will preview the worksheet and delete the entry in the left section of the header, and then you will run the macro. After the macro has been executed, you will preview the worksheet again to make sure that the keystroke shortcut and the macro ran successfully.

To test the new keyboard combination:

1. Click the **Print Preview** button on the Standard toolbar.

2. Click the **Setup** button on the Preview toolbar, click the **Header/Footer** tab, click the **Custom Header** button, delete your name from the left section of the header, click the **OK** button twice, and then close Print Preview.

   Now you will test the macro using the keyboard shortcut.

3. Press **Ctrl + Shift + H** to run the macro.

4. Click and then zoom in as necessary, to make sure that the Header macro ran successfully, placing your name in the left section of the header.

   TROUBLE? If the macro didn't insert your name in the left section of the header, return to the worksheet and press Ctrl + Shift + H again. If you hear a beep, it means that the keystroke combination hasn't been assigned to any action. You need to repeat the previous set of steps.

5. Close Print Preview.

A few of your most advanced users use keyboard shortcuts on a regular basis, but there is a larger group of users who prefer to use toolbar buttons for common commands. Clicking a button on a toolbar is easier and doesn't require memorizing combinations of keys.

Attaching a Macro to a Toolbar Button

You can assign, or attach, a macro to a new button on an existing toolbar or on a new toolbar. You can create a toolbar and add the buttons that you use on a regular basis, or in this case, you can add a button that will run a macro. You can display your customized toolbars whenever you need them and have access to all of the macros you have created. Although you can customize the existing toolbars in Excel, you should do so with caution, especially if other people use or have access to your computer.

REFERENCE WINDOW   **RW**

Creating a New Toolbar with a Macro-Assigned Button
- Click View on the menu bar, point to Toolbars, and then click Customize; or right-click any toolbar and then click Customize on the shortcut menu.
- Click the Toolbars tab, click New, enter a name for the toolbar, and then click the OK button.
- Click the Commands tab, click Macros in the Categories list, and then drag the Custom Button command from the Commands list to the new toolbar.
- Click the Modify Selection button, and then click Assign Macro on the shortcut menu.
- Click the macro name that you want to assign to the macro, and then click the OK button.
- Click the Close button.

Lynn suspects that GVR employees would use macros more often if they were added to a toolbar. Lynn wants you to create a new toolbar to contain the Header macro.

To create a new toolbar and add a macro-assigned button:

1. Click **View** on the menu bar, point to **Toolbars**, and then click **Customize**. You can use the Customize dialog box to toggle on and off existing toolbars, create and delete custom toolbars, change the buttons on existing and custom toolbars, and change the way toolbars are presented.

2. Click the **Toolbars** tab (if it is not already selected), and then click the **New** button. The New Toolbar dialog box opens.

3. Type **Printing Tools** in the Toolbar name text box, and then click the **OK** button. The new Printing Tools toolbar appears beside the Custom dialog box. See Figure 6-4. Because there are no buttons on the Printing Tools toolbar yet, it is very small.

Figure 6-4   PRINTING TOOLS TOOLBAR

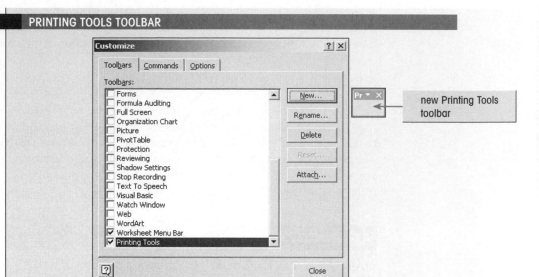

new Printing Tools toolbar

TROUBLE? If the Printing Tools toolbar already exists, select it in the Toolbars list, click the Delete button, click the OK button, and then repeat Steps 2 and 3.

TROUBLE? If the new toolbar is not visible on your screen, move the Customize dialog box so both the new toolbar and the dialog box are clearly visible.

4. Click the **Commands** tab, scroll down and click **Macros** in the Categories list, and then drag the **Custom Button** command to the new Printing Tools toolbar. As you drag the command button to the toolbar, your pointer changes to ⬚. Also, note that a black I-beam appears on the toolbar to indicate where the new button will be positioned. Once a custom button is added to the toolbar, you can attach a macro to it.

5. Click the **Modify Selection** button in the Customize dialog box, and then click **Assign Macro**. The Assign Macro dialog box opens, displaying all of the macros in the open workbooks, which at this time is only the Header macro.

6. Click **Header** in the list, and then click the **OK** button. See Figure 6-5. The Header macro has been attached to the custom button on the Printing Tools toolbar, so that when you click the button the macro will run.

Figure 6-5   CUSTOM BUTTON ADDED TO THE PRINTING TOOLS TOOLBAR

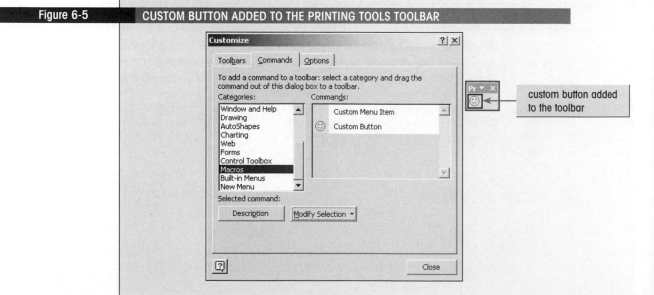

custom button added to the toolbar

7. Click the **Close** button in the Customize dialog box.

To make sure that the new button on the new Printing Tools toolbar works as intended, you need to delete the existing text in the left section of the header and then use the button to run the Header macro.

To test the custom button on the Printing Tools toolbar:

1. Click **File** on the menu bar, click **Page Setup**, click the **Header/Footer** tab (if it is not already selected), click the **Custom Header** button, delete the text in the left section, and then click the **OK** button twice.

2. Click the **Custom Button** ☺ on the Printing Tools toolbar to run the macro.

3. Click the **Print Preview** button 🔍 on the Standard toolbar, zoom in as necessary to make sure that the Header macro ran successfully, and then close Print Preview.

To make sure that the macro runs successfully in other workbooks too, you'll start a new workbook.

4. Click the **New** button 🗋, type **=TODAY()** in cell A1, and then press the **Enter** key to display today's date.

5. Click the **Custom Button** ☺ on the Printing Tools toolbar to run the macro.

6. Click the **Print Preview** button 🔍 on the Standard toolbar, zoom in if necessary to make sure that the Header macro ran successfully, and then close Print Preview.

7. Close the new workbook without saving it.

The macro ran as intended from the new custom toolbar. As long as the workbook that contains the actual macro code is open, you can run the Header macro on any other workbook, too. Lynn finds it much easier to run the Header macro by clicking a single button on a toolbar than by finding the macro using the Tools menu or remembering the keyboard combination.

Modifying a Button Image and ScreenTip

The default image for a custom button is the smiley face. That image might be acceptable if your toolbar contains only one button; however, if you continue to add custom buttons to the toolbar, you won't be able to distinguish which button runs which macro. Therefore, you'll probably want to modify the button image and its ScreenTip so that they are more representative of the given task, making the buttons easier to use. You can change a button so that it displays only text, only an image (the default setting for a button), or both text and an image. You can modify the appearance of the image on the button, create an entirely new image, and modify the ScreenTip that is displayed when you point to the image.

REFERENCE WINDOW `RW`

Modifying the Image of a Toolbar Button
- Display the toolbar that contains the button you want to change.
- Click View on the menu bar, point to Toolbars, and then click Customize; or right-click any toolbar and then click Customize on the shortcut menu.
- Click the Commands tab, click the button on the toolbar, and then click the Modify Selection button.
- Click the Edit Button Image or Change Button Image option to modify the shape or color of the image, or click the Default Style (image only), Text Only, or Image and Text option to determine whether the button displays an image, text, or both.

Lynn suspects that GVR employees would use several other small macros to automate printing processes and wants you to modify the existing custom button so that it's more obvious that it runs the Header macro. First, you'll modify the button image itself so that the image is more representative of the Header macro than the smiley face image.

To modify the image of the custom button on the Printing Tools toolbar:

1. Right-click any toolbar and then click **Customize** on the shortcut menu to open the Customize dialog box.

2. Click the **Commands** tab (if it is not already selected), click the **Custom Button** ☺ on the Printing Tools toolbar, and then click the **Modify Selection** button.

3. Point to **Change Button Image** on the shortcut menu, and study the available button images on the palette of images that appears. See Figure 6-6. If one of the existing button images is related to a header, choosing that button image would be the fastest way to modify the button. However, because none of the buttons clearly relates to customizing a header, you'll create your own image.

Figure 6-6   **AVAILABLE BUTTON IMAGES**

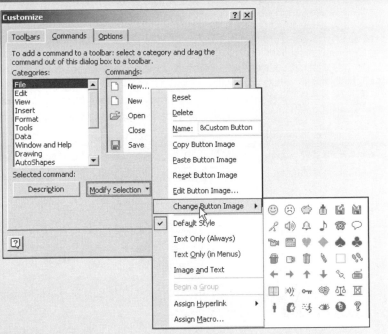

4. Press the **Esc** key twice to close the palette of button images and the short-cut menu.

   You will copy the image from the Bold button and modify it so that the "B" becomes an "H."

5. Click the **Bold** button on the Formatting toolbar, and then click the **Modify Selection** button in the Customize dialog box. Note that at the top of the short-cut menu the text "&Bold" appears in the Name field.

   TROUBLE? If the Formatting toolbar is not visible, close the Customize dialog box, right-click any visible toolbar, and then click Formatting. If the Customize dialog box covers the Bold button on the Formatting toolbar, drag the title bar of the Customize dialog box to move it so that you can see the Bold button.

6. Click **Copy Button Image** on the shortcut menu, click 🙂 on the Printing Tools toolbar, click the **Modify Selection** button, and then click **Paste Button Image**. Even though the button on the Printing Tools toolbar now displays a "B" icon, the Header macro is still assigned to the button. To modify the image so that the "B" is an "H," you'll use the Button Editor dialog box.

   TROUBLE? If you inadvertently clicked the Paste Button Image instead of the Copy Button Image, the image on the Bold button changed. Click the Modify Selection button, click Reset at the top of the shortcut menu, and then repeat Step 6.

7. Click the **Modify Selection** button, and then click **Edit Button Image**. The Button Editor opens. See Figure 6-7. You use the Button Editor to change an existing button image or to create an entirely new image. At this point, you need to change the "B" into an "H". To do this, use the color Black and the Erase option. To add a color block to the image, click a color in the color palette and then click a square in the Picture grid. To remove color from the image, click the Erase option and then click a square in the Picture grid. The Erase option applies an alternating white and gray diagonal stripe to the grid that appears as a solid gray background when the button is viewed on a toolbar.

Figure 6-7   **BUTTON EDITOR DIALOG BOX**

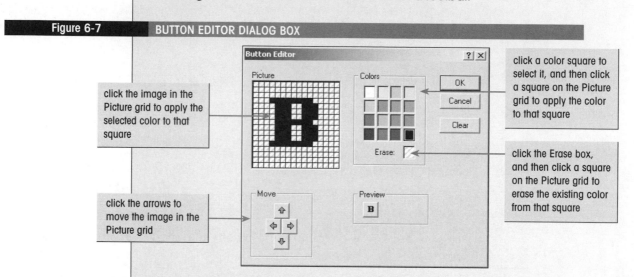

click the image in the Picture grid to apply the selected color to that square

click the arrows to move the image in the Picture grid

click a color square to select it, and then click a square on the Picture grid to apply the color to that square

click the Erase box, and then click a square on the Picture grid to erase the existing color from that square

8. Using the Black color square (last row, fourth column from left) and the Erase option, click the individual squares in the Picture grid so that the image looks like the image in Figure 6-8. Note that counting the squares in the grid will help you edit the image correctly.

Figure 6-8   **THE MODIFIED BUTTON IMAGE**

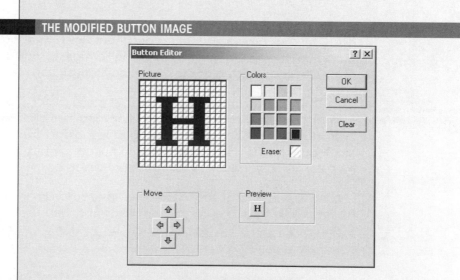

9. Click the **OK** button in the Button Editor dialog box, and then click the **Close** button in the Customize dialog box.

The new button on the Printing Tools toolbar now displays the letter *H*, which better represents the action the button will execute (in this case, modifying a header) than a smiley face icon. You could have also chosen to display the name of the macro, "Header," as the button image, but displaying the macro name makes the button wider. The wider each button becomes on a toolbar, the less room you have for new buttons. A compromise between descriptive button images and saving room on the toolbar can be reached by using a descriptive ScreenTip for a button. A **ScreenTip** is text that appears when you point to a button on a toolbar. ScreenTips are generally used to describe and clarify the purpose for the button.

REFERENCE WINDOW   **RW**

Modifying a Toolbar Button ScreenTip
- Click View on the menu bar, point to Toolbars, and then click Customize.
- Click the Commands tab, click the button whose ScreenTip you want to change, and then click the Modify Selection button.
- Select the default text in the Name box, and then type the new ScreenTip text.
- Click the Close button.

You will modify the ScreenTip text for the new button on the Printing Tools toolbar to read "Insert name in header" so that the purpose of the button is more explicit than just the "H" on the button.

To modify the ScreenTip of the H button on the Printing Tools toolbar:

1. Right-click any toolbar and then click **Customize** on the shortcut menu to open the Customize dialog box.

2. Click the **H** button on the Printing Tools toolbar, and then click the **Modify Selection** button in the Customize dialog box.

3. Select **&Custom Button** in the Name box, type **Insert name in header**, press the **Enter** key, and then click the **Close** button.

4. Point to **H** on the Printing Tools toolbar. See Figure 6-9.

Figure 6-9   **NEW TOOLBAR BUTTON SCREENTIP**

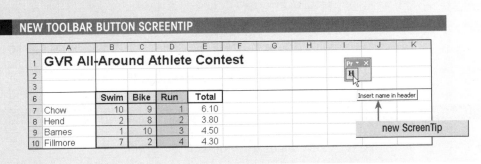

In addition to creating and modifying custom buttons that run macros, you can also add existing Excel commands (that is, menu items and toolbar buttons) to the toolbar. You can easily add existing buttons to a toolbar by using the Customize dialog box.

REFERENCE WINDOW   RW

Adding an Excel Command to a Toolbar
- Display the toolbar to which you want to add an Excel command, or create a new toolbar.
- Open the Customize dialog box, and click the Commands tab.
- Select the category that contains the Excel command that you want to add to the toolbar.
- Click the command, and then drag the selection to the toolbar.
- Release your mouse button.

Because the users at GVR work with almost all of the options in the Page Setup dialog box, you will add a button to the Printing Tools toolbar that opens the Page Setup dialog box.

To add a button that opens the Page Setup dialog box to the Printing Tools toolbar:

1. Right-click any toolbar and then click **Customize** on the shortcut menu to open the Customize dialog box.

2. Click the **Commands** tab (if it is not already selected). The Categories list shows the existing Excel command categories, organized similarly to how they are presented on the menu bar. The Commands list shows the existing Excel commands.

3. Click **File** in the Categories list (if it is not already selected), scroll down the Commands list, and then click **Page Setup**.

4. Drag **Page Setup** to the left of the **H** button on the Printing Tools toolbar. The Page Setup button is now on the Printing Tools toolbar.

   TROUBLE? If you drag the wrong button, or if you drag it to the wrong toolbar, drag the misplaced button off the toolbar to remove it. If the button appears to the right of the H button, drag the Page Setup button to the left. Note that you can only add, move, and delete toolbar buttons when the Customize dialog box is open.

   Now you will change the appearance of the Page Setup button to a smaller image.

5. With the Page Setup button still selected, click the **Modify Selection** button, click **Default Style** so the text on the Page Setup button is replaced by the default Page Setup icon, and then click the **Close** button. The Printing Tools toolbar now has two buttons. See Figure 6-10.

Figure 6-10   PRINTING TOOLS TOOLBAR WITH THE NEW PAGE SETUP BUTTON

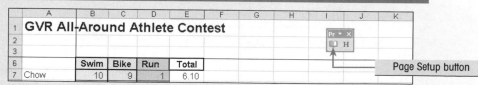

Test the new button.

6. Click the **Page Setup** button 📖 on the Printing Tools toolbar, and then click the **Cancel** button in the Page Setup dialog box.

7. Click the **Close** button ☒ to close the Printing Tools toolbar for now.

8. Right-click any toolbar, click **Customize**, click the **Toolbars** tab (if it is not already selected), select **Printing Tools** from the Toolbars list, click the **Delete** button, click the **OK** button, and then click the **Close** button.

9. Save the changes made to the workbook, and then close the workbook.

You have learned how to create new toolbars, add buttons that represent either existing Excel commands or new macros to toolbars, and modify toolbar images and ScreenTips. With these skills to make the macros that you create easy to find and use, you will now continue to learn more ways that VBA can improve Excel workbooks.

Using a Custom Dialog Box

Although macros are created with VBA statements, you know that VBA is a full programming language, capable of much more than merely automating and simplifying printing tasks. With help from a friend, you have developed a workbook that uses VBA to create a custom dialog box. The custom dialog box prompts a user for an entry and then adds the data to the appropriate location in the workbook. You are anxious to show it to Lynn so that she gets a better appreciation of what VBA can do.

To work with a custom dialog box:

1. Open the **Contestants-6** workbook from the Tutorial.06\Tutorial folder on your Data Disk, and then click the **Enable Macros** button. This workbook logs all new triathlon athletes. You have created a dialog box that prompts the user for three pieces of information: last name, birthday, and gender. (The age value is calculated based on the current date.) You can open the dialog box by clicking the Add New Contestant button.

2. Click the **Add New Contestant** button. See Figure 6-11. A small dialog box titled "UserForm1" appears, prompting for the three pieces of information you need to enter a new contestant.

| Figure 6-11 | USERFORM1 CUSTOM DIALOG BOX |

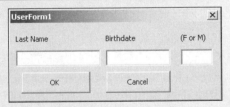

3. Type *your last name* in the Last Name text box, press the **Tab** key and enter *your birthdate* using the MM/DD/YY format, press the **Tab** key and type **F** or **M** (for female or male), click the **OK** button, and then click the **Cancel** button to close the UserForm1 dialog box.

4. Scroll down the list to row **28**. Your last name, date, age (calculated based on the date you entered), and gender now appear in row 28.

5. Print the Entrants worksheet with your name in the left section of the header.

6. Save and close the workbook.

Lynn is beginning to realize the vast potential for VBA. She tells you that she is envisioning the development of several new workbooks to be used by many GVR employees, such as one for retirement planning and another for budget planning. Knowing that VBA can not only automate redundant tasks but also create custom dialog boxes that simplify data entry, she believes that VBA will help extend Excel's advantages to many people who are not currently using the software. She suggests that you find a course on using VBA within Excel and authorizes the tuition expense. First, though, you explain to her that there is another simple example of how to use VBA within Excel and that is to create a custom function.

Using a Custom Function

You are already very familiar with Excel built-in functions, such as SUM, PMT, and IF. You are also very familiar with why you use functions, that is, to help simplify formulas. Even a formula as basic as =SUM(A1:A10) would become tedious and error prone if you had to enter it without using the SUM function, =A1+A2+A3+A4+A5+A6+A7+A8+A9+A10. Functions such as PMT and STDEV are much more complex, because the formulas that they represent include multiple mathematical operations, sometimes including exponents. For example, to find the standard deviation of a range of scores from A1 through A4, you would enter =STDEV(A1:A4). An equivalent entry, without the aid of the STDEV function would involve the following formula:

$$\sqrt{\frac{n\sum x^2 - \left(\sum x\right)^2}{n(n-1)}}$$

If you want to create your own function, such as a function called RETIRE that calculates a retirement date based on your company's unique formula or a function called COMMISSION that calculates commission earnings based on a different proportion of sales from different categories, you would use VBA to do that. Because you cannot record this type of VBA using the macro recorder, you must create VBA code for a new function directly in the Visual Basic Editor.

At GVR's Sunflower golf course, summer dues are $200, $250, or $300, depending on the person's zip code (which, in turn, estimates the public subsidy to the golf course through local taxes). If a zip code starts with 77, the annual dues are $200; if 76, annual dues are $250; and if the zip code starts with any digits other than 77 or 76, the annual dues are $300. Rather than using a formula with an IF or LOOKUP function, you will use a workbook that includes a custom function called Dues that asks for one argument, the zip code. The Dues function evaluates the zip code entry and returns the appropriate dues value of 200, 250, or 300.

To explore the custom function named Dues:

1. Open the **Sunflower-6** workbook located in the Tutorial.06\Tutorial folder on your Data Disk, and then click the **Enable Macros** button. This workbook contains a list of annual members at the Sunflower golf course. The zip code for each individual is stored in column C, and the dues are calculated in column D.

2. Click cell **C4**, type **12345**, and then press the **Enter** key. The formula in cell D4 returns a value of 300 because the zip code doesn't start with either 77 or 76.

3. Click cell **D4** and observe the Dues function in the Formula bar. There is only one argument in the Dues function, the cell reference for the zip code entry. Test the function using other zip codes.

4. In cell C4, enter **77111** and press the **Enter** key. The value in cell D4 changes to 200.

5. In cell C4, enter **76222** and then press the **Enter** key. The value in cell D4 now changes to 250.

   Now you will explore the VBA code that defines the Dues function in the Visual Basic Editor.

6. Click **Tools** on the menu bar, point to **Macro**, and then click **Visual Basic Editor**. See Figure 6-12.

   TROUBLE? If the Project Explorer and Properties windows open, close them.

Figure 6-12	VBA CODE FOR THE DUES FUNCTION

```
Microsoft Visual Basic - Sunflower-6.xls - [Module1 (Code)]
  File  Edit  View  Insert  Format  Debug  Run  Tools  Add-Ins  Window  Help        Type a question for help
                                                            Ln 1, Col 1
(General)                                          Dues

Function Dues(zip)
    If Left(zip, 2) = "77" Then
        Dues = 200
    ElseIf Left(zip, 2) = "76" Then
        Dues = 250
    Else
        Dues = 300
    End If
End Function
```

You'll enter your name as a comment in the first line of code just to become familiar with typing statements in the Visual Basic Editor.

7. Position the insertion point at the beginning of the Function statement, press the **Enter** key, press the **Up Arrow** key ↑ so that you are positioned at the beginning of the blank line, type *'your name*, and then click any other statement. The apostrophe at the beginning of the text you just typed denotes a **comment line**—text that provides information about the macro and should not be interpreted as an actual VBA instruction. Note that comment text appears in green. Other text in the Code window is color-coded as well. VBA reserved keywords are blue, and other VBA code appears in black. You'll learn more about the colors and parts of the Visual Basic Editor window as you become more proficient with VBA.

8. Click **File** on the menu bar, click **Print**, and then click the **OK** button in the Print – VBAProject dialog box.

9. Click the **Save** button on the Standard toolbar to save the changes made to the code, and then close the Visual Basic Editor.

10. Close the Sunflower-6 workbook.

Even if you don't understand each statement, you can learn more about VBA by viewing existing code. Some VBA, such as the statements that create custom forms or functions, can only be created and modified directly within the Visual Basic Editor. Another way to create VBA is to use the macro recorder to translate clicks and keystrokes into corresponding VBA statements. To modify macros, you can either rerecord them from scratch, or you can work in the Visual Basic Editor to change just those statements that need to be modified.

You have learned that once a macro is created, you can attach it to a new or existing tool-bar to make it easier and faster to run. You can also assign macros to keystroke combinations. In the next session, you'll continue expanding your awareness of how VBA can be used to automate and simplify workbooks.

Session 6.1 QUICK CHECK

1. What is the key difference between Visual Basic and VBA?

2. What are the most common uses for VBA within Excel?

3. Explain the relationship between an Excel macro, the macro recorder, and VBA.

4. Identify two uses for VBA within Excel that do not include the use of macros.

5. Once a macro is created, identify three ways to make it easier to run than by accessing it from the Tools menu.

6. What is the purpose of creating a custom form?

7. What is the purpose of creating a custom function?

SESSION 6.2

In this session, you will learn about VBA by using the macro recorder to record macros, and then using the Visual Basic Editor to examine and edit the code created by the recorder. You'll also learn key VBA terminology and fundamental concepts of the VBA programming language. You will learn how to read and simplify the code created by the macro recorder. Finally, you'll work with security levels and digital signatures to elevate the authenticity of your VBA code and to give others the information they need in order make a decision on whether to trust the code.

Using the Macro Recorder

You can create a macro by directly typing the VBA statements into the Visual Basic Editor, or you can use the **macro recorder** to convert keystrokes or mouse clicks into VBA code. Using the macro recorder has both benefits and disadvantages. The benefit is that it is a relatively fast way to write VBA to automate a repetitive function. Also, using the macro recorder, you shield yourself from having to know much about VBA. The disadvantage, however, is that the code created by the macro recorder is often much more cumbersome than if you wrote it from scratch in the Visual Basic Editor. Creating a macro using the macro recorder often creates extra VBA statements that may not be needed, thereby making things more complicated if you try to edit the code later. And don't forget that some applications of VBA, such as creating custom dialog boxes or functions, cannot be accomplished using a macro recorder because no existing feature within Excel can simulate the desired task. Still, most people start writing VBA by using the macro recorder because it is generally considered the easiest way to get started.

Creating a Macro Using the Macro Recorder

- Click Tools on the menu bar, point to Macro, and then click Record New Macro.
- Type the name of the new macro in the Macro name text box, enter a description of the macro (optional), and then click the OK button.
- Using the keyboard and mouse, complete the task or process that you want the macro recorder to capture as VBA statements.
- Click the Stop Recording button on the Stop Recording toolbar to stop the macro recorder (or click Tools, point to Macro, and then click Stop Recording).

Lynn wants you to modify the Header macro so that it also centers the worksheet on the page. Because you don't know the VBA statement to center the worksheet on the page, you'll use the macro recorder to help you figure out what VBA statements are required for this additional functionality. First, though, you'll use the macro recorder to add your name to the left section of the header, then you will run the new macro and then compare the VBA code created by the macro recorder to the statements of the existing Header macro.

To use the macro recorder to record the Header2 macro:

1. Open the **Athlete-6** workbook located in the Tutorial.06\Tutorial folder on your Data Disk. Click the **Enable Macros** button to open the workbook.

   To record the Header2 macro correctly, you must prepare the Page Setup dialog box so the recorded actions make sense.

2. Click **File** on the menu bar, click **Page Setup**, click the **Header/Footer** tab (if it is not already selected), click the **Custom Header** button, delete any text that appears in the section boxes, click the **OK** button, click the **Page** tab, and then click the **OK** button.

3. Click **Tools** on the menu bar, point to **Macro**, and then click **Record New Macro**.

4. Replace the default "Macro1" with **Header2** in the Macro name text box. Macro names cannot contain spaces, but letters, numbers, and the underscore character are valid characters. You can use the underscore character to simulate a space. Also, macro names must start with a letter rather than a number. Note that macros do not recognize the difference between upper- and lowercase letters, so you can begin a macro name with either. Capitalizing the first letter of each word in a macro name makes the macro name easier to read in the Excel dialog boxes.

5. Select the text in the Description text box, and then type **Inserts your name in the left section of the header.** See Figure 6-13.

Figure 6-13 | **RECORD MACRO DIALOG BOX**

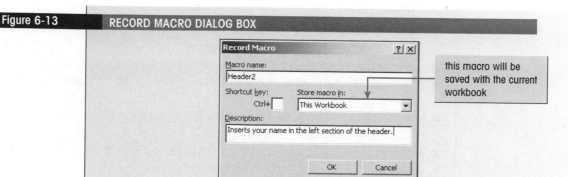

6. Click the **OK** button. The Stop Recording toolbar appears on the screen, and the status bar shows the "Recording" indicator to tell you that any action that you take from this point on will be recorded.

   TROUBLE? If the Stop Recording toolbar doesn't appear on the screen, right-click any existing toolbar and then click Stop Recording on the shortcut menu. Or click View, point to Toolbars, and then click Stop Recording to display the Stop Recording toolbar.

7. Click **File** on the menu bar, click **Page Setup**, click the **Header/Footer** tab, click the **Custom Header** button, type **your name** in the Left section box, click the **OK** button in the Header dialog box, and then click the **OK** button in the Page Setup dialog box.

8. Click the **Stop Recording** button ▣ on the Stop Recording toolbar.

Before comparing the Header2 macro to the existing Header macro, you will test the Header2 macro to make sure that it performs as intended. First, though, you must delete the current text in the header to make sure that the Header2 macro works successfully when you test it.

To test the Header2 macro:

1. Click **File** on the menu bar, click **Page Setup**, click the **Header/Footer** tab (if it is not already selected), click the **Custom Header** button, delete the text in the Left section box, click the **OK** button in the Header dialog box, and then click the **OK** button in the Page Setup dialog box. With the header clear of all text, you will run the Header2 macro to see if it enters your name in the left section of the header as intended.

2. Click **Tools** on the menu bar, point to **Macro**, click **Macros**, click **Header2** in the Macro name list, and then click the **Run** button. Depending upon the speed of your computer, you may have noticed that it took longer to run the Header2 macro than you experienced when you ran the Header macro. If you experienced that slowdown, it is a sure sign that the Header2 macro contains more lines of code than the Header macro. Right now, though, you need to check the Print Preview window to see if the header was modified correctly.

3. Click the **Print Preview** button ◩ on the Standard toolbar, and then zoom in to view the text in the left section of the header. Your name should be in the left section of the header.

4. Close Print Preview.

Working with the Visual Basic Editor

Now that you've used the macro recorder to record a macro, you can view the VBA code that it created in the Visual Basic Editor. You use the Visual Basic Editor to view and edit existing VBA code, as well as to write VBA code from scratch.

To open the Header2 macro in the Visual Basic Editor:

1. Click **Tools** on the menu bar, point to **Macro**, click **Macros**, click **Header2** in the Macro name list, and then click the **Edit** button. See Figure 6-14.

| Figure 6-14 | VISUAL BASIC EDITOR WITH THE HEADER2 MACRO CODE |

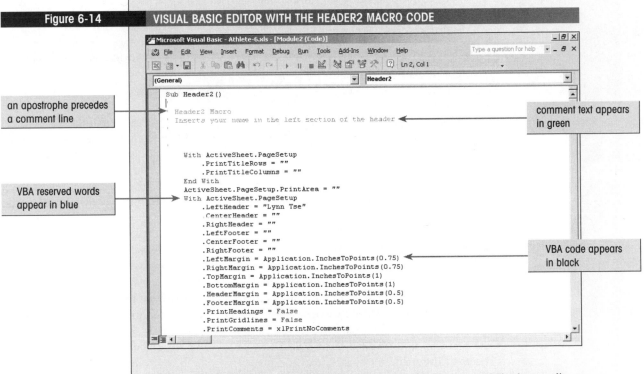

an apostrophe precedes a comment line

comment text appears in green

VBA reserved words appear in blue

VBA code appears in black

There is a big difference in the number of VBA statements between the recorded Header2 macro and the Header macro you used earlier. To view the Header macro, also contained in this workbook, you will open the Project Explorer, in which you will have access to the rest of the code stored in this and other open workbooks.

2. Click the **Project Explorer** button ◩ on the Standard toolbar to open the Project Explorer (its title bar displays Project - VBAProject), and then double-click **Module1** to view the code in the Header macro. See Figure 6-15. Depending on what add-ins you have loaded, the atpvbaenx and funcres projects may also be visible in the Project Explorer.

TROUBLE? If the VBAProject (Athlete-6.xls) project is not expanded, click the **Expand** button to the left of VBAProject (Athlete-6.xls) to open that section of the window.

Figure 6-15	PROJECT EXPLORER

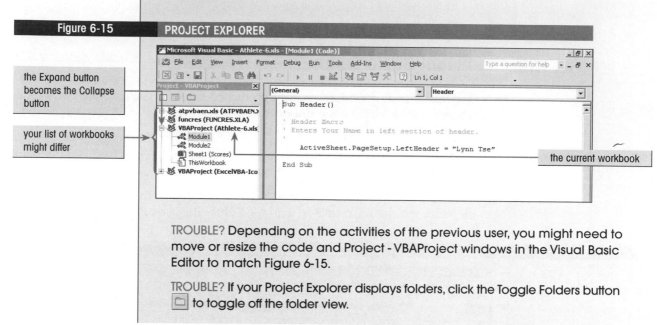

the Expand button becomes the Collapse button

your list of workbooks might differ

the current workbook

TROUBLE? Depending on the activities of the previous user, you might need to move or resize the code and Project - VBAProject windows in the Visual Basic Editor to match Figure 6-15.

TROUBLE? If your Project Explorer displays folders, click the Toggle Folders button to toggle off the folder view.

The Project window displays all of the currently open projects. A **project** is an Excel file, usually an .xls (workbook) or an .xla (add-in) file. An **add-in** is an external file that contains VBA code that enhances Excel's functionality. Add-ins provide a way for outside vendors to easily add their library of custom functions or features to an existing Excel workbook. If you click one of these add-ins, a message appears, indicating that they are both password protected. This means that you can't view or modify the code within them without knowing the password.

Within each expanded project you see the objects within the project that can contain VBA code. In this context, an **object** is either the workbook itself, a worksheet within the workbook, or a module. Each object can store VBA code, and you therefore need to know how to move between the objects in order to view and work with the VBA code stored within each. (You'll learn more about the differences between these objects and how they relate to VBA later.) To open an object and display the code within it, you must double-click the object in the Project Explorer. If you merely single-click an object, you select it, and the Code window doesn't display the VBA code for the selected object. Try moving between the objects of the Athlete-6 workbook now.

To move between objects in the Visual Basic Editor:

1. Double-click **Module2** in the Project Explorer. The VBA code for the Header2 macro appears. Each time you open a workbook and you create a new macro using the macro recorder, it is automatically stored in a new module object.

2. Double-click **Module1** in the Project Explorer. The VBA code for the Header macro appears in the Code window.

3. Double-click the **Sheet1 (Scores)** object in the Project Explorer, and then double-click the **ThisWorkbook** object in the Project Explorer. Neither the Sheet1 (Scores) nor the ThisWorkbook object currently stores any code. Also note that the title bar of the Code window displays the name of the object that you are displaying. When the Code window is maximized, the Visual Basic Editor and the active Code window share the top title bar, which is why the name of the active object (currently ThisWorkbook) is currently displayed in the top title bar.

4. Click **Module1** in the Project Explorer. Although Module1 is clearly selected in the Project Explorer, the Code window is still empty because it still displays code for the ThisWorkbook object.

5. Double-click **Module1** in the Project Explorer. With the Module1 object selected, the Code window displays the VBA code for the Header macro stored within Module1.

In order to compare the VBA code for the Header and Header2 macros, you need to rearrange the screen so that you can view the code windows for the Module1 and Module2 objects side-by-side.

Tiling Macros in the Visual Basic Editor

A **module** is a container for VBA code and can contain one or more macros. But, by default, every time you create a new macro, Excel inserts it in a new module. That's why the Header and Header2 macros are currently stored in two separate modules that display two separate code windows. You want to tile the Module1 and Module2 code windows on the screen to compare the VBA code between the Header and Header2 macros.

To tile the Header and Header2 modules in the Visual Basic Editor:

1. Click the **Close** button ☒ on the title bar of the Project Explorer.

2. Click **Window** on the menu bar, click **Tile Vertically**, and then close the blank Code windows for the Sheet1 and ThisWorkbook windows.

   Since the Sheet1 and ThisWorkbook Code windows don't contain any VBA code, there's no purpose in displaying them on the screen at this time. By closing them, you'll provide more room for the Module1 and Module2 windows.

3. Click **Window** on the menu bar, and then click **Tile Vertically**. See Figure 6-16. No wonder the Header2 macro seemed to run a little sluggishly. It obviously contains many more lines of VBA code than the Header macro.

Figure 6-16   **TILING MODULE WINDOWS**

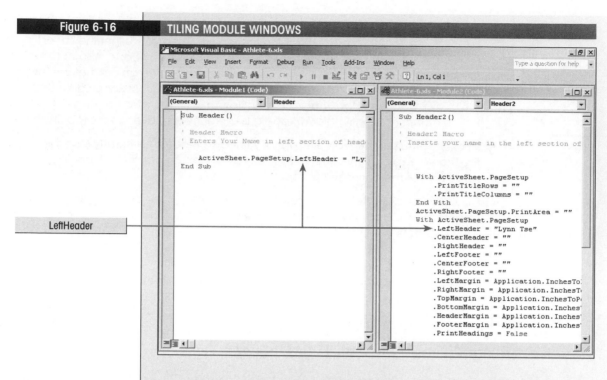

4. Scroll through the Header2 macro in the Module2 Code window and find the statements that modify the LeftHeader and your name.

Even though the macros accomplish the same thing, entering your name in the left section of the header, they are obviously much different from one another. The Header macro contains only three statements (not counting the comment statements), but the Header2 macro, the one you created using the macro recorder, contains so many statements that you can't even see all of them on the screen. After glancing through the code in the Header2 macro on the right and trying to find the statement that enters your name in the left section of the header, you quickly realize that you need to know more about VBA if you are to successfully read, edit, and use it.

VBA Terminology

Like any foreign language, learning VBA requires learning many new terms. Sometimes, learning a programming language is actually harder than learning a foreign language because you're not just learning new terms, you're also learning new meanings for existing words. Sometimes you need to "unlearn" the meaning that you previously attributed to that word, at least in the context of VBA. But the sooner you accept and internalize the specific definition of a common word within the framework of a new program or programming language, the easier it will be to read your textbook, look up information in the Help manuals, and communicate with other VBA programmers.

You've already encountered some VBA words such as project and module. Another key VBA term is "object." Within VBA, an **object** is anything that can be identified and controlled by the code. You can think of an object as a noun, such as a single cell, a range of cells, a toolbar, a worksheet, a workbook, or the entire Excel application itself. VBA is considered to be an **object-oriented** programming language because VBA statements manipulate objects.

Objects are organized in an **object hierarchy** that defines which objects can contain other objects. For example, the `Workbook` object can contain `Worksheet` objects and `Chart` objects. The `Worksheet` object can contain `Range` objects and `PivotTable` objects. All of the objects of one type are called an **object collection**. For example, the `Worksheets` object would be the object name for the collection of all of the individual `Worksheet` objects in a particular workbook.

It's important to understand what objects are, and how they are related to one another in the object hierarchy, because VBA statements use object names extensively. For example, the following portion of a VBA statement identifies the Income worksheet, which is a member of the `Worksheets` collection.

```
Worksheets("Income")
```

As you can see, to reference a single object from a collection object, you put the object's name in parentheses after the name of the collection. If you had two workbooks open, and therefore needed to further identify that the CarDealers workbook contained the Income worksheet, the statement would expand to:

```
Workbooks("CarDealers").Worksheets("Income")
```

This example shows that when you use the object hierarchy within a VBA statement, you start with the "highest" member of the hierarchy, and you separate member objects with a period, usually referred to as a **dot** by VBA programmers.

At the top of the model is the `Application` object, Excel itself. So the same VBA code could actually be expanded to:

```
Application.Workbooks("CarDealers").Worksheets("Income")
```

Because the `Application` object is not an object collection, you did not need to clarify within parentheses which member of the collection you are referring to. To refer to the cell range B1:B8 in the Inc worksheet of the Car workbook, the full VBA code would look like this:

```
Application.Workbooks("Car").Worksheets("Inc").Range("B1:B8")
```

If you omit a specific reference to an object, Excel uses the active object, so most programmers do not start the identification of the object at the `Application` object level. Rather, they start at whatever level is required for the code to run effectively. Therefore, it's important to understand object hierarchy and to anticipate all of the different environments from which you might run that VBA statement. For example, if you anticipate running a macro that bolds a range of cells when multiple workbooks might be open, you would need to start the object identification at the `Workbook` object level in order to clarify exactly where the code should run.

The Excel Objects Model

You don't have to know every menu option and feature of Excel to start using it in a productive way. You also don't need to know everything about each object within the object hierarchy, which is referred to as the **Microsoft Excel Objects model**, in order to start writing VBA code. But knowing where to find a map of the Excel Objects model can help you understand the object hierarchy and help you write VBA code later on.

To explore the Microsoft Excel Objects model:

1. Click in the Ask a Question box in the Visual Basic Editor window, type **object model**, and then press the **Enter** key.

   EXCEL 2000: Because there is no Ask a Question box in the Excel 2000 Visual Basic Editor window, click **Help** on the menu bar, click **Microsoft Visual Basic Help**, type **microsoft excel objects**, and then click the **Search** button. Click **Microsoft Excel Objects**, maximize the Help window, and then go to Step 3.

   TROUBLE? Make sure you use the Ask a Question box in the Visual Basic Editor window, and not the Microsoft Excel workbook window.

   TROUBLE? You might be prompted to install the Help feature. If so, follow the instructions on the screen, or ask your instructor or technical support person for help.

2. Click **Microsoft Excel Objects** in the list, and then maximize the Microsoft Visual Basic Help window.

3. Click the **Hide** button ⊞ on the Help toolbar to close the left navigation pane. See Figure 6-17. The Application object is at the highest level and contains the Workbooks and AddIns objects, among others. The Workbooks object contains the Worksheets and Charts objects, among others.

Figure 6-17	MICROSOFT EXCEL OBJECTS MODEL

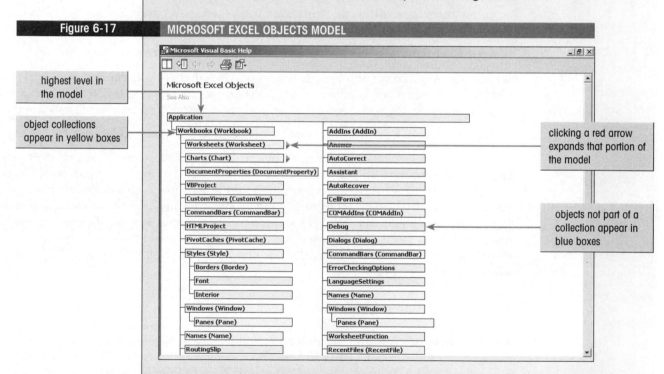

4. Scroll through the window as necessary to see the legend in the lower-left corner of the Help page. Yellow boxes represent object collections. The collection name is usually the plural form of an individual object name. Light blue boxes represent objects that are not part of a collection of similar objects. Clicking a red arrow expands that portion of the model.

5. Scroll back to the top of the window, and then click the **red arrow** to the right of the Worksheets (Worksheet) object. See Figure 6-18. The `Worksheets` object contains many objects, which, in turn, contain many other objects. To find out more about a specific object, click it.

Figure 6-18   **EXPLORING THE WORKSHEET OBJECT**

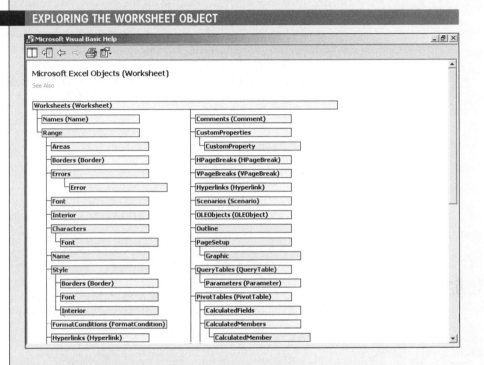

6. Click the **Range** box. The Help page that describes the Range Collection opens. The `Range` object is shown in a hierarchy both below "Multiple objects" and above "Multiple objects". That means that many objects can "contain" the `Range` object and that the `Range` object itself contains many other objects. You can click either of the "Multiple objects" boxes to find out which objects are both "above" and "below" the Range object in the object hierarchy.

   EXCEL 2000: In the Range Object page that appears, "Multiple Objects" appears only once, below the `Range` object; therefore, in any of the subsequent steps, click this occurrence of Multiple Objects when instructed to click the upper or lower occurrence of this option.

7. Click the upper **Multiple objects** box, and then scroll through the list that appears. The objects that can contain the `Range` object are listed in alphabetical order. The `Worksheet` object, which you were viewing earlier, is listed last.

   EXCEL 2000: When you click the Multiple Objects box, the Topics Found dialog box opens. Scroll through the topics.

8. Click anywhere on the Help page to close the list, click the lower **Multiple objects** box to view the objects that the `Range` object can contain, scroll through the list, and then close it.

   EXCEL 2000: Click the **Cancel** button to close the Topics Found dialog box.

9. Click the **Back** button ⇐ on the Help toolbar until you return to the first page of the Microsoft Excel Objects model.

Knowing how to access information on the Excel Objects model is important. You will be able to access this information regardless of the Office product in which you are working. Each program has its own objects model, because each software program has different objects that are only appropriate for that product. For example, you would not find the `Worksheet` object in the Word Objects model, but the concept of objects, object collections, and object hierarchy are applied consistently to VBA within all of the programs in the Microsoft Office suite.

Properties

To do something meaningful in VBA, you need to manipulate objects. For example, you might want to modify the font color for a range of cells, or you might want to change the value of a single cell. Interestingly, there is no Excel object that refers to an individual cell. A single cell is identified with the `Range` object that references only one cell such as `Range("A1")`.

Every characteristic of an object is called a **property** of that object. For example, the `Range` object has the `Value` property that determines the entry in that range. You refer to a specific property of an object by adding it to the end of the object structure code, separating the property from the object with a period. So the following statement would set the value of a range's (in this case, a single cell's) `Value` property to 3000:

```
Range("A1").Value = 3000
```

The `Range` object also contains the `Font` object, which contains many properties that identify the characteristics of the font for an object. The following statement would refer to the `Value` property for the `Range ("A1")` object (on the current worksheet in the current workbook of Excel).

```
Range("A1").Value
```

To change the `Value` property to 300, you separate the object and property identification from 300 with an equal sign as follows:

```
Range("A1").Value = 300
```

To turn on the `Bold` property for cell A1, the statement would look like this:

```
Range("A1").Font.Bold = True
```

In this case, `Bold` is a property of the `Font` object. (The `Name` property of the `Font` object sets the actual font typeface.) The `Font` object properties that can only be turned "on" or "off," including `Bold`, `Strikethrough`, and `Superscript`, are described as such by using the words `True` ("on") or `False` ("off") in VBA.

To explore object properties:

1. On the first page of the Microsoft Excel Objects model, click the **red arrow** to the right of the Worksheets (Worksheet) box, and then click the **Range** box to redisplay the Range Collection page. On each object page, you can access a list of object properties by clicking the Properties link.

   EXCEL 2000: The Range Object page is displayed.

2. Click the **Properties** link on the Range Collection, and then scroll through the list of available properties. See Figure 6-19.

   EXCEL 2000: When you click the Properties link on an object page, the Topics Found dialog box opens. Scroll through the list of available properties.

Figure 6-19	VIEWING PROPERTIES FOR THE RANGE OBJECT

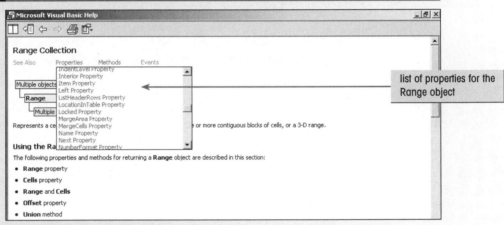

list of properties for the Range object

3. Click anywhere in the Help page to close the list, click the lower **Multiple objects** box to view the objects that the Range object can contain, and then click **Font Object** in the list. The Help information for the Font Object appears.

   EXCEL 2000: Click the **Cancel** button to close the Topics Found dialog box, click the **Multiple Objects** box, and then double-click **Font Object** in the list.

4. Click the **Properties** link on the Font Object page, and then click **Bold Property** in the list to examine the Help page for this property. See Figure 6-20. When you are examining a property in the Visual Basic Help system, the Properties link changes to the Applies To link. The Applies To link will identify all objects for which this property is available.

   EXCEL 2000: Double-click **Bold Property** in the Topics Found dialog box. The Help window for the Bold Property does not provide examples. This omission will not affect the steps.

Figure 6-20   EXAMINING THE BOLD PROPERTY

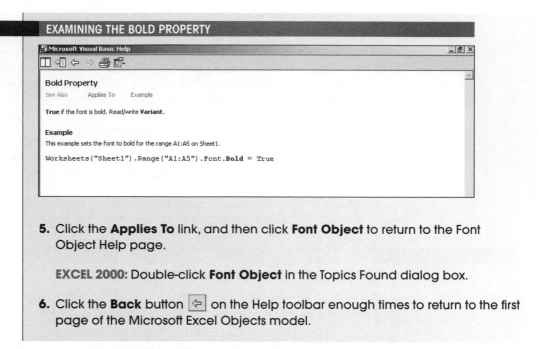

5. Click the **Applies To** link, and then click **Font Object** to return to the Font Object Help page.

   EXCEL 2000: Double-click **Font Object** in the Topics Found dialog box.

6. Click the **Back** button ⇐ on the Help toolbar enough times to return to the first page of the Microsoft Excel Objects model.

In addition to showing the object model hierarchy and available properties, the Visual Basic Help pages often provide extra explanatory text, links to related topics, and examples. Not all of that "help" will be helpful to you right now, but it is still vital that you are comfortable with the key VBA concepts of objects and properties and that you know how to look them up and move through the Visual Basic Help system.

Methods

Another way to work with an object is to perform an action with it. A **method** is an action that an object can accomplish. For example, you might want to delete the existing entry in a range of cells. To accomplish this task, you could use the `Clear` method of the `Range` object. Just as properties are added to the end of the VBA code that describes an object, so are methods. The code that applies the `Clear` method to a `Range` object would look like this:

```
Range("A1:B1").Clear
```

If you can think of an object as a noun, you would consider a method a verb.

Arguments

Many methods need additional information in order to clarify their action. These additional pieces of information are called **arguments**. (You can think of the arguments of a method in the same way you think of the arguments of an Excel function such as PMT—they are the additional pieces of information that are required to successfully complete the task.) The `Clear` method did not require arguments, but consider the `Copy` method. When you use the `Copy` method on a `Range` object, you need to supply the destination of the location to which the values will be copied. To copy the contents of cell A1 to cell A2, the statement would be:

```
Range("A1").Copy Range("A2")
```

Because there is only one argument for the `Copy` method, the argument merely follows the VBA code by a space. Note that arguments are not separated from methods using a period. If there are multiple arguments for a method, subsequent arguments are separated by using commas (just as arguments are separated in Excel functions using commas). In addition, you can use named arguments to make your code easier to read. A **named argument** separates the name of the argument from its value using a colon and an equal sign. For example, the following two VBA statements are equivalent:

```
Range("A1").Copy Range("A2")
Range("A1").Copy destination:=Range("A2")
```

Properties can also use or require arguments, although not as commonly as methods use properties. When a property contains an argument, the argument is placed in parentheses behind the property, much like the specific object name is referenced by an object collection. For example, the `Range` object has the `Address` property, which returns the range reference of the cell. The property can be clarified with up to six optional arguments. See Figure 6-21 for three examples of VBA code that uses arguments to further clarify the `Address` property of the `Range` object.

Figure 6-21	USING OPTIONAL ARGUMENTS

VBA CODE	RETURNS
Range("A1").Address	$A$1
Range("A1").Address(RowAbsolute:=False)	$A1
Range("A1").Address(RowAbsolute:=False, ColumnAbsolute:=False)	A1

Some arguments are optional, and some are required. **Optional arguments** already contain a default value and therefore do not need to be explicitly referenced if you want the property or method to use the default value for that argument. **Required arguments** must be provided a value in order for VBA to work correctly. Furthermore, if you are not using named arguments, you must reference each argument in the order in which it is defined in the Visual Basic Help system. You can insert commas as placeholders to indicate that the default value should be used for that argument. For example, if you wanted the `Address` property of the `Range` object to return the answer in the R1C1 (Row 1 Column 1) reference style versus the A1 (default, Column A Row 1) reference style, and you did not use named arguments, the statement would look like the following because the `ReferenceStyle` argument of the `Address` property of the `Range` object is the third argument in a list of five optional arguments for that property:

```
Range("A1").Address(,,xlR1C1,,)
```

As with any programming language, there are many rules, sometimes called programming **syntax**, which must be understood and followed if you are to read and write VBA code successfully. Fortunately, you don't have to understand each specific object, property, method, or argument in order to enjoy the benefits of enhancing your workbooks with VBA. You must, however, have a general sense of how a VBA statement is organized in order to write, debug, and modify simple macros, custom functions, and custom forms.

To explore methods and arguments:

1. On the first page of the Microsoft Excel Objects model, click the **red arrow** to the right of the Worksheets (Worksheet) box, and then click the **Range** box. For each object, you can click the Methods link on the Help page to access a list of object methods.

   EXCEL 2000: The Range Object page appears.

2. Click the **Methods** link on the Range Collection page, and then scroll through the list of available properties. See Figure 6-22.

   EXCEL 2000: When you click the Methods link on an object page, the Topics Found dialog box opens. Scroll through the list of available properties.

Figure 6-22	VIEWING METHODS FOR THE RANGE OBJECT

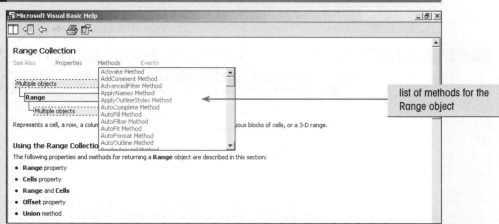

3. Click **ClearMethod** in the list, and then click the **Clear method as it applies to the ChartArea, Legend and Range objects** link. See Figure 6-23. Note that there are no arguments, required or optional, for the `Clear` method. The only requirement is that an expression that returns a Range object be identified before using the `Clear` method as shown in the example provided.

   EXCEL 2000: Click **ClearMethod** in the list, click the **Display** button, click the **Applies To** link, and then double-click the **ChartArea Object** in the Topics Found dialog box. To learn how the `Clear` method applies to the `Legend` or `Range` object, double-click the object in the Topics Found dialog box.

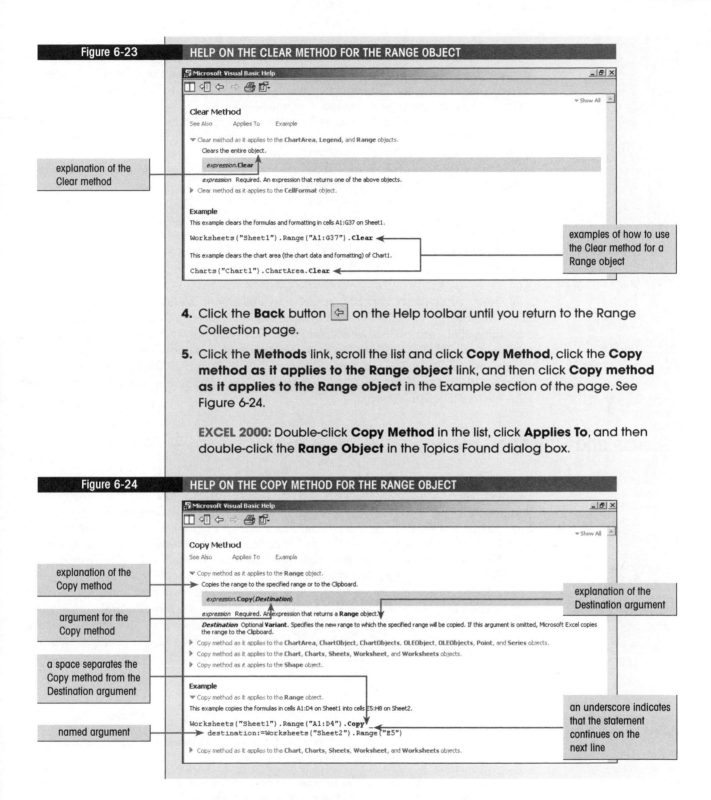

Figure 6-23   HELP ON THE CLEAR METHOD FOR THE RANGE OBJECT

explanation of the Clear method

examples of how to use the Clear method for a Range object

4. Click the **Back** button on the Help toolbar until you return to the Range Collection page.

5. Click the **Methods** link, scroll the list and click **Copy Method**, click the **Copy method as it applies to the Range object** link, and then click **Copy method as it applies to the Range object** in the Example section of the page. See Figure 6-24.

   EXCEL 2000: Double-click **Copy Method** in the list, click **Applies To**, and then double-click the **Range Object** in the Topics Found dialog box.

Figure 6-24   HELP ON THE COPY METHOD FOR THE RANGE OBJECT

explanation of the Copy method

argument for the Copy method

a space separates the Copy method from the Destination argument

named argument

explanation of the Destination argument

an underscore indicates that the statement continues on the next line

Note the general syntax for the Copy method is given as *expression.Copy(Destination)*. The Destination argument is not required, but if you do not specify a value for it, the Copy method will copy the range to the Clipboard rather than a specific destination on a workbook.

Also, note that in the example, the `Destination` argument uses the named argument option, which is separated from the `Copy` method with a space. Recall that arguments separated from properties are placed in parentheses, but arguments separated from methods are separated by a space. This syntax can help you figure out if the last item of VBA code separated by dots (periods) is a property or a method.

The underscore character serves as a **continuation character**, indicating that the single line of VBA code continues on the next line. The character is used when a single line of VBA code doesn't fit on a single line in the Visual Basic Editor, or when you simply want to shorten up the width of your lines of code for readability purposes. You must enter a space before the underscore for it to work correctly.

To close Microsoft Visual Basic Help:

1. Click the **Close** button ☒ on the Help window title bar.

By now you may have noticed that some methods can be applied to more than one object (just as some properties can be applied to more than one object). You usually don't need to read everything about that method or property in order to find out what you need for a particular statement of VBA. You only need to expand and read the sections of the Help page that apply to your situation. Once you understand some of the basics of VBA programming, including what an object, a property, a method, and an argument are, you can continue learning about VBA by studying examples of code.

Subs **and Functions**

With a better understanding of the key vocabulary used in VBA, you want to go back to the Header2 macro and review the VBA code that was created by the macro recorder. Before doing so, however, you also need to cover a few more VBA keywords, specifically `Sub` and `Function`. You might have also noticed that when you write a macro, the first line of the macro always starts with the word "Sub." **Sub** (short for subroutine or subprocedure) is a VBA keyword and is identified in a dark blue text color in the VBA Editor window. The word following `Sub` is the name of the macro.

Similarly, when you create a custom function, the first line of VBA starts with the keyword **Function**. Together, subs and functions are called VBA procedures. In other words, a VBA **procedure** is a collection of VBA statements that perform an operation or calculate an answer. One VBA module can contain as many procedures as you like, but each must start with the `Sub` or `Function` VBA keyword and end with either the `End Sub` (for subs) or `End Function` (for functions) statement.

To view Sub and End Sub statements in your macros:

1. In the Visual Basic Editor, note that the first line of the Header macro starts with `Sub Header()` and the last line is `End Sub`.

2. Note that the first line of the Header2 macro starts with `Sub Header2()`, and then scroll to the bottom of the code so that you can see that the last line is `End Sub`. The left and right parentheses are always added to the end of the sub name in the first line of a sub procedure. They do not contain a space between them.

Visual **Basic Editor Colors**

The Visual Basic Editor uses different colors for different types of VBA code. Figure 6-25 identifies the default colors used by VBA.

Figure 6-25	VBA COLORS	

COLOR	DESCRIPTION
Blue	Keyword text. Blue words are reserved by VBA and are already assigned specific meanings such as Sub, Function, With, and If.
Black	Normal text. Black words are the unique VBA code developed by the user such as those that identify the object, property, method, or arguments being used.
Red	Syntax error text. A line of code that appears red will not execute correctly because there is a syntax error (perhaps a missing parenthesis or a spelling error) in the text.
Green	Comment text. Any green text that appears after an apostrophe is used for documentation purposes and is ignored in the execution of the procedure.

Depending on the color settings on your computer, you might find it difficult to distinguish between the dark blue and black colors. You can change the default color settings to make the distinction between colors more apparent.

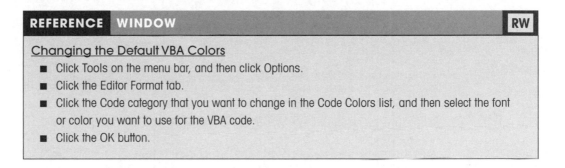

REFERENCE WINDOW   **RW**

Changing the Default VBA Colors
- Click Tools on the menu bar, and then click Options.
- Click the Editor Format tab.
- Click the Code category that you want to change in the Code Colors list, and then select the font or color you want to use for the VBA code.
- Click the OK button.

Because you are still new to VBA, but you want to clearly see the difference between the VBA reserved keywords and the normal text, you'll change the background color of the keyword text to highlight it.

To change the background color of the keyword text:

1. Click **Tools** on the menu bar, and then click **Options**. As with all Microsoft products, the Options dialog box provides default settings used by the entire program. Changes you make within this dialog box will affect all Visual Basic Editor windows within all Excel workbooks.

2. Click the **Editor Format** tab (if it is not already selected), click **Keyword Text** in the Code Colors list, click the **Background** list arrow, and then scroll down the list and click the **Yellow** option in the list. See Figure 6-26. The Sample window gives you a preview of the keyword text with the yellow background.

Figure 6-26   CHANGING DEFAULT KEYWORD TEXT OPTIONS

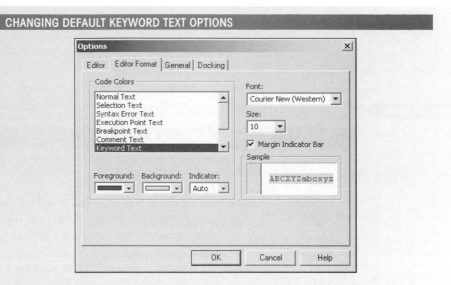

3. Click the **OK** button. VBA keywords are now displayed with a bright yellow background, making them easier to find. See Figure 6-27.

Figure 6-27   VBA KEYWORDS DISPLAYED WITH A YELLOW BACKGROUND

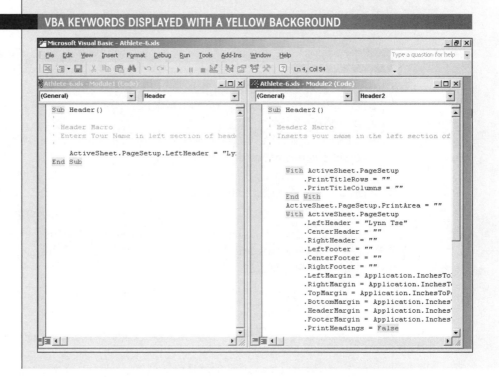

Often, new VBA programmers wonder why the default font is Courier New (Western) when Arial is used as the default font on an Excel workbook itself. The reason is that Courier New and Courier are fixed (mono-spaced) fonts that give each character the same amount of horizontal space, regardless of which character it is. In other words, five lower-case "l" characters and five uppercase "W" characters would use exactly the same width when entered using a mono-spaced font. This insures that the same number of characters can be used for every statement, which can make long statements that are copied and modified easier to read and debug. Courier fonts also use **serifs** (lines on the tops and bottoms of characters) that further define each character and make it easier to read. Also, because the default VBA Editor font is Courier New, VBA programmers are more familiar with seeing their VBA code in this font.

Documenting **VBA Code**

You will now study the Header2 macro a little more closely to determine the intent and meaning of each statement. You'll use comment lines to clarify and document the code.

To document the lines of the Header2 macro:

1. Maximize the module window that contains the Header2 macro. Note that VBA allows you to skip lines and also to indent lines to make your program more readable. Neither blank lines nor indents change the execution of the code, nor are they required for the code to run properly.

2. Click below the comment that begins "Inserts your name…" and add the new comments as shown in Figure 6-28. Be sure to enter your own name and the current date.

Figure 6-28   ADDING COMMENTS

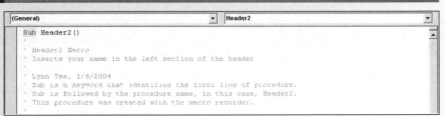

TROUBLE? To enter the text as shown in Figure 6-28, type ' (an apostrophe), press the spacebar, type the comment, and press the Enter key. Don't worry if you have extra apostrophes or blank lines, because these do not affect the functionality of the macro.

3. Click to the right of the `With ActiveSheet.PageSetup` statement, type `' With allows you to set many properties for an object` and then press the **Enter** key. By entering an apostrophe, you can add a comment to the end of an existing statement as well as to a new line.

4. Click to the right of the `End With` statement, type `' Enter End With after the last property` and then press the **Enter** key. See Figure 6-29.

Figure 6-29   ADDING A COMMENT TO THE END OF A STATEMENT

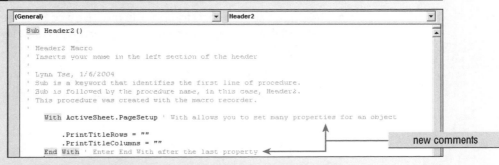

new comments

The four lines of code in the Header2 macro that start with the `With ActiveSheet.PageSetup` statement set property values for the `PrintTitleRows` and `PrintTitleColumns` properties of the `ActiveSheet.PageSetup` object. Because nothing has been specified for either property (a double set of quotation marks means that the property has been set to nothing, or an empty string), those four lines of code didn't make any changes to your workbook. Of course, if your workbook already contained row or column title settings, these statements would reset them to nothing. Because you want this macro to enter your name in the left section of the header, without changing any other existing print options, you don't need these four lines of code.

To delete the first set of unnecessary lines of code in the Header2 macro:

1. Select the four lines of code that start with the `With ActiveSheet.PageSetup` statement and end with the `End With` statement, and then press the **Delete** key.

   Next, you'll examine the rest of the statements to see if you need to add clarifying comments. You also want to delete any statements that are unnecessary for the purpose of adding your name to the left section of the header.

2. Examine the `ActiveSheet.PageSetup.PrintArea = ""` statement. If necessary, open Help and read more about these objects and properties. At first glance, this line of code may appear to be setting the print area to nothing, but in reality the statement is setting the property to an empty string, which means that the entire sheet, and not a specific range, has been selected as the print area. Therefore, everything on the current worksheet will be printed. Because this task is irrelevant to your goal of adding your name to the upper-left section of the header, you will delete this line of code.

3. Select the `ActiveSheet.PageSetup.PrintArea = ""` statement, and then press the **Delete** key.

   TROUBLE? If you click the gray bar to the left of a statement, you set a breakpoint, identified by a brown dot and highlight. You can use breakpoints when you want to examine the effect of running a few lines of code at a time. To remove the breakpoint, click the brown dot to toggle the breakpoint off. You will learn more about breakpoints in a later tutorial.

   The next two lines `With ActiveSheet.PageSetup` and `.LeftHeader = "Lynn Tse"` are the lines that add your name to the left section of the header. In VBA, the `LeftHeader` property of the `PageSetup` object of the `ActiveSheet` object is equal to whatever text is included in the quotation marks at the end of the statement. You cannot delete these lines of code. But what about the rest? Because you don't want to modify any other print setup options, you can delete many more statements.

4. Delete the statements starting with the `.CenterHeader = ""` statement through the `.PrintErrors = xlPrintErrorsDisplayed` statement. See Figure 6-30.

   EXCEL 2000: Delete the statements starting with the `.CenterHeader = ""` statement through the `.FitToPagesTall = 1` statement.

Figure 6-30 | UNNECESSARY PROPERTY STATEMENTS DELETED

```
(General)                                    Header2

Sub Header2()
'
' Header2 Macro
' Inserts your name in the left section of the header
'
' Lynn Tse, 1/6/2004
' Sub is a keyword that identifies the first line of procedure.
' Sub is followed by the procedure name, in this case, Header2.
' This procedure was created with the macro recorder.


    With ActiveSheet.PageSetup
        .LeftHeader = "Lynn Tse"
    End With
End Sub
```

Because there is now only one property statement assignment for the `ActiveSheet.PageSetup` object, you no longer need to use the `With` and `End With` statements.

5. Delete the `With`, delete `End With`, and then delete the spaces between the two existing lines so that the remaining statement is on one line. See Figure 6-31.

Figure 6-31 | UNNECESSARY WITH AND END WITH STATEMENTS DELETED

```
(General)                                    Header2

Sub Header2()
'
' Header2 Macro
' Inserts your name in the left section of the header
'
' Lynn Tse, 1/6/2004
' Sub is a keyword that identifies the first line of procedure.
' Sub is followed by the procedure name, in this case, Header2.
' This procedure was created with the macro recorder.
'

    ActiveSheet.PageSetup.LeftHeader = "Lynn Tse"

End Sub
```

6. Save and then print the code for the Header2 macro.

Now that you've effectively used color to highlight the keywords in the VBA code, you'll remove the background color for keyword text to return that option to its default setting.

7. Click **Tools** on the menu bar, click **Options**, click the **Editor Format** tab, click the **Keyword Text** entry in the Code Colors list, click the **Background** list arrow, scroll to the top of the list and click **Auto**, and then click the **OK** button.

8. Close the Visual Basic Editor.

The Header2 macro now looks very similar to the original Header macro because both now contain only one line of VBA code that makes a property assignment. Whether one is better than the other, depends upon what you are trying to accomplish. If your real goal were to add your name to the left section of the header and to not change any other printing settings, no matter what they were, the original Header macro would work best for this purpose. If, on the other hand, the goal were to capture all of the options within the Page Setup dialog box and apply them to the workbook so that all print settings such as margins, gridlines, and titles were restored to the same settings as those used at the time the Header2 macro was recorded, then the original Header2 macro with its many lines of property assignments would have been best for this task.

At this point, the main thing to realize is that the macro recorder is a wonderful tool for quickly creating VBA code, but that it often creates more code than you need for your intended purpose. With only a basic understanding of VBA, you were able to read and edit code created by the macro recorder and simplify it for your purpose. You can use the macro recorder to create code, and then copy, paste, and edit the code needed to an existing macro.

Deleting **Macros and Modules**

VBA code doesn't require a lot of extra storage space. Still, you should delete all unneeded code to keep your Excel workbook as clean as possible. If your procedures are sub procedures, you can delete them using the Macro dialog box.

REFERENCE WINDOW   **RW**

Deleting a Macro
- Click Tools on the menu bar, point to Macro, and then click Macros.
- Click the macro name in the Macro name list that you want to delete, and then click the Delete button.
- Click the Yes button.

You want to delete the macros you've created so far.

To delete the Header2 macro:

1. Click **Tools** on the menu bar, point to **Macro**, and then click **Macros**. All of the existing sub procedures are listed in the Macro name list, regardless of whether they were created by the macro recorder or written from scratch by you in the Visual Basic Editor. If there is more than one sub located in a module, each sub is displayed as a macro in the module's list.

2. Click **Header2** in the Macro name list, click the **Delete** button, and then click the **Yes** button when prompted to delete the macro.

   Now also delete the Header macro.

3. Click **Tools** on the menu bar, point to **Macro**, click **Macros**, click the **Delete** button, and then click the **Yes** button.

4. Save and close the Athlete-6 workbook, and then reopen it. The message box opens, warning you that the workbook contains macros, even though you just deleted all of them.

Although you have deleted the macros, Excel still asks if you want to disable or enable existing macros. This is because you didn't delete the modules that stored those macros. The presence of any extra module in an Excel workbook causes this prompt to appear, indicating that the workbook *may* contain macros.

<u>Deleting an Existing Module</u>
- Click Tools on the menu bar, point to Macro, and then click Macros.
- Open the Project Explorer.
- Right-click the module that you want to delete, and then click Remove Module(#).
- Click the No button to permanently delete the module, or click the Yes button to export the module to another workbook.

Because you were only using this workbook to learn how macros and VBA can be applied at GVR, you want to clean up all traces of your work so that the macro prompt doesn't appear when this workbook is reopened.

To delete the modules that are stored in the workbook:

1. Click the **Disable Macros** button in the message box. (You could click the Enable Macros button—it doesn't matter since the workbook contains no macros.) To delete the modules, you have to open the Visual Basic Editor and the Project Explorer.

2. Click **Tools** on the menu bar, point to **Macro**, and then click **Visual Basic Editor**.

3. Click the **Project Explorer** button on the Standard toolbar, and then double-click **Module1** to display it in the Code window. Because Module1 is now just an empty container, void of any VBA subs or functions, you can delete it.

4. Right-click **Module1** in the Project Explorer, click **Remove Module1** on the shortcut menu, and then click the **No** button when prompted to export it. Programmers will often develop VBA code in one workbook and then export or copy it to another workbook when they have finished testing the code. In this case, you don't need to export the modules before you delete them.

5. Double-click **Module2** to display it in the Code window. Module2 was originally created when you recorded the Header2 macro, but it doesn't contain any code now because you deleted the Header2 macro. By default, each new macro that you record is placed in its own module. You might want to organize similar macros together in their own module and then export them as a group once they are finished. For now, however, you want to delete Module2.

6. Right-click **Module2** in the Project Explorer, click **Remove Module2** on the shortcut menu, and then click the **No** button when prompted to export it. You're left with only the Sheet1 (Scores) and ThisWorkbook objects within the VBAProject (Athlete-6.xls) project, which do not contain any VBA code at this point. You cannot delete these objects because they exist due to the presence of the workbook and worksheets within the workbook.

7. Save the changes you have made, and then close the Visual Basic Editor. When you click the Save button in the Visual Basic Editor, you're saving the changes to VBA and to the Excel workbook.

8. Close the workbook, and then reopen it. You should not be prompted to enable or disable macros this time, because you deleted all of the module containers.

9. Close the Athlete-6 workbook.

Security

You might be a little concerned about clicking the Enable Macros option when you open a new workbook because of the warning about viruses. Unfortunately, hackers often use macros to spread viruses, which is why you are prompted about the potential presence of macros and viruses every time you open a workbook with VBA code or modules. To address security issues, Excel provides three **security levels**, High, Medium, and Low, which determine how macros are handled and what prompts you see. By default, the Excel security level is set to Medium, which prompts you to enable or disable unsigned macros.

An **unsigned macro** is one for which you have no legitimate way to determine the authenticity of the creator of that macro. As you know, workbooks often get passed from person to person, and malicious programs can be attached to files from outside sources. Just because you received a workbook from one person doesn't mean that a potential virus in the form of a macro hasn't been introduced into that file by another person.

You will study Excel security levels and digital signatures so that the macros that are used within the workbooks at GVR do not cause users any problems or open the door for potentially harmful viruses.

To study Excel security levels:

1. Click **Tools** on the menu bar, point to **Macro**, and then click **Security**. The Security dialog box opens. See Figure 6-32.

Figure 6-32	SECURITY DIALOG BOX

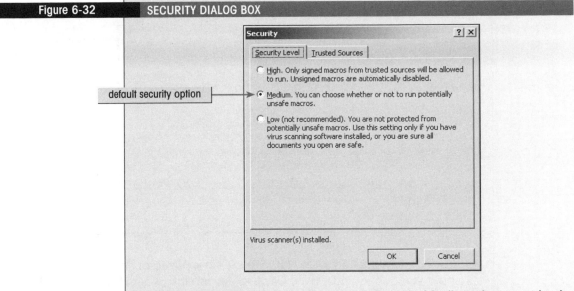

default security option

Right now the security level is probably set to Medium. A summarized version of each security level is presented. In the lower-left corner of the dialog box, a message appears indicating whether or not you have virus-scanning software installed. If you do not have virus-scanning software, and if you do not want to run unsigned macros, you could click the High security option so that unsigned macros would be automatically disabled.

2. Click the **Cancel** button.

After reading the summary statements about each security level, you realize that you need to know more about signed and unsigned macros. Signed macros appear to be a method to accept macro code from trusted sources and disable macros from unidentified sources.

Creating a Digital Signature

A **signed macro** is a macro that contains a digital signature. A **digital signature** is an electronic signature that is unique from the signer. It is also encrypted and therefore cannot be altered. The presence of a digital signature confirms that the macro came from the owner of the digital signature and that it has not been altered since it was applied. You can purchase a digital signature from a company such as VeriSign, Inc., or you can create your own digital signature using the **SELFCERT.EXE** Office XP tool. Because a digital certificate that you create using the SELFCERT.EXE tool isn't issued or guaranteed by a formal certification authority such as VeriSign, a digital certificate created with this tool is a less secure signature than one certified by VeriSign. Still, creating a self-generated digital certificate will help the user of a workbook that contains the macros you've created and signed know more about the authenticity of the macro code. Macros signed by such self-generated digital certificates are said to be **self-signed**.

To create your own digital certificate:

1. Open **Microsoft Windows Explorer**, and then navigate to the **C:\Program Files\Microsoft Office\Office10** folder in the Folders window.

2. Double-click the **SELFCERT** file. The Create Digital Certificate dialog box appears. See Figure 6-33.

Figure 6-33	CREATE DIGITAL CERTIFICATE DIALOG BOX

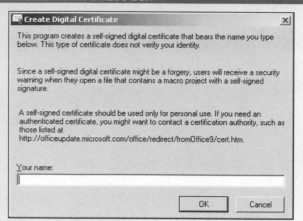

TROUBLE? The location of the SELFCERT.EXE file is based on the initial Office installation. If you cannot find it in the Office folder, use the Search tool to locate the file.

TROUBLE? If you cannot locate the SELFCERT.EXE file using the Search tool, you might have to install it. Open the Help page titled "Create your own digital certificate" for instructions.

3. Type **your name**, click the **OK** button, and then click the **OK** button when prompted that a certificate was successfully created.

Now that you've created a digital signature, you can sign your own macros. By signing the macro, you will provide more information about the macro to the person who opens the workbook—information that will help users know whether they want to trust that macro or not.

Signing a Macro

You sign a macro after you have created and tested it. You sign it right before you are ready to distribute it to others. You decide to create a small macro to horizontally center the worksheet on the page. You'll sign the macro and learn how the digital signature helps others who may use this macro.

To create a macro to horizontally center the worksheet:

1. Start a new, blank workbook. You'll create the macro using the macro recorder.

2. Click **Tools** on the menu bar, point to **Macro**, and then click **Record New Macro**.

3. Type **CenterPrintout** as the macro name, type **Center a worksheet horizontally on the page** as the description of the macro, press the **Enter** key, type **your name**, and then click the **OK** button.

4. Click **File** on the menu bar, click **Page Setup**, click the **Margins** tab (if it is not already selected), click the **Horizontally** check box, and then click the **OK** button.

5. Click the **Stop Recording** button ■ on the Stop Recording toolbar to end the macro recording session.

Now that you've created a macro, you will sign it. To sign a macro, you use the Visual Basic Editor.

REFERENCE WINDOW   **RW**

Signing a Macro
- Click Tools on the menu bar, point to Macro, and then click Visual Basic Editor.
- In the Project Explorer, double-click the module that contains the macro that you want to sign.
- Click Tools on the menu bar, and then click Digital Signature.
- Click the Choose button.
- Click the certificate you want to use for the signature in the Select Certificate dialog box, and then click the OK button.
- Click the OK button in the Digital Signature dialog box.

You will sign the CenterPrintout macro, which you created for this purpose.

To sign the CenterPrintout macro:

1. Click **Tools** on the menu bar, point to **Macro**, and then click **Visual Basic Editor**.

2. If the CenterPrintout macro is not displayed, click the **Project Explorer** button 🗔 on the Standard toolbar to open the Project Explorer, and then double-click **Module1** in the Project Explorer to display the CenterPrintout macro code contained within that macro.

3. Click **Tools** on the menu bar, click **Digital Signature**, and then click the **Choose** button. The Select Certificate dialog box opens, in which you can choose from the digital certificates stored on your computer.

4. Click the certificate with your name, click the **OK** button in the Select Certificate dialog box, and then click the **OK** button in the Digital Signature dialog box.

There is no visible difference to the macro or the Visual Basic Editor when you are viewing a signed versus an unsigned macro. The difference appears when you open the workbook with the macro.

To experience how a signed macro works:

1. Close the **Visual Basic Editor** window, save the workbook with the name **DigitalSigTest-6** to the Tutorial.06\Tutorial folder on your Data Disk, and then close the workbook.

2. Open the **DigitalSigTest-6** workbook. You are immediately presented with the dialog box shown in Figure 6-34. Using signed macros, instead of merely being able to "enable" or "disable" macros, you have also provided some information about the person or organization that signed the macro.

Figure 6-34   SECURITY WARNING DIALOG BOX

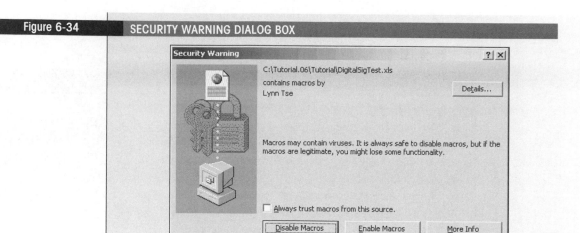

3. Click the **Details** button. You are presented with a Digital Signature Details dialog box that contains both general and advanced information about the digital signature.

4. Click the **View Certificate** button. The Certificate dialog box is presented and tells you that the signature was self-issued, and therefore the digital signature is considered a "self-signed" signature. See Figure 6-35.

Figure 6-35   CERTIFICATE DIALOG BOX

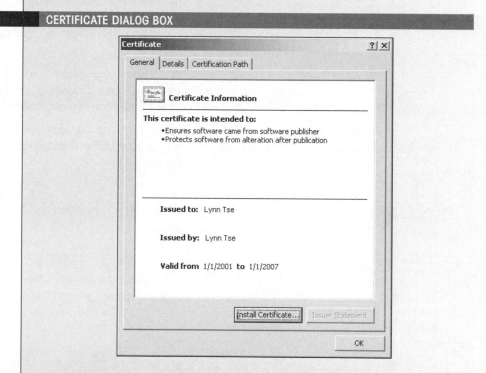

TROUBLE? Your certificate may look a little different, depending on whether or not it has been installed in the certificate store (an area on the hard drive of a computer that stores certificates). Unless you are working on your own computer, do not install the certificate in the certificate store.

> **5.** Click the **OK** button, click the **OK** button in the Digital Signature Details dialog box, click the **Always trust macros from this source** check box, and then click the **Enable Macros** button in the Security Warning dialog box. The DigitalSigTest-6 workbook opens with the CenterPrintout macro enabled.

Certificates from those companies that create digital certificates will have much more information than the digital certificates you create with the SELFCERT.EXE tool. You can use this information to determine the authenticity and safety of macros and files you receive from other users.

Trusted Sources

Because you clicked the Always trust macros from this source check box when viewing your digital certificate in the previous exercise, you will no longer be prompted to enable macros if they were signed with this digital signature, even if you changed your security level to High. Therefore, you should periodically check the trusted sources list to make sure that you are not enabling macros from authors in whom you do not have an extremely high level of confidence in the authenticity of their digital signatures.

REFERENCE WINDOW **RW**

Removing an Entry from the Trusted Sources List
- Click Tools on the menu bar, point to Macro, and then click Security.
- Click the Trusted Sources tab.
- Click the source that you want to remove, and then click the Remove button.
- Click the OK button.

You want to check the trusted sources list, both to see if your digital signature was added from the previous step and to remove it from the list for this computer for now.

To check the trusted sources list:

1. Click **Tools** on the menu bar, point to **Macro**, and then click **Security**.

2. Click the **Trusted Sources** tab.

3. Click your name in the list, and then click the **Remove** button.

4. Click the **OK** button in the Security dialog box.

5. Close the DigitalSigTest-6 workbook, and then exit Excel.

Writing VBA code takes a lot of work and patience. Knowing how to use and apply digital signatures enables you to distribute your VBA code in a safe way.

Session 6.2 QUICK CHECK

1. What are the advantages of using the macro recorder to write VBA code?

2. What are the disadvantages of using the macro recorder to write VBA code?

3. What is an add-in?

4. Explain the relationship between a macro, VBA statements, and a sub.

5. Identify which parts of speech would best describe an object and method.

6. In the following example, identify the object, method, and arguments

   ```
   Workbooks("Budget.xls").Protect "x1x2", True, True
   ```

7. What is a digital signature, and how do you get one?

REVIEW ASSIGNMENTS

Green Valley Recreation (GVR) uses Excel workbooks in a number of ways. One task that it faces on a regular basis is that of recording enrollment in various programs. Lynn asks if there is a way to automate the process of entering the names, gender, and ages of participants in various lists. She explains that everyone at GVR isn't comfortable with Excel. Almost everyone needs to be able to enter a name on an enrollment or waiting list; therefore, she wants the process to be as simple as possible. Also, in the past, GVR has recorded a child's age at enrollment, which has caused problems when children are placed in the wrong age grouping because they have had a birthday between the time they were enrolled and the time the event takes place. She asks if you could create an easy way to calculate a child's age for users with very few Excel skills. You have developed a prototype workbook to automate these tasks, but it still needs some work.

To complete this task:

1. Start Excel and open the **Registration-6** workbook located in the Tutorial.06\Review folder on your Data Disk. Enable the macros in the workbook. You have developed a sample workbook to address Lynn's requests. Now you'll use the custom form that you developed with the help of a VBA programmer.

2. Click the Add New Child button, enter your own name, the birth date of 1/1/1995, and your own gender, and then click the OK button. Click the Cancel button to close the Get Name and Gender dialog box. Now that you see how the custom form works, you will enter a formula in column E using the custom function you created to calculate the child's age.

3. In cell E3, enter the formula "=AgeYears(D3)" and then copy it through range E4:E11.

4. Open the Visual Basic Editor and view the code for the AgeYears function, which appears in the Module1 object. Add your name and the current date as a comment to the first line, and then add comment lines after every VBA statement to explain what that statement does. Be sure to point out the VBA keywords. Also point out any Excel built-in functions that are used in the formula and what role they play in the formula.

5. Save, print, and close the code for the custom AgeYears function.

6. Using the macro recorder, create a macro called PrintSettings. Use the keystroke combination of Ctrl+Shift+T as the shortcut key for the macro.

7. Record a macro that puts your name in the left section of the header, the current date code in the right section of the header, and specifies a landscape orientation for the page.

8. Edit the macro in the Visual Basic Editor by deleting all lines except those having to do with the `LeftHeader`, `RightHeader`, and `Orientation` properties of the `ActiveSheet.PageSetup` property. (*Hint*: The PrintSettings macro will be in the Module2 object.)

9. Save the code, close the Visual Basic Editor, and then use the Page Setup dialog box to remove the entries in the header and return the paper orientation to portrait.

10. Test the macro using the Ctrl + Shift + T keyboard shortcut, and then preview the printout. If the macro worked successfully, print the page. If not, edit the PrintSettings macro in the Visual Basic Editor so that the macro enters your name in the left section of the header, the current date in the right section, and provides a landscape orientation for the printout. Remember that you need to remove existing print settings before you rerun your macro in order to make sure that it works as intended.

11. Create a new toolbar named GVRMacros, and add the PrintSettings macro to the toolbar as a custom button.

12. Copy the button image from the Bold button, and then paste the image to the new custom button on the GVRMacros toolbar.

13. Modify the button image so that it appears as a capital "P" (for PrintSettings) versus a capital "B".

14. Modify the ScreenTip of the "P" button to display the text "Print Setup".

15. If your workbook is still in landscape orientation and contains header entries, delete the header entries and change the orientation back to portrait. Then click the "P" button to test the new button.

16. In the Customize dialog box, delete the GVRMacros toolbar.

17. In the Visual Basic Editor, apply your digital signature to the code, close the Visual Basic Editor, and then save and close the workbook.

18. Reopen the Registration-6 workbook to make sure that the digital signature was applied correctly, and then enable macros.

19. Close the Registration-6 workbook, and then exit Excel.

CASE PROBLEMS

Case 1. A Custom Commissions Function   As a marketing manager for a large software company, you have been asked to develop a new commission formula that rewards achievement. You have decided to create four commission percentages that, when applied to net sales, calculate earned commissions. You've asked a VBA programmer to help you write the custom function, and now you want to add clarifying comments to the VBA code so that you don't forget how the function was developed.

To complete this task:

1. Open the **Commissions-6** workbook located on the Tutorial.06\Cases folder on your Data Disk. Enable the macros in the workbook. The workbook consists of only three columns of information.

2. Review the formulas in column C. The custom Commission function uses only one argument, the sales values in range B2:B8 to calculate the commission. It is not obvious what percentage was used to calculate the commission values in column C, though.

3. To display the percentage used to calculate the commission, enter the label "Percentage" in cell D1, apply a bold format to cell D1, and widen column D to display the entire label. Then, enter the formula =C2/B2 in cell D2.

4. Format the value in cell D2 as a percentage with no digits to the right of the decimal point, and then copy the formula in cell D2 through the range D3:D8. By entering this formula, you make it obvious that the higher sales, the higher the commission rate. You decide to test the commission percentage threshold by entering different sales values for Barach.

5. In cell B2, enter 100,000, and then 200,000, 300,000, and 400,000 to see how the commissions and associated percentages change. To know where the thresholds between the four commission percentages are for sure, however, you need to view the VBA code behind the Commission function.

Explore

6. Open the Visual Basic Editor, and display the code for the Module1 object. Enter a comment line before the `Function` statement with your name and the current date, and then enter a comment line after each statement that describes what just happened in that statement. (*Hint*: Consult Microsoft Visual Basic Help for information on the new VBA key terms, such as `Const` and `Case`, that appear in the Code window for the function.) (*Hint*: Don't leave any blank lines between any of the statements in this function or the Visual Basic Editor may insert a horizontal line to visually separate what it interprets as different procedures.)

7. In the VBA statements, change the Commission rate levels to 9%, 10%, 11%, and 15%.

8. In the VBA statements, change the third level to go up to 499999.99 and the fourth level to start at 500000.

9. Save and print the code in the Visual Basic Editor window.

10. Close the Visual Basic Editor window, and notice that none of the percentages recalculated in column D, even though different percentages are used for different ranges.

11. Copy the values in range B2:B8, and then paste them back into the same range. Notice that the percentages recalculated in column D as soon as you reentered the values.

Explore

12. Print the Commissions-6 worksheet with your name in the upper-left section of the header, and write a sentence or two explaining why the percentages didn't recalculate until after you reentered the values in column B. Use the Microsoft Visual Basic Help system as needed.

13. Save and close the workbook, and then exit Excel.

Case 2. Using the Macro Recorder to Create a Chart You work at an investment brokerage firm as an information analyst. You use Excel to analyze personal portfolios and to do corporate financial analysis, and you have been asked to extend this functionality to other brokers and clients. You've noticed that even seasoned Excel users aren't always comfortable creating charts, and that the process of creating standard charts could be automated. In response to that, you've developed a small workbook with some sample financial ratios. You'll use the macro recorder to create two charts from the information, and then add the buttons to a new toolbar.

To complete this task:

1. Open the **Investments-6** workbook located in the Tutorial.06\Cases folder on your Data Disk.

2. Use the Keyboard Shortcuts page of the Microsoft Excel Help system to help you iden- tify three keystroke combinations that would be appropriate for chart creation macros and that aren't currently assigned to existing Excel commands. Write them down.

3. Use the macro recorder to create a new macro named "SalesColumnChart."

4. With the macro recorder running, select the nonadjacent range A1:B5 and E1:E5 for the chart, use a clustered column chart for the chart type, make sure that the series is in columns, enter "Sales vs. Expenses" as the chart title, add the chart as a new sheet with the default sheet name, and then stop the macro recorder.

5. Assign one of the keystroke combinations you identified in Step 2 to the SalesColumnChart macro.

6. Return to the CorpData worksheet, and create a second macro using the macro recorder named "ProfitMargins."

7. Select the nonadjacent ranges A1:A5 and F1:G5 for the chart, use a clustered column chart for the chart type, make sure that the series is in columns, enter "Profit Ratios" as the chart title, add the chart as a new sheet with the default sheet name, and then stop the macro recorder.

8. Assign another of the keystroke combinations you identified in Step 2 to the SalesColumnChart macro.

9. Switch to the CorpData sheet, and then change the values in the range A2:C5 to those shown in Figure 6-36.

Figure 6-36

	A	B	C	D	E	F	G
1	Company	Sales	Cost of Goods Sold	Operating Costs	Total Expenses	Gross Profit Margin	Net Profit Margin
2	Peabody Inc.	500,000	250,500	200,000	450,500	50%	10%
3	VirtualDays	1,000,000	550,000	650,000	1,200,000	45%	-20%
4	Project Team	2,000,000	1,600,000	156,000	1,756,000	20%	12%
5	Hangman Games	357,000	130,000	200,000	330,000	64%	8%
6							

10. From the CorpData sheet, run both the ProfitMargins and the SalesColumnChart macros, using the quick keystrokes that you assigned to them, and then print the new Chart3 and Chart4 worksheets with your name in the left section of the header.

11. Open the Visual Basic Editor, and make sure that your name is entered as a comment at the top of both the ProfitMargins and SalesColumnChart macros (they should both be found in Module1).

12. Find the property that enters "Sales vs. Expenses" for the first chart title, and change that value to "Profitability".

13. Save the changes you have made, and then print the Module1 VBA code.

14. Close the Visual Basic Editor window.

15. Save and close the Investments-6 workbook, and then exit Excel.

Case 3. Creating Macros for Common Diagnoses You are a consultant to a podiatry clinic, and the doctors have asked you for a way to automate the information they want to pro- vide to a referring physician. They explain that if they simply had enough time to send the referring physician a quick statement regarding their diagnosis and the procedures they took, they could improve patient care through better communication with the primary care doctor. Furthermore, they explain that many foot problems and procedures can be summarized with a handful of statements. You explain that using an Excel workbook, you could create macros to capture the information they want to send back to the referring physician for the most common problems.

To complete this task:

1. Start Excel and open the **Patients-6** workbook located in the Tutorial.06\Cases folder on your Data Disk.

2. Using the macro recorder, create a macro called "IngrownToenails" that enters the following text into cell A8. Be sure the Relative Reference button on the Stop Recording toolbar is selected. (In Excel 2002, the button displays a blue border when selected. In Excel 2000, the button appears depressed or pushed in when selected.) Be sure to click cell A8 before entering the text, and be sure to press the Enter key when you are finished entering the text and want to stop the macro recorder:

    Under local anesthesia, the offending portion of the nail was removed and a procedure was completed to prevent regrowth of the nail.

3. Using the macro recorder, create a macro called "Bunions" that enters the following text into cell A8. Be sure to click cell A8 before entering the text, and be sure to press the Enter key when you are finished entering the text and want to stop the macro recorder:

    The patient was measured for orthotics. Orthotics can be helpful in preventing progression of the deformity in those patients who have only a mild bunion and wish to prevent surgery.

4. Using the macro recorder, create a macro called "Warts" that enters the following text into cell A8. Be sure to click cell A8 before entering the text:

    Warts are caused by viruses. There are many ways to treat them, including lasers, topical acids, and cryotherapy. Unfortunately, reoccurrence is always possible. For now, physicians treated the wart with a topical acid.

5. Create a new toolbar named "Diagnoses," and add the three macros to it. Attach the three macros to the three new buttons, and then change the ScreenTips to the three macros to "Ingrown Toenails" for the first macro, "Bunions" for the second, and "Warts" for the third. Apply an appropriate custom icon for each button.

6. Test the three macros by simulating three new patients, each with a different diagnosis.
    a. In cell B4, enter your name, enter "Ingrown Toenails" in cell C4, click cell A8, and then click the macro button for information on ingrown toenails. Print the worksheet.
    b. Enter "Bunions" in cell C4, click cell A8, and then click the macro button for information on bunions. Print the worksheet.
    c. Enter "Warts" in cell C4, click cell A8, and then click the macro button for information on warts. Print the worksheet.

7. By default, the macros you created enter the text in the currently active cell, not always cell A8. Use the Microsoft Visual Basic Help to research how to refer directly to cell A8 using the `Range` object.

8. Replace the `ActiveCell.FormulaR1C1 = _` statement in each macro with a statement that sets the `Value` property for cell A8 to the text that describes that medical problem. (*Hint*: You have to use the `Range` object.)

9. Test each of the new macros by clicking in any cell in the workbook and then running each macro to replace the existing text in cell A8.

10. When your macros are all working properly, delete the Diagnoses toolbar.

11. Save and close the Patients-6 workbook, and then exit Excel.

Explore

Case 4. Purchasing a Digital Signature   The SELFCERT.EXE program gives you a way to create a digital signature. If you are interested in selling your work over the Internet or providing your programs to others outside of your company, you'll probably want to purchase a more credible digital signature from a central issuing authority. In this exercise, you will research digital signatures to learn more about them, how much they cost, and what legal rights they give you.

To complete this task:

1. Open your Web browser, connect to the Internet, and go to http://www.whatis.com/. Search for "digital signature," and then read and print the definition provided by that Web site.

2. Go to www.verisign.com and search for information on cost for a "Code Signing Certificate." Print that Web page.

3. Go to www.about.com/ and search for "digital signature" or "electronic signature." Find, read, and print at least one article on the legality of a digital signature and how it affects both the signer and the recipient of information that is electronically signed. Your article may involve the Electronic Signatures in Global and National Commerce Act, which went into effect on October 1, 2000.

4. In one page, summarize what you have learned about the legality of a digital signature.

QUICK | **CHECK ANSWERS**

Session 6.1

1. VBA is not a standalone programming language like Visual Basic, but rather works only from within a host application (such as Excel or Access or whichever Microsoft product you use to access VBA).

2. The most common uses for VBA within Excel are:
   - To automate repetitive processes
   - To make a workbook faster and easier with custom dialog boxes, menu bar options, toolbar buttons, or shortcut keys
   - To make the workbook more visually appealing by changing or hiding screen elements that aren't necessary to the task at hand
   - To build custom functions to simplify complex or unique calculations
   - To share data with external files such as an Access database

3. If you use the macro recorder to record a macro within Excel, the macro recorder converts your mouse clicks and keystrokes to VBA. Not all VBA is a macro, however.

4. VBA statements are also used to create custom forms and functions. VBA used for these purposes is not stored or saved as macros.

5. You can assign a quick keystroke to a macro, attach it to a toolbar button, or attach it to a graphical icon on the workbook.

6. A custom form simplifies and improves the speed and accuracy of data entry by guiding the user through the steps of completing a process.

7. A custom function simplifies formulas.

Session 6.2

1. The macro recorder is one of the fastest ways to write VBA code. Furthermore, you don't need to know VBA in order to use the recorder.

2. The macro recorder cannot write functions or create custom forms. It often adds extra statements that are not required for the task at hand.

3. An add-in is an external file that contains VBA code that enhances Excel's functionality.

4. A macro creates VBA statements. The statements start with the Sub keyword, followed by the macro name, followed by left and right parentheses.

5. object = noun, method = verb

6. `Workbooks("Budget.xls")` is the object.

   `Protect` is the method.

   `"x1x2", True, True` are the arguments.

7. A digital signature is an electronic signature that is unique from the signer. You can either buy one from a company such as VeriSign or create one on your own using the SELFCERT.EXE application.

OBJECTIVES

In this tutorial you will:

- Write and test custom functions

- Create a global function

- Work with events

- Attach a procedure to an event

- Work with the Object Browser

- Compare IF and VLOOKUP functions to a custom function

- Use the Select Case statement in a function

- Control function recalculation

- Use If statements in a function

- Create a function with optional arguments

- Learn about various types of VBA errors

- Reset and debug VBA code that displays a run-time error

CREATING CUSTOM FUNCTIONS

Developing Custom Functions for GVR

CASE

Green Valley Recreation

You have been working for Green Valley Recreation (GVR) for several months. During that time you have worked with numerous Excel workbooks. You have noticed that these workbooks use a wide variety of formulas in many different ways. You have also noticed that many of the GVR employees are not comfortable using the workbooks and struggle trying to execute the formulas correctly.

GVR organizes many different sporting and competitive programs, so there are many workbooks that contain formulas that calculate scores or statistics. Some of these formulas are quite long, such as the one that helps the baseball and softball leagues calculate batting averages. You feel that by using Visual Basic for Applications (VBA) to create customized functions you will be able to help simplify the workbooks and make the power of Excel more accessible to a wider group of users.

In this tutorial, you will learn more about VBA and how to use the Visual Basic Editor window. You will use VBA to create custom functions, which will help simplify the formulas used in GVR workbooks.

SESSION 7.1

In this session, you will learn about custom functions. You'll create and test custom functions and their arguments. You will learn how to name and store custom functions so that they are available to all open workbooks. You'll work with the Object Browser to quickly find the property, method, or event of an object that you need. Finally, you will also learn how to attach a procedure to an event, so that the procedure automatically runs when an event is triggered.

Why Use Functions?

A **function** is a predefined formula that helps you simplify workbook calculations. The values that a function uses to make the calculation are called **arguments**, and if a function contains multiple arguments, each is separated from the other by a comma. Excel provides about 400 built-in functions, such as SUM, COUNT, and PMT, to help you build formulas. To understand how functions help simplify formulas, consider the following formula that determines a monthly payment for a loan (without the help of the PMT function). The formula to calculate a monthly payment can be expressed as $P*(J/(1-(1+J)^{\wedge}(-N)))$, where:

P = principal, the initial amount of the loan

I = annual interest rate (from 1% to 100%)

L = length, in years, of the loan

J = monthly interest, I / 12

N = number of months for the loan, L * 12

Compare that formula to the formula used in the Loan-7 workbook to calculate a monthly loan payment using the PMT function, PMT(J,N,P).

To compare the full formula to one that uses the PMT function:

1. Start Excel and open the **Loan-7** workbook located in the Tutorial.07\Tutorial folder on your Data Disk.

2. Click cell **C4** and then enter the formula **=B4/12** to convert the annual interest rate to a monthly interest rate.

3. In cell C5, enter the formula **=B5*12** to convert the number of years of the loan into the number of monthly payments.

4. Click cell **B9**, enter the formula **=B7*(C4/(1-(1+C4)^(-C5)))**.

   TROUBLE? If you have trouble entering the formula, click in the Formula bar and then use the ← key and the → key to move through the formula. As you move across a left or right parenthesis, a paired set of parentheses will appear bold. Also, pairs of parentheses are color coded to make them easier to read as well. It's easy to omit or misplace a parenthesis when entering a long or complex formula.

5. In cell B10, enter the formula **=PMT(C4,C5,B7)**. See Figure 7-1. Although the two formulas calculated the same value, the PMT function calculated the number as a negative value and applied a special format.

Figure 7-1	CALCULATING A MONTHLY PAYMENT

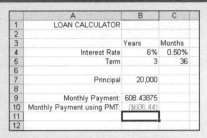

In many of the Financial functions in Excel, negative values are used to represent a "cash outflow". In other words, the positive loan principal represents a cash inflow, and the negative monthly payment represents a cash outflow. Often, however, people prefer to view both of these values as positive values. To convert the result of the formula using the PMT function to a positive value, you multiply it by negative 1.

6. Edit the formula in cell B10 so that a minus sign is inserted between the = (equal sign) and the PMT keyword, and then press the **Enter** key.

7. Save and print the Loan-7 workbook with your name in the left section of the header, and then close the workbook.

By using the PMT function to calculate the monthly payment, you didn't have to research, understand, or enter the long formula that is used to determine the actual payment. The hardest thing about using the PMT function is remembering the correct order for the three arguments (rate, term of the loan, and principal) and inserting the negative sign in front of the PMT function if you want to convert the resulting value to a positive number. Still, that effort was much less difficult than researching and entering the actual formula that it represents.

The following rules apply to all Excel functions:

- All formulas and functions in Excel start with an equal sign.
- All functions are followed by parentheses, even if the function does not use arguments, such as =Now().
- Argument values are entered within the parentheses.
- Multiple arguments are separated by commas.
- The order of the arguments is significant and determines how the function will use the arguments to make the calculation.
- Some Excel functions have optional arguments, that is, arguments that can be omitted if the default values work properly for your formula.

Creating a Custom Function

A **custom function** is one that you define in a module using VBA code. You create custom functions for the same reason that Excel provides so many built-in functions, such as SUM and PMT, to simplify the effort required to do a calculation within Excel. The result of using a custom function in a worksheet is to calculate and return a single value to the worksheet. When you create a custom function, you must identify the function name, the arguments used within the function, the order of the arguments, and the formula used to create the calculation within the Visual Basic Editor.

New functions are stored in a module, start with the `Function` statement, and end with the `End Function` statement. On the first line, after the `Function` statement, you identify the new function name as well as the function's arguments. The function name should be as short as possible to keep things simple, yet long enough to clearly identify the function. Between the `FUNCTION` and `End Function` statements, you write the code that calculates and returns the appropriate value for that function. At a minimum, the code to calculate the value for the function would include an assignment statement that assigns the name of the function you defined in the `Function` statement to the formula that calculates its value.

In your last meeting with your supervisor, Lynn Tse, you discussed the wellness programs that GVR runs. These programs are designed to help people adopt a healthy lifestyle. Often, the programs start with a basic intake form that requests some basic health statistics such as height and weight. One general health indicator that GVR uses to determine an individual's healthiness is the body mass index (BMI) statistic. BMI is used in the health field to determine whether people should be concerned about their weight. The scores generally range from 19 through about 35; the higher the score, the more concerned the person should be about his or her weight. You explain to Lynn that because GVR calculates the BMI statistic in many workbooks for many programs, and the formula that calculates BMI is somewhat complex and hard to remember, you know that calculating the BMI is a perfect candidate for a custom function.

To create a custom function called BMI to calculate the body mass index:

1. Open the **BMI-7** workbook located in the Tutorial.07\Tutorial folder on your Data Disk, and then click cell **B7**. See Figure 7-2. The formula in cell B7 is the formula used to calculate the BMI. In its generic form, the formula can be written as *(Weight*0.4535)/((Height*0.0254)^2)* where *Weight* is in pounds and *Height* is in inches.

| Figure 7-2 | BMI FORMULA |

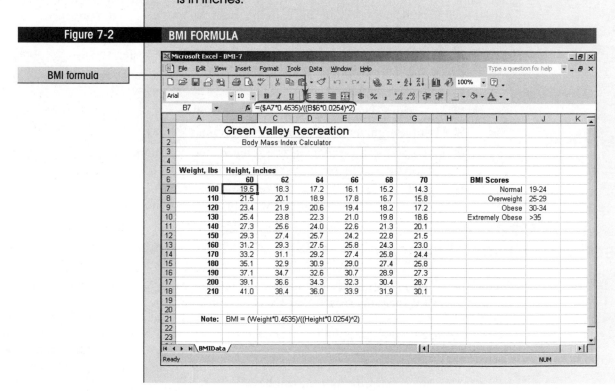

2. Click **Tools** on the menu bar, point to **Macro**, and then click **Visual Basic Editor**.

3. Click the **list arrow** for the Insert UserForm button 📋 ▾ on the Standard toolbar, and then click **Module**.

TROUBLE? If you clicked the UserForm button itself instead of the list arrow, you inserted a new UserForm instead of a new Module. To remove the new UserForm, right-click it in the Project Explorer, click Remove UserForm1 on the shortcut menu, and then click the No button when prompted to export it.

TROUBLE? The Code window and Project Explorer should be open. If the Properties window is open, close it. Maximize the Visual Basic Editor and Code windows.

By placing the VBA code for this function in its own module, the function will be available to the entire workbook rather than associated with a specific sheet. The first step is to identify the name of the new function and the number and order of arguments that it contains.

TROUBLE? If the Option Explicit statement is automatically added to the Code window, delete it. That statement requires that variables be declared before they are used. You'll learn more about declaring variables in Tutorial 9.

4. With the insertion point blinking at the top of the Code window, type `Function BMI(height, weight)` and then press the **Enter** key. The `End Function` statement is automatically entered as the last line of the function. When you enter arguments in your custom function, the argument names should be as short as possible (because you'll refer to these names later in the function) but long enough to be descriptive. Also, the order of the arguments is significant because it determines the order in which the arguments will be entered when you later use the BMI function in the worksheet. The best way to identify the arguments is in the order that makes the most sense to the user. Because you normally discuss a person's "height and weight" rather than their "weight and height", you followed this convention when defining the order of the arguments. Once the function name and arguments are identified, you enter the statement or statements that define how the custom function is going to calculate.

5. Type `BMI = (weight*0.4535)/((height*0.0254)^2)` and then press the **Enter** key. See Figure 7-3. The BMI = statement is the assignment statement that assigns the function to the value of the calculation. Note that you do not have to use the arguments in the definition of the BMI formula in the same order in which you defined them in the `Function` statement. The complexity of this formula is exactly why you're creating an easy-to-use custom function in the first place.

| Figure 7-3 | DEFINING THE BMI FUNCTION |

Toggle Folders button

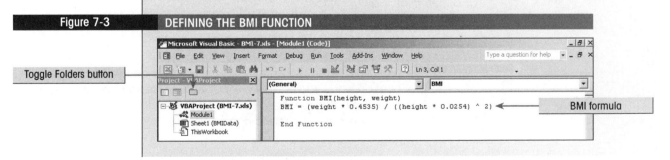

> TROUBLE? If your Project Explorer displays folders that are not shown in Figure 7-3, then the Toggle Folders option has been turned on. Click the Toggle Folders button 🗀 in the Project Explorer to turn off the view that displays the Microsoft Excel Objects and Module objects organized into different folders.
>
> 6. Click the **Save** button 🖫 on the Standard toolbar, and then close the Visual Basic Editor.

Now that the BMI function is created, you are eager to try it in the workbook. Also note that some programmers use a verb/object approach when naming new functions. In this case, the BMI function might have been named CalcBMI or CalculateBMI.

Testing a Custom Function

To test your custom function, you'll replace the long formulas in range B7:G18 that calculate the BMI statistic with formulas that use the new BMI function. To make sure that your calculation is correct, however, you'll copy the BMIData worksheet and test the BMI function on the second worksheet.

> ### To test the BMI function:
>
> 1. Right-click the **BMIData** tab, click **Move or Copy** on the shortcut menu, click the **Create a copy** check box, and then click the **OK** button in the Move or Copy dialog box.
>
> 2. In cell B7 of the BMIData (2) worksheet, type **=BMI(B6,A7)** and then press the **Enter** key.
>
>   Because you defined height as the first argument in the BMI custom function and weight as the second argument in the first line of the custom function, that is also the order in which you need to enter the arguments in this formula. The calculation appears to have worked, but in order to compare it to the value on the BMIData sheet, you want to put the worksheets side-by-side. To do this, you need to create a new BMI-7 window, and then tile the windows.
>
> 3. Click **Window** on the menu bar, and then click **New Window**. The title bar indicates that you are working in either the BMI-7:2 (second copy) or BMI-7:1 (first copy) of the BMI-7 workbook.
>
>   Tiling the two windows enables the worksheets to appear side-by-side.
>
> 4. Click **Window** on the menu bar, click **Arrange**, click the **Vertical** option button, and then click the **OK** button.
>
> 5. Click the **BMIData** tab in the left window so that the two windows display the two worksheets side-by-side as shown in Figure 7-4.
>
>   TROUBLE? It makes no difference whether BMI-7:1 appears on the left or right side of the window, but only that you have two windows that display the same workbook, and that the BMIData worksheet is selected in the left window, and the BMIData (2) worksheet is selected in the right window.

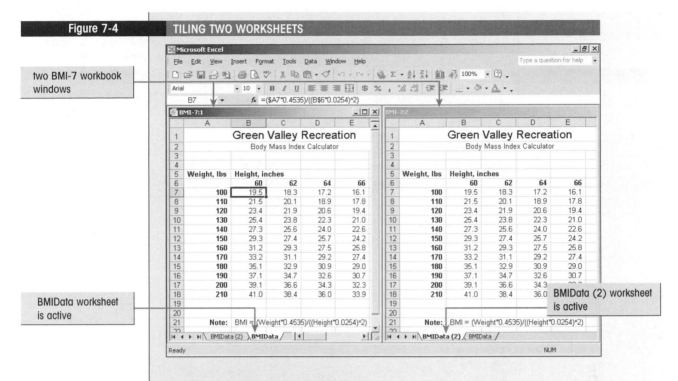

Figure 7-4   **TILING TWO WORKSHEETS**

6. Click cell **B7** on the BMIData (2) worksheet in the right window, and observe the formula in the Formula bar. The value created by the custom function appears to be working correctly. The formula in cell B7 in both worksheets calculates a value of 19.5.

7. Drag the fill handle for cell **B7** through the range **B8:B18** on the BMIData (2) worksheet in the right window. Obviously, the formula doesn't work correctly for the rest of that range of cells.

The custom BMI function is working correctly; however, notice that the `height` argument should come from cell B6 for each formula in the range B8:B18. When you copied the =BMI(B6,A7) formula through the range B8:B18, the B6 relative cell reference that identifies the weight value changed, too. Also note that the `weight` argument is always in column A. Therefore, if you copy this formula across multiple columns, you'll encounter the same type of problem with the `weight` argument. In order for the formula in cell B7 to be successfully copied down and across the table, you need to use a mixed cell reference for the cell references in the formula so that the cell reference for the `height` argument never moves out of row 6, and the cell reference for the `weight` argument never moves out of column A.

To use mixed cell references in the BMI function arguments:

1. Click cell **B7** in the BMIData (2) worksheet, click **B6** in the Formula bar, press the **F4** key twice to change the cell address to **B$6**, click **A7** in the Formula bar, press the **F4** key three times to change the cell address to **$A7**, and then press the **Enter** key. As you already know, using relative, mixed, or absolute cell references doesn't change the outcome of the formula in which they are placed. The benefit of using mixed or absolute cell references comes when you copy the formula.

2. Click cell **B7** in the BMIData (2) worksheet, drag the fill handle down the range **B8:B18**, and then drag the fill handle across the range **C7:G18**.

3. Click cell **A1** on the BMIData (2) worksheet so that you can compare several columns of values. See Figure 7-5.

Figure 7-5

| Figure 7-5 | COMPARING THE VALUES BETWEEN THE TWO WORKSHEETS |

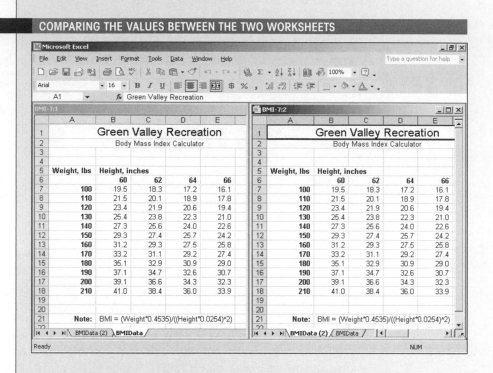

4. Maximize the window for the BMIData (2) worksheet, and then press **Ctrl + grave accent** (`) to display the formulas on the worksheet.

5. Print the worksheet in landscape orientation, scaled to fit on 1 page wide by 1 page tall with your name in the left section of the header.

6. Save the BMI-7 workbook, and then close one of the BMI-7 windows and maximize the other.

The BMI function now works as you intended, and Lynn agrees that GVR employees will appreciate using this custom function rather than entering the original formula to calculate the BMI. You also point out to Lynn that when you create a custom function, it is only available in the workbook in which the function was created because the function is stored in a module within the workbook. You explain that if GVR wants to use the BMI function in other workbooks, you need to change it into a **global function**, a function that is available for all open workbooks.

Creating **Global Functions**

By default, new functions created in modules are stored in the workbook in which you create them. But if that workbook isn't open, you can't use that custom function in that or any other open workbook. An easy way to make your functions accessible to all workbooks is to place them in a file that is automatically opened when Excel is started. Workbooks placed in the XLStart folder are automatically opened when Excel starts. The XLStart folder is usually located at this path: C:\Program Files\Microsoft Office\Office10\XLStart for Excel 2002 or C:\Program Files\Microsoft Office\Office\XLStart for Excel 2000.

Automatically Opening a Workbook When Excel Starts

■ Save the workbook (or a shortcut to the workbook) in the XLStart folder, located at either C:\Program Files\Microsoft Office\Office10\XLStart for Excel 2002 or C:\Program Files\Microsoft Office\Office\XLStart for Excel 2000.

If you don't want to move your files or create shortcuts in the XLStart folder, you can specify any other folder to be used as an additional startup folder. Files placed in an additional startup folder will automatically load after the files in the XLStart folder are loaded.

Creating Another Startup Folder

■ Click Tools on the menu bar, and then click Options.
■ Click the General tab, and then enter the path to the new startup folder in the At startup, open all files in text box. (In Excel 2000, enter the path in the Alternate startup location box.)
■ Click the OK button.

You want the BMI function to be available to all workbooks, so you'll place it in a workbook in the XLStart folder.

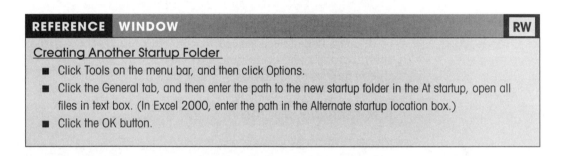

To copy the BMI function to a blank workbook:

1. Press **Alt + F11** to open the Visual Basic Editor to Module 1, click in the Code window, press **Ctrl + A** to select all of the code in Module1, and then click the **Copy** button 📋 on the Standard toolbar to place a copy of the code on the Clipboard.

2. Close the Visual Basic Editor, save and close the BMI-7 workbook, and then click the **New** button 🗋 on the Standard toolbar to open a new, blank workbook. This workbook will eventually contain your BMI custom function in a module, but nothing in the workbook portion of the file itself.

3. Press **Alt + F11** to open the Visual Basic Editor, click the **list arrow** for the UserForm button 🔳▾ on the Standard toolbar, and then click **Module**.

   The Insert Object button changes, depending on the last object inserted into the project. For example, if a user selected Module during the last Excel session, then the button appears with the Insert Module icon 🔳.

4. Click the **Paste** button 📋 on the Standard toolbar to paste the BMI function into the new module.

   TROUBLE? Be sure to delete the Option Explicit statement if it is automatically added to the code.

5. Close the Visual Basic Editor, and then click the **Save** button 💾 on the Standard toolbar.

6. Click the **Save in** list arrow, and then navigate to the C:\Program Files\Microsoft Office\Office10\XLStart folder.

   EXCEL 2000: Navigate to C:\Program Files\Microsoft Office\Office\XLStart.

TROUBLE? This path is based on the default installation of Microsoft Office XP. If you have customized the installation so that the Office files are stored in another location, you might find the XLStart folder in another location.

TROUBLE? If you are not allowed to save files in the XLStart folder on your computer, follow the instructions that were presented before this exercise to create another startup folder, and save this workbook there.

7. Enter **CustomFunctions** (no space) as the new filename, click the **Save** button, and then exit Excel. With the BMI function stored in a module within a workbook saved to the XLStart folder, the CustomFunctions workbook with the BMI function will automatically open and be available every time you start Excel.

8. Start Excel. The CustomFunctions workbook automatically opens.

Because it has been placed in a startup folder, the CustomFunctions workbook will automatically open every time Excel starts, and therefore the BMI function will be available to any other workbook that is opened, too.

Automatically Hiding a Workbook

Because you want to make the CustomFunctions workbook and the BMI function stored within it available to all other workbooks, the workbook needs to be open. Yet you don't want the GVR employees to use the CustomFunctions workbook for any other purpose than to be able to access the custom functions that are stored within it. Nor do you want the employees to enter their own data or change the CustomFunctions workbook in any way. One quick way to protect the CustomFunctions workbook is to automatically hide the workbook as soon as it opens. The VBA code in a hidden workbook is still available to all other workbooks just as if the workbook were not hidden. Hiding the CustomFunctions workbook simplifies the interface and prevents users from changing it.

REFERENCE	WINDOW	RW

Hiding or Unhiding a Workbook

- To hide a workbook, open the workbook, click Window on the menu bar, and then click Hide.
- To unhide a workbook, click Window on the menu bar, click Unhide, click the workbook that you want to redisplay, and then click the OK button.

To practice hiding and unhiding the CustomFunctions workbook:

1. Click **Window** on the menu bar, and then click **Hide**. The CustomFunctions workbook is still in memory, but the workbook no longer appears as an open workbook on the Window menu.

2. To unhide the workbook, click **Window** on the menu bar, and then click **Unhide**. The Unhide dialog box opens. All hidden workbooks would be listed in this dialog box.

3. With the CustomFunctions workbook already selected in the Unhide workbook list box, click the **OK** button.

In order to hide the CustomFunctions workbook automatically whenever you start Excel, you need to record a macro to hide the workbook that automatically runs immediately after the workbook is opened.

To record a macro to hide the CustomFunctions workbook:

1. Click **Tools** on the menu bar, point to **Macro**, and then click **Record New Macro**. The Record Macro dialog box opens.

2. Type **HideWorkbook** (no spaces) in the Macro name text box, press the **Tab** key three times (which will move the insertion point to the Description text box and select the default text), type *your name* and the *current date* as the description, and then click the **OK** button. The macro recorder starts.

3. Click **Window** on the menu bar, and then click **Hide**.

4. Click the **Stop Recording** button ▣ on the Stop Recording toolbar.

TROUBLE? If the Stop Recording toolbar is not displayed on the screen, click View on the menu bar, point to Toolbars, and then click Stop Recording.

To test your macro, you must unhide the workbook.

5. Click **Window**, click **Unhide**, and then click the **OK** button. The CustomFunctions workbook is reopened. Now test the new macro.

6. Click **Tools** on the menu bar, point to **Macro**, click **Macros**, click **HideWorkbook** (if it is not already selected), and then click the **Run** button. The Custom Functions workbook should now be hidden.

Now that you have recorded the macro to hide the CustomFunctions workbook, you explain to Lynn there is only one step left to complete: making the macro run automatically. In order to make the macro run automatically, you must connect the procedure that hides the workbook to an activity that automatically occurs within Excel, rather than running the macro in response to a user action—that is, choosing to run the macro from the Macro dialog box or from a toolbar button. Any activity that occurs within Excel that can trigger a macro is called an event.

Events

Excel monitors a wide variety of **events**, or activities that occur within Excel and that can trigger a procedure. Events are classified according to which object makes them occur. For example, workbook events include `Open` (opening a workbook) and `NewSheet` (adding a new sheet to the workbook), and worksheet events include `Change` (a cell is changed) and `Calculate` (the worksheet is recalculated).

When you want VBA code to run when an event occurs, you create a procedure with a special name that causes the VBA code within the procedure to automatically run when the event happens. The special name is the object that triggers the event, followed by an underscore, followed by the event name. For example, the procedure that is executed when a workbook is opened is called `Workbook_Open`. The procedure that is executed when a command button is clicked is called `CommandButtonName_Click` (where the actual name of the command button replaces "CommandButtonName"). Also, you must store procedures that are run by events in the Code window for that particular object, such as a workbook or worksheet object.

To make the HideWorkbook macro run automatically when the `Open` event occurs for the `Workbook` object, you must change the name of the `HideWorkbook` procedure to the `Workbook_Open` procedure. (Of course, if you knew the VBA code for hiding the workbook, you could have entered it directly within the `Workbook_Open` procedure in the first place. But because you are still learning VBA, you used the macro recorder to help create the code.) Also, you must move the VBA code from its current location in a module object to a workbook object. (Remember that the macro recorder automatically places a new procedure in a new module object rather than in a worksheet or workbook object.)

To create the Workbook_Open procedure:

1. Click **Window** on the menu bar, click **Unhide**, and then click the **OK** button to unhide the CustomFunctions workbook.

   In order to create the `Workbook_Open` procedure, you need to work in the Visual Basic Editor.

2. Open the Visual Basic Editor. The BMI function is stored in the Module1 object, and the HideWorkbook macro is stored in Module2.

3. Click the **expand button** to the left of VBAProject in the Project Explorer (if it's not already expanded), and then double-click **Module2**. The HideWorkbook macro code appears. When you create a macro, you create a procedure that starts with the Excel `Sub` keyword and ends with the `End Sub` keywords. A procedure that is triggered by an event is really no different than a macro, except for the name of the procedure. In this case, you'll edit the HideWorkbook macro with the name that causes the code to be run when the workbook `Open` event occurs.

4. Double-click **HideWorkbook** in the first line, and then type **Workbook_Open**. See Figure 7-6. If you were entering this procedure from scratch and wanted help with the procedure name, you could let the Visual Basic Editor enter the procedure name by choosing the appropriate object from the **Object list** and the appropriate event from the **Procedure list**.

Figure 7-6	WORKBOOK_OPEN PROCEDURE

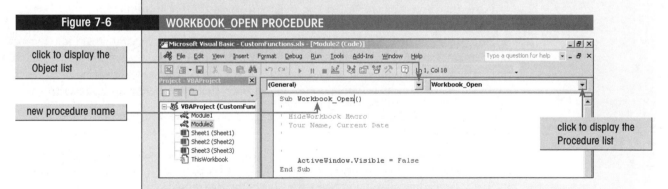

click to display the Object list

new procedure name

click to display the Procedure list

By changing the name of the sub procedure to that which includes the object name and the event name connected by an underscore, you've transformed a regular macro into a procedure that runs from an event. But you also need to move the code to the workbook object's Code window in order for it to automatically run based on the `Open` event for the workbook object.

5. Press **Ctrl + A** to select all of the code, click the **Cut** button ✂ on the Standard toolbar to move the code to the Clipboard, double-click **ThisWorkbook** in the Project Explorer, and then click the **Paste** button 📋 on the Standard toolbar to paste the code into the ThisWorkbook Code window. See Figure 7-7.

Figure 7-7	PASTING THE WORKBOOK_OPEN PROCEDURE IN THE THISWORKBOOK OBJECT

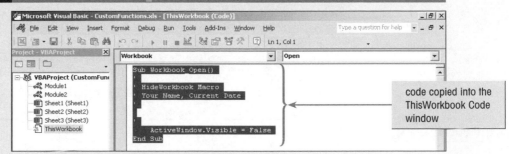

code copied into the
ThisWorkbook Code
window

TROUBLE? You need to double-click, not single-click, an object in the Project Explorer in order to open that object's Code window. The name of the object appears in the title bar.

TROUBLE? Delete the `Option Explicit` statement if it appears automatically in the ThisWorkbook object.

Now that you've moved the code to the ThisWorkbook object, you don't need Module2 anymore, because it no longer contains any code. Leaving blank modules in the workbook will not cause any problems, but removing modules that you no longer need will help you to keep the workbook as organized as possible. Also, if you record more macros in the future, it won't be as difficult to locate them if you delete empty modules.

6. Double-click **Module2** in the Project Explorer to confirm that it is blank, right-click **Module2**, click **Remove Module2** on the shortcut menu, and then click the **No** button when prompted to export Module2.

Now that you have modified the macro so that the procedure is triggered by an event, you need to test the changes you made.

To test the Workbook_Open procedure:

1. Save the changes you have made, close the Visual Basic Editor, exit Excel, and then restart it. The CustomFunctions workbook should be open, but hidden.

    Use the Window menu option to make sure that the CustomFunctions workbook is open.

2. Click **Window** on the menu bar, and then click **Unhide**. The Unhide dialog box opens, revealing the fact that the CustomFunctions workbook is open, but hidden.

3. Click the **Cancel** button.

The **Object Browser**

Lynn mentions that several GVR employees have asked if there is a way to reference the current workbook name in a cell within the workbook. They have used the File Name button in the Footer dialog box shown in Figure 7-8 to insert the &[File] code in a header or footer and want to achieve this same effect in the workbook itself.

Figure 7-8   **FOOTER DIALOG BOX**

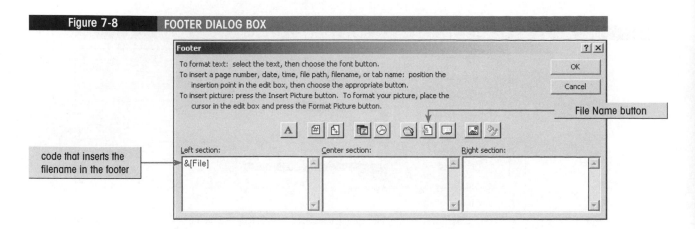

You suspect that the workbook name is a property of an object and, if so, this information could be returned to a cell by a custom function. You don't know exactly which object and property store this information. Although you could search through the Microsoft Visual Basic Help system to find this information, you have also read that the Object Browser is a great reference source and want to become more proficient at using it. The **Object Browser** is a list of all of the available objects, their properties, methods, and events. As you become more proficient with VBA, you will probably use the Object Browser more and more often to quickly locate recognizable objects, properties, methods, and events, because it gives you a quick way to search for VBA information and presents its findings in a concise list. You'll still use the Visual Basic Help system, but only when you need additional information that the more compact Object Browser does not provide. For example, the Help system provides an extensive description about the object that you are examining, helpful examples of VBA code, and hyperlinked glossary terms that are not available in the Object Browser.

To explore the Object Browser:

1. Open the Visual Basic Editor.

2. Click the **Object Browser** button 🔲 on the Standard toolbar, and close the Project Explorer. See Figure 7-9.

   TROUBLE? If the Search Results pane opens, click the Hide Search Results button ⬆ in the Object Browser.

Figure 7-9	OBJECT BROWSER

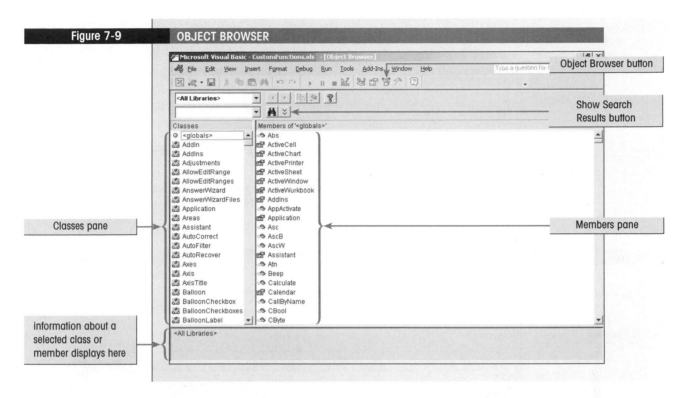

The Object Browser is divided into various panes. The items within the panes are listed in alphabetical order. The item you select in the **Classes pane** determines which **members** (properties, methods, and events) appear in the **Members pane**. The area at the bottom of the window gives you more information on what class or member you have selected. Furthermore, the Object Browser uses icons to help you identify the type of class and member you are working with. Figure 7-10 describes some of the icons you see in the Object Browser.

Figure 7-10	OBJECT BROWSER ICONS

ICON	ICON NAME	DESCRIPTION
	Class	The class determines the valid properties and methods for an object.
	Property	A property is a characteristic that you can change about an object.
	Default property	The default property for an object can be omitted from the VBA statement when you are assigning a new value to the object. For example, because Value is the default property for the Range object, the following two statements are the same: Range("A1") = 300 and Range ("A1"). Value = 3000
	Method	A method is an action that an object can perform.
	Default method	The default method is the method that is assumed if none is explicitly identified in the VBA statement. (A good programming practice clarifies all properties and methods, though, even if they are the defaults.)
	Event	An event is an activity, such as the opening of a workbook, that happens within Excel. An event can trigger a procedure.

Searching Within the Object Browser

Although you could go through the Classes list and guess at which object and property return the workbook name, it might be faster to search for that information using the **Search Text box**, where you can enter a word to search for within the Object Browser window. You can also search within different libraries. A **library** is a set of definitions for objects that pertain to a particular area. For example, there are object libraries for Excel (objects used within Excel) and Office (objects common to all Microsoft Office XP applications). You can change the library you are searching using the **Project/Library box**. Being able to access other object libraries becomes important if you want to use custom forms (described in Tutorial 8) or if you want to share Excel data with other applications that reference objects outside of Excel.

To use the Search Text box to search for information on the workbook name property:

1. Click in the Search Text list box, type **workbook** and press the **Enter** key. See Figure 7-11. The Search Results pane opens, displaying the library and class found for the search string "workbook".

| Figure 7-11 | SEARCHING WITHIN THE OBJECT BROWSER |

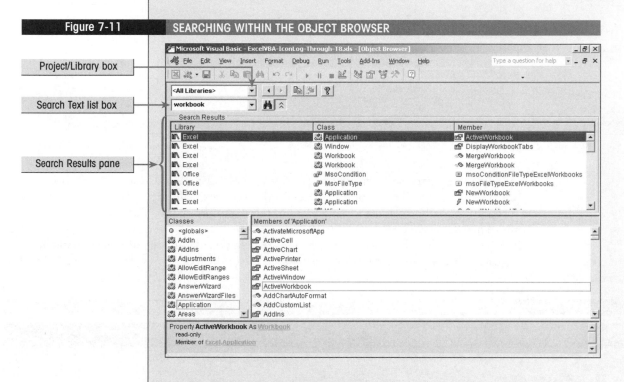

2. Scroll down the Classes list, and then click **Workbook**. Because you know that you are looking for a property (and not a method or event), you will group the members so that all of the properties are listed alphabetically in the Members pane. When you group the members of a class in this way, the properties are followed by an alphabetical list of the methods and then the events.

3. Right-click in the Members pane, and then click **Group Members** on the shortcut menu if it is not already selected.

4. Scroll within the list of members, and then click the `FullName` property. This property sounds like what you are looking for, but you need some more information on it.

   TROUBLE? If FullName does not appear in the Members pane, click Workbook in the Classes pane again, and then scroll through the list of members to locate the `FullName` property.

5. Right-click **FullName**, and then click **Help** on the shortcut menu. The Help menu appears with information on the `FullName` property as shown in Figure 7-12.

TROUBLE? You might be prompted to install the Help feature using the Office installation CD. Follow the instructions on the screen, or ask your instructor or technical support person for assistance.

Figure 7-12	VISUAL BASIC HELP FOR THE FULLNAME PROPERTY

FullName Property

See Also   Applies To   Example

Returns the name of the object, including its path on disk, as a string. Read-only **String**.

Remarks

This property is equivalent to the <u>Path</u> property, followed by the current file system separator, followed by the <u>Name</u> property.

Example

This example displays the path and file name of every available add-in.

```
For Each a In AddIns
    MsgBox a.FullName
Next a
```

This example displays the path and file name of the active workbook (assuming that the workbook has been saved).

```
MsgBox ActiveWorkbook.FullName
```

EXCEL 2000: The Help window for the `FullName` property is presented differently, but the information is the same.

6. Read the page, and then close the Microsoft Visual Basic Help window. You learned that the `FullName` property is equivalent to the `Path` property plus the `Name` property.

Now that you know what properties store the workbook name (`Name`), the path (`Path`), and both (`FullName`), you are ready to create a custom function to return this information to a cell. Then other employees at GVR can use this custom function to display the path and filename of the workbook within a worksheet, without knowing anything about VBA, objects, or properties. The Help page introduced the `ActiveWorkbook` object. You can use this object to reference the active workbook without having to know the active workbook's filename. Therefore, the `ActiveWorkbook` object helps you to write custom functions that can be used with any open workbook.

Creating a Custom Function with No Arguments

Probably the best way to become proficient at almost any software program or programming language is to use it in a wide variety of situations. The BMI function you already created for GVR has two arguments. But like Excel's TODAY() and RAND() functions, not all VBA functions require arguments. In this case you want to create a custom function called

WorkbookInfo to return the path and name of the workbook to a cell. Because there are no pieces of information that the user will have to provide for the function, you will not declare arguments when you create the function.

To create the WorkbookInfo function:

1. Close the Object Browser, return to the Visual Basic Editor, and click the **Project Explorer** button [icon] to reopen it. Note that the title bar of the Visual Basic Editor window always indicates which object's Code window you are currently viewing.

2. Double-click **Module1** in the Project Explorer to open its Code window. You can put more than one procedure, either sub or function, in a single module. To make it easier to find your global custom functions, you might want to add them to the same module.

3. Click below the End Function statement, press the **Enter** key twice to insert two blank lines, type Function WorkbookInfo(), and then press the **Enter** key. See Figure 7-13. The Visual Basic Editor automatically inserts a line between the procedures and adds the End Function statement for you.

Figure 7-13	CREATING THE WORKBOOKINFO FUNCTION

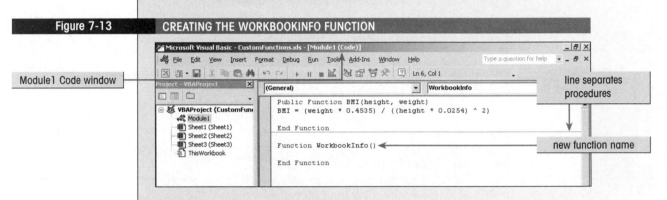

Module1 Code window

line separates procedures

new function name

4. Type WorkbookInfo = Activeworkbook. (include the period). See Figure 7-14. As soon as you type an object followed by a period, a list of available properties and methods is displayed. You can either type the specific property you want, or you can scroll and select it from the list. This list is provided when the **Auto List Members** option is selected.

TROUBLE? If the list of available members is not automatically displayed, the Auto List Members option is not selected. To select the Auto List Members option, click Tools on the menu bar, click Options, click the Editor tab, click the Auto List Members check box to select it, and then click the OK button.

Figure 7-14   **AUTO LIST**

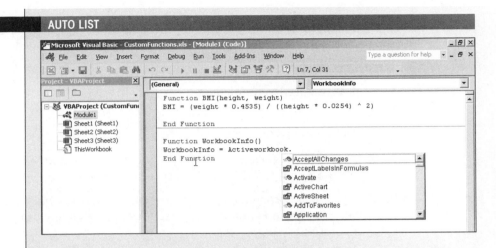

5. Press the **F** key to quickly scroll to the items in the list that start with "f", and then double-click **FullName** to insert this property into the line of code.

6. Save the changes you have made, and then close the Visual Basic Editor.

Now that the WorkbookInfo function has been created, you want to test it.

Using a Function Stored in Another Workbook

In order to use procedures stored in the CustomFunctions workbook elsewhere, the CustomFunctions workbook must be open. That is why you are storing it in the XLStart folder, because workbooks located in this folder automatically open as soon as Excel starts. If you use a function from another workbook, you must reference the workbook name followed by an exclamation point in front of the function name. For example, to reference the BMI function stored in the CustomFunctions workbook in a new workbook, the formula might be =CustomFunctions!BMI(A3,B3), if the value for the `height` argument was stored in cell A3 and the value for the `weight` argument was stored in B3. Fortunately, you don't have to remember the name of the workbook or custom function, nor do you have to type the entire reference to the custom function from the keyboard in order to use a custom function in another workbook. By default, Excel stores all custom functions in a function category called **User Functions**, which you can access from the Insert Function dialog box.

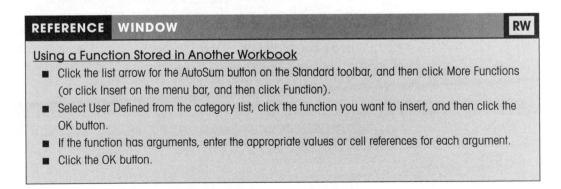

REFERENCE WINDOW   **RW**

Using a Function Stored in Another Workbook
- Click the list arrow for the AutoSum button on the Standard toolbar, and then click More Functions (or click Insert on the menu bar, and then click Function).
- Select User Defined from the category list, click the function you want to insert, and then click the OK button.
- If the function has arguments, enter the appropriate values or cell references for each argument.
- Click the OK button.

Note that in Excel 2000, the AutoSum button does not display a list arrow. You can insert a function using the Insert Function menu command or click the Paste Function button on the Standard toolbar. These methods open the Paste Function dialog box that you can use to insert a function.

Now that you've stored the BMI and WorkbookInfo functions in the CustomFunctions workbook, you need to test them.

To test the WorkbookInfo function in a new workbook:

1. Click the **New** button 🗋 on the Standard toolbar, and then save the workbook with the name **Test-7** in the Tutorial.07\Tutorial folder on your Data Disk.

2. Click the **list arrow** for the AutoSum button Σ ▾ on the Standard toolbar, and then click **More Functions**. The Insert Function dialog box opens, and Excel automatically begins a function by entering an equal sign in the Formula bar.

   EXCEL 2000: Click the **Paste Function** button on the Standard toolbar 𝑓ₓ. The Paste Function dialog box opens.

3. Click the **Or select a category** list arrow, click **User Defined**, and then click **CustomFunctions.xls!WorkbookInfo**. See Figure 7-15.

   EXCEL 2000: In the Paste Function dialog box, click **User Defined** in the Function category list, and then click **CustomFunctions.xls!WorkbookInfo**.

Figure 7-15	INSERT FUNCTION DIALOG BOX

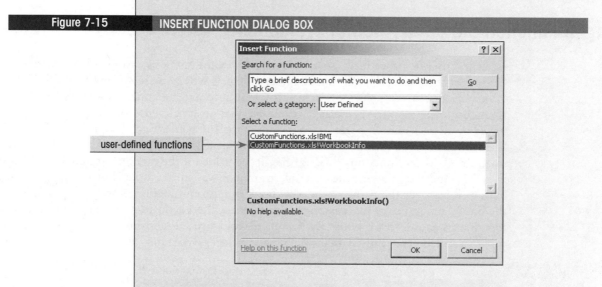

user-defined functions

4. Click the **OK** button. The selected user-defined function is automatically inserted in the Formula bar, and the Function Arguments dialog box opens.

5. Click the **OK** button. See Figure 7-16.

Figure 7-16	INSERTING THE WORKBOOKINFO FUNCTION

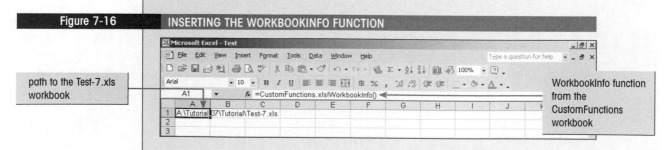

path to the Test-7.xls workbook

WorkbookInfo function from the CustomFunctions workbook

Now the users at GVR can use the WorkbookInfo function to document the workbook name within the worksheet itself. You also want to test the BMI function.

To test the BMI function in a new workbook:

1. Enter the height and weight labels and values shown in cells A5 and B5 as shown in Figure 7-17. You will use the values to test the BMI function.

Figure 7-17   **HEIGHT AND WEIGHT INFORMATION**

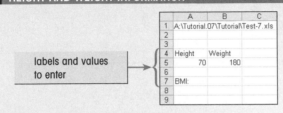

labels and values to enter

2. Click cell **B7**, click the **list arrow** for the AutoSum button , and then click **More Functions**. The Insert Function dialog box should display the last category used, the User Defined category.

EXCEL 2000: Click the **Paste Function** button 𝑓𝓍 on the Standard toolbar to open the Paste Function dialog box.

3. Click **CustomFunctions.xls!BMI** (if it is not already selected), and then click the **OK** button.

4. With the insertion point positioned in the Height reference box, click cell **A5**, click in the **Weight** reference box, and then click **B5** to enter the function arguments, as shown in Figure 7-18.

TROUBLE? If the Function Arguments dialog box covers columns A and B, move the dialog box to the right, or type the cell references in the reference boxes.

EXCEL 2000: Click the **Collapse Dialog Box** button 🔳 for the Height reference box, click cell **A5**, and then click the **Expand Dialog Box** button 🔲. Click 🔳 for the Weight reference box, click cell **B5**, and then click 🔲. The dialog box that opens looks slightly different from the one shown in Figure 7-18 but contains the same information.

Figure 7-18   **ENTERING THE ARGUMENTS FOR THE BMI FUNCTION**

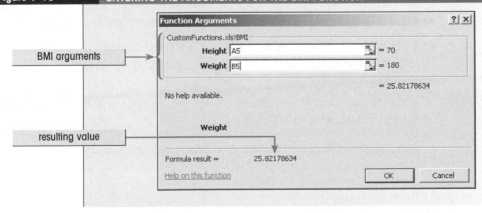

BMI arguments

resulting value

5. Click the **OK** button in the Function Arguments dialog box. See Figure 7-19.

Figure 7-19   **USING THE BMI FUNCTION**

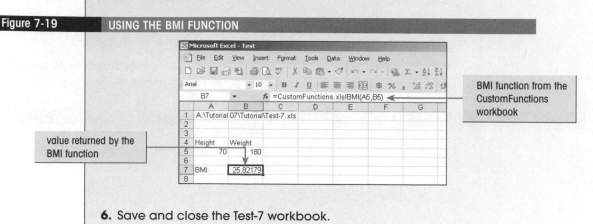

BMI function from the CustomFunctions workbook

value returned by the BMI function

6. Save and close the Test-7 workbook.

Both the BMI and WorkbookInfo functions work as intended and are ready to be used at GVR. Note that you can also store custom functions in **add-ins**, which are supplemental files that add custom functions and features to Excel. If you add functions to a workbook via an add-in file, you do not need to include the workbook name when you use the function.

Cleaning Up the XLStart Folder

If you are using your own computer and want to leave the CustomFunctions workbook in the XLStart folder, you are welcome to do so. If you are using a computer that is also used by others, you should remove the CustomFunctions workbook from the XLStart folder and restore to their default values any settings that you may have changed.

To clean up the XLStart folder:

1. Click **Window** on the menu bar, click **Unhide**, and then click the **OK** button in the Unhide dialog box to unhide the CustomFunctions workbook.

2. Click **Tools** on the menu bar, point to **Macro**, and then click **Visual Basic Editor** to open the Visual Basic Editor. The Module1 window should be displayed with the custom BMI and WorkbookInfo functions.

3. Add your name and the current date as a comment to the first line, and then save and print Module1.

4. Close the Visual Basic Editor, and then close the CustomFunctions workbook.

5. Right-click the **Start** button on the taskbar, click **Explore** on the shortcut menu, and then navigate to the C:\Program Files\Microsoft Office\Office10\XLStart folder in the Folders list.

 EXCEL 2000: Navigate to the C:\Program Files\Microsoft Office\Office\ XLStart folder.

6. Right-click the **CustomFunctions** workbook icon, click **Cut** on the shortcut menu, navigate to the Tutorial.07\Tutorial folder on your Data Disk, click **Edit** on the menu bar, and then click **Paste**. The CustomFunctions workbook is now stored on your Data Disk.

7. Close Windows Explorer and then exit Excel.

If you wanted to use the CustomFunctions workbook as the storage container for global custom functions in the future, you could always move it back to the XLStart folder on your own computer.

Session 7.1 QUICK CHECK

1. What are the advantages of using a custom function?

2. In order for Excel to automatically open a workbook when Excel is started, where does the workbook need to be located?

3. What two rules do you need to remember if you want an event to trigger a procedure?

4. Compare the Object Browser with the Microsoft Visual Basic Help system.

5. List three types of members that are presented when you click an item in the Classes pane within the Object Browser.

6. Excel automatically stores all custom functions in the function category called _____ .

SESSION 7.2

In this session, you will work more with custom function examples. You'll work with optional arguments, function recalculation, and the Select Case and If statements. You'll also work with the different kinds of VBA errors, and you will learn how to debug functions.

More Function Examples

After learning the basic terminology and getting comfortable with a new software interface, probably one of the best ways to learn any new software program or programming language is to apply it to as many new situations as possible. As with any new programming language, VBA takes a tremendous amount of time to learn, but by exploring a few more common examples, you'll be able to expand your ability to write custom functions for many new areas.

Creating a Date Function with One Argument

Excel can use dates in formulas, but many people have trouble with date formulas because they do not understand the way that Excel evaluates or formats dates. In Excel, dates are evaluated as numbers. January 1, 1900 is equal to the number 1, January 2, 1900 is equal to the number 2, and so forth. But depending on how a number is formatted, it can appear in many ways. For example, the number 1 can appear as 1, $1.00, 100%, 1/1/00, or January 1, 1900 on an Excel worksheet. Because of the general confusion that surrounds dates, date calculations are good candidates for custom functions.

Lynn wants you to develop an easy way to calculate a person's age, which is a required piece of information for successfully enrolling in many of the youth programs offered at GVR. For example, employees often have to calculate a child's age in order to put him or her in the right soccer, baseball, or football league. Because many employees are still new Excel users, you want to create a custom function called Age that calculates a person's age based on one argument, the birthdate. By providing GVR employees with the custom Age function, they won't have to worry about the actual math required to make this calculation.

To create the custom Age function:

1. Start Excel and open the **Camp-7** workbook location in the Tutorial.07\Tutorial folder on your Data Disk.

2. Open the Visual Basic Editor, and then insert a new module.

3. Type the function to calculate the age as shown in Figure 7-20. Delete the `Option Explicit` statement if it appears automatically.

Figure 7-20	AGE CUSTOM FUNCTION

type your name and the current date

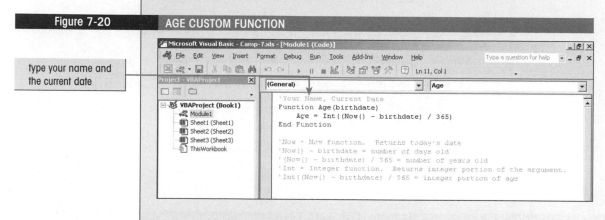

In this function, you must use the INT function to get the result you desire, the integer portion of the person's age, without regard to the remainder. (You could have also used the QUOTIENT function, which returns the integer portion of a division operation, but INT is probably more common.) At GVR, you don't want children put into the next age category until they have had that birthday. For example, if a child is 9 years old on the day a league starts, you want to place that child in the league for 9-year-olds, even if the child will have a birthday very soon after the league starts, and his or her age expressed as a decimal number is actually 9.9.

4. Save the changes you have made, and then close the Visual Basic Editor.

With the function created, you'll test it in the workbook.

To test the custom Age function:

1. Click cell **D10**, type **=age(C10)**, and then press the **Enter** key. The age for the first child in the list should appear in cell D10.

2. Copy the formula from cell **D10** through the range **D11:D22**, and then resize column D as shown in Figure 7-21. The age of each of the campers has been calculated.

| Figure 7-21 | COPYING THE AGE FUNCTION |

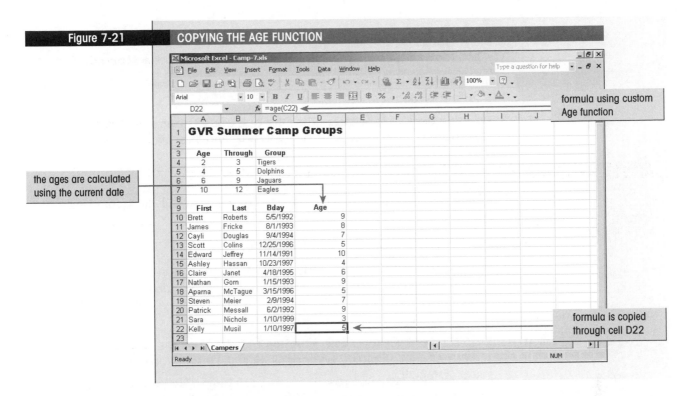

the ages are calculated using the current date

formula using custom Age function

formula is copied through cell D22

The Age function works as designed, but you can make it even easier for other GVR users by adding a function description.

Adding a Function Description

In order to make the new Age function easier for the GVR employees to use, you want to add a description to the function so that when you select it in the Insert Function dialog box, descriptive text appears that explains what the function does and how to use it. You add descriptive text to a function in the same way that you describe a macro, using the Macro dialog box.

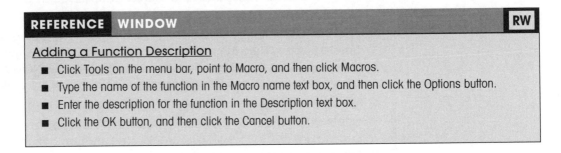

REFERENCE WINDOW   **RW**

Adding a Function Description
- Click Tools on the menu bar, point to Macro, and then click Macros.
- Type the name of the function in the Macro name text box, and then click the Options button.
- Enter the description for the function in the Description text box.
- Click the OK button, and then click the Cancel button.

You will add the description "Calculates the age based on the birthdate" to the Age function.

To add a description to the Age function:

1. Click **Tools** on the menu bar, point to **Macro**, and then click **Macros**.

2. Type **Age** as the name of the function in the Macro name text box, and then click the **Options** button.

3. Press the **Tab** key, type **Calculates the age based on the birthdate**, click the **OK** button in the Macro Options dialog box, and then click the **Cancel** button in the Macro dialog box.

Now that you've modified the function's description, you will check your work.

To review the Age function description:

1. Click cell **D10**, click the **list arrow** for the AutoSum button Σ ▾ on the Standard toolbar, and then click **More Functions** to open the Function Arguments dialog box. See Figure 7-22. The description will also appear when you use the Age function in a new cell.

   EXCEL 2000: Click the **Paste Function** button f_x on the Standard toolbar. The Paste Function dialog box opens with the description of the currently selected function.

Figure 7-22	FUNCTION ARGUMENTS DIALOG BOX

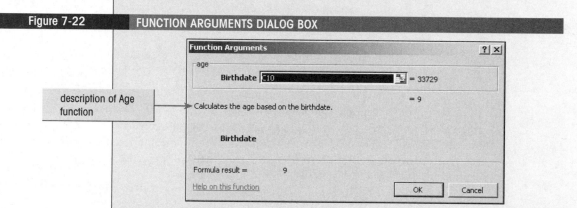

description of Age function

2. Click the **OK** button to close the Function Arguments dialog box, press the **Delete** key to delete the existing formula in cell D10, click the **list arrow** for Σ ▾ , and then click **More Functions**. See Figure 7-23. Note that the function, arguments, and description appear at the bottom of the dialog box for the selected function.

   EXCEL 2000: Click the **OK** button, press the **Delete** key to delete the existing formula in cell D10, and then click the **Paste Function** button f_x on the Standard toolbar. The Paste Function dialog box opens.

   TROUBLE? If the Age function is not displayed, click User Defined from the category list.

Figure 7-23 INSERT FUNCTION DIALOG BOX

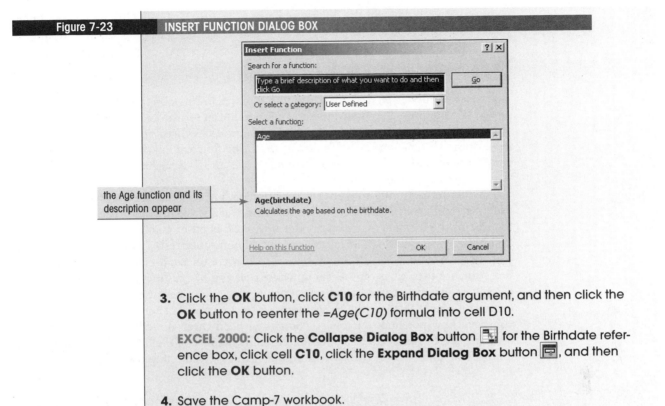

the Age function and its description appear

Age(birthdate)
Calculates the age based on the birthdate.

3. Click the **OK** button, click **C10** for the Birthdate argument, and then click the **OK** button to reenter the =Age(C10) formula into cell D10.

   EXCEL 2000: Click the **Collapse Dialog Box** button for the Birthdate reference box, click cell **C10**, click the **Expand Dialog Box** button, and then click the **OK** button.

4. Save the Camp-7 workbook.

Adding a description to custom functions is an easy way to make the function more meaningful to others.

Comparing IF, VLOOKUP, and Custom Functions

If you have ever found yourself writing a formula with several nested IF functions or been confused by the use of a VLOOKUP or HLOOKUP function, writing a custom function using the Select Case statement may help simplify the workbook.

At GVR, when a child signs up for summer day camp, the counselors place the child in one of four general groups, depending on the child's age. Although you could write a nested IF function or use a VLOOKUP function to determine the correct grouping, you know that some employees will have difficulty replicating and understanding those formulas on their own. You'll create a custom function named Camp to simplify this calculation. Figure 7-24 shows the age ranges for each group.

Figure 7-24 GVR CAMP GROUPS

AGE	GROUP
2 through 3	Tigers
4 through 5	Dolphins
6 through 9	Jaguars
10 through 12	Eagles

In order to show Lynn the difference between the IF, VLOOKUP, and custom function solutions to this problem, you'll create a workbook that compares the three techniques.

Using Nested IF Functions

The first technique you'll use to determine which team the children should be on is that of nested IF functions. The built-in Excel IF function can return one of two values, depending upon whether a test is true or false. An IF function has three arguments, and the generic form of the IF function is =IF(Test,True,False). The first argument is a test that evaluates to either true or false. If it is true, the formula returns the True argument. If it is false, the formula returns the False argument.

In order to test for more than one condition, you need to use nested IF functions. When using nested IF functions, if the first test is true, the answer to your formula is resolved and the rest of the formula is irrelevant. But if the test is false, you use the False argument to evaluate another IF function in order to conduct another test. Using nested IF functions, you always need one less IF function than you have choices, because only the last IF function provides two values for the true and false portions of the function. With nested IF functions, all tests other than the last one provide only one value for the True argument of the formula, because they use the False argument to run another IF function. In other words, if you have four potential outcomes, you would need three nested IF functions. For most users, nested IF functions are confusing, not only because of the logic, but also because they can become quite long if you have more than three or four alternative outcomes.

To make the right group assignments using nested IF functions:

1. Type **Group** in cell E9, and then press the **Enter** key.

2. In cell E10, type **=IF(D10<=B4,C4,IF(D10<=B5,C5,IF(D10<=B6,C6,C7)))** and then press the **Enter** key. The group "Jaguars" should appear in cell E10 because this is the group for ages 6 through 9.

   TROUBLE? Depending on when you are working this exercise, the ages of the children and therefore the groups to which they are assigned might change.

3. Click cell **E10**, and then click the first reference to cell **D10** in the Formula bar as shown in Figure 7-25. When you click a formula in the Formula bar, color-coded boxes identify which cells are used in the formula to help you figure out how the formula works (or why it isn't working). Because all of the cell references, with the exception of cell D10, should not move if you copy the formula, you need to make these cell references absolute cell references.

| Figure 7-25 | USING NESTED IF STATEMENTS |

nested IF functions

4. Click each cell reference (except for D10) in the Formula bar, and press the **F4** key to convert each cell reference to an absolute cell reference (for example, $B$4).

5. Copy the formula in cell **E10** through the range **E11:E22**. See Figure 7-26.

Figure 7-26	COPYING THE NESTED IF FUNCTION FORMULA

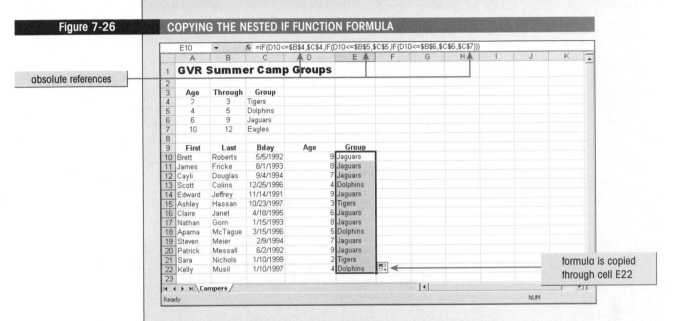

Now test the formula by changing one of the birthdates.

6. Click cell **C13** and type **5/5/91**. The new birthday should have increased Scott's age to 10 (or older), which puts him on the Eagles team.

TROUBLE? Remember, because the Age function uses the NOW function, which uses the current date, the ages calculated in column D might be older, and the groups in column E might be different, based on the date that you complete this exercise.

7. Click cell **C6**, type **Otters**, and then press the **Enter** key. Every occurrence of "Jaguars" should change to "Otters" in range E10:E22.

8. Save the Camp-7 workbook.

Now that you've used nested IF functions and seen how complex they become when multiple outcomes are available, you'll compare them to another technique to provide multiple outcomes for a formula, the VLOOKUP function.

Using the VLOOKUP Function

Anytime you find yourself nesting more than three or four IF functions, you should consider using a lookup function instead. The VLOOKUP (vertical lookup) and HLOOKUP (horizontal lookup) functions work well when you want more than three or four outcomes. When you use the VLOOKUP and HLOOKUP functions, you organize the alternative outcomes in a "lookup table". If the outcomes are organized in columns, use VLOOKUP. If the outcomes are organized in rows, use HLOOKUP. The following is the generic syntax of the VLOOKUP function, which contains three required arguments and one optional argument:

=VLOOKUP(LookupValue,LookupTable,Column,ExactMatch)

The first argument, *LookupValue*, is a cell reference or range name that contains the information you need to cross-reference with the values in the first column of the lookup table. The *LookupTable* argument is a cell range or range name, and at a minimum, references a two-column table. The first column of the LookupTable is called the lookup column, and it always contains the values that you compare with the LookupValue argument. The values in the lookup column should be arranged in ascending order. The second and subsequent columns of the LookupTable contain additional reference information for that row, similar to how fields are organized in a database record.

The *Column* argument of the VLOOKUP function determines which column of the lookup table holds the value that will be returned by the function. For example, if your lookup table is a two-column table, the *Column* argument would be 2. If the lookup table contains more columns of information, you enter the number that corresponds with the column that contains the data you want returned. The *ExactMatch* argument is an optional argument with only two options, true or false. If you do not specify an ExactMatch argument, its value is assumed to be true, and then the function will return a value even if an exact match is not made between the LookupValue and the first column of the lookup table. If you want the lookup function to return a value for a range of values, the argument should be omitted (or set the argument to true). If you want the lookup function to only return a value if it makes an exact match, the argument should be false.

The problem of assigning a child to the correct group based on age is an excellent problem for the VLOOKUP function to resolve, because the lookup table is already entered in the range A4:C7. The lookup values are in the range D10:D22.

To make the right group assignments using the VLOOKUP function:

1. Type **Group** in cell F9.

2. Select the range **A4:C7**, click the **Name Box** list arrow on the Formula bar, type **LookupTable** (no space), and then press the **Enter** key. See Figure 7-27. Although it isn't necessary to name the lookup table range in order to use the VLOOKUP function, using a range name makes the formula easier to enter and copy because you don't have to worry about referencing the lookup table with absolute references before copying the formula.

Figure 7-27 NAMING A RANGE

range name →

lookup table →

3. Click cell **F10** and enter **=VLOOKUP(D10,LookupTable,3)**. The value in cell D10 will be compared with the first column of the range identified by the LookupTable range name, A4:C7, and the value in the third column of the appropriate row will be returned by the function. Notice that the second column of the lookup table really isn't necessary for this function to work. All values from 2 through 4 return a value of "Tigers", 4 through 6 return a value of "Dolphins", and so forth. The second column in this lookup table isn't used in the function, but it does serve to help visually clarify the age groups for the user of this workbook.

4. Copy the formula in cell **F10** through range **F11:F22**. See Figure 7-28.

Figure 7-28	COPYING THE VLOOKUP FORMULA

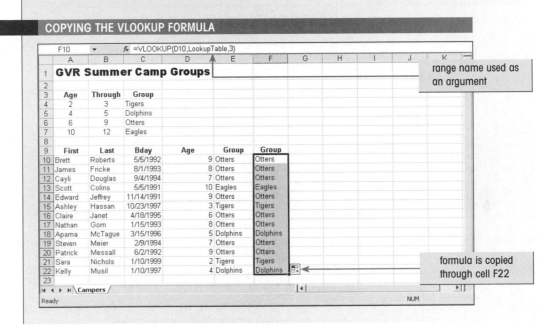

The assignments in column F were the same as those made in column E, showing that both types of formulas worked successfully. And although Excel experts have no trouble using VLOOKUP and HLOOKUP functions, most new users find them fairly daunting. Often, new users forget to sort the values in the first column in ascending order, fail to understand how the arguments within the functions work, or are unable to copy the formula because they have not mastered absolute cell references or range names.

Creating a Custom Function Using Select Case

A third way of tackling the problem of automatically assigning each child to a camp group based on their ages is to create a custom VBA function that makes the formula much simpler than using nested If statements or LOOKUP functions. You can use the Select Case statement, which allows you to enter each alternative as a "case", with the outcome determined by which case is true.

To make the right group assignments using a custom function:

1. Open the Visual Basic Editor, and then double-click **Module1** in the Project Explorer to open that Code window (if it's not already displayed).

2. Click in the Code window just below the last line of code, and then type the CAMP function to calculate the correct camp group assignment as shown in Figure 7-29. For the `Select Case` statement, the `childage` argument will be tested for four cases. The first `Case` statement tests for the `childage` argument from the value in cell A4 through the value in cell B4. If the `childage` argument is within that range, the second part of the statement, `/Camp = Range("C4")` is executed. In other words, if the date for the `childage` argument is within the ranges defined by A4 and B4, then the Camp function will return whatever value is currently stored in cell C4.

Figure 7-29   CREATING THE CUSTOM CAMP FUNCTION

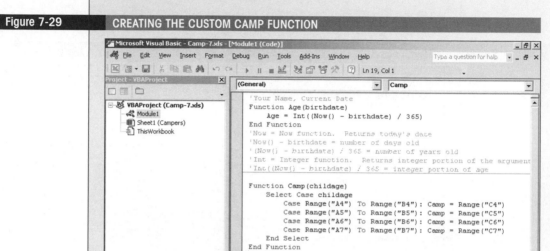

3. Save the changes you have made, close the Visual Basic Editor, and then enter **Group** in cell G9.

4. In cell G10, enter **=Camp(D10)**, and then copy the formula from cell **G10** through range **G11:G22**. See Figure 7-30.

Figure 7-30   COPYING THE CUSTOM CAMP FUNCTION

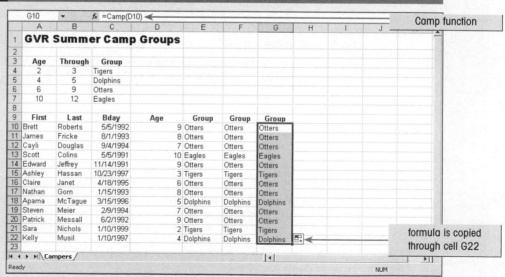

You don't have to use cell references within the Select Case statement. You could have "hard coded" the age ranges in the first part of the Case statements, and the group names (Tigers, Dolphins, and so forth) in the second part of each statement. For example, you could have entered the first Case statement as:

```
Case 2 to 3: Camp = "Tigers"
```

However, by referring to the values in cell references within the Case statements, the code is more flexible. Now, if you decide to change the age ranges or team names, the code is already equipped to handle those changes without needing to be modified.

Now test all three formulas.

To test the new formulas:

1. Click cell **C10** and then enter **5/5/90**. This birthday should make Brett Roberts at least 11 years old and place him in the Eagles group. All three formulas correctly recalculated and placed Brett in the Eagles.

   TROUBLE? If Brett Roberts is already in the Eagles group, change his birthday to a date a little more than 9 years prior to today's date so that Brett's age is calculated as 9 years old, and so that he is assigned to the Otters. Then repeat Step 1.

2. Click cell **C4** and then enter **Lions**. The nested IF function and VLOOKUP functions automatically recalculated, but the custom Camp function did not.

Custom functions, like other Excel functions, recalculate only when one of the function's arguments is modified. Because the custom Camp function has only one argument and its value is located in the Bday column, the function didn't automatically recalculate when cell C4 was modified. Because both the nested IF and VLOOKUP functions refer to cell C4 in their formulas, they recalculated.

Controlling Function Recalculation

Because functions automatically recalculate (by default) only when their arguments are changed, the functions might not recalculate as often as needed. Because the Camp function has only one argument, the child's birthdate, the function only recalculates when you change that value, and not when you change other values in the workbook. You can force custom functions to recalculate more often by adding the following statement to the function:

```
Application.Volatile True
```

This statement sets the Volatile method of the Application object to True. The Volatile method has only two settings, True or False, and the default setting is False, which forces the function to be calculated whenever recalculation occurs for any cell in the worksheet.

To make the custom Camp function recalculate automatically when any cell is changed:

1. Open the Visual Basic Editor, and then add the statement shown in Figure 7-31.

Figure 7-31   ADDING THE RECALCULATION STATEMENT

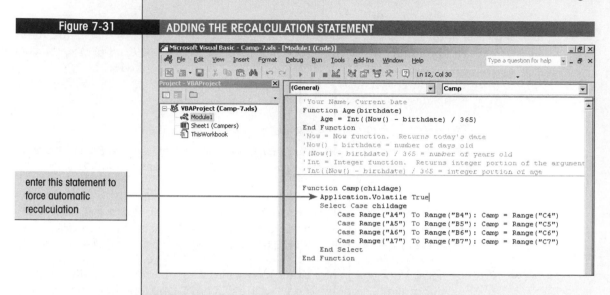

enter this statement to force automatic recalculation

2. Save the changes you have made, print Module1, and then close the Visual Basic Editor.

3. Click cell **G10**, reenter the formula **=Camp(D10)**, and then copy it to range **G11:G22**.

4. Enter **Bears** in cell C4. Now all three formulas automatically recalculate as desired.

5. Save the changes you have made, print the worksheet with your name in the left section of the header, and then close the Camp-7 workbook.

Although you may consider the complexity and effort required to build the custom Camp function to be just as great as that of creating a formula using lookup or nested IF functions, consider the effort from the user's standpoint. The following three formulas all produced the same results:

=IF(D10<=$B$4,$C$4,IF(D10<=$B$5,$C$5,IF(D10<=$B$6,$C$6,$C$7)))

=VLOOKUP(D10,LookupTable,3)

=Camp(D10)

If you were the only developer and user of this workbook, the technique that you would use would probably be based solely on your personal preferences. If you are building this workbook for less experienced Excel users, though, the custom Camp function has great appeal because it is so much easier and faster to enter.

Also note that the `Application.Volatile True` statement works well for this function because the workbooks that will use this custom function are fairly small. Therefore, the users will probably not notice any degradation in performance when this statement is used, even though it requires more processing cycles. Obviously, the larger and more complex that your applications become, the more issues you have to consider, and the more complex your VBA code becomes.

Creating a Custom Function Using If Statements

Another very common programming technique is to use `If` statements in your code to direct the flow of execution. The generic syntax of a VBA `If` statement is:

```
If Test Then TrueInstructions
```

Similar to the way the IF function within Excel works, a test must be conducted that has either a true or false outcome. If the result of the test is true, the *TrueInstructions* are executed. Both the `If` and the `Then` parts of the statement are required, and therefore `If` statements in VBA are often referred to as `If...Then` statements.

An optional part to the `If...Then` statement is the `Else` portion. The `Else` portion allows you to execute statements if the test is false and would be written as:

```
If Test Then TrueInstructions Else FalseInstructions
```

When an `If...Then` or `If...Then...Else` statement is contained in one statement, there is no need for an `End If` statement. But if the `Else` portion of the code is moved to a second line, an `End If` statement is required. Using more than one statement line is called the **block form**, and it can also include optional `ElseIf` (similar to nested IF functions within Excel) statements to expand the number of tests that can be used to determine the outcome. The generic form of the block `If` statement is:

```
If Test Then
  TrueInstructions
ElseIf Test2 Then
  TrueInstructions
Else FalseInstructions
End If
```

GVR sponsors a "Second Milers Club" for persons 60 or over. The purpose of the club is to provide fun recreational activities for retirees and their spouses. The annual dues set by the club are $60, $70, $80, and so on per person, as determined by your age. Those in their 60s pay $60, in their 70s pay $70, and so forth because there are more benefits and activities as the individual moves from age category to age category. However, those who pay $100 to join the club have a "Lifetime Membership" and pay only $10 per year after that. You'll build a custom function to help calculate annual dues based on the individual's age and Lifetime Membership decision. The `If` statement will help you control which statements are executed.

> *To create a custom function using If statements to calculate annual dues:*
>
> **1.** Open the **SecondMilers-7** workbook located in the Tutorial.07\Tutorial folder on your Data Disk, open the Visual Basic Editor, and then insert a new module.
>
> **2.** Enter the VBA code shown in Figure 7-32.

Figure 7-32	CREATING THE DUES FUNCTION

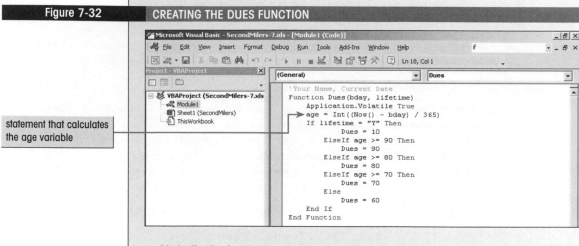

statement that calculates the age variable

Note that when you use the block form, you must end `If` and `ElseIf` statements with the `Then` keyword. If you put the TrueInstructions at the end of the `If...Then` or `ElseIf...Then` statement, the `If` statement is completed and will not recognize the next `ElseIf...Then` statement as part of the block. You will receive an error when you try to run your code, because the structure of the `If` statement is not valid.

The first thing this function does is calculate the age of the person based on the `bday` argument. In effect, you created a **variable**, a named location in memory called "age", that was then used to write the rest of the function. By calculating the `age` variable first, you enable it to be used instead of the expression it represents in the rest of the function, and therefore it helps simplify the rest of the statements.

Next, the `If` block starts executing. The first test is to see if the `Lifetime` argument is "Y". If it is true, the Dues function returns the value 10. If it is false, the first `ElseIf` statement is executed, which checks to see if the `age` argument is equal to or greater than 90. If it is true, the Dues function returns the value 90. If it is false, the next `ElseIf` statement is executed, and so forth. Because an `If` block ends when a condition is found to be true, you want to write it so that when the test is conducted and is evaluated true, no more tests need to be run. For example, it would not help to test whether an individual was older than 90 first, because you would still need to test whether the individual was a lifetime member. Similarly, it wouldn't help to test whether an individual was 60 first, because you would still have to test whether they were also older than 70, 80, and 90. Now you need to test the function.

To test the Dues function:

1. Save your work and then close the Visual Basic Editor.

2. Enter the label **Dues** in cell F4, enter **=Dues(C5,E5)** in cell F5, and then copy the formula through the range **F6:F17**. See Figure 7-33. In this workbook, the age of the individual was calculated in column D, not because it is required for the Dues function, but simply to make the resulting value from the Dues function easier to evaluate.

Figure 7-33 | COPYING THE CUSTOM DUES FUNCTION

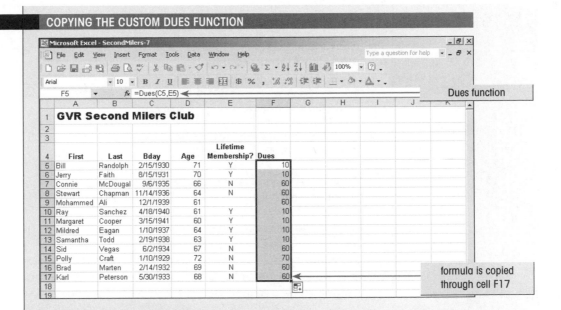

Test the Dues function by changing each of the arguments.

3. Delete the **Y** entry in cell E5. The result of the Dues function in cell F5 should have changed from 10 to 70.

4. Change the date in cell C5 to **2/15/1920**. The result of the Dues function in cell F5 should have changed from 70 to 80.

TROUBLE? If you enter only two digits in the year portion of a date entry, entries from 00 through 29 are assumed to be the years 2000 through 2029. Entries from 30 through 99 are assumed to be the years 1930 through 1999. To override these assumptions—for example if you want to enter the date 1929 or 2031—enter all four digits of the year.

Although the Dues function works as intended, in some cases you don't know whether the individual has paid a lifetime membership. In those cases, you don't use the `lifetime` argument within the function to determine the value for the Dues function. Therefore, you would like to change the function to make the `lifetime` argument an optional argument.

Creating Optional Arguments

Optional arguments are arguments that further define a function but do not need to be explicitly entered in order for a function to run successfully. Excel's built-in functions often use optional arguments that are provided to further clarify a function but are not required for every formula. The PMT function, for example, has two optional arguments, FV (future value) and Type (which determines whether the payment is made at the beginning or end of the period) that you may enter to further refine the PMT calculation, or ignore if you want to use the default values for these arguments.

To explore the PMT function's optional arguments:

1. Click the **list arrow** for the AutoSum button $\boxed{\Sigma \cdot}$ on the Standard toolbar, and then click **More Functions**.

> **EXCEL 2000:** Click the **Paste Function** $\boxed{f_x}$ button on the Standard toolbar. The Paste Function dialog box opens.

2. Click the **Or select a category** list arrow, click **Financial**, scroll and click **PMT** in the Select a function list, and then click the **OK** button.

> **EXCEL 2000:** In the Paste Function dialog box, click **Financial**, click **PMT** in the Function name list, and then click the **OK** button.

3. Click in the **Fv** reference box. See Figure 7-34. Required arguments are bold in the dialog box. Optional arguments are not bold. When you click an argument in the dialog box, a description of that argument appears at the bottom. The description of the optional arguments defines the argument as well as the default value assigned by Excel if you do not enter a value yourself.

Figure 7-34	EXPLORING OPTIONAL PMT ARGUMENTS

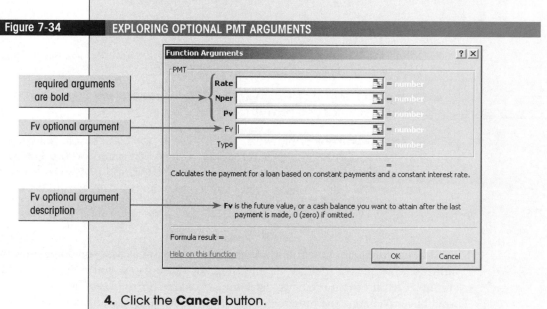

required arguments are bold

Fv optional argument

Fv optional argument description

4. Click the **Cancel** button.

Whenever you use an optional argument within a custom VBA function, you also must use the VBA `IsMissing` argument. The `IsMissing` argument will help you determine whether the argument was omitted and will help you establish a default value for the argument in that event.

Now that you have some background on optional arguments, you will change the `lifetime` argument for the Dues function to make it optional.

To change the lifetime argument within the Dues function to make it optional:

1. Open the Visual Basic Editor.

2. Modify the `Function` statement to include the **Optional** keyword in front of the `lifetime` argument and add the `IsMissing` statement to the Dues function as shown in Figure 7-35.

| Figure 7-35 | CREATING AN OPTIONAL ARGUMENT |

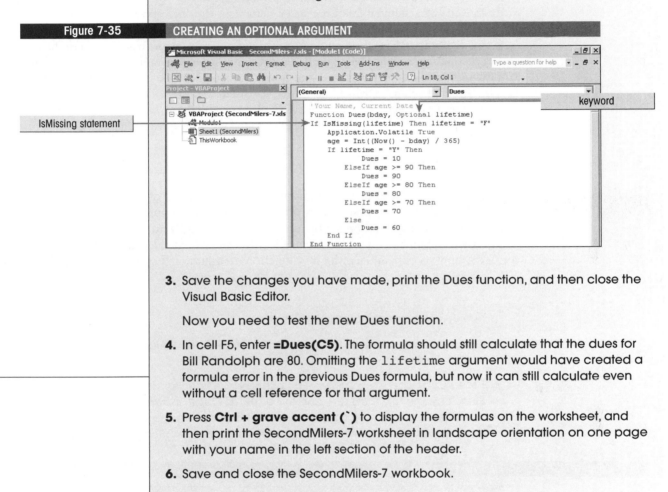

3. Save the changes you have made, print the Dues function, and then close the Visual Basic Editor.

   Now you need to test the new Dues function.

4. In cell F5, enter **=Dues(C5)**. The formula should still calculate that the dues for Bill Randolph are 80. Omitting the `lifetime` argument would have created a formula error in the previous Dues formula, but now it can still calculate even without a cell reference for that argument.

5. Press **Ctrl + grave accent (`)** to display the formulas on the worksheet, and then print the SecondMilers-7 worksheet in landscape orientation on one page with your name in the left section of the header.

6. Save and close the SecondMilers-7 workbook.

Now you can use the Dues function with or without the optional `lifetime` argument.

Debugging **Code**

As you may have already experienced, it's very difficult to write your code perfectly the first time. You're going to make a lot of mistakes, especially when you are new to any program or programming language. Sometimes you can use mistakes to learn more about the program. At other times, mistakes cause endless hours of frustration. Your ability to **debug**, or fix, code that doesn't work as intended will have a large impact on your ultimate success and productivity with VBA. Fortunately, VBA has many tools to help you figure out what is wrong and to fix broken code.

As your code becomes more complex, you'll need more sophisticated debugging tools and skills. For new VBA users, though, knowing just a little bit about the types of errors they are likely to encounter and learning a handful of debugging techniques can be of great value.

Types of Errors

There are at least three types of errors you can make when writing VBA: syntax errors, run-time errors, and logic errors. **Syntax errors** are created when you write a statement that VBA doesn't recognize. For example, you may have misspelled an argument in an expression that defines the value of a function or you may have omitted a required parenthesis. Syntax errors are the easiest to detect because your code turns red as soon as VBA detects this type of error. **Run-time errors** occur as a result of incorrectly constructed code. For example, you may have forgotten to write an `End If` statement following an `If` statement. Run-time errors are also relatively easy to debug because as you run your code, it will stop and highlight the line that it cannot resolve to help you determine where the error is. You can find run-time errors before you use the code in the workbook by clicking Debug on the Visual Basic Editor menu bar and then clicking the Compile VBAProject menu option. Note, however, that VBA code is not "compiled" first; VBA is an interpreted language, which means that each statement is interpreted and compiled each time it is run. **Logic errors** are the most difficult to troubleshoot, because they occur when the code runs without problems, but the procedure still doesn't produce the desired result.

Syntax Errors

Syntax errors are created by a wide variety of problems, many of which result from simple typos. The default color for syntax errors is red, and it will be applied to any statement that VBA cannot recognize as soon as you move to another statement.

You want to build a custom function called RetireDay that calculates the retirement date for GVR employees. You'll use this new function to intentionally experience several types of VBA errors.

To experience syntax errors:

1. Open a new, blank workbook, open the Visual Basic Editor, and then insert a new module.

2. Type `Function RetireDay(birthday, hireday` and then press the **Enter** key. The text turns red, and the error message shown in Figure 7-36 appears. The error was caused by the missing right parenthesis. Although Excel formulas will add an omitted right parenthesis automatically, VBA will not.

Figure 7-36	A SYNTAX ERROR

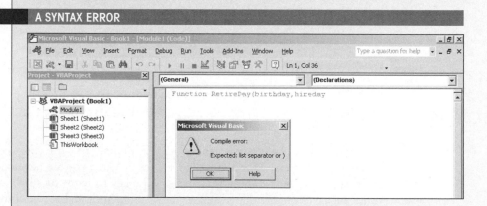

3. Click the **OK** button in the Microsoft Visual Basic dialog box, and then press the **Enter** key. The Visual Basic window will allow you to keep entering code, even though it flags the syntax error in the first line with the red text color.

4. Click immediately to the right of the `hireday` argument type **)** (a right parenthesis), and then press the **Enter** key. The code immediately changes to the blue (keyword) and black (normal text) default colors for VBA code, and the `End Function` statement appears.

5. Type `If Now() - hireday >` and then press the **Enter** key. Once again, the Visual Basic Editor was able to catch this error immediately, because it knows that the expression is not complete.

6. Click the **OK** button, and then finish the statement by typing `25*365 Then RetireDay = Now()` and pressing the **Enter** key. Your Code window should look like Figure 7-37.

| Figure 7-37 | CORRECTED IF STATEMENT |

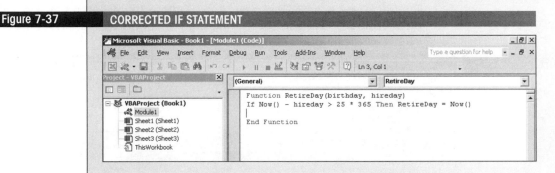

If you can't immediately determine the problem with your code, one technique that some programmers use to document various statements they have tried (so that they don't make the same mistakes over and over again) is to "comment the statement out" with an apostrophe. In other words, rather than deleting or editing a statement that doesn't work, if you precede it with an apostrophe and turn it into a comment line, you can look back at that statement and keep track of options that you did try that weren't successful. You can use this technique to document any type of error, not just syntax errors.

Run-Time Errors

Run-time errors do not cause your code to turn red like syntax errors do; run-time errors appear when the code is executing and VBA cannot determine how to complete the statement. A common run-time error would be an improperly constructed `If` statement.

To experience a run-time error:

1. Enter `ElseIf Now() - birthday > 65*365 Then RetireDay = Now()` as the next statement, and then press the **Enter** key. No syntax error was detected, but this code will not work as planned. The first `If` statement checks to see if you have more than 25 years on the job, and if so, the RetireDay is today. The `ElseIf` statement checks to see if you are over 65 years old, and, if so, the RetireDay function returns today's date. Yet the correct block form for the `If` statement was not used. To experience a run-time error, however, you'll leave the code as is and attempt to use the RetireDay function in the workbook.

2. Click the **View Microsoft Excel** button ⊠ on the Standard toolbar, and then enter the sample data shown in Figure 7-38.

Figure 7-38 | **SAMPLE DATA FOR RETIREDAY FUNCTION**

resize column to accommodate your name

	A	B	C	D	E
1	Name	Birthday	Hireday	Retireday	
2	Your name	9/7/1955	1/1/1982		
3					

Now enter the new function in a formula in cell D2 to experience the run-time error.

3. In cell D2, enter **=RetireDay(B2,C2)** and press the **Enter** key. See Figure 7-39. The error message indicates that you are using an `Else` statement without an `If` statement, which seems incorrect, because an `If` statement does exist in the line before the `ElseIf` statement. The problem is that the `If` statement is completed because the `Then` part of the statement also exists on the same line.

Figure 7-39 | **ELSE WITHOUT IF RUN-TIME ERROR**

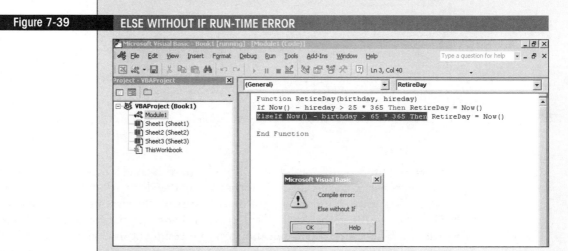

4. Click the **OK** button. A yellow arrow and yellow highlight indicate the point at which the code stopped executing. You can either continue trying to run your code by clicking the Continue button ▶ or reset the code by clicking the Reset button ■. If you see the error that you need to correct, you must click the Reset button before you can edit the code.

5. Click the **Reset** button ■ on the Standard toolbar, and then edit the code so that the portion of the statements after `Then` are moved to the next line, changing the `If` statement from a single-line statement to block form as shown in Figure 7-40.

Figure 7-40 | **USING BLOCK FORM IF STATEMENTS**

statements are now in block form

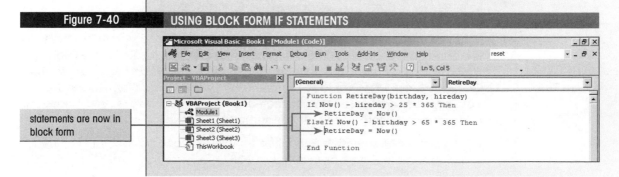

6. Click ☒, click cell **D2**, reenter the formula **=RetireDay(B2,C2)**, and then press the **Enter** key. You are presented with another run-time error. This time you are trying to create a block form `If` statement without the `End If` statement. Every block form `If` statement must be closed with an `End If` statement.

7. Click the **OK** button, click ■, and then enter **End If** on a new line just above the `End Function` statement.

8. Click ☒, click cell **D2**, reenter the formula **=RetireDay(B2,C2)**, and then press the **Enter** key. The RetireDay function now works without creating a run-time error, but unfortunately it still displays an incorrect retirement date for this test data.

Logic Errors

In this case, you are neither older than 65 nor employed for more than 25 years, so neither portion of the `If` statement is true, and the RetireDay function returned the value 0. But what you had intended for the RetireDay function to calculate is a date that you would retire. If you experience a logic error, you probably need to go back to the planning stages of your function and rethink how it should be constructed. Often, it's best to start with the outcomes that your function will provide and work backward from there. Once you know the outcomes that the function will provide, you then determine the rules and calculations needed to get those outcomes. In the case of the RetireDay function, you have only tested to see whether the person has been on the job for more than 25 years or if he or she is over 65 years of age. Most employees won't meet either of these criteria. For those employees, you want the RetireDay function to return the date of their retirement.

At GVR, an employee can retire at 65 years of age or when he or she has put in 25 years of service, whichever is sooner. Instead of having the function check to see if the employee is eligible for retirement and returning today's date as the function does now, you really need it to determine which of the two retirement dates is earlier and return that date.

To fix a logic error:

1. Return to the Visual Basic Editor, and then edit and enter the code as shown in Figure 7-41. This code uses two variables, `BirthdayRetire` and `HiredayRetire`. `BirthdayRetire` is calculated as 65 years after the birthday argument value. `HiredayRetire` is calculated as 25 years after the `hireday` argument value. Then, the two variables are compared, and whichever date is earlier is returned by the Retireday function.

TROUBLE? Be sure to delete the `Option Explicit` statement if it appears.

| Figure 7-41 | FIXING THE RETIREDAY FUNCTION |

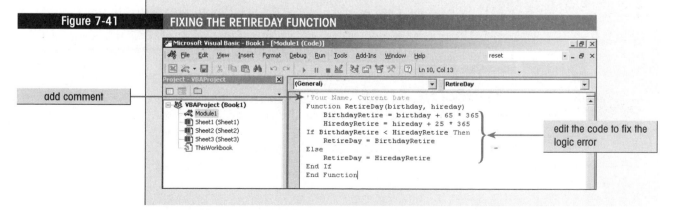

2. Click the **View Microsoft Excel** button 🗷 on the Standard toolbar, click cell **D2**, reenter the formula **=RetireDay(B2,C2)**, and then press the **Enter** key. The function returns a value (the number of days after January 1, 1900) that represents your retirement date. Formatting the value as a date will make it understandable.

3. Click cell **D2**, click **Format** on the menu bar, click **Cells**, click the **Number** tab in the Format Cells dialog box (if it is not already selected), click **Date** in the Category list, select the **M/DD/YY** date format in the Type list, and then click the **OK** button. Your workbook should look like Figure 7-42.

Figure 7-42   COMPLETED RETIREDAY FUNCTION

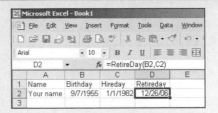

4. Save the workbook with the name **Retirement-7** in the Tutorial.07\Tutorial folder on your Data Disk, and then print the first worksheet.

5. Close the Retirement-7 workbook, and then exit Excel.

Obviously, the number and types of errors that you can make while creating VBA code is as vast as the capabilities of VBA itself. Knowing a little bit about the different types of errors that you are likely to encounter, as well as how to reset the code, is valuable when you are trying to debug it. One final tip is that you must be in Ready mode (as opposed to Edit mode) within the workbook itself in order to work in the Visual Basic Editor. Therefore, if you ever open the Visual Basic Editor but you are unable to enter any code or initiate any commands, the solution is probably to return to the workbook and press the Enter or Esc key to enter, complete, or back out of the current editing operation that returns the workbook to Ready mode.

Session 7.2 QUICK CHECK

1. Why are calculations that involve dates good candidates for custom functions?

2. If you need to test for five potential outcomes, how many nested IF functions would you have to use to cover all five alternatives?

3. What is the advantage of using VLOOKUP instead of nested IF functions?

4. What is the advantage of using a custom function with a `Select Case` statement instead of using the VLOOKUP function?

5. What is the generic syntax of the block form `If` statement?

6. What are the three general types of errors you might encounter when running VBA code? Which error is the most difficult to debug and why?

REVIEW ASSIGNMENTS

Green Valley Recreation (GVR) sponsors a variety of outdoor recreational activities. Because they are located in Illinois, the weather ranges from 100 degree Fahrenheit summer days to subzero winter days. You have been asked to develop custom Excel functions that can be used by all GVR employees to calculate the wind chill factor. You have found a couple of different formulas for this calculation and will compare the two. Because these formulas are quite long and complex, custom functions will work well to simplify the calculations.

To complete this task:

1. Start Excel and open the **Weather-7** workbook located in the Tutorial.07\Review folder on your Data Disk. Explore the WindChill worksheet. There are only two variables that go into the wind chill calculation, wind speed and temperature. However, the equation that calculates wind chill based on these two factors is quite long. One formula to compute wind chill is

    WindChill = (0.3V^0.5+0.474-0.02*V)*(T-91.4)+91.4

    where *V* equals the wind speed in miles per hour and *T* equals the temperature in degrees Fahrenheit.

2. Open the Visual Basic Editor, insert a new module, add a comment with your name and the current date, and then enter a function statement that creates a new function named WindChill that uses two arguments, `Windspeed` and `Temperature`.

3. Use the formula for wind chill provided in Step 1, which assigns the value of the calculation to the WindChill custom function.

4. In the WindChill worksheet, enter the formula using the WindChill custom function into cell B6 using mixed references for the two arguments so that you can copy the formula through the range B6:P13 without modifying the copied formula. The resulting value in cell B6 should be 38 and in cell P13 should be (99).

5. In the Visual Basic Editor, enter a new function in the existing module named WindChill2 that uses two arguments, `Windspeed` and `Temperature` based on another WindChill formula.

    A second formula to compute wind chill is

    WindChill2 = 91.4 - (0.474677 - 0.020425 * V + 0.303107 * (V)^0.5) * (91.4 - T)

    where *V* equals the wind speed in miles per hour and *T* equals the temperature in degrees Fahrenheit.

6. In the WindChill worksheet, copy the range A3:P13 to the range A15:P25. Modify the formula in cell B18 to use the WindChill2 function rather than the WindChill function, and then copy the modified formula from cell B18 to range B19:P25. The resulting value in cell B18 should be 37 and in cell P25 should be (100).

7. Save the changes you have made, and then print the WindChill sheet in landscape orientation on one page with your name in the left section of the header.

8. Use the Macro dialog box to document the source of the WindChill function formula by entering "provided by USA Today" as the description.

9. Use the Macro dialog box to document the source of the WindChill2 function formula by entering "provided by the National Weather Service" as the description. Close the Weather-7 workbook.

10. GVR workbooks often have the text "Green Valley Recreation" entered in cell A1. You'll create a new macro that records the keystrokes necessary to add this label to cell A1, and then add the macro to a workbook that automatically opens when you start Excel. Open a new workbook, and make sure that cell A1 is the active cell.

11. Using the macro recorder, record a macro with the name "GVR" that enters the text "Green Valley Recreation" in cell A1 of the current workbook. Format that label with an Arial Black font style and a 20-point font size.

Explore ▷ 12. Open the Visual Basic Editor, display the code for the GVR procedure (found in Module1), and delete the statements that are not relevant to entering the label and applying the two formatting characteristics to the selection.

13. Copy the code to the ThisWorkbook object, and then change the name of the procedure to "Workbook_Open" so that it executes when the Open event occurs for the workbook object.

14. Save the workbook with the name **GVR-7** in the Tutorial.07\Review folder on your Data Disk.

15. Delete the label and formatting in cell A1, save and close the GVR-7 workbook, and then reopen it. The Green Valley Recreation label should be reentered in cell A1, formatted in a 20-point Arial Black font.

16. Delete the label and formatting in cell A1, and then save and close the GVR-7 workbook.

17. In Windows Explorer, create a new folder named **ExcelStartup** at the C:\ location. Copy the GVR-7 workbook to the C:\ExcelStartup folder.

Explore ▷ 18. In Excel, open a new, blank workbook, open the Options dialog box, click the General tab, and then enter C:\ExcelStartup in the At startup, open all files in text box for Excel 2002 (or for Excel 2000, enter C: C:\ExcelStartup in the Alternate startup file location text box).

19. Exit Excel and then restart it. The GVR-7 workbook should have automatically opened when you started Excel.

20. In Excel, open the Options dialog box, and remove the C:\ExcelStartup entry from the startup option on the General tab to return to the default settings for that option. In Windows Explorer, delete the C:\ExcelStartup folder.

21. Open the **ParkingLot-7** workbook located in the Tutorial.07\Review folder on your Data Disk. In this workbook, you'll create a custom function to help determine which employees get the parking spots next to the building (there are three spots next to the building), which employees get the parking spots across the street (there are five spots across the street), and which employees must use satellite parking. The parking assignments are based on seniority.

22. Create a custom function in a new module called ParkingLot with one argument, Rank. The function should use the Select Case statement and assign the employees with the ranks 1 through 3 to the "Building" parking lot. Assign the employees with the ranks 4 through 8 to the "Street" parking lot. Assign the employees with ranks of 9 to 100 to the "Satellite" parking lot. In this instance, you are comfortable hard coding the Case statement values into the function because neither the number of parking spots nor the names of the parking lots are very likely to change.

23. In cell C4, enter the formula that uses the custom function to determine to which parking lot each employee is assigned, and then copy the formula through range C5:C19 as shown in Figure 7-43.

Figure 7-43

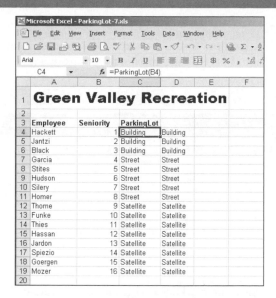

24. Create a custom function in the same module called ParkingLot2 with one argument, Rank. This time, use a block form If statement to determine which parking lot assignment should be made to each employee.

25. Add your name and the current date as a comment to the module, and then print it.

26. In the workbook, use the ParkingLot2 function in cell D4 to determine the parking lot assignments for the first employee. Copy the formula from cell D4 to range D5:D19. The results of the formula using the ParkingLot2 function should be the same as those in range D4:D19 where you used the ParkingLot function.

Explore 27. Write a one-page, double-spaced paper comparing the Select Case and If statements. Use Visual Basic Help to provide more information about each statement. To find information about the statements in the Help system, open the Help window, click the Contents tab, and then expand the Visual Basic Language Reference and Statements areas of the Contents list. The If statement is in the A-L section, and the Select Case statement is in the M-Z section. Conclude your paper with a recommendation of when to use the Select Case statement and when to use the If statement.

28. Display the formulas on the Parking worksheet of the ParkingLot-7 workbook, and then print the worksheet in landscape orientation on one page. Make sure that your name is in the left section of the header.

29. Save and close the ParkingLot-7 workbook, and then exit Excel.

CASE PROBLEMS

Case 1. Going Metric Your business supplies rose bushes to customers in the United States and Canada. Because Canada uses metric measurements, you are often asked to convert English measurements to metric measurements and vice versa. You have decided to create four custom functions to handle the often-needed conversions from Celsius to Fahrenheit, Fahrenheit to Celsius, meters to feet, and feet back to meters within a blank workbook so that you can use the functions within all other workbooks.

To complete this task:

1. Start Excel and start a new, blank workbook.

2. Using the Internet or any other reference source, research and find the formulas to create the following custom functions in a new module as described in Figure 7-44.

Figure 7-44

DESCRIPTION	CUSTOM FUNCTION NAME	ARGUMENT(S)
Converts Fahrenheit degrees to Celsius degrees	ToCelsius	Fahrenheit
Converts Celsius degrees to Fahrenheit degrees	ToFahrenheit	Celsius
Converts feet to meters	ToMeters	feet
Converts meters to feet	ToFeet	meters

3. Enter your name and the current date as a comment in the module, and then print it.

4. Save the workbook with the name **Metric-7** in the Tutorial.07\Cases folder on your Data Disk. Leave the Metric-7 workbook open.

5. Open the **Roses-7** workbook located in the Tutorial.07\Cases folder on your Data Disk. Use the functions you created in the Metric-7 workbook to convert the existing statistics to complete the table so that you have both Fahrenheit and Celsius measurements for all of the low and high temperatures, and for the typical height statistics expressed both in feet and meters.

6. Print the Stats worksheet with your name in the left section of the header. Also print the formula view of the Stats worksheet.

7. Save and close both workbooks, and then exit Excel.

Case 2. Revamping the Gold Club The Gold Club at your school is an honorary club that is based on dedication to community service, high academic achievement, and participation in extracurricular activities. Unfortunately, the standards for the club have not been applied equitably for all new members. The club has asked if you can help them determine if a student is eligible for the club, and if not why.

To complete this task:

1. Open the **Gold-7** workbook located in the Tutorial.07\Cases folder on your Data Disk.

2. Create a custom function called Membership that includes three arguments, `service`, `GPA`, and `extra` (for extracurricular activities).

Explore   3. Use the following rules to guide your creation of `If` statements within the Membership function to determine whether the person is eligible for the Gold Club.

To be eligible for the Gold Club, the member must:

- Complete at least 15 hours of community service work
- Maintain a 3.25 GPA
- Participate in at least two extracurricular activities

Explore   4. Add enough `ElseIf` statements to test for each condition that might occur (any combination of hours of community service, GPA, and extracurricular activities that allow the student to qualify or not qualify for the Gold Club) so that the Membership function returns a descriptive message indicating whether the student qualifies, or if not, why. To account for all combinations, you'll need a total of eight tests, which are equal to one `If` statement and seven `ElseIf` statements. Use the following example as a guide to entering the Membership function:

```
Function Membership(service, GPA, extra)
If service >= 15 And GPA >= 3.25 And extra >= 2 Then
  Membership = "Yes"
ElseIf service >= 15 And GPA >= 3.25 And extra < 2 Then
  Membership = "Low extra"
```

5. Add your name and the current date as a comment at the end of the code in the module, and then print it.

6. In cell E4 of the Candidates worksheet, enter a formula using the new Membership function that returns a message stating whether or not the individual is eligible for the Gold Club, and if not, why. Copy the formula through range E5:E13.

7. Print the Candidates worksheet with your name in the left section of the header.

8. Display the formulas on the Candidates worksheet, and print it again.

9. Save and close the Gold-7 workbook, and then exit Excel.

Case 3. Finding Information About VBA on the Web Microsoft provides a tremendous amount of information, sample code, and support at its Web site. In this exercise, you'll research what information and conventions are available for VBA developers.

To complete this task:

1. Start your Web browser, connect to the Internet if not already connected, go to http://msdn.microsoft.com/vba/, and then wait as your browser loads the Web page.

2. Explore the links in the navigation area on the left side of the screen. Your goal is to navigate to the FAQ (Frequently Asked Questions) page. At the time of this writing, the FAQ link was located within the Product Information category.

3. Find and click the What are the differences between Visual Basic, VBA, and VBScript? When would I use one over another? link, and read the explanation.

4. Find and click the Which Microsoft applications include Visual Basic for Applications? link, and read the explanation.

5. Find and click the Does VBA include any security features? link, and read the explanation.

6. Explore any other FAQ articles or any other area of the Web site.

7. Based on your exploration of the FAQ articles, write a one-page, double-spaced paper listing the things you learned from the FAQ articles.

8. Find a Web site for an upcoming Microsoft Office XP or VBA developer conference. Try http://www.devconnections.com/office/ and www.microsoft.com/usa/events.

9. Find and print the descriptions of the sessions on VBA.

10. Close your Web browser and, if you are using a dial-up connection, disconnect from the Internet.

Case 4. Creating a Custom Function to Calculate the Heat Index You work in the research department for a seed company, and you want to start a series of experiments that determine how various plants react to changes in the heat index. Because the heat index is calculated based on a complex formula that combines humidity and temperature, you decide to create a custom function for it so that you need to create the formula only once.

To complete this task:

1. Start Excel and open the **HeatIndex-7** workbook located in the Tutorial.07\Cases folder on your Data Disk. Notice that a table that compares temperature and humidity is already set up for you to use to calculate the heat index factors.

2. Use the Internet to research the formula for the heat index. When you find a Web site that shows how the actual formula is calculated, print it.

Explore

3. In the HeatIndex-7 workbook, open the Visual Basic Editor. Insert a new module, and then create a new function called HeatIndex with two arguments, H (humidity) and T (temperature).

   Enter the formula you found on the Internet for calculating the heat index, replacing the variables used on the Web site for humidity and temperature with the H and T arguments you defined for the HeatIndex function. Note that the character for exponentiation in Excel is the caret (^).

4. After you have created the function, use the continuation characters to break the formula into several lines so that you can see the entire formula on the screen.

5. Enter your name and the current date as a comment on the first line of the module, and then print it.

6. In cell B6 of the HeatIndex worksheet, enter a formula using the new custom HeatIndex function and mixed cell references for the humidity and temperature arguments.

7. Copy the formula through range B6:P17. The value for cell B6 should be about 80, and the value for cell P17 should be about 245.

8. Save and print the workbook on one page in landscape view. Print the formula view of the workbook on one page and in landscape orientation. Be sure to include your name in the left section of the header. Close the workbook and exit Excel.

QUICK | CHECK ANSWERS

Session 7.1

1. A custom function helps you simplify and standardize a long or complex formula.

2. The workbook (or a shortcut to the workbook) needs to be located at C:\Program Files\Microsoft Office\Office10\XLStart for Excel 2002 and C:\Program Files\Microsoft Office\Office\XLStart for Excel 2000.

3. When you want to run VBA code when an event occurs, you create a sub procedure with a special name that causes the code within the procedure to automatically run when the event happens. The special name is the object that triggers the event, followed by an underscore, followed by the event name. Also, you must store procedures that are run by events in the code window for that particular object.

4. The Object Browser is a list of all of the available objects, their properties, methods, and events. As you become more proficient with VBA, you will probably use the Object Browser to quickly locate recognizable objects, properties, methods, and events. The Visual Basic Help system is more extensive, providing more information and examples on the single item that you are working with.

5. properties, methods, and events

6. User Defined

Session 7.2

1. Dates are good candidates for custom functions, because dates are confusing to new Excel users for at least two reasons. First, new users don't understand that dates are really numbers, formatted as dates. Second, new users don't know how to switch between a number format, such as 32700, and a date format, such as September 2, 2002.

2. Four. When using nested IF functions to resolve a problem, you always need one less IF function than the number of alternatives.

3. The VLOOKUP formula is much shorter, and it can accommodate more alternatives than nested IF functions.

4. A custom function is a lot easier and faster to enter than using a VLOOKUP function.

5. The generic form of the block form If statement is:

```
If Test Then
TrueInstructions
ElseIF Test2 Then
TrueInstructions
Else FalseInstructions
End If
```

6. Syntax, run-time, and logic errors. Logic errors are generally the hardest to debug because there is no tool or feature to help you to fix code that works correctly but not as intended.

OBJECTIVES

In this tutorial you will:

- Learn the benefits of using a custom form

- Learn the terminology associated with an Excel UserForm

- Design a UserForm

- Learn about the controls available to a UserForm

- Add various controls to a UserForm including the Label, TextBox, SpinButton, ListBox, ComboBox, and CommandButton controls

- Modify control and UserForm properties

- Change the tab order for a UserForm

- Write event-handler procedures

- Use VBA functions, including FormatNumber and MsgBox

- Use VBA methods, including InputBox, Show, SetFocus, and Copy

- Use an Excel function in a VBA procedure

- Validate entries on a UserForm

CREATING CUSTOM FORMS

Developing Customized Forms for GVR

CASE

Green Valley Recreation

Green Valley Recreation (GVR) is a community agency that organizes sports and performing arts programs to help build the physical and mental skills of the residents of Green County, Illinois. Lynn Tse, the director of GVR, hired you as a business analyst. After working at GVR for a few months, you have worked with a wide variety of Excel workbooks. You have noticed that GVR uses workbooks to record a wide variety of statistics, enrollments, and facts regarding their programs. You feel that by using Visual Basic for Applications (VBA) to create some custom forms, you will be able to simplify the workbooks and make the often tedious process of data entry much faster, easier, and more accurate.

In this tutorial, you will learn more about VBA and how it is used to create custom forms, and you will further your knowledge of VBA objects, properties, methods, and events. You will use VBA to create a variety of custom forms that contain many different types of controls including labels, text boxes, option buttons, combo boxes, list boxes, and command button controls that will simplify the user interface for GVR workbooks.

SESSION 8.1

In this session, you will learn about the benefits of using custom forms within Excel. You'll learn the terminology associated with custom forms, and you'll create and modify a UserForm by adding different types of VBA controls to a form, including TextBox and Label controls. You'll learn how to open a UserForm using a Command Button control placed on a worksheet. You will also learn how to work with an InputBox control to prompt a user for information.

Why Use Custom Forms?

A **custom form** is a dialog box that you can create to address a function, such as data entry, within Excel. Just as you can use an Excel dialog box to enter, modify, and manipulate information in an Excel workbook, you can use a custom form to complete the same tasks. You are already very familiar with Excel's extensive system of built-in dialog boxes and have used them to complete a wide variety of tasks. For example, you have already used the Format Cells dialog box to apply formatting changes and the Page Setup dialog box to change print settings many times.

The benefits of creating a custom form are very similar to those of creating a custom function. Both tools serve to simplify, clarify, and improve the speed at which a user can accomplish a given task within Excel. The primary difference in purpose is that custom functions focus on simplifying complex or long formulas, whereas custom forms simplify the user's interface with the workbook itself. Custom forms are also more extensive. You can create a custom form to accomplish almost any user task, such as entering and editing data, navigating through a large workbook, or organizing various print definitions.

To define how a custom form interacts with the workbook, you use VBA. To the user, however, the custom form is simply a new, easy-to-use and easy-to-understand dialog box. To the VBA programmer, the custom form is actually a set of controls that are tied to underlying VBA code.

Designing a Custom Form

A **control** is any item on a dialog box. Figure 8-1 displays the Format Cells dialog box with the Font tab selected. This dialog box uses many different types of controls.

Figure 8-1   CONTROLS ON THE FORMAT CELLS DIALOG BOX

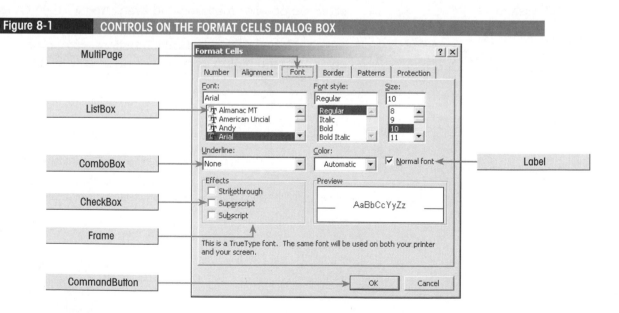

Figure 8-2 displays the Page Setup dialog box with the Page tab selected. This dialog box uses other types of controls.

Figure 8-2 | **CONTROLS ON THE PAGE SETUP DIALOG BOX**

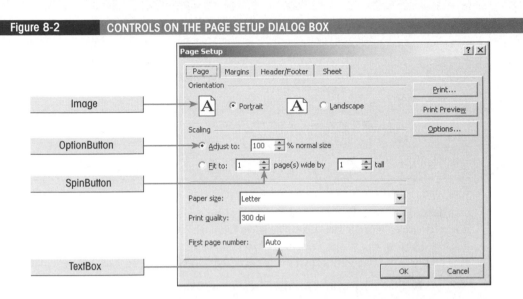

A major step in designing a new custom form is determining which controls you will use and how they will be organized on the form. Figure 8-3 identifies and describes the available controls.

Figure 8-3 | **CUSTOM FORM CONTROLS**

ICON	CONTROL NAME	DESCRIPTION
A	Label	Displays descriptive text that identifies a control on a form.
abl	TextBox	Displays a rectangular box in which you enter text and numbers.
	ListBox	Presents a list of items from which you can select a choice.
	ComboBox	Combines a TextBox control and a ListBox control because the ComboBox control displays a rectangular box in which you can enter information and a list of values from which you select from the available choices. A ComboBox is commonly called a drop-down box.
☑	CheckBox	Displays a small square that enables you to make one of two choices (yes or no), depending on whether the CheckBox is checked (yes) or clear (no).
◉	OptionButton	Displays a small circle that enables you to make a single selection from a small number of alternatives, each of which is an OptionButton control. OptionButton controls that are placed in a frame are mutually exclusive so that when one OptionButton control is selected, the others are deselected. An OptionButton is commonly called an option or radio button.
	Frame	Displays a panel in which groups of related controls, such as OptionButton, are organized.
	ToggleButton	Displays a button that enables you to make one of two choices, either yes or no, depending on if the ToggleButton control is pressed (yes) or not pressed (no).
	CommandButton	Displays a button that initiates an action when clicked. For example, the OK CommandButton applies the choices made within the dialog box, and the Cancel CommandButton closes the dialog box, canceling the choices made.
	TabStrip	Displays a tab that you can use to organize other controls on a multipage dialog box.

Figure 8-3   **CUSTOM FORM CONTROLS (CONTINUED)**

ICON	CONTROL NAME	DESCRIPTION
	MultiPage	Displays a page (or tabbed page) that enables you to organize other controls on a multipage dialog box. (The MultiPage control is very similar to the TabStrip control but offers more options for multipage dialog boxes.)
	ScrollBar	A vertical or horizontal bar that enables you to change the value by dragging a button along the ScrollBar control.
	SpinButton	A set of up and down arrows that enables you to change a value by clicking the arrows to either increase or decrease the value.
	Image	Displays a graphic image.
	RefEdit	Button that when clicked enables you to select a range in a worksheet.

You add controls to a dialog box by creating a UserForm in the Visual Basic Editor window. In other words, the **UserForm** is what the form designer sees in the Visual Basic Editor window, but when viewing a UserForm from within the workbook itself, it appears as a dialog box. The general steps involved with creating a new custom form are these:

- Plan what you want the UserForm to do.
- In the Visual Basic Editor, insert a new UserForm.
- In the Visual Basic Editor, add controls to the UserForm, and modify and adjust their properties as needed.
- In the workbook, add a Command Button to a worksheet.
- In the Visual Basic Editor, write a procedure that displays the UserForm when the Command Button is clicked. This procedure is located in the Code window for the worksheet that contains that Command Button.
- Check and modify the tab order of the UserForm as necessary.
- In the Visual Basic Editor, write procedures for the controls that are executed when various control events occur (such as when the form is displayed or when you enter text into a TextBox control). These procedures are located in the Code window for the UserForm.

Planning a UserForm

The first step in creating a UserForm is planning it. Planning the UserForm involves identifying the need for the form and determining what information the form requires to accomplish its goal. You may want to sketch out the form, which helps you determine which control would be most appropriate for each input item. A sketch also helps you plan out the overall layout for the form.

At GVR, you have noticed that many employees and coaches have trouble calculating the batting averages for their teams. In its simplest form, a batting average is a ratio of hits divided by the official number of times the batter got a chance to hit. A batter who gets one hit every two tries would be "batting 500", which is usually presented as a decimal number to the hundredths place, .500. But although the actual batting average calculation is quite simple, there are underlying complexities that not all users understand. Hits are calculated as singles plus doubles plus triples plus home runs which is fairly easy to understand. But the number of official times the batter got a chance to hit is confusing for most people. The official times the batter got the chance to hit is not the total number of times they got a chance at bat. The number of times a batter got a chance to bat is called **plate appearances**. **Official at bats** are calculated as plate appearances minus the batter's walks, hit by pitches, and sacrifices. Because the official number of "at bats" is often not clear to those who are not baseball enthusiasts, you decide to create a custom form to help simplify this calculation.

Figure 8-4 defines the baseball terms, including those that are used to calculate a batting average.

Figure 8-4	BASEBALL TERMINOLOGY USED TO CALCULATE A BATTING AVERAGE	
TERM	**COLUMN HEADING**	**DESCRIPTION**
Plate appearances	PlateApp	The number of times a batter gets up to bat.
Hits	Hits	The number of times a batter successfully reaches base calculated as the number of singles plus doubles plus triples plus home runs.
Base		There are four bases in baseball, organized in the form of a diamond: **home plate** (where the batter goes to bat), first base, second base, and third base. When a hit occurs, the batter runs from first to second to third and back to the home plate.
Single	1B	A hit that results in the batter gaining first base.
Double	2B	A hit that results in the batter gaining second base.
Triple	3B	A hit that results in the batter gaining third base.
Home run	HR	A hit that results in the batter gaining home plate. A home run scores at least one run (from the batter) and may score additional runs if other runners are on base when the home run occurred. A home run that scores four runs (the batter and runners on first, second, and third bases) is called a **grand slam**.
Run		When a batter crosses home plate, his or her team scores one run. The score of the game is determined by how many runs each team gets.
Runner		A batter becomes a runner when he or she successfully reaches a base.
Walks	Walks	The number of times a batter gets four pitches outside of the strike zone before getting out or getting a hit. A batter who gets a walk automatically advances to first base.
Strike zone		The area between the batter's knees and shoulders and as wide as the home plate. If a batter does not swing at a pitch in the strike zone, the batter is charged with a strike; if a batter swings at a pitch and misses, he or she is charged with a strike. When the batter has three strikes, the batter is "out".
Hit by pitches	HitPitch	The number of times the pitcher hits the batter with the baseball (for example, if the pitcher makes a wild pitch that hits the batter in the shoulder). When a pitch hits a batter, the batter automatically advances to first base.
Sacrifices	Sac	The number of times the batter advances existing runner(s) to the next base(s) but does not reach base himself; examples include bunts (in which the runner[s] are advanced to the next base, but the batter is thrown out at first base) and long fly balls (in which the runner[s] advance, but the batter is out because the fielder catches the fly ball).

Only two values are used to make the actual batting average calculation, Hits/Official At Bats, but they are not well known by most people who are not baseball enthusiasts. You'll create a UserForm that calculates the batting average based on information in an existing workbook.

Inserting a UserForm

In the Visual Basic Editor, you insert a new UserForm to create custom forms similar to the way in which you inserted new modules when you wanted to create a custom function.

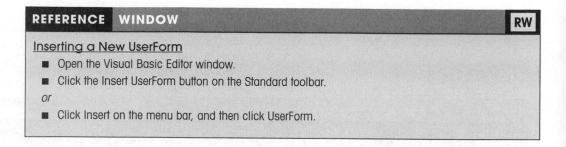

REFERENCE WINDOW | **RW**

Inserting a New UserForm

- Open the Visual Basic Editor window.
- Click the Insert UserForm button on the Standard toolbar.

or

- Click Insert on the menu bar, and then click UserForm.

You want to create a custom form to help users calculate the batting average.

To insert a UserForm to help calculate the batting average:

1. Start Excel and then open the **Batting-8** workbook located in the Tutorial.08\Tutorial folder on your Data Disk.

2. Press **Alt + F11** to open the Visual Basic Editor window, click the **Insert UserForm** button on the Standard toolbar, and then maximize the window. See Figure 8-5. A new UserForm object is created with the default name of UserForm1, and the Toolbox toolbar automatically appears.

Figure 8-5	INSERTING USERFORM1

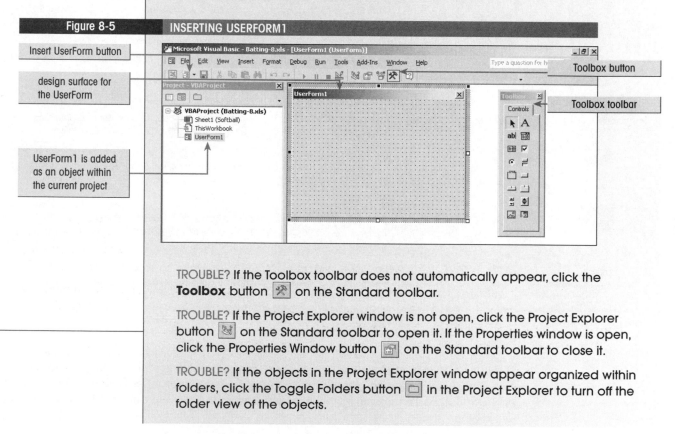

TROUBLE? If the Toolbox toolbar does not automatically appear, click the **Toolbox** button on the Standard toolbar.

TROUBLE? If the Project Explorer window is not open, click the Project Explorer button on the Standard toolbar to open it. If the Properties window is open, click the Properties Window button on the Standard toolbar to close it.

TROUBLE? If the objects in the Project Explorer window appear organized within folders, click the Toggle Folders button in the Project Explorer to turn off the folder view of the objects.

Notice that the UserForm1 is displayed as an object within the current VBA project in the Project Explorer.

Adding **Controls to a UserForm**

You work with the buttons on the Toolbox toolbar to add controls to the UserForm design surface. Every item, from a simple line to a complex command button, is a control. Controls are categorized as either unbound or bound. **Unbound** controls are not related to the actual data in the workbook and will not change as you work with the data. The most common unbound control is the label control that displays descriptive text. In contrast, a **bound** control is connected to the data in the workbook. A bound control allows you to enter, display, or edit the values that are used within the workbook itself and are therefore much more complex than unbound controls. To add any control to a form, you click the button that represents the control on the Toolbox toolbar, and then click on the UserForm where you want the control to appear.

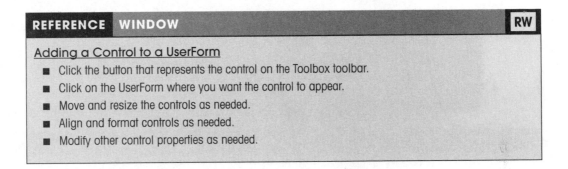

REFERENCE WINDOW   **RW**

Adding a Control to a UserForm
- Click the button that represents the control on the Toolbox toolbar.
- Click on the UserForm where you want the control to appear.
- Move and resize the controls as needed.
- Align and format controls as needed.
- Modify other control properties as needed.

Now that the UserForm is created you're ready to add controls to it.

Adding a Label Control

The first controls you add to a form are usually Label controls. Label controls on a form are used for the same purpose as labels that you enter into a worksheet cell—to clarify and identify the other parts of the worksheet or form.

To add a Label control to UserForm1:

1. Click the **Label** button A on the Toolbox toolbar, and then click the upper-left corner of the UserForm1.

2. Click in the **Label** control to edit the text, double-click **Label1**, type **Batting Average Calculator**, and then resize the label so that all of the text is clearly displayed as shown in Figure 8-6.

   TROUBLE? If you double-click the label control itself rather than the Label1 text, you'll start a new sub, Label1-Click(). Right-click UserForm1 in the Project Explorer, and then click View Object on the shortcut menu to return to the form.

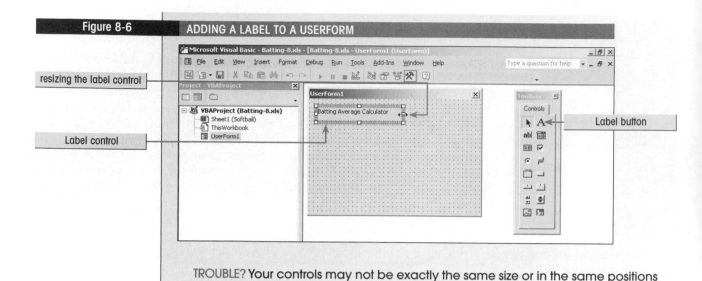

Figure 8-6 ADDING A LABEL TO A USERFORM

TROUBLE? Your controls may not be exactly the same size or in the same positions as the ones in the figures. Later, you'll modify the controls to match the figures.

Although you were able to modify the text for the label by working directly within the control, there are many other characteristics of the control that you may want to modify as well that go beyond just editing the default text. To see a complete list of all of a control's properties, you open its Properties window.

Properties Window

The characteristics of the control are called its **properties**. To see all of the properties for the selected control, you open the Properties window by clicking the Properties Window button on the Standard toolbar or selecting Properties Window on the View menu. You can change a control's properties in many ways. You can make a change directly in the Properties window, or you can apply a property change by using a quick keystroke, manipulating the control using the pointer, or initiating a menu command. Some properties, however, are only available through the Properties window. For example, you can only change the Name property of a control using the Properties window, but you can change the Width property of a control by entering a value in the Width property in the Properties window, dragging a handle on the selected control using the pointer, or selecting a spacing option from the Format menu.

You will explore the properties that are available for the Label control.

To view the properties for the Label control:

1. Click the **Properties Window** button 🔲 on the Standard toolbar to open the Properties window. Note that the Toolbox toolbar disappears when the Properties window or the Project Explorer is the active window. The Toolbox toolbar will redisplay when you click in the UserForm.

You can resize the components of the Visual Basic Editor to create an environment that suits your preferences.

2. Drag the top edge of the Properties window up so that more of the Properties window or less of the Project Explorer window are displayed, as shown in Figure 8-7. The property sheet displays an alphabetical list of the properties for the currently selected control. (The currently selected control displays sizing handles.) The title bar of the Properties window also displays the name of the control whose properties you are currently inspecting.

Figure 8-7 | **PROPERTIES WINDOW**

Properties Window button

drag pointer to resize the window

Properties window for Label1

property sheet displays an alphabetical list of the properties for the selected control

sizing handles show that this label is selected

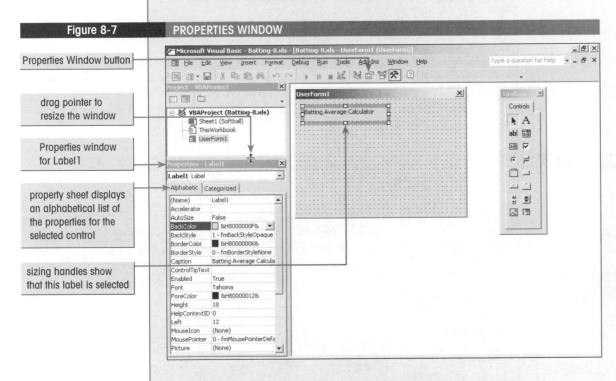

3. Click the **UserForm** to display its properties in the Properties window, and then click the **Label** control to observe the changes in the Properties window. The first property in the property sheet displays the name of the control, which in this case is Label1. Also note that the Caption property now displays the text you entered to replace the default text. You can change or modify the text of the Label control by modifying the Caption property or by typing directly in the Label control.

TROUBLE? If you double-clicked the control, its Code window opened. Close the Code window and then click the control once to select it.

4. Click the **Categorized** tab in the Properties window. The Categorized tab lists the same properties, but organizes them by function. All properties that apply to the appearance of the control are grouped together, all properties that apply to the control's behavior are grouped together, and so forth. You can make changes to a property in either the Alphabetic or Categorized list, and your changes will automatically be applied to the other list.

5. Double-click **Label1** in the (Name) property box, type **Title**, and then click the **Alphabetic** tab. Title appears as the (Name) property entry on the Alphabetic list as well.

All objects have properties, including the UserForm itself. If you plan to have several custom forms in your workbook, you should change their generic names from UserForm1, UserForm2, and so on to more meaningful names so that they are easier to identify in the Project Explorer.

To modify the properties of the UserForm:

1. Click anywhere on UserForm1 to select it (do not click the Label control). The property sheet displays the properties for the UserForm1 control.

2. Double-click **UserForm1** in the Name property box, type **BatAvg**, and then press the **Enter** key. See Figure 8-8. The new Name property of the form now appears in the Project Explorer. This will make it easier to identify this form in the future. You can modify the names of the other objects in the current project using the Properties window.

Figure 8-8   **CHANGING THE NAME PROPERTY OF USERFORM1**

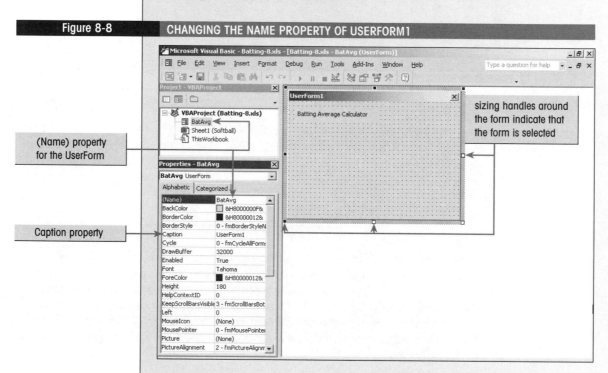

(Name) property for the UserForm

Caption property

The Caption property for the form controls the text in the title bar of the form. Changing the Caption property of the UserForm1 control will make the form easier to recognize.

3. Click the **Caption** property, double-click **UserForm1** in the Caption entry, and then type **What's your batting average?**

Note that the text in the title bar of the UserForm automatically changes as you change the Caption property for the control.

Now that you've added a descriptive label and changed the Caption property of the form so that the title bar also displays descriptive text, you're ready to add more controls to the form.

Adding a TextBox Control

The TextBox control is probably the most common bound control for a form because it accepts almost any type of data entry (text, numbers, dates). Any time you are working with a workbook value that has an indeterminate number of values (such as a name, street, or telephone number field), the TextBox will probably be the control you'll use because it allows you to enter or edit almost any type of entry.

To add a TextBox control to the BatAvg UserForm:

1. Click the **BatAvg** UserForm to redisplay the Toolbox toolbar, click the **TextBox** button abl on the Toolbox toolbar, and then click below the Batting Average Calculator label on the UserForm.

   TROUBLE? If the Toolbox toolbar does not redisplay, click View on the menu bar, and then click Toolbox.

   The process of adding a TextBox control to the UserForm is very similar to that of adding a Label control. The main difference is making sure that you click the TextBox button versus the Label button on the Toolbox toolbar. Point to the buttons on the Toolbox toolbar and read the ScreenTips to make sure you are working with the right control.

2. In the Properties window, double-click **TextBox1** in the (Name) property box, and then type **TextBoxHits**. You'll need to refer to this control later as you complete the VBA code for calculating the batting average. You might find it helpful to include the name of the control as part of the (Name) so that you don't get Label and TextBox controls mixed up when you are manipulating them with VBA code.

3. Click the **BatAvg** UserForm to redisplay the Toolbox toolbar, click the **Label** button A on the Toolbox toolbar, and then click to the left of the TextBoxHits control.

4. Modify the (Name) property of the new Label to **LabelHits** and the Caption property to **Hits**, and then resize LabelHits as shown in Figure 8-9.

Figure 8-9   HITS LABEL CONTROL

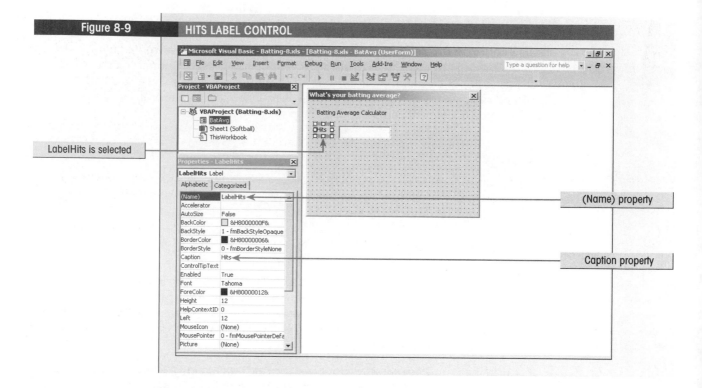

LabelHits is selected

(Name) property

Caption property

Modifying a Control

Depending on your experience working on a design surface such as a UserForm, you may be very familiar with the actions you can take to modify existing controls on a UserForm. Figure 8-10 organizes many tips that will help you select, move, align, and resize controls on a UserForm.

Figure 8-10   TIPS FOR MODIFYING CONTROLS

ACTION	TIP
Select a control	Click to select a control.
Select multiple controls	To select multiple controls, click the first control, and then press and hold the Shift key while you click the subsequent controls.
	Drag a selection box (sometimes called a "lasso") over the controls you want to select.
	When you select multiple controls, the first control you select appears with white sizing handles rather than black ones, and is used to determine how the other controls will adjust when you choose an alignment or spacing command.
	Press the ← or → key, or press the Tab key or press Shift + Tab to select the multiple controls.
Move a control	To move a control, click to select it and then use the ↔↕ pointer to drag the control to another location. By default, controls "snap" to the grid displayed on the UserForm when you release the mouse button. To change the grid settings, click Tools on the menu bar, click Options, click the General tab, and then modify the Form Grid Settings.
	You can move more than one control at a time by selecting them first.

Figure 8-10	TIPS FOR MODIFYING CONTROLS (CONTINUED)

ACTION	TIP
	To move a control with more precision, select the control or controls, click Format on the menu bar, and then use the available options: Horizontal Spacing and Vertical Spacing (Make Equal, Increase, Decrease, Remove), and Center in Form (Horizontally, Vertically).
Align controls	To align controls with respect to each other (by their left, center, right, top, middle, or bottom edges), select the control or controls, click Format on the menu bar, point to Align, and then select an appropriate alignment command.
Resize a control	Select the control, and then drag a sizing handle to resize the selected control. Drag a corner sizing handle to resize both the control's height and width. Drag a middle sizing handle to resize only the control's height or width.
	Select a control or controls, click Format on the menu bar, and then use the available Make Same Size options: Width, Height, Both.
Delete a control	Select the control or controls, and then press the Delete key.

In addition to the techniques and method shown in Figure 8-10, you can right-click a control and then use the options on the shortcut menu to copy, align, size, and move the control.

Now you will add two more TextBoxes and associated Label controls to identify the official at bats and batting average values. Figure 8-11 shows the completed form.

Figure 8-11	BATAVG USERFORM WITH LABEL AND TEXTBOX CONTROLS

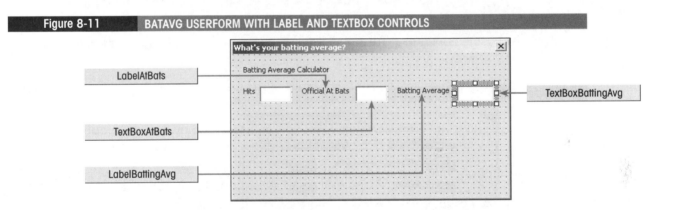

To add the rest of the controls to the BatAvg UserForm:

1. Click the **BatAvg** UserForm to redisplay the Toolbox toolbar, click the **Label** button A on the Toolbox toolbar, click to the right of the TextBoxHits control.

2. Change the (Name) property to **LabelAtBats** and the Caption property to **Official At Bats**, and then resize the control to accommodate the caption.

3. Click the **TextBox** button ab| on the Toolbox toolbar, click to the right of the Label control you created in Step 1, and then change the (Name) property to **TextBoxAtBats**.

4. Resize and reposition the controls and BatAvg form to accommodate the new control.

5. Add the third Label control and change its (Name) property to **LabelBattingAvg** and its Caption property to **Batting Average**.

6. Add the third TextBox control and change its (Name) property to **TextBoxBattingAvg**.

7. Use the techniques presented in Figure 8-10 to move, reposition, and align the controls as needed. See Figure 8-11 for the sizes and locations of the controls.

Because many properties can be modified in many different ways, the techniques that work best for you will probably come from practice and experience. To change the font settings of a Label control, you must use the Properties window.

To modify the controls on the BatAvg form:

1. Click the **Batting Average Calculator** label to select it, and then click the **Categorized** tab in the Properties window.

You will change the foreground color of the control, to display the text in the color you select.

2. Click the **ForeColor** property, click the **list arrow** that appears to the right of the ForeColor property entry, click the **Palette** tab, and then click the **Red** box (third row down from the top, second column from the left) from the color palette. The color of the text in the Title control changes to red. If you knew that the code for red was &H000000FF&, you could type that code directly into the ForeColor property box, but most users will probably find it much easier to select a color from the color palette.

TROUBLE? Resize the Properties window as desired in order to clearly view property values.

3. Double-click the **Font** property to open the Font dialog box, click **Bold** in the Font style list, click **12** in the Size list, and then click the **OK** button.

TROUBLE? Scroll down the list of properties to display the Font property rows. If only one row is displayed, click its **expand** button to display the Font properties. Double-click the **Font** property within the Font group to open the Font dialog box, and then continue with Step 3.

4. Resize and move the Batting Average Calculator control so that the entire caption is clearly visible and does not crowd the other controls on the UserForm.

5. Drag to create a selection box that includes the three Label and three TextBox controls that appear below the Batting Average Calculator control to select the six controls as shown in Figure 8-12.

Figure 8-12   SELECTING MULTIPLE CONTROLS

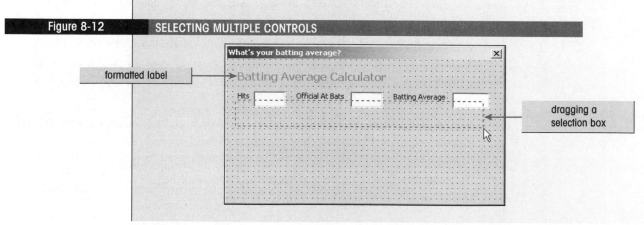

formatted label

dragging a selection box

6. Click **Format** on the menu bar, point to **Align**, and then click **Tops**. The top edges of the six controls are now perfectly aligned. When controls are in a horizontal arrangement as they are in the BatAvg UserForm, you often align the top or bottom edges. When controls are in a vertical arrangement, you align their left or right edges to make them align in a column.

7. With the six controls still selected, click **Format** on the menu bar, point to **Horizontal Spacing**, and then click **Make Equal**.

8. Click in the **BatAvg** UserForm (but do not click a control) to deselect all the controls.

The number and type of font and formatting property enhancements that you can choose to make to your UserForm is vast. At some point, however, you'll want to check the form to see how it will appear in the worksheet to the user.

Displaying a UserForm in a Worksheet

To display the BatAvg UserForm in a worksheet, you will need to write a VBA procedure that opens the form in a worksheet and attaches the code to the Click event of a Command Button. In other words, you want the BatAvg UserForm to open when a user clicks a Command Button located on a worksheet. Procedures that run in response to events are called **event handler procedures**. For now, however, you will just test the UserForm to see how it will appear to a user before writing the code. You can display a UserForm without writing a procedure by clicking the Run Sub/UserForm button on the Standard toolbar in the Visual Basic Editor.

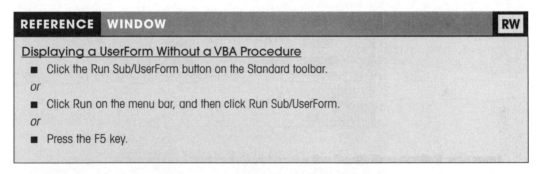

REFERENCE WINDOW **RW**

Displaying a UserForm Without a VBA Procedure
- Click the Run Sub/UserForm button on the Standard toolbar.

or
- Click Run on the menu bar, and then click Run Sub/UserForm.

or
- Press the F5 key.

At this point, your form is not connected with values in the workbook, but you want to see how the form will appear to the user.

To display the BatAvg UserForm:

1. Click the **Run Sub/UserForm button** ▶ on the Standard toolbar, and then press the **Tab** key several times to move through the TextBox controls on the form. Depending on how you added the TextBox controls to the UserForm, the **tab order**, the sequence in which the controls receive the focus as the user presses the Tab key to move through the controls, may not match the order in which the controls are positioned on the UserForm. A control is said to have the **focus** when it is the active control. (For example, a TextBox control has the focus when the insertion point appears in the control and you can enter a value into it. A CommandButton control has the focus if it initiates an action when you press the Enter key.) In Figure 8-13, the insertion point appears in the Hits text box.

Figure 8-13   **DISPLAYING THE BATAVG USERFORM**

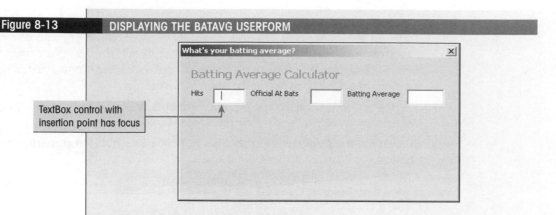

TextBox control with insertion point has focus

2. If the Hits text box does not have the focus, press the **Tab** key to move to the Hits text box, or click in the Hits text box.

3. Type **10** into the Hits text box, type **20** into the Official At Bats text box, and then type **.500** into the Batting Average text box just to practice using the form.

4. Close the form. You are returned to the Visual Basic Editor window.

At this point, the values that you entered into the UserForm were not saved with the workbook or used in any way, but later, you'll add the VBA code to save the entries made in the UserForm to the workbook. Displaying the UserForm as you develop it will help you to get a feel for how the user is going to react to the form. It also gives you a chance to test the tab order.

Changing the Tab Order

By now, you see how important the tab order is to the overall ease of use of the form. If the tab order causes the users to skip around on the form, they may become frustrated and unproductive. You check the tab order of a UserForm and change the order if you feel that a specific order will help ensure ease of use and accurate data entry.

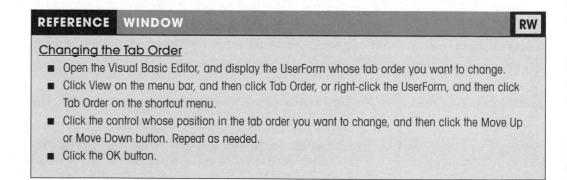

REFERENCE WINDOW   **RW**

Changing the Tab Order
- Open the Visual Basic Editor, and display the UserForm whose tab order you want to change.
- Click View on the menu bar, and then click Tab Order, or right-click the UserForm, and then click Tab Order on the shortcut menu.
- Click the control whose position in the tab order you want to change, and then click the Move Up or Move Down button. Repeat as needed.
- Click the OK button.

You will check the tab order on the BatAvg UserForm to make sure that it's organized in a way that works best for both the form user and you as the form designer.

To check the tab order on the BatAvg UserForm:

1. Click **View** on the menu bar, and then click **Tab Order**. The Tab Order dialog box opens, showing the (Name) property of all of the controls on the UserForm. Because unbound controls, such as Labels, cannot have the focus, the tab order for Labels and other unbound controls has no effect on the user. But Labels can still be selected when you are working in the Visual Basic Editor. Therefore, you want to organize the controls in the Tab Order window not only by how a user would tab through them, but also by how you want to tab through them in the Visual Basic Editor.

2. Click each control in the Tab Order list, and then click the **Move Up** or **Move Down** button to organize the tab order as shown in Figure 8-14.

Figure 8-14	TAB ORDER DIALOG BOX

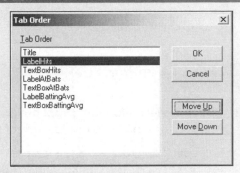

3. Click the **OK** button, and then press the **Tab** key enough times to tab through all of the controls.

You have completed the first phase of the UserForm. The controls have been added to the UserForm, the controls have been moved, resized, and formatted, and you have set an appropriate tab order. Now you're ready to add a Command Button on the worksheet to open the UserForm. You also need to write procedures for the controls to save the data that you enter in the UserForm to the workbook.

Creating a Command Button on the Worksheet to Open a Form

After the form is created, you can display it in response to almost any event in the workbook. Usually, though, you open a form in response to the Click event for a Command Button that you have placed on the worksheet for the specific purpose of opening the form. You can add a Command Button control to a worksheet using the Control Toolbox toolbar.

When you add a Command Button to a worksheet using the Control Toolbox toolbar, the label on the inserted control displays the two words, "Command Button". The ScreenTip for the Command Button button on the Control Toolbox toolbar also appears as two words (that is, "Command Button"). Note, however, the ScreenTip for the CommandButton button on the Toolbox toolbar in the Visual Basic Editor appears as one word "CommandButton".

REFERENCE WINDOW   **RW**

Adding a Command Button to a Workbook

- Display the worksheet on which you want to add a Command Button control.
- To display the Control Toolbox toolbar, click the View menu, point to Toolbars, and then click Control Toolbox, or right-click any toolbar within the workbook, and then click Control Toolbox.
- Click the Command Button button on the Control Toolbox toolbar, and then click the location in the worksheet where you want to place the control.
- To change the label on the Command Button control, click the Properties button on the Control Toolbox toolbar, and then modify the Caption property.
- Resize, format, and modify the Command Button control as needed.

You will add a Command Button control that when clicked will display the BatAvg UserForm. You will position the Command Button control to the right of the labels in cells A1 and A2 of the worksheet.

To add a Command Button control to display the BatAvg UserForm:

1. Click the **View Microsoft Excel** button 🖾 on the Standard toolbar in the Visual Basic Editor window to display the Softball worksheet of the Batting-8 workbook.

2. Right-click any toolbar, and then click **Control Toolbox** to display the Control Toolbox toolbar. The Control Toolbox contains buttons that represent controls that you can place directly on the workbook. This toolbar works similarly to the Toolbox toolbar within the Visual Basic Editor used to add controls to a UserForm.

3. Move your pointer over the controls on the Control Toolbox and observe the ScreenTips for each control.

4. Click the **Command Button** button 🔲, and then click cell **F1** to insert the control at that location. See Figure 8-15. The Command Button control appears with the default caption "CommandButton1". To change the text on the control, you open its Properties window and change its Caption property, just as you changed the Caption properties for controls in the Visual Basic Editor.

| Figure 8-15 | ADDING A COMMAND BUTTON CONTROL TO A WORKBOOK |

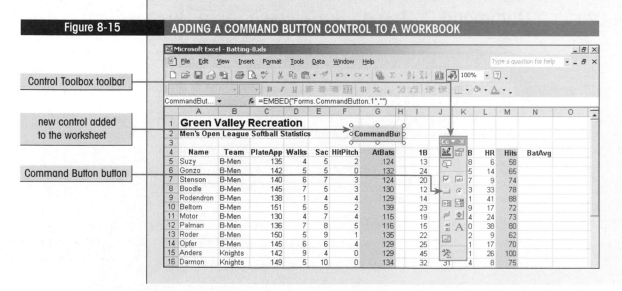

5. Click the **Properties** button 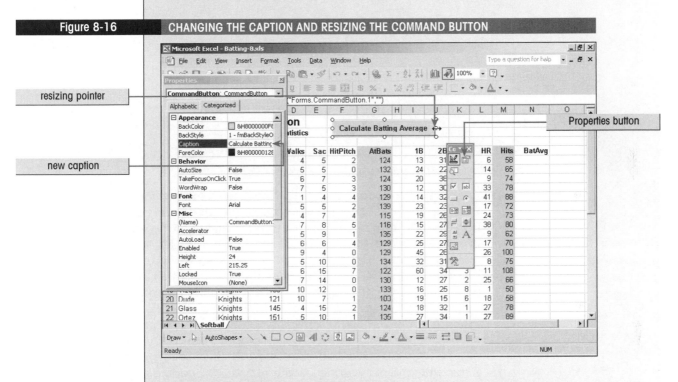 on the Control Toolbox, click the **Caption** property, double-click **CommandButton1**, and then type **Calculate Batting Average**.

TROUBLE? If you cannot read the text in the Caption property field, widen the Properties window. The number at the end of the CommandButton property represents the sequential number of controls that were added in a particular session, so it may vary from the figures in this book.

To view the entire caption on the Command Button, you need to widen it.

6. Resize the Command Button control so that the entire caption is visible as shown in Figure 8-16.

Figure 8-16	CHANGING THE CAPTION AND RESIZING THE COMMAND BUTTON

The Properties window for the selected control may appear. For now, you don't need to change any more properties for the Command Button.

7. Close the Properties window.

Now that the Command Button is added to the workbook, you need to add VBA code so when you click the Command Button, it opens the correct form.

Displaying a UserForm from a Command Button

The procedure that opens a UserForm when a Command Button is clicked should be located in the current worksheet object in the Visual Basic Editor. As you already know, there are many ways to open the Visual Basic Editor window, including using menu commands or the Alt + F11 shortcut keystrokes. When building the code that you want to run when a control is manipulated on a workbook, the best way to open the module is to either double-click the control, right-click the control and then click View Code on the shortcut menu, or click the View Code button on the Control Toolbox. If you use any of these techniques, Visual Basic will automatically open the Code window for the current worksheet, create the first and last lines of your sub procedure, and name your procedure with the name of the control so that it will execute the code you add when the `Click` event occurs for that control.

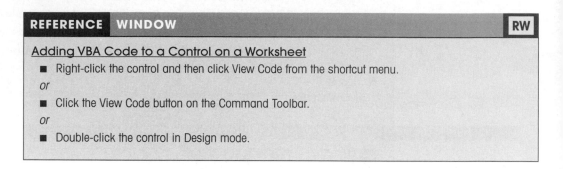

REFERENCE WINDOW | RW

Adding VBA Code to a Control on a Worksheet

- Right-click the control and then click View Code from the shortcut menu.

or

- Click the View Code button on the Command Toolbar.

or

- Double-click the control in Design mode.

Now that you have the UserForm and the Command Button created, you want to create the VBA code that opens the UserForm when the Command Button is clicked.

To add the VBA code that opens the UserForm from the Command Button:

1. Click the **View Code** button 🔲 on the Control Toolbox toolbar. The Visual Basic Editor opens the Code window for the current worksheet named Softball. Because this code applies to a Command Button on the worksheet, the code needs to be in the `Sheet1(Softball)` object. The first line of the procedure `Private Sub CommandButton1_Click()`. `Private` means that the procedure can only be used in the current workbook. Either `Sub` or `Function` must precede the procedure name. Because this procedure completes an action rather than returning a value, it is a `Sub` procedure verses a `Function` procedure. `CommandButton1` is the name of the Command Button (found in the (Name) property, not the Caption property), and `Click` indicates what event will run this code. All procedures end with a set of parentheses. The `End Sub` command must be the last line of a `Sub` procedure just as the `End Function` command must be the last line of a `Function` procedure.

2. With the insertion point positioned between the `Sub` and `End Sub` statements, type **BatAvg.Show**. This statement invokes the `Show` method of the `BatAvg` UserForm to display the form. See Figure 8-17.

Figure 8-17 | **CREATING A PROCEDURE TO RUN ON A CLICK EVENT**

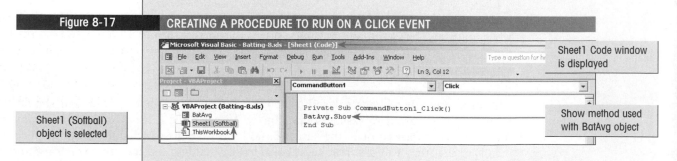

TROUBLE? When you type a period (.), the Auto List of properties and methods appears. You can select the property or method you want from the list, or enter a property or method from the keyboard.

When you type the period (.), a drop-down list of properties and methods appears. You can select the desired property or method from the list, or enter it from the keyboard.

3. Close the Visual Basic Editor, click the **Exit Design Mode button** 🖾 on the Control Toolbox toolbar, and click the **Calculate Batting Average** button on the worksheet. See Figure 8-18.

| Figure 8-18 | USING THE COMMAND BUTTON TO OPEN THE BATAVG USERFORM |

clicking the button displays the form

button toggles between Design View and Exit Design View

BatAvg UserForm

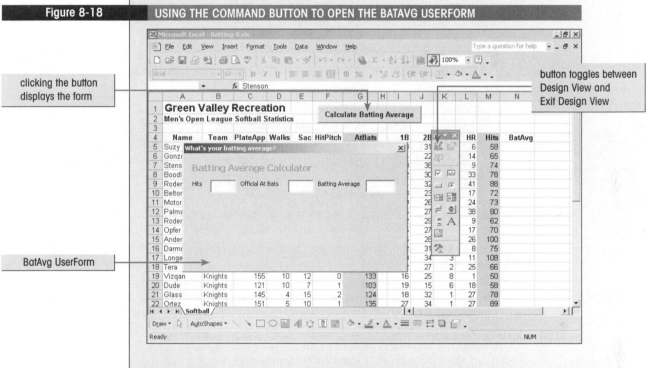

You don't need to close the Visual Basic Editor to test the Command Button, but testing the Command Button with only the workbook window open simulates the environment of the user.

4. Close the form, and then save the Batting-8 workbook.

The Exit Design Mode button is a toggle that moves you back and forth between **Design mode** (which occurs automatically when you are adding controls to a workbook, and which you use to select and modify controls) and the normal workbook Ready mode. In Design mode, if you click the Command Button, you select it. You know when you are in Design mode because the selected Command Button (or any other control) displays sizing handles indicating that it is selected. When the Command Button is selected, you can move, resize, delete, or otherwise modify it. When you are not in Design mode, clicking the Command Button initiates the Click event for the button.

Writing a Procedure for the UserForm

Now that you have the form created and can open it from a Command Button placed in the workbook, you need to write a procedure so that the TextBoxBattingAvg calculates the batting average using the value in the TextBoxHits control divided by the value in the TextBoxAtBats control. You want the value for TextBoxHits to come from column M of the row for the active cell, and you want the value for TextBoxAtBats to come from column G of the row for the active cell. In other words, you want the user to be able to click any name in column A and then be able to use the BatAvg form to quickly calculate the batting average.

The code for the controls on the UserForm is stored within the UserForm object itself. To access the code behind each control, you either double-click the control when viewing the UserForm in the Visual Basic Editor window or right-click the control and then click View Code from the shortcut menu.

The VBA code you'll write for the UserForm depends on what you want it to do. Often, you use TextBox controls for data entry purposes, and you use the UserForm as a data entry tool. In this case, though, you want the TextBox to get its value from column M of the row for the active cell, so that if you click a player's name in column A, and then click the Command Button on the workbook, the batting average is calculated for that individual. Because you want to feed the custom form values from the workbook, one important issue that you must resolve is determining which cells contain the values you want to send to the form. You'll tackle this issue by using the `ActiveCell` property of the `Application` object to identify the active cell (the player's name that you click in column A). Then, you'll use the `Offset` property to find the associated cells for the Hits and AtBats values for that player. The `Offset` property allows you to find a cell an offset number of columns and rows from the current cell. Once you find the values for the Hits or AtBats cells relative to the active cell, you'll use those values in a simple calculation of Hits/AtBats to determine the value for the TextBoxBattingAvg text box in the form.

To write the VBA code for the UserForm:

1. Press **Alt + F11** to return to the Visual Basic Editor (if it isn't already displayed), and then double-click the **BatAvg** UserForm object in the Project Explorer window to display the BatAvg UserForm in the Visual Basic Editor window.

2. Double-click the **TextBoxHits** control. The Code window for the BatAvg UserForm appears as shown in Figure 8-19. The object name and event name are displayed in the first line of the procedure `Private Sub TextBoxHits_Change()`. The **Object list box** also displays the object with which you are currently working, and the **Procedure list box** displays the current event that defines this procedure. In other words, if you entered code

within the two existing statements, the code would run when the `Change` event for the `TextBoxHits` object occurred. Although this may be the appropriate event to trigger the code if you were using the TextBox to enter data, you want the TextBox to accept the appropriate entry from the workbook as soon as the BatAvg UserForm is displayed. Therefore, you need to change both the object and the event that makes this code occur.

Figure 8-19   **CODE WINDOW FOR BATAVG USERFORM**

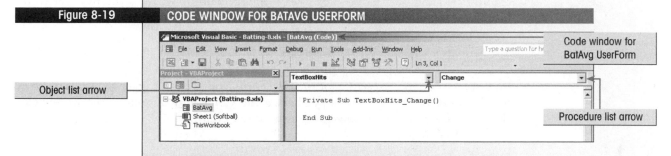

3. Select the existing code, and press the **Delete** key to delete it.

To write a procedure that runs when the UserForm is displayed, you can either write the code directly in the Code window or use the Object list box and Procedure list box to help you select the right object and event.

4. Click the **Object** list arrow, and then click **UserForm**. The VBA Editor attempts to anticipate the event that you want, and immediately provides two lines of code:

```
Private Sub UserForm_Click()
End Sub
```

The code entered between these two statements will run when the `Click` event occurs for the `UserForm`. Instead of running the code when the `UserForm` is clicked, however, you want the code to run when the UserForm is opened, which is represented by the `Activate` event.

5. Click the **Procedure** list arrow, and then click **Activate**. The VBA Editor added two more lines, the first and last lines of the `UserForm_Activate` procedure. In other words, the code that is entered between these two lines will automatically run when the form is activated.

6. Delete the `Private Sub UserForm_Click` and `End Sub` statements (which are not needed for this procedure), and then enter the code shown in Figure 8-20.

Figure 8-20   **VBA CODE TO DETERMINE BATTING AVERAGE**

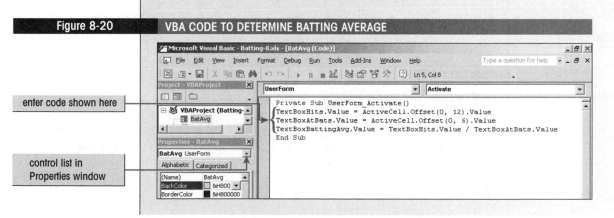

> TROUBLE? Controls must be referenced in VBA code exactly as they are identi-
> fied by their (Name) property. To see a list of control names, click the control list
> arrow in the Properties window and then select the control whose properties
> you want to inspect from the list.

Now that the `UserForm_Activate()` procedure is written, you're eager to test it using the Command Button on the workbook.

Testing the UserForm Procedure

To test the code you just wrote for the UserForm, you need to trigger the `Activate` event for the UserForm. You do this by clicking the Command Button on the workbook that shows the UserForm that triggers the `Activate` event.

To test the UserForm_Activate procedure:

1. Click the **View Microsoft Excel** button on the VBA Standard toolbar, click cell **A5**, and then click the **Calculate Batting Average** Command Button. The BatAvg UserForm is activated, which causes the UserForm_Activate procedure to run. See Figure 8-21.

| Figure 8-21 | TESTING THE USERFORM_ACTIVATE PROCEDURE |

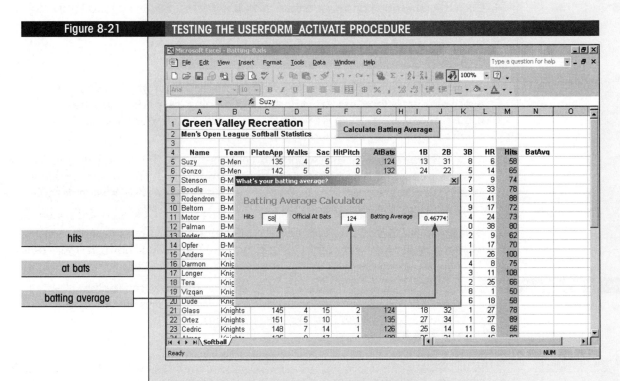

> TROUBLE? If your code doesn't run successfully, click Debug in the Microsoft
> Visual Basic dialog box, compare your code to Figure 8-20, click the Reset
> button, and then repeat Step 1.

2. Close the BatAvg custom form.

One of the most difficult things about learning VBA is getting a grasp of the vast number of ways to accomplish a task, but a bit of documentation to explain what each line of VBA code accomplishes can help. Over time, you'll work with enough examples that you'll gain the experience required to write the code from scratch.

To document the VBA code for the UserForm and the rest of the workbook:

1. Press **Alt + F11** to open the Visual Basic Editor, right-click the **BatAvg** UserForm in the Project Explorer, and then click **View Code** to display the Code window for the UserForm if it isn't already displayed.

2. Press **Ctrl + Home** to move the insertion point to the upper-left corner of the code window for the BatAvg UserForm, and then press the **Enter** key.

3. Close the Project Explorer and the Properties window (if they are open) to allow more room on the screen, and then add the following comments as shown in Figure 8-22.

Figure 8-22	DOCUMENTING THE VBA CODE FOR THE USERFORM

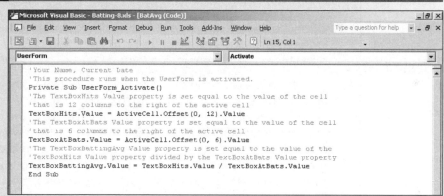

4. Save the changes you have made, and then print the code for the UserForm.

5. Click the **Project Explorer** button on the VBA Standard toolbar, double-click **Sheet1(Softball)** in the Project Explorer to display the code window for that object, and then add your name and the current date as a comment above the `Private Sub CommandButton1_Click()` statement.

6. Save the workbook. Clicking the Save button on the Standard toolbar in either the Visual Basic Editor or the Excel workbook window saves the entire workbook, including any VBA code that it may contain.

Although you have a working UserForm, users need to be trained to click on a name in column A before they click the workbook Command Button to calculate the batting average for that individual. This requirement may or may not be acceptable to them. Furthermore, as the batting average calculation stands now, it is calculated within the UserForm, but it isn't transferred to the workbook. You'll address both of these issues next.

Using an InputBox

Once you have the basic functionality of a UserForm working correctly, you will probably find a number of improvements that you would like to make. It's always a good idea to test your custom forms with a user as soon as possible, too. Testers can provide valuable feedback on how to improve the form—ideas that you as the form designer may not have considered.

After testing the UserForm with a colleague at GVR, you see that it's hard for the user to remember to select a name in column A before clicking the Command Button to calculate the batting average. You'll use the `InputBox` method of the `Application` object to prompt the user to select the player for whom they desire to calculate the batting average. The `InputBox` method creates a dialog box for you to enter information that is used in the procedure. The data that you enter into the dialog box can be any type of information such as text, a value, a date, or a range. The `InputBox` method has only one required argument, `Prompt`, which represents the message to be displayed in the dialog box. It has a number of optional arguments that further define characteristics of the argument and dialog box itself. To force the argument to be a special type of value, such as a cell reference, you use the `Type` argument. If the `Type` argument is set to 8, the entry must be a valid range such as B1.

To add an InputBox to the BatAvg UserForm:

1. Open the Visual Basic Editor if it's not already open, double-click **BatAvg** in the Project Explorer to open the UserForm, and then double-click the **UserForm** to open the code window for the form.

2. Add three lines of code shown in Figure 8-23. Normally, you would not need to include the `Set` keyword in order to assign a value to a variable, but in this case, you want the `NameCell` variable to be set to the cell reference rather than the value within the cell reference. The `Set` keyword accomplishes this. Also, this code includes a named argument. A **named argument** is an argument name followed by a colon followed by the argument value. Because the `InputBox` method has eight possible arguments, most of which are optional, it is easier to explicitly name the arguments you are using than to worry about the syntax required to specify eight arguments.

| Figure 8-23 | ADDING THE CODE TO THE USERFORM |

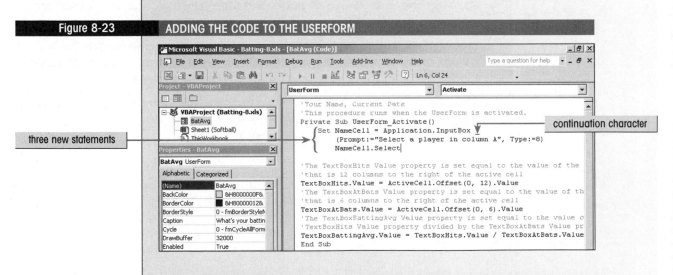

TROUBLE? Press the spacebar and type an underscore character (_) at the end of a line that you want to continue on the next line.

3. Close the Visual Basic Editor to return to the Batting-8 workbook, and then click the **Calculate Batting Average** Command Button.

See Figure 8-24.

Figure 8-24   **INPUTBOX PROMPT**

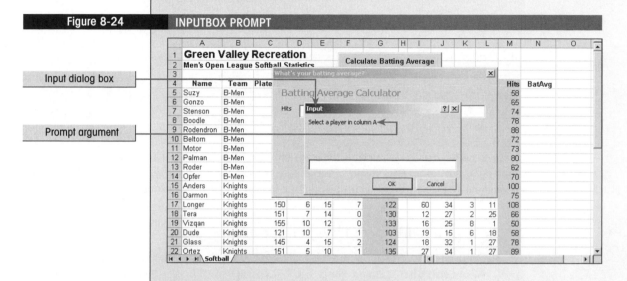

Input dialog box

Prompt argument

4. Click cell **A6** and then click the **OK** button. The batting average for Gonzo is calculated and displayed within the custom form.

5. Close the form.

Adding the `InputBox` statement provided a big improvement for the UserForm because users no longer need to remember to click the name of the individual they want to select before clicking the Command Button on the workbook.

VBA Functions

By now you have probably used the Microsoft Visual Basic Help system on a variety of occasions to provide additional information on a variety of VBA concepts or subjects that may be new to you. Of special note is the section that lists VBA functions. VBA, being a programming language, has its own set of functions, whose purpose it is to return a value (just as Excel has its own built-in set of functions). In many cases, the VBA functions such as `Int` (find the integer portion of a value), `Round` (round a value to a given number of digits to the right of the decimal point), and `Pmt` (find a monthly payment given the principal, interest rate, and term of a loan) are very similar to their counterparts in Excel. In other cases, though, you'll use VBA functions to manipulate values in a way that you have not used Excel functions before. One such example of a new way to use a function is to format a value. In Excel, you'd use the Formatting toolbar or Format menu options to format values. In VBA, you must use functions to control the formatting characteristics of how a value is returned to the user. Because functions are used in a somewhat broader context in VBA than in Excel, you'll want to become familiar with finding and using them.

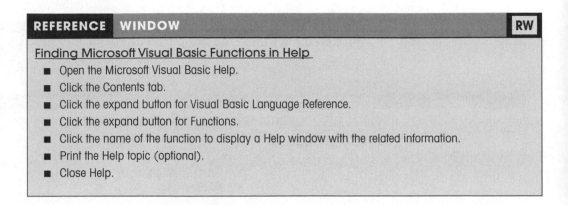

REFERENCE WINDOW | **RW**

Finding Microsoft Visual Basic Functions in Help
- Open the Microsoft Visual Basic Help.
- Click the Contents tab.
- Click the expand button for Visual Basic Language Reference.
- Click the expand button for Functions.
- Click the name of the function to display a Help window with the related information.
- Print the Help topic (optional).
- Close Help.

You need to find a function that returns the value of the TextBoxBattingAvg value formatted as a number that displays three digits to the right of the decimal point. You'll use the Visual Basic Help system to find the name and syntax for the function you need.

To find a VBA formatting function:

1. Return to the Visual Basic Editor, click **Help** on the menu bar, and then click **Microsoft Visual Basic Help**. The Microsoft Visual Basic Help window opens.

2. Click the **Show** button ⊞ (if it is not already selected) on the Help toolbar to display the navigation window, click the **Contents** tab (if it is not already selected), click the **expand** button for the Visual Basic Language Reference topic, and then click the **expand** button for the Functions topic. See Figure 8-25.

Figure 8-25   USING THE HELP SYSTEM TO FIND INFORMATION ON VBA FUNCTIONS

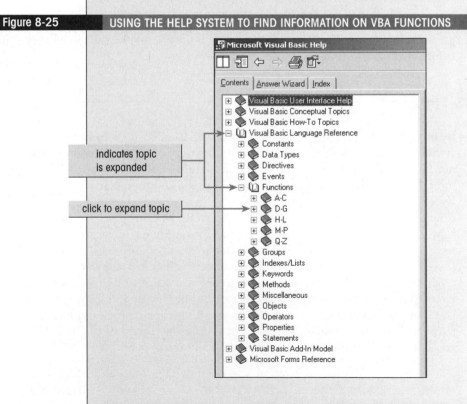

3. Click the **expand** button for the D–G topics, and then scroll and click the **FormatNumber Function** entry in the list of functions. See Figure 8-26.

Figure 8-26 | HELP FOR THE FORMATNUMBER FUNCTION

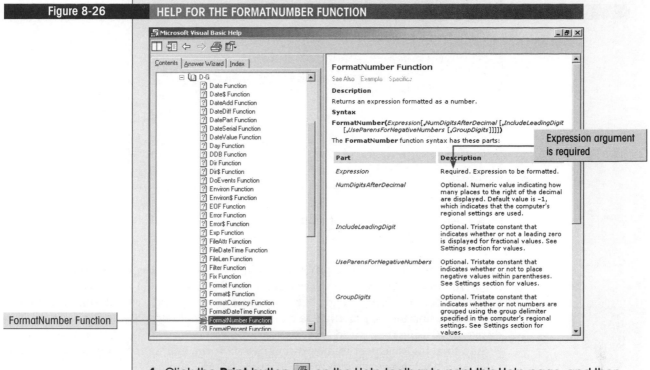

FormatNumber Function

4. Click the **Print** button 🖨 on the Help toolbar to print this Help page, and then click the **OK** button to print the selected topic.

5. Close the Microsoft Visual Basic Help window.

Excel has no counterpart function to the `FormatNumber` function within VBA. The `FormatNumber` function has one required argument, `Expression`, as well as a number of optional arguments including `NumDigitsAfterDecimal`, which determines the number of digits to display after the decimal point, and `IncludeLeadingDigit`, which determines whether a leading zero is displayed for values that are less than 1.

Using a VBA Function to Format a Value

Although the custom form does calculate the batting average correctly, the value is not rounded to three digits to the right of the decimal point, as is common when discussing batting averages. There are a number of formatting functions used to format values calculated on a custom form. The one you need is `FormatNumber`, which returns an expression formatted as a number. You'll use `FormatNumber` to format the value calculated in the `TextBoxBattingAvg` control to show three digits to the right of the decimal point.

To format the value of the TextBoxBattingAvg:

1. Close the Project Explorer and Properties window so that you have more room to view the code, and then modify the second to the last statement from `TextBoxBattingAvg.Value = TextBoxHits.Value / TextBoxAtBats.Value` to `TextBoxBattingAvg.Value = FormatNumber(TextBoxHits.Value / TextBoxAtBats.Value, 3)`.

2. Click the **View Microsoft Excel** button 🗷 on the Standard toolbar, click the **Command Button**, click **A8**, and then click the **OK** button. See Figure 8-27.

Figure 8-27   TEXTBOXBATTINGAVG VALUE IS FORMATTED

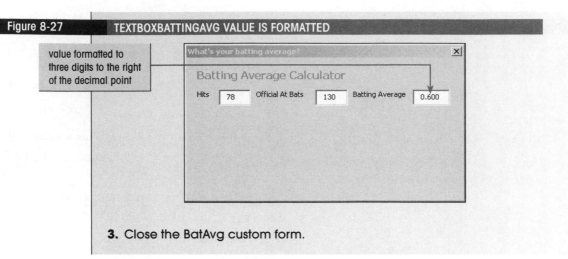

value formatted to three digits to the right of the decimal point

3. Close the BatAvg custom form.

Another way to solve this problem would have been to use VBA's `Round` function to round the value to three digits to the right of the decimal point. The `FormatNumber` function was a better choice, though, because a batting average such as .600 still displays the last two zeros using the `FormatNumber` function, but would drop the insignificant digits and display as .6 using the `Round` function.

As a final improvement to the existing custom form, you want to automatically enter the calculated batting average into the appropriate cell in column N.

Using **Assignment Expressions**

An **assignment expression** is a VBA statement that sets the value of an object, variable, or property to the result of an expression. In other words, an assignment expression is read as "Set this equal to that", where "this" is the object, variable, or property that is being assigned a value, followed by an equal sign that is followed by "that", the expression that determines the value. To use the custom form to enter a value in the workbook, you'll use an assignment expression to assign a cell in a workbook to the value of the TextBoxBattingAvg control. You have already used assignment expressions to set the values of the TextBoxHits.Value property and TextBoxAtBats.Value property to the values their corresponding cells found in the workbook. Now you'll use an assignment expression in the opposite way, to set the value of a cell in a workbook to the value stored by the TextBoxBattingAvg control on the UserForm.

> *To assign the value of the TextBoxBattingAvg control to a cell in the workbook:*
>
> 1. Open the Visual Basic Editor to display the code behind the BatAvg UserForm, and then add the following statement immediately before the `End Sub` statement:
>
>   `ActiveCell.Offset(0, 13).Value = TextBoxBattingAvg.Value`
>
> 2. Save your changes, close the Visual Basic Editor, and then click the **Command Button** in the workbook.
>
> 3. Click cell **A7** in the workbook, click the **OK** button, and then close the BatAvg custom form. See Figure 8-28.

Figure 8-28	ASSIGNING THE VALUE IN A USERFORM TO A CELL REFERENCE

active cell

TextBoxBattingAvg value is assigned to the cell 13 columns to the right of the active cell

	A	B	C	D	E	F	G	H	I	J	K	L	M	N
1	**Green Valley Recreation**						Calculate Batting Average							
2	Men's Open League Softball Statistics													
3														
4	**Name**	**Team**	**PlateApp**	**Walks**	**Sac**	**HitPitch**	**AtBats**		**1B**	**2B**	**3B**	**HR**	**Hits**	**BatAvg**
5	Suzy	B-Men	135	4	5	2	124		13	31	8	6	58	
6	Gonzo	B-Men	142	5	5	0	132		24	22	5	14	65	
7	Stenson	B-Men	140	6	7	3	124		20	38	7	9	74	0.597
8	Boodle	B-Men	145	7	5	3	130		12	30	3	33	78	
9	Rodendron	B-Men	138	1	4	4	129		14	32	1	41	88	

With the new assignment statement, the value displayed in the TextBoxBattingAvg is assigned to the appropriate cell (0 rows above and 13 columns to the right of the active cell) in the worksheet.

4. Save the workbook, open the Visual Basic Editor, click the **Project Explorer** button on the Standard toolbar to open that window (if it is not already open), double-click **BatAvg** in the Project Explorer, double-click the form itself to display the Code window for that object, and then print the code for the BatAvg UserForm.

5. Double-click **Sheet1 (Softball)** in the Project Explorer window to display the Code window for that object, and then print the code for Sheet1.

6. Close the Visual Basic Editor, and then print the first page of the workbook in portrait orientation with your name in the left section of the header.

7. Save and close the Batting-8 workbook, and then exit Excel.

Now that you've demonstrated how a custom UserForm can be used to simplify and guide a user through a calculation, Lynn wants you to focus your future UserForm development on new workbooks.

Session 8.1 QUICK CHECK

1. What is the primary purpose of creating a custom form?

2. Compare and contrast the use of a custom form to the use of a custom function within an Excel workbook.

3. List the steps required to create a UserForm that is opened using a Command Button placed in a workbook.

4. Is a Label control bound or unbound? Is a TextBox control bound or unbound?

5. Explain the difference between the Caption and (Name) properties for a Label control.

6. How can you display a UserForm without writing code using the Show method for the UserForm object?

7. Where should you store the procedure that runs when a Command Button on a worksheet is clicked? Where should you store the procedure that runs when a CommandButton on a UserForm is clicked?

SESSION 8.2

In this session, you will plan and build a new UserForm to guide the users in a data entry activity. You'll learn how to work with the MsgBox function, and you will use several other types of UserForm controls, including SpinButtons, ComboBoxes, and ListBoxes.

Creating a UserForm for Data Entry

Lynn is pleased with your ability to build a UserForm that prompts the user for the player name and then calculates the batting average. Because all of the official at bat and hits statistics were previously recorded in the workbook you used, all you needed to calculate the batting average were two cell values from the workbook. Lynn explains that she wants you to develop a workbook that starts at the beginning of the process. She wants you to build a user form that prompts the user for baseball or softball statistics, enters that data into the workbook, and then lets the workbook calculate the batting average based on this information.

Because the BatAvg UserForm was one of the first UserForms you created, you decide to review the complete development process when creating a new form. You want to create a form that includes all of the statistics required to calculate Hits and Official At Bats and use that form for data entry purposes. You review the steps of creating a UserForm and then use them to build the new form.

- Plan what you want the UserForm to do.
- In the Visual Basic Editor, insert a new UserForm, add controls to the UserForm, and modify and adjust the properties of the controls as needed.
- In the worksheet, add a Command Button to a worksheet.
- In the Visual Basic Editor, write a procedure that displays the UserForm when the Command Button is clicked.
- Check and modify the tab order of the UserForm as needed.
- In the Visual Basic Editor, write procedures for the controls that are executed when various control events occur.

Step 1: Plan What You Want the Form To Do

There are 10 pieces of data you need to gather for each new batter as shown in Figure 8-29. You'll use the sketch as a reference as you develop a custom form.

| Figure 8-29 | SKETCH OF NEW FORM TO CALCULATE THE BATTING AVERAGE |

Once you've gathered these statistics using a form, you can then build formulas within the workbook to calculate the statistics you need.

- Hits = singles (1B) + doubles (2B) + triples (3B) + home runs (HR)
- Official At Bats = Plate Appearances - Walks - Hit By Pitches - Sacrifices
- Batting Average = Hits / Official At Bats

Step 2: Insert a New UserForm

In order to create this custom form in a workbook, you need to create a design surface, the UserForm.

To create a UserForm to enter batting statistics:

1. If you took a break from the previous session, start Excel and open the **League-8** workbook from the Tutorial.08\Tutorial folder of your Data Disk.

2. Open the Visual Basic Editor, open the Project Explorer (if it is not already opened), and click the **Insert UserForm** button 🔲 on the Standard toolbar.

With the UserForm object in place, you're ready to add controls to the form.

Step 3: Add Controls to the UserForm

You add controls to a UserForm using the Control Toolbox toolbar. The type of control you choose determines the control's behavior. TextBox controls are commonly used to enter data on a form. CommandButtons are used to initiate actions such canceling the form, or transferring the data from the form to the workbook.

To add controls to a new UserForm to enter batting statistics:

1. Add the controls to the form using Figures 8-29 and 8-30 for the layout and information about the controls and properties. One way to create duplicate controls very quickly is to select the control you want to duplicate, click the Copy button 🔲 on the Standard toolbar, click the UserForm, and then click the Paste button 🔲 on the Standard toolbar.

Figure 8-30	CONTROLS AND PROPERTIES FOR DATA ENTRY USERFORM		
TYPE OF CONTROL	**NAME PROPERTY**	**CAPTION PROPERTY**	**FONT PROPERTY**
Label	LabelName	Name	Tahoma, Bold, 10 points
TextBox	TextBoxName		
Label	LabelTeam	Team	Tahoma, Bold, 10 points
TextBox	TextBoxTeam		
Label	Label1B	1B	Tahoma, Bold, 10 points
TextBox	TextBox1B		
Label	Label2B	2B	Tahoma, Bold, 10 points

Figure 8-30 | CONTROLS AND PROPERTIES FOR DATA ENTRY USERFORM (CONTINUED)

TYPE OF CONTROL	NAME PROPERTY	CAPTION PROPERTY	FONT PROPERTY
TextBox	TextBox2B		
Label	Label3B	3B	Tahoma, Bold, 10 points
TextBox	TextBox3B		
Label	LabelHR	HR	Tahoma, Bold, 10 points
TextBox	TextBoxHR		
Label	LabelPA	Plate Appearances	Tahoma, Bold, 10 points
TextBox	TextBoxPA		
Label	LabelWalks	Walks	Tahoma, Bold, 10 points
TextBox	TextBoxWalks		
Label	LabelHP	Hit by Pitches	Tahoma, Bold, 10 points
TextBox	TextBoxHP		
Label	LabelSac	Sacrifices	Tahoma, Bold, 10 points
TextBox	TextBoxSac		
CommandButton	OKButton	OK	
CommandButton	CancelButton	Cancel	

Step 4: Modify the Properties of the Controls

No doubt you'll need to move, resize, and format the controls on your form in order to get them to look the way you want. Some of these modifications are purely personal preference, but formatting a form in an orderly and professional way can also improve productivity and data entry accuracy.

To modify the controls:

1. Resize the form as necessary and use Figure 8-31 as a guide for how the final form is supposed to look.

2. Save the workbook.

Figure 8-31   **SOFTBALL STATISTICS DATA ENTRY USERFORM**

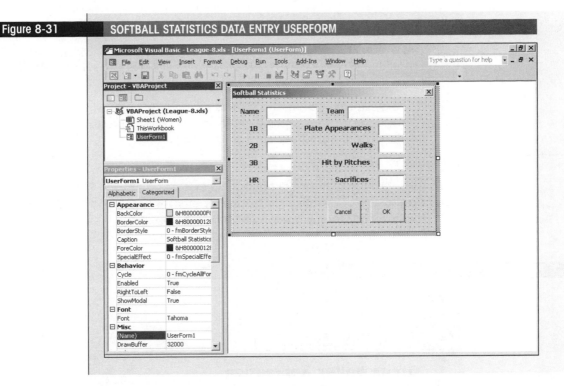

Step 5: Add a Command Button to the Workbook

With the controls in place, you're ready to add a Command Button to the workbook to open the custom form.

To add a Command Button to the workbook to open the UserForm:

1. Click the **View Microsoft Excel** button ⊠, right-click any existing toolbar, and then click **Control Toolbox** to display the Control Toolbox toolbar if it is not already visible.

2. Click the **Command Button** button ▱ on the Control Toolbox toolbar, and then click in cell **J1**. Now you will change the caption to read "Add Statistics".

3. Click the **Properties** button 🖺 on the Control Toolbox toolbar, and then change the Caption property for the Command Button to **Add Statistics**.

Now that the Command Button is in place in the workbook, you need to add the underlying code so that it opens the UserForm when it is clicked.

Step 6: Write a Procedure for the Command Button

To write a procedure that opens the UserForm from the Command Button:

1. Double-click the **Command Button** to open the code window for the Sheet1 (Women) worksheet, and then enter the following VBA statement between the Sub and End Sub statements as follows:

   `UserForm1.Show`

2. Close the Visual Basic Editor, click the **Exit Design Mode** button 🔄 on the Control Toolbox toolbar, close the Properties window and the Control Toolbox toolbar, and then click the **Add Statistics** Command Button in the workbook. See Figure 8-32.

Figure 8-32	OPENING THE SOFTBALL STATISTICS FORM WITH THE COMMAND BUTTON

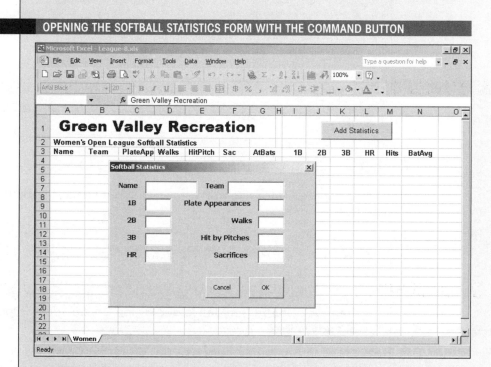

3. Test the tab order by pressing **Tab** enough times to move the focus through all of the controls on the form. Notice that focus also moves through the OK and Cancel buttons on the UserForm.

Depending on how you created the controls on the UserForm, you may or may not be pleased with the tab order. You can change the tab order so the focus moves from one text box to another in an order that will make data entry easy and logical.

Step 7: Modify the Tab Order of the UserForm as Needed

You change the tab order in the Visual Basic Editor window. In this case, you want to tab from the Name TextBox to the Team TextBox, and then through the rest of the first column and second column.

To check the tab order for the new UserForm:

1. Close the UserForm by clicking its **Close** button, return to the Visual Basic Editor, and then double-click **UserForm1** in the Project Explorer.

2. Click **View** on the menu bar, and then click **Tab Order**.

3. Use Figure 8-33 and 8-34 to set the tab order for the controls on the form, and then click the **OK** button.

   TROUBLE? The UserForm itself, not its Code window nor the Code window for any other module, must be selected in order for the Tab Order option to appear on the View menu.

Figure 8-33	TAB ORDER FOR FIRST 12 CONTROLS ON THE CUSTOM FORM

Figure 8-34	TAB ORDER FOR LAST 12 CONTROLS ON THE CUSTOM FORM

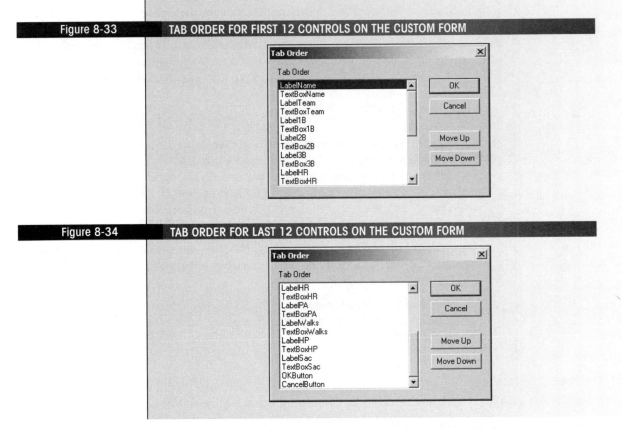

As you just experienced in creating the new UserForm, creating it, adding and modifying controls to it, creating a Command Button on the workbook that opens it, and modifying its tab order are fairly straightforward tasks. The last step in the UserForm creation process, however, that of writing procedures for the controls on the UserForm, requires the most extensive VBA skills. These procedures determine how the controls on the UserForm are going to behave.

Step 8: Write Procedures for the Controls on the UserForm

In this case, instead of sending information on the existing worksheet to the UserForm as soon as the UserForm is opened as you experienced with the BatAvg UserForm, you want to fill in the TextBoxes with data entered by the user, and then send that data to the workbook. Typically, you send the data or the decisions that you make using a dialog box to the application by clicking an OK CommandButton on the dialog box. Similarly, you want the OK CommandButton on the UserForm to send the entries in the TextBoxes to the workbook. These activities require that you write VBA code connected to events on the UserForm. The rest of this session will be devoted to writing the procedures for the controls on the UserForm.

Using CommandButtons on UserForms

When you want to use a UserForm for data entry, you will almost always want to add OK and Cancel CommandButtons to the UserForm to initiate the action of sending the data in the UserForm to the worksheet or to cancel the activity. You connect the VBA code necessary to turn this UserForm into a data entry tool to the `Click` events of the CommandButtons. Although the VBA code to transfer the entries in the TextBoxes to the workbook is involved, the VBA code for the Cancel CommandButton is fairly straightforward. All you want to happen when the Cancel CommandButton is clicked is for the UserForm to close, which can be accomplished with one statement. Because the code behind the Cancel CommandButton is simpler, you'll write that code first.

To write the procedure for the Cancel CommandButton:

1. In the Visual Basic Editor with the UserForm displayed, double-click the **CancelButton** control. The Code window for the UserForm appears, and the first and last lines of the procedure are already entered. Because the name of the procedure is `CancelButton_Click()`, you know that this procedure will run when the `Click` event occurs for the `CancelButton`, just as you want it to.

2. Enter the statement `Unload UserForm1` between the first and last lines of the `CancelButton_Click()` procedure. The `Unload` statement removes the identified object from memory. With the statement in place, you'll run the form and test the Cancel button.

3. Click the **Run Sub/UserForm** button ▶ on the Standard toolbar, and then click the **Cancel** CommandButton. The form closes and the Visual Basic Editor with the UserForm redisplays.

With the code for the Cancel CommandButton in place, you'll turn your attention to what needs to happen when the OK CommandButton is clicked. When the OK button is clicked, you want to transfer all of the values from the TextBoxes on the UserForm to the workbook.

Using the CountA Function

One challenge you have is to determine exactly where you want to insert data that is entered into the UserForm in the workbook. In this case, since you're creating a list of information that will grow over time, you need to search for the next blank row, and insert the new data in the next blank row. In order to find the next blank row, you will need the help of the VBA CountA function. The **CountA** function counts the number of nonblank cells in a given range and returns that value. In this case, you'll use the CountA function to count the number of entries in column A and then use that number plus one to identify the next blank row for data entry purposes. First, you will give column A a range name so that you can use that range name in the VBA code you write for the UserForm.

To range name column A:

1. Click the **View Microsoft Excel** button ▣ on the Standard toolbar to return to the worksheet, click the **column heading** for column **A** to select the entire column, click the **NameBox**, type **ColA**, and then press the **Enter** key. See Figure 8-35.

Figure 8-35 **RANGE NAME FOR COLUMN A**

range name is ColA

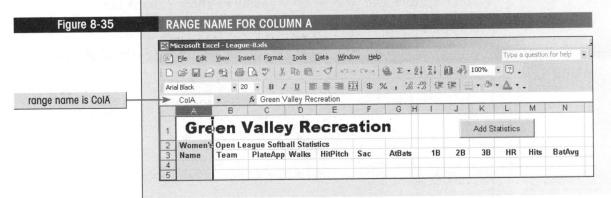

With the range name of ColA for column A in place, you'll return to the UserForm and add the code to count the number of entries in the ColA range.

To use the CountA function to determine the next blank row:

1. Return to the Visual Basic Editor, double-click **UserForm1** in the Project Explorer to open the UserForm (if it is not already open), and then double-click the **OK CommandButton** to open the Code window for the UserForm. The `Private Sub OKButton_Click()` and `End Sub` statements are automatically added to the Code window. As you know by now, the name of this procedure indicates that it will run when the `Click` event for the `OKButton` occurs.

2. Close the Project Explorer and Property window to make more room to display long statements, maximize the Visual Basic Editor and Code window if they are not already maximized, and then enter the following statement between the first and last lines of the `OKButton_Click()` procedure:

```
NextBlankRow = Application.WorksheetFunction.CountA
(Range("ColA")) + 1
```

TROUBLE? This statement should fit on one line. If you see two lines, use the continuation character, an underscore (_), to connect the lines into one statement.

This statement assigns the `NextBlankRow` variable to the value determined by the CountA function as applied to the `Range` defined by the `ColA` range plus one. Because cells A1, A2, and A3 contain entries in column A of the workbook, you expect this assignment to return the value of 4, the row number of the first blank row in the workbook.

Sometimes, when making assignment statements, it's helpful to know what value the variable has after the assignment statement is made. One way to know what value the `NextBlankRow` variable contains is to use VBA's `MsgBox` function.

The MsgBox Function

The MsgBox function creates a dialog box that can be used to display the results of a variable. It has only one required argument, Prompt, that determines the message displayed in the dialog box. In this case, the Prompt argument will be the NextBlankRow variable so that the dialog box displays the value of the variable at that point in the code.

To add the MsgBox function to the procedure:

1. Just before the End Sub statement, enter MsgBox (NextBlankRow). See Figure 8-36.

Figure 8-36	ADDING THE MSGBOX FUNCTION

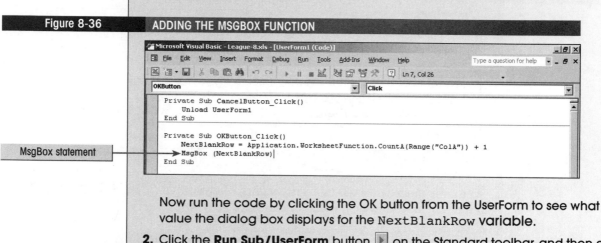

MsgBox statement

Now run the code by clicking the OK button from the UserForm to see what value the dialog box displays for the NextBlankRow variable.

2. Click the **Run Sub/UserForm** button ▶ on the Standard toolbar, and then click the **OK CommandButton** on the UserForm. See Figure 8-37. The MsgBox function created a dialog box that displays the current value of the NextBlankRow variable. You expected the result to be 4 and it is.

Figure 8-37	THE RESULT OF THE MSGBOX FUNCTION

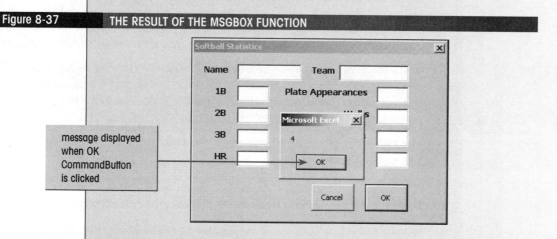

message displayed when OK CommandButton is clicked

3. Click the **OK** button in the message box, and then close the UserForm.

TROUBLE? If prompted that a variable is not defined, delete the Option Explicit statement in your code, and then repeat Steps 2 and 3.

Now that you know that the assignment statement to calculate the row number for the NextBlankRow variable works correctly, you'll add the code that transfers the entries in the dialog box to the appropriate cells in the workbook.

Transferring Data from a UserForm to the Workbook

You have already used assignment statements to assign values to variables, values of TextBoxes on the UserForm, and cell values within the workbook itself. Now that you have figured out a way to identify the next blank row in the workbook, you'll use assignment statements to transfer data from the UserForm to the workbook.

To add the code to transfer data from the UserForm to the workbook:

1. Return to the Visual Basic Editor, right-click **UserForm1** in the Project Explorer, and then click **View Code** on the shortcut menu.

   TROUBLE? If you open the Code window for the UserForm by double-clicking the form, the Visual Basic Editor assumes that you are adding a new procedure `UserForm_Click()` and provides the first and last lines of the procedure. If this happens, delete these extra lines of code.

2. Type ' (an apostrophe) before the `MsgBox` statement to convert it into a comment.

3. After the `MsgBox` statement, enter the VBA code shown in Figure 8-38. The `Cells` object is used to locate the `NextBlankRow` row number and given column number. This cell is set equal to the `Text` or `Value` property of the associated `TextBox` control on the form. Don't forget to use copy and paste techniques to speed up the process of entering several similar statements.

| Figure 8-38 | CELL ASSIGNMENT STATEMENTS |

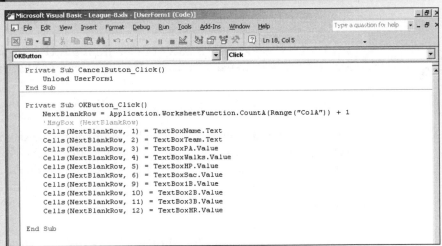

Test the procedure by displaying the form, entering values into the `TextBoxes`, and clicking the OK CommandButton.

4. Click the **Run Sub/UserForm** button , and then enter the data shown in Figure 8-39.

Figure 8-39   TESTING THE DATA ENTRY CAPABILITIES OF THE USERFORM

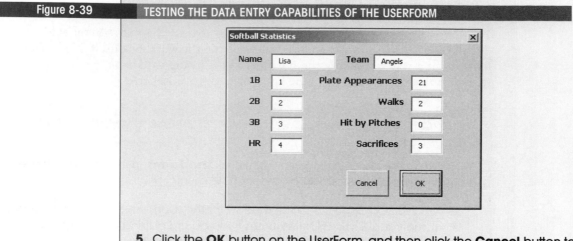

5. Click the **OK** button on the UserForm, and then click the **Cancel** button to close it. Your workbook should now look like Figure 8-40.

Figure 8-40   DATA TRANSFERRED FROM THE DIALOG BOX TO THE WORKSHEET

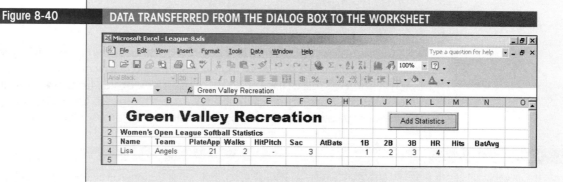

Now that you have the transfer of data from the UserForm to the workbook working correctly, and have tested it, you see a few improvements that you'd like to make.

Clearing the UserForm for the Next Entry

Because the statistics for each team's players are generally submitted as a list, you want the UserForm to clear the current values, in anticipation of the next entry, as soon as you click the OK CommandButton and transfer the data from the dialog box to the workbook. Using assignment statements, you can set the properties of the controls on the form to nothing, also known as **null**.

To add VBA code to reset the values of the TextBoxes to null:

1. Return to the Visual Basic Editor window, right-click **UserForm1** in the Project Explorer window, and then click **View Code** from the shortcut menu.

2. After the last `Cells` statement, enter the VBA code as shown in Figure 8-41.

Figure 8-41 | RESETTING THE TEXTBOXES

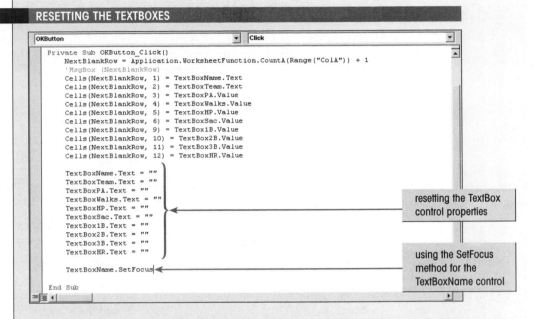

resetting the TextBox control properties

using the SetFocus method for the TextBoxName control

Each line resets a property for the identified `TextBox` control to nothing. The last new line uses the `SetFocus` method for the `TextBoxName` control to set the focus in that `TextBox` once all of the given properties are reset to nothing so that you'll be in a position to start typing the next name. Test the new code.

3. Click the **Run Sub/UserForm** button , and then enter the data shown in Figure 8-42.

Figure 8-42 | ENTERING TEST DATA

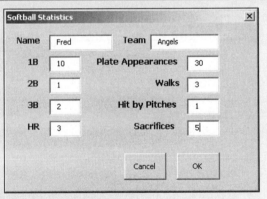

4. Click the **OK CommandButton** on the UserForm. The data transfers to row 5 of the workbook, all of the TextBox controls clear, and the focus moves to the TextBoxName control, ready for you to make the next entry.

5. Click the **Cancel CommandButton** on the UserForm.

The last embellishment that you want to make is the automatic calculation of the statistics (total hits, official at bats, and batting average) for each player as soon as the statistics are entered in the UserForm.

Copying a Formula Using VBA

To copy a formula from one row to the next, you will enter the formula you want in the first row of the workbook, and then use the Copy method to copy the formula to the next row. In that way, the formula will not appear in a new row until data is entered via the UserForm.

First, you'll reset the workbook and seed the first row to contain the formulas that you want to copy. Then, you'll enter the appropriate VBA code in the UserForm so that the formulas are copied to the new row when data is entered into it.

To add the starting formulas to the workbook:

1. Return to the Excel workbook, click **row heading 5**, and then press the **Delete** key so that only one row of data is currently entered into the workbook.

2. Click cell **G4**, click the **AutoSum** button Σ on the Standard toolbar, and then press the **Enter** key to accept the formula of *=SUM(C4:F4)* into the cell.

3. Click cell **M4**, click Σ, and then press the **Enter** key to accept the formula of *=SUM(I4:L4)* into the cell.

4. Click cell **N4**, and then enter the formula **=M4/G4** into the cell. The workbook should look like Figure 8-43.

Figure 8-43 | **ENTERING THE STARTING FORMULAS**

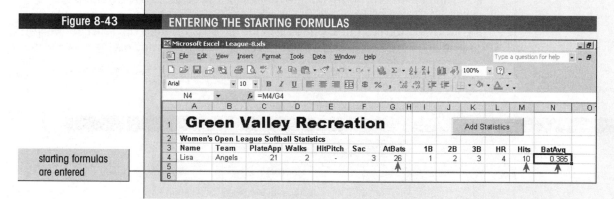

starting formulas are entered

With the starting formulas in place, you now need to add the VBA code that copies the formulas from the previous row to the current row for columns G, M, and N when the OK button is clicked.

To add VBA code to copy the formulas:

1. Return to the Visual Basic Editor window, right-click **UserForm1** in the Project Explorer window, and then click **View Code** from the shortcut menu.

2. After the last `Cells` statement, enter the VBA code as shown in Figure 8-44.

Figure 8-44   ADDING VBA CODE TO COPY THE FORMULAS FOR EACH NEW LINE

```
OKButton                                    ▼   Click                                ▼

Private Sub OKButton_Click()
    NextBlankRow = Application.WorksheetFunction.CountA(Range("ColA")) + 1
    'MsgBox (NextBlankRow)
    Cells(NextBlankRow, 1) = TextBoxName.Text
    Cells(NextBlankRow, 2) = TextBoxTeam.Text
    Cells(NextBlankRow, 3) = TextBoxPA.Value
    Cells(NextBlankRow, 4) = TextBoxWalks.Value
    Cells(NextBlankRow, 5) = TextBoxHP.Value
    Cells(NextBlankRow, 6) = TextBoxSac.Value
    Cells(NextBlankRow, 9) = TextBox1B.Value
    Cells(NextBlankRow, 10) = TextBox2B.Value
    Cells(NextBlankRow, 11) = TextBox3B.Value
    Cells(NextBlankRow, 12) = TextBoxHR.Value

    PreviousRow = NextBlankRow - 1

    Cells(PreviousRow, 7).Copy Cells(NextBlankRow, 7)
    Cells(PreviousRow, 13).Copy Cells(NextBlankRow, 13)
    Cells(PreviousRow, 14).Copy Cells(NextBlankRow, 14)

    TextBoxName.Text = ""
    TextBoxTeam.Text = ""
    TextBoxPA.Text = ""
    TextBoxWalks.Text = ""
    TextBoxHP.Text = ""
    TextBoxSac.Text = ""
    TextBox1B.Text = ""
    TextBox2B.Text = ""
```

new lines of code

In these statements, the `PreviousRow` variable is assigned the value one less than the `NextBlankRow` variable. Then the `Copy` method is used to copy the contents from the appropriate cell in the `PreviousRow` to the same column in the `NextBlankRow`.

3. Click the **Run Sub/UserForm** button ▶, and then enter the data shown in Figure 8-45.

Figure 8-45   ENTERING TEST DATA

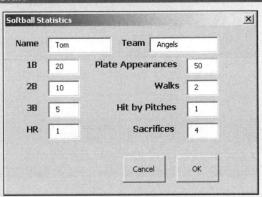

Softball Statistics			
Name	Tom	Team	Angels
1B	20	Plate Appearances	50
2B	10	Walks	2
3B	5	Hit by Pitches	1
HR	1	Sacrifices	4

Cancel   OK

4. Click the **OK CommandButton** on the UserForm. The data should have been transferred to row 5 of the workbook. The TextBox controls clear, and the focus moves to the TextBoxName control, ready for you to make the next entry.

5. Click the **Cancel CommandButton** on the UserForm. The formulas in cells G5, M5, and N5 were added.

6. Save the workbook, and then print it on one page in landscape orientation with your name in the left section of the header.

7. In the Visual Basic Editor window, enter your name and the current date in the first line of the code for the UserForm, and then print both the code and the image for the UserForm.

8. Close the Visual Basic Editor window, and then save and close the League-8 workbook. Exit Excel.

At this point you might be thinking that creating a custom form is a lot of work, and learning a new programming language is going to take a long time. If so, you would be correct. Remember, using VBA to automate and enhance a workbook generally isn't for *your* benefit. If you're the only one using a workbook and you have the skills to create custom forms, you probably have very extensive Excel skills as well. And unless you're going to use the workbook over and over again, it may be more work to create custom forms than the effort involved in entering the data directly into the workbook. On the other hand, if you're creating a workbook to be distributed across a wide range of users or used for an extensive period of time, almost any productivity or ease-of-use improvement that you can program into the workbook will pay back tremendous benefits.

Session 8.2 QUICK CHECK

1. Which statement is typically attached to the Click event of the Command Button used to open a UserForm from within a workbook?

2. What must you do before you can open the Tab Order dialog box for an existing UserForm?

3. When you are using a UserForm for data entry purposes, what two CommandButtons are almost always placed on the UserForm, and what do they do?

4. What object do you use within VBA code to call an Excel workbook function?

5. How can the MsgBox function help you write code?

6. It is worth the time and effort to develop custom forms when what conditions are true?

SESSION 8.3

In this session, you will learn how to use different types of form controls including the SpinButton, ListBox, and ComboBox. You'll also learn how to validate data and use the MsgBox to prompt users for missing data.

The **SpinButton Control**

Generally, most users like to point and click rather than enter data from a keyboard. Many of the UserForm controls such as the SpinButton allow the user to make an entry using the pointer rather than entering a value directly from the keyboard. The SpinButton has other benefits as well, including the ability to limit the values you allow the user to enter to a list. By limiting the range of available entries, you help keep bogus data from being entered into the workbook. A SpinButton can only be used for numeric values, though.

A SpinButton is often used in conjunction with a TextBox or Label that displays the current value of the SpinButton. Whether you choose the TextBox or Label control for this role is based on whether or not you want to also allow the user to make an entry from the keyboard (in which case you need to use a TextBox control), or whether you want the control to do nothing more than display the value that is currently selected based on the user's interaction with the SpinButton (in which case you need to use a Label control).

Because the values for the TextBoxHR (home runs) are always between 0 and 50, you will use a SpinButton connected to the existing TextBox to let users enter that value using either the SpinButton or the TextBox.

To create a SpinButton for the UserForm:

1. If you took a break after the last session, start Excel and open the **League-8** workbook from the Tutorial.08\Tutorial folder of your Data Disk, and enable the macros.

2. Open the Visual Basic Editor, and then double-click **UserForm1** in the Project Explorer window to display the UserForm if it is not already displayed.

3. Click the **Toolbox** button 🔧 on the Standard toolbar to display the Toolbox toolbar (if the toolbar is not already displayed), click the **SpinButton** button ⬍ on the Toolbox toolbar, and then click to the right of the **TextBoxHR** on the UserForm to add the SpinButton control in that location.

   See Figure 8-46.

| Figure 8-46 | ADDING A SPINBUTTON CONTROL TO A USERFORM |

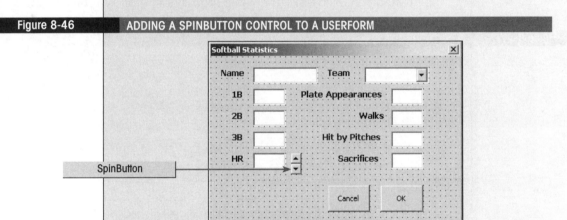

To set the minimum and maximum values for the SpinButton control, you modify the SpinButton's properties.

4. Click the **Properties Window** button 📄 on the Standard toolbar to open the Properties window (if it is not already open), double-click **100** in the Max property, and then type **50**.

   Because you want the SpinButton to move between the values of 0 and 50, you don't need to modify the Min property, which is already set to 0.

Now that the SpinButton is added to the UserForm, you need to add code to it so that it is connected to the TextBoxHR.

Connecting a SpinButton to a TextBox

To connect the SpinButton to the TextBox, you need to make sure that the value in the TextBox always displays the value of the SpinButton. You can accomplish this by writing an event-handler procedure that changes the value of the TextBox whenever the value of the SpinButton also changes.

To set the value of the TextBox to that of the SpinButton:

1. Right-click **UserForm1** in the Project Explorer, and then click **View Code** on the shortcut menu.

2. Press **Ctrl + End** to quickly move to the bottom of the Code window, and then press the **Enter** key twice to insert two blank rows after the `End Sub` line for the `OKButton_Click()` procedure.

3. Enter the following code to set the value of the `TextBoxHR.Value` property equal to that of the `SpinButton1.Value` property based on the `Change` event for the SpinButton control (which by default, is named `SpinButton1` unless you change the (Name) property in the Properties window):

```
Sub SpinButton1_Change()
TextBoxHR.Value = SpinButton1.Value
End Sub
```

Now test the form.

4. Click the **Run Sub/UserForm** button ▶ on the Standard toolbar, and then enter the data shown in Figure 8-47. Be sure to click the arrows on the SpinButton control to test it. The value should not go above 50 or below 0.

Figure 8-47	ENTERING TEST DATA

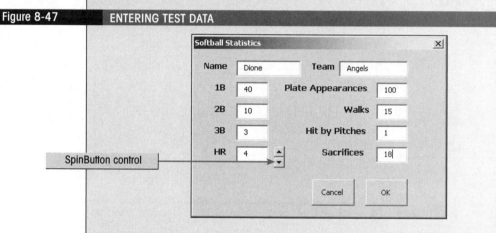

5. Click the **OK Command Button** on the UserForm, and then move the form to see the data entered in the worksheet. The data was successfully transferred to the workbook using a SpinButton control to determine the value of the TextBoxHR control.

6. Click the **Cancel CommandButton**, and then return to the Visual Basic Editor.

In addition to testing a SpinButton control, you want to try out other controls to experience how they can make data entry easier, faster, or more accurate.

The **ListBox Control**

Because there are only four team names in this league, you could easily change the TextBoxTeam control into a ListBox control so that you could provide a list of possible teams for the user to click. If the workbook contains a list of items that you want the ListBox control to display on the workbook, you can enter the cell range that contains the values (such as B1:B10) in the RowSource property of the ListBox to populate the list. You can also add items to the ListBox using VBA code.

Because there are only four existing softball teams for which you will report statistics, providing the users with a list of the available teams via a ListBox control will help them make the entry for the Team information.

To create a ListBox for the UserForm:

1. Click the **TextBoxTeam** control, and then press the **Delete** key to remove it from the UserForm.

2. Click the **ListBox** button 📧 on the Control Toolbox toolbar, and then click to the right of the Team Label control to add a new ListBox control to the form. Move and resize the new ListBox as shown in Figure 8-48. A ListBox control looks very similar to a TextBox control when you are designing a UserForm. Don't forget that you can look at the Properties window to see the type and name of the selected control.

| Figure 8-48 | ADDING A LISTBOX CONTROL |

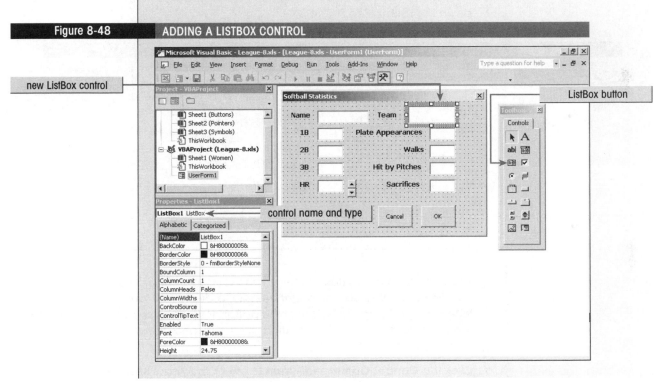

Now that you have the ListBox added to the form, you want to populate the values of the list. Instead of writing VBA code to fill the list, you'll enter the list values in the workbook and reference the range using the ListBox's RowSource property.

To populate the values for the ListBox control:

1. Click the **View Microsoft Excel** button 📧 on the Standard toolbar, scroll to the right so that you can clearly see column P, and then enter the following labels in the range P3:P7:

Cell P3: **Teams**
Cell P4: **Angels**

Cell P5: **Twisters**
Cell P6: **Diamonds**
Cell P7: **Stars**

2. Save the workbook, and then return to the Visual Basic Editor window with the UserForm still displayed.

3. Click the **ListBox** control (if it is not already selected) to display its properties in the Properties window.

4. Enter **P4:P7** in the RowSource property box for the control, and then click any-where on the UserForm. The values from the range P4:P7 of the worksheet fill the ListBox in the UserForm. A vertical scroll bar appears on the right side of the control.

5. If a horizontal scroll bar appears in the ListBox control, widen the control until it disappears. The horizontal scroll bar will not display if all of the text within the control can be clearly displayed. Now test the form.

6. Press the **F5 key** to display the form in the workbook, and then scroll up and down the ListBox. See Figure 8-49.

| Figure 8-49 | TESTING THE LISTBOX CONTROL |

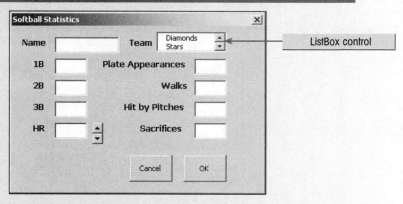

You can make the ListBox as tall as you like, depending on the available size of your form. In this case, you might be able to display all four values at the same time by expanding the height of the ListBox. If you can see all of the values in the list, there is no need for a vertical scroll bar, and it also disappears from the ListBox control.

7. Click the **Cancel CommandButton** to return the Visual Basic Editor.

Now that you've successfully added the ListBox control and populated its values, you need to revisit the VBA code that transfers the values from the form to the workbook. Recall that the TextBoxTeam control was formerly used to collect and then transfer the Team information. You've deleted that control and replaced it with the ListBox control, so you also need to alter your VBA code that is executed when you click the OK CommandButton to respect this change.

To change the code behind the OK CommandButton:

1. Right-click **UserForm1** in the Project Explorer window, and then click **View Code** on the shortcut menu.

2. Change the `Cells(NextBlankRow, 2) = TextBoxTeam.Text` statement to `Cells(NextBlankRow, 2) = ListBox1.Value`.

3. Change the `TextBoxTeam.Text = ""` statement to `ListBox1.Value = ""`.

4. Close the Visual Basic Editor, click the **Add Statistics Command Button** on the workbook, enter the sample data shown in Figure 8-50 using both the SpinButton and the ListBox.

| Figure 8-50 | ENTERING DATA USING THE LISTBOX |

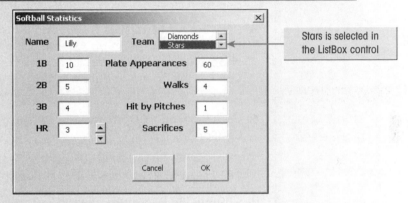

5. Click the **OK CommandButton** and then click the **Cancel CommandButton**.

6. Scroll as necessary to observe the new entry in row 7. The choice you selected in the ListBox, Stars, appears in cell B7.

Both the SpinButton and ListBox controls give the users the ability to make entries using the pointer rather than using the keyboard. For many, this is a faster and more accurate way to enter data.

The **ComboBox Control**

Another very popular control is the ComboBox control. This control is a combination of the TextBox and ListBox controls. In other words, you can use the ComboBox to select a choice from a list or to enter data from the keyboard. Because of this ability, the ComboBox is more flexible than the ListBox control which only allows users to make a selection from the list. When users are choosing from a list for most of their responses, such as in a City or Country field, yet they also need the ability to make a unique entry, the ComboBox control is the perfect candidate. Since you believe that more teams could be established in the future, you'll replace the existing ListBox control with a ComboBox control.

To replace the ListBox with a ComboBox:

1. Return to the Visual Basic Editor, and then double-click **UserForm1** in the Project Explorer.

2. Click the **ListBox** control, and then press the **Delete** key to remove it from the UserForm.

3. Click the **ComboBox** button 📇 on the Control Toolbox toolbar, and then click to the right of the Team Label control to add a ComboBox control to the form. A ComboBox control looks very similar to a ListBox control, except that the ComboBox also contains a list arrow on the right side of the control. Like the ListBox control, you need to specify the RowSource property of the ComboBox so that it knows where the values are that will populate its list.

4. With the ComboBox still selected, enter **P4:P7** in the RowSource property box and then close the Visual Basic Editor. Test the ComboBox.

5. Click the **Add Statistics Command Button**, click the **Team list arrow**, click **Diamonds**, and then type **Asteroids**. The ComboBox allows you to either choose an option from the list or make an entry from the keyboard. Before you can use this control to transfer data to the workbook, however, you need to modify the code behind the OK CommandButton on the form.

6. Click the **Cancel CommandButton** and then display the Code window for the UserForm.

7. Change the `Cells(NextBlankRow, 2) = ListBox1.Value` statement to `Cells(NextBlankRow, 2) = ComboBox1.Value`.

8. Change the `ListBox1.Value = ""` statement to `ComboBox1. Value = ""`.

9. Close the Visual Basic Editor, click the **Add Statistics Command Button** on the workbook, enter the sample data shown in Figure 8-51 using both the SpinButton and the ComboButton, click the **OK CommandButton**, and then click the **Cancel CommandButton**.

Figure 8-51   USING A COMBOBOX TO ENTER DATA

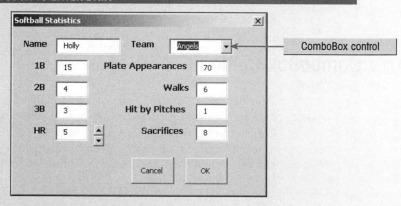

10. Scroll the worksheet as necessary to observe the new entry in row 8. The choice you selected, Angels, from the ComboBox should be the entry in cell B8.

Because of its versatility as both a ListBox and a TextBox, and its "drop-down" behavior, the ComboBox control is often a favorite among users.

Validating Data

Obviously, the more you know about which controls work best for your data and which ones your users prefer, the faster you can create custom forms. As you saw, changing controls from one type to another after the form is already completed causes extra work because you had to edit and adjust the code behind the OK CommandButton each time you changed a control. In addition, you have to recheck the tab order for the form every time a new control is added to make sure that the tab order still works as intended.

One other common problem that form designers commonly forget is how to handle erroneous or incorrect user activities. For example, if you want to make sure that the user provides an answer for a particular TextBox control, you need to add some sort of code that prompts the user to enter a value if it is left blank. Also, you need to enter that code before the values are transferred to the workbook.

You'll tackle the problem of requiring that the user provide an entry in the TextBoxName control by using an `If` statement combined with a `MsgBox` function that prompts the user for an entry if the TextBoxName control is left blank.

To enter the code to validate that an entry is made in the TextBoxName control:

1. Open the Code window for the UserForm, and then enter the following four lines of code immediately after the first line for the `OKButton_Click()` procedure:

```
If TextBoxName.Text = "" Then
MsgBox "Please enter a name."
Exit Sub
End If
```

The `If` statement checks to see if the `Text` property of the `TextBoxName` control is empty, and if so, presents the message "Please enter a name." in a dialog box. Whenever you use the `MsgBox` function, the procedure is temporarily halted, until you click the OK CommandButton in the dialog box, indicating that you have seen the message. At that point, control is returned to the next line of the `OKButton_Click()` procedure, which exits the procedure with the `Exit Sub` command. This gives you the opportunity to make an entry in the TextBoxName control, and click the OK CommandButton again.

To test the validation code for the TextBoxName control:

1. Switch to the workbook, and then click the **Add Statistics** button.

2. Without entering a value in the TextBoxName, enter a value in each of the other TextBoxes in the UserForm, and then click the **OK CommandButton**. The `MsgBox` provides a dialog box with the specified message as shown in Figure 8-52.

Figure 8-52   VALIDATING DATA USING THE MSGBOX FUNCTION

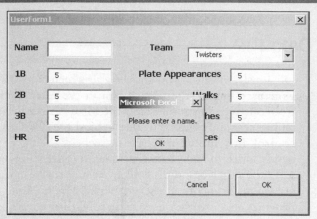

3. Click the **OK** button in the message box, type *your first name* in the TextBoxName control, and then click the **OK CommandButton**.

4. Click the **Cancel CommandButton** on the form, and then save the workbook.

5. Print the workbook on one page in landscape orientation with your name in the left section of the header.

6. Return to the Visual Basic Editor, display the UserForm, and then print both the code and the image for the UserForm.

7. Close the Visual Basic Editor, close the League-8 workbook, and then exit Excel.

There are a number of further improvements that you could make to this custom form. For example, if your users like SpinButtons, you might add them to the right of each TextBox that displays a value. Not only do the SpinButtons provide a way to make an entry without using the keyboard, they limit the possible entries to numeric values.

After you develop the custom form to the best of your ability, your next step is to pilot it with a small number of trusted users. Not only will they give you valuable feedback on ways to improve your form before making it available to others, they will test it in ways that you may not think about on your own. The main thing in any custom form development process is that the form makes sense to the user. Remember, the goal of a custom form is to improve productivity and ease of use, and the people who are using the form itself are the best judges of that.

Session 8.3 QUICK CHECK

1. What are the benefits of using a SpinButton control on a form?

2. What are the limitations of using a SpinButton rather than a TextBox for entering data on a form?

3. What is the benefit of connecting a SpinButton control to a TextBox rather than to a Label?

4. Compare and contrast a ListBox control with a ComboBox control.

5. What does the `Exit Sub` statement do?

6. Why would you use the `Exit Sub` statement?

REVIEW ASSIGNMENTS

GVR runs several golf courses and has been asked by their members to help them establish handicaps. How to calculate a golf handicap is not well understood by most of the GVR employees, so Lynn has come to you to see if you can help them find a way to make this calculation easier.

First, Lynn wants you to examine an existing workbook that already logs golf handicap indexes for the local golf league members. She wants you to use this information to calculate the course handicap for a particular golf course for an upcoming tournament. Secondly, she wants you to build a new custom form that prompts the user for the entries needed in order to track the statistics required to calculate a golf handicap for new league members.

To complete this task:

1. Start Excel and open the **Golf-8** workbook located in the Tutorial.08\Review folder on your Data Disk. The Women worksheet represents the current handicap indexes.

2. In the Visual Basic Editor, insert a new UserForm and change the UserForm's Caption property to "Women's Course Handicap Calculator".

3. Create the UserForm shown in Figure 8-53.

Figure 8-53

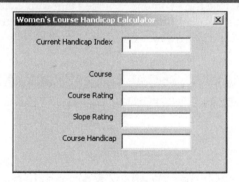

4. Use the following (Name) properties for the TextBoxes (from top to bottom):

    ```
    TextBoxCHI
    TextBoxCourse
    TextBoxCR
    TextBoxSR
    TextBoxCH
    ```

5. Make sure that the tab order is set in such a way that it moves through the TextBox controls from top to bottom.

6. In the workbook, using the Control Toolbox toolbar, add a Command Button to the workbook positioned at cell E1. Change its Caption property to "Calculate Course Handicap", and then widen the Command Button so that the full caption is visible.

7. Double-click the Command Button to open the Code window for the Sheet1 (Women) worksheet, and then create an event-handler procedure that opens the UserForm1 custom form when the Command Button is clicked. Return to the workbook, exit Design mode, and close the Properties window and the Control Toolbox toolbar.

Explore   8. In the Code window for the UserForm, add the code that executes on the **Activate** event for the UserForm as shown in Figure 8-54. (*Hint*: You might find it helpful to open the Batting-8 workbook, so that you can compare the code needed for this UserForm with the code you created in that workbook. You can move between the UserForms for each workbook in the Project Explorer.)

Figure 8-54

```
'Your Name, Current Date
'This procedure runs when the UserForm is activated.
Private Sub Userform_Activate()
    Set Namecell = Application.InputBox _
    (Prompt:="Select a name in column A", Type:=8)
    Namecell.Select

TextBoxCHI.Value = ActiveCell.Offset(0, 1).Value
TextBoxCourse.Text = Range("F5")
TextBoxCR.Value = Range("F6")
TextBoxSR.Value = Range("F7")
TextBoxCR.Value = Round(TextBoxCHI.Value * TextBoxCR.Value / 113, 0)
ActiveCell.Offset(0, 2).Value = TextBoxCH.Value

End Sub
```

Explore   9. Close the Visual Basic Editor, click the Calculate Course Handicap Command Button on the worksheet, select cell A4 when prompted, and then click the OK button.

10. Close the Women's Course Handicap Calculator UserForm, and then click the Command Button again to calculate the course handicap for the name in cell A7. Repeat this process for the names in cells A11 and A12 as shown in Figure 8-55.

Figure 8-55

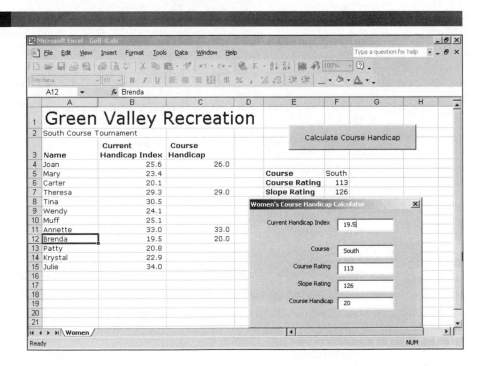

11. Close the Women's Course Handicap Calculator UserForm, enter your name in cell A17, and then print the workbook on one page. Open the Visual Basic Editor, and print the code and form image for the UserForm.

12. Save and close the Golf-8 workbook.

13. Open the **Handicap-8** workbook located in the Tutorial.08\Review folder of your Data Disk. In this workbook, you'll create a data entry form similar to the one shown in Figure 8-56 to enter the statistics you need to calculate a golf handicap.

Figure 8-56

14. Create a new UserForm and change the Caption property to "Enter Golf Statistics".

15. Change the Caption property for the Label and CommandButton controls to the captions shown in the figure.

16. Use the following (Name) properties for the bound controls (from top to bottom):

```
TextBoxName
TextBoxDate
TextBoxScore
SpinButtonScore
ComboBoxCourse
TextBoxCR
SpinButtonCR
TextBoxSR
SpinButtonSR
OKButton
CancelButton
```

17. Make sure that the tab order is set in such a way that it moves through the controls from top to bottom. Test the tab order, and then return to the Visual Basic Editor.

18. The Min property for the `SpinBoxScore` control should be 50 and its Max property should be 150.

19. The Min property for the `SpinBoxCR` control should be 50 and its Max property for the `SpinBoxCR` control should be 90.

20. The Min property for the `SpinBoxSR` control should be 55 and its Max property should be 155.

21. The RowSource property for the `ComboBoxCourse` should be H4:H9.

22. In the workbook, enter the following labels in range H3:H9 to populate the **ComboBoxCourse** control:

Courses
Northland
Cedar Hill
Sycamore Hill
Perry
Copper
Willow Creek

23. In the workbook, using the Control Toolbox toolbar, add a Command Button to the workbook postioned at cell G1. Change its Caption property to "Enter Golf Statistics", and then widen the Command Button so that the full caption is visible.

24. Double-click the Command Button to open the Code window for the Scores worksheet, and then create an event-handler procedure that opens the UserForm1 custom form when the Command Button is clicked. Return to the workbook, exit Design mode, and close the Properties window and the Control Toolbox toolbar.

25. In the Code window for the UserForm, add the code that executes on the **Click** event for the **CancelButton** as shown in Figure 8-57. The code should unload the UserForm.

Figure 8-57

```
'Your Name, Current Date
'CancelButton procedure
Private Sub CancelButton_Click()
Unload UserForm1
End Sub
```

26. In the workbook, assign the range name "ColA" to column A.

Explore

27. In the Code window for the UserForm, add the code that executes on the **Click** event for the **OKButton**. (*Hint*: You may find it helpful to also open up the League-8 workbook, so that you can compare the code needed for this UserForm with the code you created in that workbook. You can move between the UserForms for each workbook in the Project Explorer window.) The code is documented with comments as shown in Figure 8-58.

Figure 8-58

```
'OKButton procedure
Private Sub OKButton_Click()
'Validate that an entry has been made in the TextBoxName control
    If TextBoxName.Text = "" Then
        MsgBox "You must enter a name."
        Exit Sub
    End If
'Count the number of entries in column A, and set that value plus 1 equal to NextBlankRow
    NextBlankRow = Application.WorksheetFunction.CountA(Range("ColA")) + 1
'Transfer the values in the UserForm to the workbook.
    Cells(NextBlankRow, 1) = TextBoxName.Text
    Cells(NextBlankRow, 2) = TextBoxDate.Text
    Cells(NextBlankRow, 3) = TextBoxScore.Value
    Cells(NextBlankRow, 4) = ComboBoxCourse.Text
    Cells(NextBlankRow, 5) = TextBoxCR.Value
    Cells(NextBlankRow, 6) = TextBoxSR.Value
'Reset the controls to null
    TextBoxName.Text = ""
    TextBoxDate.Text = ""
    TextBoxScore.Value = ""
    ComboBoxCourse.Text = ""
    TextBoxCR.Value = ""
    TextBoxSR.Value = ""
'Set focus in the TextBoxName control
    TextBoxName.SetFocus
End Sub
```

28. In the Code window for the UserForm, add the code that executes on the Change event of the three SpinButton controls as shown in Figure 8-59

Figure 8-59

```
'Connect the value of TextBoxCR to SpinButtonCR
Sub SpinButtonCR_Change()
    TextBoxCR.Value = SpinButtonCR.Value
End Sub

'Connect the value of TextBoxScore to SpinButtonScore
Sub SpinButtonScore_Change()
    TextBoxScore.Value = SpinButtonScore.Value
End Sub

'Connect the value of TextBoxSR to SpinButtonSR
Sub SpinButtonSR_Change()
    TextBoxSR.Value = SpinButtonSR.Value
End Sub
```

29. Save the workbook, close the Visual Basic Editor, and then test the UserForm by clicking the Enter Golf Statistics Command Button in the worksheet and entering the information shown in Figure 8-60.

Figure 8-60

30. Click both the OK CommandButton and then click the Cancel CommandButton on the UserForm.

31. Print the workbook in portrait orientation on one page. In the Visual Basic Editor, print both the code and the image for the UserForm.

32. Save and close the Handicap-8 workbook, and then exit Excel.

CASE PROBLEMS

Case 1. Creating a Dialog Box to Organize Workbook Reporting If you need to print a workbook in many different ways, you can use a dialog box to organize and automate the various ways you print it. A small business that offers public seminars has asked you to help with an Excel problem it faces before each board meeting. The bottom line profits are very closely aligned with the number of participants. The company keeps a spreadsheet for each seminar it offers with the number of participants for each month. For its monthly board meeting, the company doesn't need a printout of all of the details for each seminar; therefore, much time is wasted hiding columns and rows to create the necessary reports. The company prints each workbook in three ways: showing all details, showing quarterly details for all line items, and showing quarterly details for only the Total Revenue, Total Expense, and Total Profit lines. You have been given a sample workbook and asked if you can automate the monthly printing process.

To complete this task:

1. Start Excel and open the **Seminar-8** workbook from the Tutorial.08\Cases folder on your Data Disk.

2. Record a macro called "QuarterlyDetail" that hides columns C, D, E, G, H, I, K, L, M, O, P, and Q; prints the workbook with your name in the left section of the header; and then redisplays all of the columns.

3. Record a macro called "QuarterlySummary" that hides columns C, D, E, G, H, I, K, L, M, O, P, and Q and rows 5 through 12 and 16 through 26; prints the workbook with your name in the left section of the header; and then redisplays all of the columns and rows.

4. In the Visual Basic Editor, create a new UserForm with two CommandButtons. Change the Caption property for the UserForm to "Print Board Reports", change the Caption property for CommandButton1 to "Print Quarterly Detail Report", and change the Caption property for CommandButton2 to "Print Quarterly Summary Report".

5. Resize the CommandButtons as needed to clearly display the entire captions.

6. In the workbook, using the Control Toolbox toolbar, add a Command Button to the workbook postioned at cell E1. Change its Caption property to "Print Board Reports", and then widen the Command Button so the caption is visible.

7. Double-click the Command Button to open the Code window for the Projections worksheet, and then create an event-handler procedure that opens the UserForm1 when the Command Button is clicked. Return to the workbook, exit Design mode, and close the Properties window and the Control Toolbox toolbar.

Explore

8. In the Code window for the UserForm, write the code that executes on the Click event for CommandButton1 and CommandButton2 to run the following two macros:

```
Private Sub CommandButton1_Click()
Application.Run ("QuarterlyDetail")
End Sub

Private Sub CommandButton2_Click()
        Application.Run ("QuarterlySummary")
End Sub
```

9. In the worksheet, click the Print Board Reports button to open the UserForm. Click both buttons in the UserForm to create the two printouts. If you have trouble with your macros or if your macros run slow, compare the code in the Module1 object for your workbook to the following solutions.

```
Sub QuarterlyDetail()
'
' QuarterlyDetail Macro
' Macro recorded on current date by your name
'
' Hide columns
Columns("C:E").Select
Selection.EntireColumn.Hidden = True
Columns("G:I").Select
Selection.EntireColumn.Hidden = True
Columns("K:M").Select
Selection.EntireColumn.Hidden = True
Columns("O:Q").Select
Selection.EntireColumn.Hidden = True

'Print workbook with your name in the left section of the
'header
ActiveSheet.PageSetup.LeftHeader = "Your Name"
ActiveWindow.SelectedSheets.PrintOut Copies:=1, Collate:=True

'Unhide columns
Columns("A:T").Select
Selection.EntireColumn.Hidden = False
End Sub

Sub QuarterlySummary()
'
'QuarterlySummary Macro
'Macro recorded on current date by your name
'
'Hide columns and rows
Columns("C:E").Select
Selection.EntireColumn.Hidden = True
Columns("G:I").Select
Selection.EntireColumn.Hidden = True
Columns("K:M").Select
Selection.EntireColumn.Hidden = True
Columns("O:Q").Select
Selection.EntireColumn.Hidden = True
Rows("5:12").Select
```

```
    Selection.EntireRow.Hidden = True
    Rows("16:26").Select
    Selection.EntireRow.Hidden = True
    Rows("1:31").Select

    'Print workbook with your name in the left section of the
    'header
    ActiveSheet.PageSetup.LeftHeader = "Your Name"
    ActiveWindow.SelectedSheets.PrintOut Copies:=1,Collate:=True

    'Unhide columns and rows
    Rows("1:30").Select
    Selection.EntireRow.Hidden = False
    Columns("A:T").Select
    Selection.EntireColumn.Hidden = False
    End Sub
```

10. In the Visual Basic Editor, print the code for both Module1 and the image for the UserForm.

11. Save and then close the Seminar-8 workbook, and then exit Excel.

Case 2. Using a Custom Form to Help with Financial Ratio Analysis You work for an investment firm that uses a standard Excel workbook format into which it enters income statement and balance sheet values. You have been asked to create a custom form to help users do financial analysis. Specifically, the company wants you to use a sample workbook to help its employees calculate various profitability ratios using a custom form.

To complete this task:

1. Start Excel and open the **Ratios-8** workbook from the Tutorial.08\Cases folder on your Data Disk.

2. Examine the values on the IncomeStmt and BalanceSheet worksheets.

3. In the Visual Basic Editor, create a new UserForm with four OptionButtons and one TextBox. The final form is shown in Figure 8-61.

Figure 8-61

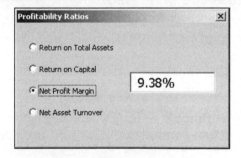

Change the Caption property for the UserForm to "Profitability Ratios". The (Name) and Caption properties for the four OptionButtons should be as follows:

(Name)	Caption
ROTA	Return on Total Assets
ROC	Return on Capital
NPM	Net Profit Margin
NAT	Net Asset Turnover

4. Change the (Name) property of the TextBox to "TextBoxRatio", and change the Font property to 14-point, regular Tahoma.

5. Resize the OptionButtons as necessary to clearly display the captions.

6. In the workbook, using the Control Toolbox toolbar, add a Command Button to the IncomeStmt worksheet positioned at cell D5. Change its Caption property to "Calculate Profitability Ratios", and then resize the Command Button so its caption is visible.

7. Double-click the Command Button to open the Code window for the IncomeStmt worksheet, and then create an event-handler procedure that opens the UserForm1 when the Command Button is clicked. Return to the workbook, exit Design mode, and close the Control Toolbox toolbar.

Explore

8. In the Code window for the UserForm, enter the following code that executes each time an OptionButton is clicked. This code uses `If` statements to determine which financial ratio you want to calculate and returns the value formatted as a percentage to the TextBox on the form. The comments in the code help you understand what values are being used in each calculation.

```
'Your Name, Current Date
Sub ROTA_Click()
'If the ROTA (Return on Total Assets) option button is
'selected
        If ROTA.Value = True Then
'Then TextBoxRatio.Value property is set to the ratio of
'Net profits before taxes/total assets
'Use the FormatPercent function to display the value as a
'percentage.
            TextBoxRatio.Value = _
FormatPercent(Worksheets("IncomeStmt").Range("B6") / _
Worksheets("BalanceSheet").Range("D13"))
        End If
End Sub


Sub ROC_Click()
'If the ROC (Return on Capital) option button is selected
        If ROC.Value = True Then
'Then TextBoxRatio.Value property is set to the ratio of
'Net profits before taxes/total capital
            TextBoxRatio.Valuef= _
FormatPercent(Worksheets("IncomeStmt").Range("B6") / _
Worksheets("BalanceSheet").Range("D23"))
        End If
End Sub


Sub NPM_Click()
'If the NPMf(Net Profit Margin) option button is selected
        If NPM.Value = True Then
'Then TextBoxRatio.Value property is set to the ratio of
'Net profits before taxes/Sales revenue
            TextBoxRatio.Value = _
FormatPercent(Worksheets("IncomeStmt").Range("B6") / _
Worksheets("IncomeStmt").Range("B5"))
        End If
```

```
End Sub

Sub NAT_Click()
'If the NAT (Net Asset Turnover) option button is selected
        If NAT.Value = True Then
'Then TextBoxRatio.Value property is set to the ratio of
'Sales/Capital
            TextBoxRatio.Value = _
FormatPercent(Worksheets("IncomeStmt").Range("B5") / _
Worksheets("BalanceSheet").Range("D23"))
        End If
End Sub
```

9. Save the code. Return to the Excel workbook, and click the Calculate Profitability Ratios button. Click each option button to view the calculation for each of the four profitability ratios, and then close the Profitability Ratios form.

10. In the Visual Basic Editor, print the code for both Module1 and an image for the UserForm.

11. Save and close the Ratios-8 workbook, and then exit Excel.

Case 3. Creating a Splash Screen   You work for a software development company that wants to present a **splash screen**, an introductory dialog box that appears for a few seconds when the company's program loads. To create a splash screen for an Excel workbook, you use a UserForm. You have been asked by the company to learn how to create splash screens so that you can attach them to the future Excel applications you develop.

To complete this task:

1. Start Excel and start a blank workbook.

2. Open the Visual Basic Editor and insert a new UserForm. Change the Caption property of the UserForm to "Quality Software Developers". Change the BackColor property of the UserForm to a color of your choice.

3. Add a label to the form with your name as the Caption property. Change the ForeColor, BackColor, and Font properties of the label to colors and styles of your choice.

Explore   4. Add an Image control to the UserForm, and then use the Picture property to find a graphic image that you could use for the purposes of this project. The image should have something to do with computers. Look in the C:\Program Files\Common Files\Microsoft Shared\Clipart folder for Microsoft-supplied clip art, or create a graphic of your own to use for this project.

Explore   5. Set the AutoSize property of the Image control to True, and then resize the form and the image so that you can clearly see the graphic.

6. Make any additional formatting embellishments that you deem appropriate to create a pleasing splash screen.

7. Write the following procedure in the code window for the ThisWorkbook object. This is an event-handler procedure that will run when the Open event occurs for the Workbook object.

```
Sub Workbook_Open()
    UserForm1.Show
End Sub
```

8. Open the Code window for the UserForm, and insert the following procedure that runs the `CloseSplashScreen` procedure four seconds after the UserForm `Activate` event occurs:

```
Sub UserForm_Activate()
      Application.OnTime Now + TimeValue("00:00:04"), _
"CloseSplashScreen"
End Sub
```

9. Insert a new module, and then insert the following procedure that closes the UserForm as follows:

```
Private Sub CloseSplashScreen()
      Unload UserForm1
End Sub
```

10. Save the workbook with the name **SplashScreen-8** in the Tutorial.08\Cases folder on your Data Disk, and then close the workbook.

11. Open the **SplashScreen-8** workbook to observe the splash screen.

12. In the Visual Basic Editor, print the code and form image for your splash screen UserForm.

13. Close the editor, save and close the workbook, and then exit Excel.

Case 4. Studying the Use of Controls in Excel Dialog Boxes   One of the best ways to determine which control to use on new UserForms is to examine how Microsoft has used similar controls in existing dialog boxes. In this exercise, you'll find and study examples of the controls on the Toolbox toolbar described in Figure 8-3 in Excel's own dialog boxes.

To complete this task:

1. Start Word and open the **Tutorial8-Case4** document located in the Tutorial.08\Cases folder on your Data Disk.

2. Start Excel. Your goal is to find an example of each of the controls documented in the first column of the Word document in an existing Excel dialog box. When you find an example of that control, fill in the second and third columns describing the dialog box and purpose for the control in the dialog box. Do not use the examples provided in Figures 8-1 and 8-2 of this tutorial.

3. Document a picture of each dialog box by pressing Alt + Print Screen when the dialog box is displayed. (This keystroke combination will capture an image of the dialog box to the Clipboard.)

4. In your Word document, paste an image of each dialog box that you reference in the table at the bottom of the Word document.

5. Save, print, and close the document, and then exit both Word and Excel.

QUICK CHECK ANSWERS

Session 8.1

1. A form is used to simplify, clarify, and improve the speed at which a user can accomplish a given task within Excel.

2. The primary difference in purpose is that custom functions focus on simplifying complex or long formulas. Custom forms focus on simplifying the user's interface with the workbook itself. Custom forms are also more extensive. Although functions always return a value to the workbook, custom forms can be developed to accomplish almost any user task, such as entering and editing data, helping a user navigate through a large workbook, or organizing various print definitions.

3. (Students might combine some of the actions.)

   ■ Plan what you want the UserForm to do.

   ■ In the Visual Basic Editor, insert a new UserForm.

   ■ In the Visual Basic Editor, add controls to the UserForm.

   ■ In the Visual Basic Editor, modify and adjust the properties of the controls as needed.

   ■ In the workbook, add a Command Button to a worksheet.

   ■ In the Visual Basic Editor, write a procedure that displays the UserForm when the Command Button is clicked. Check and modify the tab order of the UserForm as necessary.

   ■ In the Visual Basic Editor, write procedures for the controls that are executed when various control events occur.

4. A Label is an unbound control. A TextBox is a bound control.

5. The (Name) property is the name you must use if you refer to the control using VBA. The (Name) property is also how you identify controls when you open the Tab Order dialog box. The Caption property controls the text that the Label displays.

6. Click the Run Sub/UserForm button on the Standard VBA toolbar, click Run on the menu bar, and then click the Run Sub/UserForm menu option; or press the F5 key.

7. The procedure that runs when a Command Button on a worksheet is clicked is stored in the worksheet object. Double-click the worksheet object in the Project Explorer to enter, view, or modify procedures stored in that object. The procedure that runs when any control on a UserForm (including a CommandButton) is clicked is stored within the UserForm object. Double-click the UserForm object in the Project Explorer to view the UserForm, and then double-click the UserForm itself to open the code window for procedures associated with that form.

Session 8.2

1. `UserForm1.Show`

2. In order to open the Tab Order dialog box, you must open the Visual Basic Editor and select the UserForm. You cannot access the Tab Order dialog box from the Code window for the UserForm.

3. When you want to use a UserForm for data entry, you will almost always want to add OK and Cancel CommandButtons to the UserForm to initiate the action of sending the data in the UserForm to the worksheet or to cancel the activity.

4. `Application.WorksheetFunction`

5. The MsgBox function creates a dialog box that can be used to display the results of a variable at that point in the execution of your VBA code.

6. If you're creating a workbook for a wide range of users or one that will be used over an extended period of time, the productivity and improved accuracy that custom forms can provide can pay back tremendous benefits.

Session 8.3

1. The SpinButton control allows the user to make an entry using the pointer rather than entering a value directly from the keyboard. The SpinButton also limits the range of available entries, which helps you keep bogus data from being entered into the workbook.

2. A SpinButton can only be used with numeric entries.

3. By connecting a SpinButton to a TextBox versus a Label, you can also enter a value from the keyboard into the TextBox.

4. A ListBox control displays a list of values from which you can choose. A ComboBox control not only displays a list of values, but also a TextBox into which a user can enter a value. Also, a ComboBox displays its values as a drop-down list, whereas a ListBox has no drop-down behavior associated with the list.

5. The `Exit Sub` statement stops execution of the procedure at that point.

6. You could use the `Exit Sub` statement to stop execution of a procedure that didn't pass a validation test.

OBJECTIVES

In this tutorial you will:

- Declare variables with specific data types

- Work with relative versus absolute cell references within VBA

- Work with the Range object

- Use the GoTo statement

- Use the On Error statement

- Use the If...Then...Else control structure

- Use the Select Case control structure

- Use the For...Next loop structure

- Use the Do...Loop structure

EXAMINING
VARIABLES AND RANGES AND CONTROLLING CODE EXECUTION

CASE

Green Valley Recreation

As a business analyst for Green Valley Recreation (GVR), you have been working to improve and automate several Excel workbooks. Now you have been asked to build more sophisticated procedures that will require programming logic, the ability to manipulate ranges in different ways, and the ability to mask error messages.

In this tutorial, you will learn more about variables, data types, and absolute versus relative cell references within VBA. Since much of your VBA code deals with manipulating ranges, you'll learn different ways to identify and select ranges using VBA. In addition, you will also work with many control structures such as GoTo, If...Then, Select Case, and For...Next statements, used to redirect or repeat statements within your procedure.

**SESSION
9.1**

In this session, you will learn the purpose and need for variables and data types. You'll learn how to declare variables within a VBA procedure. You will also study how VBA handles absolute versus relative cell referencing, and you will learn many ways to reference the Range object.

Variables

A **variable** is a named storage location, used within the execution of your VBA code. You use variables within VBA in a way similar to how you use cell references within an Excel formula. For example, in the formula =*A1+B1*, *A1* and *B1* are variables, dependent upon the current value entered into those cells. You create formulas in Excel using cell references rather than raw data to preserve the ability of your formula to automatically recalculate. By creating a formula using the =*A1+B1* format, if the values of A1 and/or B1 change, the value of your formula changes automatically as well. Using variables to make your VBA code more flexible works in a similar way.

For example, if your company calculated commissions using a unique and complex formula, you might want to create a custom function called Commission to simplify this calculation. Furthermore, if you used the variable name of "Sales" to represent the sale amount within the function, it would be far more flexible than writing the VBA code to calculate the commission for a single sales value such as $10,000. By using a variable name, the same code can be used to calculate the commissions for any number of sales values, not just the commission on a sale for $10,000. Although you are already familiar with entering values in cells and using those cell references in a workbook, you may not be as familiar with how to create and assign values to variables used within VBA.

Declaring Variables

To **declare** a variable means to define it by giving it a name and data type before you use it. You declare variables for a sub procedure using the DIM statement. You declare variables for a function procedure by naming them as arguments in the Function statement. The name of a variable must adhere to the following rules:

- The first letter must be alphabetic, although you can use numbers and some special characters such as the underscore in variable names.
- Because VBA is not case sensitive, MORTGAGERATE, mortgagerate, Mortgagerate and MortgageRate are the same variable name. Because variable names are easier to read if the first character of each word is capitalized, some VBA programmers prefer to use mixed-case names such as MortgageRate for variables.
- Variable names cannot include spaces or periods, but underscores are allowed. For example, Mortgage_Rate is an acceptable variable name.
- You cannot use #, $, %, &, or ! characters in variable names.
- Variable names can be up to 255 characters in length.

You need to create another custom function to determine the annual golf membership fee, and you have decided to create the custom function with the name GOLFFEE. At GVR, two variables, your zip code (which determines whether or not you already support the golf courses through local property taxes) and your age, are used to determine your annual golf membership fee. Within the VBA code, you will name the variables ZipCode and BDay. You will create this custom function in a new workbook.

To create a new function called GOLFFEE:

1. Start Excel and open a new, blank workbook.

2. Press **Alt + F11** to open the Visual Basic Editor, click the **list arrow** for the Insert UserForm button [icon] on the Standard toolbar, and then click **Module**.

   TROUBLE? The Insert UserForm button on the Standard toolbar might appear as the Insert Module, Insert Class Module, or Insert Procedure button depending upon the activities of the last user.

3. Enter the following code for a custom function:

   ```
   Function GOLFFEE(ZipCode, BDay)
         GOLFFEE = 500
   End Function
   ```

4. Click the **Save** button on the Standard toolbar, navigate to the Tutorial.09\Tutorial folder on your Data Disk, type **Golf-9** as the filename, and then click the **Save** button.

At this point, neither the `ZipCode` nor the `BDay` variable were used in the calculation for the GOLFFEE function. Later, you'll add logic to your VBA code to use these variables so that different values are returned by the GOLFFEE function based on different values for these variables.

Data Types

The **data type** of a variable identifies the type of data that the variable can store. Figure 9-1 lists the available data types, their storage sizes, and their range of values.

Figure 9-1	DATA TYPES	
DATA TYPE	**STORAGE SIZE IN BYTES**	**RANGE OF VALUES**
Byte	1	0 to 255
Boolean	2	True or False (Yes or No, On or Off)
Integer	2	-32,768 to 32,767
Long	4	-2,147,483,648 to 2,147,483,647
Single	4	Numbers in the range of -3.4 to the 38th power to 3.4 to the 38th power
Double	8	Numbers in the range of -1.798 to the 308th power to 1.798 to the 308th power
Currency	8	-922,337,203,685,477.5808 to 922,337,203,685,477.5807
Decimal	14	Positive or negative numbers in the range of 29 digits total (28 digits might be to the right of the decimal point)
Date	8	January 1, 0100 to December 31, 9999
Object	4	Any object reference
String (variable length)	10 + string length	0 to about 2 billion
String (fixed-length)	length of string	1 to about 65,400
Variant (with numbers)	16	Any number up to the range of numbers in the Double data type
Variant (with characters)	22 + string length	1 to about 65,400

VBA does not require you to declare the variables you use, but if you don't declare a specific data type for a variable, VBA will assign the Variant data type. The **Variant** data type can store either numeric or text information. While this may sound convenient, look at the storage size of the Variant data type in Figure 9-1 as compared to the storage size of other data types. Because the Variant data type requires so much more storage, your programs will run slower if you allow VBA to automatically define variables with the Variant data type rather than explicitly declaring the variable name as well as its data type. In general, you want to use the data type that uses the smallest number of bytes yet still accommodates the range of data it may represent.

You want to declare the variables in the GOLFFEE function with a specific data type, so that the storage requirements for the variables as well as for the result of the GOLFFEE function are smaller than those used by the Variant data type.

To declare the variables in the GOLFFEE function with a specific data type:

1. Declare the `ZipCode` variable as a `String` data type, the `BDay` variable as a `Date` data type, and the resulting value as a `Currency` data type by modifying the first line of the function as follows:

   ```
   Function GOLFFEE(ZipCode As String, BDay As Date)
   ```

2. Type `As Currency` at the end of the first statement to declare the result of the GOLFFEE function with the Currency data type.

   You don't need to worry about capitalizing "As" or the data type itself. VBA will automatically capitalize these keywords as well as enter spaces in certain parts of the statement to make it easier to read.

Because the Currency and Double data types require only 8 bytes compared to the Variant data type that requires 16 bytes for numeric information, you've cut the storage requirements for your variables in half. By cutting the storage requirements down, you'll increase the speed for this function.

Option Explicit Statement

To require that all variables be declared before they are used in a sub procedure, you enter the `Option Explicit` statement as the first instruction in your VBA module. The benefit of this statement is that by requiring that all variables be declared before they are used in your sub procedures, you prevent the problem of misspelling a variable by mistake. Without the `Option Explicit` statement, a misspelled variable name would not be considered an error—the misspelled variable name would be treated as a new variable and assigned a Variant data type, which makes debugging your code more difficult. To automatically insert the `Option Explicit` statement as the first statement in a new VBA module, make sure that the Require Variable Declaration check box is selected on the Editor tab of the Options dialog box.

REFERENCE WINDOW RW

Automatically Entering the Option Explicit Statement

- Click Tools on the menu bar, and then click Options.
- Click the Editor tab, and then click the Require Variable Declaration check box to select it.
- Click the OK button.

You decided that it's a good idea to require that all variables be declared before using them in a procedure. You'll change the Visual Basic Editor's options so that the `Option Explicit` statement is entered as the first statement for every new module.

To automatically insert the Option Explicit statement:

1. Click **Tools** on the menu bar, and then click **Options**. The Options dialog box opens.

2. Click the **Editor** tab (if it is not already selected), and then click the **Require Variable Declaration** check box to select it (if it is not already selected).

3. Click the **OK** button.

4. Click the **Insert Module** button 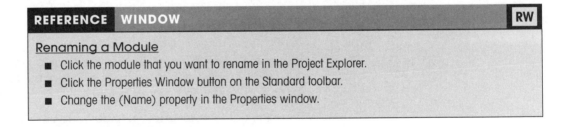 on the Standard toolbar. Module2 appears with the `Option Explicit` statement as the first statement of the module.

5. Click **Window** on the menu bar, click **Golf-9.xls-Module1 (Code)**, click before the `Function` statement, press the **Enter** key, press the ↑ key, and then type `Option Explicit` (if it doesn't already appear above the GOLFFEE function code).

6. Click **Tools** on the menu bar, click **Options**, click the **Editor** tab, click the **Require Variable Declaration** check box to deselect it, and then click the **OK** button.

Now you have two modules, one that contains a partially created new function, GOLFFEE and one that contains nothing more than an `Option Explicit` statement. You'll use Module1 to store new functions and Module2 to store new sub procedures. Sometimes it's helpful to give your modules meaningful names so that they are easier to recognize in the Project Explorer.

Renaming Modules

To rename a module to something more meaningful than Module1 or Module2, you work with a module's properties. You can access a module's properties by opening the Properties window.

REFERENCE WINDOW   **RW**

Renaming a Module
- Click the module that you want to rename in the Project Explorer.
- Click the Properties Window button on the Standard toolbar.
- Change the (Name) property in the Properties window.

Because you plan to use Module1 to store custom functions for this workbook and Module2 to store custom sub procedures, you will rename the modules to help identify their contents.

To rename Module1 and Module2:

1. Click the **Project Explorer** button 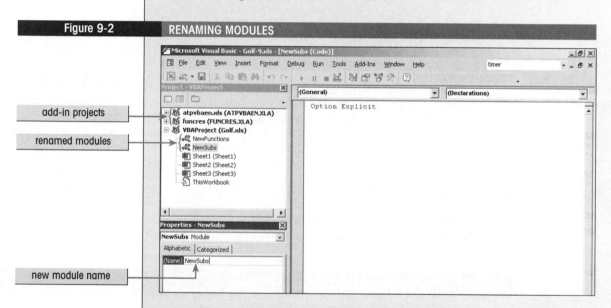 on the Standard toolbar to open the Project Explorer if it is not already visible, and then click **Module1** in the VBAProject (Golf-9.xls) object list.

2. Click the **Properties Window** button on the Standard toolbar to open the Properties window if it is not already visible.

3. Double-click **Module1** in the (Name) property box in the Properties window, type **NewFunctions**, and then press the **Enter** key. The name of the module automatically changes in the Project Explorer.

4. Drag the top edge of the Properties window down as necessary to see all the entries in the Project Explorer, and then double-click **Module2** in the Project Explorer.

5. Double-click **Module2** in the (Name) property box in the Properties window, type **NewSubs**, and then press the **Enter** key. Your Visual Basic Editor should look like Figure 9-2.

Figure 9-2	RENAMING MODULES

add-in projects

renamed modules

new module name

TROUBLE? Depending upon the number of add-ins you currently have installed on your computer, you might see more or fewer projects displayed in the Project Explorer. Add-ins will be covered in Tutorial 10.

TROUBLE? If your Project Explorer displays folders, then the folder view has been enabled. Click the Toggle Folders button in the Project Explorer to turn the folder view on or off.

Now the new functions and subs that you write for this workbook will be a little easier to find because their modules have been renamed to identify their contents. Also, you've added the `Option Explicit` statement to both modules, which will require that all variables be declared before they are used.

Variable Scope

Scope determines which modules and procedures can use a variable. Figure 9-3 identifies how to declare a variable within a particular scope. Both the `Dim` and `Private` VBA keywords can be used to declare a **local variable**, which is a variable used only within a single procedure, and a **module-wide variable**, a variable available to every procedure in a module. Note, however, the `Dim` keyword is more common. It is also used with other programming languages, including BASIC. The `Private` keyword is more descriptive of the actual scope of the variable.

Whether a variable is declared for use within a single procedure or for an entire module is determined by the placement of the statement. If the statement comes between the `Sub` and `End Sub` statements, it is a local variable. If the statement is placed before the first line of the first procedure, it is a module-wide variable.

Figure 9-3	VARIABLE SCOPE
SCOPE	**VARIABLE DECLARATION STATEMENT**
Within a procedure (local variable)	Enter `Dim` variable declaration statements to declare the variables and data types *within* the procedure, usually immediately after the `Sub` statement. *or* Enter `Private` variable declaration statements to declare the variables and data types *within* the procedure, usually immediately after the `Sub` statement.
Within an entire module (module-wide variable)	Enter `Dim` variable declaration statements before the first procedure in a module. *or* Enter `Private` variable declaration statements before the first procedure in a module.
All modules	Enter `Public` variable declaration statements before the first procedure in a module.

You want to create a small sub routine to display a message box to practice declaring variables within a procedure using the `Dim` keyword.

To create the Greeting sub:

1. Click below the `Option Explicit` statement in the NewSubs Code window, and then enter the following VBA statements that include the declaration of local variables:

```
Sub Greeting()
    Dim FName As String
    Dim LName As String
    FName = "Lynn"
    LName = "Tse"
    MsgBox ("Greetings from " + FName + " " + LName)
End Sub
```

You can also use the ampersand character (&) to concatenate text in the `MsgBox` argument as follows:

```
MsgBox ("Greetings from " & FName & " " & LName)
```

2. Click in any statement of the `Greeting` sub procedure, and then click the **Run Sub/UserForm** button ▶ on the Standard toolbar. Running the code produces the small dialog box as shown in Figure 9-4.

3. Click the **OK** button to return to the Greeting sub procedure, and then click the **Save** button on the Standard toolbar.

Although you can also declare multiple variables on one line, the syntax is somewhat tricky. For example, the following statement is valid but declares only the LName variable with a String data type. The FName variable is not declared with a data type and therefore is given the Variant data type.

```
Dim FName, LName As String
```

To declare more than one variable on the same statement line, you have to identify the data type for each variable. For example, you could declare both the FName and LName variables with a String data type by using this single statement:

```
Dim FName As String, LName As String
```

As a convention, most programmers declare all of the variables for one procedure immediately after the Sub statement and use a single statement for each variable. Using these conventions makes it easy to find, read, and understand what variables are used in the procedure. Also, be sure to use local variables whenever possible because VBA frees up the memory for those variables when the procedure ends, thus increasing the efficiency of your code.

Object Variables

Object variables are variables that represent any object, such as a range or a worksheet. Object variables help simplify your code. Consider the following two examples of VBA code. Both enter "Clark CCC" in cell A1, and then bold the value and change the font color to red. The first example is an object variable.
Example 1:

```
Sub ClarkCCC()
      Worksheets("Sheet1").Range("A1").Value = "Clark CCC"
      Worksheets("Sheet1").Range("A1").Font.Bold = True
      Worksheets("Sheet1").Range("A1").Font.ColorIndex = 3
End Sub
```

By declaring an object variable to refer to Worksheets("Sheet1").Range("A1"), you can use the variable name instead of referring to Worksheets("Sheet1") .Range("A1") in the rest of your procedure. Example 2 declares School as an object variable and then uses that variable name in the rest of the statements instead of Worksheets("Sheet1").Range("A1").
Example 2:

```
Sub ClarkCCC()
      Dim School As Range
      Set School = Worksheets("Sheet1").Range("A1")
      School.Value = "Clark CCC"
```

```
        School.Font.Bold = True
        School.Font.ColorIndex = 3
    End Sub
```

Lynn has decided that she wants to help users standardize the first label in a workbook. She wants all GVR workbooks to have the label "Green Valley Recreation" in cell A1, formatted in a Times New Roman, 24 point, blue font color. Because this will be a repetitive process that will be used over and over again, you will create a procedure to automate this process. You could use the macro recorder, but at this point, you want to practice declaring object variables, so you'll enter the VBA code to accomplish this task directly into the NewSubs module.

To use an object variable to refer to a range object:

1. Insert two blank lines after the End Sub statement of the Greeting procedure, and then enter the following code to enter "Green Valley Recreation" in cell A1 and to format the text with the Times New Roman font, 24-point font size, and a blue font color:

```
Sub GVREntry()
    Dim GVR As Range
    Set GVR = Worksheets("Sheet1").Range("A1")
    GVR.Value = "Green Valley Recreation"
    GVR.Font.Name = "Times New Roman"
    GVR.Font.Size = 24
    GVR.Font.ColorIndex = 5
End Sub
```

This procedure declares GVR as a Range variable and then uses the variable in four statements to simplify the code.

2. Click in any line in the GVREntry sub, click the **Run Sub/UserForm** button ▶ on the Standard toolbar to run the sub, and then click the **View Microsoft Excel** button ⊠ on the Standard toolbar to return to the Excel workbook. See Figure 9-5.

| Figure 9-5 | RESULTS OF GVRENTRY SUB |

The GVREntry sub entered the "Green Valley Recreation" label in cell A1 in a blue, 24-point, Times New Roman font.

Using the Macro Recorder to Help Edit Existing Procedures

At this point, you might wonder how you'll ever learn all of the correct property names to use for each statement. Although much of your comfort with VBA is directly tied to your experience, Excel provides some excellent tools to help write code. One of those tools is the macro recorder, which you can use to create new sub procedures and to edit existing ones. For example, Lynn wants to change the color of the label "Green Valley Recreation" to green. You don't know the number that represents this color, so you'll record a little macro using the macro recorder to determine this information. You'll then use that information to edit the existing GVREntry sub procedure so that the label is green instead of blue.

To use the macro recorder to determine the color number for green and edit the GVREntry sub procedure:

1. Click **Tools** on the menu bar, point to **Macro**, and then click **Record New Macro**.

2. Change the default name in the Macro name text box to **Green**, enter the *current date* and *your name* in the Description text box, and then click the **OK** button.

3. Click cell **A1** (even if it is already the active cell), click the **list arrow** for the Font Color button ⏬ on the Formatting toolbar, and then click the **Sea Green** box (third row from the top, fourth column from the left) from the color palette.

4. Click the **Stop Recording** button ⏹ on the Stop Recording toolbar. Now that you've recorded a macro that changes text to the color of green that Lynn wants, you'll look at the code and see what number was assigned to the Color property.

5. Click **Tools**, point to **Macro**, and then click **Macros**. Even though you didn't create the Greeting and GVREntry sub procedures using the macro recorder, they are listed as macros in the Macro dialog box because they start with the Sub statement.

6. Click **Green** (if it is not already selected), and then click the **Edit** button. See Figure 9-6. As with other sub procedures created by the macro recorder, you may see extra statements that you do not need. Look through the statements for the Selection.Font.ColorIndex statement. The number 50 represents the sea green color.

| Figure 9-6 | GREEN MACRO |

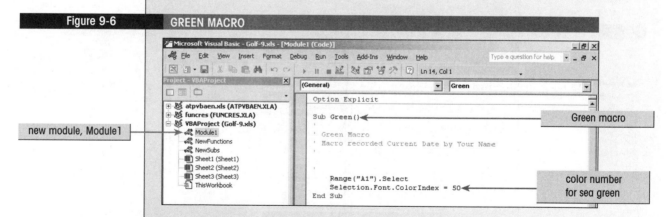

new module, Module1

Now that you know what value equals sea green, you don't need the Green macro anymore. To delete it, as well as the new module named Module1 that was created to store it, you'll delete Module1 from the Project Explorer.

7. Right-click **Module1** in the Project Explorer, click **Remove Module1** on the shortcut menu, and then click the **No** button when prompted about exporting the module before removing it.

8. Double-click the **NewSubs** module in the Project Explorer to display the existing subs (if the module isn't already displayed).

9. Click to the right of the GVR.Font.ColorIndex = 5 statement, type **0** so that the statement becomes GVR.Font.ColorIndex = 50, and then click the **Save** button 🔲 on the Standard toolbar.

To test whether the updated GVREntry subroutine works as intended, you need to rerun it. First, however, you'll delete the existing row 1 to make sure that both the label and formatting options are removed from that row.

To test the new color number for the GVREntry sub:

1. Click the **View Microsoft Excel** button 🔲 on the Standard toolbar to return to the workbook.

2. Right-click the **row heading** for row **1**, and then click **Delete** on the shortcut menu to delete the row.

3. Return to the Visual Basic Editor, click anywhere in the GVREntry sub, and then click the **Run Sub/UserForm** button ▶ on the Standard toolbar.

4. Click 🔲. The "Green Valley Recreation" label appears in cell A1 formatted in a sea green, 24-point Times New Roman font.

You see that using the macro recorder to help write or edit certain statements within an existing procedure is a handy tool.

Relative **Versus Absolute Cell References**

In Excel you need to know how to build formulas using both relative and absolute cell references in order to control how a formula is changed when it is copied or moved. In VBA, you need to know how to write code that references cells using both relative and absolute cell references so that your code works as intended. By default, VBA records absolute cell references to cells. In other words, it wouldn't matter what the active cell is when you run the GVREntry sub; the Green Valley Recreation label will always be entered in cell A1. You will return to the workbook and test this.

To test the absolute cell reference to A1 in the GVREntry sub:

1. Right-click the **row heading** for row **1**, and then click **Delete** on the shortcut menu to delete the row.

2. Click any cell in the Sheet1 worksheet other than cell A1. Because all sub procedures are considered to be macros, you can run the GVREntry sub from within the workbook using the Macro dialog box.

3. Click **Tools** on the menu bar, point to **Macro**, and then click **Macros**.

4. Click **GVREntry** in the Macro name list, and then click the **Run** button. The formatted "Green Valley Recreation" label is inserted in cell A1 as expected.

It doesn't matter which cell is the active cell when you run the GVREntry procedure because it references cell A1 as an absolute cell reference and will always enter the label in that cell.

To make the VBA code enter a label relative to the location of the active cell, you can either enter the appropriate statements directly in the Visual Basic Editor or use the macro recorder to create the code.

Lynn wants you to create a macro that inserts the text "For internal use only" at the location of the active cell, wherever it may be. You'll record this macro using relative cell referencing so that no matter what cell is currently active, the text will be placed in that cell.

To record a macro using relative cell referencing:

1. Click cell **D7**, click **Tools** on the menu bar, point to **Macro**, and then click **Record New Macro**.

2. Type **Internal** as the macro name, edit the text in the Description text box to include the *current date* and *your name*, and then click the **OK** button.

3. Click the **Relative Reference** button [image] on the Stop Recording toolbar.

   TROUBLE? If the Stop Recording toolbar doesn't automatically appear when you start recording a macro, right-click any toolbar and then click Stop Recording on the shortcut menu.

4. Type **For internal use only**, press the **Enter** key, and then click the **Stop Recording** button [image] on the Stop Recording toolbar.

To test whether the macro was recorded using the active cell, rather than referencing cell D7 as an absolute cell reference, you need to run the Internal macro.

To run the Internal macro:

1. Click cell **D10** to make it the active cell.

2. Click **Tools** on the menu bar, point to **Macro**, and then click **Macros**.

3. Click **Internal** in the Macro name list, and then click the **Run** button. See Figure 9-7.

Figure 9-7   RUNNING THE INTERNAL MACRO

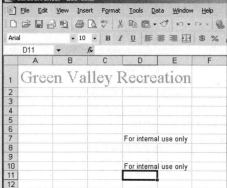

Unlike the GVREntry sub, which always entered "Green Valley Recreation" in cell A1, the Internal sub will enter "For internal use only" in whichever cell is active.

The Relative Reference Button

Interestingly, the Relative Reference button on the Stop Recording toolbar remains toggled "on," even when you have finished recording the macro. Therefore, the next time you record a macro, you will be recording it using the relative cell referencing mode unless you click the Relative Reference button again to return to the default, absolute cell referencing mode. Figure 9-8 shows how the Relative Reference button looks when it is selected (when relative cell referencing is turned on) in both Excel 2000 and Excel 2002.

| Figure 9-8 | STOP RECORDING TOOLBAR WITH THE RELATIVE REFERENCE BUTTON SELECTED |

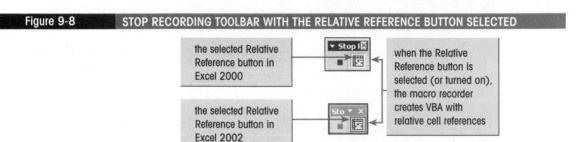

When the Relative Reference button is selected in Excel 2000, the button looks pressed in, or depressed. In Excel 2002, selected buttons appear with a blue square around the outer edge of the button. The ScreenTip for the button (whether it is selected or not) is "Relative Reference." By default, the Relative Reference button is *not* selected, which means that the macro will record using absolute cell references for all ranges. When the Relative Reference button is selected, the macro will write VBA using relative cell references for all ranges. Therefore, you need to check the state of the Relative Reference button each time you start recording a macro to make sure it represents the state of cell referencing that you want to record. If you want to return the button to an unselected, absolute cell reference mode before you record the next macro, you need to display the Stop Recording toolbar and check the Relative Reference button before you record the next macro. To display the Stop Recording toolbar when you are not recording a macro, select it from the Toolbars list within the Customize dialog box.

Checking the Relative Reference Button Status
- Click View on the menu bar, point to Toolbars, and then click Customize.
- Click the Toolbars tab, and then click the Stop Recording check box in the Toolbars list.
- Click the Close button in the Customize dialog box.

You will check the Relative Reference button even though you are not recording a macro and then return the button to its default mode, absolute cell referencing.

To check the mode of the Relative Reference button when you are not recording a macro:

1. Click **View** on the menu bar, point to **Toolbars**, and then click **Customize**. You must open the Customize dialog box, which shows you all of the available tool-bars within Excel, to display the Stop Recording toolbar when you are not in the process of recording a macro.

2. Click the **Toolbars** tab if it isn't already displayed, scroll down the list of avail-able toolbars, and then click the **Stop Recording** toolbar check box to select it, as shown in Figure 9-9. The Stop Recording toolbar appears.

Figure 9-9	CHECKING THE STATUS OF THE RELATIVE REFERENCE BUTTON

3. Click the **Close** button in the Customize dialog box.

4. Click the **Relative Reference** button [▦] on the Stop Recording toolbar to unse-lect it so that you are back to an absolute cell reference mode.

5. Click the **Close** button [X] for the Stop Recording toolbar to close it.

You can click the Relative Reference button to switch from one state to another as you begin to record a new macro, after you have recorded a macro, or in the middle of record-ing a macro. Recording macros in either an absolute or relative reference mode makes a dif-ference in how the VBA statements are written, which in turn determines what the macro will do. You will view the new code for the Internal macro and compare the VBA statements that use relative cell referencing with those that use absolute cell referencing in the GVREntry sub procedure.

To view the code for the Internal macro:

1. Click the **Microsoft Visual Basic** program button on the taskbar to return to the editor, and then double-click **Module1** in the Project Explorer. Recall that the code for each new macro is recorded in a new module. You will cut and paste that code to the NewSubs module, so that you can more easily compare the code for the Internal macro that uses relative cell referencing with that of the GVREntry sub that uses absolute cell referencing.

2. Select all of the code from the `Sub Internal()` statement through the `End Sub` statement, and then click the **Cut** button ✂ on the Standard toolbar. You've transferred the code for the `Internal` sub to the Windows Clipboard. Now you will paste it into the NewSubs module.

3. Double-click the **NewSubs** module in the Project Explorer, click below the last `End Sub` statement, press the **Enter** key twice, and then click the **Paste** button 📋 on the Standard toolbar.

4. Delete all of the comment lines in the `Internal` sub so that you can more easily compare the code with that of the `Greeting` and `GVREntry` sub procedures as shown in Figure 9-10. If you have any extra lines of code, or if there are any differences between your `Internal` sub and that shown in Figure 9-10, modify your code to match the figure.

Figure 9-10	COMPARING THE GVRENTRY AND INTERNAL SUB PROCEDURES

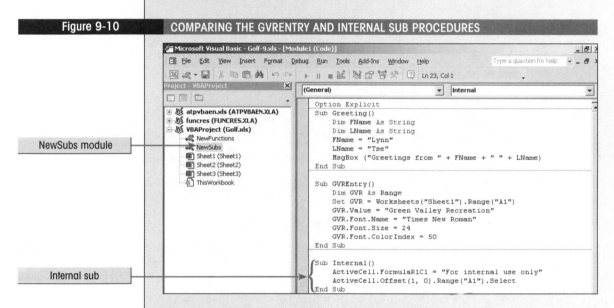

Now delete Module1, which is no longer needed, to keep your Project Explorer as organized as possible.

5. Right-click **Module1** in the Project Explorer, click **Remove Module1** on the shortcut menu, and then click the **No** button when prompted about exporting the module before removing it.

6. Double-click the **NewSubs** module in the Project Explorer (if it isn't already displayed), and then click the **Save** button 💾 on the Standard toolbar.

In the `GVREntry` macro, `GVR` was declared as a range object and set equal to `Worksheets("Sheet1").Range("A1")`, an absolute reference. In the `Internal` macro, the `ActiveCell` object uses the `FormulaR1C1` and `Offset` properties to identify cells. Because these statements are so different and because you spend so much time identifying and manipulating the contents of cells in Excel, you will study the `Range` object.

Working with Range Objects

Because Excel workbooks arrange data in single or multiple-cell ranges, much of the VBA code that you will create involves manipulating `Range` objects. As you have already seen in the GVREntry and Internal macros, there is more than one way to refer to a `Range` object.

Understanding how to work with `Range` objects requires that you have an excellent command of VBA terminology. To review, a `Range` object is contained within a `Worksheet` object and may consist of one or more cells on a single worksheet.

There are multiple ways to manipulate a `Range` object in VBA code, including:

- Using the `Range` property of the `Worksheet` object
- Using the `Range` property of a `Range` object
- Using the `Cells` property of a `Worksheet` object
- Using the `Cells` property of a `Range` object
- Using the `Offset` property of a `Range` object

Since you are sure that a better understanding of `Range` objects will be important to your success with VBA at GVR, you've decided to study each way of working with a `Range` object.

The Range Property of the Worksheet Object

The `Range` property of a `Worksheet` object returns a `Range` object. In general, the syntax for the `Range` property is:

```
object.Range(cell1, cell2)
```

Applying this syntax to the problem of assigning the value of 50 to six cells, A1, A2, A3, B1, B2, and B3, on the Sheet1 worksheet object, you could use the following statement:

```
Worksheets("Sheet1").Range("A1:B3").Value = 50
```

An equivalent way of writing this statement is to identify the first and last cell reference of the range as shown in the following statement:

```
Worksheets("Sheet1").Range("A1", "B3").Value = 50
```

Also note that you could use a range name in your VBA code. For example, instead of referencing cells A1 and B3 as the corners of your range, you could select the range, give it an appropriate name, and use the range name in the statement. The benefit of using range names is that you will have less work to do in maintaining your code later, if you add new rows or columns that affect the cell addresses of the range.

Applying this syntax to the problem of assigning the value of 50 to two cells, A1 and A3, on the Sheet1 worksheet object, you could use the following statement:

```
Worksheets("Sheet1").Range("A1,A3").Value = 50
```

You will practice writing statements that use the `Range` property of the `Worksheet` object by inserting a new module, and then writing the code to select three different ranges and assigning values to them in the Sheet2 worksheet of the current workbook. You'll use a common set of entries required by workbooks that deal with pay levels for golf course employees to practice working with the `Range` property of the `Worksheet` object.

To work with the Range property of the Workbook object:

1. Click the **Insert Module** button 🔲 on the Standard toolbar. A new module named Module1 is inserted with the `Option Explicit` statement in the first line.

   TROUBLE? If the Insert Module button isn't displayed, click the list arrow for the button, and then click Module.

2. Enter the following VBA statements. To facilitate the process, enter the first four statements, copy and paste the `Range` statements, and then edit the arguments and the assignment values as needed.

```
Sub PayScale()
    Worksheets("Sheet2").Activate
    Range("A1").Select
    Range("A1").Value = "Level"
    Range("B1").Select
    Range("B1").Value = "Hourly Rate"
    Range("A2").Select
    Range("A2").Value = "Entry"
    Range("B2").Select
    Range("B2").Value = 10
    Range("A3").Select
    Range("A3").Value = "Level 1"
    Range("B3").Select
    Range("B3").Value = 11
End Sub
```

3. Click the **Save** button on the Standard toolbar.

This code uses the Range property of the Worksheets object to select and then assign a value to the identified cell. To see how this code works, statement by statement, you will step through the macro one statement at a time, as you are watching the result of the code in Excel.

To step through the PayScale procedure:

1. Click the **Restore** button 🗗 for the Visual Basic Editor, (if it is not already restored) and then position and resize the Excel and Visual Basic Editor windows as needed. See Figure 9-11.

Figure 9-11   POSITIONING THE EXCEL AND VISUAL BASIC EDITOR WINDOWS SIDE-BY-SIDE

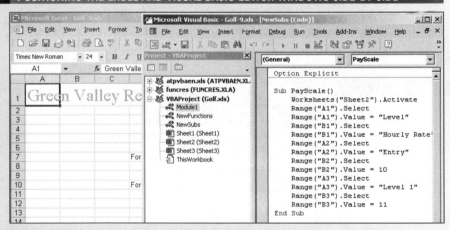

2. Click anywhere in the first line of the Sub PayScale() statement, click **Debug** on the menu bar, and then click **Step Into**. The first line of code is high-lighted in bright yellow.

3. Press the **F8** key (the quick keystroke for the Step Into command) three times to move to the fourth statement. Notice that cell A1 of the Sheet2 worksheet is the active cell in the Excel window.

4. Press the **F8** key as many times as necessary to complete the procedure. The yellow highlight indicates which statement you are about to step into. When you have completed the procedure, no statements will be highlighted. Your Excel window should look like Figure 9-12.

Figure 9-12   STEPPING THROUGH THE ENTIRE PAYSCALE PROCEDURE

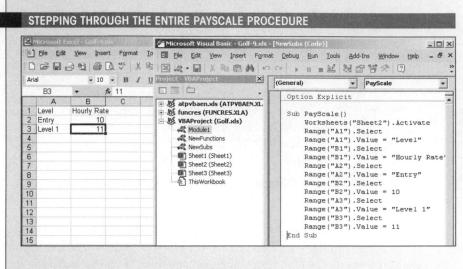

5. Maximize the Visual Basic Editor.

You used the `Select` method to select a particular `Range` object. This made it very easy to step through the code and see exactly what was happening in the Excel workbook. In VBA, however, you don't have to select a cell before you enter data into it. Therefore you can shorten the `PayScale` procedure by deleting the `Select` statements.

To shorten the PayScale procedure:

1. Delete every statement that ends with the `Select` method. Your simplified procedure should look like Figure 9-13.

Figure 9-13   SIMPLIFIED PAYSCALE PROCEDURE

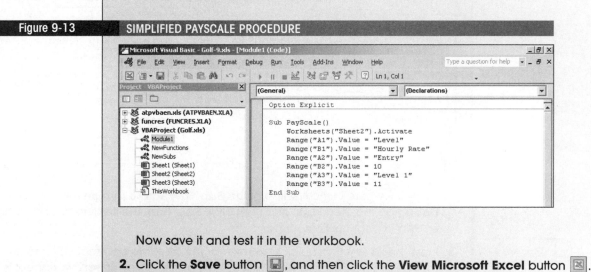

Now save it and test it in the workbook.

2. Click the **Save** button , and then click the **View Microsoft Excel** button .

You will delete the entries on the Sheet2 worksheet so that you can retest the updated `PayScale` procedure.

3. Maximize the workbook (if it isn't already maximized), select range **A1:B3** on the Sheet2 worksheet, press the **Delete** key, and then switch to the **Sheet1** worksheet so you can retest the PayScale procedure including the statement that activates Sheet2.

4. Click **Tools** on the menu bar, point to **Macro**, and then click **Macros**.

5. Click **PayScale** in the Macro name list, and then click the **Run** button. The six entries are reentered in the range A1:B3 of the Sheet2 worksheet.

The `Range` property of a `Worksheet` object is one of the most direct and common ways to work with a cell or range of cells using VBA.

The Range Property of the Range Object

You can also work with cells by using the `Range` property of a `Range` object such as `ActiveCell`. The syntax of the `Range` property of the `Range` object can be written as follows:

```
object.Range(cell1)
```

For example, consider the statement:

```
ActiveCell.Range("B1") = "Lynn Tse, Director"
```

This statement assigns the label "Lynn Tse, Director" to the cell that is one column to the right and in the same row as the active cell. In this case, "B1" doesn't refer to the cell B1 on the worksheet, but rather, to whatever column is one column to the right and the same row as the active cell. To refer to the cell two columns to the right and two rows below the active cell, you'd enter the statement:

```
ActiveCell.Range("C3") = "Lynn Tse, Director"
```

To practice using the Range property of the ActiveCell object, you'll modify the `Internal` sub.

To modify the Internal sub to use the Range property of the ActiveCell object:

1. Return to the Visual Basic Editor, and then display the code for the **NewSubs** module.

2. Modify the `Internal` sub by entering the following statement immediately above the `End Sub` line:

   ```
   ActiveCell.Range("A2") = "GVR"
   ```

   This statement will assign the label "GVR" to the cell that is in the same column, but one row below, the active cell. Now you'll test the `Internal` sub to see how the new statement works.

3. Switch to the Sheet1 worksheet in the Golf-9 workbook, delete the "For internal use only" labels in column D, and then click cell **B5**. You'll test the updated `Internal` sub in cell B5.

4. Click **Tools** on the menu bar, point to **Macro**, and then click **Macros**.

5. Click **Internal** in the Macro name list, and then click the **Run** button. Your screen should look like Figure 9-14. The "For internal use only" label appears in the cell that was active (cell B5) when the macro started. The "GVR" label appears in the cell that is in the same column and one row below the cell that was active.

Figure 9-14 | **USING THE RANGE PROPERTY OF THE ACTIVECELL OBJECT**

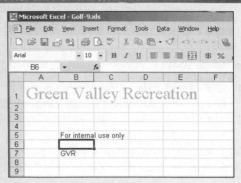

You will modify the `Internal` sub so that both statements use the `Range` property of the `ActiveCell` object so that the labels are entered at the active cell and the cell below the active cell without a blank line in between them.

6. Return to the Visual Basic Editor, and then replace the first two statements in the `Internal` sub that start with `ActiveCell` with a single statement that uses the `Range` property of the `ActiveCell` object as follows:

```
ActiveCell.Range("A1") = "For internal use only"
```

Figure 9-15 shows the final `Internal` sub.

Figure 9-15 | **INTERNAL SUB**

```
Sub Internal()
    ActiveCell.Range("A1") = "For internal use only"
    ActiveCell.Range("A2") = "GVR"
End Sub
```

7. Return to the Excel workbook, delete all the labels in column B, click cell **B5**, and then rerun the **Internal** macro. The macro entered the first label "For internal use only" in the active cell (represented by the `Range ("A1")` property) and the second label "GVR" in the cell in the same column and one row below the active cell (represented by the `Range ("A2")` property).

When you want to work with cells that you can define in relationship to the current cell, the `Range` property of the `ActiveCell` object is very useful.

The Cells Property of the Worksheet Object

Yet another way to reference a cell is to use the `Cells` property of the `Worksheet` object. The syntax of the `Cells` property of the `Worksheet` object can be written as follows:

```
object.Cells(rowIndex, columnIndex)
```

The `Cells` property uses two placeholders, `rowIndex` and `columnIndex`, to identify the row and then the column number, numbered consecutively from row 1 through row 65536 and from column A to column IV (numbers 1 through 256) of the cell you are referencing. For example, the following assignment statement would enter the value 500 in the cell that is two rows down (row 2) and three columns to the right (column C):

```
Worksheets("Sheet1").Cells(2,3) = 500
```

Because the `Cells` property of the `Worksheet` object can reference a variable for the column and row values, you will find it is useful when working with code that loops through a range of cells. Looping will be covered later in this tutorial.

The Cells Property of the Range Object

The `Cells` property of the `Range` object is similar to working with the `Range` property of the `Range` object. Both help you work with cells *in relation to* the active range object. The syntax of the `Cells` property of the `Range` object can be written as follows:

```
object.Cells(rowIndex, columnIndex)
```

For example, the following two lines of VBA code both assign the value 5 to the cell one column to the right and one row below the current cell. The first uses the `Range` property of a `Range` object, and the second uses the `Cells` property of a `Range` object:

```
ActiveCell.Range("B2") = 5
ActiveCell.Cells(1,1) = 5
```

The Offset Property of the Range Object

The `Offset` property only applies to a `Range` object. Its general syntax is as follows:

```
object.Offset(rowOffset, columnOffset)
```

For example, `ActiveCell.offset(0,1)` refers to the cell one column to the right and in the same row as the active cell. `ActiveCell.offset (1,0)` refers to the cell one row down and in the same column as the active cell.

You may have noticed in the Internal macro, that when you record a macro using relative cell reference mode, Excel used the `Offset` property. Because the `Offset` property can reference both positive and negative values, it is extremely flexible. Positive values refer to cells to the right and below the active cell. Negative values refer to cells to the left and above the active cell.

You'll record one more macro using the macro recorder to practice working with range objects. Since your users are often comparing statistics from GVR's four golf courses, they are often entering four labels into four consecutive cells in the workbook. Lynn has asked you to build a macro that helps the users quickly enter those labels. Since you don't always want the labels to be entered in exactly the same place on the workbook, you need to record it using relative cell referencing. You'll call the new macro GolfCourses.

To record the GolfCourses macro:

1. Click cell **A2** in the Sheet1 worksheet.

2. Click **Tools** on the menu bar, point to **Macro**, and then click **Record New Macro**.

3. Type **GolfCourses** as the macro name, and then click the **OK** button.

4. Click the **Relative Reference** button on the Stop Recording toolbar to turn the option on.

5. Type **Sun Valley** and press the **Enter** key, type **Blue Hills** and press the **Enter** key, type **Indian Hills** and press the **Enter** key, type **Shadow Glen** and then press the **Enter** key.

6. Click the **Relative Reference** button on the Stop Recording toolbar to turn the option off, and then click the **Stop Recording** button on the Stop Recording toolbar to stop the macro.

Now you'll study the code, to examine how the macro recorder uses the `Offset` property of the `Range` object to work with relative cell references.

To study the code created by the macro recorder for the GolfCourses macro:

1. Return to the Visual Basic Editor.

2. Double-click **Module2** in the Project Explorer.

3. Modify the comment to include today's date and your name.

   As you've already learned, the macro recorder often doesn't create the most efficient code. Now that you know how to work with range objects, you can edit this code to make it easier to read (and faster as well).

4. Edit the code to use the `Offset` property of the `Range` object as shown in Figure 9-16. Each statement refers to a cell reference in a consecutive row of the same column.

| Figure 9-16 | EDITING THE GOLFCOURSES MACRO |

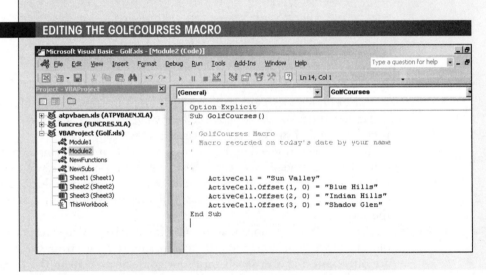

As always, it's important to test your changes.

To test the edited GolfCourses macro:

1. Switch to Sheet1 of the Excel workbook, delete any existing entries on the worksheet except for the label in cell A1, click **B8**, and then run the **GolfCourses** macro. The four labels have been inserted in the workbook at the location of the current cell and the next three cells below the current cell, as shown in Figure 9-17.

Figure 9-17 **TESTING THE GOLFCOURSES MACRO**

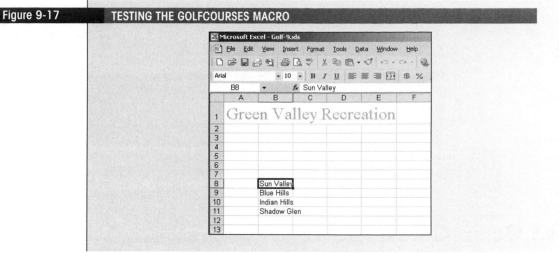

As a final activity, you'll copy the `GolfCourses` and `PayScale` subs into the NewSubs module and then delete the extra modules that were created when you used the macro recorder.

To clean up the Golf-9 workbook:

1. Select range **A1:B11**, press the **Delete** key, click the **Sheet2** tab, select range **A1:B3** (if it isn't already selected), and then press the **Delete** key.

   Now move the new macros into the NewSubs module.

2. Return to the Visual Basic Editor, and then double-click **Module1** in the Project Explorer.

3. Select all of the statements from the `Sub PayScale()` statement through the `End Sub` statement, and then click the **Cut** button ✂ on the Standard toolbar.

4. Double-click the **NewSubs** module in the Project Explorer, insert two blank lines after the `Internal` sub, and then click the **Paste** button 📋 on the Standard toolbar. A horizontal line, a procedure separator, appears between the last statement of the `Internal` sub and the first line of the `PayScale` sub. With the `PayScale` sub successfully transferred to the NewSubs module, you can delete the empty Module1 module.

5. Right-click **Module1** in the Project Explorer, click **Remove Module1** on the shortcut menu, and then click the **No** button when prompted about exporting Module1 before removing it.

   Now transfer the `GolfCourses` sub to the NewSubs module.

6. Double-click **Module2** in the Project Explorer, select all of the statements from the `Sub GolfCourses()` statement through the `End Sub` statement, and then click ✂.

7. Double-click the **NewSubs** module in the Project Explorer, insert two blank lines after the `End Sub` statement for the `PayScale` sub, and then click 📋.

8. Print the **NewSubs** module.

9. Right-click **Module2** in the Project Explorer, click **Remove Module2** on the shortcut menu, and then click the **No** button.

10. Click the **Save** button 🖫 on the Standard toolbar, close the Visual Basic Editor, and then close the Golf-9 workbook.

Now that you have more fundamental VBA skills in the area of declaring variables and data types, recording macros using absolute versus relative cell referencing, and manipulating range objects, you'll be in a better position to read and write meaningful VBA code.

Session 9.1 QUICK CHECK

1. What rules must the name of a VBA variable follow?

2. What data type does a variable assume if you do not explicitly declare it?

3. By default, how does the macro recorder reference cell addresses?

4. Identify five ways to manipulate a range object.

5. What technique of working with ranges does the macro recorder use when you are using relative cell referencing?

SESSION 9.2

In this session, you will expand your knowledge of the If...Then and Select Case control structures. You will use and compare many different techniques to control execution, including the GoTo statement used in conjunction with the On Error statement. Finally, you will work with For...Next, and Do...Loop structures.

Controlling Code Execution

When you record a sub procedure using the macro recorder, the statements execute from top to bottom, finishing at the End Sub statement. There are times, however, when you may want to skip statements, branch to another location in your code, or repeat a set of statements depending on a given condition. For example, you may want to immediately stop execution of a procedure (skip the rest of the steps and run the End Sub statement) if your code encounters a run-time error. Or, you may need to repeatedly loop through a series of statements to calculate information for each item in a list of data. You can't create this type of code using the macro recorder. To add "logic," or the ability to determine which statements will be executed, and how many times they will be executed, you need to add the statements directly in the Visual Basic Editor.

On Error Statement

Use the On Error statement to specify what should happen in your procedure when a run-time error occurs. The On Error statement gives you two choices, to continue running the code or to jump to a special section of your code. The statement to continue running the code is:

```
On Error Resume Next
```

The syntax for jumping to a different location in your code is:

```
On Error Resume GoTo ErrorHandler
        statements
ErrorHandler:
        statements
```

Often, when an error is encountered, you'll use the GoTo statement to redirect code to another part of the procedure.

GoTo Statement

One way to change the order in which the statements of a procedure execute is to use the GoTo statement. A label follows the GoTo keyword, which is then repeated in another section of the procedure and identifies where the execution of the code should be transferred after executing the GoTo statement.

The most common place you see the GoTo statement is in conjunction with handling errors. It is not considered a good programming practice to use the GoTo statement in other situations, because it creates spaghetti code. **Spaghetti code** is programming code that has more than one entry or exit point, making it much more difficult to debug and maintain. **Structured programming** rules, a set of standards developed over time that help programmers to develop high-quality programs, encourage programmers to write procedures with only one entry and exit point. Most programmers, therefore, only use the GoTo statement for stopping a program when it hits a run-time error.

If your code hits a run-time error, you are presented with a dialog box that displays information about the error. Although you try to predict and eliminate as many conditions that will create a run-time error as possible, it's impossible to predict absolutely everything a user might do that could cause the code to encounter a run-time error. And, you don't want most users to see run-time error dialog boxes. So, you might use an error-handling technique such as the On Error statement combined with the GoTo statement to provide a meaningful message to a user if and when a run-time error occurs, rather than presenting them with the default error message. The general syntax of the GoTo statement is:

```
statement GoTo Label
        statements
Label:
        statements
```

When you want to jump to a new location in your code when an error occurs, you use the GoTo statement to identify a label name that you will go to when the error occurs. Upon executing the GoTo Label statement, the code immediately jumps to the Label: statement in the procedure. Note that the label name that identifies where the code will continue is followed by a colon.

You will use the On Error and GoTo statements to capture a common error and redirect execution to a new area of the procedure that calculates golf handicaps. The first thing you'll do, however, is intentionally create a run-time error to experience what happens when you don't handle errors with On Error statements.

To experience a run-time error:

1. If you took a break after the previous session, start Excel and then open the **GolfHandicap-9** workbook located in the Tutorial.09\Tutorial folder on your Data Disk.

2. When you are prompted that the workbook contains macros, click the **Enable Macros** button.

You want to create the error that would occur if the user attempted to calculate a course handicap for a row that doesn't contain data. To experience this error message, intentionally run the code on a row that doesn't contain the necessary data, row 16.

3. Click the **Calculate Course Handicap** button to open the Input dialog box, click cell **A16** to enter this cell as the name in column A, and then click the **OK** button. You are presented with the error message shown in Figure 9-18. The "Type mismatch" error indicates that you are attempting to execute an operation with data that is incapable of being handled in that way. This error usually means that you are trying to calculate with text or nonexistent data rather than with numeric data.

Figure 9-18	MICROSOFT VISUAL BASIC ERROR MESSAGE

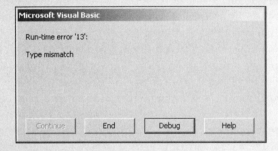

4. Click the **Debug** button. The Visual Basic Editor opens and highlights the line of code that created the run-time error in bright yellow. Clicking the End button in the message box would have stopped the procedure, and you would have returned to the workbook itself.

5. Click the **Reset** button ■ on the Standard toolbar to stop executing the code and to remove the yellow highlight.

Encountering a run-time error when running VBA code and then clicking the Debug button in the error message dialog box helps you find and determine the exact cause of the error. In this case, though, you know why the error occurred. It occurred because you are trying to do a calculation on a row that contains no data.

To insert an On Error statement to mask the run-time error:

1. Click above the `TextBoxCH.Value = Round(TextBoxCHI.Value * TextBoxCR.Value / 113, 0)` statement, and then press the **Enter** key to insert a blank row.

2. Type the statement `On Error Resume Next`, and then press the **Enter** key. See Figure 9-19.

Figure 9-19   **USING THE ON ERROR RESUME NEXT STATEMENT**

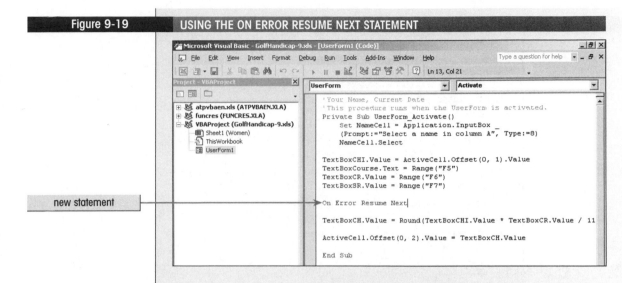

new statement

3. Save the code and then return to the Excel workbook.

   To test the new statement, you will first run the procedure using appropriate data to see how the procedure is supposed to work, and then run the procedure using row 16 (which is empty) to see how the new statement handles the error.

4. Click the **Calculate Course Handicap** button, click cell **A15**, and then click the **OK** button. The Course Handicap value is calculated and displayed in the dialog box; this information is also transferred to cell C15 of the worksheet, as shown in Figure 9-20.

Figure 9-20   **RUNNING THE PROCEDURE SUCCESSFULLY**

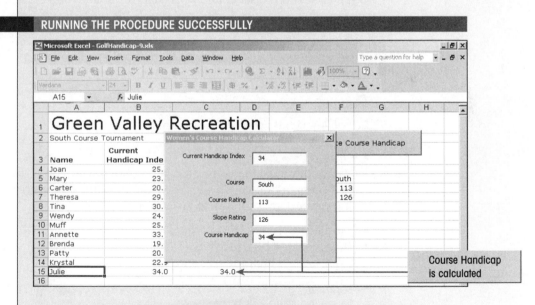

Course Handicap is calculated

5. Close the Women's Course Handicap Calculator dialog box.

   Now run the procedure using inappropriate data from a blank row.

6. Click the **Calculate Course Handicap** button, click cell **A16**, and then click the **OK** button. See Figure 9-21. Using the On Error Resume Next statement in the code merely skipped the statement that created the run-time error and continued with the next statement. In this case, the TextBoxCH.Value calculation statement was skipped, which means that the value of ActiveCell.Offset(0, 2) (in this case, A16), is null.

Figure 9-21 RUNNING THE PROCEDURE USING THE ON ERROR RESUME NEXT STATEMENT

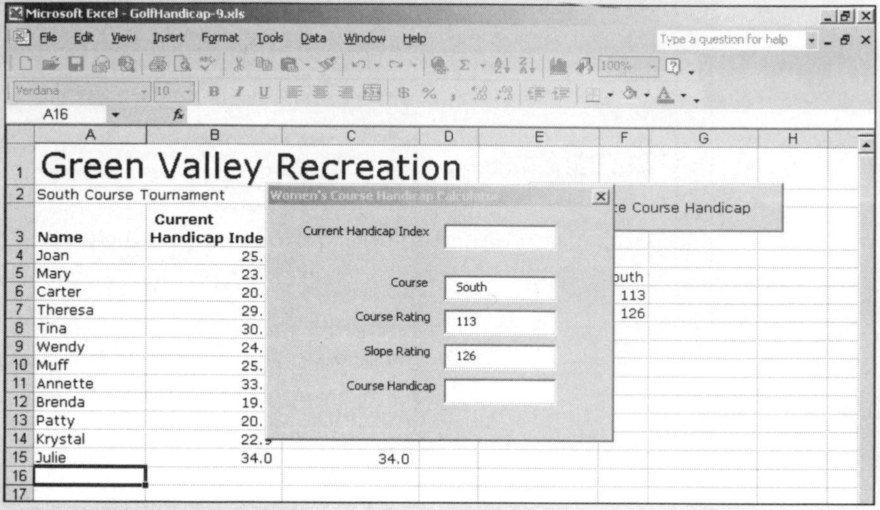

7. Close the Women's Course Handicap Calculator dialog box.

The `On Error Resume Next` statement provides a way for the procedure to continue in the event of an error so the user won't be tempted to try to debug the code in the Visual Basic Editor. A better way to handle an error is to redirect the code to a new location in the procedure that gives information to users that helps them deal with the error.

You'll use the `GoTo` statement when an error occurs to redirect the execution of the code to statements that provide feedback about the error to the user.

To use the GoTo statement to redirect code execution on a run-time error:

1. Return to the Visual Basic Editor.
2. Edit the `On Error Resume Next` statement so it becomes

   ```
   On Error GoTo ErrorHandler
   ```

   `ErrorHandler` is the name of the label that you want the procedure to jump to if an error occurs. Now you need to add the statements that will execute if the procedure is passed to the `ErrorHandler` label.
3. Modify the `End Sub` statement so it becomes **`Exit Sub`**. The `Exit Sub` statement will be executed if the error does not occur. The `Exit Sub` statement causes the procedure to end at that statement.
4. Click after the `Exit Sub` statement, press the **Enter** key, and then type the following statements, as shown in Figure 9-22:

   ```
   ErrorHandler:
       MsgBox "You must select a name in column A."
       UserForm1.Hide
   End Sub
   ```

Figure 9-22	DEFINING THE GOTO LABEL

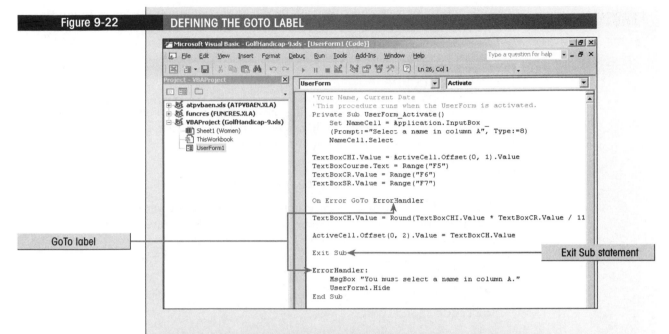

Now, when a run-time error is encountered, the `MsgBox` statement will provide a reason why the command button didn't work as intended. The `UserForm1.Hide` statement will close the Women's Course Handicap Calculator dialog box.

Now test the new code.

5. Click the **Save** button 🖫, and then return to the worksheet.

6. Click the **Calculate Course Handicap** button, click cell **A16**, and then click the **OK** button. The dialog box created by the `MsgBox` statement appears, as shown in Figure 9-23.

Figure 9-23	MSGBOX INFORMATION

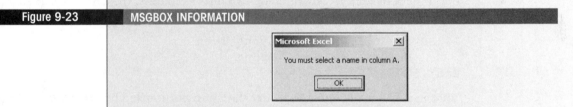

7. Click the **OK** button. The dialog box closes and the Women's Course Handicap Calculator dialog box, which is no longer needed, automatically closes too.

8. Return to the UserForm1 module in the Visual Basic Editor, click **File** on the menu bar, click **Print**, make sure the **Form Image** and **Code** check boxes are selected, and then click the **OK** button to print both the form image and code.

9. Close the Visual Basic Editor, and then close the GolfHandicap-9 workbook.

Although you cannot foresee every potential problem that a user might encounter, by piloting your applications with a few typical GVR users you can gain tremendous insight about how the rest of the employees will react to the system. You can use that feedback to improve and refine your code. By masking the most common problems with informational `On Error` statements, you can increase the productivity, shorten the training curve, and improve the overall satisfaction of your work.

If...Then Structure

The `If...Then` structure is perhaps the most common way to add logic to programming code. This structure gives the code a way to make a decision to run a set of statements depending on whether a condition is true or not. The general syntax of the `If...Then` structure is as follows:

```
If condition Then true_instructions
```

The `condition` portion of the statement is a test, the answer to which is either true or false. For example, the following three portions of VBA statements would be valid conditional expressions in an `If` statement:

```
Quantity >=1000

Range("A1").Value < 50

ActiveCell.Column <256
```

If the test evaluates "true," then the `true_instructions` portion of the statement is executed. If not, the `true_instructions` portion is skipped.

The `If...Then` structure has a several optional parts, including `Else`, `ElseIf`, and `End If` statements. The `Else` statement allows you to execute a set of statements if the test evaluates "false," the `ElseIf` statement allows you to test another condition, and the `Else` statement allows you to execute a set of statements if no previous condition is true.

The `End If` statement is required as the last statement in an `If...Then` structure when it spans multiple statements. For example, the following statement requires no `End If` statement because the entire `If...Then` structure is contained in one statement:

```
If ActiveCell.Value = "Lynn" Then MsgBox "Welcome, Lynn"
```

But if the statement were written on two lines as follows, the `End If` statement would be required:

```
If ActiveCell.Value = "Lynn" Then
      MsgBox "Welcome, Lynn"
End If
```

You can add as many statements after the `Then` portion and before the `End If` portion of the `If...Then` structure as you need, knowing that they will only be executed if the `condition` is true.

The general syntax of the `If...Then` structure that uses the `Else` and `ElseIf` structures follows:

```
If condition1 Then
      true_instructions for condition1
ElseIf condition2 Then
      true_instructions for condition2
Else
      instructions if neither condition is true
End If
```

You can test multiple conditions by using the `ElseIf` statement. This approach enables the code to decide which statements to run when there are more than two possible outcomes.

`If` statements are commonly used to control the execution of custom functions. They are also used in sub procedures to check for common conditions that help the code determine where entries or actions should occur in the workbook.

GVR is planning a golf tournament to raise money for the renovation of public golf facilities, and a few pledges come in every day. Lynn has asked you to automate the entries of the golf tournament pledges. You'll use VBA code to determine the row that represents the next available row at the end of the list. You want to prompt the user with dialog boxes created by `InputBox` statements for the next entry in the list. You'll use an `If...Then` structure to exit the procedure if the users decide that they don't want to make an entry. You'll call the new sub `EnterPledge`.

To create the EnterPledge sub:

1. Open the **GolfTournament-9** workbook located in the Tutorial.09\Tutorial folder on your Data Disk.

2. Press the **Page Down key** to view the list of last names and pledges on the Members worksheet. The first blank row is row 42. You want to build a VBA procedure that prompts the user for the values for the LastName and Pledge columns and inserts the values in the next blank row.

3. Press **Ctrl + Home** to return to cell A1, and then press **Alt + F11** to open the Visual Basic Editor.

4. Click the **list arrow** for the Insert UserForm button , and then click **Module**.

5. Enter the VBA code for the `EnterPledge` sub shown in Figure 9-24.

| Figure 9-24 | VBA CODE FOR ENTERPLEDGE SUB |

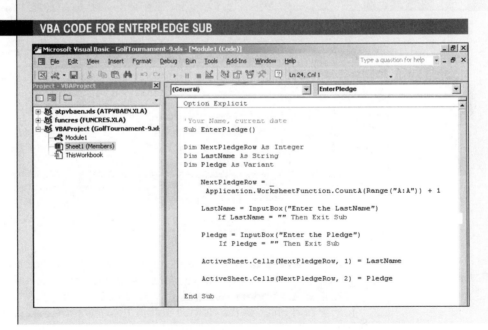

The `Dim` statements declare three variables used in the `EnterPledge` sub. The reason that you declared the `Pledge` variable with the `Variant` data type is because the `InputBox` function always returns a string value. Later, you may want to use the `Pledge` variable in a calculation, so you'll declare it with the versatile (yet memory intensive) Variant data type rather than declare it as a String data type. The `NextPledgeRow` statement uses the `WorksheetFunction` object, contained in the `Application` object, to call the Excel COUNTA function, which counts the number of cells that are not empty in the given range, column A. Unlike the COUNT function (which only counts numeric entries), COUNTA also counts labels. Therefore, the `NextPledgeRow` variable will hold the integer that represents the number of entries in column A plus one, which should represent the next blank row.

The `LastName =` and `Pledge =` statements assign the value entered through the `InputBox` statement into those variables. If the user does not enter anything, the `If` statement executes the `Exit Sub` statement. But, if the user makes an entry, it is assigned to the range identified by the `ActiveSheet.Cells` statements.

Note that in the `ActiveSheet.Cells` statements, the row is determined by the value of the `NextPledgeRow` variable. Now you need to test the sub, but first you will add a command button to the GolfTournament workbook to make the `EnterPledge` sub easy to run.

To add a command button to run the EnterPledge sub:

1. Click the **Save** button 🖫, and then return to the Excel workbook.

   To make the `EnterPledge` sub easier to run than running it as a macro from the Tools menu, you'll add a command button to the workbook that executes the `EnterPledge` sub.

2. Right-click any toolbar and then click **Forms**. The Forms toolbar appears.

3. Click the **Button** button 🔲 on the Forms toolbar, and then click cell **E1**. The Assign Macro dialog box appears, as shown in Figure 9-25, prompting you to attach a macro to the button.

Figure 9-25   ASSIGN MACRO DIALOG BOX

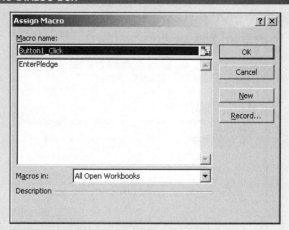

4. Click **EnterPledge** in the Macro name list and then click the **OK** button. With the command button added to the workbook that will run the `EnterPledge` sub, it will be easier to test the new macro. But, first, you will make the button larger and change the default Button 1 text to something more meaningful.

5. Drag the lower-right corner of the button to cell **G4**, select the **Button 1** text, and then type **Enter New Pledge**.

6. Close the Forms toolbar and then click on any cell in the workbook. The new button is shown in Figure 9-26.

Figure 9-26	ENTER NEW PLEDGE BUTTON

Now you'll test the `EnterPledge` sub using the new button.

To test the EnterPledge sub:

1. Click the **Enter New Pledge** button. The dialog box that prompts you for the value for the last name appears. Test the true condition of the first `If` statement by entering nothing.

2. Click the **OK** button. Because there was no entry for the `LastName` variable, the condition of the first `If` statement evaluated to true, and the `Exit Sub` statement was executed, ending the subroutine.

   Now test the second `If` statement.

3. Click the **Enter New Pledge** button.

4. Type *your last name*, and then click the **OK** button. The dialog box that prompts you for the value of the pledge appears. Test the true condition of the second `If` statement by not entering a pledge amount in this dialog box.

5. Click the **OK** button. Because there was no entry for the `Pledge` variable, the condition of the second `If` statement evaluated to true, and the `Exit Sub` statement was executed, ending the subroutine. Now test the function when both `If` statements evaluate to true (when there is an entry in the `InputBox` dialog box for both prompts).

6. Click the **Enter New Pledge** button. The dialog box that prompts you for a last name appears.

7. Type *your last name*, and then click the **OK** button. The dialog box that prompts you for the pledge value appears.

8. Type **500** and then click the **OK** button.

9. Press the **Page Down** key to view row 42. Your last name appears in cell A42 and 500 in cell B42.

When you use `If` statements, you should test each potential condition. In this case, there are three possible ways that a user could execute this code: The first `If` statement could evaluate to false, which should execute the first `Exit Sub` statement. The first `If` statement could be true, but the second `If` statement could evaluate to false, which should execute the second `Exit Sub` statement. Or both `If` statements could evaluate to true, which should execute the `ActiveSheet.Cells` statements. When both `If` statements evaluate to true, the `ActiveSheet.Cells` statements take the entries from the `InputBox` values and enter them into the workbook.

Select Case Structure

Although the `If...Then` structure is the most popular choice for choosing between two alternatives, the `Select Case` structure is very useful when you have three or more options. The general syntax of the `Select Case` structure is:

```
Select Case TestExpression
     Case expression1
          instructions when TestExpression = expression1
     Case expression2
          instructions when TestExpression = expression2
     Case expression3
          instructions when TestExpression = expression3
     Case Else
          instructions when no expressions are true
End Select
```

GVR has set up three levels of charitable contributions. The names of the members who donate at each level will be printed in the annual report. Members who give $1000 or more are part of the Gold Club. Members who give $500 to $999 are part of the Silver Club, and members who give $1 to $499 are part of the Bronze Club. You'll use the `Select Case` structure to automatically enter the club membership for each pledge in column C. You'll add this code to the end of the `EnterPledge` sub so that as new pledges are recorded, the club is automatically recorded in column C, based on the pledge amount in column B.

To add the Select Case structure to the EnterPledge sub:

1. Return to the Visual Basic Editor.

2. Add the code shown in Figure 9-27 to the end of the `EnterPledge` sub. The statements will select and then execute the appropriate statement based on the value of the `Pledge` variable.

| Figure 9-27 | ADDING THE SELECT CASE STATEMENTS TO THE ENTERPLEDGE SUB PROCEDURE |

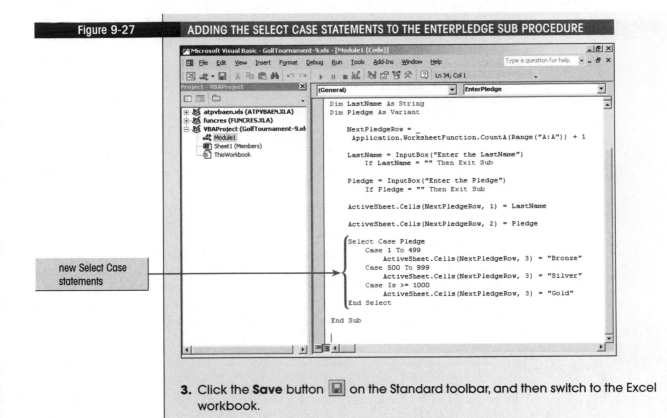

new Select Case
statements

```
Dim LastName As String
Dim Pledge As Variant

    NextPledgeRow = _
        Application.WorksheetFunction.CountA(Range("A:A")) + 1

    LastName = InputBox("Enter the LastName")
        If LastName = "" Then Exit Sub

    Pledge = InputBox("Enter the Pledge")
        If Pledge = "" Then Exit Sub

    ActiveSheet.Cells(NextPledgeRow, 1) = LastName

    ActiveSheet.Cells(NextPledgeRow, 2) = Pledge

    Select Case Pledge
        Case 1 To 499
            ActiveSheet.Cells(NextPledgeRow, 3) = "Bronze"
        Case 500 To 999
            ActiveSheet.Cells(NextPledgeRow, 3) = "Silver"
        Case Is >= 1000
            ActiveSheet.Cells(NextPledgeRow, 3) = "Gold"
    End Select

End Sub
```

3. Click the **Save** button 🖫 on the Standard toolbar, and then switch to the Excel workbook.

Now test the new Select Case statements.

To test the Select Case statements by entering three pledges:

1. Click the **Enter New Pledge** button.

2. Type **Smith**, click the **OK** button, type **50**, and then click the **OK** button.

3. Click the **Enter New Pledge** button.

4. Type **Washington**, click the **OK** button, type **500**, and then click the **OK** button.

5. Click the **Enter New Pledge** button.

6. Type **Lahey**, click the **OK** button, type **1000**, and then click the **OK** button.

7. Scroll down to view rows 43 through 45. See Figure 9-28. "Bronze" appears in cell C43 because the value in cell B43 is between 1 and 499. "Silver" appears in cell C44 because the value in cell B44 is between 500 and 999. "Gold" appears in cell C45 because the value in cell B45 is greater than or equal to 1000.

Figure 9-28   TESTING THE SELECT CASE STATEMENTS

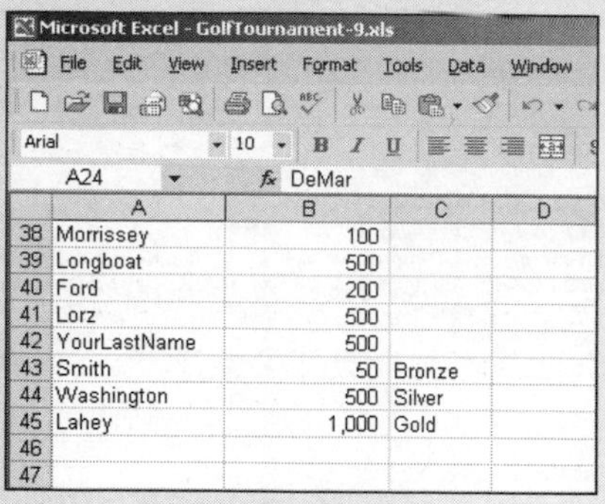

VBA exits the `Select Case` structure as soon as a true condition is found and that statement is executed. Therefore, you might want to enter the most common condition first. You can nest `Select Case` structures just as you can nest `If` statements. Just as a multiline `If` statement needs an `End If` statement to mark the end of that structure, each `Select Case` structure needs a corresponding `End Select` statement.

Creating Loops

A **loop** is a set of VBA statements that are repeated until some condition is met or some condition is true. There are two basic looping structures: `For…Next` and `Do…Loop`.

For…Next Loop

The `For…Next` loop structure uses a counter to determine how many times a set of instructions should be executed. The general syntax of the `For…Next` loop is:

```
For Counter = StartValue to EndValue
        instructions for each value from StartValue to EndValue
Next Counter
```

In other words, the instructions between the `For` and `Next` statements will be executed as many times as it takes the `Counter` variable to move from the `StartValue` through the `EndValue`.

You want the `EnterNewPledge` sub to prompt you for the next entry, without having to go back and click the Enter New Pledge button between each new pledge. You'll surround the code with a `For…Next` loop so that it continues to run until you encounter one of the two exit points, an empty entry in either dialog box created by the `InputBox` statements.

To create a For…Next loop in the `EnterPledge` *sub:*

1. Return to the Visual Basic Editor, and then edit the code so that it looks like Figure 9-29. The three statements added are the `Dim Count As Integer` statement, the `For Count = 1 To 50`, and the `Next Count` statements. The GVR employees typically enter anywhere from 1 to 10 new pledges into this workbook at a time. Therefore, you arbitrarily chose 50 as the upper value for the counter to optimistically anticipate 50 consecutive entries. You want the upper value to be larger than the maximum number of entries that you would

anticipate so that the code doesn't stop before the user has entered the final pledge. Yet you don't want the value to be so high that it would cause a long wait if the code were broken and had to loop through each value for the `Count` variable before it stopped. Also, note that blank lines have been deleted, and code has been indented to make the procedure easier to read on one screen.

| Figure 9-29 | ADDING A FOR...NEXT LOOP |

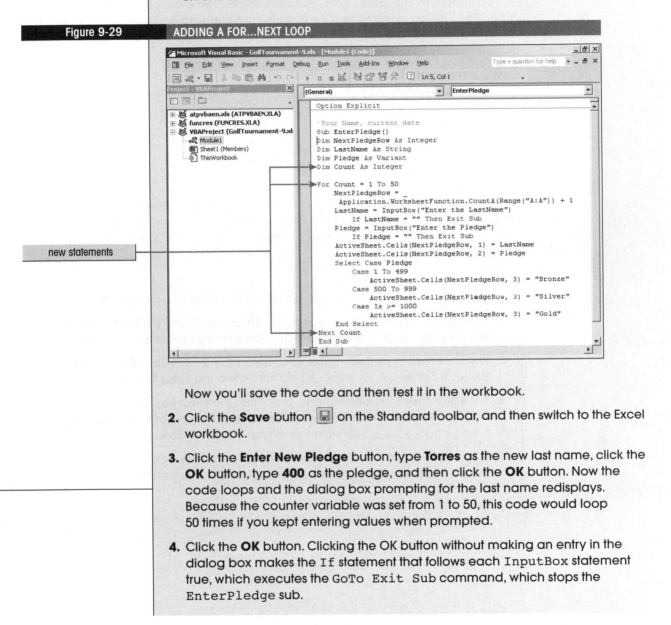

new statements

Now you'll save the code and then test it in the workbook.

2. Click the **Save** button 🖫 on the Standard toolbar, and then switch to the Excel workbook.

3. Click the **Enter New Pledge** button, type **Torres** as the new last name, click the **OK** button, type **400** as the pledge, and then click the **OK** button. Now the code loops and the dialog box prompting for the last name redisplays. Because the counter variable was set from 1 to 50, this code would loop 50 times if you kept entering values when prompted.

4. Click the **OK** button. Clicking the OK button without making an entry in the dialog box makes the `If` statement that follows each `InputBox` statement true, which executes the `GoTo Exit Sub` command, which stops the `EnterPledge` sub.

Use the `For...Next` structure to loop through statements a given number of times. Closely related to the `For...Next` structure is the `For...Each` structure. Use the `For...Each` structure to loop through all of the objects in a collection. In other words, you could use the `For...Each` loop to apply the same command to each worksheet in the worksheets collection. For example, you might want to apply the same page setup commands to each worksheet in the worksheets collection. Any time you want to do the same set of statements multiple times, there is a looping structure that will help you.

Do...Loops

A Do...Loop is sometimes called an "indefinite" loop because you don't set a specific number of times for the loop to repeat as you did with the For...Next structure. Instead, a Do...Loop continues processing until a certain condition is true. There are two variations of the Do...Loop: Do While and Do Until.

As indicated by the names, a Do While loop executes *while* a specified condition is true. A Do Until loop executes *until* a specified condition is true. Therefore, your decision to use one of these structures often depends on how you want to state the condition itself. The general syntax of a Do...Loop is:

```
Do Until condition is true
        instructions
Loop
```
or

```
Do While condition is true
        instructions
Loop
```

To practice using a Do...Loop, you will build a procedure that will test whether or not the Club membership label has been entered in column C. You want the code to loop for each row in which an entry hasn't already been made. You'll call the procedure ClubMembership.

To create the ClubMembership sub using a Do...Loop:

1. Click cell **C1**, type **Club**, and press the **Enter** key. "Club" will be the column heading for the entries you want to automatically create for column C.

2. Return to the Visual Basic Editor, click below the End Sub statement for the EnterPledge sub procedure, and then press the **Enter** key twice.

3. Type **Sub ClubMembership** and then press the **Enter** key. The Visual Basic Editor automatically enters the parentheses at the end of the sub procedure's name and the End Sub statement in the Code window.

4. Enter the VBA code shown in Figure 9-30 between the Sub and End Sub statements. Note that the ClubCellRow variable is incremented by 1.

Figure 9-30   **ENTERING CODE FOR CLUBMEMBERSHIP SUB PROCEDURE**

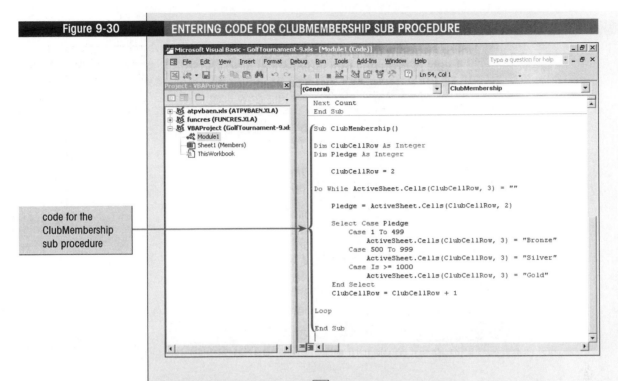

code for the
ClubMembership
sub procedure

```
Next Count
End Sub

Sub ClubMembership()

Dim ClubCellRow As Integer
Dim Pledge As Integer

    ClubCellRow = 2

Do While ActiveSheet.Cells(ClubCellRow, 3) = ""

    Pledge = ActiveSheet.Cells(ClubCellRow, 2)

    Select Case Pledge
        Case 1 To 499
            ActiveSheet.Cells(ClubCellRow, 3) = "Bronze"
        Case 500 To 999
            ActiveSheet.Cells(ClubCellRow, 3) = "Silver"
        Case Is >= 1000
            ActiveSheet.Cells(ClubCellRow, 3) = "Gold"
    End Select
    ClubCellRow = ClubCellRow + 1

Loop

End Sub
```

5. Click the **Save** button 🖫 on the Standard toolbar, and then return to the Excel workbook.

   Because you only need to run this procedure once to fill the existing pledge rows that have not been assigned to a club, you won't create a button to run this procedure. Instead, you'll run it from the Tools menu.

6. Click **Tools** on the menu bar, point to **Macro**, and then click **Macros**.

7. Double-click **ClubMembership** to run the macro. The values in range C2:C41 are automatically filled in with the appropriate club designation as shown in Figure 9-31.

Figure 9-31   RUNNING THE CLUBMEMBERSHIP SUB PROCEDURE

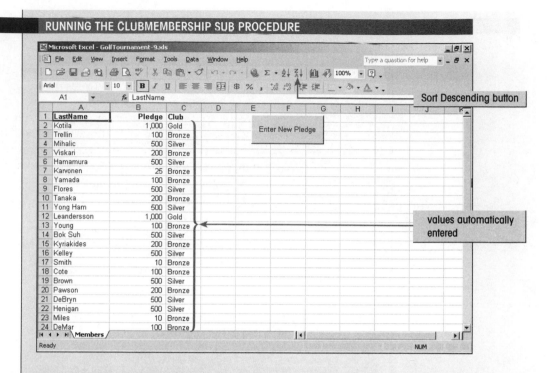

To make sure that the clubs were assigned correctly, you'll sort the records.

8. Click any value in column **B**, click the **Sort Descending** button [Z↓] on the Standard toolbar, and then scroll down column C to view all of the new entries.

9. Save the workbook, and then print the worksheet with your name in the left section of the header.

10. Switch to the Visual Basic Editor, and then print Module1.

11. Close the Visual Basic Editor, and close the GolfTournament-9 workbook.

A Do...Loop is very flexible because it allows the procedure to loop through code as many times as a condition is true or until a condition is true. Knowing how to control statement execution using GoTo, If...Then, For...Next, and Do...Loop statements will greatly expand your abilities as a VBA programmer.

Session 9.2 QUICK CHECK

1. You most often see GoTo statements in conjunction with what situation?

2. In what situation do you *not* need to follow an If statement with an End If statement?

3. When would it make more sense to use the Select Case statement than the If statement?

4. What is the difference between the For...Next and For...Each structures?

5. What is the difference between the Do While and Do Until loops?

REVIEW ASSIGNMENTS

Lynn wants you to use the new skills you've learned about variables, data types, and control structures to finish the GOLFFEE function that calculates the annual golf fee for each member. GVR offers discounts to certain age groups as well as to those members who live in certain zip codes. To calculate the appropriate discounts, you've declared two variables to be used as arguments within the function: `ZipCode As String` and `BDay As Date`. To complete the GOLFFEE function, you need to add logic statements that will evaluate the `ZipCode` and `BDay` arguments and apply the appropriate discounts to the golf fee calculation.

To complete this task:

1. Start Excel and open the **GolfFee-9** workbook located in the Tutorial.09\Review folder on your Data Disk. Enable macros. The worksheet presents some of the information used to determine actual golf fees. The standard fee is in cell C4, $500, but discounts may be applied if a person is within a certain age group and lives within a certain zip code.

   The age discounts are: for members who are 0 to 5 years of age, 100%; ages 6 to 12, 50%; ages 13 to 18, 25%; and ages 70 and up, 25%.

   GVR also offers another 10% discount if the individual lives in a zip code 77000, 77001, or 77002. This discount is applied to the golf fee after the applicable age discount is applied.

2. Open the Visual Basic Editor and view the start of the GOLFFEE function in Module1. Your task is to create the code necessary to calculate the appropriate value for the GOLFFEE function based on the rules identified in Step 1. Use the following guidelines:

   - Enter your name and the current date as a comment at the top of the module.
   - Set `GOLFFEE` equal to 500 at the beginning of the function. $500 is the base golf membership fee, before any appropriate discounts are applied.
   - Declare another variable named `Age` with a `Date` data type.
   - Calculate the `Age` variable using the following formula:

     `Age = Int((Now() - BDay) / 365)`

   - Use `Select Case` statements to determine if the member's age is 0 to 5, 6 to 12, 13 to 18, or greater than 70 and apply the appropriate discount to the GOLFFEE function.
   - Add an `Exit Function` statement at the end of the Case 0 to 5 section. (*Note*: The `Exit Function` statement is necessary so that the additional discount for the zip code isn't applied when the golf fee is already equal to 0 for ages 0 to 5.)
   - Use the `If...Then...ElseIf` code to apply the 10% discount for those members who live in zip codes 77000, 77001, or 77002.

3. Save the changes you have made, and then switch to the GolfFee-9 workbook.

4. Make the following entries in the workbook to test the GOLFFEE function:

   A7: 77000
   B7: 5/5/2000
   C7: =Int((Today()-B7)/365)
   D7: =GOLFFEE(A7,B7)

(*Hint*: The ages in column C will vary based on the current date, but the value in cell D7 should be 0 if the individual is in the 0 to 5 age group.)

5. Now you want to test all combinations. You have five different age groups to test and four different zip codes for a total of 20 groups. First, set up the zip code tests for each of the five age groups. Enter "77001" in cell A8, "77002" in cell A9, and "77003" in cell A10. Copy the range A7:A10 to the ranges A11:A14, A15:A18, A19:A22, and A23:A26.
6. Now you need to set up the birthdays so you can test each age group for each of the four zip codes. Copy cell B7 to range B8:B10.
7. Copy the formula in cell C7 through range C8:C26 to help you quickly calculate the rest of the ages and golf fees for the birthdates you are about to enter.
8. Copy the formula in cell D7 through range D8:D26.
9. In the range B11:B14, enter a birthdate that calculates an age between 6 and 12 (the age will be displayed in the range C11:C14).
10. In the range B15:B18, enter a birthdate that calculates an age between 13 and 18 (the age will be displayed in the range C15:C18).
11. In the range B19:B22, enter a birthdate that calculates an age between 19 and 69 (the age will be displayed in the range C19:C22).
12. In the range B23:B26, enter a birthdate that calculates an age greater than 70 (the age will be displayed in the range C23:C26).
13. Format column D with the Currency Style format, and widen the columns as shown in Figure 9-32. Depending upon the date that you complete this exercise, you may have to use different birthdate values in column B to calculate ages within each age group.

Figure 9-32

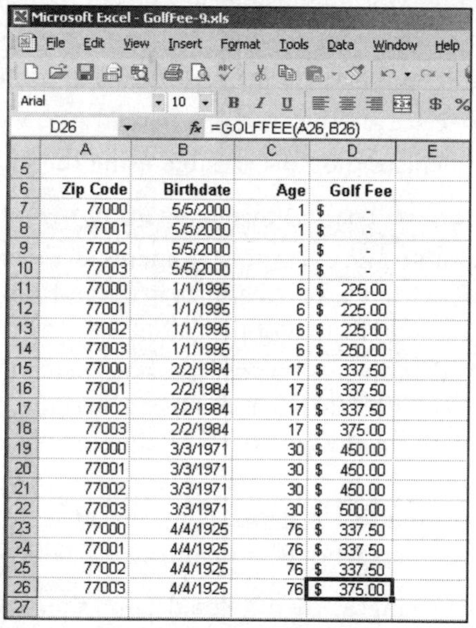

	A	B	C	D	E
5					
6	Zip Code	Birthdate	Age	Golf Fee	
7	77000	5/5/2000	1	$ -	
8	77001	5/5/2000	1	$ -	
9	77002	5/5/2000	1	$ -	
10	77003	5/5/2000	1	$ -	
11	77000	1/1/1995	6	$ 225.00	
12	77001	1/1/1995	6	$ 225.00	
13	77002	1/1/1995	6	$ 225.00	
14	77003	1/1/1995	6	$ 250.00	
15	77000	2/2/1984	17	$ 337.50	
16	77001	2/2/1984	17	$ 337.50	
17	77002	2/2/1984	17	$ 337.50	
18	77003	2/2/1984	17	$ 375.00	
19	77000	3/3/1971	30	$ 450.00	
20	77001	3/3/1971	30	$ 450.00	
21	77002	3/3/1971	30	$ 450.00	
22	77003	3/3/1971	30	$ 500.00	
23	77000	4/4/1925	76	$ 337.50	
24	77001	4/4/1925	76	$ 337.50	
25	77002	4/4/1925	76	$ 337.50	
26	77003	4/4/1925	76	$ 375.00	
27					

14. Save the GolfFee-9 workbook, and then print the Sheet1 worksheet with your name in the left section of the header.
15. Return to the Visual Basic Editor, and then print the GOLFFEE function stored in Module1.
16. Close the Visual Basic Editor, close the GolfFee-9 workbook, and then exit Excel.

CASE PROBLEMS

Case 1. Exploring How Data Types Affect Processing Speed You've enrolled in a VBA class at a local community college. One of the assignments is to create a procedure that clarifies the value of declaring your variables with specific data types as it relates to processing speed. To complete this task, the instructor has asked that you use the VBA Timer function to determine the time that it takes to execute the same statements in two different procedures: one that declares its variables with a specific data type, and one that does not declare its variables.

To complete this task:

1. Start Excel, open a new, blank workbook, and then save it with the filename **Test-9** in the Tutorial.09\Cases folder on your Data Disk.

Explore 2. Open the Visual Basic Editor, and then use Visual Basic Help to research the Timer function that you'll use for this exercise.

3. Read the information that explains the Timer function, print the page, and then close Help. You will build a procedure that tests the speed of a long loop by capturing the value of the Timer function before and after completing the loop, and then calculating the difference. You'll run the loop with variables declared and with variables not declared so that you can capture the difference in the time it takes the procedure to run.

Explore 4. Insert a new module and then enter the `DataTypeTest` sub as shown in Figure 9-33. Notice the syntax for declaring more than one variable in a single statement. The code in the loops manipulates the values of `Variable1` and `Varible2` to create three results. The calculations and loops themselves are meaningless. They are used only to create enough computer cycles so that the difference in speed between using declared and undeclared variables within the procedure is significant.

This sub will return the difference between the `StartTime` and `EndTime` variables to cell A5 in the workbook with all of the variables used in the subroutine declared. Be sure to delete the `Option Explicit` statement if it is automatically entered in the Code window. You can't use the `Option Explicit` statement when you test code that doesn't declare the variables used in the procedure, so you eliminate it from the test altogether.

Figure 9-33

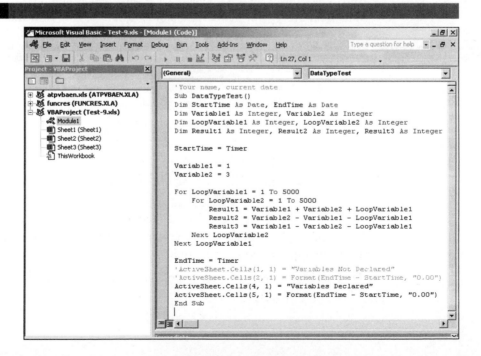

5. Save the code, switch to the Excel workbook, and then run the `DataTypeTest` sub. Obviously, the results of this test will be highly influenced by the speed of your computer. Even with a current computer, though, the test will probably take a few seconds. When the procedure has finished, the difference between the `EndTime` and `StartTime` will be inserted in the `ActiveSheet.Cells(5,1)` object, cell A5.

6. Return to the Visual Basic Editor, and then remove and add apostrophes as needed so that the `DataTypeTest` sub looks like Figure 9-34. This sub will return the difference between the `StartTime` and `EndTime` variables to cell A2 in the workbook without declaring any of the variables.

Figure 9-34

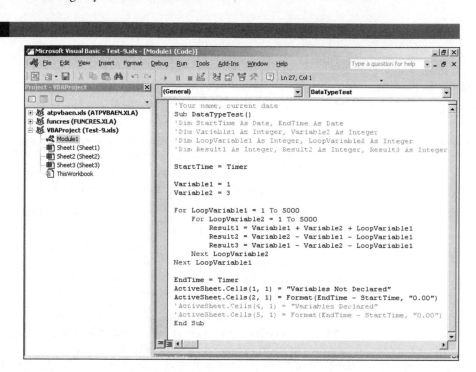

7. Save your changes, switch to the Excel workbook, and then run the `DataTypeTest` sub. The values that are calculated will vary, depending on the speed of your computer. The final Test-9 workbook should look similar to that shown in Figure 9-35.

Figure 9-35

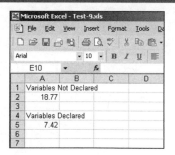

8. Print the Test-9 workbook with your name in the left section of the header, and then print the `DataTypeTest` module.

9. Save and close the Test-9 workbook, and then exit Excel.

Case 2. Adding Up an Unknown Range of Values Just as it's common for an Excel workbook to include a formula that adds up a column or row of cells, you often need to simulate this action within a VBA procedure as well. When you insert a formula in a workbook that adds up a column of values, you have the benefit of knowing which cell should contain the formula, as well as which range of cells should be added. Therefore, when you click on the AutoSum button to insert the formula, you can visually verify whether the correct range was selected for the SUM function. When you are creating a formula in VBA, though, the code will have to determine where to insert the formula, as well as how many cells are in the range of values to be added. Because you know that this type of problem is common to VBA programmers, you want to study the code that adds up the values of a variable range of numbers. In this exercise, you'll build such a procedure.

To complete this task:

1. Start Excel and then open a new, blank workbook.

2. Open the Visual Basic Editor, and then insert a new module.

Explore

3. Enter the following code, shown in Figure 9-36.

Figure 9-36

```
Option Explicit
'Your Name, current date
Sub AddColumn()
    'Declare the two range variables
    Dim ColumnRange As Range
    Dim ColumnTotal As Range

    'Set ColumnRange equal to the range surrounding the active cell
    Set ColumnRange = ActiveCell.CurrentRegion

    'Set ColumnTotal equal to the cell that is offset the same number of rows
    ' as contained within the ColumnRange, and offset 0 columns
    ' Use the .Resize(1) property to resize the range to only one row tall
    Set ColumnTotal = ColumnRange.Offset(ColumnRange.Rows.Count, 0).Rows(1)

    'Use the .Formula property to build the final formula
    ' using the range returned by the Address property of the ColumnRange variable
    ColumnTotal.Formula = "=SUM(" & ColumnRange.Address & ")"

End Sub
```

4. Save the workbook with the name **AddColumn-9** in the Tutorial.09\Cases folder on your Data Disk, and then switch to the Excel workbook.

5. Enter the ranges shown in Figure 9-37. You will use these values to test the `AddColumn` sub.

Figure 9-37

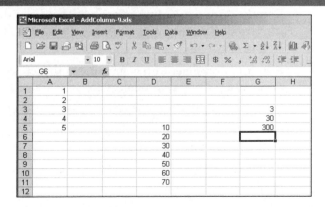

6. Test the **AddColumn** sub by clicking any value in the range A1:A5 and then running the sub. The value of 15 should have been entered in cell A6.

7. Test the **AddColumn** sub by clicking any value in the range D5:D11 and then running the sub. The value of 280 should have been entered in cell D12.

8. Test the **AddColumn** sub by clicking any value in the range G3:G5 and then running the sub. The value of 333 should have been entered in cell G6.

9. Save the workbook and then examine the formulas in cells A6, D12, and G6. Display the formulas in the worksheet, and then print it with your name in the left section of the header.

10. Print the module that contains the **AddColumn** sub, and then close the Visual Basic Editor.

11. Close the AddColumn-9 workbook, and then exit Excel.

Case 3. Using the For Each Statement to Convert Uppercase Values to Proper Case Values As a business analyst for an insurance company, you regularly work with data that is imported from an outside information bureau. The text entries of the imported data are all uppercase or lowercase letters. You'll use the **For Each** statement to loop through each cell and convert it to proper case.

To complete this task:

1. Start Excel and open the **PatientAssignmentList-9** workbook located in the Tutorial.09\Cases folder on your Data Disk. Note that all of the data in columns A, B, C, and D is entered in all uppercase. The field names for data records are entered in row 1.

2. Open the Visual Basic Editor, insert a new module, and then enter a comment line with your name and the current date.

3. Start a new sub as shown here:

```
Sub ConvertToProper()

Dim Cell As Range
Dim ConversionRange As Range

Set ConversionRange = ActiveCell.CurrentRegion
  For Each Cell In ConversionRange
  Cell.Value = Application.WorksheetFunction.Proper(Cell.Value)
  Next Cell
End Sub
```

4. Save the code, switch to the Stats worksheet in the workbook, and then click in any cell in the range A2:E41.

5. Run the **ConvertToProper** sub. All values in the range A2:D41 should have been converted to proper case. The numeric values in column E are not affected by the Proper function.

6. Print the worksheet with your name in the left section of the header, and then print the **ConvertToProper** module. Close the Visual Basic Editor.

7. Save and close the PatientAssignmentList-9 workbook, and then exit Excel.

Case 4. Exploring Optional Arguments of the MsgBox Function You have heard from other VBA programmers that they use the VBA MsgBox function as a debugging tool to pause code and display the result of a calculation or assignment while they are writing it. You want to write a subprocedure that incorporates an If...Then structure and the MsgBox function so that you can learn more about the MsgBox function and its optional arguments.

To complete this task:

1. Start Excel, open a new, blank workbook, and then save the workbook as **MessageBox-9** in the Tutorial.09\Cases folder on your Data Disk.

2. Open the Visual Basic Editor, and then use the Visual Basic Help to research the MsgBox function that you need to use. Print the MsgBox Function page.

3. Click the Example link on the MsgBox Function page, and then print the MsgBox Function Example page.

4. Select all of the code from the Dim statement through the End If statement on the MsgBox Function Example page, right-click within the selection, click Copy on the shortcut menu, and then close Help.

5. Insert a new module, enter the starting statement Sub MsgBoxExample( ), press the Enter key to insert the ending statement End Sub, and then paste the example code in between the Sub and End Sub statements.

6. Run the procedure from within the Visual Basic Editor, and then click the Yes button when presented with a message box asking if you want to continue. Switch to the Excel workbook, run the sub again, and click the No button when asked to continue.

Explore   7. Return to the Visual Basic Editor, and then modify the code so that the variable used as the Style argument defines the buttons so that they display "Yes", "No", and "Cancel"; the icon displays a Warning Message icon; and the first button is selected by default. (*Hint*: Use the information you printed about the MsgBox function for assistance.)

Explore   8. Modify the code so that the variable used as the Title argument reads "*Your name's* test".

Explore   9. Modify the code so that the variable used as the Msg argument reads: "This is only a test".

10. Delete the statements used to assign variable values to the Help file and context arguments, Help and Ctxt.

11. Delete the portion of the Dim statement that declares the Help and Ctxt variables, and delete the use of those variables in the Response assignment statement.

12. Replace the MyString = "Yes" and MyString = "No" statements with the appropriate MsgBox statement as follows:

```
MsgBox ("Execute Yes statements")
MsgBox ("Execute No statements")
```

13. Delete the MyString variable in the Dim statement because the variable is no longer used in the code.

14. Run the MsgBoxExample sub to test it. See Figure 9-38 for the dialog box that should result.

Figure 9-38

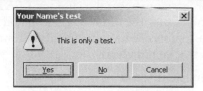

15. Press the Print Screen key when you see the dialog box shown in Figure 9-38, start a word processing program, paste the image of the screen into a blank document, and then print it. On the printout, draw lines to identify the elements of the dialog box that the `Msg`, `Style`, and `Title` arguments have created. Close the word processing program without saving the document.

16. Click the Yes button to make sure that the "Execute Yes statements" message is displayed, and then click the OK button.

17. Rerun the `MsgBoxExample` sub, and then click the No button to make sure that the "Execute No statements" message is displayed. Click the OK button.

18. Rerun the `MsgBoxExample` sub, and then click the Cancel button. The code ran the `Else` portion of the statement, which is the same result as clicking the No button.

Explore 19. Modify the `If...Then...Else` structure as follows:

```
If Response = vbYes Then      ' User chose Yes.

      MsgBox ("Execute Yes statements")

ElseIf Response = vbNo Then     ' User chose No.

      MsgBox ("Execute No statements")

Else      'User chose Cancel.

      MsgBox ("Execute Cancel statements")

End If
```

20. Rerun the `MsgBoxExample` sub three times, testing the Yes, No, and Cancel buttons. Make sure that in each case the appropriate `MsgBox` message appears.

21. Save the changes, print the `MsgBoxExample` sub, and then close the Visual Basic Editor.

22. Close the MessageBox-9 workbook, and then exit Excel.

Quick Check Answers

Session 9.1

1. A VBA variable name must adhere to the following rules:
   - The first letter must be alphabetic, although you can use numbers and some special characters such as the underscore in variable names.

- Because VBA is not case sensitive, MORTGAGERATE, mortgagerate, Mortgagerate and MortgageRate are the same variable name, but since variable names are easier to read if the first character of each word is capitalized, some VBA programmers like to use mixed-case names such as MortgageRate for variables.

- Variable names cannot include spaces or periods, but underscores are allowed. Therefore, some VBA programmers like to create variable names with an underscore between words such as Mortgage_Rate.

- You cannot use #, $, %, &, or ! characters in variable names.

- Variable names must be less than 255 characters long.

2. If you don't declare a specific data type for a variable, VBA will assign the Variant data type.

3. By default, VBA records absolute cell references for cells.

4. To manipulate a range object, you can:

- Use the `Range` property of the `Worksheet` object

- Use the `Range` property of a `Range` object

- Use the `Cells` property of a `Worksheet` object

- Use the `Cells` property of a `Range` object

- Use the `Offset` property of a `Range` object

5. The macro recorder uses the `Offset` property of the `Range` object to work with relative references.

Session 9.2

1. The most common place you see the `GoTo` statement is in conjunction with handling errors.

2. An `If` statement that uses only one line does not need to be closed by an `End If` statement.

3. You should use the `Select Case` structure when you have three or more options because embedded `If` statements can be more confusing than a series of `Select Case` statements.

4. Use the `For...Next` structure to loop through statements a given number of times. Use the `For...Each` structure to loop through all of the objects in a collection.

5. A `Do While` loop executes *while* a specified condition is true. A `Do Until` loop executes *until* a specified condition is true.

SHARING EXCEL DATA WITH OTHER PROGRAMS

Importing, Linking, and Using VBA to Share Excel Data with Access Databases and the Web

CASE

Green Valley Recreation

Green Valley Recreation (GVR) has grown rapidly over the past few years. Like most companies, users have created various solutions to departmental data management issues. Depending upon the amount of data they need to manage and their own skills with various software programs, they have created a variety of solutions involving Excel workbooks and Access databases. Now many of those departments would like to share information. Lynn Tse, the director of GVR, needs your help in evaluating each situation and implementing an appropriate solution.

In this tutorial, you will use many Excel and VBA features to import, link, and embed information from other data sources. You'll also load and install add-ins, Excel programs that add new functionality to an existing Excel workbook.

SESSION 10.1

In this session, you will learn about the various sources of data that an Excel workbook can import. You'll work with various import tools including Microsoft Query. You'll also use VBA to import Access data to an Excel workbook, and you'll study the VBA statements required to make a connection to an external file and to select the appropriate data to import.

Importing Data

Importing is the process of bringing data from another program file into an Excel workbook. You can import data into an Excel workbook using different techniques. For example, some types of files can be directly imported into Excel by selecting the Open option on the File menu, just as you would open an existing Excel workbook. Other file types, however, require the use of special tools such as the Data Connection Wizard, which starts when you use the Data menu, in order to successfully pass data from one file format to another. Figure 10-1 shows the list of files that can be directly opened within Excel 2002 using the Open command on the File menu and a list of those that can be imported using the Import External Data command on the Data menu.

Note: To import data in Excel 2000 you use the Get External Data command on the Data menu.

Figure 10-1	BRINGING EXTERNAL FILES INTO EXCEL
FILES OPENED USING THE OPEN COMMAND	**FILES IMPORTED USING THE IMPORT EXTERNAL DATA COMMAND:**
• Microsoft Excel Worksheets, .XLS	• Excel Workbooks, .XLS
• Microsoft Excel Macros, .XLM, .XLA	
• Microsoft Excel Charts, .XLS	
• Microsoft Excel 4.0 Workbooks, .XLW	
• Microsoft Excel Workspaces, .XLW	
• Microsoft Excel Templates, .XLT	
• Microsoft Excel Add-Ins, .XLA, .XLL	
• Microsoft Excel Toolbars, .XLB	
• Microsoft Excel Backup Files, .XLK, .BAK	
• Office Database Connections, .ODC	• Office Database Connections, .ODC
• Access Databases, .MDB, .MDE	• Access Databases, .MDB, .MDE
	• Access Projects, .ADP, .ADE
• Microsoft Data links, .UDL	• Microsoft Data links, .UDL
• ODBC File DSNs, .DSN	• ODBC File DSNs, .DSN
• Web Pages, .HTM, .HTML, .MHT, .MHTL	• Web Pages, .HTM, .HTML, .ASP, .MHT, .MHTL
• Text Files, .TXT, .PRN, .CSV	• Text Files, .TXT, .PRN, .CSV, .TAB, .ASC
• Lotus 1-2-3 files, .WK?	• Lotus 1-2-3 files, .WK?, .WJ?
	• Paradox Files, .DB
• DBase Files, .DBF	• DBase Files, .DBF

Figure 10-1	BRINGING EXTERNAL FILES INTO EXCEL (CONTINUED)
FILES OPENED USING THE OPEN COMMAND	**FILES IMPORTED USING THE IMPORT EXTERNAL DATA COMMAND:**
• Web Queries, .IQY	• Web Queries, .IQY
• Database Queries, .DQY, .RQY	• Database Queries, .DQY, .RQY
• OLAP Queries, .OQY	• OLAP Queries/Cube Files, .OQY, .CUB
• XML Files, .XML	• XML Files, .XML
• Quattro Pro/DOS Files, .WQ1	
• Microsoft Works 2.0 Files, .WKS	
• SYLK files, .SLK	
• Data Interchange Format, .DIF	

The method that you use to import data doesn't always make a difference in the final result. For example, if you import a text file using either the Open command on the File menu or the Import External data command from the Data menu, you will invoke the **Text Import Wizard**, a tool that helps you import a text file. A **text file** is a file that contains only text and numbers, with no special formatting or graphics. Sharing data using a text file is a common way to pass information between different computer systems, and no matter whether you import the data using the File menu or Data menu, you'll end up with the same final result.

Sometimes, however, the method that you choose to import data makes a big difference in the final result. Some import methods will retain a link to the original data, allowing you to refresh the imported copy with up-to-date data from the original source. Other import methods are nothing more than an automated way to copy and paste data. These processes do not save a link between the imported copy and the original data, and therefore they do not allow you to refresh the imported copy at a later time. Several import processes that retain a link to the original data will be highlighted in this tutorial.

Using text files to pass information to Excel has some limitations. For example, perhaps the data that you want to import is already stored in a relational database such as an Access, SQL Server, or Oracle database. Because a text file is a single list of data, and a relational database stores data in multiple lists that are linked together, a single text file cannot store the information in the same way a relational database does. The process of preparing a text file by exporting data from a database to a text file format is tedious, too.

There is another important difference between opening a file within Excel and using the options on the Data menu. The Data menu provides you with expanded options. For example, if you want to import a set of data from an Access database to an Excel workbook on a regular basis, you can save the definition of the import process as a **database query**, and you can simply rerun the saved database query the next time you want to import the data. The Data menu options allow you to edit the query definition and import the data as a PivotTable. When you import data using the File menu, you don't have these advanced options. Rather, the data is simply placed in the Excel workbook just as if it were copied from the original data source and pasted into the Excel workbook.

At GVR, the Human Resources (HR) department has a small Access database that it uses to track information about employee names and addresses. Other departments often ask HR to share its data for use in Excel workbooks. You'll show the HR employees two different ways to import data from an Access database into an Excel workbook so that they can choose the best tool for the job.

Importing Access Data Using the File Menu

When you import data from an Access database using the Open command on the File menu, the Select Table dialog box opens. You use this dialog box to import tables or views from a selected database. In Access, a **table** stores a list of data. Each column represents a **field** and each row represents a **record**. Because Access is a relational database, many tables can be "related" to share data. The benefit of using multiple related tables is that data does not need to be duplicated as your database grows. For example, in an Access database, you may have one table that stores customer records and one that stores sales records. By relating the two tables, you do not need to duplicate all of the customer information, such as name, address, credit card number, and so forth, each time the same customer makes a purchase as you would if all of the information for each sale were listed in only one table.

Because data is separated in multiple related lists (tables) in an Access database, yet you often want to view only a few fields or records at a time, Access provides a tool called a query that you use to create a **view** of the data. In Access, a **query** is a stored set of SQL (Structured Query Language) statements that select fields and records from one or more tables. For example, you might want to see all of the sales records for all of the customers from Colorado. To do that, you'd need to select fields from both the Customers and Sales tables, as well as use limiting criteria so that only those records where the State field equaled "CO" were selected. In Access, queries give you the ability to collect the specific data that you want to view in one list. When you import data from an Access database, you may choose to import data from all of the tables and views (queries) stored in that Access database.

REFERENCE WINDOW   **RW**

Importing Access Data Using the File Menu
- Click File on the menu bar, and then click Open (or click the Open button).
- Click the Look in list arrow, and then navigate to the folder where your Access database is located.
- Click the Files of type list arrow, and then click Access Databases.
- Click the database in the files list, and then click the Open button.
- Click the table or view (query) that you want to import, and then click the OK button.

The HR employees want to know how to import queries they have created in an Access database into an Excel workbook. You'll show them how to do this using the File menu.

Note: You cannot open an Access database file directly into Excel 2000. You must use Microsoft Query to import the data from an Access database. Therefore, if you are using Excel 2000, read this exercise without performing the steps. You will import data using Microsoft Query later in this tutorial.

To import a query from the Employees Access database into an Excel workbook using the File menu:

1. Start Excel and open a new, blank workbook.

2. Click **File** on the menu bar, click **Open**, navigate to the T10\Tutorial folder on your Data Disk, click the **Files of type** list arrow, scroll down the list, click **Access Databases**, click **Employees**, and then click the **Open** button. The Select Table dialog box opens as shown in Figure 10-2.

Figure 10-2	SELECT TABLE DIALOG BOX

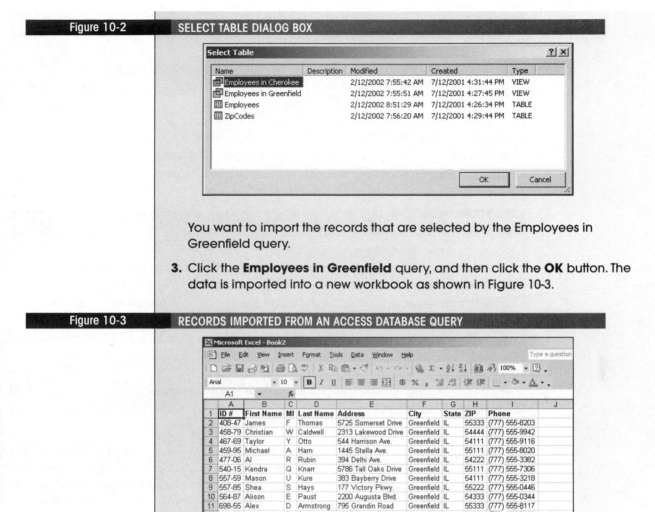

You want to import the records that are selected by the Employees in Greenfield query.

3. Click the **Employees in Greenfield** query, and then click the **OK** button. The data is imported into a new workbook as shown in Figure 10-3.

Figure 10-3	RECORDS IMPORTED FROM AN ACCESS DATABASE QUERY

4. Close the workbook without saving it.

Importing Access Data Using the Data Menu

The HR department likes the quick and easy steps used to import an Access table or query using the File menu. However, you also want to show these employees the advanced features that are available if they use the Data menu. They can use the Data menu to import new data as well as a previously defined data source.

REFERENCE WINDOW

Importing New Access Data Using the Data Menu
- Click Data on the menu bar, point to Import External Data, and then click Import Data.
- Click the Look in list arrow, and navigate to the folder that contains the Access database you want to import.
- Click the Files of type list arrow, and then click Access Databases.
- Click the name of the database, and then click the Open button.
- Click the table or view (query) that you want to import, and then click the OK button.

REFERENCE WINDOW

Importing a Previously Defined Data Source
- Click Data on the menu bar, point to Import External Data, and then click Import Data.
- Click the data source file that you want to import, and then click the Open button.
- Click the Properties button in the Import Data dialog box to edit the import properties, and then click the OK button.
- Select the location to which you want to import the data, and then click the OK button in the Import Data dialog box.

or

- Click the Create a PivotTable report link to import the data as a PivotTable.

To demonstrate the differences between importing Access data using the File and Data menus, you'll import the same query, the Employees in Greenfield query, from the Employees Access database. This time, however, you'll examine the import properties and will also import the data as a PivotTable instead of a list of records using the Data menu.

Note: You cannot open an Access database file directly into Excel 2000. You must use Microsoft Query to import the data from an Access database. Therefore, if you are using Excel 2000, read this exercise without performing the steps. You will import data using Microsoft Query later in this tutorial.

To import a query from the Employees Access database into an Excel workbook using the Data menu:

1. Click the **New** button 🗋 on the Standard toolbar to create a new workbook.

2. Click **Data** on the menu bar, point to **Import External Data**, and then click **Import Data**. The Select Data Source dialog box opens as shown in Figure 10-4.

Figure 10-4	SELECT DATA SOURCE DIALOG BOX

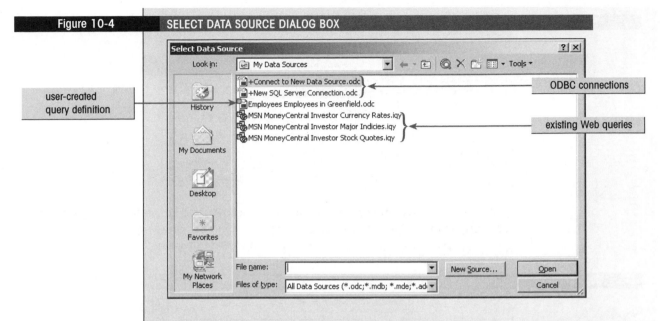

user-created query definition

ODBC connections

existing Web queries

The first two options, +Connect to New Data Source.odc and +New SQL Server Connection.odc, are provided by Excel to help you connect to a new database that follows **Open Database Connectivity (ODBC)** standards. The last three options are saved Web queries that help you import current information about currency rates, major stock indices, and stock quotes from the Microsoft MoneyCentral Investor Web site. Also notice that because you previously imported the Employees in Greenfield query from the Employees table using the File menu, an .odc file has been automatically saved in the My Data Sources folder, in order to make it easier for you to import this data again.

TROUBLE? When working with new file types, you might find it helpful to display the file extensions, which provide additional information about the files. If you do not see the file extensions in the Select Data Source dialog box, open Windows Explorer, click Tools on the menu bar, click Folder Options, click the View tab, clear the Hide file extensions for known file types check box, click the OK button, and then close Windows Explorer.

3. Click **Employees Employees in Greenfield.odc**, and then click the **Open** button. The Import Data dialog box opens, presenting advanced importing features as shown in Figure 10-5. You can specify where you want to import the data, in the current worksheet beginning with a specific cell reference or on a new worksheet. You also import the data as a PivotTable report. Finally, you change the properties of the import process or to edit the query. You'll explore the properties.

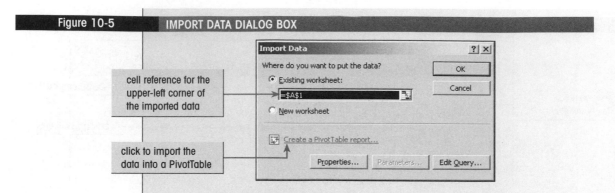

Figure 10-5   IMPORT DATA DIALOG BOX

cell reference for the upper-left corner of the imported data

click to import the data into a PivotTable

4. Click the **Properties** button. The External Data Range Properties dialog box opens as shown in Figure 10-6. In addition to renaming the query, you can change the way data is refreshed, formatted, and imported using this dialog box.

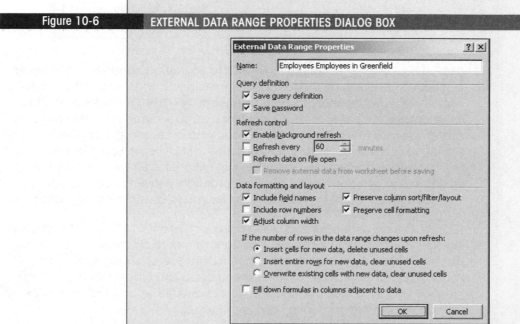

Figure 10-6   EXTERNAL DATA RANGE PROPERTIES DIALOG BOX

5. Click the **Refresh data on file open** check box, and then click the **OK** button.

6. Click cell **A1** to select it as the location for the imported data (if cell A1 is not already selected), and then click the **OK** button. At this point, the data looks the same as the data imported using the File Open command.

Importing Data as a PivotTable

A PivotTable enables you to view data in a variety of ways. To compare the difference between importing the data as a list and importing the data as a PivotTable, you will import the data as a PivotTable now.

Note: In Excel 2000, you can import external data as a PivotTable when you use the Microsoft Query Wizard. You'll use the Query Wizard later in this tutorial. Therefore, if you are using Excel 2000, read the steps on directly importing data as a PivotTable, but do not perform them.

To import data as a PivotTable:

1. Click cell **A16**.

2. Click **Data** on the menu bar, point to **Import External Data**, click **Import Data**, click **Employees Employees in Greenfield.odc**, and then click the **Open** button.

3. Click the **Create a PivotTable report** link in the Import Data dialog box, and then click the **Finish** button. The layout for the PivotTable, the PivotTable Field List, and the PivotTable toolbar appear.

4. Drag **City** to the Drop Row Fields Here area, **Zip** to the Drop Column Fields Here area, and **Last Name** to the Drop Data Items Here area.

5. Close the PivotTable Field List and the PivotTable toolbar. See Figure 10-7. This PivotTable counts the number of people in each zip code for each city in the data source that was also imported as a list in rows 1 through 12.

Figure 10-7	PIVOTTABLE OF IMPORTED DATA

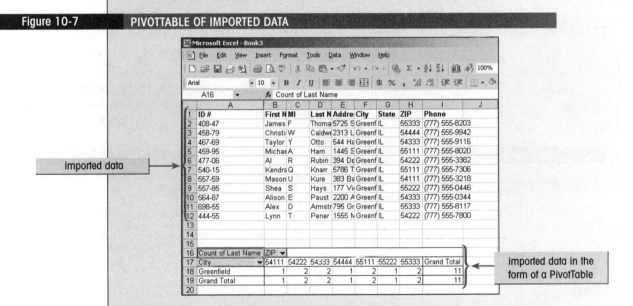

6. Save the workbook as **Greenfield-10** in the Tutorial.10\Tutorial folder on your Data Disk, and then print the PivotTable with your name in the left section of the header.

7. Close the Greenfield-10 workbook.

The HR employees appreciate that you showed them the difference between using the Data menu and using the File menu to import data. They are particularly intrigued by the ability to automatically refresh the imported data each time the workbook is opened as well as the ability to import data as a PivotTable. You'll test the refresh feature of the import by adding a record to the Employees database and then reopening the Greenfield-10 workbook.

Note: This is a continuation of the previous exercise. If you are using Excel 2000, read through the steps without performing them.

To test the automatic refresh ability of the imported PivotTable:

1. Start Access and open the **Employees** database located in the T10\Tutorial folder of your Data Disk. Access starts with its Database window displayed. There are two tables in the Employees database. You'll add your own name as an employee to the Employees table.

    TROUBLE? If you didn't close the Greenfield-10 workbook in the previous exercise, you'll be prompted to open the Employees database in read-only mode. Click the **OK** button, close Access and the Employees database, close the Greenfield-10 workbook, and repeat Step 1.

2. Double-click **Employees** to open the Employees table in its own window, and then click the **Maximize** button on the Employees Table window (if the window is not already maximized).

3. Click the **New Record** button ▶* on the Table Datasheet toolbar, and then enter a new record using the data shown in Figure 10-8. Notice that there is no city information recorded in the Employees table. The Employees table has a one-to-many relationship with the ZipCodes table where the corresponding City and State fields are recorded for each unique zip code.

Figure 10-8	ADDING A NEW RECORD TO THE EMPLOYEES TABLE

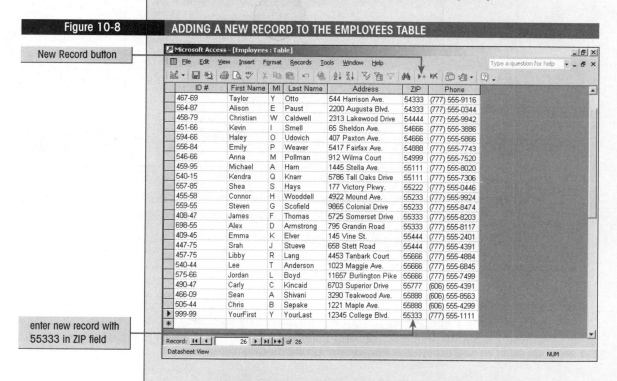

4. Close the Employees table, double-click the **ZipCodes** table, and then click the **expand** button to the left of the **55333** zip code. See Figure 10-9. By relating one record in the ZipCodes table to many records in the Employees table, you avoid having to enter the City and State values for each employee. Rather, the entry in the ZIP field in the Employees table relates that record to the appropriate city and state stored in the ZipCodes table.

| Figure 10-9 | ONE ZIP CODE IS RELATED TO MANY EMPLOYEES |

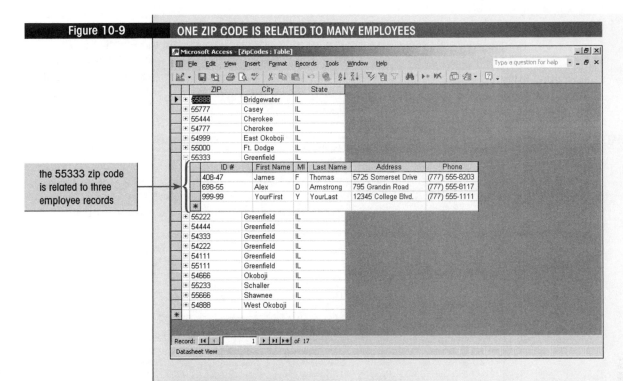

the 55333 zip code is related to three employee records

5. Close the ZipCodes table, click the **Queries** button on the Objects bar, and then double-click **Employees in Greenfield** to observe the results of the query in Access. The purpose of a query is to select fields and records from one or more tables. In this case, the query selected several fields from the Employees table and the City and State fields from the ZipCodes table into one view. The query also selected 12 records in which the value of the City field was equal to "Greenfield". Therefore, the Employees database has been updated successfully.

6. Close the Employees in Greenfield query, close the Employees database, and then exit Access.

7. Return to Excel and open the **Greenfield-10** workbook from the Tutorial.10\Tutorial folder on your Data Disk. The Query Refresh dialog box appears, as shown in Figure 10-10.

| Figure 10-10 | QUERY REFRESH DIALOG BOX |

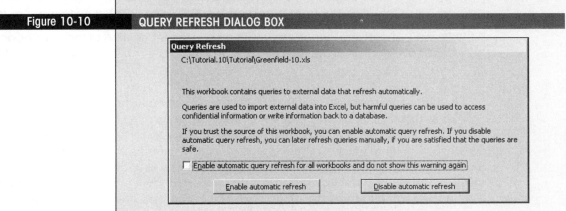

8. Click the **Enable automatic refresh** button. See Figure 10-11. Your name was automatically added to the list of imported records, but the PivotTable was not automatically refreshed. There are 12 records in the list, just as there were in the Employees in Greenfield query in Access. As you may already know, the data in a PivotTable doesn't automatically refresh unless you set the PivotTable's properties to automatically refresh, too.

Figure 10-11 | PIVOTTABLE DOES NOT REFLECT REFRESHED DATA

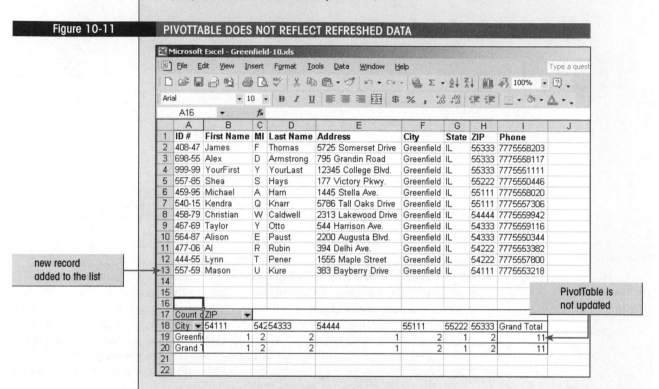

new record added to the list

PivotTable is not updated

9. Right-click the **PivotTable** and then click **Refresh Data** on the shortcut menu. The PivotTable is now automatically updated with 12 records (as indicated by the Grand Total count value), three with the zip code value of 55333.

10. Right-click the **PivotTable** and then click **Table Options**. Click the **Refresh on open** check box, and then click the **OK** button. Now both the PivotTable and the list will automatically refresh every time the Greenfield-10 workbook is opened.

11. Print the Sheet1 worksheet with your name in the left section of the header, and then save and close the Greenfield-10 workbook.

The HR employees thank you for the quick lesson on importing data from Access. They now know that they can import data using two different menu options. They also know that using the Import External Data command on the Data menu saves the import definition and enables them to quickly refresh imported data. Using this method also provides many more importing options, such as the ability to import data as a PivotTable. The HR department uses many PivotTables, so learning that imported PivotTable data doesn't automatically refresh without executing the Refresh Data command or changing the PivotTable's properties is essential knowledge.

While working with the Select Data Source dialog box, however, the HR employees noticed the MSN MoneyCentral Investor queries and want to know if these queries could be used to help provide up-to-date investment information for GVR pension benefit programs. You will demonstrate the three Microsoft MoneyCentral Web queries for the HR department.

Importing Data Using Microsoft MoneyCentral

The Microsoft Money Web site (http://moneycentral.msn.com/) is devoted to providing information on all types of money matters. A few of the services that the Web site provides include:

- Investment portfolio management
- Market news, information, and research
- Stock and mutual fund quotes
- Budget planning
- Investment planning
- Tax information
- Online trading
- Automated bill payment
- E-mail money

In addition to these services, the Web site is connected to Excel via three saved Web queries in the subject areas of currency rates, major investment indices, and stock quotes.

REFERENCE WINDOW   **RW**

Using the MSN MoneyCentral Investor Web Queries
- Connect to the Internet.
- Click Data on the menu bar, point to Import External Data, and then click Import Data. (In Excel 2000, click Data on the menu bar, point to Get External Data, and then click Run Saved Query.)
- Click the MSN MoneyCentral Investor Web query that you want to use, and then click the Open button. (In Excel 2000, click the Get Data button.)
- Specify the location for the imported data, and then click the OK button.

You'll use all three Web queries to show the HR department how saved Web queries work.

To work with the MoneyCentral Web queries:

1. Connect to the Internet if you are not already connected, and then create a new, blank workbook.

2. Click **Data** on the menu bar, point to **Import External Data**, and then click **Import Data**.

   EXCEL 2000: Click **Data** on the menu bar, point to **Get External Data**, and then click **Run Saved Query**.

3. Click **MSN MoneyCentral Investor Currency Rates.iqy** and then click the **Open** button. The Import Data dialog box opens.

   EXCEL 2000: Click **Microsoft Investor Currency Rates.iqy** and then click the **Get Data** button. The Returning External Data to Microsoft Excel dialog box opens.

4. Click the **OK** button in the dialog box to import the data to cell A1 of the existing worksheet as shown in Figure 10-12. The current currency rates as provided by the MSN MoneyCentral Investor are automatically imported into the workbook. Because the data was created through a Web query, it was defined and saved in the Select Data Source dialog box, so you can refresh the data to display the most up-to-date data. The currency types in column A are hyperlinks. Clicking a hyperlink takes you to a Web page at MSN Money, which provides more information about that currency type.

EXCEL 2000: The layout of the imported data might differ from that shown in Figure 10-12, but the latest currency rates should appear.

Figure 10-12	CURRENCY RATES PROVIDED BY MSN MONEYCENTRAL INVESTOR

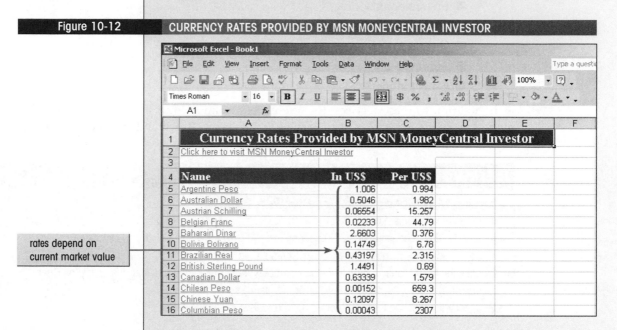

rates depend on current market value

5. Right-click any value in the table, and then click **Refresh Data** on the shortcut menu. As the Web query is working, a globe appears in the status bar indicating that information is being downloaded from the Web to your workbook. The values update with the latest information from the MSN Money Web site.

TROUBLE? If the data did not change, refresh it at a later time to prove that the refresh process works.

6. Click the **Sheet2** tab, click **Data**, point to **Import External Data**, and then click **Import Data**.

EXCEL 2000: Click **Data**, point to **Get External Data**, and then click **Run Saved Query**.

7. Click **MSN MoneyCentral Investor Major Indices.iqy** and then click the **Open** button.

EXCEL 2000: Click **Microsoft Investor Major Indices.iqy** and then click the **Get Data** button.

8. Click the **OK** button in the dialog box to import the data to cell A1 of the existing worksheet as shown in Figure 10-13. Financial information about current market indices, including the Dow Jones Industrial Average and the S&P 500, is imported into your workbook.

Figure 10-13	MARKET INDEX INFORMATION PROVIDED BY MSN MONEYCENTRAL INVESTOR

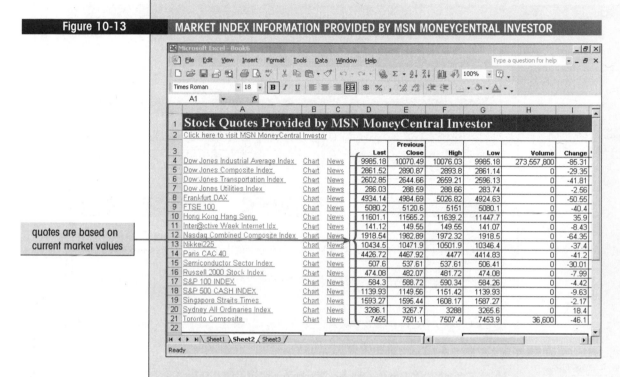

quotes are based on current market values

9. Click the **Chart** link for the Dow Jones Industrial Average Index. The link takes you to a Web page at MSN MoneyCentral that shows a one-year graph of that index.

10. Click the **Microsoft Excel** program button in the taskbar to return to your workbook.

11. Click the **Sheet3** tab, click **Data**, point to **Import External Data**, and then click **Import Data**.

 EXCEL 2000: Click **Data**, point to **Get External Data**, and then click **Run Saved Query**.

12. Click **MSN MoneyCentral Investor Stock Quotes.iqy** and then click the **Open** button.

 EXCEL 2000: Click **Microsoft Investor Stock Quotes.iqy** and then click the **Get Data** button.

13. Click the **OK** button in the dialog box to import the data to cell A1 of the existing worksheet. The Stock Quotes query displays the Enter Parameter Value dialog box in which you can enter the investor symbol(s) for which you want information displayed. The symbols you enter will determine which investment information is imported into the Excel workbook. If the workbook already contained the stock symbols, you could use the Collapse Dialog Box button to select the symbols you want to use.

14. Type **MSFT, IBM** (which are the stock quote symbols for Microsoft and IBM), and then click the **OK** button. Financial information about the current price of Microsoft and IBM stock is imported into the workbook as shown in Figure 10-14.

Figure 10-14   IMPORTED STOCK QUOTE INFORMATION

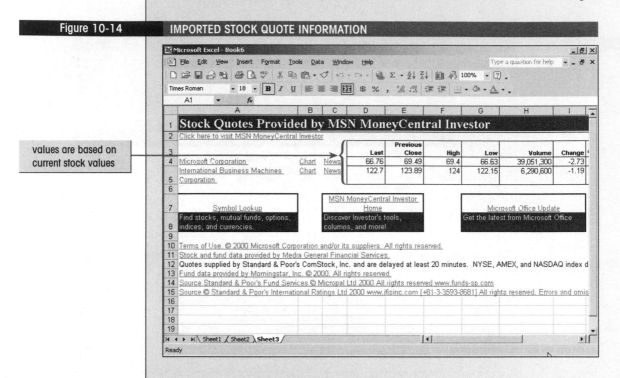

values are based on current stock values

15. Type *your name* in cell **A3** of the worksheet, and then save the workbook with the filename **Investments-10** in the Tutorial.10\Tutorial folder on your Data Disk.

16. Print the entire Investments-10 workbook, and then close it.

The HR employees are pleased with their new ability to provide up-to-date investment information for employees and the GVR investment club in a workbook format.

Importing Access Data Using Microsoft Query

Another tool you may need to use to import data from an Access database is Microsoft Query. **Microsoft Query** provides advanced query capabilities, such as the ability to:

- Filter rows or columns of data before they are imported
- Create a parameter query that prompts you for the criteria used to determine which records will be imported
- Sort data before it is imported
- Join multiple tables of related data

If you are already familiar with Access, you'll recognize that the query object within Access does all of these functions as well. If you can define the view of data that you want to import in Access before you attempt to import it, you don't need to use Microsoft Query. On the other hand, if your data source is an Access database and you have no direct access to the database file (which means that you have no ability to create queries within the Access database itself), you'll want to use Microsoft Query to make sure that you're importing only the data that you need and want and in the most productive way possible.

REFERENCE WINDOW   **RW**

Importing Data Using Microsoft Query
- Click Data on the menu bar, point to Import External Data, and then click New Database Query to open the Choose Data Source dialog box. (In Excel 2000, click Data on the menu bar, point to Get External Data, and then click New Database Query.)
- Select the correct type of database on the Databases tab, and then click the OK button.
- In the Select Database dialog box, navigate to the folder that contains the database from which you want to import data, select the database, and then click the OK button.
- Follow the steps of the Query Wizard to select the fields, criteria, and sort order that you want to define, and then click the Finish button.

Because not everyone in the HR department can build queries in the Employees database, you decide to show the employees how to use Microsoft Query. This will allow them to import only the fields and records they need, even if the data has not been saved as a view within Microsoft Access.

Note: Microsoft Query cannot import data from a database stored in a folder structure that includes a period. Therefore, the Employees database is stored in the T10\Tutorial folder on your Data Disk rather than in the Tutorial.10\Tutorial folder.

To use Microsoft Query to import data from the Employees database to a new Excel workbook:

1. Start Excel and open a new, blank workbook.

2. Click **Data** on the menu bar, point to **Import External Data**, and then click **New Database Query**. The Choose Data Source dialog box opens, presenting you with a list of existing ODBC drivers. An **ODBC** (Open Database Connectivity) driver is a file used to connect to a particular database. Microsoft Query automatically installs the set of drivers as shown in Figure 10-15.

EXCEL 2000: Click **Data** on the menu bar, point to **Get External Data**, and then click **New Database Query**.

TROUBLE? If the Microsoft Query program has not been installed on your computer, you need to install it now. Close all open dialog boxes and close Excel. Insert the Office Installation CD in the appropriate drive, and then follow the installation instructions for installing Microsoft Query within Excel.

Figure 10-15	ODBC DRIVERS

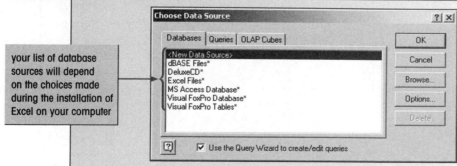

your list of database sources will depend on the choices made during the installation of Excel on your computer

3. Click **MS Access Database*** and then click the **OK** button. The Select Database dialog box opens.

4. Navigate to the T10\Tutorial folder on your Data Disk, click **Employees.mdb** in the Database Name list, and then click the **OK** button. The Query Wizard appears with the tables and queries in the Employees database listed on the left. For your query, you want to select the First Name, Last Name, City, and State fields. The First Name and Last Name fields are in the Employees table, and the City and State fields are in the ZipCodes table.

5. Click the **expand** button to the left of the Employees table, click **First Name**, click the **Select Single Field** button [>], click **Last Name**, and then click [>]. Now add the two fields you need from the ZipCodes table.

6. Scroll down the list box, click the **expand** button to the left of the ZipCodes table, click **City**, click [>], click **State**, and then click [>]. See Figure 10-16.

| Figure 10-16 | SELECTING FIELDS FROM MULTIPLE TABLES IN THE QUERY WIZARD |

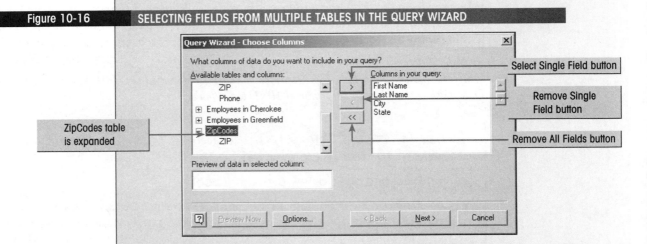

7. Click the **Next** button. Because you're only interested in those records where the City field equals "Shawnee", you'll specify that criterion in the Filter Data step of the Query Wizard.

8. Click **City** in the Column to filter list, click the **City** list arrow, click **equals**, and then type **Shawnee** as shown in Figure 10-17.

| Figure 10-17 | SPECIFYING CRITERIA TO FILTER THE RECORDS IN THE QUERY WIZARD |

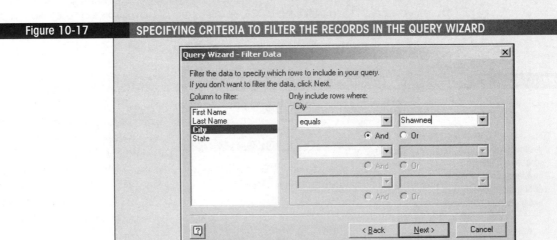

Next, you will sort the records so that they are imported in the order in which you want to work with them.

9. Click the **Next** button, click the **Sort by** list arrow, click **Last Name**, and then click the **Next** button. This step of the Query Wizard provides three choices that determine where the data will be returned: to Excel, to Microsoft Query itself (to define the query even further before importing it), or to an **OLAP (Online Analytical Processing)** Cube, a technology that allows you to create a multi-dimensional database with just the data you need to work with. At this point, you could save the query with a given name, so that you could access it from the Select Data Source dialog box with the other saved queries. For now, you just want to import the data to the current Excel workbook.

10. Make sure that the **Return Data to Microsoft Excel** option button is selected, click the **Finish** button, and then click the **OK** button to finish the import process. Three records, as shown in Figure 10-18, have been imported. Note that these records meet the criteria that you specified in the Query Wizard. You selected the First Name and Last Name fields from the Employees table, selected the City and State fields from the ZipCodes table, filtered for records where the City field value was equal to "Shawnee", and sorted the records in ascending order based on the contents of the Last Name field.

Figure 10-18	RECORDS IMPORTED USING THE QUERY WIZARD

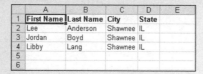

	A	B	C	D	E
1	First Name	Last Name	City	State	
2	Lee	Anderson	Shawnee	IL	
3	Jordan	Boyd	Shawnee	IL	
4	Libby	Lang	Shawnee	IL	
5					
6					

11. Enter your own name in cell A6, print the worksheet, and then close the workbook without saving it.

Now the HR employees know how to import data using the File menu and the Select Data Source dialog box and have expanded their knowledge of Web queries. They feel confident that they can use Excel to import any data from Access databases as well as from the Web. To help the department to work more efficiently and effectively, you want to show them how to automate these processes using VBA.

Importing **Access Data Using VBA**

Yet another way to import Access data to an Excel workbook is to use VBA. You could either research the statements necessary to enter this code directly into the Visual Basic Editor or use the macro recorder to help figure it out. You decide to first use Microsoft Query to create a stored database query (.dqy) file, which selects the fields necessary to create an employee address from the Employees table. Because a complete address will require fields from both the Employees and ZipCodes tables of the Employees database, and no existing query in the Employees database currently provides this view of the data, you'll have to use Microsoft Query to create the database query from within Excel. You will then run the query using the macro recorder and examine the VBA code in the Visual Basic Editor.

To use Microsoft Query to build the employee address database query:

1. Start a new, blank workbook.

2. Click **Data** on the menu bar, point to **Import External Data**, and then click **New Database Query**. The Choose Data Source dialog box opens.

   EXCEL 2000: Click **Data** on the menu bar, point to **Get External Data**, and then click **New Database Query**.

3. Click **MS Access Database*** and then click the **OK** button.

4. Navigate to the T10\Tutorial folder on your Data Disk, click **Employees.mdb** in the Database Name list, and then click the **OK** button. The Query Wizard starts.

5. Click the **expand** button to the left of the Employees table, and then move the **First Name**, **Last Name**, and **Address** fields to the Columns in your query list.

6. Click the **expand** button to the left of the ZipCodes table, and then move the **City**, **State**, and **ZIP** fields (in that order) to the Columns in your query list. See Figure 10-19. You will use the fields that you have selected to build an employee address.

Figure 10-19   **FIELDS FOR EMPLOYEE ADDRESS DATABASE QUERY**

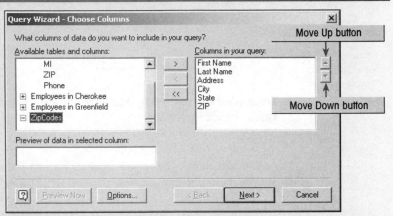

TROUBLE? If the fields are not in the order shown in the figure, click the field in the Columns in your query list, and then click the Move Up or Move Down button to reposition the field.

7. Click the **Next** button to move to the next step, and then click the **Next** button to bypass the Filter Data step.

8. Click the **Sort by** list arrow, click **Last Name**, and then click the **Next** button. In order to run this query later from the Choose Data Source dialog box, you need to save the query.

9. Click the **Save Query** button, type **EmployeeList** in the File name text box, click the **Save** button, and then click the **Finish** button. Note that the query is saved in the Queries folder by default.

10. Click the **OK** button to import the data starting at cell A1.

11. Save the workbook with the filename **EmployeeAddressList-10** in Tutorial.10\Tutorial folder on your Data Disk.

Now that the database query has been defined and saved, you can record a macro that runs the EmployeeList database query.

To create a macro to run the EmployeeList database query:

1. Click the **Sheet2** tab to move to a blank worksheet.

2. Click **Tools** on the menu bar, point to **Macro**, and then click **Record New Macro**.

3. Type **ImportEmployee** in the Macro name text box, enter *your name* and the *current date* in the Description text box, and then click the **OK** button. The macro is now recording your actions as indicated by the status bar and the presence of the Stop Recording toolbar.

4. Click **Data** on the menu bar, point to **Import External Data**, and then click **Import Data**. The EmployeeList database query file that you just saved should now be listed as a data source list.

EXCEL 2000: Click **Data** on the menu bar, point to **Get External Data**, and then click **Run Saved Query**.

5. Click **EmployeeList.dqy** and then click the **Open** button.

6. Click the **OK** button to import the data to cell A1 of the existing worksheet, and then click the **Stop Recording** button ▣ on the Stop Recording toolbar. Now test the macro on another worksheet.

EXCEL 2000: Click the **Get Data** button, click the **OK** button, and then click the **Stop Recording** button ▣ on the Stop Recording toolbar.

7. Click the **Sheet3** tab.

8. Click **Tools**, point to **Macro**, click **Macros**, and then click the **Run** button to run the selected ImportEmployee macro. The database query runs and returns the data to the workbook as shown in Figure 10-20.

Figure 10-20 RESULTS OF EMPLOYEELIST DATABASE QUERY

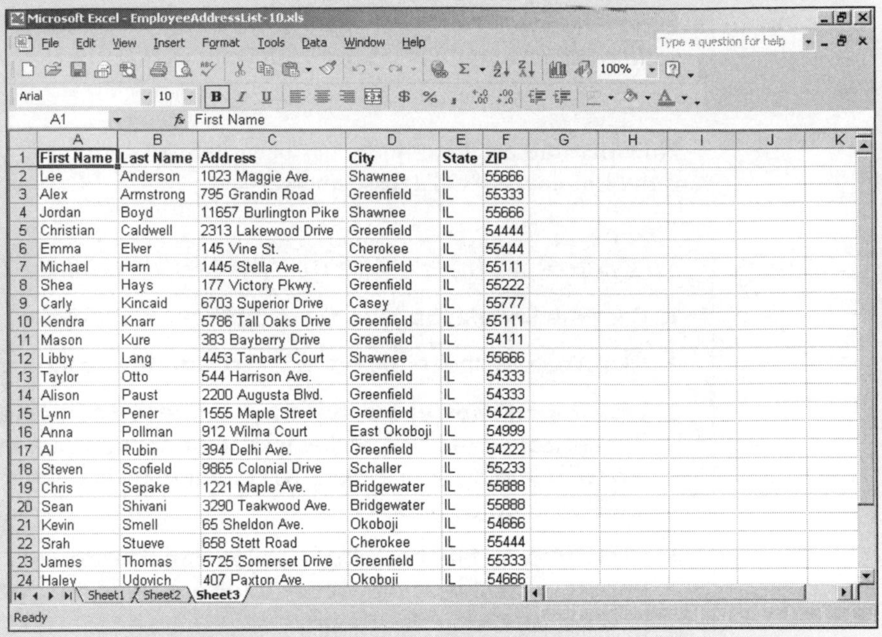

	A	B	C	D	E	F
1	First Name	Last Name	Address	City	State	ZIP
2	Lee	Anderson	1023 Maggie Ave.	Shawnee	IL	55666
3	Alex	Armstrong	795 Grandin Road	Greenfield	IL	55333
4	Jordan	Boyd	11657 Burlington Pike	Shawnee	IL	55666
5	Christian	Caldwell	2313 Lakewood Drive	Greenfield	IL	54444
6	Emma	Elver	145 Vine St.	Cherokee	IL	55444
7	Michael	Harn	1445 Stella Ave.	Greenfield	IL	55111
8	Shea	Hays	177 Victory Pkwy.	Greenfield	IL	55222
9	Carly	Kincaid	6703 Superior Drive	Casey	IL	55777
10	Kendra	Knarr	5786 Tall Oaks Drive	Greenfield	IL	55111
11	Mason	Kure	383 Bayberry Drive	Greenfield	IL	54111
12	Libby	Lang	4453 Tanbark Court	Shawnee	IL	55666
13	Taylor	Otto	544 Harrison Ave.	Greenfield	IL	54333
14	Alison	Paust	2200 Augusta Blvd.	Greenfield	IL	54333
15	Lynn	Pener	1555 Maple Street	Greenfield	IL	54222
16	Anna	Pollman	912 Wilma Court	East Okoboji	IL	54999
17	Al	Rubin	394 Delhi Ave.	Greenfield	IL	54222
18	Steven	Scofield	9865 Colonial Drive	Schaller	IL	55233
19	Chris	Sepake	1221 Maple Ave.	Bridgewater	IL	55888
20	Sean	Shivani	3290 Teakwood Ave.	Bridgewater	IL	55888
21	Kevin	Smell	65 Sheldon Ave.	Okoboji	IL	54666
22	Srah	Stueve	658 Stett Road	Cherokee	IL	55444
23	James	Thomas	5725 Somerset Drive	Greenfield	IL	55333
24	Haley	Udovich	407 Paxton Ave.	Okoboji	IL	54666

To expand your understanding of VBA, you'll explore the code that was created by the ImportEmployee macro.

To explore the VBA code created by the ImportEmployee macro:

1. Click **Tools** on the menu bar, point to **Macro**, click **Macros**, and then click the **Edit** button to open the Visual Basic Editor for the selected ImportEmployee macro. The code for the sub procedure named `ImportEmployee()` appears.
2. Close the Project Explorer and Properties window (if they are open) so that you have more room on your screen to view the Code window as shown in Figure 10-21.

Figure 10-21 | IMPORTEMPLOYEE SUB

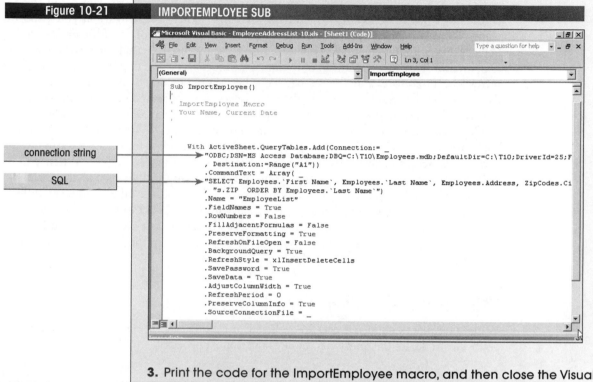

connection string

SQL

3. Print the code for the ImportEmployee macro, and then close the Visual Basic Editor.

4. Save the EmployeeAddressList-10 workbook.

There are two important new elements in this code that are required to retrieve data from an external file, the connection string and the query string, which are both critical parts of the Add method for the QueryTables property of the ActiveSheet object. A **connection string** describes the type of data source and the file name. In this example, the connection string specified an ODBC (Open Database Connectivity) data source, a Microsoft Access database named Employees located in the T10 folder. A **query string** is an **SQL (Structured Query Language)** statement that identifies which fields and records are returned and how they will be sorted. Most SQL statements start with the SELECT command. The rest of the VBA code sets values for other properties.

Even though you may not be an experienced VBA or SQL programmer, reading the code that was created by the macro recorder helps you learn how it works. And in the future, if the location of the database changed or if you wanted to select a new field, you could read the pattern used by the connection string and query string to change or modify the VBA code necessary to select the correct data from the correct location rather than rebuilding the database query and sub procedure from scratch.

Imported **Data Versus Linked Data**

Historically, when you imported data you followed an automated process to copy data from one location and to paste it into another location. No connection between the original source and the new copy was retained. This definition of *imported* still applies to many import processes within the Microsoft Office XP suite. When you import Access data into Excel, however, no matter whether you use the Open command on the File menu or the Import External Data command on the Data menu, you not only create a copy of the data but also save a definition of the import process. When you import data using the Open command, you create an **.odc** (open database connectivity) file, and when you import data using Microsoft Query, you create a **.dqy** (database query) file. Both files are visible in the Select Data Source dialog box when you select the Import External Data command on the Data menu. Because a definition of the import process is retained, the imported data can be refreshed. Therefore, a link exists between the original data and the copy of the imported data in Excel that can be used to update and refresh the imported copy of data. That link is referred to as a **query** within Excel, no matter whether it is an .odc or a .dqy file.

Contrast this with the traditional definition of linked data. When you *link* data from one application file to another, only one copy of the data exists. For example, you can link Excel data to an Access database using the linked table feature within Access. When you use a linked table within Access, the single copy of the data physically exists in the Excel workbook, but it can be updated and edited from within the Access database. The key difference between imported data and linked data is that with linked data only one copy of the data exists. You cannot link Access data into an Excel workbook, but creating a refreshable copy of imported Access data does help you keep the copy of data in the Excel workbook updated with the copy you imported from Access.

Deleting Imported Data

When you delete imported data in an Excel workbook, you are also asked whether or not you want to delete the query that defines the import process.

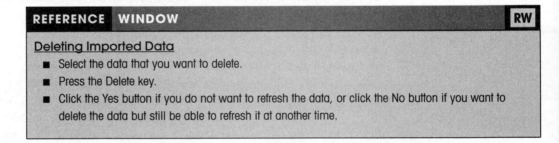

REFERENCE WINDOW   **RW**

Deleting Imported Data
- Select the data that you want to delete.
- Press the Delete key.
- Click the Yes button if you do not want to refresh the data, or click the No button if you want to delete the data but still be able to refresh it at another time.

In the process of creating the EmployeeAddressList-10 workbook, you created three copies of the data on three worksheets. You will delete the extra copies of the data from the workbook to better understand the difference between deleting just the data and deleting the query that defines the import process.

To delete the imported employee address data and query:

1. Click the **Select All** button above row 1 and to the left of column A to select all of the data on Sheet3, and then press the **Delete** key. A message appears, asking whether you want to delete the query in addition to the data. See Figure 10-22.

Figure 10-22   MESSAGE BOX WITH INFORMATION ABOUT DELETING IMPORTED DATA

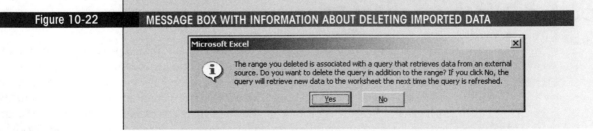

2. Click the **No** button. When you click the No button, only the data is deleted. Because imported data is a copy of data, modifying or deleting this data has no effect on the data in the original data source, the Access database.

3. Click the **Sheet2** tab.

4. Click the **Select All** button to select all of the data on Sheet2, and then press the **Delete** key. This time, you'll delete both the data and the query that defines the data.

5. Click the **Yes** button. Although the data on both the Sheet2 and Sheet3 worksheets appears to be deleted, you did not delete the query on the Sheet3 worksheet. That means that you can refresh the data later, even if the imported copy was deleted.

6. Click the **Sheet3** tab, click cell **A1** or any cell within the original range of imported data, click **Data** on the menu bar, and then click **Refresh Data**. An up-to-date copy of the data in the Access Employees database is imported again into Sheet3 of the EmployeeAddressList-10 workbook. Now try the same process on Sheet2.

7. Click the **Sheet2** tab, click cell **A1**, and then click **Data** on the menu bar. The Refresh Data menu option is dimmed, meaning that it can't be used at this time. Because you deleted both the data and the query when you deleted the data on Sheet2, you can't use the Refresh menu option to import the data.

8. Press the **Esc** key to close the Data menu, delete the **Sheet2** worksheet, delete the **Sheet3** worksheet (because this data also exists on Sheet1), and then save and close the EmployeeAddressList-10 workbook.

Each copy of imported data has an associated query that can be selectively deleted or not, depending upon whether you want to refresh the data at a later time. Deleting imported data and its associated query is different from deleting the data source file in the Select Data Source dialog box.

Deleting the Data Source File

When you import Access data into an Excel workbook, a data source file is created and made available in the Select Data Source dialog box so that you can use the query definition in other workbooks as well. Deleting imported data and its associated query does not delete this file.

REFERENCE WINDOW   **RW**

Deleting a Data Source File

■ Click Data on the menu bar, point to Import External Data, and then click Import Data. (In Excel 2000, click Data on the menu bar, point to Get External Data, and then click Run Saved Query.)

■ Click the data source file that you want to delete, and then press the Delete key.

■ Click the Yes button to confirm the deletion of the file.

In teaching the HR employees about the various ways to import data, you have created two data source files, Employees Employees in Greenfield.odc and EmployeeList.dqy, which you now want to delete.

To delete the data source files:

1. Open a new, blank workbook, click **Data** on the menu bar, point to **Import External Data**, and then click **Import Data**.

   EXCEL 2000: Click **Data** on the menu bar, point to **Get External Data**, and then click **Run Saved Query**.

2. Click **Employees EmployeeList.dqy**, press the **Delete** key, and then click the **Yes** button when asked if you want to delete this file.

   EXCEL 2000: Skip Step 3 because you did not create the Employees Employees in Greenfield.odc query file.

3. Click **Employees Employees in Greenfield.odc**, press the **Delete** key, and then click the **Yes** button when asked if you want to delete this file.

4. Click the **Cancel** button to close the dialog box.

5. Close the workbook without saving it, and then exit Excel.

The terms import, query, and link are used in different ways in different programs. Learning how they are used within Excel to import data from an Access database or the World Wide Web will help you to keep information current and accurate.

Session 10.1 QUICK CHECK

1. Identify three ways that you can import data from an external data source into Excel.

2. Identify two benefits of importing data using the Import External Data command on the Data menu versus using the Open command on the File menu.

3. What is Microsoft MoneyCentral?

4. What is the purpose of the three MoneyCentral Web queries provided in the Select Data Source dialog box?

5. For what reasons would you need to use Microsoft Query to select data from an external data source?

6. What are the two critical components of a VBA statement that imports data from an external data source?

SESSION 10.2

In this session, you will learn how to install, download, and use add-ins to add new functionality to Excel. You'll work with the Analysis ToolPak and Conditional Sum Wizard, which are default Excel add-ins, and you will download the AccessLinks add-in from the Web. You will use then the AccessLinks add-in to analyze data. You will also learn how to unload and delete an add-in you now longer need to use.

Using **Add-Ins**

An **add-in** is a program that provides additional features to Microsoft Excel. Some add-ins are provided within a default installation of Excel, and more are available from the Microsoft Office Web site. You can create your own add-ins using VBA or many other programs. You can see which add-ins are available and which are installed by clicking the Add-Ins option on the Tools menu to open the Add-Ins dialog box as shown in Figure 10-23.

Figure 10-23	ADD-INS DIALOG BOX

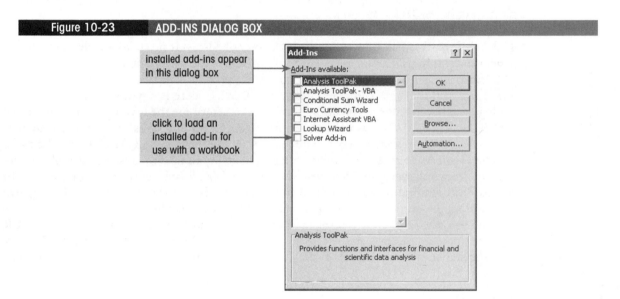

installed add-ins appear in this dialog box

click to load an installed add-in for use with a workbook

If an add-in is listed in the dialog box and its check box is not selected, the add-in has been installed but not yet loaded. Descriptions of the default add-in programs that are available through the standard installation of Excel are shown in Figure 10-24.

Figure 10-24	DEFAULT ADD-INS FOR EXCEL

ADD-IN	DESCRIPTION
Analysis ToolPak	Adds statistical and engineering analysis tools and functions such as advanced correlation, regression, and sampling analysis tools. These tools are available within the Data Analysis command on the Tools menu.
Analysis ToolPak - VBA	Provides VBA functions that were created for use within the Analysis ToolPak in workbook formulas.
Conditional Sum Wizard	Creates a formula that adds the data in a list based on criteria you specify.
Euro Currency Tools	Formats values as eurodollars, or euros, and provides the EUROCONVERT worksheet function, which converts currencies to eurodollars.
Internet Assistant VBA	Enables users to publish Excel data to the Web by using Internet Assistant syntax.
Lookup Wizard	Creates a formula to look up data in a list by using another known value in the list.
Solver Add-In	Calculates solutions to what-if scenarios based on assumptions and constraints.

To use the default add-ins, you must load them from the Add-Ins dialog box. If they are not listed in the Add-Ins dialog box, you must install them from the Office installation CD. Because an add-in is an extra program that you might not need for every workbook, you usually don't load an add-in unless you need it. The Add-Ins dialog box allows you to load the available add-ins for the current workbook.

REFERENCE WINDOW   **RW**

Loading an Add-In
- Click Tools on the menu bar, and then click Add-Ins.
- Click the check box for the add-in that you want to use with the workbook.
- Click the OK button.

Analysis ToolPak

The **Analysis ToolPak** is one of the most popular add-ins. It provides a wide range of statistical analysis tools that create a variety of statistical reports very quickly.

GVR has been asked by the community to provide a facility to offer the GMAT (Graduate Management Admission Test). The GMAT score is a national measurement of academic achievement, used by business schools to determine the qualifications of potential applicants. The GMAT tests writing, quantitative, and reading skills, and returns a cumulative score for the examinee between 200 and 800. The higher the GMAT score, the more qualified the candidate. In addition to offering a facility to take the test, GVR is also interested in providing preparatory classes to help GMAT candidates score higher on the test. To do this, the organization has requested and received a list of GMAT scores for the past five years for people who have taken the test at the next closest facility.

Lynn has asked if you will help analyze this data, so that as this program progresses, GVR can determine if its efforts are helping local patrons gain higher GMAT scores. You'll work with the statistical analysis tools available through the Analysis ToolPak add-in to accomplish this task.

To load the Analysis ToolPak add-in:

1. If you took a break after the previous session, start Excel, open a new, blank workbook, click **Tools** on the menu bar, and then click **Add-Ins**. The Add-Ins dialog box opens.

2. Click the **Analysis ToolPak** check box, and then click the **OK** button.

   TROUBLE? If the Analysis ToolPak program has not been installed on your computer, you need to install it now. Click the OK button in the Add-Ins dialog box, close Excel, insert your Office CD in the appropriate drive, and then follow the installation instructions for installing the program.

   When the Analysis ToolPak is loaded, the Data Analysis command appears on the Tools menu.

3. Click **Tools** and then click **Data Analysis**. The Data Analysis dialog box opens. This menu option and these advanced statistical analysis features are not available unless the Analysis ToolPak add-in is installed.

4. Click the **Cancel** button to close the dialog box.

With the Data Analysis tools available, you're ready to use them to analyze the GMAT data. The Graduate Management Admission Council provided the GMAT scores in a text file. You'll import the data in the text file and then analyze the data.

To import the GMAT-10 text file:

1. Click the **Open** button 🖼 on the Standard toolbar, click the **Files of type** list arrow, click **Text Files**, navigate to the Tutorial.10\Tutorial folder on your Data Disk, make sure the **GMAT-10** text file is selected, and then click the **Open** button. The Text Import Wizard starts as shown in Figure 10-25. The Wizard indicates that there is one column of data provided, the GMAT scores.

Figure 10-25	STEP 1 OF TEXT IMPORT WIZARD

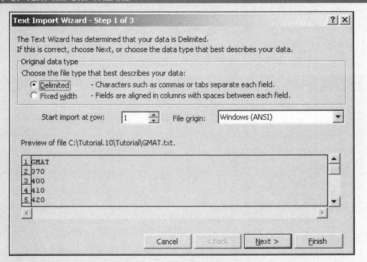

2. Click the **Next** button twice to move to the third step of the Wizard. Because you are importing only one column of data, the delimiter (the character that separates the columns in a text file) will not affect this data.

3. Click the **Finish** button. The values are imported, apparently sorted from lowest to highest, as shown in Figure 10-26.

Figure 10-26	IMPORTED GMAT SCORES

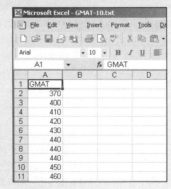

To make the range of values easier to work with, you'll assign the values in the list a range name.

4. Click cell **A2**, press **Shift + Ctrl + End** to quickly select the range **A2:A725**, click the **Name Box**, type **Scores**, and then press the **Enter** key.

5. Press **Ctrl + Home** to make cell A1 the active cell.

With the Analysis ToolPak add-in loaded and the data imported and given a range name, you're ready to use the analysis tools provided by the add-in to analyze this data. The new analysis tools that are available create a wide variety of new statistical reports.

To analyze the GMAT scores using the Analysis ToolPak tools:

1. Click **Tools** on the menu bar, and then click **Data Analysis**. The Data Analysis dialog box opens providing a list of 19 different statistical reports that you can create.

2. Click **Descriptive Statistics** in the Analysis Tools list, and then click the **OK** button. The Descriptive Statistics dialog box appears as shown in Figure 10-27.

Figure 10-27	DESCRIPTIVE STATISTICS DIALOG BOX

3. Type **Scores** in the Input Range reference box, click the **Summary statistics** check box, click the **Confidence Level for Mean** check box, click the **Kth Largest** check box, and then click the **Kth Smallest** check box. The Summary Statistics option calculates a wide range of statistics for the range including mean, standard error, median, and mode. The Confidence Level for Mean option calculates the confidence level of the mean (average) according to the percentage shown. The Kth Largest and Kth Smallest options calculate the Kth largest and Kth smallest values in the list, where K can represent any number between one and the total number of values in the list. If K is 1, the Kth largest value is the maximum value and the Kth smallest value is the minimum value.

The New Worksheet Ply option inserts the results of the choices made in the Descriptive Statistics dialog box into a new worksheet. Because this file is currently a text file, which doesn't support storing data on multiple worksheets, you'll need to insert this statistical report on the same worksheet that contains the GMAT scores.

4. Click the **Output Range** option button, type **C1** into the Output Range reference box, and then click the **OK** button.

5. Double-click the line separating the column headings **C** and **D** to resize the columns so that you can clearly see the labels in column C, and then click cell **D3**. A report that provides descriptive statistics on this column of data has been created on a worksheet as shown in Figure 10-28. Excel provides built-in functions, such as SUM, AVERAGE, COUNT, and STDEV, which you also could have used to create many of these statistics. If your data is **static** (doesn't change), using the Descriptive Statistics tool is faster than using Excel formulas to create each of these statistics.

Figure 10-28 **DESCRIPTIVE STATISTICS REPORT**

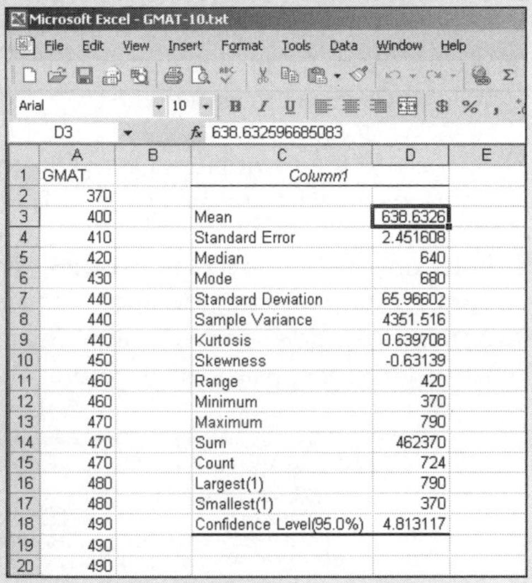

6. Press the ↓ key while observing the values in the Formula bar. Note that each of these values is a raw value and would not be recalculated if any of the data in your original list of scores changed. Therefore, be aware that if your raw data changes, you need to rerun the Analysis Tools report in order to get an up-to-date report of statistics.

7. Print the worksheet with your name in the left section of the header.

8. Click the **Save** button 💾 on the Standard toolbar, click the **Yes** button when prompted, and then close the GMAT-10 text file.

EXCEL 2000: Click the **Save** button when prompted.

If you use Excel to conduct extensive statistical analysis, the tools in the Analysis ToolPak and advanced statistical functions made available through the Analysis ToolPak VBA add-in can make your job much easier.

Conditional Sum Wizard

The **Conditional Sum Wizard** is an add-in that provides a wizard interface to add a column of numbers based on criteria that you supply. You can use the Conditional Sum Wizard to help you find subtotals of numbers.

GVR has conducted an extensive fundraiser to raise money for new facilities. You've logged the donations into an Excel spreadsheet and have used Excel's DSUM function in the past to subtotal the donations based on criteria. You will load and then use the Conditional Sum Wizard to see if it makes this task easier.

To load and use the Conditional Sum Wizard:

1. Open the **FundRaiser-10** workbook located in the Tutorial.10\Tutorial folder on your Data Disk.

   TROUBLE? Change the option in the Files of type list box to All Microsoft Excel Files if it isn't already displayed.

2. Click **Tools** on the menu bar, and then click **Add-Ins**. The Add-Ins dialog box opens.

3. Click the **Conditional Sum Wizard** check box (if it is not already selected), and then click the **OK** button. Now that you have the data and the Conditional Sum Wizard ready to go, you'll use it to find subtotals in the amount column based on criteria that you enter.

   TROUBLE? If the Conditional Sum Wizard doesn't appear as an add-in, you'll need to install it from your Office CD.

4. Click any cell in the range **A6:C26**, click **Tools**, and then click **Conditional Sum**. As soon as you installed the Conditional Sum add-in, the Conditional Sum option was added to the Tools menu. The first step of the Conditional Sum Wizard appears as shown in Figure 10-29.

Figure 10-29	STEP 1 OF THE CONDITIONAL SUM WIZARD

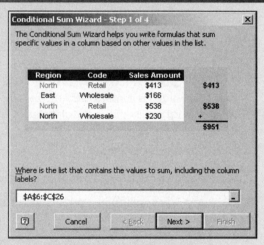

EXCEL 2000: Click any cell in the range **A6:C26**, click **Tools**, point to **Wizard**, and then click **Conditional Sum**.

5. Click the **Next** button. In the second step of the Wizard, you specify which column to sum and what conditions you want to apply. You want to sum the tuition for all colleges in the state of Illinois.

6. Click the **Column** list arrow, click **Purpose**, click the **This value** list arrow, click **Community Center**, and then click the **Add Condition** button. See Figure 10-30. If you wanted to specify additional conditions, you would do so now.

| Figure 10-30 | ADDING CONDITIONS IN THE CONDITIONAL SUM WIZARD |

Conditional Sum Wizard - Step 2 of 4

Which column contains the values to sum? Select the column label.

Column to sum: Amount

Next, select a column you want to evaluate, and then type or select a value to compare with data in that column.

Column: Is: This value:

Purpose   =   Community Center

Add Condition   Remove Condition

Purpose=Community Center

Cancel   < Back   Next >   Finish

7. Click the **Next** button, click the **Copy the formula and conditional values** option button, click the **Next** button, type **E6** in the reference box to specify where you want the conditional value copied, and then click the **Next** button.

8. Type **E7** in the reference box to specify the cell where you want the conditional sum formula copied, and then click the **Finish** button. Community Center appears in cell E6 and 14,150, appears in cell E7. Cell E7 represents the sum of the donations for the Community Center fund. The benefit of adding both the conditional value to cell E6 and the conditional formula to cell E7 is that now you can use them to find other statistics.

9. Click cell **E6**, type **General**, and then press the **Enter** key. The value in cell E7 changes to 22,650 as shown in Figure 10-31. The value in E7 now represents the total of the values in the Amount field that have "General" in the Purpose field. Notice that the formula for cell E7 is displayed in the Formula bar.

| Figure 10-31 | RESULTS OF THE CONDITIONAL SUM WIZARD |

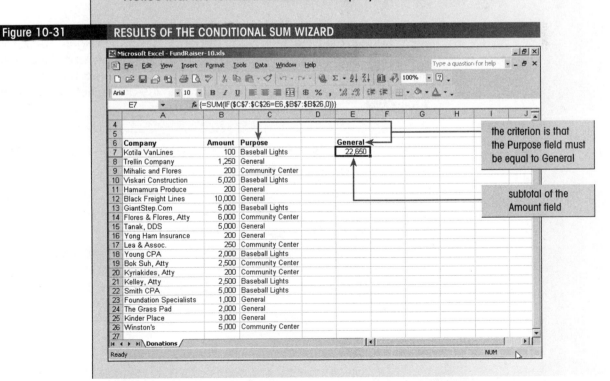

the criterion is that the Purpose field must be equal to General

subtotal of the Amount field

10. Print the Donations worksheet with your name in the left section of the header.

11. Save and close the FundRaiser-10 workbook.

Like the functions of the Analysis ToolPak add-in, the features of the Conditional Sum Wizard are not impossible to reproduce using existing Excel functions. However, for users who are not familiar with advanced statistical functions or DSUM, both tools provide easy ways to create the desired result.

Downloading **Add-Ins from the Web**

In addition to the add-ins provided with Excel, new ones are being developed all the time. Some add-ins are specific to an individual company's purposes. Others have a wider audience and are available for free or for a fee from the developer. Microsoft Corporation provides several additional free add-ins that you can find and download from its Web site.

Always looking for ways to make Excel workbooks faster, easier, and more productive for the users at GVR, you will explore the free add-ins available at the Microsoft Web site to see how they might apply to your needs. One of the easiest ways to find the appropriate Web page at the Microsoft Web site is to access it through the Excel Help.

To download an add-in available from the Microsoft Web site:

1. Click in the **Ask a Question** box, type **add-in**, and then press the **Enter** key.

EXCEL 2000: Click **Help** on the menu bar, and then click **Office on the Web** to display the Assistance Center at the Microsoft Web site, click the **Download Center** link on the left side of the Web page, and then continue with Step 4.

EXCEL 2000: Links and Web pages often change. If these steps don't work, go directly to http://office.microsoft.com/Downloads/.

2. Click the **Add-in programs included with Excel** link. The Add-in programs included with the Excel Help page appears as shown in Figure 10-32. You can use this page, or other related Help pages, to learn more about the add-ins supplied by Excel such as the Euro Currency Tools or Internet Assistant VBA add-in. For now, however, you're interested in the additional add-ins supplied on the Web.

Figure 10-32 HELP PAGE FOR EXCEL ADD-IN PROGRAMS

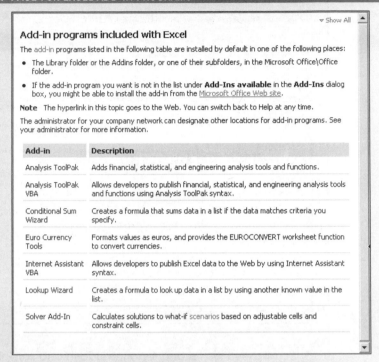

▾ Show All

Add-in programs included with Excel

The add-in programs listed in the following table are installed by default in one of the following places:

- The Library folder or the Addins folder, or one of their subfolders, in the Microsoft Office\Office folder.

- If the add-in program you want is not in the list under **Add-Ins available** in the **Add-Ins** dialog box, you might be able to install the add-in from the Microsoft Office Web site.

Note The hyperlink in this topic goes to the Web. You can switch back to Help at any time.

The administrator for your company network can designate other locations for add-in programs. See your administrator for more information.

Add-in	Description
Analysis ToolPak	Adds financial, statistical, and engineering analysis tools and functions.
Analysis ToolPak VBA	Allows developers to publish financial, statistical, and engineering analysis tools and functions using Analysis ToolPak syntax.
Conditional Sum Wizard	Creates a formula that sums data in a list if the data matches criteria you specify.
Euro Currency Tools	Formats values as euros, and provides the EUROCONVERT worksheet function to convert currencies.
Internet Assistant VBA	Allows developers to publish Excel data to the Web by using Internet Assistant syntax.
Lookup Wizard	Creates a formula to look up data in a list by using another known value in the list.
Solver Add-In	Calculates solutions to what-if scenarios based on adjustable cells and constraint cells.

3. Click the **Microsoft Office Web site** link, and then if prompted to select a country, click the appropriate link.

4. Click the **Product** list arrow, click **Excel**, click the **Version** list arrow, click **2002/XP** (if it is not already selected), clear the **Updates** check box, click the **Add-ins and Extras** check box to select it, and then click the **Update List** button. A Web page appears that identifies the add-ins and extras available for Excel 2002/XP as shown in Figure 10-33.

EXCEL 2000: Click the **Product** list arrow, click **Excel**, click the **Version** list arrow, click **2000**, clear the **Updates** check box, click the **Add-ins and Extras** check box to select it, and then click the **Update List** button.

Figure 10-33   WEB PAGE FOR EXTRA EXCEL ADD-IN PROGRAMS

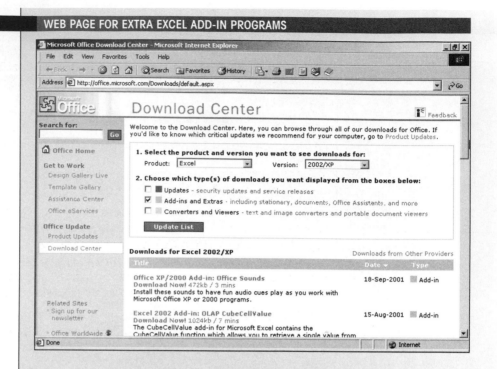

5. Scroll down the list and read the add-in and sample file descriptions. Notice in the title and description of the add-in that some of the add-ins are applicable to the entire Office suite, and some are specific to Excel. Also, based on the Type column, some of the downloads are add-ins, and some are sample workbooks (Documents). Because GVR uses both Access and Excel and you've already had several requests to share data between those two types of files, you'll download the AccessLinks add-in. Note that this add-in is only available for Excel 2002 users.

6. Click the **Excel 2002 Add-in: Access Links** link. A page opens that describes the add-in.

   EXCEL 2000: Select another add-in to download and install, or read the rest of this exercise without performing the remaining steps.

7. Click the **Download Now** button, and then click the **Save** button.

8. When prompted to save the program to disk, navigate to your Desktop, click the **Save** button, and then click the **OK** button if prompted that the download is complete. The add-in is downloaded to your Desktop as file ACCLNK.EXE.

   TROUBLE? Your instructor or technical support person might want you to download the file to a location other than the Desktop. If so, note the location of that folder so that you can find the downloaded file later.

   EXCEL 2000: Note the filename of the add-in that you have downloaded.

Now that the AccessLinks Add-In installation file has been downloaded to your computer, you'll use it to install the actual files on your computer that provide the new AccessLinks functionality.

To install the AccessLinks add-in on your computer:

1. Minimize all of your open program windows so that you can view your Desktop (or navigate to the folder that you used in Step 8 of the previous exercise), and then double-click **ACCLNK.EXE**, which is the file you just downloaded from the Microsoft Web site.

   EXCEL 2000: Double-click the file of the add-in you selected to download. If you did not download an add-in, read the remaining steps without performing them.

2. Follow the steps to install the add-in, including the steps to read and accept the license agreement if one is presented.

3. Note the folder location in which the AccessLinks add-in is being installed, click the **OK** button to install the AccessLinks add-In, and then click the **OK** button to acknowledge that the add-In was installed successfully. This process creates a file named ACCLINK.XLA and stores it in the given folder location. The ACCLINK.XLA file provides the actual functionality for the AccessLinks add-In. Once the add-in is installed, you don't need the downloaded installation file acclnk.exe anymore.

4. Minimize all of your open program windows so that you can view your Desktop (or open the folder that stores the acclnk.exe file in Windows Explorer), and then delete the acclnk.exe file.

   EXCEL 2000: Delete the file of the add-in you downloaded.

5. Close the Excel Help window, and if using a dial-up connection, disconnect from the Internet.

Now that the AccessLinks add-in has been downloaded and installed on your computer, you still need to load it within Excel by selecting it in the Add-Ins dialog box.

To load the AccessLinks add-in:

1. Start a new, blank workbook (if one isn't already open).

2. Click **Tools** on the menu bar, and then click **Add-Ins**.

3. Click the Microsoft **AccessLinks Add-In** check box.

   TROUBLE? If the AccessLinks add-in is not listed, click the Browse button, navigate to the folder that you noted when you were installing the program, and then double-click the ACCLINK.XLA file.

   TROUBLE? If the AccessLinks Add-In is already installed, you will be prompted to replace it. Click the Yes button.

4. Click the **OK** button.

With the AccessLinks add-in downloaded and installed, you're ready to use the new functionality provided by this add-in.

AccessLinks Add-In

The **AccessLinks** add-in provides several advanced features for sharing data between Access and Excel. This add-in provides the Convert to MS Access, MS Access Report, and MS Access Form commands on the Data menu. Figure 10-34 provides a short description of each.

Figure 10-34	ACCESSLINKS FEATURES

FEATURE	DESCRIPTION
Convert an Excel list to an Access database	To directly convert an Excel list to an Access database file
Create an Access report from Excel data	To design an Access report from Excel data
Use an Access form to enter Excel data	To create a customized form to enter, find, or delete data in an Excel list

Now that you've downloaded and installed the AccessLinks add-in, you want to see how it will work with existing Excel data. Being able to use the AccessLinks add-in will help you to share data between the GVR Access and Excel users and bring the power of Access forms and reports to existing Excel workbooks. You have some survey data in an Excel workbook that you want to convert to an Access database for the Human Resources department.

Note: If you are using Excel 2000, read through the steps without performing them.

To convert survey data in an Excel workbook to an Access database:

1. Open the **Survey-10** workbook from the Tutorial.10\Tutorial folder on your Data Disk.

2. Click any cell in the range **A1:E41**, click **Data** on the menu bar, and then click **Convert to MS Access**. The Convert to Microsoft Access dialog box opens as shown in Figure 10-35. You want to export this data to a new database.

Figure 10-35	CONVERT TO MICROSOFT ACCESS DIALOG BOX

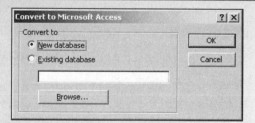

3. Click the **OK** button. An Access database is created and the Import Spreadsheet Wizard starts as shown in Figure 10-36.

| Figure 10-36 | IMPORT SPREADSHEET WIZARD DIALOG BOX |

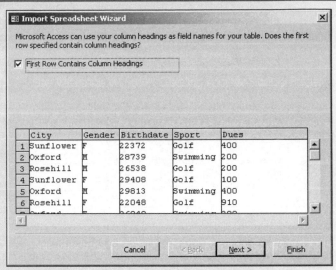

4. Click the **Next** button four times to move through the Wizard dialog boxes, accepting the default values and options, click the **Finish** button to import the Survey-10 table to the Survey-10 database, and then click the **OK** button in the dialog box that indicates that the Import Spreadsheet Wizard has finished importing the file. An Access database named Survey-10 has been created with a single table called Survey-10 also. See Figure 10-37.

| Figure 10-37 | SURVEY-10 ACCESS DATABASE |

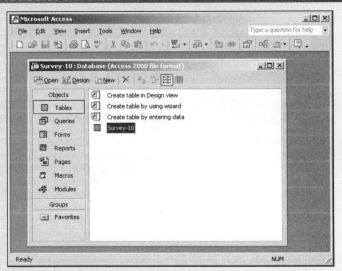

5. Double-click the **Survey-10** table to open it, and then press the **Tab** key several times to move through the fields of several records. At the bottom of the Table window, you can see that 40 records were imported from Excel into this table.

6. Click the **Close** button ☒ on the Survey-10 Table window, close the Survey-10 database, and then exit Access.

7. Return to the Survey-10 workbook. A text box has been added to the original list of data that provides information about the conversion as shown in Figure 10-38.

Figure 10-38 **TEXT BOX WITH CONVERSION INFORMATION**

text box provides
information on the
data that was converted
to an Access database

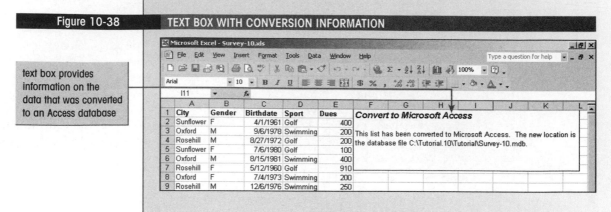

8. Print the survey data in portrait orientation with your name in the left section of the header. Use the scaling options to print the worksheet on one page.

9. Save and close the Survey-10 workbook.

Now you know how to import Access data into an Excel workbook as well as export Excel data to an Access database. With these capabilities, you can choose the best tool for the job rather than be limited by the constraints of the program into which the data was first entered.

Unloading an Add-In

You might think that since add-ins provide additional functionality, there's no reason not to load all of them at one time. But like all programs, unless you really need them and are using them, you should not load them into memory. Loading only those programs that you really need will help keep your computer running as fast as possible.

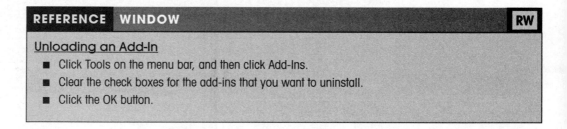

REFERENCE WINDOW   **RW**

Unloading an Add-In
- Click Tools on the menu bar, and then click Add-Ins.
- Clear the check boxes for the add-ins that you want to uninstall.
- Click the OK button.

You know that for the majority of your Excel workbooks, you don't need all the add-ins installed. Therefore, you'll uninstall all Excel add-ins for now to improve the performance of your overall system and selectively install specific add-ins as needed for future tasks.

To unload the new add-ins:

1. Start a new, blank workbook, click **Tools** on the menu bar, and then click **Add-Ins**.

2. Clear the check boxes of the add-ins that are currently installed.

3. Click the **OK** button.

4. Exit Excel.

In most current computer systems, there is plenty of extra hard drive space to store small files such as the ACCLNK.XLA file, which provides the AccessLinks add-in functionality. The size of this file is 233 KB, so the storage requirements for keeping the file on your computer are minimal. Loading any program, such as an add-in, requires some memory, which affects the overall performance of your computer. Therefore, you generally don't need to concern yourself with the number of add-ins that are installed and available on your system, but you do probably want to keep track of which add-ins are currently loaded so that you can maximize performance.

Deleting an Add-In

To delete the actual AccessLinks add-in file, you delete the ACCLNK.XLA file, which is found in the C:\Program Files\Microsoft Office\Office10\Library folder (or in the folder you specified for the add-in earlier during the installation of the add-in). You will delete the AccessLinks add-in from the computer you are using so that it is set up for the next student who uses this computer.

To delete the AccessLinks add-in:

1. Start Windows Explorer, and then navigate to and open the **C:\Program Files\Microsoft Office\Office10\Library** folder in the Folders pane, and click the **ACCLNK.XLA** file, as shown in Figure 10-39. Your screen might look different, depending on the current operating system on your computer, the folders stored on your hard drive, and other Windows Explorer settings. Figure 10-39 shows Windows Explorer within Windows 2000 Professional with the Details view applied.

| Figure 10-39 | DELETING THE ACCLNK.XLA FILE |

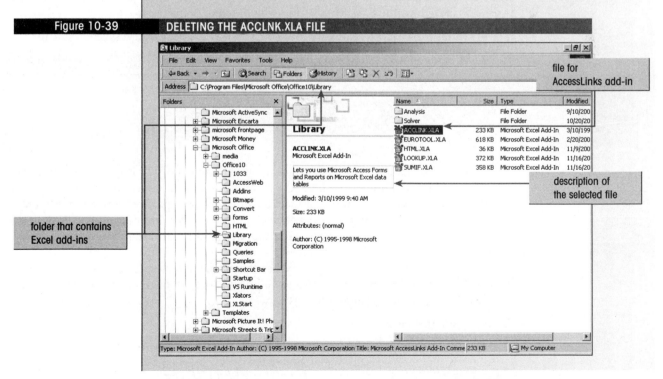

TROUBLE? If you saved the program to a different folder during the installation of the AccessLinks add-in, navigate to that folder to locate and select the ACCLNK.XLA file.

EXCEL 2000: Select the file for the add-in that you downloaded.

2. Click the **Delete** button ⊠ on the Standard Buttons toolbar, and then click the **Yes** button to send the file to the Recycle Bin.

Usually, you do not delete programs or functionality by deleting them directly in the Windows Explorer window. Whenever possible, use an uninstall program or the Add/Remove Programs utility within Control Panel to make sure that you delete all of the appropriate files for a particular program successfully. In this case, however, the AccessLinks add-in did not come with an uninstall program and is not shown as a separate entry in the Add/Remove Programs window. Therefore, to delete the ACCLNK.XLA file that provides the AccessLinks functionality, you had to locate and delete it manually from within Windows Explorer.

Comfortable with the steps required to find, install, and load add-ins, you're ready to tackle problems beyond the capabilities of the standard Excel application. You'll use your new knowledge of add-ins to extend the capabilities of Excel to support the business of Green Valley Recreation.

Session 10.2 QUICK CHECK

1. What is the purpose of the Analysis ToolPak add-in?

2. The Conditional Sum Wizard automates the process of which Excel built-in function?

3. When you load the Analysis ToolPak add-in and the Conditional Sum Wizard add-in, which commands are added to which menu?

4. What three new features are available when you load the AccessLinks add-in?

5. When you load the AccessLinks add-in, which commands are added to which menu?

REVIEW ASSIGNMENTS

Green Valley Recreation (GVR) manages many different sporting leagues. Depending on which director at GVR is in charge of the program, some employees use Access and some use Excel to manage the teams. The adult bowling league is particularly difficult to manage because players have to pay a $50 or $100 per month bowling fee for each month that they participate in the league. Because of the number of records required to manage the bowling league, the director in charge of the bowling league kept track of the data using a relational Access database. The database has three related tables: teams, players, and payments. Now, however, the director wants to import some of the data into Excel in order to use Excel's what-if and graphing features.

To complete this task:

1. Start Excel and open a new, blank workbook.

Note: Excel 2000 users should read Steps 2 and 3 but not perform them.

2. Open the **Teams-10** database located in the T10\Review folder of your Data Disk, and then import the Players table into the Excel workbook.

3. Add a new worksheet to the workbook.

4. Use Microsoft Query to import data from the **Teams-10** database located in the T10\Review folder of your Data Disk. Select the FName and LName fields from the Players table, the TeamName field from the Teams table, and the Amount and Date fields from the Payments table.

5. Filter the records so that only those records where the TeamName equals Angels are selected, and sort the records in ascending order based on the LName field and then the Date field.

6. Save the query with the name **Angels** in the Tutorial.10\Review folder on your Data Disk, return the data to cell A1 of the existing worksheet, and then rename the worksheet "Angels".

7. Insert a new worksheet, and then name the worksheet "PivotTable".

Note: Excel 2000 users should read Steps 8, 9, and 10, but not perform them.

8. Import the data defined by the Angels database query as a PivotTable starting in cell A4 on the PivotTable sheet.

9. Move the LName field to the Drop Page Fields Here area, the TeamName field to the Drop Column Fields Here area, the Date field to the Drop Row Fields Here area, and the Amount field to the Drop Data Items Here area.

10. Close the PivotTable toolbar and the PivotTable Field List, and then use the Page field to filter for only those records for Cahill.

11. Save the workbook with the name **Bowling-10** in the Tutorial.10\Review folder of your Data Disk, and then close the workbook.

12. Open the **Teams-10** database in Access from the T10\Review folder on your Data Disk, and then double-click the Players table to open the table.

13. Find the record for Percy Cahill, and then modify the record with your own first and last names. Close the Players table, close the Teams-10 database, and then exit Access.

14. Open the **Bowling-10** workbook from the Tutorial.10\Review folder on your Data Disk, and then switch to the Angels sheet.

15. Refresh the data on the worksheet.

16. Filter the list for your own last name, and then print that worksheet.

Explore 17. Add a new worksheet and name it "AllPayments". On the AllPayments sheet, start the import process to import the Angels data source from the Select Data Source dialog box. (Excel 2000 users should import the Angels query from the Run Query dialog box.)

Explore 18. You want to import the same fields as defined by the Angels data query, but you don't want to include any filters. To edit the Angels query, click the Edit Query button in the Import Data dialog box. (Excel 2000 users should click Data on the menu bar, point to Get External Data, and then click Edit Query.) Move to the Filter Data dialog box of the Query Wizard, and then remove the filter for TeamName field.

Explore 19. Use the same sort order for this query, save it with the name **AllPayments**, and then return the data to Microsoft Excel starting in cell A1 of the AllPayments worksheet.

20. Load the Conditional Sum Wizard add-in.

Explore

21. Use the Conditional Sum Wizard to sum all payments that were made for the Eggheads team.

22. Copy both the formula and the conditional values to the workbook in cells G2 and G3.

23. Change the value in cell G2 to "T-Bones" to make sure that the conditional sum works. Print the first page of the AllPayments worksheet with your name in the left section of the header.

24. Click a blank cell in the workbook, and then open the Select Data Source dialog box. (Excel 2000 users should open the Run Query dialog box.) Delete all of the new queries you've created, including the AllPayments and Angels data queries and the Teams-10 Players ODC file created when you opened the Players table.

25. Unload the Conditional Sum Wizard add-in, and then save and close the Bowling-10 workbook.

26. Start a new, blank workbook, and then use the MSN MoneyCentral Investor Stock Quotes Web query to import stock quote information for two investor symbols of your choice (but do not use MSFT or IBM) to cell A1 of the new workbook.

27. Use the Chart link for both stocks, and then print the charts. Explore any other aspect of the links or the MoneyCentral Web site that you desire. Based on the one-year trend for this stock, and any other news or information you may have researched for this company, write a brief paragraph explaining whether or not you think this stock is a good buy right now or not.

28. Save the workbook with the name **Invest-10** in the Tutorial.10\Review folder on your Data Disk, and then close the workbook.

29. Use Excel Help to go to the Microsoft Office Download Center Web site, and search for and then download the Excel 2002 Sample: PivotTable Reports document to your Desktop. (Excel 2000 users should download the Excel 2000 Tutorial: PivotTable Reports 101 add-in.)

30. Double-click the Reports.exe file icon that appears on your desktop to install the program, read and accept the license agreement, and extract the files to the T10\Review folder on your Data Disk or if using floppy disks, extract the files to a new, clean floppy. (Excel 2000 users should double-click the XCrtPiv.EXE file icon, extract the files to the T10\Review folder. If using floppy disks, extract the files to a new, clean floppy, and then follow the instructions provided to work through the tutorial to finish this Review Assignment exercise. Do not complete Steps 31 through 35 of the Review Assignments because they pertain to the SampleCustomReports workbook with which the Excel 2002 users are working.)

31. Open the SampleCustomerReports workbook from the T10\Review folder on your Data Disk.

32. On the Source Data worksheet, change the product named "Alice Mutton" to "Your Name's Product" in cell A2, and then copy the new product name to range A3:A14.

33. Switch to the Top Q1 Customer worksheet and refresh the PivotTable. Although customer RATTC didn't purchase any of Your Name's Product in quarter 1, a listing for the product appears in the PivotTable. Print this sheet.

34. Explore the other worksheets, and read the text boxes for each worksheet to learn more about PivotTable functions.

35. When you are done, close the SampleCustomerReports workbook without saving it, and then exit Excel.

CASE PROBLEMS

Case 1. Converting Euros to Native Currencies You work for an international investment firm. Often you need to be able to convert money expressed in euros to other currencies and vice versa. You'll use Excel's Euro Currency Tools add-in to work with a business plan expressed in euros to convert it to Italian lira.

To complete this task:

1. Start Excel and open the **ProfitLoss-10** workbook from the Tutorial.10\Cases folder on your Data Disk. The workbook shows a new business income projection. The currency symbol € is euros.

2. Copy the values in range A4:B11 to range A14:B21. Enter the label "Italy" in cell A13.

Explore 3. Use Excel Help to search for the function EUROCONVERT, and then print that page.

4. Install and load the Euro Currency Tools add-in.

Explore 5. Enter the formula in cell C14 to convert the euros shown in C4 to lira (the basic unit of currency for Italy). Do not worry about the two optional arguments.

6. Copy the formula from cell C14 through the range C14:G21.

Explore 7. Format the values in range C14:G21 with the L. Italian (Standard) symbol. Resize the columns as needed to clearly display the values in the range.

8. Enter your name in cell A2, and then print the workbook.

9. Unload the Euro Currency Tools add-in.

10. Save and close the ProfitLoss-10 workbook, and then exit Excel.

Case 2. Finding Your District Number Using the Lookup Wizard You're working as a volunteer in an information booth in Washington, D.C. Because state representatives change frequently, many of the services and information provided to tourists are listed by district number within each state. Tourists who visit the national's capital sometimes don't know what district they live in, but they do know the name of their representative. Your job is to help tourists determine their district number. You'll install the Lookup Wizard add-in to help you with the job of locating a district number based on a representative's name.

To complete this task:

1. Start Excel, and then open the **Congress-10** workbook from the Tutorial.10\Cases folder on your Data Disk.

2. Load the Lookup Wizard add-in. The District column contains the value that you want to find, and Crenshaw is the name of the representative whose district number you need to find.

Explore 3. Use the Lookup Wizard to find the district number of Representative Crenshaw. Copy the formula, the lookup parameters, and the lookup formula to cells F1, F2, and F3, respectively. (*Hint:* Use the Lookup option on the Tools menu.)

4. Sort the records by state, scroll through the list to find your own state representative, and then replace the last and first names of your state representative with your last name and first name in columns A and B of that record. Note in which district you live.

5. In cell F2, enter your own last name. Cell F3 should now display the district you live in for your state.

6. Save the workbook, and then print the first page.

7. Unload the Lookup Wizard.

8. Close the Congress-10 workbook, and then exit Excel.

Case 3. *Importing Medical Statistics from an Access Database* You work with a small diabetes clinic that tracks a variety of statistics on their patients. Since diabetes patients make several visits to your clinic each year, you've elected to manage the data in a relational database so that patient demographic information such as name and address are entered only once, in a Patients table, and summary statistics for all patients are very easy to create. Now, however, you need to import some of the data into Excel for further analysis.

To complete this task:

1. Start Excel and start a new, blank workbook.

2. Using Microsoft Query, create a new database query using the **Patients-10** MS Access database located in the T10\Cases folder on your Data Disk. Select the following fields from the appropriate tables in the order as shown:

   City and Gender from the Patients table

   Cholesterol from the Visits table

   LName from the Employees table

Explore 3. You selected fields from multiple tables of the database, and in this case, Microsoft Query cannot determine how those tables are joined. Click the OK button when prompted to manually join the tables in your query.

Explore 4. Drag the SSN field from the Patients table field list to the SS # field in the Visits table field list to join the Patients and Visits tables. Drag the Code Number field from the Employees table field list to the Case Manager Code field in the Visits table field list to join the Employees and Visits tables. The data that you are about to return in this query is shown in the lower half of the Microsoft Query window.

5. Click the Return Data button on the Microsoft Query toolbar, and then click the Create a PivotTable report link in the dialog box that appears. (If you are using Excel 2000, click the PivotTable report option button in the dialog box that appears.) Select cell A3 as the starting location for the PivotTable report. Organize and format the fields as shown in Figure 10-40. The values have been formatted with Comma Style format and no digits to the right of the decimal point. The Cholesterol field displays the average cholesterol value. (*Hint*: Double-click the Sum of Cholesterol field button, and select Average in the Summarize by list.)

Figure 10-40

	A	B	C	D
1	LName	(All)		
2				
3	Average of Cholesterol	Gender		
4	City	F	M	Grand Total
5	Cherokee	250		250
6	Greenfield	200	241	219
7	Independence	242		242
8	Leavenworth	302		302
9	Leawood		206	206
10	Lee's Summit		157	157
11	Liberty	229		229
12	Lindale		189	189
13	Raytown	278	159	238
14	Grand Total	217	226	221
15				

6. Print the PivotTable with your name in the left section of the header of the worksheet.

7. Save the workbook with the name **Cholesterol-10** in the Tutorial.10\Cases folder on your Data Disk.

8. Close the workbook, and then exit Excel.

Case 4. Importing and Charting Volunteer Hours You are the president of a local philanthropic club whose members volunteer time for community activities. Right now, you're tracking the activities and hours for which each member volunteers in an Access database, but you want to create some charts of the data in Excel. You'll import the required data into Excel using Microsoft Query, and then make the appropriate chart you need.

To complete this task:

1. Start Excel and start a new, blank workbook.

2. Using Microsoft Query, create a new database query using the **Club-10** MS Access database located in the T10\Cases folder on your Data Disk. Select the following fields from the appropriate tables:

Last from the Names table

ActivityDate and Hours from the Activities table

City from the Zips table

3. Do not apply any filters or sort orders, and return the data to cell A1 of the current Excel worksheet without saving the query definition.

 Explore

4. Create a PivotChart using the data in a new worksheet with the fields in the PivotChart positions as shown in Figure 10-41 by using the PivotTable and PivotChart Report option on the Tools menu. Filter the data for the cities of Blue Springs, Kansas City, and Lee's Summit. (*Hint*: You might have to change the chart type or sub-type.)

Figure 10-41

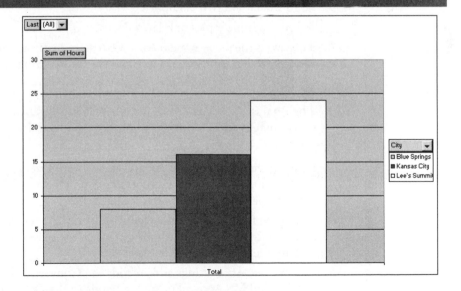

5. Save the workbook with the name **Club-10** in the Tutorial.10\Cases folder on your Data Disk.

6. Print the PivotChart with your name in the left section of the header.

7. Save and close the Club-10 workbook, and then exit Excel.

QUICK CHECK ANSWERS

Session 10.1

1. You can import data into Excel in any of these ways:

   - Use the Open button on the Standard toolbar (or select the Open command on the File menu). (This option is not available in Excel 2000.)
   - Use the Import External Data command on the Data menu. (In Excel 2000, use the Get External Data command on the Data menu.)
   - Use a Web query.
   - Use a database query.

   Write or record VBA statements that include data import statements.

2. The Import External Data command on the Data menu provides many more options for how and where you can import the data, including the ability to import the data as a PivotTable. The queries that you build using the Import External Data command are saved, so you can quickly and easily rerun them at a later time to refresh imported data.

3. Microsoft MoneyCentral is a Web site (http://moneycentral.msn.com/) devoted to providing information on all types of money matters.

4. The three MoneyCentral Web queries that are provided by default in the Select Data Source dialog box import currency rates, major stock market index figures, and stock quote information.

5. Microsoft Query gives you additional data import features that are not provided by the other import tools. These features include the ability to:

   - Filter rows or columns of data before they are imported
   - Create a parameter query that prompts you for the criteria used to determine which records will be imported
   - Sort data before it is imported
   - Join multiple tables of related data

6. The two critical components of a VBA statement that select data from an external source are the connection string and the query string.

Session 10.2

1. The Analysis ToolPak provides statistical and engineering analysis tools and functions, such as advanced correlation, regression, and sampling analysis tools.

2. DSUM

3. Loading the Analysis ToolPak add-in adds the Data Analysis command to the Tools menu. Loading the Conditional Sum Wizard add-in provides the Conditional Sum option to the Tools menu.

4. The three features available when you load the AccessLinks add-in are: Convert an Excel list to an Access database, Create an Access report from Excel data, and Use an Access form to enter Excel data.

5. Loading the AccessLinks add-in adds the Convert to MS Access, MS Access Report, and MS Access Form commands to the Data menu.

TASK	PAGE #	RECOMMENDED METHOD/NOTES
Access data, import a table or view	EX 532	See Reference Window: Importing Access Data Using the File Menu
Access data, import new	EX 534	See Reference Window: Importing New Access Data Using the Data Menu
Access data, import previously imported data	EX 534	See Reference Window: Importing a Previously Defined Data Source
Add-in, load	EX 556	See Reference Window: Loading an Add-In
Add-in, unload	EX 568	See Reference Window: Unloading an Add-In
AutoFormat, apply	EX 102	See Reference Window: Applying an AutoFormat
Cells, unlock	EX 23	Select the cells to be unlocked, click Format, click Cells, click the Protection tab, clear the Locked check box
Chart, add a data table	EX 198	See Reference Window: Adding a Data Table to a Chart
Chart, add a new data series using the Chart Wizard	EX 143	See Reference Window: Adding a New Data Series Using the Chart Wizard
Chart, add a new data series using copy and paste	EX 144	Select the new data series, click 📋, click the chart, click 📋
Chart, apply a custom chart type	EX 159	See Reference Window: Applying a Custom Chart Type to an Existing Chart
Chart, apply a cylinder, cone, or pyramid chart type	EX 179	See Reference Window: Applying a Cylinder, Cone, or Pyramid Chart Type to an Existing Chart
Chart, apply right-angle axes to a 3-D chart	EX 175	See Reference Window: Applying Right Angle Axes
Chart, change 2-D to 3-D	EX 171	See Reference Window: Changing a 2-D Chart to a 3-D Chart
Chart, change options using the Chart Wizard	EX 133	Click the chart, click 📊, go to Step 3 in the Chart Wizard, modify the available options
Chart, change the chart type or sub-type	EX 147	See Reference Window: Changing a Chart Type or Sub-Type
Chart, change the data series order	EX 173	See Reference Window: Changing the Data Series Order
Chart, create using Chart Wizard	EX 130	Select cells to be charted, click 📊, complete the steps in the Wizard
Chart, delete a user-defined custom	EX 160	See Reference Window: Deleting a User-Defined Custom Chart Type
Chart, format element	EX 154	See Reference Window: Formatting a Chart Element Using Its Format Dialog Box
Chart, modify data series or x-axis labels	EX 140	See Reference Window: Modifying the Data Series or X-Axis Labels on an Existing Chart
Chart, modify elevation or rotation on a 3-D chart	EX 176	See Reference Window: Modifying the Elevation or Rotation of a 3-D Chart

TASK REFERENCE

TASK	PAGE #	RECOMMENDED METHOD/NOTES
Chart, modify source data using the Chart Wizard	EX 131	Click the chart, click ▥, go to Step 2 in the Chart Wizard, click the Series tab, specify the options
Chart, modify values	EX 151	See Reference Window: Modifying Chart Values
Chart, move	EX 138	Click the chart, point to the Chart Area, drag the chart to a new location
Chart, remove data series	EX 133	Click the chart, click ▥, go to Step 2 in the Chart Wizard, click the Series tab, click the value in the Series list that you want to remove, click Remove
Chart, resize	EX 138	Select the chart, drag the selection handles to resize it
Chart, select	EX 138	Click the chart
Chart type, change default	EX 160	See Reference Window: Changing the Default Chart Type
Chart type, create custom	EX 158	See Reference Window: Creating a Custom Chart Type
Column and row headings, print	EX 20	See Reference Window: Printing Row and Column Headings on a Printout
Command Button, add to a workbook	EX 428	See Reference Window: Adding a Command Button to a Workbook
Command Button, add VBA code	EX 430	See Reference Window: Adding VBA Code to a Control on a Worksheet
Command Button, change text	EX 428	With the Command Button selected, click ▤ on the Control Toolbox toolbar, modify the Caption property
Conditional formatting, apply	EX 33	Click the cell to which you want to apply the conditional formatting, click Format, click Conditional Formatting, specify the criteria and formatting for each condition
Control, add to a form	EX 417	See Reference Window: Adding a Control to a UserForm
Control, modify	EX 422	In the Visual Basic Editor, click the control, modify the values on the control's property sheet
Custom calculation, create in PivotTable	EX 109	See Reference Window: Creating a Custom Calculation
Data, delete imported	EX 552	See Reference Window: Deleting Imported Data
Data, import from a Web page	EX 72	See Reference Window: Importing Data from a Web Page
Data, import using Microsoft Query	EX 545	See Reference Window: Importing Data Using Microsoft Query
Data, refresh imported	EX 74	Click any cell that contains imported data, click ▯ on the External Data toolbar
Data source, change for PivotTable	EX 106	See Reference Window: Changing the Range of the Source Data for the PivotTable
Data source file, delete	EX 553	See Reference Window: Deleting a Data Source File

TASK	PAGE #	RECOMMENDED METHOD/NOTES
Excel Objects model, explore	EX 330	Search for "object model" in the Visual Basic Help
Errors, trace	EX 240	See Reference Window: Tracing Errors
Folder, create a startup folder	EX 367	See Reference Window: Creating Another Startup Folder
Formulas, display	EX 19	See Reference Window: Displaying Formulas in Worksheet Cells
Formulas, hide	EX 22	Press Ctrl + grave accent (`)
Function, add a description	EX 383	See Reference Window: Adding a Function Description
Function, find in Visual Basic Help	EX 438	See Reference Window: Finding Microsoft Visual Basic Functions in Help
Function, use a function stored in another workbook	EX 377	See Reference Window: Using a Function Stored in Another Workbook
Gridlines, print	EX 20	See Reference Window: Printing Gridlines on a Printout
List, analyze with PivotChart	EX 90	See Reference Window: Analyzing a List with a PivotChart
Macro, assign to a keyboard shortcut	EX 308	See Reference Window: Assigning a Macro to a Keyboard Shortcut
Macro, assign to a new toolbar	EX 311	See Reference Window: Creating a New Toolbar with a Macro-Assigned Button
Macro, create with the macro recorder	EX 323	See Reference Window: Creating a Macro Using the Macro Recorder
Macro, delete	EX 344	See Reference Window: Deleting a Macro
Macro, edit	EX 306	See Reference Window: Editing an Existing Macro
Macro, run	EX 305	See Reference Window: Running an Existing Macro
Macro, sign	EX 349	See Reference Window: Signing a Macro
Module, delete	EX 345	See Reference Window: Deleting an Existing Module
Module, rename	EX 483	See Reference Window: Renaming a Module
Option Explicit statement, automatically enter	EX 482	See Reference Window: Automatically Entering the Option Explicit Statement
Pie chart, change a color of a slice	EX 192	See Reference Window: Changing a Slice Color
Pie chart, create an exploded	EX 183	See Reference Window: Creating an Exploded Pie Chart
Pie chart, create an extracted	EX 188	See Reference Window: Creating an Extracted Pie Chart
Pie chart, move data points in an extracted	EX 190	See Reference Window: Moving the Data Points in an Extracted Chart

TASK	PAGE #	RECOMMENDED METHOD/NOTES
PivotChart, create	EX 90	See Reference Window: Analyzing a List with a PivotChart
PivotTable, create a custom calculation in	EX 109	See Reference Window: Creating a Custom Calculation
PivotTable, apply an AutoFormat	EX 102	See Reference Window: Applying an AutoFormat
PivotTable, change the default settings	EX 111	See Reference Window: Changing PivotTable Defaults
PivotTable, change the range of source data	EX 106	See Reference Window: Changing the Range of the Source Data for the PivotTable
PivotTable, change the structure	EX 97	See Reference Window: Changing the Structure of a PivotTable
PivotTable, drill down	EX 112	Double-click any value in the Data Item area of a PivotTable
PivotTable, format data field	EX 96	See Reference Window: Formatting a Data Field in a PivotTable
PivotTable, show or hide detail	EX 100	See Reference Window: Showing or Hiding Detail on a PivotTable
PivotTable and PivotChart Wizard, start	EX 90	Click any cell in an Excel list, click Data, click PivotTable and PivotChart Report
Procedure, write for UserForm	EX 429	See Reference Window: Writing a Procedure for a UserForm
Properties window, display	EX 418	In the Visual Basic Editor, click 🖼
R1C1 reference style, apply	EX 245	See Reference Window: Applying the R1C1 Reference Style
Records, group in PivotTable	EX 104	Right-click the field on the PivotTable whose records you want to group, point to Group and Show Detail, specify the grouping option, click OK
Relative Reference button, check status	EX 591	See Reference Window: Checking the Relative Reference Button Status
Row and column headings, print	EX 20	See Reference Window: Printing Row and Column Headings on a Printout
R-squared value, add to scatter chart	EX 42	See Reference Window: Adding a R-Squared Value to a Scatter Chart
Scatter chart, add a R-squared value	EX 42	See Reference Window: Adding a R-Squared Value to a Scatter Chart
Scatter chart, add a trendline	EX 42	See Reference Window: Adding a Linear Trendline to a Scatter Chart
Scatter chart, change type of trendline on	EX 50	See Reference Window: Changing the Type of Trendline Displayed on a Scatter Chart
Scatter chart, create	EX 37	See Reference Window: Creating a Scatter Chart
Scenario, apply	EX 29	See Reference Window: Applying a Scenario

TASK REFERENCE

Excel 2002 with Visual Basic for Applications File Finder

Location in Tutorial	Name and Location of Data File	Student Creates New File
Tutorial 1		
Session 1.1	Tutorial.01\Tutorial\CashFlow-1.xls	
Session 1.2	Tutorial.01\Tutorial\T-Shirts-1.xls	
	Tutorial.01\Tutorial\Expansion-1.xls	
Session 1.3	Tutorial.01\Tutorial\PoolStats-1.xls	
Review Assignments	Tutorial.01\Review\Analysis-1.xls	
Case Problem 1	Tutorial.01\Cases\ProfitLoss-1.xls	
Case Problem 2		Tutorial.01\Cases\JobAnalysis-1.xls
Case Problem 3	Tutorial.01\Cases\RainGrain-1.xls	
Tutorial 2		
Session 2.1	Tutorial.02\Tutorial\ChildrensBooks-2.xls	
	Tutorial.02\Tutorial\BostonLists-2.xls	
	Tutorial.02\Tutorial\BostonLists-2B.xls	
Session 2.2	Tutorial.02\Tutorial\Survey-2.xls	
Review Assignments	Tutorial.02\Review\Tennis-2B.xls	
Case Problem 1	Tutorial.02\Cases\Representatives-2B.doc	Tutorial.02\Cases\Representatives-2.xls
Case Problem 2	Tutorial.02\Cases\Census-2B.xls	
Case Problem 3	Tutorial.02\Cases\TechnologyStore-2.xls	
Case Problem 4	Tutorial.02\Cases\BookClub-2.xls	
Tutorial 3		
Session 3.1	Tutorial.03\Tutorial\CallAnalysis-3.xls	
	Tutorial.03\Tutorial\Billiards-3.xls	
Session 3.2	Tutorial.03\Tutorial\Billiards-3.xls	
	(continued from Session 3.1)	
Review Assignments	Tutorial.03\Review\Registrations-3.xls	
Case Problem 1	Tutorial.03\Cases\Grades-3.xls	
Case Problem 2	Tutorial.03\Cases\WeMakeIt-3.xls	
Case Problem 3	Tutorial.03\Cases\KentuckyDerby-3.xls	
Case Problem 4	Tutorial.03\Cases\Turnover-3.xls	
Tutorial 4		
Session 4.1	Tutorial.04\Tutorial\Tests-4.xls	
	Tutorial.04\Tutorial\MgmtSurvey-4.xls	
	Tutorial.04\Tutorial\Southside-4.xls	
Session 4.2	Tutorial.04\Tutorial\LifeguardReport-4.xls	
	Tutorial.04\Tutorial\T-ShirtShop-4.xls	
	Tutorial.04\Tutorial\GolfCourses-4.xls	
	Tutorial.04\Tutorial\BMI-4.xls	
	Tutorial.04\Tutorial\StockWatch-4.xls	
Review Assignments	Tutorial.04\Review\Consult-4.xls	
	Tutorial.04\Review\Research-4.xls	
Case Problem 1	Tutorial.04\Cases\SalesPerformance-4.xls	
Case Problem 2	Tutorial.04\Cases\Baker-4.xls	
Case Problem 3	Tutorial.04\Cases\HeatIndex-4.xls	
Case Problem 4		
Tutorial 5		
Session 5.1	Tutorial.05\Tutorial\GVRGrowth-5.xls	
Session 5.2	Tutorial.05\Tutorial\DepreciationCalculator-5.xls	
	Tutorial.05\Tutorial\HealthClub-5.xls	
	Tutorial.05\Tutorial\FundRaiser-5.xls	
	Tutorial.05\Tutorial\RockRoad-5.xls	

Excel 2002 with Visual Basic for Applications File Finder

Location in Tutorial	Name and Location of Data File	Student Creates New File
Session 5.3	Tutorial.05\Tutorial\Pitching-5.xls Tutorial.05\Tutorial\MathCamp-5.xls Tutorial.05\Tutorial\ComputerCamp-5.xls Tutorial.05\Tutorial\BBRegistration-5.xls Tutorial.05\Tutorial\Golfers-5.xls	
Review Assignments	Tutorial.05\Review\UsersGroup-5.xls	
Case Problem 1		Tutorial.05\Cases\Mortgage-5.xls
Case Problem 2	Tutorial.05\Cases\BusinessPlan-5.xls	
Case Problem 3	Tutorial.05\Cases\Conversion-5.xls	
Case Problem 4	Tutorial.05\Cases\MathTest-5.xls	
Tutorial 6		
Session 6.1	Tutorial.06\Tutorial\Athlete-6.xls Tutorial.06\Tutorial\Contestants-6.xls Tutorial.06\Tutorial\Sunflower-6.xls	
Session 6.2	Tutorial.06\Tutorial\Athlete-6.xls (continued from Session 6.1)	Tutorial.06\Tutorial\DigitalSigTest-6.xls
Review Assignments	Tutorial.06\Review\Registration-6.xls	
Case Problem 1	Tutorial.06\Cases\Commisions-6.xls	
Case Problem 2	Tutorial.06\Cases\Investments-6.xls	
Case Problem 3	Tutorial.06\Cases\Patients-6.xls	
Case Problem 4		
Tutorial 7		
Session 7.1	Tutorial.07\Tutorial\Loan-7.xls Tutorial.07\Tutorial\BMI-7.xls	Tutorial.07\Tutorial\ CustomFunctions.xls (Excel 2002 only) Tutorial.07\Tutorial\ CustomFunctions.xls (Excel 2000 only) Tutorial.07\Tutorial\Test-7.xls
Session 7.2	Tutorial.07\Tutorial\Camp-7.xls Tutorial.07\Tutorial\SecondMilers-7.xls	Tutorial07\Tutorial\Retirement-7.xls
Review Assignments	Tutorial.07\Review\Weather-7.xls Tutorial.07\Review\ParkingLot-7.xls	Tutorial.07\Review\GVR-7.xls
Case Problem 1	 Tutorial.07\Cases\Roses-7.xls	Tutorial.07\Cases\Metric-7.xls
Case Problem 2	Tutorial.07\Cases\Gold-7.xls	
Case Problem 3		
Case Problem 4	Tutorial.07\Cases\HeatIndex-7.xls	
Tutorial 8		
Session 8.1	Tutorial.08\Tutorial\Batting-8.xls	
Session 8.2	Tutorial.08\Tutorial\League-8.xls	
Review Assignments	Tutorial.08\Review\Golf-8.xls Tutorial.08\Review\Handicap-8.xls	
Case Problem 1	Tutorial.08\Cases\Seminar-8.xls	
Case Problem 2	Tutorial.08\Cases\Ratios-8.xls	
Case Problem 3		Tutorial.08\Cases\SplashScreen-8.xls
Case Problem 4	Tutorial.08\Cases\Tutorial8-Case4.doc	
Tutorial 9		
Session 9.1		Tutorial.09\Tutorial\Golf-9.xls
Session 9.2	Tutorial.09\Tutorial\GolfHandicap-9.xls Tutorial.09\Tutorial\GolfTournament-9.xls	
Review Assignments	Tutorial.09\Review\GolfFee-9.xls	
Case Problem 1		Tutorial.09\Cases\Test-9.xls
Case Problem 2		Tutorial.09\Cases\AddColumn-9.xls

Excel 2002 with Visual Basic for Applications File Finder

Location in Tutorial	Name and Location of Data File	Student Creates New File
Case Problem 3	Tutorial.09\Cases\PatientAssignmentList-9.xls	
Case Problem 4		Tutorial.09\Cases\MessageBox-9.xls
Tutorial 10		
Session 10.1	T10\Tutorial\Employees.mdb	Tutorial.10\Tutorial\Greenfield-10.xls
		Tutorial.10\Tutorial\Investments-10.xls
		Tutorial.10\Tutorial\EmployeeAddressList-10.xls
Session 10.2	Tutorial.10\Tutorial\GMAT-10.txt	
	Tutorial.10\Tutorial\FundRaiser-10.xls	
	Tutorial.10\Tutorial\Survey-10.xls	
Review Assignments	T10\Review\Teams-10.mdb	Tutorial.10\Review\Bowling-10.xls
		Tutorial.10\Review\Invest-10.xls
Case Problem 1	Tutorial.10\Cases\ProfitLoss-10.xls	
Case Problem 2	Tutorial.10\Cases\Congress-10.xls	
Case Problem 3	T10\Cases\Patients-10.mdb	Tutorial.10\Cases\Cholesterol-10.xls
Case Problem 4	T10\Cases\Club-10.mdb	Tutorial.10\Cases\Club-10.xls